The Bumper Book of Vitali's Travels

Thirty Years of Globe-Trotting (1990 – 2020)

Vitali Vitaliev

For [illegible], with all best wishes! [illegible]

Vitali 27/11/21

ISBN: 1-912741-09-1
ISBN-13: 978-1-912741-09-0 (Thrust Books)

Photos by Christine Bohling

'A good traveller is one who does not know where he is going to, and a perfect traveller does not know where he came from.'
Lin Yutang

Contents

Ian Mayes: Vitali in the Guardian

(instead of a foreword)

In the autumn of 1988 a thirty-four-year-old Kharkov-born writer and journalist, Vitali Vitaliev, arrived at the *Guardian* to start a month-long 'educational' visit. Vitaliev was an award-winning journalist in the Soviet Union, contributing investigative articles to several leading journals such as Ogonyok,[1] but especially to the satirical weekly *Krokodil* for which he was a special correspondent. Alan Rusbridger had invited him to England at the suggestion of Martin Walker, the *Guardian*'s man in Moscow. 'Martin Walker and the *Guardian* changed my life,' Vitaliev declared.[2] The features and reviews he contributed to the *Guardian* in the four weeks of his visit – the first time he had been anywhere outside the Soviet Union – led to a book offer and a regular slot reporting from Moscow in Clive James's television show, *Saturday Night Clive*. A little over a year after his return to Russia, prompted by the deteriorating situation there as crisis followed crisis and by the increasing risk to which his journalism was exposing him and his family, he 'defected,' bringing his wife and son to start life in the West ...

Walker had first met Vitaliev four years earlier, in 1987, when he went to the offices of *Krokodil* to interview him. 'We had lunch and became friends. At the time he was passionately pro-Gorbachev and pro-perestroika and one night over vodka even thought aloud about joining the Party. I got to know his wife and son, and when he had the use of a *Krokodil* dacha my family would go out and spend Sundays in the country with them. By early 1988, when the economic disruption and the internal party counter-attack against Gorbachev were emerging, Vitali became very depressed about the future, convinced that the hard-liners were coming back, along with more antisemitism. Skinheads were becoming a problem, tough young nationalists who would beat up blacks and people from Abkhazia, and Jews as well if they recognised them.' Walker himself was arrested and beaten up on the Arbat in Moscow while

[1] See The Best of Ogonyok, edited by Vitaly Korotich (the magazine's editor) and Cathy Porter, 1990, which contains several of Vitaliev's contributifons. An editorial note says that by 1990 it was selling about 3m copies a week. See also Cathy Porter, Flame burns anew, an interview with Korotich, *Guardian* 27 March 1989.

[2] Email to the author 11 September 2012.

covering what he described as a 'dignified and silent' demonstration by Jews who were protesting at the length of time they were being made to wait for exit visas.

'We talked endlessly, as I did with other Russian friends, about perestroika and its prospects and the way it was going wrong. [These were what Vitaliev called "Russian-style kitchen sessions"] I knew from economist friends that the economy was going badly awry, and from my pro-Gorbachev contacts in the central committee and other officials that Gorbachev was facing intense opposition. They were baffled that the US and the West, after Reagan's famous visit to Red Square [May 1988], were not being more supportive. In retrospect, I doubt that any kind of Western aid would have helped; the economic system was fundamentally rotten, the farms unproductive, the infrastructure crumbling and industrial output declining.'

Vitaliev's view was equally gloomy and becoming gloomier. The contrast with the life he found in England on that first visit, where everyone seemed to smile, struck him forcibly. Walker recalled, 'When he came to London, I met him [off the boat train] at Liverpool Street station, drove him around the sights, took him to his first supermarket and [a day or two later] down to my parents-in-laws' place on Church Square in Rye. It was like watching someone fall in love: the old town, the medieval church, the cobbled streets and teashops, the shops in general, and visiting the *Guardian*. He was spectacularly happy.'[3]

In the office he was placed in the care of John Cunningham, a staff feature writer, who took him on various excursions – he was keen to experience Soho – and arranged assignments for him, including a day with Thames Valley police in Oxford that deeply impressed him. He found he shared with the chief constable a great admiration for Charles Dickens (one of the things he took back to Russia was a policeman's helmet). He went to an Arsenal match at Highbury with Roger Alton and Alan Rusbridger whose home was within earshot of the ground. With Bill Webb he visited the Traveller's club, where the doorman provided the necessary tie. Inspired and chastened by this experience he went out the following day and bought a sensationally glittery suit. He only understood the reaction to it when a couple of years later he saw another shiny suit exactly like his in a Hollywood comedy thriller, worn by a Harlem drug dealer. At that time he was a non-smoker, but he mingled happily with *Guardian* journalists in the sweaty smoke-laden atmosphere of the Coach and Horses, just a few yards from the back door of the office. By the time he left at the end of his month he had been given a richly flavoured taste of England. His impressions of the *Guardian* itself have been a recurring element in his work ever since:

[3] Vitaliev's own recollection of these first few days in England may be found in his *Dreams on Hitler's Couch*, published by Richard Cohen, London 1997.

'Here dozens of journalists were sitting next to each other, yet the huge room was immersed in silence, strangely enhanced by softly purring telephones and whispered conversations. No one bothered raising their voice. Twice a day a food trolley was rolled into the newsroom by a white-robed young man from the canteen. The journalists bought their tea and sandwiches and consumed them there and then at their desks. When the trolley was about to leave, the young man shouted: 'Trolley going!' at which point the hacks would look up from their computers and chant in chorus: 'Bye-bye, trolley!' This little ritual was as sweet and spontaneous as only a children's game could be. Can it be that they are all adult children who have forgotten to grow up? I wondered then.'[4]

Russia upon his return provided an even sharper contrast. The economic situation had deteriorated further, crime was on the increase, food shortages were growing. Russia seemed to be moving rapidly towards the dystopian society imagined by his close friend Alexander Kabakov, whose publication in print as opposed to clandestine circulation in samizdat had, paradoxically, been one of the portents that led to early optimism about glasnost.[5] Vitaliev and his colleagues were shaken when Gorbachev launched an attack on press and publishers, including the editors of Ogonyok and *Krokodil*, accusing them of exaggerating the difficulties that perestroika was encountering. By the spring of 1989 the editor of Ogonyok, such was the magazine's vulnerability, was asking all his journalists to sign every fact and figure: 'If they make one mistake they can't work for us any more.'[6] There were personal difficulties for Vitaliev. His phone was bugged: he heard KGB voices on the line once while talking to Jonathan Steele, the *Guardian* correspondent who had taken over from Martin Walker in Moscow. He started to get threatening calls, implicitly directed not just at him but also at his son, Mitya, then aged six. He became a heavy smoker again. About a year after his return he made up his mind to defect. There was a tearful family gathering at which he told his mother he was planning to leave. Early in December when he went to Kharkov with Kabakov he took the opportunity to visit his father's grave.

On 26 December, Vitaliev heard of the execution of Ceausescu: he had taken to his bed in Moscow, in pain from a gastric ulcer. He should have been in Latvia but his talk in Riga had been cancelled when it transpired that local gangsters were planning to settle accounts with him for exposing their lucrative racket in fake jeans, carried on in collusion with corrupt high officials.[7] On 30 January 1990 he said a final

[4] Vitaliev, op cit.

[5] Vitaliev was later to profile Kabakov as 'a Russian Orwell,' for the Guardian 2 April 1990. Kabakov's dystopian novella quoted by Vitaliev in his profile was published in the United States by William Morrow, New York, later in the year under the title *No Return*. The chaotic crime-ridden society Kabakov imagined was supposed to exist in the Moscow of 1993.

[6] Cathy Porter, Korotich interview, *Guardian* 27 March 1989.

[7] Vitaliev gives a long account of this investigation and its consequence in *Special Correspondent* 1990.

goodbye to his mother. The following day his train crossed the border into Poland at Brest.[8]

This time when he arrived in Britain on the ferry from the Hook of Holland, his wife and son were with him, and Alan Rusbridger was at Harwich to meet them, waving an advance copy of Vitaliev's first book in English, *Special Correspondent*. For the first few weeks after his arrival Vitaliev and his family lived with the Rusbridgers in Highbury. 'He supported me strongly in my decision not to return to the USSR and said that if "they" tried to do anything to my Mum in Moscow in revenge, the *Guardian* people would demonstrate at the Soviet Embassy! The *Guardian* played an enormous role in building up my self-confidence – as a journalist, as a writer and as a free human being.'

Vitaliev wrote for the *Guardian* for the next five months when, encouraged by Rusbridger and Clive James, he took up an offer to go to Australia to become a senior staff writer for the *Melbourne Age* and the *Sydney Morning Herald*. His weekly column for Fairfax newspapers became, according to the *Age* editor Mike Smith, the most popular in the history of Australian journalism (he was getting 100 to 200 readers' letters a day). Vitaliev continued to write for the *Guardian* from time to time from Australia, correctly seeing Eduard Shevardnadze's resignation as Gorbachev's foreign minister in December 1990 as a signal of the imminent end of the Soviet Union (although Shevardnadze re-joined Gorbachev briefly before that actually happened). 'His resignation is the surest sign that the leaking ship of the Soviet empire is finally about to sink … It may well be that it won't survive until the end of the year …'[9] It lasted in fact until the end of the following year. Before that came the unsuccessful coup attempt and the enforced isolation of Gorbachev in his Crimean dacha, where he was reached by the *Guardian*'s Jonathan Steele to secure one of the great journalistic scoops of the period.

Vitaliev returned to the UK from Australia in October 1992 on Peter Ustinov's advice and joined *The European* as a staff columnist. That was followed by another spell in Australia before he returned to work in England again. He worked in Scotland and Ireland too. He seemed for a long time very much an exile in search of a home. In 1997 he was given a regular column in the *Guardian* that ran for about year under the title Outside Eye, a name – suggested by Roger Alton – that Vitaliev never liked because by then, he said, he no longer felt like an outsider. Nevertheless, the title fairly described the special perspective he brought to his work in the West. He wrote more than fifty Outside Eye columns.

[8] On Martin Walker's advice Vitaliev kept a diary of his last days in the Soviet Union. Large parts of it appear in his book *Dateline Freedom*, 1991 in a chapter headed The Cursed Days, a title taken from Ivan Bunin's record of his last days in the Soviet Union during the civil war that followed the 1917 revolution.
[9] Vitali Vitaliev, A political suicide that presages death, *Guardian* 22 December 1990.

One was prompted by the deportation from Britain of several hundred Romany people who were being sent back to former Czechoslovakia, to the Czech Republic and Slovakia. In noting their banishment from the somewhat idealised society that was Vitaliev's England at that time, he described from personal observation the appalling discrimination to which they would be returning. And he concluded, 'As a former refugee myself, I fully agree with Benjamin Franklin's pronouncement: "Where liberty dwells, there is my country" … Romanies had no future in the land where they lived. That is why they came to Britain. Like us, they have the right to freedom and the right to dance on a Tube platform without fear. Too late. Their train has gone, the station is closed, and the lights are out. They are left alone in the dark.' The contrast of light and dark was a recurring theme in his work, as was the sudden backward glance.

This was nowhere more evident than in the Outside Eye column he wrote on the death of Diana, whom he had met three and a half years earlier when she gave the impression of 'a caged animal or a troubled teenager.'[10] He was one, apparently among few, who smelled something not so sweet rising from the massed flowers in Kensington Gardens. 'Let's face it: the Princess of Wales was bullied to death – and not by the media alone. She was bullied by the society as a whole – the press, the politicians, the royal family and the crowd, the same crowd which is now shedding tears over her death and which – only days ago – greedily digested every bit of Diana gossip, thus boosting the fees of the hacks and the paparazzi. It was bullying on a national scale, for bullying, after all, is but a violent intrusion of privacy … The mentality can best be described as totalitarian, for robbing people of their private lives is the very first thing every totalitarian regime does after grabbing power … Diana, an unstable and confused Western woman … could not cope with this brutal force … A deeply vulnerable human being who had largely lost control of her life, simply couldn't survive a leering crowd of totalitarian bullies …' He concluded, 'Diana is gone. Who will be next?'

Just a little over a year later, Vitaliev wrote perhaps his most moving piece for the *Guardian*, beneath the headline Russia's Lost Soul.[11] 'My friend Galina Starovoitova, the soul of Russian politics, was gunned down in a dark doorway in St Petersburg on Friday night … Galina, the last example of decency in Russian politics, could no longer exist in a country where political murder has become the norm, where everything from a human life to a government can be bought and sold.' Vitaliev had first met her, a dynamic and indefatigable campaigner for minority rights, in London, oddly or appropriately on the day of the failed Communist putsch in Moscow, a failure they had seen as a rare cause for celebration. He had last met

[10] Vitaliev: Diana – bullied to the end, *Guardian* 8 September 1997.
[11] Vitaliev: Russia's Lost Soul, *Guardian* 24 November 1998.

her at a media conference in Istanbul taking what she called a short break from politics, just two months before she was murdered. She had told Vitaliev of her intention to contest the governorship of the Leningrad region. Was that, he wondered, the ambition that had cost her her life?

… As for Vitaliev himself, finally released and able to enjoy the freedom he had already tasted, he became a great traveller and a wonderful travel writer, immune from stereotypes and clichés …[12]

Ian Mayes is a former associate editor of the* Guardian *and was the paper's first readers' editor. He wrote this article about Vitali to include in* The History of the Guardian *from 1986 on which he was working at the time

[12] Only his second piece for the *Guardian*, Bike and Berlitz, 21 October 1988, was a scathing and very funny review of a book by Brian Hall, *Stealing from a Deep Place: Travels in South-Eastern Europe.*

Confessions of a Dromomaniac

A little intro to a bumper book

All through my childhood and youth in the Soviet Union, by far the world's largest country, I had been secretly preoccupied with little things. Purely out of the spirit of contradiction, I guess …

Our Soviet life was characterised by a severe case of megalomania on a national scale. Starting from kindergarten we were led to believe that our country was the greatest, the freest and the largest in the world (the latter was true, by the way). At school we were taught that Russia always conducted only just wars; that everything – from the wheel to the electric bulb – had been invented by the Russians; that all Russian writers (except for those who were banned or shot, of course) were great and cared for the 'common people.' 'A poet in Russia is more than a poet!' Yevgeny Yevtushenko once wrote. '*More*? Or *less*?' I couldn't help wondering.

The first powered aircraft, of course, was plagiarised by Wilbur and Orville Wright from the Russian scientist Zhukovsky. Wireless telegraph was discovered not by Guglielmo Marconi, but by Alexander Popov. The steam-engine was a creation of Ivan Polzunov's genius, and James Watt simply nicked his idea. And so on and so forth. By the age of twelve, a Soviet child could be forgiven for thinking that there was no real life west of Kaliningrad and east of Khabarovsk. I must confess that even at a fairly mature age, I used to experience serious doubts as to whether the Western world existed at all and was not just another KGB invention to keep the Soviet people on the alert.

As I have just said, there was one little grain of truth in this otherwise mendacious flow of indoctrination. With an area of 22,402,202 square kilometres, the USSR was by far the world's largest country, and that was a popular excuse for food shortages and inefficiency. 'You see, our land is so vast that we simply cannot provide for all hungry mouths, like they do in Switzerland, ha-ha.' Switzerland, for some reason, was a common butt of jokes and unfavourable (to Switzerland, of course) comparisons (luckily they seemed to be unaware of Liechtenstein or Andorra). Maybe it was because Switzerland was 543 times smaller than the Soviet Union. And 543 times more prosperous and efficient.

The very vastness of the USSR was the system's first, last and only real argument in its favour. Statistics might have been blown out of all proportion; 'elections,' even with only one candidate to choose from, might have been rigged, but one thing was indisputable: it was the largest country in the world. This added an aura of trustworthiness to heaps and heaps of meaningless propaganda.

A popular semi-official rebuff to growing pro-independence movements in the Soviet Union's smaller dominions (Estonia, Moldavia, Lithuania etc) was: 'How can you possibly exist without us, being so small? You simply won't survive on your own!' A typical Big Brother attitude. The fact that countries like Belgium, Iceland or Luxembourg not only survive, but even prosper was either forgotten or ignored (or both) as if none of them actually existed.

But we were not easily fooled. Every force breeds counterforce, as proved by one great Russian physicist and later repeated by Sir Isaac Newton. Very few were prepared to believe seriously in any 'final truth' the system was trying to impose on its seemingly submissive subjects. In fact, the harder it tried, the less we believed …

One winter day, when I was six, I saw a tiny yellow toy truck in a shop window on the way from the kindergarten, and froze in my step. My mother, who was holding me by the hand, froze too, which was not difficult since it was freezing anyway. With my nose flattened against the window, I stood there for a good half-hour, tearfully begging my mother to cough up. She didn't feel like coughing, despite the cold weather. I had lots of toys at home, and a whole fleet of almost life-size toy trucks among them. But this one was special: the size of a matchbox, it was all bright and gleaming, like a clot of condensed sunlight. I managed to persuade my mother eventually (I usually did), and triumphantly went home, clutching my (or rather my mother's) little purchase in my little hand, clad in a little *varezhka* – a Russian woollen glove with thumb but no fingers. The fact that the truck had two pairs of miniscule rotating wheels and could actually move added to my childish delight.

The sheer magic of motion. I didn't know then it was called travelling.

I would play with this toy for hours, until I got bored with it finally, and the beautiful mini-truck ended up in the pile of discarded toys in a big cardboard crate under my bed – its first and last garage.

As I grew up, my fascination with little things grew accordingly. Looking back now, I can see that this was most likely just a spontaneous, and often subconscious, protest against the officially cultivated gigantomania. As a boy I was addicted to midget tin soldiers, micro steam-engines and tiny 'one-tooth' lollies. My favourite book was Jonathan Swift's *Gulliver's Travels*, where the protagonist alternately travels among the Lilliputians or turns into a Lilliputian himself (in the land of giants). As a youngster I was keen on microscopes and the life of African pigmies. As a mature man (still far from a giant) I am attracted to small screen, short stories and (let's face it) diminutive (petite) women.

Having never suffered from illusions of grandeur, I nevertheless failed to avoid another mental disease – dromomania. Don't hurry to put me away in a psychiatric asylum: among all manias, phobias and brain disorders, dromomania is probably the most innocent. It is a *medical condition characterised by an irrepressible itch to travel.*

Journalists and writers are passionate travellers (read *dromomaniacs*) as a rule, and I am no exception.

I contracted dromomania at an early age, shortly after acquiring the miniature yellow truck, or so I guess. 'If you have the doubtful happiness of being born, you must at least see the world' – these words from Konstantin Paustovsky's romantic novel *The Black Sea* kept echoing in my soul. It was easy for Paustovsky to say … I suspect he was a dromomaniac, too.

I was gradually going mad (I didn't know that my madness had a medical name then). I collected maps and train schedules. I treasured a tarred wooden chip that I covertly peeled off a cargo car at a railway station. My parents didn't mind, only shrugged. I kept the chip in a special box which I would open and sniff from time to time: it smelled of journeys and adventures.

At school they would tease me for carrying this fancy snuff-box with me and nicknamed me Engine Driver. I was secretly proud of that nickname.

In the evenings, before falling asleep on my old-fashioned narrow bed, I would knock its nickel-plated leg gently (so as not to wake up my parents) with my knuckles: Ta-ta, ta-ta; ta-ta, ta-ta; ta-ta, ta-ta – to imitate the rattling of train wheels. I was falling asleep to the sweet music of the railroad.

Trains were so special to me simply because I travelled seldom. Forbidden fruit. I had no idea what freedom of movement was. Without knowing it, by the age of fourteen I had turned into a typical 'armchair buccaneer,' a vicarious traveller with no prospect of ever seeing the world.

The city where I lived could not boast any architectural masterpieces or historic monuments, apart from a regulation statue of Lenin with his outstretched hand pointing either to the bright future or, as local wits assured, to the nearest vodka shop. The only monument it could take some fiendish pride in was a huge railway terminal – an ugly, pompously decorated building, dominating the cityscape. Inside, on the walls and even on the ceiling, were frescoes in the best traditions of socialist realism: heroic workers and peasant women with bulging eyes clutching red banners in their sinewy muscular hands. This particular style of architecture and interior design was privately (in whispers) called 'Stalin Gothic.'

Indeed, the station building had something to do with Stalin. When, in 1951, 'The great leader and teacher' was travelling by rail to one of his dachas in the south and was passing through our city (there were usually three identical trains in the procession, and no one, not even Stalin himself perhaps, knew exactly which of them carried the paranoid dictator), he allegedly peeped out of the window and saw the old decrepit building of the terminal. 'What a disgrace to have a station like this in our socialist country! I don't want to see it again!' he remarked angrily to one of his aides in his broken Russian aggravated by a heavy Georgian accent.

A month later, when Stalin was returning to Moscow, the new grandiose station building was already there. The builders in their ardour (or rather fear) must have broken all-time records to construct the architectural monster which was destined to stand for ages as an impressive monument to totalitarianism.

Despite its ugliness and intimidating proportions, the railway station attracted me like an oversized magnet. Playing truant, I used to go there with my best friend and a fellow-dromomaniac, Sasha. We would stand on a wooden footbridge hanging above the tracks and gape at the moving trains below for hours on end, until our heads started spinning and we had the illusion that it was we who were moving, floating in the air above immobile trains.

It was from there that we ventured on our first real journey one day. 'Real' meant that we travelled on our own, without parents or any other adults to keep an eye on us. Of course, the whole venture was planned and undertaken in utter secrecy, under cover of a normal school day. It was just a forty-minute journey by a shuttle train, but to us it was no less dangerous and revealing than the first round-the-world voyage of Magellan. In line with the forced and all-permeating patriotic zeal, almost all whistle-stops on our way had the word *krasniy* (red) in their names: Red Village, Red Field, Red Corner, Red Excavator, even Red Whitewash, as far as I can recall.

We got off the train in the sleepy suburban town of Lyubotin, bought a couple of elderly, wrinkled meat-pies at the station and headed back. It was an unforgettable feeling – looking through the window of the moving (or rather crawling) train, chewing meat pies and being on our own.

I can still feel the oily smack of those cheap (and not very fresh) meat pies on my lips.

Our small and guilty Earth, in the form of a tattered old globe, stood on the bookshelf in my room. It might just as well have been the Atlas of the Moon. We had to be happy with what we had. Travelling, especially outside the country, was reserved for party functionaries and big shots – not little boys. In the well-oiled mechanism of privilege, the main moving force behind the system, this was one of the main gears. The corruptive value of a trip abroad was on a par with an out-of-town dacha or a personal Volga sedan.

We were all encaged. True, ours was the biggest cage in the world, occupying one sixth of the planet's territory, but it didn't make much of a difference to those who were inside it.

Much later, when already a journalist in Moscow, I was able to travel all over the Soviet Union. I would board a plane in Moscow and fly for ten hours non-stop, with my knees stuck in the back of the seat in front and someone else's sharp knees stuck into my back from behind ('prop my back and I'll prop yours' could be Aeroflot's official logo), only to disembark in precisely the same country, in an almost identical city somewhere in the Soviet Far East, with exactly the same buildings; the same newspapers, full of the same inflated lies; the same never-ending queues; the same downtrodden people with bleak expressionless eyes. It was mind-boggling.

I am lucky, at least luckier than most of my compatriots. Luckier than my father, who died prematurely in 1982 without ever catching a glimpse of the outside world. Luckier than Leonid Prudnikov, my omniscient University professor of English, fluent in eighteen languages, who also died young having never been abroad. Wherever I go, I am looking at the world with their eyes too. Wherever I travel, they travel with me.

Yes. I am lucky: in my thirty-odd years in the West not only have I travelled the world, I have even managed to buy a second-hand Volvo sedan, my very first car. Its colour was bright-yellow, like the toy-truck of my childhood. I happily smashed it against a fire hydrant during one of my first self-driving (ie without an instructor) drives in Melbourne, Australia. But that was not enough to disrupt my travels, which continue – in reality, or in the mind – daily.

I am now proud to report that from a 'good traveller' who, according to Lin Yutang, doesn't know where he is going to, I am slowly but surely turning into a 'perfect' one, who forgot where he had come from!

But it is up to you, my dear readers, to judge whether the latest transformation has really taken place. This collection of my travel stories will, hopefully, help you to make such a judgement. Or if not – it will at least offer you a good opportunity for the armchair travels of memory and imagination when – for one reason or another – you are unable to travel properly.

Happy journeys!

Vitali Vitaliev, August 2020

Part One
Travels on the Wrong Side of the Iron Curtain

'Pineapples in Champagne'

As a teenager in the old Soviet Union, I had a fascination with the poetry of Igor Severianin, an early twentieth century Russian symbolist, whose work was branded 'decadent' and 'anti-social' by Soviet officialdom. In all the seventy years of Soviet power, only a couple of his books were published. They immediately became bibliographic rarities.

I particularly enjoyed Severianin's collection of poems under the title *Pineapples in Champagne*, which, to me, did sound 'decadent' and therefore irresistible – largely due to the fact that pineapples in the USSR were as rare as snowstorms in the Sahara desert and as exotic as an Eskimo in the streets of Abu Dhabi …

I had my first pineapple at the age of ten at my friend's birthday party. His father had just returned from Moscow where he acquired this exotic tropical fruit from a street vendor after four hours of queuing.

We had never seen a pineapple before, only read about it in the poem by Vladimir Mayakovsky, which was compulsory learning in our school curriculum:

'Gobble up pineapples
And much hazel-hens –
Your final hours are approaching,
You vicious capitalist!'

The magic 'capitalist' fruit was cut into a dozen thin, almost transparent, slices – one for each guest. I will never forget the taste. How shall I describe it? Blissful? Divine? I didn't know the word 'orgasmic' then …

I had my second, third and fifty-fifth pineapples twenty years later, in 1984, when on a journalistic assignment to the town of Blagoveshchensk in the Soviet Far East, a ten-hour flight from Moscow.

Blagoveshchensk was a curious place. Situated on the bank of the Amur River, along which the border with China ran, it faced the Chinese city of Heihe on the opposite side of the river. From the room of my *Yubileyniy* Hotel, I had a clear visa-free view of Red China, just a couple of hundred metres away across the Amur. I could see ramshackle clay houses with small blast furnaces on the roofs – the aftermath of the Great Leap Forward when every Chinese household was forced to melt iron. It was seven years since the death of Mao Tse-tung, and the Cultural Revolution was effectively over. That's why there were no more 'lets-pull-together' slogans on the buildings, and the countless finger-shaped chimneys of the useless in-house furnaces were sticking out into the sky like peculiar phallic obelisks on the mass grave of human stupidity.

I could even see the people – all dressed in dark-blue or dark-grey fatigues and riding antediluvian bicycles. My first ever glimpse of the world outside the Soviet Union ... Although visa-free, it was not particularly inspiring.

The shops in Blagoveshchensk were as bare as everywhere else in the USSR. Probably even slightly barer. Practically nothing was on sale. 'Milk is available only to the sick in possession of a doctor's prescription,' ran the handwritten signs in shop-windows. But ... A couple of weeks before my arrival, a stray foreign freighter had been stranded in the town's port. She was carrying a load of Vietnamese pineapples, which were starting to rot. There was little choice but to unload all several hundred tons of this sensitive cargo in Blagoveshchensk and sell it through local shops. That was how the God-forsaken town – almost overnight – became the pineapple capital of the Soviet Union, if not of the whole world.

As a result of that sudden tropical windfall, pineapples were sold on every street corner. They were piled in the windows of all the town's stores, even bookshops. The air smelt of rotting pineapples, which became the main (and often the only!) component of the locals' diet. School kids were having pineapple sandwiches for their school lunches. Drunks in parks and gateways were munching on pineapples to chase their glasses of vodka – a substitute for herring and pickled cucumbers, not seen in Blagoveshchensk since the 1950s.

Whether I wanted it or not, I suddenly had to eat pineapples three times a day.

After a week of such enforced tropical diet my tongue felt rough and rigid as a piece of sandpaper stuck into my mouth. I was also suffering from a permanent thirst that was impossible to quench: due to the breakdown of the town's plumbing system, only boiling water was coming out of both taps in my hotel room.

It was then that I recalled the title of Igor Severianin's collection – *Pineapples in Champagne* – and decided to diversify my monotonous pineapple menu by adding a touch of 'decadence' to it.

The immediate problem was champagne – not just unseen, but also unheard of in Blagoveshchensk. Instead, I had to satisfy myself with a bottle of cheap sparkling plonk which I put into a permanently empty fridge in my room.

The fridge did a good job, and by the time of my ultimate 'decadent' experience, the plonk was frozen stiff, and I had to melt it by leaving the bottle on a hot windowsill for a while.

I chopped the pineapple into small rectangular lumps and tossed them into the glass. The plonk started bubbling and foaming. You can observe a similar chemical reaction if you drop a piece of chalk into a cup of vinegar. The chemical composition of the plonk was probably close to that of sulphuric acid.

Without waiting for the foaming to subside, I gulped the glass down, choking simultaneously on the icy plonk and on a pineapple chunk.

When I stopped coughing, I felt as if I had just swallowed an ice-cold grater, made of stainless steel. Yet I heroically, with a truly Soviet stoicism better known as stupidity, carried on with my 'decadent' experiment until both the plonk and the pineapple were gone. In fact, they didn't disappear completely, but – in accordance with the preservation of matter law – continued their boisterous struggle in my stomach throughout the night. By the following morning, their battle had reached truly revolutionary dimensions. A civil war between two utterly incompatible substances was under way inside my tummy. I had also lost my voice and was suffering from the severest flu I had ever had. Lying on my bed, I was sweating, shivering and moaning silently.

I was saved by the editor of a local rag who popped in unannounced for a courtesy chat. Having appraised the situation with one quick glance at the mess on the table and at my wriggling supine body that continued to be mutilated from inside, he asked briskly: 'What have you drunk?'

'Pineapples in champagne,' I whispered.

'Don't move!' he barked and rushed out.

Five minutes later, he returned with a bottle of vodka and a huge leaking packet of table salt. He poured vodka into a glass, added a generous handful of salt, stirred it violently with his rough, nicotine-stained index finger (I nearly threw up at the sight) and handed it over to me.

'Drink!'

I tried to protest, but he forced the glass down my throat.

A flash of lightning pierced my brain. A Krakatoa volcano erupted in my stomach. I don't remember how I reached the bathroom.

Two hours later I was cured and felt as fresh as a proverbial Russian cucumber. Looking through the window at the hardworking Chinese across the Amur River, I couldn't help feeling that they were laughing at me. They obviously had no idea of what 'decadence' was about …

Now you will understand why, when living in Australia, I had no problem resisting the mind-boggling displays of tropical fruit on street stalls and in shop windows …

My own fruity (if not fruitful) 'experiment' was a success after all: it taught me that good things should only be enjoyed in moderation and that overindulging in them could be ruinous and even life-threatening.

As Buddhists say, all in moderation, including moderation …

The memories of that fateful and near-lethal research into 'decadence' linger in my memory until now. Whenever I see a pineapple, I am reminded not of Igor Severianin but rather of Mayakovsky:

'Gobble up pineapples
And munch hazel-hens –
Your final hours are approaching,
You vicious capitalist!'

I now know exactly what he meant.

Chernobyl: Inside the Innermost Zone

Putting on my face mask during the Coronavirus pandemic, I often recall the only other occasion in my life when I had to have my face covered …

I visited the site of the Chernobyl tragedy several years after the disaster with a Channel 4 UK TV crew while making a documentary about Ukraine. The fact that my father, a nuclear physicist, died prematurely in 1982 of the long-term effects of radiation, added a special personal significance to that trip.

Sasha, a young local dosimetrist assigned to our film crew, was making a point of ignoring radiation and, with considerable bravado, refusing to wear a protective mask. With his every step forward, towards the grey bulk of the leaking reactor, his antediluvian Geiger counter showed great jumps in the level of background radiation. At times it was four to five thousand times higher than the accepted 'norm' of five micro-roentgens per hour.

I couldn't tear my eyes from the faded slogan crowning the building next to reactor number four: 'The victory of communism will come!' They had tried to paint over this tragically ironic slogan several times, but the stubborn white letters were still clearly visible through layers of paint. 'The victory of communism will come!' they were screaming.

Down below, shift workers fished patiently in the reactor's cooling pond. Even the normally unperturbed Sasha couldn't refrain from commenting acerbically: 'They must be mad! Eat that fish and you'll lose all your hair within hours.'

Channel 4 bosses were unable to insure our small crew of three (director, cameraman and writer/presenter, ie me) for that particular day of the shoot: no insurance company was prepared to give us cover for filming in one of the world's most dangerous places.

On arrival, we had to cough up $800 for the 'tour' plus a further $100 for each hour of filming. In addition to lunch and an English-speaking guide, the 'package' included a chauffeured Chaika limo. Usually reserved for top government apparatchiks, this particular vehicle was abandoned in the contaminated zone by some visiting dignitary: it was too 'dirty' (read: irradiated) to be taken back to the outside world. As I discovered, the Chernobyl tour was open to any reckless foreigner with a half-decent excuse for being interested. And with plenty of dollars of course.

We were granted a brief interview with an official from the Ministry of Chernobyl (there is such a Ministry in Ukraine), who told us, among other things, that the Chernobyl Museum had just opened in Kiev to publicise 'achievements' made in tackling the catastrophe.

Alcoholic Decontamination

At the entrance to the ten kilometre interior (heavily contaminated) zone, we were offered sets of baggy 'protective' clothing, which were merely pre-used battle fatigues. We were given face masks called *lepestok* (petal) to protect our lungs against radiation. The guide cheerfully informed us that within the ten kilometre exclusion zone the level of radiation was on average a thousand times higher than the accepted maximum, which made me think that the only outfit that could provide proper protection was probably a complete set of medieval knight's armour, lined with lead. We exchanged black jokes and nervous cackles, made even more uneasy by the knowledge that an even bigger radioactive leak than usual had been reported the day before our visit.

Chernobyl, we were told, leaked all the time.

Standing there, in front of the reactor, in my ridiculous khaki outfit and with a flimsy white mask over my mouth, I was confronted again with the frightening melodrama of the situation.

'If there's another explosion here, it would mean ultimate disaster, not only for Ukraine but for the whole of Europe,' the guide announced in a tone of unmistakable pride.

Earlier, at the entrance to the outer thirty kilometre zone, we had seen a busload of workers returning from their fifteen-day shift at the reactor. The workers were getting off the 'dirty' zone bus and boarding a 'clean,' decontaminated one to take them to the neighbouring town of Slavutich for a fortnight's rest. They literally fell out of the bus, drunk out of their minds.

Many reactor workers, it seemed, started working in a state of mild inebriation and continued drinking throughout their shift in the mistaken but officially encouraged belief that alcohol could fend off radiation. The realisation that Europe's future was in the unsteady hands of these drunken men and women sent shivers down my spine.

Deception

There was another old slogan in Pripyat, the nearest town to Chernobyl, half a kilometre away: 'Let us translate the historic decisions of the 27th Soviet Communist Party Congress into life!'

The 'historic decisions' had indeed been translated. Pripyat once had a population of 50,000, but it was dead and empty now. The explosion of reactor number four, which had affected fifty-five million people worldwide, was in some ways the last nail in the coffin of Soviet-style communism. The whole of Pripyat was evacuated in one day, thirty-six hours after the April 1986 explosion, though for most of the evacuees it was already too late.

As it has been revealed by the protocols of the Politburo's secret meetings, Kremlin bosses, instructed by Gorbachev, fell over themselves to keep quiet about what had happened. Ukrainian Communist Party leaders promptly reassured the population there was no danger, while hastily (and secretly) evacuating their own families from the Kyiv area. Had it not been for the Swedes, who noticed a sharp rise in radiation levels in their country and raised the alarm, the truth about the explosion might have been concealed for much, much longer, and many more people would have been lethally contaminated.

Pripyat was eerie.

The motor of our camera whirred on in utter silence.

Flowerbeds had vanished beneath thick vegetation.

In the town funfair, nestling between abandoned high-rise apartment blocks, the wind slowly propelled a rusty merry-go-round and leafed through the pages of the March 1986 issue of the children's magazine *Vesyoliye kartinki* ('Merry Pictures'), discarded beneath a park bench.

Here, was an overturned go-cart; there, a broken LP of 1980s Soviet musical hits trampled in the ground.

'Long live the First of May!' proclaimed the faded signs in dusty shop windows. The disaster happened on 26 April 1986. They had no time to celebrate 1 May in Pripyat, and they never will. Walking around this dead town, I could almost feel the radiation in the stale mosquito-ridden air.

I entered an empty pillaged flat on the second floor of one of the defunct apartment blocks, and froze. Its layout was a standard pre-fab Soviet type – exactly the same as my last flat in Kharkiv, another Ukrainian city where I lived as a child. The same corridor with door-less closets in the wall; the same crudely tiled bathroom; the same tiny kitchen with broken gas-stove and heaps of rubbish on the scratched wooden floor. It felt like trudging through the ruins of my childhood.

Flowers of Hope

Leaving the thirty kilometre zone, we passed through several villages, now populated by samosyoli ('self-settlers'), the people who had flouted every ban to return, by choice, to their contaminated dwellings.

In the village of Opachichi, an old wrinkled man offered me a glass of water from his well. Overwhelmed with gruesome impressions of the day, I stupidly drank it without thinking, and only then the realisation struck: what am I doing? I am in Chernobyl!

The old man spotted the fear on my face. 'Don't worry about the radiation, son,' he said, reassuringly. 'They have pumped it all out.'

Two weeks before, he told me, there had been a wedding in Opachichi – the first one inside the exclusion zone.

I looked up at the straw roof of his house, where a stork had built a nest – a symbol of procreation, an omen of life. The people who had withstood history's worst nuclear disaster, the people who chose to live and marry in the contaminated zone, the people who sincerely believed that radiation could be 'pumped out,' deserved such an omen more than anyone else.

Through the murky window of the ruined house of my childhood, I could see timid flowers of hope and life stubbornly breaking through radioactive rubble.

The Town that Didn't Exist

In the USA's National Atomic Museum in Albuquerque, New Mexico, which I visited while researching a book on America, I once saw a map of the Soviet 'secret cities.'

Collectively, these secret cities were known as *zakrytye administrativno-territorial'nye obrazovaniia* (ZATO), or 'post boxes,' and many were built by slave labour from the Soviet GULAG. During the cold war many of Russia's towns and cities, including some of its largest, were 'closed.' Anyone with a foreign passport was forbidden to enter, and many were even out of bounds to Soviet citizens. These closed cities provided the technical foundation for Soviet military technology including chemical, biological and nuclear weapons research and manufacturing, enrichment of plutonium, space research, and military intelligence work. Large numbers of highly qualified scientists and researchers were concentrated in these geographical areas, developing new technologies but isolated from the global research community.

Such 'secret cities' were known only by a postal code, identified with a name and a number.

To me, the map seemed incomplete for one simple reason: I spent the first three years of my life in one of the 'secret cities' near Moscow, to where my parents, young scientists (Mum – a chemical engineer, Dad – a nuclear physicist) and the newly-married graduates of Kharkov University, were dispatched in the early 1950s to work at a top-secret Soviet government facility, developing nuclear and hydrogen bombs. The town of 40,000 people – both unmapped and unnamed (it was referred to as 'Military Unit BA/48764,' or something similar) – was definitely NOT on the map.

I approached the Atomic Museum's Director and told him about the omission. He got very curious and asked how I could prove 'my' secret town's existence.

Of course, I didn't remember much from those distant years; I was too young.

But strangely enough I could recall some smells, vague impressions and feelings. I remember the chiming of church bells (the nearby town of Zagorsk was the centre of Russia's Orthodox Church – then heavily corrupted and KGB-controlled), black-robed priests, holy water springs in which the area abounded, and brand-new portraits of Stalin (who died one year before I was born), displayed in the windows of log-cabins next to faded icons of Holy Mary.

I can clearly evoke a walk in the wintry forest when I – for the first time in my life – saw a wild hare jumping away from us along the snow.

We lived in a so-called 'communal flat' having to share bathroom and kitchen with several other families.

One of our neighbours, an engineer who worked at my parents' laboratory, used to keep his motorbike in the corridor (our apartment was on the fifth floor of a standard block of flats, and there was no lift, so the motorbike owner had to drag his vehicle up the stairs every evening). That mechanical monster once fell on top of me as I was playing in the communal corridor. My screams must have been heard all over the town …

Because my parents were at work all day, they had to hire a child-minder to look after me. She was an ancient woman (*babushka*) in a kerchief and looked very much like Baba Yaga – a long-nosed witch from Russian folk tales who lives in a hut standing on chicken's legs.

Once, coming home from the laboratory, my parents saw the Baba Yaga with me in a bundle standing near the church and asking for alms to feed 'the poor little orphan' that was me. It was the 'orphan' bit of her whining mantra that must have offended my parents more than anything else (I don't blame them), and the begging Baba Yaga was sacked the same day …

I visited the town with my mother shortly before my defection from the USSR – in late 1989, after thirty-three years of absence.

The devilish 'facility' was still there. It was still located in the grounds of the old monastery, only instead of crosses, the factory buildings had faded metallic red stars mounted on the onion domes.

The town was still surrounded by the thick concrete wall with barbed wire. You could only get in through a couple of check-points, provided you had an invitation from someone living inside the compound.

A young military guard, having carefully scrutinised our credentials, gave us a one-day pass into my childhood and Mum's youth – equally constrained and repressed.

We were invited by a woman who worked with my parents many years before. She was the only person still alive of those who had worked with my father. The treacherous effects of radiation, dormant for many years, finally came to the surface and destroyed them all (including my Dad) one by one. And the woman herself? Yes, she was alive, but was no more than a skeleton covered with skin. In her late fifties, she looked at least eighty years old. Her hands were trembling incessantly, and her skull was practically bald. What a far cry from the smiling plump laboratory assistant of a girl on the old yellowish photo my mother had shown me. And, God, what a miserable life she led. Alone in the whole world, without any relatives or friends, she was dwelling in a tiny one-room kitchenette. Books were piled everywhere: on the bedstead and under the table. Among them – not a single romance or thriller, nothing that could pass as pulp or easy reading, but almost exclusively art, history or philosophy. She offered us tea and produced a small packet from the drawer saying it was her monthly ration. Having wasted all her life for the sake of the system, what did she get in return? A seventy-five-ruble pension, a tiny hole of a flat and one packet of tea a month!

But she said she was happy. 'I have lots of books and lots of memories – what else do I need?'

'The place hasn't changed a bit,' my mother noted sadly on the way back.

The early 1950s were tough. Stalin wanted to develop nuclear weapons by hook or by crook to achieve military parity with the West and then, ultimately, superiority over it. My parents had to work for twelve hours a day and there was practically no protection against the excessive radiation.

My mother recalled how skin peeled off her palms when she was pregnant with me (so I must have got my share of the stuff too). According to her, some of her colleagues literally expired in front of her eyes from overdoses, and my father was particularly affected, since he dealt directly with radioactive substances and often used to travel to 'Lemonia' – a secret nuclear weapons testing range in Kazakhstan. He died of a heart attack at the age of fifty-six. None of his co-workers had lived to see his or her sixtieth birthday …

How could I prove it?

I said to the Atomic Museum Director that I'd ask my mother to pen down her memories of the place and post them to him.

My Mum was then already living in Australia. She agreed to write some notes on the 'secret city' of her youth and started working on them.

Shortly after that she fell ill and had to be moved to a hospital.

Sorting out her papers in her miniature Melbourne bed-sit which she had left forever, I found several notebooks with her characteristic scribbles. Some of them were the Notes she had written for the Atomic Museum.

I've translated them into English:

'Zagorsk, 1951.

Winter. Early morning. I open the door to my laboratory. The room is lit up with some strange fluorescent light. Where is it coming from? The lead-lined fume cupboard contains retorts with radioactive substances, and it is they that emanate this weird light. My first thought is: 'How beautiful!' A colleague arrives, and together we admire the sight, not realising immediately that those fluorescent solutions carry colossal radioactivity doses. They were sent to us for research purposes from a range in Kazakhstan, where nuclear bombs are being tested. This highly radioactive glow accompanies us on most of our working days. The only 'protection' we have is a pair of rubber gloves …

Midday. We are staring at Geiger counters showing the quantity of radioactive particles in the substances that we analyse. Suddenly, all the counters go into 'red' indicating a massive radiation dose. Where did it come from? People from other laboratories complain in the corridors that their counters show the same picture, and everyone is concerned about the source. At this point, in the end of the corridor there appears Major Gramolin, a young and capable scientist, a recent graduate of Moscow Chemical Defence Academy. He is short, muscular and has a noble 'aristocratic' face of a Pushkin times hussar. He is dressed in a protective suit he wore while working in the contaminated (or 'dirty,' as we used to call it) zone of increased radioactivity. It was the radioactivity of his suit that has made our Geiger counters go crazy – despite the 'special' decontamination shower he had to take before leaving that horrible zone. His suit had to be incinerated. As for Gramolin himself, he died suddenly of a heart attack in his early forties.

Olya and Raya – two girls from Ukraine – worked as our laboratory assistants. They were sent to us straight from a Poltava comprehensive school. Olya was a tall green-eyed blonde, and Raya – a plump, short and brown-eyed joker. They both worked in a Drinking Water Decontamination Laboratory. Radioactive water was decontaminated with the help of a chromatographic column, and that was why they always kept three separate vessels with normal drinking water, radioactive water and water decontaminated in the column. Once – in a rush to get to the factory's canteen during a lunch break – the girls mixed up the vessels and drank some radioactive water. It was tragic. They were soon diagnosed with radiation sickness. Hospitals, disability and slow painful deaths followed.

I will never forget it, never!

A young colleague of ours, with whom we shared a communal flat, once brought home a Geiger counter to measure the radiation background. It transpired that all our personal belongings: clothes in wardrobes, cushions, blankets, even handkerchiefs were radioactive – the fact, however, did not worry us in the least. We were young and naïve, despite being scientists. Besides, what was the point of worrying when we lacked effective means of protection; our clothes and bodies were not properly decontaminated after work. Protection of the staff was never the authorities' concern: the only thing that mattered was the order of 'our great leader and teacher Comrade Stalin' to come up with the Bomb as soon as possible. After that, several of our co-workers, having armed themselves with dosimeters, measured radioactivity levels in the forest outside the factory (formerly, the monastery) walls. All the trees, the grass, the flowers and the ground were emanating the invisible deathly rays. It was the same in the residential part of the town only half a kilometre away …'

My mother passed away in Melbourne in 2006.

Vodka Travels in the USSR Part One: The Importance of a Glass

A Russian (or Polish) vodka-drinker will give anything for a glass. Even the most degraded of alcoholics wouldn't drink vodka from a bottle, for this would be like severing his last remaining connection with the breed of civilised humans. I don't know whose sick fantasy created the stereotype of a Russian (or a Pole) smashing his vodka glass against a wall after emptying it. A glass is too precious a commodity to be disposed of in such a barbaric way.

Here are a couple of real-life illustrations.

Once, waiting for a train at a Moscow railway station I got talking with a man who had just been freed from a labour camp, where he had served an eleven-year stretch for murder. At that time, I was researching an article about the appalling conditions in Soviet labour camps, and the ex-convict was an invaluable source. He happened to have a bottle of vodka on him, and he insisted we drank together as a precondition of a conversation. The only problem was where to drink it: we were in the midst of the Gorbachev-induced anti-alcoholism campaign when drinking in any public place could (if you were caught) lead to a hefty fine with subsequent loss of one's job. For my ex-convict friend this would almost certainly mean returning to the labour camp, a scenario to which he did not particularly look forward.

After a quick reconnaissance, it was decided that the safest place would be a stretch of railway track behind a stationary cargo train. We were about to uncork the bottle when a derelict red-nosed type, with two weeks' stubble on his hollow cheeks, materialised in front of us. 'Are you planning to have a drink, guys?' he enquired, hypnotising our bottle with his faded yellowish eyes. We mumbled something incoherent. 'You are not going to drink vodka from the bottle, like savages, are you?' he asked us, and without waiting for a reply to this largely rhetorical question, added, 'Give me one rouble, and I shall provide you with a glass!'

And although the type did not inspire the slightest degree of trust, although the ex-convict, who had had to imbibe glue and glass-cleaning fluid during his eleven-year incarceration, was clearly not a proponent of civilised drinking, we gave the type a rouble. Drinking tepid vodka from the bottle was out of the question, and the bottle was there waiting to be emptied. We didn't have a choice.

The type took the rouble and disappeared like greased lightning, having told us to wait. We waited for an hour, suspecting that he wouldn't come back. And he didn't, of course. The ex-convict blurted out a prolonged and hard-hitting burst of sophisticated underworld curses aimed at the unshaven liar (which would have definitely brought the crook to his knees had he been around), after which we said goodbye to each other and split up. The vodka remained undrunk, and the conversation never took place. What else could we do? We couldn't drink vodka from the bottle like uncultured brutes, could we?

The second incident took place at about the same time in Byelorussia, where I was sent by the satirical magazine *Krokodil* to write a 'rosy' piece glorifying the republic's achievements in procuring some food for its population at a time when the rest of the country was literally starving.

There was indeed some food in Byelorussia's shops (I remember being particularly impressed by the availability of two different sorts of cheese, whereas the shops in Moscow remained totally cheese-less). Throughout my trip, I was accompanied by the republic's minister of agriculture, who had kindly offered to let me travel in his chauffeured black Volga limo.

On the last day of our trip, the minister was visibly restless and agitated. He was looking around like a troubled bird, and kept winking at me conspiratorially from the front seat of the Volga. At last, after a visit to a collective farm near the town of Orsha, he leant towards me and whispered, 'Vitali Vladimirovich, do you feel like having a rest?'

I knew this was a euphemism for having a drink. On my journalistic missions I had to be careful not to fall into the trap of drinking with potential heroes of my satirical pieces who were only waiting for a chance to compromise me and to ruin my credibility. I remember one bureaucrat in the Zaporozhie region following me with a string bag full of booze wherever I went for three days. 'Let's have a drink, Vitali Vladimirovich,' he kept whining. Of course, I refused to be provoked: a written denunciation, substantiated with the photos of me drinking with a potential target of the article, would have reached Moscow before I did.

But this case was different: the article was to be a positive one. There was no immediate harm in drinking with the minister, except for the danger of being caught doing so in a public place (restaurants included), in which case even he would have lost his ministerial job before he could say '*Vashe Zdorovie*!' ('To your health!')

A popular joke of those times was about a director preparing to make love to his secretary on a sofa in his office. 'Have you closed the door?' she asks him. 'What for? We aren't drinking, are we?' he replies.

I agreed to have a drink with the hospitable minister and suggested that we should do this in the privacy of my hotel room. 'Are you mad or what?' the minister objected. He told me that several voluntary stooges were constantly on duty near the hotel. When they spotted a group of men with carefully wrapped parcels entering the building, they would wait for half an hour, and then burst into the newcomers' room without knocking. If they saw the men drinking, they would blackmail them: pay us a hundred roubles, or we shall report you to the management. Normally people paid the blackmailers off rather than risk exposure: alongside non-alcoholic restaurants (they were *all* non-alcoholic under Gorby), a hotel room was classified as a public place, too.

Having stuffed the Volga boot with booze and drink, on the minister's recommendation we headed for a nearby forest, which he thought was the safest place. It was late November. For a good hour we drove along a narrow forest path in complete darkness, with wild rabbits jumping from under the mud-covered wheels of our car. The forests are thick in Byelorussia. During the Second World War, they gave excellent shelter to the partisans, and the Nazis were scared of entering them. But we were neither Nazis nor partisans. We simply wanted to have a drink.

'Can't we stop here? It looks perfectly safe,' I said from time to time, like a tired child in the back of the car who keeps pestering his parents with the question, 'Are we nearly there?' 'No, it's not safe enough,' the minister would reply. For some reason, we communicated only in whispers.

Eventually, we reached the end of the forest path. The car could not go any farther. It was a real no-man's-land, and we could hear wolves howling somewhere close by, behind the bushes.

'It's OK,' the minister said to his driver. We climbed out of the car. The driver switched on the headlights and started laying food and vodka on the top of the boot. When everything was ready and we were about to 'have a rest,' it turned out that we had forgotten the glasses.

On the way back, none of us uttered a word. We could hear the unopened vodka bottles clinking merrily in the boot, as if they were giggling at us.

Vodka Travels in the USSR Part Two: The Soviet Version of a Driverless Train

I am often asked at parties and public talks to share my most incredible travel story – not an easy thing to choose after decades of (often purposeless) wanderings in over seventy countries. Yet, there is one episode that stands out.

The year was 1972 or 73. As a second-year university student in the Soviet Ukraine, I took a summer job (we all had to) as a sleeping-car attendant of the train that ran between Novorossiysk on the Russian Black Sea coast to Kaliningrad in the Baltics – a forty-eight hour journey.

Each carriage had two attendants working alternate shifts. My fellow worker, Mitrich, was an old man (probably in his late forties which seemed ancient to me then), with an amazing capacity for vodka. He drank two half-litre bottles three times a day, locking himself in his compartment and gulping each one down within the space of five to ten minutes. Then he would attend to his chores: checking tickets, sweeping the carriage floors and taking small bribes (usually in the form of vodka) from stowaways. A litre of vodka didn't seem to have much effect on him, though his normally expressionless eyes would start gleaming. 'Wine is bad for you, but vodka is very healthy,' he would say then. 'Doctors recommend it!'

Officially, the railway was a no-drinking zone. But this did not inhibit the staff on our train. The chief attendant, my boss, would routinely ransack the compartments of his subordinates in search of a drink and would confiscate (and consume on the spot) anything with an alcohol content: vodka, beer, perfume, shampoo, toothpaste or even shoe polish, which he used to spread on a slice of bread. Shoe-polish sandwiches were supposed to give you a mildly inebriated feeling (I didn't try one myself, mind you!).

One night, when I was on duty in carriage thirteen, smoking a cheap Cuban cigar (one of the unlikely consumer items from 'brotherly' Cuba that were never in short supply in USSR) so as not to fall asleep, a very drunk and unshaven man in a soiled railway uniform stumbled into my tiny service compartment. He said, stuttering, that he was an engine driver.

'Enjoying your holidays?' I asked him politely thinking he was one of the passengers in my carriage.

'Which h-holidays, you fool?!' he shouted. 'I am the d-driver of this very train! Let's have a drink!'

He then showed me his train driver's ID and a pocket logbook which left me in no doubt that he was telling the truth.

The train kept chugging ahead through the dark at a high speed.

Before I started to panic, the driver explained that he had left the engine on ATO as there were no scheduled stops for the next 200 kilometres. He also tried to calm me down by saying that his young assistant was still in the driver's cabin, 'in case of em-mergency,' although the latter was apparently so drunk that he couldn't even stand (or sit) upright and was sleeping on floor after they had celebrated his wife's birthday together.

'I hope his wife is not in the cabin with him,' I muttered to myself.

Having locked the delirious driver in my compartment, I dashed out in search of the chief attendant, who, luckily, was a bit less drunk than usual. Together, we dragged the semi-conscious driver all through the thirteen carriages back to his cabin. We woke up the assistant, who was indeed slumbering on the floor, lifted him, shook him well and installed him behind the train controls … I suggested we pressed the emergency stop button, but the chief attendant refused saying that it could affect his approaching salary bonus.

The train continued to fly ahead and reached the next station, at which the locomotive crew was replaced, without an incident …

If you look at me now, you'll see the mane of snow-white hair on my head. I can tell you with certainty – as I made sure myself, having looked in the cracked mirror above the sink in my carriage's smelly toilet the following morning – that my first ever grey hairs sprang up during that very night, on board that very vodka-propelled train rattling ahead unstoppably through the starry Soviet darkness …

The Zone of Fear and Hope

In November 2018, I briefly stepped back onto the 'wrong,' communist (read totalitarian) side of the Iron Curtain for the first time since my defection from the USSR. The Soviet Union as such no longer existed, but the so-called 'Democratic People's Republic of Korea,' better known as 'North Korea,' still did …

Several days before I sat down to write this feature, a sudden glimmer of hope appeared in the seemingly endless North-South Korea standoff: on 3 January 2018, after two years of lying dormant, a direct telephone hotline between the North and the South at the border village of Panmunjom was reopened for possible negotiations about North Korea's participation in the 2018 Winter Olympics in the South Korean province of Gangwon. There was even talk of a face-to-face meeting between the representatives of the two warring sides (for the truth is that, although the Korean War ended in July of 1953, North and South Korea are still technically at war, interrupted by the armistice agreement of 1953) – the first in a couple of years. As I am writing these lines, such a meeting already took place and North Korea's participation in the Olympics has been agreed upon – a real breakthrough the world had been waiting for!

The technical side of that unexpected change was limited to an ordinary secure phone line deemed a far safer option than internet communications. In general, it has to be said that, apart from the cutting-edge electronic surveillance and warning systems, the technology of the North-South Korea cross-border relations remains traditional, and, apart from the 'hot' telephone lines, is limited to good old loudspeakers through which both sides (particularly the North) keep pouring propaganda at their respective neighbours.

I was able to hear snippets of Northern loudspeaker-enhanced broadcasts, brought in by the wind, during my recent visit to the Demilitarised Zone (DMZ) – a 250-kilometre-long and four-kilometre-wide buffer, cutting the Korean peninsula in half. Those ecstatic, almost inhuman in their aggressiveness, sounds, were mixing with the jolly carefree rings, bleeps and jingles of the rides and merry-go-rounds of the funfair on the Southern side, from where I was listening – an amazing cacophony of confrontation and defiance.

The South, it has to be said, often responds in kind. In a recent episode, they bombarded the North with the loud recording of the latest K-Wave pop-music. As a member of the US Army military contingent inside the DMZ told me, the North Koreans hated the music so much that they pleaded for it to be stopped in exchange for turning down the volume of their own broadcasts in turn.

In 2016, South Korea, reportedly, purchased a new stereo system to outshout the North.

'The Mother of All Borders'

I can clearly visualise the historical 9 January 2018 meeting of the North and South Korean military envoys. It happened in the Joint Security Area (JSA), or to be more specific, inside the Military Armistice Commission Conference Building, the so-called 'Peace House' (the better name for which – until very recently – would be 'War House' of course) sitting astride the Military Demarcation Line – a paved narrow stretch of ground which leads to a row of blue United Nations huts straddling the border. Inside the 'Peace House,' this line runs straight through a small polished conference table dissecting it in the middle. I managed to stand on both sides of that permanently unattended (if you don't count the tourists) piece of furniture, marking the spot of the world's most volatile frontier, which, with the collapse of the Berlin Wall, has every reason to be called 'The Mother of All Borders.'

As Paragraph 1 of the July 1953 Armistice Agreement goes: 'A Military Demarcation Line shall be fixed and both sides shall withdraw two (2) kilometres from this line so as to establish a Demilitarized Zone between opposing forces.' Behind those dry lines – years of suffering and grief, thousands of separated families, hundreds of defectors on both sides (yes, in the 1960s, several American soldiers chose to escape to the North!) as well as killings and kidnappings. Among the defectors from the North, was twenty-two-year-old Russian Vasily Matuzok, a Soviet citizen and a trainee with the Soviet Embassy in Pyongyang, now living in California, who, in his own words, used his life's very first opportunity to escape to the West, when he sprinted across the border to the South Korean DMZ sector, chased by North Korean soldiers, firing Soviet-made pistols and AKMs at him, in 1984.

That was one of the very few 'lucky' escapes, with the main legacies of the DMZ remaining gruesome: fear and mutual distrust that still keep the Korean nation apart. That is why the initial peacefulness of my DNZ excursion was a surprise. Our coach rolled through the endless suburbs of Seoul and soon entered the DMZ, less than fifty kilometres away.

After the first Korean Army checkpoint, our coach drove across the so-called no man's land. In nature, everything is balanced, and while the buffer zone was literally dotted with the unexploded landmines from the Korean War and hence became a no-go area for humans, it had turned into a sanctuary for wildlife. Never before have I seen so many herons, cranes and other rare birds and animals. Hundreds of majestic wide-winged Siberian eagles were floating in the skies above our heads. I later read that Asiatic black bears, leopards, Goral sheep and the near-extinct Amur tigers have all rebuilt their populations in the DNZ.

At the same time, it was impossible to ignore countless watch towers and observation masts at hilltop points, from where South Korean, American and UN soldiers kept a constant lookout across the border for any signs of suspicious military activity.

I noticed some white-marked stones pushed into the endless wire fence along the road. Those were simple detection devices that would fall out if anyone tried to climb over.

Three passport controls later, we arrived at Camp Bonifas, the USA Army base just outside the DMZ. 'In Front of Them All' was written (with a touch of bravado) in large white letters on top of a round control tower dominating the Camp, named after the USA Army Captain Arthur Bonifas, one of the two victims of the so-called 'Axe Murder Incident' on 18 August 1976. On that day, the Camp commanders, having preliminarily agreed with their North Korean counterparts, sent a small group of soldiers and officers on a fairly mundane mission – to trim the branches of a tall poplar tree in the buffer zone next to the Bridge of No Return (through which POWs were exchanged during the war) which blocked the direct line of sight to the next Allied Forces checkpoint. Despite the agreement, they were brutally attacked by axe-wielding North Korean soldiers, who killed Captain Bonifas and his colleague First Lieutenant Mark Barnett. Three days later, the Americans returned in force and, backed by helicopters and fighter planes, completed the tree pruning.

Inside the 'Peace House'

Having received a thorough briefing from a couple of young American soldiers, both speaking with a distinctive Texan drawl, and having signed a somewhat bizarre Visitor's Declarations (see panel), we proceeded to the actual border line, from where we were able to eyeball a motionless North Korean officer in a vast Soviet-style peaked cap who was eyeballing us in return from on the steps of a grey and dull office building. 'We call him Bob,' US Army Private Earp, our guide, explained. 'And inside there's another dude whom we call Jack.'

He explained that more 'Bobs' and 'Jacks' were staring at us from the dimmed office building windows. I could almost feel their heavy unblinking stares on my face.

Private Earp then gave permission (which sounded more like a command) to take photos, having forewarned against using cameras with over 90mm zooming lenses.

We entered the 'Peace House,' guarded inside exclusively by the USA military policemen of Korean origins. Private Earp explained that they were all Taekwondo black belts and added somewhat mysteriously that as Koreans they were 'less likely targets in case of an attack.' 'But there will be no attack of course, and you are safe here with me,' he hastened to add with a smile.

Inside the building, I stepped over the invisible Demarcation Line and thus found myself *de facto* back in a totalitarian state for the first time since my defection from the USSR in 1990! The sensation was ticklish …

On the way back to the Camp, I asked Private Earp about the latest North Korean defector, who survived but had to undergo five operations at the hospital. 'We'll check him for being a spy, and if not, will give him citizenship, flat and freedom,' the soldier shrugged. Well, by all counts, it sounded like a risk well worth taking.

We toured a number of other DMZ 'venues.' Each had a regulation Souvenir Shop doing brisk trade in 'DMZ vinegar,' 'I've done the DMZ' t-shirts, DMZ chocolates, laminated North Korean banknotes, and such like. Interestingly, the plastic statuettes of North Korean soldiers on sale in those stores looked kindly, benign and even smiley. Those plastic good will ambassadors … And they were not the only ones around. I noted that South Koreans rarely spoke badly of their Northern neighbours. In a truly Buddhist manner, which requires to treat everyone, even your enemies, with *metha* (kindness), they talked about the northerners as parents about unruly children and would never forget to mention that yes, they (the North Koreans) seemed to truly love their leader; that their lives appeared to be improving, that in North Korea they didn't pay taxes and health care and education were free …

Not once did I feel an outright hostility, albeit most people would regard any prospect of re-unification with scepticism. To quote our DMZ Korean guide: 'There won't be war. Stock prices in the South are the highest ever. Businessmen would not invest in a potential war zone! In future we'll have co-operation with the North, but not reunification. Yes, co-operation as a precondition for co-existence is the most we can expect in the future!'

Touring the DMZ

Below, I will briefly describe several DMZ sites.

Infiltration Tunnel 3

In 1970, Kim Il-Sung, the Supreme Commander of the (North) Korean People's Army, ordered construction of two tunnels under the DMZ to be used for infiltration and possible invasion of the South. In September 1974, Kim Bu-seong, a North Korean military engineer, who defected to the South, said he was a surveyor on the construction of a tunnel underneath the UN Command Guard post on Mt. Dora and indicated the approximate path of the tunnel. The South Korean Army then drilled 107 bore holes deep into the ground and placed PVC pipes in each. Due to the use of granite-blasting explosives by the North Koreans, high-pressure charges of air were sent through the holes, and the pipes were promptly filled with water thus confirming the tunnel's location. Having established that, the South Korean soldiers started digging an interception tunnel. Knowing that their tunnel had been discovered, the North Koreans painted the sides of their tunnel black, rubbed coal dust on its walls and claimed that the South must have found an old coal mine.

This 1,635-metre-long and 2.1 metre-high tunnel, known as Infiltration Tunnel 3 (three more similar tunnels were eventually discovered by South Koreans), runs seventy-three metres below ground and is capable of letting through a division of 30,000 soldiers with their weapons within an hour. It is now a museum. Ironically, to keep it in line with safety regulations, it has been extended by South Korean engineers, and electric lighting has been installed. Tourists are now able to walk safely underneath North Korean territory.

Mt Dora Observatory and the 'Propaganda Village'

The Observatory is one and a half kilometres south of the MDL. A former UN Command guard post, it is now a civilian security education centre, with a briefing room and a diorama of the entire DMZ area. From an observation platform on the 2nd floor, equipped with powerful pay-for-view binoculars, visitors can clearly see the North Korean territory, including the outlines of Kaesong, North Korea's third-largest city, with its industrial complex, and the village of Kijung-dong, better known in the South as 'Propaganda Village' – a scattering of neat and permanently empty modern buildings, where lights are automatically switched on after dark making it obvious that the houses, designed to dupe the South with the picture of 'socialist paradise,' do not even have floors!

Above that real-life manifestation of the 'Potemkin Villages' metaphor, and next to the thirty-metre-high regulation statue of 'the great leader' Kim Il-sung, one of the 35,000 identical ones across North Korea, flies an enormous North Korean flag, which, reportedly, took fifty men to hoist. The flag is atop of a 160-metre-high pole, the third tallest in the world. Holding a 272-kilogram fourteen-metre-high and thirty-metre-wide banner, it is substantially taller than the competitive South Korean flagpole across the border.

The Bridge of No Return

This bridge crossing the MDL was the venue for POW exchange after the Korean War in 1953. It also features in a James Bond movie 'Die Another Day' (filmed elsewhere of course). The last time the Bridge was the venue for prisoner exchange was in 1968 when the crew of USS Pueblo, captured by the North, was released and allowed to cross back into South Korea. The use of the bridge was discontinued after the 'Axe Murder Incident' of 1976 (see above).

Dorasan Station

This northernmost station of the Gyeongui railway line (in the South) that once connected Seoul to China is only fifty-six kilometres away from Seoul and 205 kilometres away from the North Korean capital Pyongyang. Opened for traffic towards North Korea in 2007, at the time of the so-called 'Sunshine Policy' – a temporary thaw in the North-South relations under Kim Jong-Il, it was meant to become a working symbol of Korea's reunification. In 2016, the last freight and passenger services on the line came to a stop, and only platform tickets are now on sale in the station's solitary ticket office under a large 'Road to Unification' sign. The 'road to unification' so far remains the line of division, and looking at the empty track stretching into nowhere, I was tempted to brand Dorasan the saddest train station in the world.

Yet, who knows: with all the recent developments, it could be galvanised back to life in the near future and one would be able to board again a 10.21 train to Pyongyang!

* * *

We were leaving the Demilitarized Zone, to which Bill Clinton once referred as the scariest place on earth, and I had the last view of North Korea on the opposite bank of the Imjin River. There were trees on the Southern side, yet none on the opposite North Korean bank. Our ever-smiling guide explained that all the trees in the North had been cut and used as fuel …

The North Korean side, in stark contrast to the South, however, had plenty of the most beautiful mountains, clearly silhouetted against the setting sun. There was some vague and hard-to-explain hope in those mountains, which couldn't be used for fuel and were therefore indestructible.

Our coach kept rolling along smoothly through the burning sunset, towards Seoul …

Appendix: Rules and Dress Code for DMZ Visitors

From Visitor Declaration UNC REG 551-5:

- Fraternization, including speaking, making gestures or associating with personnel from the Korean People's Army/Chinese People's Volunteers (KPA/CPV) side is strictly prohibited.

- Visitors will not point, make gestures or expressions like scoffing, abnormal action which could be used by the North Korean side as propaganda material against the United Nations Command

- There is no drinking alcohol, and those who consumed alcohol in the last 12 hours will not be accepted …

The following civilian attire and accessories are strictly prohibited within the UHC MACHA:

1. Shirts/tops without sleeves or which expose the midriff
2. Ripped jeans or trousers which expose undergarments or private parts of the anatomy
3. Shorts or skirts which are shorter than knee length
4. Shower shoes, sandals or open-toe shoes
5. Oversized clothing or excessively baggy trousers
6. Sports uniforms, logos or athletic clothing of any kind
7. Umbrellas (except for during periods of precipitation)
8. Tripods (except for authorized media) …

Part Two
Travels on the 'Right' – Post-Communist – Side of the Freshly Lifted Iron Curtain

A Short Intro to Part Two

In 1995-96 I spent eleven months travelling around Eastern and Central Europe to research my book *Borders Up! Eastern Europe Though the Bottom of a Glass*, first published by Simon & Schuster. It was a journey not so much through the countries, whose old political borders had largely become blurred, ill-defined and often irrelevant, but rather through drinks – through vodka and beer, palinka and slivovitz, Zubrovka and Riesling, Tokaji and Cabernet Sauvignon – whose spheres of influence and areas of consumption were as stable and impregnable as ever before. By that time, for many Westerners, Eastern Europe had largely lost its attraction. At least under the communists it was different and hence exciting (so they thought). That kind of attitude prevailed among the Western travel writers, who chose to keep feasting on familiar clichés and stereotypes.

A stereotypical paragraph from a stereotypical Western travel book on Eastern Europe would read approximately like this:

> On a dull rainy morning, my Hungarian (Polish, Czech) unemployed friend Gyula (Stanislaw, Bohumil) kindly – for just a hundred US dollars, the equivalent of his salary for ten years – offered me a lift to Warsaw (Bucharest, Bratislava) in his dilapidated Skoda (Dacia, Polish Fiat). We are chugging towards the drab capital city along a bumpy, pot-holed dirt-track, lined with destitute prostitutes, prostituting destitutes and corrupt, bribe-seeking policemen in their grey uniforms. We drive past gloomy apartment blocks with peeling stucco on their facades and filthy washing hanging from the balconies. Hungry, skeleton-like children, dressed in rags, play in the debris and follow with their sad eyes the gleaming BMWs of the new rich and the mafiosi – with sub-machine-guns and rocket launchers sticking out of their bullet-proof windows.

And so on.

And although you might think this was a pretty adequate description of some parts of the 1990s Romania or Bulgaria, nothing could be further from reality, for Eastern Europe was then an extremely interesting and (yes!) exciting place balancing precariously – like a drunk on a tightrope – between the past and the future, between so-called socialism and the so-called free market, between the so-called East and the so-called West.

In an amazing twist of history, many post-communist countries were again ruled by the communists, who had been voted back into power by the very people who overthrew them. The post-communist hangover was being cured by a 'hair of the dog,' a proven recipe.

And although the communists, who used to call themselves 'communists,' started calling themselves democrats and champions of the free market, their mentality remained unaltered.

A traveller in the late 1990s Eastern and Central Europe had therefore a unique opportunity to watch the edifice of history being built in front of his eyes. If lucky, as I was, he might even be allowed to hold a trowel.

In Part Two you will find a small selection of my impressions of that fascinating world which was to be soon – finally and irretrievably – sucked into the whirlwind of Western consumerist society, like a fallen autumn leaf into a drainage pipe.

A Kick in the Baltics Part One: Talinn Unjammed

What a curious substance, human memory! It can be compared to an overflowing rubbish-bin, which our brain, this amnesiac dustman, chronically forgets to empty. Having forgotten many useful addresses, I still remember this one in Tallinn: 12, Sakala Street. It was there that the city's only camera repair shop was located in 1966, when our family was spending summer holidays in the Tallinn suburb of Pirita. At the age of twelve, I was already a keen amateur photographer and kept snapping right and left, especially on vacations, with my crude *Smena* photo-camera. When it started malfunctioning – due to over-exploitation, I assume – my mother and I had to have it repaired.

It took us hours to find the place.

Tallinn passers-by, whom we repeatedly stopped for guidance (due to an inexplicable Soviet paranoia, city maps were non-existent), would politely direct us elsewhere. We ended up criss-crossing the whole town before accidentally stumbling upon the blasted shop.

Unbeknown to us, we had found ourselves on the receiving end of the so-called 'passive protest' – the only way the natives of the Baltic republics of the USSR (Lithuania, Latvia and Estonia) could voice their angst at what they rightly perceived as the Soviet occupation: the three republics were forcibly 'annexed' by the Soviet Union in 1940 in the wake of the treacherous Molotov-Ribbentrop Pact.

Apart from sending visitors to the opposite end of town when asked for directions in Russian, the locals practised another form of the 'passive protest' by totally ignoring Russian speakers at a public place, be it a restaurant or a morgue.

The staff would simply look through you, as if you were an empty space, which once made my granddad, an old Bolshevik and the Civil War veteran, lose his temper. 'Russians and dogs are not welcome here, are they?!' he exploded in the face of a dispassionate doorman of a Pirita restaurant who had staunchly refused to take any notice of us.

Despite this obvious downside of holidaying in the Baltics, we used to do so often. It was the closest one could come to the West, still firmly out of our reach. In defiance of blatant 'russification,' the three small nations were desperately clinging to their national identities, languages and culture and kept surprising visitors from elsewhere in the USSR with higher living standards, civility and style they had somehow managed to preserve.

It was in Estonia, in the late sixties, that I had my first experience of a self-service 'supermarket' – an establishment unheard of in the rest of the Soviet Empire. The thing that baffled me most was a special shopping basket for every customer. 'How come the baskets don't get stolen?' I was wondering.

Among few other 'Western-looking' products, they sold jam in tubes. And although the jam, when squeezed (or, in my case, sucked) out, had a distinct taste of lead, I could not have enough of it and kept walking around with the tube protruding from my mouth cigar-like – as once captured on film by my mother, when I inadvertently allowed her to hold my faithful *Smena*.

All black-and-white snapshots of my childhood have been lost for good, yet many of them are so firmly imprinted in my memory that it only takes closing my eyes to bring them back to life. This is probably why I couldn't help the constant feeling of recognition during my trip to Tallinn and Riga, my first experience of Estonia and Latvia as independent states.

Tallinn, the capital of Estonia, to where I returned after thirty-odd years of absence, was covered with melting snow, and thawed patches of black earth were showing through the white slush here and there.

Like in my childhood photos, the city was all black-and-white!

And not just in terms of colour. Whereas Russian signs, cars and monuments have disappeared completely, it was Russian that most people in the streets were fearlessly speaking.

The 'passive protest' has gone. In a free market society, ruled not by a dogma, but by the mammon, it was unnecessary. Money speaks no languages, except for the language of profit – its own internationally accepted Esperanto. It has no prejudice, except for that of a class.

The predominance of Russian speech in the streets of Tallinn, where only about forty per cent of the population were officially Russian-speaking, could be explained by the fact that Estonians are generally taciturn and, like their neighbours the Finns, prefer meaningful silence to idle verbal exchanges. No wonder if we remember that Estonian, a tongue-breaking Finno-Ugric language, has fourteen case endings; two different infinitives, yet just one word for 'he' and 'she'; no future tense, and, to cap it all, something called 'the partitive plural.'

This is not to mention ubiquitous double vowels and consonants, as if the alphabet itself suffers from a chronic stutter.

Tallinn's Old Town, where my five-star Schossle Hotel was located (it was skilfully built into the robust frame of a thirteenth century mansion), remained one of the best-preserved in Europe. And one of the cosiest too. There were amazingly few cars, and parking was hardly a problem.

With the proliferation of well-stocked shops and brand-new restaurants of all imaginable cuisines and with prices four to five times lower than in London, modern Tallinn had few visible signs of poverty, endemic to most European capitals.

Crumbling and neglected in Soviet times – it is now a secret tourist paradise, a living proof of the creative might of capitalism.

In this all-embracing and somewhat idealistic world, a place was found for The House of Russian Culture – a grim 'Stalin Gothic' structure in Mere Street. Inside, one can spot the Soviet national emblem – the last remaining in Estonia, and the sullen-faced patrons still addressing each other as 'Comrade.'

'Undress! Are you deaf, or what?! Undress immediately!' Piotr Nikolayevich, an old, ruddy-faced doorman of the 'Ostap' restaurant bellowed (in Russian of course) at an unsuspecting Estonian, who tried to sneak inside in his overcoat ('*razdet'sya*' – 'to undress' in Russian means both 'to strip naked' and 'to take off one's coat' – the doorman obviously meant the latter). I thought that his manners and appearance betrayed an ex-Soviet serviceman, possibly a KGB officer, and I was right.

'We were sent here in 1946,' he said, having finally dragged the coat off the recalcitrant Estonian's shoulders. 'Stalin told us: stay here and serve our Motherland – and that's what we did: stayed and served for fifty-odd years …'

For patrons of 'Ostap', irrespective of their nationality, there was no danger of being ignored by this vigilant doorman, for whom every deposited coat meant a tip.

Standing on Toompea Hill, I was looking down at Tallinn's impressive panorama, mentally comparing it with my long-lost photo, taken from the same spot thirty-five years ago.

At first glance, little has changed, and the main landmarks: tiled Gothic roofs; church-spires; the guard towers Fat Margaret and Kik in de Kok (Peep into the Kitchen); the medieval Town Hall, topped with the weather-vane figure of Vaana Toomas (Old Toomas), Tallinn's main mascot, were still in place – as was the Soviet-style railway station (railway stations all over the world are resistant to change).

Yet something was definitely missing. I recalled that my old photo had been largely ruined by three tall ugly masts sticking out of the ground and spoiling the view. Those were special jamming towers built by the KGB to interfere with 'corruptive' radio and TV broadcasts from neighbouring Finland – just eight miles away across the gulf (the fourth one was hidden inside the spire of the magnificent twelfth century St Olaf's Church!). The town's tallest structures, they were eye-sores in more than one sense: the over-intensive round-the-clock jamming was also affecting the quality of reception of the politically correct programmes from Moscow, and the picture on the locals' TV screens was constantly blurred and jumpy.

The towers had gone, and the vision and sound on all twenty-odd TV channels (a couple of Estonian, a dozen German and only one Russian) in my hotel room were crystal-clear, although at times I wished they were not. Estonian news featured such ground-breaking stories as:

- Tallinn Mayor's (unofficial) visit to a well-known striptease bar, also housing an underground brothel. 'But there was no show there that day,' he said when confronted.

- Estonian Prime Minister using the photograph of the opposition leader as his target during a shooting exercise. Unlike the hapless Mayor, the Prime Minister admitted the misdeed and publicly apologised.

And so on. In despair, I flicked over to the Russian channel, on which a professorial bespectacled weatherman was delivering a forecast: 'Tomorrow the temperature will fluctuate between five and zero degrees, snowfall is not excluded, but if a woman becomes pregnant she can rely on Pregnavit!'

It took me a while to realise that they have turned the weather forecast into a commercial, at which point I felt a momentary pang of nostalgia for the jamming towers of yesteryear!

A Kick in the Baltics Part Two: Baker Street, Riga

'…but what am I going to do with fallen yellow leaves in the park? …'

The poignant refrain of a song, performed by a Russian busker, was echoing in the freshly painted Art Nouveau facades of Riga's Old Town …

It was late afternoon in March. Stray cats were copulating frantically on time-beaten cobbles. A plush Volvo of the latest make was crawling up a narrow lane squeezing itself into the gap between houses like a gleaming dagger into a tight sheath.

The sedan's owner must have been wealthy enough to afford paying 5 Lats (£5,50) per hour for entering the Old Town. He obviously did not belong to the Russian busker's metaphoric 'fallen leaves' – those by-passed by Latvia's post-Communist boom.

Or could it be that by 'yellow leaves' the busker meant his numerous fellow-Russians (sixty per cent of Riga's population are officially Russian-speaking)? Indeed, Russians in Riga have been turned into an overwhelming ethnic minority.

Even menus in Russian restaurants were printed exclusively in Latvian, the republic's only official tongue. Russian schools were being closed down at an alarming rate, and a respected Riga publishing house had launched a students' competition for the best project for the Russians' deportation.

Such nationalistic excesses could be partly explained by the fact that out of the three Baltic republics of the USSR Latvia had suffered most from 'russification.'

By the 1980s, Latvian language and culture were on the verge of extinction, and some drastic measures were needed to galvanise them after independence.

Latvian nationalism was like a forcefully depressed spring: the tighter you press it (and the longer you hold it) – the higher it will jump when released.

My old photos of Riga were much clearer in my memory than those of Tallinn.

I often came to Riga on holidays and on journalistic assignments in the 1980s. During one of those assignments I met Borya, a Riga-born satirist of Jewish origins, who had become one of my best friends.

The hotel, where I was put up, had no water (hot or cold), and Borya kindly offered to let me to stay in his flat, located in an exclusive apartment block for party functionaries in Lenin Street.

Not a functionary himself, he lived there courtesy of his mother-in-law, who worked at Latvia's Communist party Central Committee.

Ironically, this house was now an equivalent of a council estate, inhabited by the poor.

Its smelly littered courtyard was the only place in Riga where I spotted a dozen rusty Ladas.

As for Borya, he lived in Israel with his family (including his once influential mother-in-law).

Lenin Street had been renamed Liberty Street, and 'Shalom,' a small Jewish restaurant, was doing brisk trade in the basement of the house next to Borya's – a little Israel on his former doorstep.

Unlike Borya, his elder brother Sasha still lived in Riga and had the official status and passport of an 'un-citizen,' due to the fact that his parents 'only' came to Riga after World War II.

His whole salary went on rent, and he had to rely on his wife's casual earnings to survive. A 'fallen leaf' in the blooming park of capitalism, Sasha still spoke about 'us' and 'the West,' not realising that 'the West,' with all its pros and cons, had returned to Latvia after fifty years of exile, and he had found himself there without emigrating.

Jauniela, a quiet and unremarkable Art Nouveau street in Riga, used to be the Soviet Latvia's most photographed site (I remember using a whole roll of film in it once).

The reason was simple: the hard-currency-starved Soviet cinema industry chose it as a natural film location for the movies set in the 'decaying' West.

It was there that Sherlock Holmes' Baker Street flat from the popular Soviet TV serial was located.

It was there that Geneva and Berlin-set scenes of *Seventeen Moments of Spring*, a blockbuster spy-thriller, were shot by the inventive Moscow film-makers.

All it took was removing the 'Let's Pull Together' slogans from the facades, sweeping the pavement – and bingo – 'the West' was there, with all its seductively un-Soviet neatness.

The most photographed Riga attraction these days was the Freedom Monument, also known as Milda – Latvia's own Statue of Liberty.

Built in 1935, it survived untouched all fifty years of Soviet domination, even if those who ventured to lay flowers to it were whisked away to the nearby KGB headquarters.

The monument was undergoing a face-lift and was covered with scaffolding. Looking at the solid wooden box, hiding bashful Milda from public view and trying to remember what she looked like, I had to summon up in memory another old photo of mine which featured the statue of a graceful Latvian girl, holding three stars, representing three provinces of Latvia, high above her head.

I was hoping that Milda would emerge from under the scaffolding in all her unscathed beauty – as she once appeared on one of my black-and-white holiday photos.

Only after re-visiting the Baltics, I no longer saw these photos as black-and-white: they had gained colours – the dazzling and often conflicting colours of the free world …

Pub-Crawling in Prague

Some countries take a perverse pride in their beer-drinking statistics. The Germans maintain that they consume 251 pints per head a year, the Danes 225 pints, whereas the British average intake is a modest 180. The indisputable leadership here, however, is claimed by the Czechs, each of whom (including new-born babies and octogenarians), allegedly, gulps down a staggering 283 pints, or 150 litres, of beer annually. And although Bavarians assert that their per capita average consumption is 350 litres, we have to take into account Australian visitors to the Bierfest, whose contribution to the overall Bavarian figure, as witnessed by myself, must be close to ninety per cent.

I was looking forward to my time in the Czech Republic not so much because of its beer-drinking records, but rather because former Czechoslovakia was the first ever foreign country I visited while still living in the Soviet Union. The impressions of that trip in 1986 could be best described as shopping shock. I was stunned by the abundance of goods in the shops, by the fact that beer was always on sale and could be acquired easily – almost without queuing. I remember bringing proudly back to Moscow such flagrantly Western souvenirs as chewing gum, chocolate Easter eggs and strawberry-flavoured milk powder. For months after the trip, I was a welcome guest in many a Moscow flat on the condition that I shared with the hosts my impressions of the Czechoslovakian paradise and some of the milk powder, too.

Interestingly, a couple of my London friends who visited communist Czechoslovakia at approximately the same time, from the other side of the Berlin Wall, were genuinely appalled by 'near absence of everything' (in their words), unsmiling people and never-ending queues. What better proof of Einstein's theory of relativity?

An old Soviet joke makes the point even better than Einstein. An American and a Russian head off to Paris from their respective countries. By mistake, both end up in Prague (Warsaw, Budapest, East Berlin etc), and both think that they have reached their destination.

Czechoslovakia had changed a lot since my last visit. After the KGB-inspired 'velvet revolution' of 1989, it was no longer communist; and after the 'velvet divorce' from Slovakia in 1993, it was no longer Czechoslovakia, but simply the Czech Republic.

If formerly I was advised not to speak Russian while in Prague (after the events of 1968, the locals were not exactly head over heels in love with Russians – and I didn't blame them), now a Prague-based Russian friend instructed me to speak exclusively Russian to taxi drivers as the best guarantee against being fleeced. 'If you speak Russian, they will think that you are a member of the Russian mafia and will be afraid to charge you a fortune,' he said. I did speak Russian to a glib taxi driver who picked me up at the station, but ended up being taken for a ride anyway. Having paid 350 crowns for a two-minute lift, I consoled myself that it was due to my total lack of resemblance to a Russian mafia gangster.

Post-communist Prague is a robber-city. Especially if you are a foreigner. They charge you 60 crowns (about $2) for a glass of watery orange juice or for a cup of decent coffee with an 'all-inclusive' hotel breakfast (the coffee that *is* included tastes like bad orange juice). They charge you extra for washing your hands at a public toilet. They make foreigners pay up to ten times the locals' fare for visiting the same tourist attractions. What's worse, they try to camouflage this injustice in a rather clumsy way.

Fluent in Russian and Ukrainian, I had no problem reading Czech street signs. I wished I had. Walking in Prague's Old Jewish Quarter, I spotted the following sign – in English and in Czech – near the entrance to the Old New Synagogue:

The Old New Synagogue –	**adults – 150 kc**
	children – 100 kc
Staronova Synagoga –	**dospeli – zdarma**
	deti – zdarma

As you have probably guessed, '*dospeli*' means 'adults,' and '*deti*' means 'children.' What you might not have guessed is that '*zdarma*' means 'free.'

In other instances, they would indicate the foreigners' fare in figures (340 kc for 'entrance to the Jewish Quarter,' say) and the locals' fare in Czech letters: *padesat* kc – fifty crowns for the same 'entrance.' A simple, yet pretty nasty, ruse.

Yes, in the ten years since my last visit, Prague had become an exemplary capitalist city, where everything was on sale, including human flesh. Every newspaper kiosk prominently displayed a glossy pinkish brochure, enticingly entitled *Prague Sex Guide*, in three languages, featuring photos of naked women with languorous raunchy eyes, and brothels with names like Club Apollon ('entrance includes a complimentary bottle of champagne'), Satanella ('designed to look like a hospital room, contains a chair with stirrups, and all the necessary tools for fantasy clinic sex') and Lotos Club ('if you wish to indulge, there are plenty of beautiful girls to choose from – the one you pick will take you to a tastefully decorated private room, the best of which is a jungle-theme room with a particularly large whirlpool bath'). To be on the safe side of AIDS, the Sex Guide provided potential clients of Prague brothels with such useful tips as 'A sore or chafed penis dramatically increases your risk of infection' and 'If you have any cuts on your fingers, don't insert them into your partner.' Nice and clear.

Don't get me wrong. Prague is still breath-takingly beautiful, and the new spirit of Western commercialism has added some entrepreneurial buzz to its narrow cobbled streets, lined with old baroque houses and churches. Baroque architecture, by the way, strikes me as somewhat beer-inspired: this extensive ornamentation, this profusion of curved and interrupted lines, these heavy and solid – almost stout – facades, this beer-foam-like multitude of cupolas and turrets … And isn't it true that the best examples of baroque can be found in beer-loving countries? Please correct me if I am wrong (which I probably am).

Let's get back to beer, as Australians say. As a reluctant beer-drinker, I made sure I memorised one very useful Czech expression, '*Uz nepiju*' ('I don't drink any more') before starting my pub-crawl. Saying that I didn't like beer in a Prague pub would have been tantamount to confessing to being impotent in a brothel.

Of course, my starting point had to be U Fleku, Prague's oldest and most famous beer hall, which has been brewing its own dark and strong brand Flekovsky Lezak since 1499. I am not sure about 1499, but when I came to U Fleku in 1986 during my first foreign trip from the beerless Soviet Union, I was seriously worried that they would run out of beer before I had time to be served. I also remember that the pub was full of swinging and mug-wielding East Germans.

U Fleku was easy to find. An uninterrupted line of neatly parked tourist buses led me to its entrance from Karlovo Namesti. Just as ten years before, the place was bursting with tourists, mostly Germans, although this time there were streaks of Americans and Japanese among them. A musician, dressed in the military uniform of the times of Good Soldier Svejk, was playing an accordion in one of the cavernous rooms. Just as I had ten years ago, I went out into the beer garden. It was cold outside, and the long wooden benches were half empty. Only some cold-resistant Scandinavians and several legless Germans were there. I sat next to a drunken German sugar daddy snogging his blonde and red-eyed young girlfriend. She was massive – Brünhilde-like – and had a thick bovine neck. They both stank of beer.

Somewhere from above there came a voice '*Pivo*?' ('Beer?'). It was the waiter, and I suddenly realised why in the Czech Republic and in Slovakia they call waiters *Pan Vrchny* (Mister Upper). U Fleku's Mr Upper, sporting a short-sleeved white shirt under a black vest, was towering above me holding an enormous tray with several dozen beer mugs on it. His question was rather a rhetorical one: why on earth would someone come to U Fleku, if he didn't want beer? To play snooker? To board a flight to Bratislava? Or to scribble away in a WH Smith recycled notebook, as I did?

Thump! A weighty mug with dark brown liquid landed on the table in front of me. It was followed by Mr Upper's dexterous hand which made one quick notch on a piece of paper, stuck under my coaster. Before I could say '*Dekuji*!' ('Thanks!'), another Mr Upper's hand was stretching towards me with a shot of Becherovka liqueur. But I was well prepared for the trick. Gently pushing his hand away, I told him resolutely '*Ne*!' ('No!'), as the Pub Etiquette section of the *Prague Post* newspaper advised.

'*Perche*?' Mr Upper asked in unexpected Italian.

'Because I don't want it!' I replied in English.

'But it is very good with beer,' the obstinate polyglot insisted.

'I don't think so. Take it away!'

The reason for Mr Upper's persistence was that they charged you 200 crowns (£5) for a shot, the price of a three-course meal (with beer) in a good Prague restaurant, whereas a 0.4 litre mug of beer at U Fleku was 'only' 39 crowns – by far the most expensive in the Czech Republic. Besides, contrary to Mr Upper's assurances, mixing the vomitingly sweet Becherovka with beer was like eating a pickled herring topped with raspberry jam. Ten years ago they didn't do this to unsuspecting tourists. Capitalism can sometimes be pushy.

I took a couple of sips from my mug and found the beer surprisingly pleasant. Its bitter-sweet taste reminded me of kvass, a drink of my Ukrainian childhood. Kvass is a mildly alcoholic (not stronger than yoghurt) drink made of yeast and black bread. It is the same dark brown and is – or used to be – sold by fat Ukrainian women from huge yellow tanks on every street corner. I stopped drinking kvass when one day I saw a tank break into two and all its contents pour out on to the asphalt: the streams of brown kvass were swarming with white intestinal worms …

Meanwhile, my neighbours were busily gulping their Becherovkas, washing them down with beer. Several happy Mr Uppers were hovering above them like butterflies, and the rows of pencilled 'notches' on their beer slips were as thick as hedges in Devon. A group of German students at the next table tried half-heartedly to sing, but quickly gave up. The sugar daddy was quarrelling with his bovine-necked Brünhilde, whose face was by now pretty bovine, too.

The famous U Fleku, which claims to be the oldest beer pub in the world, was clearly no longer a place where one could find much local colour.

Not far from U Fleku, in Kaprova Street, I spotted a small pub called U Mestkiy Knihovni (At a Local Bookshop). What an ingenious name! Imagine an angry wife questioning her wayward husband: 'Where have you been all evening?' 'At a local bookshop,' he answers meekly. In Finland, by the way, they have gone even farther in pacifying angry wives: they have pubs called At My In-Laws and At My Brother's. The best pub name I have ever seen was in Scotland: The Why Not?

I didn't venture into A Local Bookshop, but through the window I could discern several fat, red-faced men drinking beer. And not a single book!

My next destination was U Pravdu, which translated as The Truth. My guidebook promised a nice beer garden and a convivial Svejk atmosphere. The beer garden was closed (it was too cold to sit in it anyway), the pub was totally empty, and this was the whole truth about The Truth.

I was luckier at U Cerneho Vola (At a Black Ox), although the name of this pub near Prague Castle would have been an immediate give-away for a beer-loving husband.

The atmosphere inside the pub was warm and brotherly: under low, beamed ceilings, the patrons were sitting next to each other on long dark-wood benches.

They were drinking Kozel (Goat) beer and chasing it with traditional 'Pivni syr,' a strong, spicy goat cheese. The balance, as I soon discovered, was perfect: my mouth was set on fire after each bite of the heavily peppered cheese, and the only way to put the flames out was to wash them down with a good gulp of Kozel. The man next to me had six notches on his slip already, and was thirstily approaching his seventh. A large mug of beer cost just 8.40 crowns (about 20p) – a big difference from U Fleku.

Through a small leaded window, I could see the palatial Foreign Ministry building across the road. It was there, in the courtyard, that the dead body of the country's democratically elected President Jan Masaryk was found beneath an open window on 10 March 1948. It was officially announced that he had killed himself by jumping to his death. Interestingly, the first doctor to arrive at the scene also committed suicide a fortnight later.

The death of Masaryk was the final episode in the communist takeover of Czechoslovakia. Rather than a suicide, it was the last (so far) case of a centuries-old Czech political tradition of defenestration (from the Classical Latin 'fenestra' – window), which means chucking an undesirable politician out of a window and making it look as if he has taken his own life. The first defenestration, a collective one, was in 1419, when several over-zealous Prague town councillors were hurled out of their office windows by a group of bullish religious reformers. Since then there have been three more (including the famous one during the Thirty Years War – uncannily similar to that of 1419 – and, of course, Masaryk's). In August 1996, the Czech news agency CTK reported that two Chinese men were tied up and thrown from the ninth floor of a block of flats in Prague, but both survived, which showed that the age-old defenestration tradition was very much alive.

Who is going to be the victim of the next great defenestration of Prague? It is hard to say, although when I was there many Czechs were inclined to believe it was likely to be Vaclav Havel, beer-loving former dissident, playwright and incumbent President of the Republic. Some time ago, he even won the honorary (if somewhat dubious) title of The-Most-Likely-to-be-Defenestrated Person in Prague.

After a mug of strong, pale Kozel, I started clearly seeing human bodies – in suits and ties – flying out, one by one, from the Foreign Ministry's windows. I needed a cup of coffee.

'What will happen if I order a coffee here?' I asked my beer-swilling neighbour, who happened to speak some English.

'They will think that you are an alcoholic,' he replied, finishing off his tenth mug.

The Inglorious End of Bohumil Sol, the Father of Semtex

In June 1997, I read in a London newspaper about a suicide of a sixty-three-year-old Czech by the name of Bohumil Sol. He chose an unusual way to die: by blowing himself up in a psychiatric sanatorium where he lived. The reason? The hospital personnel tried to stop him firing off rockets that scared his fellow patients and aggravated their condition.

Who was he? A jingoistic arsonist? A suicidal madman? An infantile pyromaniac with a crazy hobby of blasting holes in the frozen Labe river? Yes, he was all these – and more. Bohumil Sol, the former Czechoslovakia's leading explosives expert, was also known as 'the father of Semtex.'

I don't have to explain what Semtex means: every British (and especially Northern Irish) schoolboy has this word at his fingertips. Just a couple of reminders to refresh your memory.

The favoured plastic explosive of terrorists worldwide, including the IRA, Semtex has always been produced exclusively by the Synthesia (formerly Explosia) factory in the East Bohemian city of Pardubice, about a hundred miles east of Prague. Along with Pilsner Urquell and Budvar lagers, Semtex remained one of the best-known Czech trademarks and export items. Unlike the famed beer capable (allegedly) of reaching the remotest parts of human body, Semtex is capable of blowing this very body apart. The Pan Am flight over Lockerbie was destroyed by Semtex, of which more than a thousand tons were sold to Libya in the late 1980s. Thousands of tons went to Iraq and North Korea. It was used in many IRA bombs on the territory of Britain and has taken hundreds of innocent lives. Not much is needed. Experts say a piece of Semtex the size of a fist would blow a hole in the side of an aircraft.

In 1991, Synthesia was forced to add to the explosive a chemical almond-like 'smell' that can be detected by airport security machines, but, miraculously, the stocks in terrorist hands remain odourless, and their Semtex caches do not seem to be suffering from shortages.

'TIME FOR ENERGY DRINK. SEMTEX FORTE' was written on a billboard I spotted in Prague's Argentinska Street.

Yes, Semtex, the Italian-made fizzy drink, had blasted into Prague. The billboard showed a young woman blissfully tasting the explosive drink in front of a KLM airline poster. Was there some hidden meaning there? Whatever it was, I doubted that either KLM or CSA, the Czech national airline, was likely to offer Semtex to passengers on its flights. It also occurred to me that Synthesia, the manufacturers of the solid, not liquid, Semtex, must have been pretty annoyed by such flippant abuse of their awe-inspiring trade mark.

Callers to a popular Prague radio show unanimously concluded that the new Semtex soft drink was tasteless (not half as much as the billboard, I am sure). But for my purposes this didn't matter. There was only one little thing left: to visit Synthesia. As far as I knew, no Western journalist had ever been allowed to do so.

I decided to be persistent. My rationale was simple: if indeed, as Synthesia kept publicly asserting, the production of Semtex had been wrapped up since 1991 and they had nothing to hide any longer, why couldn't they show me round – as they did at, say, Staropramen, Prague's largest brewery?

'Hopeless. Forget about it!' I was rebuffed at the offices of the *Prague Post*, where I popped in one day in search of advice. 'We have tried it many times, but they've never allowed us to come close to Synthesia. The only thing they were willing to give us was their glossy brochure on environmental protection – and even that only by post. Communism or free market, Synthesia's policy remains unchanged: strictly no press visits.'

The journalists also assured me that if I phoned Synthesia myself they would feign inability to communicate in English. But, having dealt in the past with the Soviet mafia and the KGB, I was not easily discouraged. I asked a Czech acquaintance, a respected Prague businessman, to make the initial contact with Synthesia. 'Let them try and pretend they don't speak Czech,' I thought venomously.

Next morning the following fax message from my go-between was waiting for me at my hotel: 'Regarding your visit to the Semtex producer, I was trying to arrange a meeting for you, but the notice was very short for some people, and others are just not available at the time you were suggesting. However, should you still be interested in contacting them, they are ready to handle your questions at least.' A phone number and the name of a 'contact person' – a certain Mr Mokren – followed. Not bad for a start.

My call was answered by a woman ('Pani Misova') whose English was limited to just two words: 'not possible.' Remembering an old bureaucratic dictum – 'If you can't convince them, confuse them' – I switched to Russian. Pani Misova's Russian was only marginally better, just good enough to convey that Mr Mokren was unavailable. Having lost patience, I decided to take advantage of our lack of a lingua franca and told her clearly in English that I was leaving the Czech Republic the day after next (which was true) and that I would be coming to Pardubice the following day. 'Call us tomorrow morning,' she replied in unexpectedly correct English.

Next morning I dialled the same number. 'Can you call me back in a month?' Pani Misova asked nonchalantly.

'Look, I am taking a train to Pardubice in half an hour,' I told her firmly. 'Would you be so kind as to pick me up at the station?' The line went dead for a while. 'Not possible,' she mumbled after a long pause. 'OK, I will take a taxi,' I said, and hung up. I decided that I had managed to confuse Pani Misova, if only a little.

Two hours later I was shifting from one foot to the other on the cobbled station square of Pardubice. It was raining. I had a cold. My nose was running, but taxis weren't: there were none in sight. The unknown town around me was bleak and uninviting. The people looked bleak and uninviting too, quite a contrast to the bubbling and bustling Prague.

I was hoping to flag down a private car (a normal thing anywhere in Eastern Europe), but had to give up the idea after fifteen minutes of fruitless hand-waving. Having returned to the station building, I found a public telephone and dialled the Synthesia number. This time I was lucky enough to get Mr Mokren himself on the line. His English was much better than Pani Misova's. 'I am sorry, the working day is over,' he told me curtly.

'So this is your famous Czech hospitality!' I exploded, Semtex-like. I was fed up with their ridiculous cat-and-mouse game. 'Here I am in Pardubice, having come all the way from London to ask you a couple of simple questions, and you are telling me off!'

'OK, I shall be with you in seven minutes,' said Mr Mokren all of a sudden. He obviously didn't want to appear inhospitable.

Ten minutes later, a battered Lada stopped in the far end of the square. A round-faced young man wearing a suit and tie got out and angrily paced towards me. In his hand he was clutching a glossy pamphlet, probably a brochure on environmental protection.

'You must go back to Prague now,' said Mr Mokren, giving me the brochure (it *was* on environmental protection) and his business card which said simply: 'Ales Mokren, Manager.'

'You can't do this to me!' I insisted, flashing my press card in his moon-like dispassionate face. 'Your factory is not protected by any official secrecy acts, and as a member of the press in a free democratic country, which you now claim to be, I am entitled to see it. Besides, the next train to Prague leaves only in two hours.'

My last statement was an outright lie, but, fortunately for me, Mr Mokren was not too familiar with train schedules. He scrutinised me carefully for a couple of minutes. Soaking wet and shivering in the wind, I must have looked pitiful enough to inspire some trust. 'All right,' he said finally. 'I shall take you to Synthesia for half an hour, but you won't see anything, because the working day is over.' From the expression on his face it was plain that he couldn't wait to get rid of me.

Promptly (before he had time to change his mind) I climbed into his Lada. Mr Mokren took out a map of Pardubice. 'Synthesia is here,' he said, pointing to an unmarked blank area at the map's edge. 'We'll be there in ten minutes.'

We drove past smoking chimneys, naked pipelines and shabby houses, dotted here and there with Marlboro and Coca-Cola signs, a familiar city-scape of post-communist Eastern Europe.

'I am sorry,' said Mr Mokren from behind the wheel. 'We have to be careful with journalists. In all our history, only a couple of local ones have been allowed into the factory.'

'Why such secrecy?' I enquired.

'Terrorism,' he said gravely. 'We are a chemical factory, you know.'

He went on to explain that Semtex was only one of their hundreds of products and he couldn't understand why everybody was so interested in it. 'We stopped shipments of Semtex to Libya in 1981, and that was the end of the matter.

'We are now a joint-stock company with thousands of shareholders,' he babbled on. 'Privatisation of the factory was completed in 1995.'

I couldn't care less about privatisation.

We were already driving across Synthesia's territory. Contrary to my escort's assurances, the factory didn't give the impression that the working day was over. Chimneys were belching out clouds of yellow smoke into the uncomplaining Bohemian skies. Cargo trains were rattling along the viaducts, criss-crossing on several levels above our heads. Trucks and tanker-lorries were driving in and out of the gates, guarded by security men in grey uniforms. Business was clearly booming at the world's only Semtex factory.

'We are the largest industrial enterprise in eastern Bohemia,' Mr Mokren commented in a guide-like manner. 'The factory consists of a thousand buildings connected by two hundred kilometres of road and sixty kilometres of rail tracks. We employ seven thousand workers.' There was genuine pride in his voice.

We stopped near an unmarked red-brick house, overgrown with acacias. Mr Mokren opened the front door with his own key. It was probably an administrative building. Its long, dark, Soviet-style corridors were lined with anonymous plate-less doors. 'This is my office,' said Mr Mokren letting me into a spacious room with an oblong table in the middle and bookshelves along the walls.

'I'll ask my secretary to make us coffee,' he said and went out.

So his secretary was still at work, despite the 'end of his working day.'

Left alone in Mr Mokren's office, I picked up a couple of brochures from a shelf. One was the company's annual report for 1995. On page 18 I found a 'Production of Explosives' section with parallel texts in Czech and stilted English:

> Despite of a continuing decrease of sales in the sector of military production, the sales of explosives show a steady increase of sales. This was contributed by an increase in sales of nitrocellulose and also owing to the sales of explosives and smokeless powders. The assortment of the latter products was

> innovated and their production modernised. In the division of explosives the export-oriented sales amount to nearly 65%.

On the following page, there were some tables and diagrams. One of the latter – 'Export of products by the Sectors' – showed a steady growth in the export of explosives, from 9.8 per cent in 1993 to fourteen per cent in 1995. 'The most significant increase was recorded in the sales of organic substances and explosives,' ran the caption. Another diagram – 'The most significant export destinations' – listed, among others, Great Britain (3.8 per cent), Italy (8.5 per cent), Austria (3.3 per cent) and 'Other Countries,' to which unnamed destination 12.1 per cent of Synthesia's export products were dispatched.

The second pamphlet was a 1996 edition of the factory's list of products. It included several different types of Semtex: Semtex 1A, Semtex 1AP, Semtex 2P and Semtex ZPN, all described as 'plastic explosives for special blasting operations.'

The secretary brought in a coffee tray. I hastily replaced the brochures. Mr Mokren returned and sat down behind his desk looking at me with impatience.

'To which countries do you export Semtex these days?' I asked him.

'I don't know,' he said briskly, and he looked at his watch. 'The only thing I can say is that our export of explosives keeps going down.'

'Not according to the annual report,' I thought.

'Do you have many incidents of theft at your explosives department?'

'Not many. One or two a year.'

'And who are the thieves?'

'Workers. We have recently cut our workforce by three hundred people.'

'What do you export to Britain?'

'Everything.'

'Including Semtex?'

No reply.

I looked at the smoking chimneys behind the window. 'Is it possible to see a Semtex production line?'

'Out of the question. You have to go back to the station now.'

There was no point in continuing this fruitless verbal exchange.

'Can I take a couple of your brochures?' I asked. Unexpectedly, Mr Mokren nodded. I took the annual report and the list of products and stuffed them hurriedly into my shoulder-bag.

'I am sorry I was unable to tell you much,' said Mr Mokren as we shook hands near the station. 'I am not an expert in explosives.'

'What are your areas of expertise?' I asked.

'Well, I am not a chemist,' he replied enigmatically and went back to his Lada.

On the train back to Prague, I tried to make some sense out of my impromptu visit to Synthesia.

It was obvious they hadn't wanted me to go to Pardubice in the first instance. It was no less clear that when I did get to Pardubice they hadn't wanted me to see the factory, an abnormal attitude for a freshly privatised 'joint-stock' company which, theoretically, should grab every opportunity for media exposure.

It was also evident that the facts and figures in their brochures, targeting prospective buyers, were in stark contradiction of what Mr Mokren was prepared to tell a visiting 'member of the press.'

Or could it be that Mr Mokren – in defiance of his bosses (whoever they were), or for some other unknown reason – actually *wanted* me to visit Synthesia and to see the brochures?

One thing was certain: Semtex, the deadly substance invented by Bohumil Sol, was being produced in huge quantities at Synthesia, and the bulk of it was exported to countries which the factory was not willing to reveal.

A week later, police in London seized a cache of Semtex destined to be used in IRA attacks on British targets.

Now you will understand why I wasn't inclined to shed any tears over the inglorious death of Bohumil Sol, the father of Semtex, who blasted himself to smithereens in a psychiatric asylum near Pardubice.

Hotel 'Libido'

My train from Krakow to Gdansk was called the Malopolska Express. The journey across the whole of Poland was to take seven hours, and I was not particularly looking forward to it. My new Krakow friends had inundated me with frightening stories about careless travellers who were either robbed or killed or both (first robbed and then killed, or vice versa) on the sinister Malopolska Express. 'Don't go to sleep, not even for a moment,' they warned me. 'Watch your luggage constantly. And under no circumstances should you agree to drink with fellow-passengers: they add drugs to vodka, you fall asleep, and when you come to – your luggage is gone.'

I got very upset when I saw that my carriage was a *Wagon dla Nepalyacich*, that is, a non-smoking one. Bracing myself for seven hours of extreme nicotine deficiency, I entered the carriage and immediately smelt the beautiful stale stench of burnt tobacco. Half the passengers were smoking. This made me realise again that in Poland things are often poles apart from what you expect them to be. As I could clearly see several hours later, this includes rumours, too: it was the safest journey I had had in Eastern Europe, with not even a hint of devilishly cunning robbers waiting to pump you with poisoned vodka, so as to nick your shoulder-bag containing your most precious possession, the *Lonely Planet Guide to Eastern Europe*.

The most 'dangerous' moment of the journey was when an angry-faced five-year-old Serbian beggar peeped into my compartment and tugged me by the sleeve, asking for money. He was followed by a moustachioed young Pole with an English sign on his chest: 'Good morning! My name is Yarek. I am hungry.' 'So am I,' I was tempted to say. I wondered whether he carried with him several different chest-signs for different times of the day. At midday he would probably replace the 'Good morning' sign with a 'Good afternoon' one, and so on.

My neighbours were a young Polish couple: an effeminate youngster who spoke in a falsetto voice and was reading the memoirs of Pope John Paul II, and his girlfriend (or sister), immersed in the Polish edition of *Hello!* magazine. In frequent intervals between reading, they ate (in Eastern Europe people like eating on trains). I was salivating, unable to abandon my suitcase to go for lunch at a restaurant car until hunger took the upper hand. Having returned from lunch, I was surprised to discover that my suitcase was still safely in its place on the luggage rack.

In Gdansk I was met by a fussy official of the local branch of the Polish Tourism Promotion Agency. 'We have decided to put you up at one of our new hotels as a sort of … er … experiment,' he chuckled. I never enjoy being a guinea-pig, but there wasn't much choice.

The hotel was just five minutes' walk from the station. It was an unremarkable freshly painted two-storey building. 'Lido. Restaurant – Night Club' ran a bright pink sign on its roof. Two burly security guards with square shoulders and broken noses blocked my way. I tried to explain that I had a booking, but they kept pushing me away from the door.

A huge gorilla-like man ran out of the building. He threw the guards aside with a brisk wave of his hairy left hand (he was twice as thick and robust as either of them) and – simultaneously – extended his right palm, the size of an excavator's digging bucket. 'Maciek, the hotel owner,' he introduced himself in Russian. 'You are our very first guest. Welcome.'

We climbed a narrow, dark staircase and found ourselves in a small room, lit with a treacherous pink light. An empty bar stand was in the corner. There were no spirits or wines on the shelves above, only bottles with mineral water and … an impressive selection of condoms. 'This is our Reception,' said Maciek.

A stunning long-haired blonde, wearing a transparent blouse and such a short mini that one could be forgiven for thinking that she had forgotten her skirt at home, materialised from one of the room's dark corners. 'This is Angela, our receptionist,' explained Maciek.

The sight of my dog-eared Australian passport, which I had dutifully produced for registering, made Angela all gooey-eyed. 'Ah, Australia. It is my dream!' she sang in passable English.

Maciek told me that they had six rooms in the hotel, and as the special first-ever guest of honour I was assigned the best luxury suite, which he (Maciek) normally used himself.

The 'suite' consisted of two rooms, a lounge with an old, squeaky sofa covered with cigarette burns, and a bedroom. The furniture was drab and battered. The TV set was firmly tuned to one channel showing an erotic movie in German. The menu on the coffee table informed me that the nightclub downstairs was open from 1am to 6am, which didn't bode well for a good night's sleep. It also listed several alcoholic drinks and basic Polish dishes, with blank spaces instead of prices. To make a phone call, I had to give a number to Angela, who would dial it for me from the Reception and then transfer the call to my room. There was no fax.

I have seen many hotels in my life, but I was nevertheless puzzled in the extreme. Pondering the mystery of the Lido, I sat on the bed and – Some unknown force suddenly pushed me on to my back, then threw me up in the air and – after a brief levitation – deposited me on the floor. I felt like a hapless American cowboy trying to harness an obnoxious wild mustang on the prairie.

Rubbing a fresh lump on my head, I crawled to the offensive bed on my knees and cautiously, as if I were testing the temperature of bath water to make sure it was not boiling hot, touched the mattress with my index finger. The mattress recoiled and began rocking up and down, as if it was riding a sea-wave.

'Do you like your water-bed?' Maciek's voice sounded from behind my back. He had entered the room without knocking.

'I think it's fine for anything – except sleeping,' I replied.

'Nonsense! You will sleep like a baby,' he said. 'Our ex-president Lech Walesa has six water-beds in his Gdansk home.'

'That is probably why he lost the last elections,' I muttered.

Maciek then told me to beware of muggers and pickpockets while I was in Gdansk and suggested that I should leave all my valuables at the Lido. I was not sure whether the hotel's wild-looking security guards (to say nothing of the owner himself) were less dangerous than street muggers and mumbled something incoherent in response.

'As you wish,' Maciek said before leaving. He paused near the door and added gravely, 'But remember: Gdansk is not London.'

And it certainly wasn't. The centre of Gdansk was one huge flea market: it was the time of the annual St Dominic's Trade Fair. The innumerable street stalls selling souvenirs made of amber blocked out the sights of this pretty Hanseatic town, which looked more German or Scandinavian than Polish. Indeed, for many years it was known by its German name of Danzig and was prominent in the Hanseatic League, a medieval commercial union of north German and Baltic towns. In the fourteenth and fifteenth centuries it even rivalled Lübeck, the capital of the Hanseatic League, in size and richness.

In more recent times, Gdansk became famous for two momentous beginnings. It was there that the Second World War broke out at 4.45am on 1 September 1939, when a unit of 210 Polish soldiers was fired on by the German battleship *Schleswig-Holstein* cruising near the Westerplatte peninsula. Thirty-one years later, in December 1970, the Solidarity movement, which triggered the destruction of the communist system all over Eastern Europe nineteen years later still, was born at the Gdansk Shipyard. One of its leaders, a modest shipyard electrician called Lech Walesa, was eventually catapulted to international stardom and became the first democratically elected president of Poland and one of the world's most charismatic politicians, who forged unlikely friendships with the Queen and with the Pope.

In an ironic twist of fate and fortune, by the mid-1990s Walesa had fallen into political disfavour. Having been voted out of office, he was replaced by the reformed communist Alexander Kwasniewski in December 1995. Walesa then returned to Gdansk, where he reportedly resumed his employment as an electrician at the money-starved shipyard. His life had turned full circle, although certain things were never going to be the same. First, his work at the shipyard was a media hoax, for he spent all his time running the so-called Walesa Foundation, whose headquarters were just a stone's throw from my Lido Hotel, and fighting with the authorities over the tax from the $1,000,000 dollars he had received from Hollywood (for a film about his life) which he refused to pay, claiming that 'it was a gift.' Second, the house where he lived was a far cry from his former electrician's abode, and not just because of its (allegedly) plush six-water-bed interior. Situated in Oliva, one of Gdansk's most prestigious areas, it was a well-maintained cottage which stood in a spacious garden surrounded by a security fence with video cameras and barbed wire on top. The low-built, stocky cottage looked very much like its podgy, broad-shouldered post-presidential owner. To complete the simile, the thick rows of barbed wire along the perimeter of the fence could easily pass for Walesa's famous long and droopy moustache.

There was nothing much left in Gdansk to remind the visitor of the heroic times of Solidarity, except for a tacky avant-garde monument on the shipyard's territory and Solidarna vodka on shop shelves …

Before retiring for the night, I went to the nearby seaside town of Sopot, which together with Gdansk and Gdynia constitutes a three-city agglomeration called Trojmiasto. There I had a quiet dinner in a totally empty (it was too expensive for the locals) John Bull, The Real English Pub, which looked the spitting image of a pub almost anywhere in England. The only difference was that one could get Polish borscht (beetroot soup with soured cream) there (which I did). It is probably the world's only English pub where they serve this peculiar East European delicacy.

Shortly before midnight I got out of a taxi near the Lido Hotel. And again my way was blocked by the security guards, who let me inside only after I showed them the key to my 'luxury suite.' A different, yet equally skirtless, receptionist stood behind the bar. I asked her whether it was possible to make a phone call to London. She said that it wasn't, but for me she would try.

The prospect of spending the night on the undulating water-mattress was not particularly enticing. Having taken a sleeping pill, I carefully approached my bed and lowered myself on to it gently. I tried my best not to stir or make any sharp movements, but whenever I turned over, the obnoxious bed would give me a kick in the ribs before tossing me up in the air, and it would take several minutes for the rolling and pitching to subside. Finally, having found a more or less quiet corner (or should I say haven?), I dozed off.

I was awoken by deafening music, played somewhere underneath. The sound was so loud that it filled my 'luxury suite' to the brim and rocked my water-bed. I looked at my watch. It was past 1am, the time when the basement nightclub was due to open. In the short intervals between the blasts of music, other noises reached me from the hotel's corridor: doors slamming, women screaming playfully. I thought I could even hear a dog barking. From the street there was the distinctive clap-clap of multiple gunshots: the vigilant security guards were probably reasoning with some pushy late-comers.

At the bottom of my bag, I found several cotton-wool balls which I stuck into my ears. The moment I lay down there came a phone call: the skirtless girl had managed to put me through to London.

Soon I had to give up all hope of falling asleep and I started leafing through the hotel's glossy brochure, which had probably been brought to my room in my absence by the hospitable Maciek. I learnt that the hotel's nightclub offered 'erotic show, striptease, women mud and oil wrestling, sexy excitement, charming company of beautiful hostesses, pig's feet with beer, and pig's feet with shaved [sic] horseradish.'

My last doubts as to the nature of the Lido evaporated: it was a brothel, thinly camouflaged as a hotel. I thought that it would have been more appropriate to rename it the Libido.

At 6am the music at the nightclub suddenly stopped and I was able to steal a short nap on the floor, next to the water-bed.

Angela – as skirtless as the day before – was back at her post behind the bar. 'Did you have a good sleep?' she asked me with a sadistic smile before presenting me with a bill for my three-minute phone call to London. A Polish friend told me later that the sum amounted to her total phone bill for six months. I paid it, consoling myself with the thought that by doing so I was contributing a further boost to the growing Polish economy, although in this case it was most likely the black economy which would benefit from it (brothels are illegal in Poland, hence the desire to disguise the Libido as a hotel).

Angela was very surprised when I asked whether I could have breakfast. 'It is too early for breakfast,' she muttered. It was almost 10am.

'And what's on your breakfast menu? Shaved radishes? Oily hostesses? Condoms with eggs? And what's your tart of the day?' I asked. Without waiting for her reply, I ran down the stairs and out into the street.

I thought that the experiment of my Gdansk hosts, who had put me up at a brothel, was probably a success, from their point of view, that is.

Ostalgie Hotel

Masochism has become a feature of modern travel. Luxury suites, candle-lit dinners and first-class flights are no longer enough to satisfy the demands of discerning holidaymakers, now looking for danger spots (even if imaginary), where their nerves and egos can undergo some pleasant titillation. They need trials, hardship and horror-stories, which could be later recounted to friends in the safety of their lounge-rooms. This trend has already brought to life all sorts of mass-market survival manuals and guides to 'the world's most dangerous places,' numerous hotel rooms replicating cabins of the Titanic and even guided tours of Chernobyl (I thoughtlessly went on one in 1994 and, as my friends like to tease me, my body still glows in the dark).

One such place is Hotel Sittavia in the outskirts of the East German town of Zittau, on the Czech border. Its owner, Guenter Ziemann, went out of his way to recreate inside his establishment the atmosphere of the former GDR.

'Halt! You are leaving the territory of the Federal Republic of Germany!' announces a sign in strict Gothic characters, next to a striped sentry booth at the hotel's entrance. Situated in the building of the former GDR military academy, with grim long corridors and squeaky doors, Sittavia is stuffed with Communist memorabilia and samples of GDR products – from Vita Cola (a politically correct 'Communist' version of Coke) to Tutsi toothpaste and 'F6' – foul-smelling 'proletarian' cigarettes. The walls are adorned with photos of tin-shaped Trabants, much ridiculed East German cars, and the hotel's 'Best People': Herr Ziemann himself, his wife and two receptionists.

Each room has its own East German theme. Mine was dedicated to ORWO – a factory that used to produce low-quality films and photographic paper. There are rooms celebrating German-Soviet Friendship Society, Young Pioneers Organisation, Union of German Communist Youth and victorious East German athletes (where they probably serve you steroids for breakfast). At the Reception, guests are asked to fill in a formidable GDR entry form and are issued with a grey East German 'Personalausweis' (passport).

All prices are in now-defunct East German marks, and the food in the basement canteen tastes as if it was produced at a plan-dominated state 'nutrition factory' at the end of a month.

Drinks are also charged with the nostalgia for communist times, or *Ostalgie*, as it had come to be known in the German press. Among them was *Erichs Rache* (Eric's Revenge) – a peculiar *Schnaps* (or *Schnap**ps***, if you had a double – only joking), poured from a bottle with a portrait of the late East German communist leader Erich Honecker, whose portrait hangs above Sittavia's spartan reception desk.

At dusk, thousands of black crows would descend on the hotel's secluded grounds. Their piercing screams made the place look and feel even spookier than it was in reality. For lack of anything else to do, I would entertain myself by goose-stepping for hours along the deserted military academy's marching '*platz*,' now used as the hotel's car-park, and wondering how long it would be before I myself turned into a goose.

The owner assured me that the whole idea was but a joke, but as someone who had spent thirty-five years of his life in the totalitarian Soviet Union, I didn't find it particularly funny. Ten years after the collapse of the Berlin Wall, the former East Germany is still struggling with the aftermath of its forty-year-long Communist past. The level of unemployment in Zittau is twenty-five per cent – three times higher than in Germany's Western lands, social services are in a mess, and every year thousands of locals migrate to the West. In short, the wound is still bleeding, and laughing at it now is like inviting guests to a 'Titanic suite' while the Titanic is still sinking.

My brief stay at this peculiar hotel was nevertheless useful. The fact that I was the only guest there was encouraging: it showed that, even among the new breed of masochistic Western tourists, whom the proprietor is obviously trying to target, there is no great demand for the crude symbols of totalitarianism.

'Bruderschaft' Sneezing in Budapest

'Ah-tishoo!' I was woken by my own sneeze and realised, with horror, that I had flu. I looked out of the window. It was early morning. My train, the Pannonia Express, was stationary. There was a sign with a frightening word, 'Szekesfehervar,' in front of me. A station name like that could exist only in one country: Hungary.

With an effort, I remembered that the night before I had been drinking with my Prague-based friend Igor in the Palffy House; that I had then dashed around Prague Central Station in search of a pharmacy (I could feel a cold approaching) and failed to find one; that the unending passport controls had kept me from sleeping during the night as the train was crawling across the brand-new East European borders, from the Czech Republic into Slovakia and then into Hungary.

I recalled that at 3am a Slovak border-guard, a slim young woman in baggy uniform and with a gun dangling from her belt, asked me in Russian to translate to a visa-less Australian in the next carriage that he had to pay the fine. I enquired whether I would be eligible for the Meciar Cross, Slovakia's highest award (invented by me), for that and advised her to shoot the recalcitrant Aussie straight from her lovely hip (I didn't remember whether I had said the last five words out loud).

Later, the Australian, who had eventually agreed to cough up, came to my compartment to complain (and woke me up again). He was red-eyed and dishevelled, and had the peculiar disgruntled look of a man who had just been mugged. I tried to comfort him by saying that he was lucky not to have been shot, according to my advice.

'Ah-tishoo!' My nose was blocked. An uninterrupted buzzing noise from the headphones, which I wasn't wearing, resounded in my clogged ears. A didgeridoo was playing inside my brick-heavy head. I felt dizzy, queasy and uneasy. Evgeny Bulavin, the drinking supervisor of my youth, used to like having colds, because, he asserted, they made him feel as if he was drunk. I might have enjoyed my cold, too, had it not been for several days of intensive wine-tasting which lay ahead of me. In this condition, I couldn't tell a Bordeaux from a *bormotukha* – the cheapest Soviet plonk (to be honest, I was not sure whether I could have done that even if completely healthy).

I asked an attendant for some Panadol pills. He was Hungarian and didn't understand: the word for Panadol was probably not dissimilar to 'Szekesfehervar' in Hungarian – the mind-boggling Finno-Ugric language, in which '*ugly*' means 'galoshes.'

At Keleti, the main station of Budapest, I was greeted by a lanky young man in a baseball cap, a driver from the Tourism Bureau.

'A-ah-tishoo!' he sneezed, shaking my hand.

'Ah-tishoo!' I replied.

'My name is Attila,' he said.

'What?' I asked, thinking that he had sneezed again.

'Attila,' he repeated. 'Like Attila the Hun – ah-tishoo! Sorry, I have a cold.'

'It makes two of us. At least we won't infect each other. Let's sneeze '*Bruderschaft*,'' I suggested.

We decided to go to one of Europe's most famous cafés, Budapest's Café New York, for a welcome-to-Hungary drink. Having squeezed ourselves into Attila's battered Suzuki, we drove off, all three of us (including the Suzuki) constantly sneezing.

Like his distant ancestor and namesake, the legendary Hunnish king, nicknamed 'the Scourge of God' by his contemporaries, Attila was a bit of a daredevil. If Attila the Hun was notorious for his belligerence, grim disposition and reckless horse-riding, Attila the Hungarian was the wildest car-driver I had ever come across.

'I am taking you along the same road that our president normally travels,' he told me proudly in his amazingly good American English (he had spent a year in the USA), swerving his jalopy to the right and nearly hitting a traffic policeman. I was sincerely hoping that the incumbent Hungarian president, Arpad Goncz, was not travelling along his favourite road at the same time as we were: all wine-tastings were likely to be cancelled if Hungary was suddenly thrown into several days of national mourning.

Attila's driving was such that, for the first time in years, I rejoiced in having grey hair: had it not been grey already, it would have certainly gone snow-white after a ride in his Suzuki. He took short-cuts across parks, street pavements and shopping malls. He zig-zagged through the narrow lanes of Buda, the old town. He would stop in the middle of a busy thoroughfare for a chat with his 'university mate.' Besides, he kept talking non-stop on his mobile phone, letting go of the wheel and gesticulating wildly with both hands.

'To drive in Budapest, you need fast reactions and smartness,' he told me, chasing an old lady with shopping bags along the pavement. The lady was waddling away from his barmy Suzuki with the speed of a hurricane.

'Honk! Why don't you *honk* at her?' I screamed.

'I never beep at pedestrians. The police do not allow beeping in the city,' he replied calmly.

'But they obviously don't mind running over old ladies,' I thought.

When we stopped near a pharmacy to buy us some Panadol (I noted with fiendish satisfaction that the Hungarian word for pharmacy was '*gyogyszertar*'), Attila triple-parked his car in such a way that it blocked three lanes of moving traffic, which came to a halt and became honking traffic for all the ten minutes we spent at the pharmacy. Attila listened to the honking with unhidden delight, as if it was the famous 'Faust' Symphony by the great Hungarian composer Ferenc List.

'In Budapest, you can park anywhere. I normally park on the pavement,' he explained. Indeed, all the places on the pavement near the pharmacy had already been taken by mechanical stallions driven by other wild descendants of the lugubrious king of the Huns.

When we were crossing the impressive Erzebet Bridge, I looked down and was upset to see that the water in 'the blue Danube' was actually not blue but brown. 'They add paint to the water to make it blue during festivals and national celebrations,' Attila reassured me, narrowly avoiding a head-on collision with a tram.

The dreary Soviet-style facades and formerly grand *fin-de-siècle* boulevards of Pest, Budapest's newer area, which, surprisingly, was much more run-down than its older part, Buda, were – like the Danube – in need of repainting. They were somewhat animated by the newly erected advertising cylinders, covered with ads for Marlboro and Pepsi.

'Hungary is the only country in the world where the sales of Pepsi are almost as high as those of Coca-Cola, and their competition is fierce,' said Attila.

According to him, Pepsi targeted Budapest trams and covered them with its logo. In retaliation, Coca-Cola had set its sights on the historic graffiti-ridden Chain Bridge, having offered to scrub it clean and replace graffiti with Coca-Cola ads and decorations.

'Can it be that an explanation for the brown waters of the 'blue Danube' lies in this unscrupulous rivalry?' I thought, remembering that blue was the 'official' Pepsi colour. I wouldn't have been particularly surprised to learn that it was indeed Coca-Cola which – in an advertising frenzy – had repainted the great European river brown. If so, the Pepsi manufacturers could console themselves with the fact that when Coke first went on sale in China under the name Ke-kou-ke-la, it turned out that in some Chinese dialects this means 'female horse stuffed with wax.'

I was a bit wary of Budapest restaurants and cafés. My fears had been triggered by multiple stories in London newspapers about the large-scale fleecing of foreign visitors by charging them thousands of dollars for no more than modest meals and drinks. Four Danish tourists were, reportedly, presented with a bill for a million forints (£3,400) – enough to buy a nice new car in Hungary (which was probably their waiter's dream) – for a humble non-alcoholic dinner at a Budapest restaurant. 'These are our night prices. We charge what the market will bear,' the restaurant manager explained. Even if the market could bear it, the determined, cold-blooded Danes could not. Their complaint led to an investigation, the subsequent closure of several dozen 'guilty' restaurants and an official warning by the US embassy in Budapest, urging Americans 'to beware cafés and night-clubs where bills can require a second mortgage.' (As to non-Americans, the embassy did not seem to mind them being robbed.) A useful tip from the Union of Hungarian Restaurateurs was that 'a good meal in a Budapest restaurant should not cost more than £5 (about 1,600 forints).' What exactly they meant by 'a good meal' remained a mystery. What if the meal was 'very good,' or (improbably) 'excellent?' Clearly, Hungarians were taking the words 'free market' at their face value. Or maybe, in accordance with the old Hungarian saying 'We are poor but we live well,' they were all desperate to get themselves new cars?

The other sign of the emerging Hungarian qualms-free market was the introduction of package dental tours of Budapest, which had received a lot of publicity in Britain. Prices started at £175 for three nights including flight, hotel, a consultation with a dentist and examination. If the dentist thought treatment was necessary (it was highly unlikely that he would determine otherwise), a tourist had to cough up a further £280 for dentures and a mere £22 to have a tooth extracted. In between filling and drilling sessions, guided tours of Budapest were offered to the travellers (or rather to the patients) – for an additional price of course. In short, anyone subscribing to these package holidays, which were sinisterly advertised as 'dental breaks,' faced the cheerful prospect of returning to his home country not only broke but also toothless.

It was 11am, and the Café New York in Andrassy Street was half empty: the breakfast patrons had already left and the early lunchers had not turned up yet. The *belle époque* interior of the place was grand: mirrors, columns, chandeliers, furniture of polished mahogany. It reminded me of the famous casino at Monte Carlo. I hoped that the resemblance stopped there and that having a drink at the Café New York wouldn't be much of a gamble: unlike some wealthy Americans, I couldn't afford a second mortgage. To be honest, I couldn't afford the first one either.

We sat down at a heavy dark-wood table and swallowed a couple of Panadols each before reaching for the menus.

'Czechs have beer in their veins, Austrians coffee, and Hungarians – wine!' Attila chanted nasally (his nose was as firmly blocked as mine).

He was probably right, for even the weather forecast in one of Budapest's English-language weeklies, which I had read on the train, contained the following advice: 'Sunday will be partly cloudy again with occasional showers. We'd recommend warming some wine.'

But the idea of what Attila's driving might be like when he was drunk was so terrifying that it defied contemplation.

'I would rather you be an Austrian just for now,' I muttered.

A tuxedo-clad waiter-boy, who was fifteen (we had asked him) but looked eleven, brought us coffee and bread, but no butter.

'We don't serve butter before dinner,' he explained.

The coffee was excellent and fully corresponded to the Hungarian proverb 'Coffee should be black like the devil, hot like hell, and sweet like a kiss.' A group of chain-smoking young girls sat in the corner, living proof of the fact that Hungary is the eighth heaviest smoking nation in the world, and every statistical Hungarian smokes 3,177 cigarettes a year, slightly fewer than an average resident of the United Arab Emirates (3,218), but more than a happy citizen of the world's wealthiest state, Brunei (3,158). In front of our eyes, the girls were quickly approaching their annual smoking quotas.

At the turn of the century, the New York was the liveliest of Budapest's four hundred cafés and one of the best in the whole of the Austro-Hungarian Empire. On its opening day, a group of satisfied customers threw its key into the Danube so that it would stay open day and night. In 1910-30 it became the favourite haunt of Budapest literati. Struggling Budapest writers scribbled away on the free paper provided by the café. A special (and fairly frugal) 'writer's platter,' consisting of cold meat, cheese and bread, was the most popular item on the menu. Here, the aspiring authors could also catch up on the latest news, for the café proudly stocked 'all the dailies and arts journals of the world.' Writers were followed by journalists (after all, as one of my Moscow friends used to say, a writer is a journalist who can't get his copy into print), and some of Budapest's best-known newspapers and magazines were edited in the café's first-floor gallery.

Among the café's old-timers was Ferenc Molnar, the renowned Hungarian playwright of Jewish origin. In the New York, he had his favourite chair, in which he would sit for hours, drinking coffee and writing. After the 1938 Anschluss, when neighbouring Austria was annexed by Germany and got fully incorporated into Hitler's Reich, a friend asked Molnar, who was sitting in his beloved café New York chair: 'Ferenc, aren't you afraid? Why don't you save yourself by emigrating to America?' 'It is easy to emigrate to America,' replied Molnar, 'but it is difficult to get up from this chair.'

After the Second World War, the New York became a shoe-shop before re-opening as a café in 1954, two years prior to the Soviet military invasion, as a result of which real writers disappeared from the café (and from Hungary in general) for many years to come. The New York survived the thirty-two years of Janos Kadar's rule, popularly known as 'goulash communism,' when certain economic freedoms, unheard of in other Soviet-bloc states, were preserved by the cunning communist leader. Nowadays, some of the writers have returned to the New York. And although the 'literary waiters' of the twenties and thirties, who used to call all their clients by their first names and read all their works, had vanished for good, the café still boasted a 'literary toilet attendant,' a well-read elderly lady, who did not charge her favourite writers for the use of her vital facility. She did charge me, but that was probably because she didn't know English and hence hadn't had a chance to read any of my books.

In the ante-room of the café's grand literary toilet, I picked up a promotional leaflet saying, 'Welcome to Budapest. Congratulations! You are in the right place at the wrong time – but that's our job!' This reminded me not just of the peculiar

Hungarian sense of humour but also of another place that I wanted to see in Budapest, a place which was closely connected with the caustic and self-deprecating Hungarian wit.

A couple of months before my trip to Hungary, several London newspapers had run a story about a certain Ferenc Kovacs, who had opened the world's first and only joke shop in Budapest. The shop was aimed at relieving the famous Hungarian depression and pessimism. According to the papers, the entrepreneurial Kovacs charged 3 forints (1.5p) for making a customer smile, 7 forints for provoking a grin, 9 for a chuckle, and 12 (plus VAT) for making one laugh one's pants off.

There was even an example of a 9-forint joke: 'A policeman is shaving in the bathroom, when his wife comes in. 'You have cut yourself, darling,' she says. 'I know,' replies the policeman. 'I did it deliberately when you came in, just so I know where to start again when you leave.'

The joke shop (reportedly) sold musical condoms with the choice of two tunes – an old communist song called 'Arise, You Red Proletarian' and 'You Sweet Little Dumbbell' – which played as the condom was unrolled.

'What does a joke shop, with all these singing condoms, have in common with exploring Hungarian wines?' you might ask. The connection is both simple and logical. Hungarian Panadol didn't seem to work, and since the next day I had to be ready for the wine-tasting in the Tokaji region, I had to get rid of my cold by hook or by crook. And nothing cures a cold as efficiently as a good laugh.

Unfortunately, the papers did not give the address of the joke shop, and the street-wise Attila expressed total ignorance not just of its whereabouts but of its very existence, too. He rang several of his friends at the Tourism Bureau on his mobile, but none of them had ever heard of either Ferenc Kovacs or his joke shop, which only increased my desire to find it.

In Attila's faithful Suzuki we combed the whole of central Budapest. Several times we whooshed past the newly reopened Great Synagogue, Europe's largest, in Dohany Street. Every two minutes, Attila would jump out of the car and start questioning passers-by about the joke shop and Kovacs Ferenc.[13] The pedestrians only shook their shoulders, and one of them remarked in truly Hungarian fashion, 'You can pay me, and I'll tell you a joke!'

Having quadruple-parked the car in the middle of a pedestrian crossing, we began door-knocking, but the result was the same: the residents of Budapest had never heard of Ferenc Kovacs – sorry: Kovacs Ferenc – and/or his joke shop.

[13] In Hungarian, not only are prepositions added on to the end of the words, but last – family – names precede first ones, which would make me into 'Vitaliev Vitali' and, say, Boutros Boutros Gali into 'Gali Boutros Boutros'.

After a couple of hours, it dawned on me that the joke shop had never existed, and the whole idea, fed to gullible and news-hungry British journalists who had spread it all over the UK without checking, was but a product of the elusive Kovacs Ferenc's imagination and his typically Hungarian sense of humour. At this point, I burst out laughing. Soon I was joined by Attila. We laughed our pants off until we both stopped abruptly, having realised that we had just earned Kovacs Ferenc 24 forints plus VAT.

Late in the afternoon, Attila dropped me at Honved Hotel in Pest. He was to come back tomorrow morning to give me a lift back to Keleti station, from where I was to take a train to Tokaji.

My room was filthy, and the bathroom sink was blocked. 'Our Hotel is taking care on [sic] environment' said a sign on one of the dirty, fly-stained walls with peeling wallpaper. 'Not *on* its own environment though,' I thought ruefully.

The hotel restaurant was closed, which was probably for the best.

'There is a good restaurant nearby,' said the receptionist. 'It is called the Goldfish.'

The area around the hotel was unkempt and rundown. The familiar Ikarus buses (we had plenty of them in the Soviet Union) rattled past me nonchalantly as I trudged along the rugged pavement trying to spot any place that distantly resembled a restaurant called the Goldfish. It was hopeless. For a good ten minutes I stood in front of a sign saying 'Kerjuka Kaput Belsukni,' trying to guess what on earth it could mean.[14]

The only readable sign in the vicinity was above a chocolate shop. 'Bon Hemingway,' it said in English. I thought that Hemingway himself would not have been pleased to see a shop selling chocolates, not booze, named after him.

I finally located the Goldfish, having spotted a picture of a fish in its window (how very clever!). You will never guess what its name looked like in Hungarian: 'Aranigal Vendeglo.'

Sitting in the cosy, small restaurant surrounded by locals, whose language remained a total enigma for me, I was slurping a hot and spicy fish soup (good for my sore throat). Everything was fine until I asked the waiter for a bottle of mineral water. To be on the safe linguistic side, I said it in four languages: 'mineral water' in English, '*mineralnaya voda*' in Russian, '*l'eau minérale*' in French, and even – God knows why – '*aqua minerale*' in Italian. The waiter nodded and promptly brought me … a Hungarian newspaper, which I couldn't read, let alone drink.

[14] In reproducing Hungarian words, I deliberately omit accents above the vowels: nearly all Hungarian vowels are accented, and all the accents are different. So – just as in other parts of this book – I decided to take pity on its British typesetters, and on the readers, too.

I slept badly during the night. Cockroaches rustled matter-of-factly behind the peeling wallpaper. The blocked bathroom sink stank. At about 3am. I was woken up by the sound of bursting fireworks from behind the window. Next morning, the receptionist told me that those were Michael Jackson's fans celebrating after his concert at Budapest's Nepstadion – the same music-loving fans who later that day smashed the windows of a record store where the king of pop was shopping. The Great Friend of Children (especially boys) did not want to leave me alone on my East European journeys. Could it be that he had somehow come to fancy me and was following me around?

I got up at 6am. My cold was no better. In fact, it had got worse. My nose which had been firmly, almost bathroom-sink-like, blocked the day before, was now – unlike the sink – running (God knows where to) and flooding me with snot.

Ten minutes later Attila rang up to say that he was not coming, because – surprise, surprise – he had had a car accident the night before. He was calling from a hospital, but assured me that he was OK – a broken leg and a couple of bruises, that was all. From the way he sounded, it was plain that his cold had not improved either.

'Get well soon! Ah-tishoo!' I said.

'Ah-tishoo!' echoed he, before hanging up.

Dinner with Sceptics in Sofia

The new private restaurant where I dined on my last night in Sofia with Christo and Nikolai, two young executives of Domaine Boyar, Bulgaria's first independent wine merchants, was called Across the Road Behind the Cupboard. One of the dishes on its English-language menu was Cock in Red Wine with Green Rice. None of us ventured to order it.

The otherwise delightful meal could be described in just three words: dinner with sceptics. My hosts started by sceptically sniffing the cork of the bottle of Merlot Suhindol they had ordered. They made faces, wrinkled their noses and exchanged disgruntled remarks like 'Disrupted taste' and 'Acidic palate.' With horror, I realised that I had forgotten all the wisdom grasped in London from my invaluable book *Wine for Dummies.*

'Wineries often send bad bottles to restaurants,' explained Nikolai, returning the wine to the waiter and ordering another bottle of the same brand. 'Also, in restaurants, they don't store them properly.'

'In general, our best wines go to the West, and the worst stay in Bulgaria,' added Christo. 'Despite this, the British attitude to Bulgarian wines can be described as negative ignorance: I don't know and I don't want to know. Bulgaria's bad image affects consumption.' Having finished his tirade, Christo opened the second bottle, which proved excellent.

Throughout the evening, I had to play the unlikely role of an optimist trying to disperse the impenetrable doom and gloom emanating from my dinner companions.

My points were:

1. There was no more KGB in Bulgaria.
2. There was no real censorship and the elections were more or less democratic.
3. The reforms were slow but irreversible.
4. Bulgaria had a bright future.
5. My Sofia InterContinental Hotel was superb, even by Western standards.
6. (my last and weightiest argument) It takes a highly civilised country to produce such a beautiful wine (I meant the second bottle, not the first one).

Christo and Nikolai's counter-points were:

1. The West had forgotten Bulgaria.
2. Bulgaria was surrounded by enemies.
3. Bulgaria was very corrupt: the moment Domaine Boyar made public its production figures, the mafia knocked on their door.

4. They couldn't improve the quality of their wines until they had control of vineyards, which they didn't.
5. There was no real market in Bulgaria and no one knew who the land belonged to.
6. Things were still reversible, and Stalinism could come back.
7. Bulgarians could still be seen barbecuing meat (a sign of prosperity in Bulgarian folklore), but it was 'the meat of their fellow Bulgarians.'

As you see, their arguments outweighed mine. At least, in quantity they did. I knew that they had good reason to be negative. But negativity could only create more negativity and their sad prophecies could easily become self-fulfilling, whereas a bit of optimism and 'hope against hope,' as I knew only too well from my thirty-five years in the Soviet Union, could work miracles.

My enthusiasm was, to a large extent, faked. Looking back on my first few days in Bulgaria, I thought I could be forgiven for having succumbed to some cautious pessimism myself.

'Be alert,' I had been instructed at the small London offices of Domaine Boyar a week before. The series of adverse happenings in Bulgaria prior to my departure was so extraordinary that I was seriously thinking of putting the trip off.

Three days before my scheduled arrival in Sofia, Andrei Lukanov, Bulgaria's former prime minister and one of the country's leading reformist politicians, was assassinated in a mafia-style killing, which looked almost like a copy-cat version of the murder of Russia's leading TV journalist, Vladislav Listjev, in Moscow two years earlier. The assassin, camouflaged as a tramp, was waiting outside Lukanov's house and shot him in the heart and in the head – precisely as in Listev's case.

Lukanov was an outspoken critic of the slow pace of reform in Bulgaria. Some time before his death, he claimed publicly that he had evidence pointing to a 'return to Stalinist methods' to be introduced by Bulgaria's ruling Socialist Party. His murder sparked off rumours of troops in the streets of Sofia, of an impending state of emergency and even of a possible military coup.

Almost simultaneously, nine of Bulgaria's biggest private banks collapsed, effectively destroying the country's financial network. Inflation reached truly cosmic proportions. According to a London broadsheet, ruthless leather-clad gangsters, nicknamed 'wrestlers,' swarmed all over the place and 'have transformed Sofia's cityscape.' And my recently published *Lonely Planet* guidebook warned that 'foreigners are robbed by locals who invite them for a drink,' which didn't bode well for the purposes of my wine-familiarisation trip.

As if all that were not enough, an epidemic of meningitis, triggered by the plummeting living standards, was raging in many areas of the country – a fact that made me carry water-purification pills in my luggage.

I learnt more bad news from the Bulgarian newspapers offered on my Balkan Airlines flight from Heathrow to Sofia. The Bulgarian language is similar to Russian, and uses the same Cyrillic alphabet, so I could understand almost everything, although, on that occasion, I wished I couldn't.

The papers led with speculations about possible motives for Lukanov's murder: economic, political or mafia-connected. These were followed by the news of yet another death (this time, natural and non-violent), that of Bulgaria's legendary clairvoyant and fortune-teller Baba Vanga (Granny Vanga), reputedly consulted at various times by Hitler, Brezhnev, Gorbachev, as well as by generations of Bulgarian leaders, who all wanted to know what the future had in store for them.

In 1943 the blind peasant oracle, who lost her sight at the age of twelve during a whirlwind, allegedly told Hitler 'to leave Russia alone or face defeat.' In 1992, she assured Yeltsin of his forthcoming landslide election victory. She was also able to brief many grieving parents as to the exact whereabouts of their runaway offspring. And so on. Blind Baba Vanga was one of the country's few remaining optimists (probably just because she was blind): she predicted the onset of bright and plentiful times for Bulgaria, without specifying when they were going to come. But the undisputed fact that she had been able to foretell correctly the time of her own death was encouraging.

There seemed to be no end to negative newspaper stories. One was entitled 'Plovdiv Residential Area Attacked by Worms.' It was too much, and I put the papers aside.

A sumptuous in-flight meal, washed down by a glass of excellent Bulgarian red wine, cheered me up a bit. 'Surely, things cannot be that hopeless in a country that can produce such refined wine,' I mused in self-consolation.

From what I knew, despite all the political mess and economic instability, the wine-making industry of Bulgaria, one of the World's four top wine exporters, was doing well. Brits alone were drinking more than three million cases of Bulgarian wine a year. My research files were bursting with recent press cuttings, in which snooty and hard-to-please British wine critics described Bulgarian wines as 'fine,' 'unbelievably good,' 'gloriously juicy' and 'safest choice,' while Bulgarian wine-makers were credited with 'delivering great wine under incredibly difficult conditions.'

The plane gently probed the ground with its wheels, as if to check whether it was firm enough for landing. In a few minutes, it taxied up to a dimly lit terminal with a 'SOF A' neon sign on its roof.

'I' was missing from the sign, but *I* was in Sofia – there was little doubt about it. And in 'SOF A,' too.

'Don't lose it!' the immigration officer blurted out handing me a dreaded 'statistical card' – a leftover from totalitarianism. The card was supposed to be stamped in every hotel I was to stay at. The punishment for its loss was probably a prison sentence. Or a firing squad. It all made sense: communists calling themselves 'Socialists' were still in power in Bulgaria.

A stooping young man in a leather jacket took a step towards me the moment I stumbled into the arrivals lounge. Still under the influence of the gory newspaper stories, I decided he was a 'wrestler.' Having dropped my suitcase, I frantically tried to recall the latest Taekwondo moves we had learnt at my martial arts class in London.

'Are you Vitali?' he asked me in perfect Russian, picking up my suitcase from the floor.

'Yes, and you must be from Domaine Boyar,' I said in English with relief.

He shook his head.

I was about to wrench my suitcase from the cheeky Russian gangster's grip, when I remembered that shaking one's head in Bulgaria means 'yes.'

The young man's name was Christo. A Domaine Boyar official, he had studied in Moscow and was married to a Russian woman. He spoke Russian with a good Moscow accent.

'Has the situation in Sofia stabilised a little?' I asked him in the car.

He nodded, which, in the peculiar Bulgarian body language, meant 'no.'

It was late afternoon, but the dark streets of Sofia were already deserted. Very few cars were on the road. Most traffic lights didn't work. The kerb was lined with hundreds of wheel-less and door-less Soviet-made Ladas abandoned by their owners, who could not afford to maintain them. Flags were flying at half-mast on lampposts with no lamps. It looked as if the whole city had retired into itself, waiting for more troubles to come.

'At this spot a bomb exploded the other day,' said Christo pointing at an intersection of two wide streets.

'No one knows why.'

At the money-exchange office of my InterContinental hotel, I was given a thick wad of greasy lev banknotes in exchange for £20 – an average monthly salary in Bulgaria, which I intended to use as a couple of days' pocket money. The exchange rate was in the region of 350 lev per pound.

'Yesterday, the lev suddenly rose slightly against the US dollar, for no reason. It's chaos,' commented Christo.

All telephones at the hotel were switched off by the city council as a punishment for a neighbouring factory, which had refused to dispose of its rubbish and dumped it in the street. The hotel had nothing to do with the slovenly factory, but was unfortunate enough to share the same telephone line.

The famous fountains of Sofia had been dead for over five years. 'No one cares any more,' explained a street bookseller, whose wobbly stall in the former 9th of September (the start of communist rule in 1944), now 3rd of March (the victory over the Turks) Square sagged under glossy Bulgarian translations of Western pulp which nobody was buying.

Old men, with tearful eyes and faces of brown parchment, sat on benches under acacia trees surrounded by begging gypsy kids, whom they waved away without looking – like flies. Khaki-painted military jeeps were parked here and there.

The faded totalitarian grandeur of Sofia's centre reminded me of Moscow in the eighties. The only restored building was that of the Bulgarian People's Bank. A long line of queuers eager to withdraw their shrinking savings was snaking towards its entrance. The nearby Italian embassy was besieged by crowds of visa-seekers. In a small park around the church of Alexander Nevsky, grannies were selling portraits of Lenin, old samovars and 'The KGB is Alive' badges. And on the opposite side of the former Russian – now King the Liberator – Street, there was a strip club. Posters of the forthcoming Miss Erotic and Miss Lingerie competitions were stuck to its walls.

Weeping female voices could be heard from the magnificent Byzantine St Sofia Cathedral, where a morning liturgy was under way. 'Dear foreigners. We thank you with gratitude for your donation,' said a handwritten English sign on its front door. The moan-like Orthodox prayer floated above the empty mausoleum of Georgy Dimitrov (the founder of the Bulgarian Communist Party had been reburied at Sofia's Central Cemetery); above the Stalinist wedding cake of the Communist Party headquarters; above the former Park of Freedom, renamed the Garden of Tsar Boris; above the statue of a lion put up in 1981 to commemorate thirteen hundred years of the Bulgarian state. A stray dog sniffed the ground around the stone lion, then lifted one leg and desecrated the symbol of once-glorious Bulgarian statehood. The lion was unperturbed. Battered and unkempt, he himself had come to resemble an oversized homeless dog.

From the centre, I took a tram to the suburb of Vitosha, on the outskirts of the city, where Bulgaria's Communist Party elite used to reside, separated from the real world by the natural wall of the Vitosha hill. This exclusive area was now occupied by Sofia's new rich, many of whom were the former party elite, so they didn't even have to move out of their ivy-covered cottages with stunning mountain views.

There, in quiet Sekvoya Street, stood the villa of Todor Zhivkov, Bulgaria's communist dictator for thirty-five years, from 1954 to 1989. His rule was marked by unquestioning loyalty to the Soviet Union, to which he referred as Bulgaria's elder brother. This tanks-enforced 'brotherhood' was the subject of many sad jokes. Here's one. At an international exhibition the Soviet Union showed a red elephant carrying a slogan: 'The Soviet elephant is the best elephant in the world!' And Bulgaria displayed a smaller elephant under the placard: 'The Bulgarian elephant is the younger brother of the Soviet elephant!'

After the popular uprising of 1989, the ageing Zhivkov was charged with nepotism (among other things, he appointed his daughter, Lyudmila, Bulgaria's minister of culture), corruption and the dictatorial abuse of power; he was put on trial, but his failing health saved him from a prison sentence. A frail octogenarian, he now lived under house arrest in Vitosha with his middle-aged granddaughter.[15]

Zhivkov's villa, half hidden from view by thick foliage, was surrounded by a fence with security cameras on top. I wondered whether they were there to protect Zhivkov from the anger of the Bulgarian people whom he had tormented for thirty-five years, or to protect the people from the nasty Stalinist ghost lurking behind the walls of this nice-looking mansion in Vitosha.

Through my Sofia contacts, I obtained Zhivkov's telephone number, and I dialled it from my hotel as soon as its telephone lines were restored. The phone was answered by a woman, probably his granddaughter. I introduced myself and asked whether I could have a word with Mr Zhivkov (with the stress on 'Mister'). I wanted to ask him only one question: whether or not he had any regrets. 'Comrade Zhivkov is ill,' the woman said after a pause (with the stress on 'Comrade'). 'He is in bed and does not give interviews.' I was not particularly upset, for I knew what the answer to my intended question would have been. Speaking at his trial several years before, Zhivkov had blamed the Kremlin and staunchly refused to repent.

My farewell-to-Sofia dinner at Across the Road Behind the Cupboard was coming to an end. After the fourth bottle of wine, the mood of my hosts had improved dramatically.

'There are no rules, but the game goes on,' said Nikolai. 'Nature is on our side, and the quality of our wines keeps going up.'

'This year's vintage is especially good, which means that politics does not affect wines,' concluded Christo.

'Grape types tend not to recognise political borders,' Angela Muir once noted in *Decanter* magazine. Whether wines were immune from politics or not, they were definitely capable of turning incorrigible pessimists into cautious optimists. If only until the following morning.

[15] Todor Zhivkor died in May, 1998.

Ceausescu's Plonk

At Vrancea winery, not far from the Romanian town of Focsani, I was offered a tasting of Galbena Odobesti, a locally produced sweet white.

'This is our best-selling brand, the so-called "*grand cru*", although you might not like its taste,' said the winery's director, somewhat apologetically. 'Before the revolution, we made only small quantities of it for the VIPs. It was the favourite wine of Ceausescu, Romania's communist dictator, and we used to send regular consignments of it to all his residences. We had to do it secretly, because Ceausescu never drank in public and tried to portray himself as ascetic and teetotal. Galbena is very popular in Romania now, because it is cheap and also because in people's minds it is associated with Ceausescu's lifestyle. We sell one hundred thousand bottles of it a day. Shop owners come here pleading for it, and it brings us a lot of profit.'

I was not in a hurry to take a sip from my glass. I already knew that the dictator's tastes in architecture and interior design were tacky, unsophisticated and reeking of megalomania. I was wondering what his favourite wine would taste like, and hoping that Galbena's amazing popularity in the impoverished post-communist Romania had more to do with its low price than with Ceausescu himself. After a guided tour of 'Ceausescu's Bucharest' several days before, I was finding it hard to imagine that anyone in Romania could feel nostalgic about him.

We had started with the House of the Republic (also known as Ceausescu's Palace), the world's second-largest building after the Pentagon, although much uglier.

The Italians have an interesting way of conveying the size of an object with the help of suffixes alone. For example, '*casa*' is a normal house, '*casetta*' or '*casino*' is a smallish house, '*casaccio*' is a huge house, and '*casuccio*' is a huge, ugly house. The Palace of the Republic, which jumped at us in all its mind-boggling monstrosity at the end of Bucharest's Unirii Boulevard, was an archetypal casuccio. The 101-metre-high building was the shape of a giant wedding-cake disfigured by drunken guests (Ceausescu had copied its design from a much smaller palace of the North Korean dictator, Kim Il Sung, in Pyongyang). For six years, twenty thousand workers and four hundred architects toiled twenty-four hours a day on its construction. Only Ceausescu's execution in December 1989 stopped him completing the project.

Next to the Palace of the Republic, stood the somewhat smaller Palace of Science, housing the National Institute for Science and Technology, of which Ceausescu's semi-literate wife, Elena, a virago with a passion for French champagne, American fur coats and expensive jewellery, had been president.

Even after their death, the vicious Ceausescu couple dominated Bucharest's city-scape, if now only in stone.

I was surprised at the entry charge to the Palace of the Republic: 3,000 leu ($1) for the locals and 15,000 leu for foreigners, who were also allowed to use photo- and video-cameras inside the building for the additional fee of 100,000 lei. Charging people for looking at the excesses of Romania's recent tragedy did not seem right and was made even more bizarre by the fact that the post-Ceausescu Romanian government had made the palace a venue for conferences, receptions and other state occasions. To me, this partially explained why democratic reforms had not taken off in Romania: how could the government take reformist decisions in houses swarming with the ghosts of the country's not-so-distant totalitarian past?

'Welcome to the Palace!' said an unsmiling female guide, addressing our small English-speaking group, which, apart from Cornel and myself, consisted of two bewildered Indians with camcorders.

Leading the way along the 150-metre-long, eighteen-metre-high neo-Baroque gallery, with marble floors and mahogany walls, she bombarded us with astounding statistics. The total volume of the palace's interior was 2,500,000 cubic metres, more than that of the largest Egyptian pyramid. The 330,000 square metres of flooring were covered with 220,000 square metres of handmade Transylvanian carpets. Three thousand massive crystal chandeliers, on which Elena Ceausescu had been especially keen, hung from the ceilings. The foundations of the palace, which was connected by underground tunnels with numerous Ceausescu residences around Bucharest, were 500 metres deep, and housed an earthquake-resistant bomb-shelter. A special underground mini-train was always ready to take Ceausescu and his wife to their private airport in case of emergency.

With a touch of pride in her voice, the guide informed us that the Ceausescus were the palace's main architects and interior designers: every single detail had to be approved by them.

'How many rooms are there in the palace?' asked one of the dumbfounded Indians.

'No one counted,' she answered.

The interiors of the sumptuous palaces of the Russian tsars, of which I had seen many, looked like barren peasants' huts in comparison with this cornucopia of tasteless extravagance. With disgust, I looked at tacky golden roses hanging from the chandeliers, at curtains embroidered with gold and silver, at columns made of pink marble, at flowery patterns on the carpets, repeating in minute detail the ornamentation of the ceilings above them. The crude 'little girl's' hand of Ceausescu's overbearing wife was felt everywhere. If architecture was indeed music in stone, the palace was a dull and pretentious cacophony played by a madman. It was the world's biggest monument to wasteful, aggressive and authoritarian kitsch, created by imbecile parvenus. The illusion of the Ceausescus' ominous presence was almost complete under its lavish ceilings. Being there was like conversing with the horrible couple at a pompous and meaningless reception.

Feeling tiny and humiliated, I looked out of the window. Debris and devastation were everywhere. In front of the palace, the building of the former Radio Centre lay in ruins, its dark glassless windows gaping at the world like empty eye-sockets. Next to it stood the iron and concrete carcass of an unfinished fast-food factory, another crazy project of the Ceausescus, who had ordered that dozens of such factories, popularly known as 'starvation clinics,' be built in Bucharest (one could still see their abandoned stone skeletons with protruding fittings here and there). The idea was that people would pop in there after work to buy pre-cooked and pre-packaged warm meals, which they would consume in their dark, cold flats, thus saving precious energy. Under Ceausescu, Romania, which had supplied the whole of the Luftwaffe with petrol during the Second World War, was able to offer its citizens water, heating and electricity for just two hours a day. All the country's resources went to accommodate the perverse needs and tastes of the Ceausescus – rulers whom the Romanian people did not deserve.

'Have a good stay in *my* country!' the guide said with a scowl and with emphasis on 'my.' It made me start with recognition: her farewell remark could have been borrowed from Dracula, who, in Bram Stoker's book, ended one of his letters to Jonathan Harker with 'I trust that you will enjoy your stay in *my* beautiful land!'

'You know why I don't want to take my two sons to the palace? I don't know what to tell them.' Cornel, my Romanian escort, said to me, back in the car. 'They will ask me, "How come all this money was wasted? How come you, Daddy, were a member of the Communist Party? How come you kept silent all those years?" I don't know what to say.'

We were heading for Ceausescu's last abode: two cubic metres of solid earth – and no chandeliers. His wife, Elena, was buried in the same cemetery. Only a couple of weeks before my tour of 'Ceausescu's Bucharest,' the vicious couple were joined there by their wayward son Nicu, an alcoholic and a skirt-chaser, who had died of cirrhosis of the liver in a Viennese hospital.

I felt as if I had known the Ceausescu family for years. It all started in Moscow in the late eighties, when, quite by chance, I bought several English books, printed in the US, from a drunken Soviet ex-diplomat. One of them was called *Red Horizons*. It was written by Ion Pacepa, Ceausescu's closest adviser and former head of the Romanian intelligence service, who had defected to the West. For many years, General Pacepa was a trusted confidant of the Ceausescu family and was able to observe their everyday life from behind the scenes. The stupidity, grotesque drunkenness, nepotism, scheming, brutality, greed and corruption described in the book were hair-raising and bordering on wild fantasy, even for someone like myself, hardened by many years of life in the USSR, which did not look half as terrifying as Ceausescu's Romania as portrayed by Pacepa.

The self-proclaimed Romanian president, referred to by his underlings as 'the Comrade' (what an irony), was shown routinely ordering assassinations, masterminding global terrorism, dancing with anger when things went wrong and drinking unchilled wine in generous quantities. He wore his suits only once, fearful that devious Western intelligence services would impregnate them with a cancer-inducing agent. He made his beloved black Labrador, Corbu, a colonel in the Romanian army and gave him his own car and driver. And so on ...

Elena, officially dubbed 'The Romanian people's most esteemed daughter,' was portrayed as an alcoholic, a nymphomaniac, a devious ignoramus and a compulsive hoarder, who was firmly in control of her weak-spirited husband and, through him, of Romania. It was not she who was Ceausescu's second-in-command, but the other way round.

The most disgusting real-life character in Pacepa's book was Nicu, who spent his time carousing at nightly saturnalia, smashing whisky bottles against walls, abusing everyone around him and screwing everything that moved.

My drinking trainer Evgeny Bulavin used to go to the neglected and run-down Kharkov zoo in the moments of despair which usually coincided with hangovers: the sight of the poor caged animals never failed to reassure him slightly. As he used to say, it was good to see living creatures whose lives were even more miserable than his own. Prior to getting hold of *Red Horizons*, I used to rely for the same purpose on the North Korean magazine *Korea Today*, readily available at Soviet news-stalls, after which a *Pravda* editorial read almost like an erotic novel.

Everything was relative indeed, and nothing could evoke the life-saving feeling of the relativity of suffering like Ion Pacepa's extraordinary book. It was one of the few treasured volumes of my Moscow library which I took with me when I had to defect to the West. It survived my numerous moves between Britain and Australia. Bedraggled and dog-eared, it lies on my desk as I am writing these lines.

A kiosk at the cemetery's gate was selling flowers and crude wooden coffins. I wondered what type of customers the florist-cum-undertaker could attract. Someone who wanted to buy a bunch of flowers to put on the grave of a loved one and suddenly decided to get a coffin, too – for himself? Or someone who came to bury a relative and forgot to bring a coffin?

Behind the gate, two rough types sat on a bench, taking turns to swig a brownish liquid that looked very much like the Biomedicine of my youth, from the all-too-familiar 'fire-extinguisher' bottle, the size and the shape of a surface-to-air missile. They turned out to be grave-diggers enjoying their break between burials. One of them volunteered to take us to the Ceausescus' graves, located in three different parts of the cemetery.

A simple stone cross with a red star on top stood on the grave of one of the twentieth century's vilest dictators. The cross was half covered with flowers and faded wreaths. 'Ceausescu Nicolae 1918-1989' was written on it. Half a dozen grave-faced and black-clad women huddled around. They crossed themselves frantically and stuck burning candles – a sign of respect – into the mellow soil.

'He was a very good man,' whispered one of them, and her eyes under her black kerchief filled with tears.

How much suffering do people have to go through to reach the point at which they stop worshipping their dead tyrants?

A handwritten note on a sheet of paper from a school notebook lay under the cross. I asked Cornel to translate it for me. 'Personal experience is an expensive school. Those who are not very clever study at this school. Clever people learn from the experience of others,' it said.

This meaningful note on the grave of Nicolae Ceausescu, whose monument in the shape of the monstrous Palace of the Republic still dominated Bucharest and whose vicious ghost had not been exorcised from the country's mutilated soul, gave hope that the people of Romania would one day be able to draw the right lessons from their own tragic past.

Elena's grave was in the cemetery's opposite corner. Inseparable during their lifetime, the Ceausescu couple were finally separated in death. This arrangement corresponded to the popular perception of Elena as a manipulating witch, who held the main blame for Ceausescu's crimes. At least in death Nicolae was spared the constant presence of his dominating wife. There were neither mourners nor flowers at her grave, which was decorated only with a bare stone cross. It was strange to see crosses on the graves of the couple, who didn't believe in anything but power and made sure that hundreds of Romanian churches were blown up. Was it a truly Christian attempt at forgiveness of the atrocious sinners who had died unrepentant and as such were impossible to forgive?

On Elena's grave, there was a note, too. 'Oh, Mother, sweet Mother, when leaves fall down from the trees, you are calling for me. Your beloved son, who has made lots of mistakes in his life.'

The fresh grave of Nicu, the Ceausescus' maverick son, was overlaid with wreaths, most of which hadn't had time to fade, and was surrounded by a crowd of mourners.

'Nicu is widely perceived as his parents' victim and a good guy,' explained Cornel. 'Tens of thousands turned up at his recent funeral.'

Standing at Nicu's grave, also decorated with a cross, though only a wooden one, I remembered a scene from *Red Horizons* describing a state banquet, at which drunken Nicu, 'a good guy,' was enjoying himself in his habitual manner. I knew it almost by heart:

> A waiter came in with a silver platter full of oysters. 'Put it here, in the middle,' ordered Nicu, pointing toward the table. 'Is there any seasoning on them?'
> 'They are just fresh and raw, Comrade Nicu,' replied the waiter.
> 'They need seasoning, you idiot …'
> He precariously climbed up on to the table and started urinating on them, careful to 'season' every oyster. 'Come on, comrades. Let's have an oyster,' he urged the guests …

> 'Nobody's eating? Who doesn't like my seasoning? Nobody? Then I'll wash them off.' And Nicu started squirting with a siphon bottle over the oysters and over the rest of us sitting around the table …
> We left Nicu pushing a waitress toward the edge of the table while tearing off her blouse. 'I want to f– you here. Right here on this table, you slut.'

Having had to share a Moscow communal flat with the drinking and womanising son of a top Soviet functionary for several years, I knew how correct this seemingly improbable description was.

Unlike the mourners, I didn't feel like paying my respects to Nicu Ceausescu, simply because I didn't have any.

Having paid the grave-digger off with enough leu to allow him to buy another surface-to-air alcohol-fuelled rocket, capable of briefly propelling him and his colleague-in-spade away from the earth they had to dig, we drove to the Memorial Cemetery of the victims of the 1989 revolution, during which eleven hundred people were killed in Bucharest alone. Romania's recent history went hand-in-hand with death.

The fresh burial ground in north Bucharest was surrounded by hideous beehive-like apartment blocks. It was deserted, except for packs of hungry stray dogs scouring among the graves, pissing and copulating on them.

The 'victims of the revolution' were mostly teenagers, brutally killed by the Securitate during pro-democracy demonstrations in November-December 1989. Their faces looked reproachfully out from mass-produced obelisks (not crosses), as if saying, 'What have you done to us? We do not belong here. Our photos should be in school albums, not on tombstones.'

They could now communicate with this world through epitaphs only.

'I didn't leave this life because I wanted to. What I am now, you will become. My dear parents and brothers, please forgive me for leaving you when I was only 13. Octavian Burcioaila – "Tavi" ' (a young bespectacled boy, with a know-it-all look on his face, who was probably bullied at school as a nerd).

'His train of life had only two stops – Revolution and Death. Stan Bogdan, 1970-1989' (a rugby ball lay on his grave).

'She was killed by the tyrants of the Ceau clan when peacefully demonstrating for free Romania. Gabriela Popescu, 1968-1989' (what a stunningly beautiful girl she was).

'We thank you and wait for you to be born again – sister, mother, father. Elin Marinescu, 1976-1989.'

'I loved my country. Vali-Valeriu Miu, 27 years old. Student. Died December 1989.'

I wished the nagging Swedish wine writer with whom I had had dinner on my first night in Bucharest were there with me. But he was elsewhere – probably eating lunch, paid for by his Romanian hosts, and complaining of the lack of toilet paper at his hotel and of the abundance of unwashed cars in the unswept, dirty streets. He didn't realise that it was not dirt that the cars and the streets of Bucharest were covered with. They were soaked in human blood.

Nursing a glass of Ceausescu's favourite drink in the tasting room of Vrancea winery, I recalled another passage from *Red Horizons*, in which Ion Pacepa described a typical drinking evening with Ceausescu in one of the dictator's personal wine cellars:

> Before we were able to reach a table, a waiter in black tie materialised out of nowhere holding a tray with a newly opened bottle of wine and one large glass. Known as 'Odobesti Galbena' ['Odobesti' means 'Yellow'], it is Ceausescu's favourite, a flavourful wine of the same colour and consistency as sunflower oil, which is made in very limited quantities in Odobesti, a Moldavian village renowned for its wines. Ceausescu downed two glasses on his feet, then sat down in his favourite easy chair beside a heavy, round oak table. The waiter refilled Ceausescu's glass and set the bottle down beside him in an ice bucket containing no ice – Ceausescu does not want his drinks cold, in order to protect his vocal cords.

When I finally tasted the drink, I realised that Ceausescu's favourite wine was indeed similar to sweetened sunflower oil, not just in 'colour and consistency' but in taste as well. If the kitsch interior of his Palace of the Republic could be somehow liquidised and expressed in wine-making terms, it would result in Galbena Odobesti.

My Prague-based friend Igor Pomerantsev was right: wines – just like humans – could be immoral.

'Can you find me a spittoon, please?' I asked the winery's director.

In the Land of Dracula

A sign saying 'Motel Dracula' flashed outside the windows of our car. We had entered Romania's Dracula country, the area around the medieval Castle Bran, which should have been long ago renamed Castle Bram, for it was Bram Stoker's wild imagination that made it into the residence of the world's most famous vampire, Count Dracula.

Due to the extraordinary popularity of Bram Stoker's book, Count Dracula became an international superstar. Over 250 feature films, 800 documentaries, over 1,000 scholarly studies as well as hundreds of novels, ballets, musicals and operas were inspired by Dracula, or rather by the original Bram Stoker book. There are also thousands of Dracula societies world-wide, which include the New York Count Dracula Fan Club and the Bram Stoker International School in Dublin. The so-called 'Drakpaks' actually explain how to become a vampire ('the first qualification for a vampire is that you have to be dead') and these are mailed around the globe by a certain Jeannie Youngson, president of the International Dracula Fan Club. There is even an international chain of 'Transylvania' restaurants serving 'Hot Bat' burgers, 'Blue Blood' cocktails and 'Dead Body' buns (one of them – in London's West Hampstead – cordially invites customers to celebrate their own funerals there: no wonder it is permanently empty).

Bram Stoker's Irish descendants still happily live off the proceeds from the book, for which the author was paid no advance in 1897 and only received 1s. 6d. after the first 100 copies were sold.

Bram Stoker based his creation on Vlad Tepes, a fifteenth century Romanian prince and a founder of Bucharest, nicknamed 'Dracul' (which means 'devil' in Romanian), who had a predilection for impaling his enemies on wooden stakes. In Romania, Vlad the Impaler was always regarded as a national hero, a connoisseur of good wines and a keen bat-keeper, whose cruelty and the number of impalees had been crudely exaggerated by vilifiers. In Bucharest, I bought a Romanian tourist brochure on Bran Castle, which was trying to shift Dracula's blood-drinking habits onto the sixteenth century Hungarian Countess Elisabeth Bathor, who lived in Transylvania and, allegedly, enjoyed biting into the flesh of her female servants.

It is interesting that in the years of Ceausescu's rule, all references to Dracula were strictly taboo, probably because the analogies between the two were too strong. In the eyes of ordinary Romanians, Count Dracula became a double victim – of Bram Stoker's vilification and of Ceausescu's paranoia.

Shortly after the revolution, a campaign to restore Dracula's good name was launched by Vlad Tepes enthusiasts. It was soon joined by Romanian tourist authorities, who decided to capitalise on Dracula's dark fame and began promoting Transylvania as 'Dracula Land' to attract foreign visitors. The Transylvanian Society of Dracula was formed 'as a reaction to the multitude of sub-human, cheap productions, draped in blood and blind terror, in the generic name Dracula.'

The society proclaimed itself 'a non-political, non-governmental, non-profit organisation' with the twofold aim: 'the analysis of the penetration of the Western myth of Dracula into Romania and the world at large,' and the establishment of Prince Vlad Dracula's true role. The alleged 'non-profit' character of the society caused me some doubt, since half of the Articles of its 'Statute' dealt with membership fees and control over Dracula paraphernalia.

Under the auspices of the society, Dracula tours of three different grades were drafted. They promised fearful initiation rites, live witch-hunts, visits to haunted cemeteries, 'goblins, trolls and pixies roaming the domain.' The tips for the courageous included:

- Hope nothing
- Trust your guide more. Not that we see another choice
- Take an umbrella

In the end, each visitor was guaranteed a Dracula Certificate saying: 'This is to certify that the courageous (so-and-so) has followed a Grade (such-and-such) Twilight Zone Dracula Tour and survived.'

This over-the-top PR campaign ended in a spectacular failure. It succeeded in frightening the potential tourists away *before* they had a chance to visit 'Dracula Land.'

The closest I ever came to a real-life vampire was in Australia. In 1991, all Australian newspapers wrote about Tracy Wiggington, a dysfunctional young woman from Brisbane who avoided mirrors (she was ugly, too) and once on a beach – probably out of boredom – stabbed a drunken businessman and drank some of his blood. Engrossed in blood-sucking, she didn't notice how her credit card, which was later picked up by the police, fell out of her pocket. She was arrested on the following day.

My advice to all would-be vampires is this: before venturing on a blood-sucking expedition, make sure you have left your credit card at home. I hope Jeannie Youngson will include it in her 'Drakpak.'

In 1995, Castle Bran was the venue for the first World Dracula Congress, which lasted for five days and brought together Dracula experts from all over the globe, but mostly from the USA. Among the papers presented to the Congress were 'The Image of Dracula in Juvenile Literature,' 'The Cult of Dracula and the New Age Religions,' 'Links Between Vampirism and Satanic Scares,' 'Dracula as a Classic Wandering Jew Figure' and (last but not least) 'Bram Stoker's Work as a Book of Menstrual Taboos.' The titles alone make it clear that the congress was a treasure-trove for an ambitious clinical psychiatrist.

Castle Bran was eerie. For half an hour we trudged along its squeaky floorboards and climbed its dark, winding staircases. I was most impressed by Dracula's own spacious four-poster bed, made of black wood. And although I knew that Bram Stoker had chosen Castle Bran at random and described it from photos he had found in the British Library, the illusion of the count's presence was almost complete, and I wouldn't have been surprised had he suddenly emerged from under the bed and greeted us 'in excellent English, but with strange intonation': 'Welcome to my house! Enter freely and of your own will!'

At the museum shop downstairs, they sold statuettes of Dracula, with his lips heavily covered either in blood or in raspberry jam, Dracula Vodka (which was red, of course), Dracula goblets, and Draculina soft drinks.

I opted for a modest postcard with a portrait of Vlad Tepes (alias Count Dracula) a plain-looking moustached man in a silly hood. His typically Romanian brown eyes had the puzzled and somewhat peevish expression of a grossly misunderstood person.

The nearby Peles Castle had seen many more real-life vampires and blood-suckers than Castle Bran. Built by King Carol I in 1883, it was used as a private retreat for leading communists under Ceausescu. It had 365 rooms, one for each day of the year. And further up the mountain stood the Villa Foisor, one of the many summer residencies of 'the Comrade' himself, who had made sure he was properly segregated even from his closest factotums and was always on top of them.

Our climb to the villa was blocked by a very young corporal of the Romanian army, with a Kalashnikov behind his back.

'You can't enter,' he told us sternly. 'The villa is closed to public.'

A bottle of wine (we had some in the boot) softened his protective resolve.

'Sorry, but I still can't let you pass,' he said accepting the gift (which was clearly intended as a bribe). 'But I have been inside, and I am prepared to tell you what I saw.'

It was raining. We stood under a tree in the middle of a thick Transylvanian forest, listening to the youthful corporal.

'The things you can see there ... ' he started with a dreamy expression on his childish face. 'It is a different world ... Swimming pools in each room ... Artificial water-falls ... Mirrors ... A greenhouse with lemon and orange trees ... It is like a dream ... I simply cannot express it.'

'What is there now?' I asked him.

'No one knows. The house belongs to the government. Prime Minister Vacaroiu stayed there recently with his family for ten days.'

As we walked away, I looked back. The corporal stood at attention, with a radiant smile of recollection on his round peasant face. In his imagination, he was still moving through the mirrored interior of the villa.

His Kalashnikov sub-machine-gun no longer looked threatening, for the corporal had a bottle of good wine in his hand.

In Dresden with 'Princess Diana'

On my first visit to Dresden in October 1992, I was mistaken for a Princess Di's bodyguard. I came there to report on the Queen's first trip to the former East Germany for the now-defunct European newspaper. With a young lady from Her Majesty's press office (who vaguely resembled the Princess of Wales), we stepped off the Royal Train and got immediately separated from the rest of the 'rat pack.' To be in time for the next Royal function, we had to run across Dresden at random stopping every now and then to ask for directions. A pedestrian whom we questioned on how we could get to the Rathaus (Town Hall), squinted at my companion and said in English: 'I know who you are. You are Princess Diana.' Despite the lady's ardent denial, he didn't budge: 'Don't try to fool me,' he insisted. 'You are Diana!' 'And who do you think I am? Prince Charles?' I demanded impatiently. 'No,' he uttered firmly. 'You must be Diana's bodyguard!'

I shall never forget that first flying visit to Dresden. The mutilated capital of Saxony, once known as the Florence on the Elbe and the realm of the glorious Saxon kings, had only just started recovering from the forty-odd years of Communist rule. The roads were rugged, the houses looked dreary and unkempt. But what saddened me most was the painfully familiar expression on people's faces, the one that I used to call 'the seal of oppression' – a peculiar haunted look, brought about by years of life under totalitarianism, with its fear, shortages, hypocrisy and daily struggle for survival. It made them look as if they were constantly expecting a blow from behind their backs. Two years of re-united Germany were not enough to erase it. And Dresden itself was carrying that 'seal of oppression' too.

The locals showed little enthusiasm for the Royal visit. The Queen was even booed briefly when attending the service of reconciliation at the Kreuzkirche. This came as no surprise to those remembering the horrors of the Anglo-American fire-bombing raids of 13 February 1945, during which Dresden, an officially designated Red Cross City , with no significant industry, was raised to the ground, and thousands of innocent people (135,000 by German estimates, and 35,000 according to one modern British source!) lost their lives. The famous baroque Frauenkirche in Neumarkt got a direct hit and was literally erased from the face of the earth. The Communists, installed in power by the Soviets after World War II, chose not to restore it and turned it into a 'war memorial.' In 1992, the inspired creation of architect George Bahr remained what it became in 1945 – a big pile of rubble.

Apart from the booing episode at the Kreutzkirche, the locals didn't show much hostility towards us. The long-suffering people of Dresden knew the dangers of being blatantly blamed for the crimes of previous generations.

'Go through my backside and then turn left!' the buxom blonde receptionist of my Dresden hotel said curtly when I asked her for directions to the Neumarkt.

That was how my second encounter with Dresden started in 1996: through the backside of the hotel receptionist (she meant the hotel's back door, of course).

It was like coming back to an entirely different, yet still recognisable, place. The huge statue of Lenin that used to dominate the cityscape had disappeared. I was told that the costs of its removal were so high that the city fathers had to appeal to the hard-up Dresden residents for donations.

The city tidied itself up by replacing a number of 'Communist' facades with new, 'Western' ones, although multiple scars of the past were still visible everywhere. Some of these 'scars' were mobile: clumsy GDR-made Trabants (or 'Trabbies,' as they were affectionately called in East Germany), these much-ridiculed snuffboxes on wheels, were coughing defiantly amongst gleaming Western limos. And 'the seal of oppression,' enhanced by the inevitable pains of re-unification, was still imprinted on people's faces. My guide, a sad-eyed middle-aged woman, complained of the trials of her daily life, spent in fear of losing her job and being replaced by a machine. 'That's what they are going to do to all the guides soon,' she asserted. My other contact, a local businessman, proudly wore a solar watch, totally useless in permanently overcast Saxony, and kept asking me the time every five minutes. He wouldn't part with this 'Western' toy of his for love or money …

Having successfully negotiated the receptionist's ample backside, which stretched for a good couple of miles, I finally reached the grassy Neumarkt Square and froze in disbelief: the foundation and some of the supports of the destroyed Frauenkirche were back in place! What's more, all its remaining fragments (about 10,000) were dug out, numbered and neatly piled under canvas tents around it. Non-existent only a couple of years before, the magnificent church was now being reborn in front of my eyes, put back together bit by bit like a giant jigsaw puzzle, with truly German meticulousness and precision.

Sitting at the Espresso Café next to the Square, I was thinking about the phenomenal resilience of Dresden – twice destroyed, twice disfigured, but never dispirited – when my attention was drawn to an opening hours sign on the Café's door:

'Samstag: 10.01 – 02.02
Sonntag: 10.01 – 22.21
Montag – Dienstag: 10.01 – 00.31'

Reading this, convinced me even further that the Frauenkirche was going to be fully restored one day, with not a single fragment gone missing.

My chance of being taken for Di's bodyguard on my third and last (so far) visit to Dresden was, mercifully, close to zero: the faces or real heroes and anti-heroes of the never-ending soap-opera of the British Royalty have become too familiar in the former East Germany.

Despite high unemployment, the creeping economic recession and the rise of the Far Right, Dresden's 'westernisation' was going ahead full speed. Asthmatic 'Trabbies' have all but vanished, and the only 'Communist' car I could spot was an abandoned coffin-like Skoda. A new, state-of-the art Volkswagen factory was being built in Neustadt area. Its main assembly line was being placed under a huge glass dome which would allow passers-by to observe the goings-on inside. The brand-new cars will be stored in a special tower, also made of glass and visible from afar. The whole project was about space, openness and accessibility – a daring architectural decision for Dresden, the city that values its newly re-acquired freedom.

The headquarters of the Stasi, the GDR's much-feared secret police, on the bank of the Elbe River, have been turned – quite symbolically – into a disco. Almost all the city facades, even the old Soviet-style apartment blocks, have been re-painted in bright 'Western' colours. It is amazing how much difference a bright paint can make. It puts a smile on the city's face.

Nowhere else have I seen so many travel agencies. Their 'density' in Dresden can only be compared with that of pubs and hairdressers in a small town somewhere in Kent. Residents of the former East Germany are making up for the years of enforced immobility by becoming the world's most adventurous travellers. You bump into them anywhere, even as far as in the Falklands, where I once met a group of fishermen from Dresden!

This time, I was put up at a brand-new hotel in Radebeul, a leafy Dresden suburb. The staff were helpful, yet unsmiling and tense. It was with sadness that I had to admit: 'the seal of oppression' was still there and was probably going to be the last totalitarian trait to disappear, for painting houses and changing street names is much easier than altering human mentality.

Speaking of street names, I was pleased to observe that Dresden did not take part in the name-changing frenzy which seized East Germany in the wake of the re-unification. In one city, they even re-named Spartacus Street, although, as far as I know, the ill fated Thracian slave and gladiator never tarnished himself by collaborating with the Communists. A convinced opponent of Marxism (I have always been of the opinion that Marks & Spencer is the only sort of Marxism that works) and never a fan of 'the great proletarian writer' Maxim Gorky, I was nevertheless pleased to see that both Karl Marx Street and Maxim Gorky Street still existed in Dresden. The latter, by the way, was next to my hotel, and it was in Maxim Gorky Street in Radebeul, Saxony, that I had one of the best Greek meals in my life ('Zorbas' – an extremely successful Greek restaurant, had Greek staff, the manager named Staphis, and all products – from ouzo to yoghurt – daily flown in from Athens).

Street names are part of history, and Dresdeners have learnt to treat history with care.

Eager to see how the restoration of the Frauenkirche was progressing, I took a tram from Radebeul to the city centre. I love trams, these moving wrinkles on the faces of modern cities. In Dresden, they have recently replaced the squeaky Czechoslovakian-made trams with much smoother German ones.

Despite the brand-new tram, my ride was slow and bumpy. According to the official statistics, six per cent of Dresden roads get 'upgraded' (read 'smoothed up' and 'Westernised') every year, yet it felt as if our tram was deliberately avoiding them. Also, every couple of minutes it would grind to a long halt at one of the countless sets of traffic lights that seemed to display three variations of one and the same colour – red. During one such stop, the driver entered the salon to announce: '*Tram Kaput!*,' and everyone had to get off. I did it without regret thanking Dresden's erratic electricity supply for interrupting my endless journey and giving me an excuse to get a cab.

My joy, however, was premature. The taxi was almost immediately stuck in the worst traffic jam I have ever experienced. Narrow and not-yet-'upgraded' streets of central Dresden were more suited for compact Trabants than for modern Western cars. Standing in a traffic jam, however, was much safer than moving. In the five minutes that it took us to reach Neumarkt, I witnessed two nasty collisions, both taken by the participating drivers with truly German sang-froid. What a striking contrast to the dull and nearly car-less streets of the GDR!

The piles of numbered stones in the middle of Neumarkt have melted away considerably since my previous visit, whereas the church itself, its regenerating carcass covered with scaffolding, has become several metres higher. I stood there for a while, mesmerised by the slow and painstaking process of restoration. Like the growth of a flower, it was invisible to the eye, and yet continuous and unstoppable. It was like witnessing the rebuilding of Democracy itself – a laborious task that cannot be completed overnight. Stone by stone, fragment by fragment, is the only way it can be done.

The restoration of the Frauenkirche is due to be completed by 2006 to coincide with the 800th anniversary of Dresden. Don't ask me why, but somehow I am sure that the moment the last piece of the church is fitted neatly into its niche, 'the seal of oppression' will be erased forever from the beautiful face of Dresden.

I'll have to come back again and see for myself.

Two Returns to Ukraine

In 1994, when I was living in London, a Channel 4 documentary gave me the opportunity to briefly return to Ukraine, my newly-independent, long-suffering motherland that I had originally left in 1978.

That was my very first glimpse of it as a separate country, no longer a province of the Soviet Empire where one could go to prison just for uttering the words 'independence' or 'Ukrainian passport' or for displaying a blue-and-yellow flag. I will never forget how two of my friends were expelled from the University of Kharkiv, Ukraine's second-largest city, simply for speaking Ukrainian to each other. They were accused of 'Ukrainian bourgeois nationalism.' What was so nationalistic, let alone 'bourgeois,' about speaking their own language in their own country? Only God, or possibly Brezhnev, knew ...

In 1994, my mother country seemed desperate, impoverished and confused. An oblong dusty mirror – part and parcel of every Soviet immigration point – hung above my head in the narrow passage of the Kiev airport passport control. The purpose of that overhead mirror had been a mystery. Was it designed to allow the border guard to scrutinise the crown of your head for signs of a toupee, or help him intercept your dissident thoughts? Or was its purpose to make every visitor feel like a trespasser?

One scene has been firmly imprinted in my memory from that visit: a beggar girl, no more than seven years old, sitting on the ground in Kiev's newly renamed Independence (formerly October Revolution) Square – the same square where 100 protesters, the so-called 'heavenly hundred,' would perish during the Maidan uprising twenty years later in 2014. Since coins had become victims of hyperinflation and no longer in use, passers-by tossed Ukrainian coupons, a kind of temporary currency, at the girl and she was half-submerged underneath those rumpled confetti-like pieces, not worth the paper they were printed on. In more poetical moments, I thought then that the beggar girl could be the young independent Ukraine reincarnated.

After another twenty-odd years of absence, I have returned once more and in the process have experienced a shock from which I am still reeling. My native country, or at least its capital Kiev, has become a different place. Having half-expected to find a bedraggled war-torn city, I was stunned by its impeccably clean streets and countless bars, coffee-shops and restaurants full of locals; by its shady boulevards and parks where, just like in my childhood, young families promenaded of an evening while older folks were engrossed in seemingly endless chess games on benches under acacia trees. The whole of Khreshchatik, Kiev's main thoroughfare, would get pedestrianised at weekends, with children playing in all ten of its empty traffic lanes.

The city appeared safe, calm and relaxed, with the only reminders of the ongoing war in Donbass to be found in newspapers and in fresh memorial plates on some of the buildings. People were reluctant to talk about the war, just taking it in their stride, as if still refusing to believe that their largely Russian-speaking nation had seen a large chunk of its territory annexed.

The biggest change, however, has befallen the Ukrainians themselves. I had always been of the opinion that it would take several generations to shake off that haunted Soviet look from peoples' faces, that peculiar I-am-waiting-to-be-hurt expression which I used to call 'the seal of oppression.' In 2016 Kiev, it is all but gone: its residents appear confident and relaxed – a Westernised, if not quite 'Western' crowd in Westernised, if not quite 'Western' streets, dotted with 'Censorship is banned by law' posters and banners promoting human rights. It was indeed a 'brave new world' born out of war, hypocrisy and centuries of oppression.

Ukraine was no longer a desperate beggar girl. A new emerging dignity could be felt everywhere – the dignity of a young and courageous nation confident of its future. 'It is Maidan that gave us this new confidence,' a Kiev friend told me. 'We believe that everything will be okay, that somehow we'll survive.'

Let's face it: modern Ukraine, one of Europe's largest and most populous countries, rich in both history and geography, remains a 'mystery wrapped in an enigma' for many a Westerner. As someone who happens to be Ukrainian by birth, I am often (much too often) mistaken for a person of an uncertain identity at best, and for a 'Russian' in all but name – in the worst and most frequent of scenarios. 'So, as a Ukrainian, you must be thrilled with Russia's World Cup progress?' I was asked the other day by one not-too-discerning a British colleague, to whom I had to explain patiently that supporting (even in soccer) a country which has annexed a chunk of my native land and is also conducting a proxy war against it would be … erm … unusual, if not to say masochistic, or wouldn't it? Forget about the over-curious 'colleagues' – even Her Majesty the Queen,' the UK's Head of State (if only a token one) insisted on my 'Russian-ness' when I was first introduced to her as 'originating from Ukraine' at press reception in Berlin in 1992! 'Oh, you were born in Russia then,' she muttered before moving on …

As for the books, particularly good books, on Ukraine available in the UK, there are probably more of them on offer than on say, Kiribati, yet definitely considerably fewer than those on Estonia …

'From Moscow's perspective, it is vital to prove that our people can't prevail over corruption, can't determine their own future and can't prosper without bowing to a foreign leader. But in Kiev we are proving every day that the Kremlin is wrong,' my namesake Vitali Klitschko, former world boxing champion and then the Mayor of Kiev, stated recently.

Of course, a flying visit is not enough to draw far-reaching conclusions. The country is still awash with problems; the government is weak, the economy is erratic, and corruption is rife. But as a travel writer, I have always believed that one can tell a lot about the state of a nation by simply mingling with morning commuters in city streets.

As I was leaving Kiev from the newly refurbished Zhuliany airport, waiting for my British passport to be stamped at the border control, I looked up: the overhead mirror – a hiccup of Soviet times – was still there. But it seems to have become much, much smaller …

Part Three
Travels To and in Blighty

My First Trip to Britain

Of all anniversaries, memorable dates, jubilees and birthdays, I never forget to mark one – 8 October 1988. It was on that warm autumn afternoon that – at the tender age of thirty-four – I arrived in Britain – and in the West – for the first time ever.

Uncharacteristically, I travelled to the UK by train – in a Moscow-Hook of Holland Soviet carriage (built in East Germany) which kept being attached to different trains (Moscow-Brest, Brest- Warsaw, Warsaw-Berlin and so on) during its forty-hour long journey, and then by ferry to Harwich.

It was my first ever trip outside the USSR, my first ever contact with the long-forbidden Western world and my first introduction to the then mysterious and alien Western way of life, including the technology of which the impressive Dutch ferry Queen Beatrix was the first shining example. But let's come back to it, or rather to her (I mean the ferry), a bit later.

I decided to take a train for one simple reason: I wanted my long-awaited journey to the West to be as long as possible, just to be able to savour it quietly, without rush ...

Even when already on the train, I was still finding it hard to believe that the journey, which I had always thought would never take place, was actually happening. But the fact remained: as a well-known Moscow journalist I was invited to England by the *Guardian* newspaper.

It was still more than two years before, under the growing pressure from the Soviet authorities, I'd have to defect, ie to leave the USSR for good. The first of several trips to follow prior to the ultimate defection, that first one was still very special, albeit I didn't know then that it would herald the beginning of my new life ...

And here I am, on board the soothingly rattling train, sharing the comfy sleeper compartment with the fellow train buffs – two Ukrainian lads on their way to visit relatives in Manchester. It is their first trip to the West too.

One of the lads immediately confides in me that he is trying to smuggle some cucumber and potato seeds for his brother in Manchester, having hidden then inside wooden *Matrioshka* dolls.

'Don't they have their own seeds in Britain?' I ask him.

'They probably do, but I want my brother to have genuine seeds from the soil of our mother Ukraine,' he says.

In my wallet, I carry £200, the maximum amount of foreign currency I am allowed to carry, solemnly given to me at Moscow's only exchange office. It feels like a real fortune and should be sufficient to sustain me for four weeks, to buy souvenirs (a contact lens holder for my editor's wife, a Bic razor blade for the editor himself – 'just one would do,' he had assured me gracefully; a supply of Alka Seltzers for a colleague; a watch for a mildly cooperative visa office clerk, a pair of jeans for my son, a sheep-skin coat for my wife and a hi-fi system) and, if I still have some money left, a cheap VHS player …

To minimize my food expenditure, I am carrying half-a-dozen cans of meat and fish preserves plus a huge chunk of *salo* – pure pork lard to be sliced and eaten with bread, with each slice containing enough calories to keep me going for a whole day …

Having survived the stern-faced sadism of the Soviet passport and customs control (with the latter asking routinely if anyone is carrying 'Bibles and pornography') in Brest the following morning, I and my two travel companions, felt a comradely bond, as if we have somehow been drawn into a perfectly legal, yet somewhat improper and shameful, collusion of leaving our great Soviet motherland, even if for a short while. The Ukrainian seed-smuggler was happy to have got away with his little innocent trick …

When after the seemingly endless change of bogies (from the Soviet 1,520 millimetre-wide gauge to the 1,435-millimetre-wide Polish and West European), when every carriage – with passengers inside – had to be lifted off the track by giant railway jacks, the train finally clattered across the patch of ploughed neutral land, which was no longer the USSR, all three of us felt both relieved and a bit worried: it was good to see that the seemingly limitless empire did have its limits after all, and yet, the uncertainly of the unknown that lay behind the barbed wire was unsettling.

Polish and later East German frontier guards – all withdrawn and coldly polite – kept boarding the train to stamp our uncomplaining Soviet 'foreign passports.' We knew they were not important and were bracing ourselves for the encounter with the Berlin Wall – the ultimate outpost of the Soviet empire, the Mother of All Borders.

At Berlin Friedrichstrasse Station the whole platoon of East German *Grenzsoldaten* (frontier guards), with snarling dogs straining at their leashes, got into our carriage. Like a bunch of uniformed plumbers, they were carrying screwdrivers, torches and portable ladders.

And the great search began.

They unscrewed everything that could be unscrewed and opened everything that could be opened in the carriage. One was shining his torch on the insides of the toilet.

What were they looking for? Bombs? Rocket launchers? Books by Solzhenitsyn? Or the same notorious 'Bibles and pornography?'

Finding nothing, they eventually got off – all but one, probably the most trusted soldier, who – as the train was crawling slowly towards the Wall – was peeping out of the window to make sure that nobody was riding outside the carriage hanging on by the door rails. Once reassured, he jumped out too …

For several minutes our carriage rode in pitch darkness. Then suddenly – a flood of lights which nearly blinded us. Flags fluttering in the wind. Myriads (or so it seemed) of gleaming rocket-shaped cars flying along the Spree River embankment in both directions.

The lights of West Berlin, the lights of Freedom – this is what they had been trying to hide from us behind the Berlin Wall …

For the rest of the journey I was as if in a trance. We rattled through bafflingly, almost lifelessly, clean and inspiringly dynamic West Germany. We rode through equally sterile, yet sleepy and toy-like, Holland. When the train stopped in Utrecht, I was the only passenger to venture onto the empty platform, only to be shooed back into the carriage by our carriage's ever-vigilant KGB steward.

My first step onto the Western soil. A small step for a man, it was completely unnoticed by mankind. But for me it was no less significant than Neil Armstrong's 'giant leap' onto the rough surface of the Moon.

At Hook of Holland, we boarded *Queen Beatrix*, a huge 161-metre-long and twenty-eight-metre-wide Cross-Channel ferry which to me looked like a floating Intourist hotel, packed with nice-smelling and ever-smiling foreigners. I stood speechless and dumbfounded at the entrance to the ship's small and poorly stocked (as I realise now) duty-free shop, not daring to step inside. There seemed to be many more goods in it than in all Moscow's supermarkets taken together.

I did gain courage, however, to pop in one of the ferry's toilets and, overwhelmed by mirrors and the entirely unfamiliar smells of deodorants and air-fresheners, rushed promptly out, convinced I had wandered into a hairdressing salon by mistake …

By the time we disembarked in Harwich three hours behind schedule I was so exhausted – both physically and emotionally – that I almost overlooked a helmeted policeman, a real-life and life-size English 'bobby,' who stood near the gang-plank. The first human being I saw in Britain, he was shifting from one foot to another and yawning, probably bored out of his mind.

It took me a good half-hour to drag my abnormally heavy bags, full of food tins and souvenirs, to the immigration area. I was sweating like a pig and that was probably why I seemed suspicious to the customs officers who asked me to open my suitcases.

'No drugs, sorry,' I tried to joke, frantically looking for the keys to my suitcases and unable to find them.

It was a mistake of course. I didn't know then that one should never test the customs (or immigration) officers' sense of humour.

'I appreciate it,' a woman customs inspector said cutting my suitcase open with a pen-knife.

That crude intrusion was the last thing I expected to happen during my first moments in the 'free' world.

Matrioshka dolls, my socks, underwear and tins were all piled together onto a low metallic table. By then, half a dozen customs inspectors, having materialised out of nowhere, were rummaging matter-of-factly through my possessions.

Who knows how long this humiliation could have lasted were it not for a man in civilian clothes who was standing nearby and watching the search silently.

'It's ok. Let him go,' he muttered.

And immediately, as if on command (it *was* actually on command!), customs inspectors started stuffing my belongings back into bags, patching my hara-kiri-ed suitcases with Sellotape and apologising reluctantly.

'Quick!' said the woman. 'You will miss your train to London!' And something that could pass on for a smile lit up her face …

The moment I puffingly dragged my bags into a carriage of a waiting train, its doors were slammed behind me by a woodpecker-like station master in a red cap. Despite being called 'Intercity Express,' it seemed unexpectedly ancient, almost antediluvian, even if compared with Soviet suburban trains. And yet, the moment it started moving, I immediately felt in my element, and soon the unpleasant customs incident was forgotten.

The train was carrying me to London.

The whole new world lay ahead.

Baedeker Raids

In 1999, to commemorate the end of one millennium and the beginning of a new one, I decided to travel around Britain armed with a 100-year old Baedeker guidebook.

My rationale was as follows:

Travelling back in time has always been one of humankind's most cherished dreams. This explains the preoccupation of science-fiction writers with time machines or any other device which allows us to peep behind the curtain of our own past.

Science fiction aside, I have discovered real vehicles capable of taking me many decades back into the past. I mean old guidebooks – Baedekers, Murrays, Bradshaws, Cooks. For me, these pocket-size tattered volumes are full of time-travel magic, especially when I find an old London Tube map (with a curtailed pink 'Northern Line' ending at Highgate), a faded landing card, or just a dried-out hundred-year-old flower in between their tattered pages. Touching such books is like touching eternity itself, for bygone realities and small practicalities of the distant past come to life in their estranged, meticulous and matter-of-fact style. In this respect, old guidebooks are preferable to fiction: they provide me with an ossified time carcass, which I am free to fill with the contents of today's reality, or with that of my own imagination.

A casual pencil mark, left by a long-deceased anonymous traveller of yesteryear on the margins of 1873 *Murray's Handbook to France*, opposite one particular ferry route from Dover to Calais; or a tick next to the cheapest horse carriage rate from the railway station to the city centre in my native Kharkiv (*Baedeker's Russia, 1914*); or the underlined exact departure time of a train from Sienna to Milan in a last century's *Bradshaw's Railway Guide for Europe*, do more for my imagination (and therefore – for my time-travels) than heaps of post-Victorian novels. When I see (and touch) these faint, yet curiously assertive, marks of time, I – for a fleeting moment – become a turn-of-the-century traveller myself.

No matter how busy I am, I make sure I open an old guidebook every day thus (literally) staying in touch not only with eternity, but also – with reality.

Baedeker Handbooks, or 'Baedekers,' are the most famous guidebooks in the world. Started by an Essen-born and Heidelberg-educated publisher Karl Baedeker in 1829, they remain unsurpassed in their authority and precision of detail. Unlike the half-baked tips of my omniscient Moscow friends, Baedeker's advice was always based on first-hand experience. Even when saying – somewhat peremptorily – that 'Europeans as a rule should never inquire after the wives of a Muslim' (I like this overcautious 'as a rule') in the early editions of his *Egypt Handbook*, he sounded as if he knew exactly what he was talking about, and the reader was led to believe that

Baedeker himself had made numerous 'inquiries' after Muslims' wives before coming to the conclusion that they should be best avoided.

It was very seldom that Baedeker allowed his personality (having travelled so much, he should have been a clandestine romantic) to come through. In one his Handbooks to Paris, he calls the French capital 'a temptress of a city which no one leaves without regret.' In the words of Alan Wykes, the compiler of *Abroad* – a comprehensive anthology of English travel writing, Baedeker 'was Schubert to the life, though without the glasses, and he had music in him which emerged through a clarinet; but nothing like as much as the information he and his successors have compiled over the years for the benefit of the practically-minded tourist.'

Baedeker himself used to travel under an assumed name, checking on hotels and restaurants, so that the information which he gave could be relied upon utterly. After his death in 1859 his sons continued his work. The first English translation appeared in 1861, the first French one fifteen years earlier. The English translation of *Baedeker's Russia, 1914* is one of the rarest: it was never reprinted. 1914 was clearly not a good year to publish a guidebook, not even a Baedeker.

The popularity of Baedeker's guidebooks was such that the following paragraph had to be added to the Introduction of some of them:

> 'To hotel-keepers, tradesmen, and others the Editor begs to intimate that a character for fair dealing and courtesy towards travellers forms the sole passport to his commendation, and that no advertisements of any kind are admitted to his Handbooks. Persons calling themselves agents for Baedeker's Handbooks are impostors.'

'Impostors' were clearly one of Baedeker's main concerns, and he always kept his eyes open for them. 'We need hardly caution newcomers against the artifices of pickpockets and the wiles of impostors, two fraternities which are very numerous in London. It is even prudent to avoid speaking to strangers in the street.' (*Baedeker's London, 1900*).

Baedeker was the first writer to add stars after hotels to pinpoint the best and most luxurious; he also used this system for especially beautiful views.

The name Baedeker became a dictionary word, not only for the excellence of its guides, but also for a sadder reason. In World War Two, British aircraft made raids on Cologne and Lubeck. In reprisal, the Germans staged a series of raids on Britain which were called 'Baedeker Raids.' They were trying to stamp out famous historic cities mentioned in Baedeker such as Bath, Exeter, Canterbury, Norwich and so on. The phrase was first used in 1942. Ironically, it was in Germany under the Nazis that Baedeker guides – for the first and the last time – were subjected to censorship: strategic areas, such as railways and bridges, were removed from the 1936 edition of *Baedeker's Berlin and Potsdam*, published for the Berlin Olympic Games.

The best Baedeker guidebooks came out between 1897 and 1909 – the years known as the Golden Age of Baedeker. Among them, were annual editions of *Baedeker's Great Britain* and *Baedeker's London and Its Environs* – the pride of my ever-growing collection. I can see no better way of celebrating the end of the century (and that of the Millennium) than travelling around 1999 Britain armed with 1900 editions of these two guides in what can be called 'Peaceful Baedeker Raids.'

In my travels, I shall – as far as possible – stick to the advice of good old Baedeker which, in certain cases, should not be a problem: 'when the traveller is in a hurry, and his route does not coincide with that of an omnibus, he had better at once engage a cab …' although, in other instances, this may prove rather tricky: 'People of moderate requirements … will have little difficulty, with the aid of the information in the Handbook, in travelling comfortably [in Britain] with a daily expenditure of 20-25s, while the pedestrian of moderate requirements may reduce his expenses to 10-15s per diem, or even less in some of the remoter districts.'

I shall board at Baedeker-recommended hotels, which 'as compared with Continental hotels, … may be said to excel in beds, cleanliness and sanitary arrangements, while their cuisine is on the whole inferior … the culinary art of hotels off the beaten track of tourists scarcely soars beyond the preparation of plain joints, steaks, chops, vegetables and puddings.'

For the purposes of maximum authenticity, I shall totally avoid modern cars, planes, computers, faxes, television, telephone and even radio, and will rely for news on newspapers – preferably broadsheets, for, according to *Baedeker's London, 1900*, 'portable drugs in the form of tabloids' were prepared by Messrs Burroughs, Wellcome & Co, Manufacturing Chemists of Hill Buildings, Holborn Viaduct. I shall have to be careful not to get an overdose.

Having put on the imaginary Dom Pedro water-proof boots of a turn-of-the-century traveller and donning a no-less-imaginary Octagon Crown tourist cap (as opposed to an unpractical bowler hat of old stereotypes which can be easily blown away by the sweeping winds of Cornwall and Devon), I shall look for the 1900 Britain – the fairy land of wagonettes, carriages and early stream trains, drawn by the white swans of my childhood dreams …

PS. My Baedeker Raids appeared regularly in the *Daily Telegraph* in the year 2000 and generated a great readers' response. And a decade or so later, the idea was nicked by Michael Portillo and the BBC for their seemingly endless (carrying on until now!) series of rather mediocre (from my point of view) TV travelogues. Below you will find several of my original 'Baedeker Raids.' VV

London Docklands

My *Baedeker's London 1900* offered three ways of getting to London Docklands: by steamer from London Bridge, by omnibus, or by railway, which, in April 1999, left me with only one option.

Sandwiched between sullen morning commuters on a Bank-bound Northern Line tube train, I was re-reading my precious old travel guide: 'One of the most interesting sights of London is the Port, with its immense warehouses ... Ships bearing the produce of every nation under the sun here discharge their cargoes, which previous to their sale, are stored, subject to customs, in large bonded warehouses ...

'Below these warehouses, which form small towns of themselves ... are extensive cellars for wine, oil, etc, while above ground are huge magazines, landing stages, packing-yards, cranes, and every kind of apparatus necessary for the loading, unloading, and custody of goods.'

At Bank station, we were urged to mind the gap, and, with a 100-year-long time gap firmly on my mind, I rattled down the stairs to catch a Docklands Light Railway (DLR) train. As I ran, Baron Karl Baedeker kept whispering in my ear in his curiously inverted, outdated English with a strong German accent:

'At times upwards of 3,000 men are employed at these docks in one day. Every morning ... there may be seen waiting at the principal entrance a large and motley crowd of labourers, to which numerous dusky visages and foreign costumes impart a curious and picturesque air.'

A number of men (and women) on the DLR platform, the 'principal entrance' to the end-of-the-Millennium Docklands, had 'dusky visages,' although 'foreign costumes' were few and far between. Most were heading for Canary Wharf, where some were indeed employed by 'huge magazines.'

Following Baedeker's suggested itinerary, I started my exploration from St Katharine's Dock, which used to 'admit vessels up to 250ft in length and 24ft of draught' until they fell victim to the tongue-breaking word 'containerisation' and closed down in 1968.

The only vessels one can see there now are pleasure boats of the super-rich (imagine owning a boat moored next to the Tower of London!) in a makeshift marina, dominated by drab office blocks and the grey bulk of the Tower Thistle Hotel, which reminded me of the Moscow International Trade Centre – by far the ugliest building in the world.

In 1900, St Katharine's Steamboat Wharf, adjoining the Docks, was 'a landing stage for steamers from the continent.' According to Baedeker's *Traveller's Manual of Conversation*, the following verbal exchanges between happily disembarking passengers could be taking place there: 'You must have all your trunks, portmanteaus, parcels, and effects carried to the custom-house, to see if there is any thing contraband in them, before they are taken to the inn …'

'Will it last long? The sea has fatigued me very much, and I should like to go to the inn to rest …'

Not counting the Tower Thistle and Dickens Inn, there are no inns in the vicinity now, and public catering is provided by a handful of dodgy cafés and the new, touristy Medieval Banquet restaurant offering 'a regal night with fighting knights, jesters and witches' (it offers nothing during the day). An ornate old weathervane on one of the wharf's turrets remains the only true reminder of the past.

A thorough reader of *Baedeker's London, 1900* can be forgiven for thinking that Baedeker was a committed drinker: on just one page of his description of Docklands, wine and wine cellars are mentioned five times. He clearly admires 'these enormous vaults with their apparently inexhaustible quantities of wine' – a rare manifestation of emotion for the notoriously reserved and meticulous writer.

He even comes up with a useful tippler's tip: 'Those who wish to taste the wines must procure a tasting order from a wine-merchant. Ladies are not admitted after 1pm. Visitors should be on their guard against the insidious effects of 'tasting' in the heavy vinous atmosphere.'

The Docks' main wine cellars used to be under the vaults of the New Tobacco Warehouse in Tobacco Dock (a ten-minute walk from St Katharine's), whose entrance is still decorated with stone wine barrels lined with two wild boars' heads (a warning against 'the insidious effects' of excessive tasting?).

These stone barrels are the only indication of the area's bibulous past, and Tobacco Dock itself is now being converted into a modern (and strictly non-smoking, no doubt) shopping centre.

True, tobacco smoke as well as some other sweet odours of the past can no longer be sniffed in Docklands, where petrol fumes came in their stead. To my considerable chagrin, I failed to locate another smelly old landmark, lovingly described by Baedeker as 'a furnace in which adulterated tea and tobacco, spurious gold and silver wares, and other confiscated goods used to be burned. The long chimney is jestingly called the Queen's Tobacco Pipe.'

I always believed in the power of smell as the most evocative ambassador of the past. Smells also have considerable longevity and often outlive their carriers. I remember sniffing Chekhov's old medicine chest in his house-museum in Melikhovo, near Moscow: the faint aroma of medicines still lingered there, eighty-odd years since the writer's death.

That is why I was pleased to learn that at least some of the historic Victorian smells were going to be recreated inside another Docklands landmark, the octopus-like Millennium Dome. The Dome's Learn and Work zones are going to bask in the aromas of a turn-of-the-century English school: floor polish, boiled cabbage and 'the rotten-eggs stench of a stray stink bomb or two.'

There is a place in Docklands, however, where genuine, not computer-generated, old smells and sounds still come to life. It is the new Billingsgate fish market in Poplar – where the best of British seafood disappears, never to be seen again after being sold in bulk to wholesale buyers.

Even Baedeker wouldn't have been able to explain why this country, being an island, boasts the worst choice and quality of seafood in Europe, with the possible exceptions of Russia and Albania.

It was 8am, and the market was already wrapping up. Fish dealers, foul-mouthed and foul-aproned, were hosing slimy floors with water, while hurling eel-like (long and supple) curses at each other.

The nauseating stench of rotting fish was hanging in the air. Outside, in the market's soiled car-park, agitated seagulls were picking up fish remains from greasy trolleys. The gulls were swearing, too.

Well, it was good to know that at least one place, although relocated, remained unchanged: it was Baedeker who labelled old Billingsgate market (in 1900, it was located near London Bridge) 'as interesting in its way as Covent Garden, though pervaded by far less pleasant odours' as well as 'the chief fish-market of London, the bad language used at which has become proverbial.'

I was returning to the real world in proud solitude. All other passengers were driven out of my DLR carriage by the fishy smells of Billingsgate emanating from my clothes and shoes.

Through the window, I could see the impressive panorama of this 'alternative' mini-London, interspersed with graceful old churches, which stood out among derelict warehouses and housing estates like pieces of amber among pebbles. I threw a last glance at the Dome – which features in the next James Bond movie – and suddenly understood why modern property buyers are prepared to cough up £300,000 for a two-bedroom flat in a converted warehouse overlooking it.

Lit by the last rays of the setting sun, the Dome looked weightless and fragile, almost transparent. Momentarily, it reminded me of a huge overturned wine-glass.

Baedeker would have loved that.

Berwick-upon-Tweed

'They talk about England and Scotland indeed,
But it's England, and Scotland, and Berwick-upon-Tweed!'
an old adage

Reading old Baedeker guidebooks is like following a well-trodden familiar trail, strewn with unexpected jewels of timeless insight and observation. In contrast to modern guides, flooding the reader with torrents of relevant and irrelevant facts and figures, Karl Baedeker often left things unsaid and semi-disclosed, as if to tease the traveller's imagination and to spark off a quest. Journeying with a Baedeker was therefore not simply informative, but also creative – the aspect that has been largely (and sadly) lost with the advent of package tours and continent-hopping holidays leaving little time for 'looking under the lid.'

Passing through the Scottish town of Montrose last April, I habitually opened my turn-of-the-century *Baedeker's Great Britain* and was baffled to learn that the 'clean little seaport at the mouth of the South Esk, with 14,800 inhabitants' was 'the first place in Scotland where Greek was taught.' That was all he had to say about the place. Greek and Montrose, the town that has gone through a good deal of decay since 1900 and was no longer even 'clean' ... An unlikely match which seemed all Greek to me until, after repeated enquiries, I found out that ancient Greek was indeed taught in the Montrose Academy, the centre of medieval Scottish enlightenment, founded by John Erskine in 1554!

The same edition of *Baedeker's Great Britain* carries a rather laconic description of Berwick-upon-Tweed (Baedeker spelled it as 'Berwick-on-Tweed') – 'an old town with 14,000 inhab., at the mouth of the Tweed,' which 'was for ages a constant object of contention between England and Scotland, while it is still regarded as a neutral county belonging officially to neither of these countries ...'

It made me wonder what the town's current status was like. Was it still 'neutral,' and if so, was it a member of the United Nations and has it joined the EU? Queries, addressed mostly to my London friends, brought little result, until a knowledgeable colleague of mine said: 'Berwick-upon-Tweed? Isn't it the English town on the Scottish border which is still officially at war with Russia?'

My curiosity went through the roof. Baedeker in hand, I raced to Kings Cross and boarded the first GNER train to Berwick.

As a professional traveller, I was familiar with several other historical and geographical anomalies. A couple of years ago, I visited Campione d'Italia, an Italian town, which – due to some medieval ecclesiastical dispute – is situated on the territory of Switzerland and therefore manages to combine the best (and the worst) traits of both countries. A similar, yet a much less known, case of displacement can be found closer to home – at the very heart of London. Ely Place – a little cul-de-sac off Charterhouse Street at Holborn Circus – is still officially part of … Cambridgeshire, and letters addressed to 'Ely Place. Holborn Circus. Cambridgeshire' still get delivered to its residents. Just like in the early fourteenth century, when Ely Place became the town residence of the Cambridgeshire Bishops (hence the confusion), the street still enjoys 'freedom from entry by the police, except by invitation!' At least, on paper it does. No wonder that Karl Baedeker, who always kept his sharp eyes wide open for historical idiosyncrasies, aptly characterised Ely Place as 'a strangely quiet nook amid the roar of Holborn' in his *London And Its Environs, 1900,* although even he was probably unaware of the street's bizarre Cambridgeshire connection.

But neither Campione nor Ely Place were 'neutral,' or at war with Russia.

The train arrived in Berwick late at night. Cold and unfamiliar Northern stars were shining in the Scotch-coloured sky above totally deserted streets. The town looked alien and uninviting. I was ready to believe that it was indeed fairly 'neutral' – neither fish nor flesh …

This late-night impression proved deceptive the following morning, when Berwick was flooded with gentle late-autumn brightness, as if its Northumbrian houses of pink sandstone were oozing sunlight. The town no longer looked hostile. Overnight, it must have signed a truce, if not with the whole of Russia, then, at least, with one of her prodigal sons.

I looked up: dextrous Russian MIGs were nowhere to be seen. Kids were cheerfully running to (or, maybe, away from) their schools across the town's three magnificent bridges spanning the Tweed. Grey-haired ladies in tartan skirts were chatting amicably on street corners. To me, their peculiar Northumberland vernacular, the so-called 'Geordie,' sounded like a particularly thick Glaswegian accent.

'Scottish Power' ran a sign on top of an electric goods store in the main street. An agreeable shop assistant explained that the English town of Berwick was getting its electricity supplies through the Scotland Electricity Board.

Berwick's electricity of ambivalence seemed limitless. The town was pasted with posters announcing a forthcoming game of Berwick Rangers, the local soccer team, which, for some reason, was part of the Scottish Football League. Books on Scotland were on sale in Local History sections of all Berwick's bookshops. Wandering past the beautifully preserved Elizabethan Walls, I spotted the still-functioning headquarters of the Scottish Borderers Legion.

The only conspicuously un-Scottish presence in town (apart from my own that is) was an old Russian cannon, a trophy from the Crimean War, on one of the ramparts – showing that Berwick was not doing too badly in its (allegedly) on-going military confrontation with Russia, whose hands were probably too tied up with Chechnya to give sufficient attention to the obscure and remote Berwick Front.

Lest the locals should mistake me for an enemy scout (*a la guerre comme a la guerre!*), I retreated to the town's Public Library. And this is what I learnt there:

Berwick's dual status was a direct result of its chequered history. A thriving Scottish international port, it was plunged into decline when taken by Edward I of England in 1296 – the decline, from which it has never fully recovered.

In the next 200 years, the town changed hands at least thirteen times. After it fell for the last time to the English in 1482, it was still not regarded as a proper English town, but rather as a foreign outpost, like Calais. In a treaty of 1502, Berwick was acknowledged as a neutral or independent state **of** the Kingdom of England, but not **within** it. It was only in 1836 that the town was legally incorporated into England, but only *de jure*, for it kept being regarded as a separate entity and continued to print its own banknotes. The last **formal** traces of Berwick's distinct identity disappeared as recently as in 1974, with the formation of the Town Council and the extension of Berwick borough boundaries deep into North Northumberland. Yet even now it still enjoys the rare status of a royal borough, which, among other perks, enables Berwick to have a Sheriff, to run its own Records Office and to send two representatives to the Parliament, whereas the Mayor of Berwick, dressed in traditionally Scottish (!) purple ceremonial robes, takes the coveted third place next to the Queen (after the Mayors of London and York) in royal processions and at state banquets.

The mystery of Berwick's war with Russia proved simpler than I thought. Throughout the nineteenth century (even after its official incorporation into England) Berwick used to be mentioned in treaties and Acts of Parliament as a separate part of the Queen's (or the King's) realm. As such, it was included in the declaration of hostilities at the outbreak of the Crimean War in 1854, but was forgotten and omitted from the peace treaty two years later. A similar mishap once befell the Principality of Monaco, which, due to its miniscule size, was overlooked and removed from the redrawn map of Europe in the aftermath of the Napoleonic wars. Luckily, Monaco was later remembered, whereas Berwick wasn't …

I went to see Councillor WN Ferguson, the Mayor of Berwick-upon-Tweed , and the only person in town who could clarify with authority whether or not the war with Russia was still raging, if only in theory.

According to him (and to my considerable relief), Berwick's own Crimean War officially ended in 1976, when a facetious Russian (Soviet) diplomat came from London and, tongue-in-cheek, exchanged all necessary peace protocols and formalities – only 120 years overdue – with the town's authorities.

'So the Russians can now sleep quietly,' the Mayor reassured me with a grin.

'Are Berwickers English or Scottish?'

'Neither. We speak of ourselves as borderers, and we are proud of our unique identity. Unfortunately, Berwick is not close to the hearts of the British government, or even to the authorities of the region – it makes no sense for them. We have a low-wage economy, high unemployment and bad roads. It is a shame that such a nice part of the country, with talented people and lots of space, seems to be forgotten again, like in 1856 ...'

'A part of which country?' I wanted to ask, but restrained myself ...

With Derek Sharman, a local historian and a tour guide, we took an evening stroll in the side lanes of the old town. We were surrounded by handsome Victorian buildings, completely unspoilt by modern development – one positive result of the British government's long-lasting neglect of Berwick which, paradoxically, made it one of the most architecturally pleasing towns in the country. It was also one of Britain's best-kept secrets, for its Victorian splendour was carefully tucked away behind the uninspiring facades of the town's main traffic arteries. In a way, Berwick itself was not unlike an old *Baedeker Handbook*, where the sheer beauty of discovery was hidden in-between the seemingly dry-ish antiquated lines. This beauty was visible only to those willing to venture into side lanes.

'Being a guide in Berwick, whose very split personality is part of its mystique, is a dream job,' Derek said and added with a sigh: 'If only we had more tourists ...'

At 8pm, we heard the curfew bell ring from the Town Hall steeple, as it has been doing for centuries – a reminder of the days when the gates of the town had to be locked every night.

We walked down to the quay. From there, through the sticky all-permeating darkness of the November night, I could clearly discern two twisted silhouettes of white swans rocking gently on the black wavy surface of the Tweed – like two more question marks in the never-ending mystery of Berwick ...

Lake District

For all the detachment and meticulousness of his famous guidebooks, Karl Baedeker did have his favourite spots, and the Lake District, with its 'wealth of charmingly diversified scenery,' was definitely one of them.

The Lake District chapter in *Baedeker's Great Britain, 1900* is by far the longest, and most detailed, in the book. It is also the most vibrant, for here Baedeker excels in his limited choice of praising epithets – from 'fine' and 'picturesque' to 'delightful,' 'charming' and (especially) 'romantic' – while describing the mountains and the lakes, whose 'picturesqueness and even wildness are far greater than their size would lead one to expect.'

Baedeker was equally generous in bestowing his coveted stars on the Lake District hotels, which, in his words, 'are generally good and not exorbitant, while even the smallest inns, almost without exception, are laudably clean,' and on the area's scenic views. Nowhere else in Baedeker handbooks have I come across a scenic vantage point with two stars attached to it, as was the case with 'The View' from the top of Orrest Head in Windermere.

Working my way through this overpowering chapter while on a train from Euston was almost as exhausting as climbing the highest of the Lake District peaks (or – in Lake-District-speak – 'pikes,' as Baedeker pointed out in his small glossary of 'local names'). Nevertheless, I marked the ascent to Orrest Head as my first priority on arrival: it is not often that one gets a chance to admire a view with two Baedeker stars.

The impressions of my only previous visit to the Lake District, nine years ago, were rather fragmentary. I could recall a muscular young man with a bare torso chained, Prometheus-like, to a lamppost in Keswick. Fresh from the Soviet Union, I was about to call an ambulance (or a blacksmith?), but was pacified by my local friends who explained that the Lake District had become a popular venue for stag parties, and the topless Prometheus was most likely the victim of some wild stag night fun.

So it was with some trepidation that I stepped off the train in 'the village of Windermere … delightfully situated among trees at the foot of Orrest Head, affording fine views of the lake' and looked around: to my great relief, no one was chained to the trees, among which 'the village' was still 'delightfully situated.'

The ascent to Orrest Head, however, had to be postponed due to intermittent rain and heavy mist, which were bound to stop me from appreciating the two-star View. Instead, I opted for a Windermere Lake cruise on board the MV Tern, which has been plying its waters since 1891. Scrawny seagulls (or were they lake-gulls?) were screaming piercingly, almost human-like, as they certainly did in Baedeker times.

Some of the present-day features of Windermere Lake, however, would have been all Greek to Baedeker: water-skiers, small hovercraft and hundreds of Japanese tourists, mostly young women, criss-crossing the lake impassively in their hired paddleboats, which the dextrous MV Tern kept narrowly avoiding.

These gooey-eyed young women were worshippers of Beatrix Potter – allegedly a cult figure in Japan, where her books are used for teaching English. And I saw many more of them (is teaching English in Japan restricted to girls-only schools?) inside 'The World of Beatrix Potter Attraction' in Bowness, where they walked – mesmerised – through Squirrel Nutkin's old oak tree and gaped in courteous disbelief at 'top quality Beatrix Porter merchandise,' from Peter Rabbit lunch bags to Peter Rabbit wellington boots, in a 'specialist' souvenir shop.

I am pleased to say that I found two umbrellas in my room at Miller Howe Hotel, between Windermere and Bowness. The sight of the two brollies, discreetly tucked away in a wall closet, made me feel immediately at home in this plush Edwardian country house, which became a hotel only in 1971 and therefore could not be recommended (and starred) by Baedeker in 1900.

Last year it was purchased by Charles Garside, former editor of *The European* newspaper, who decided that the hotel had become too formal and stuffy and needed some gentle 'editing,' which has included redesigning the house and garden to make them look even more authentically Edwardian. 'A hack is always a hack,' I thought, browsing through the First and the Main Editions of the now flexible dinner menu and choosing the glorious sunset over the Langdale Peaks as my sumptuous natural dessert. After the meal, I sat in the hotel's conservatory and watched a lonely red carnation on the garden hedge blend slowly with the fading sun …

The stunning view of the lake and the mountains that I enjoyed from my room the day before had all but disappeared by next morning, blocked by a curtain of rain. The two umbrellas in the closet proved handy, but, with visibility close to zero, there was no point in climbing Orrest Head even if I took both of them with me and turned the double-starred View into the double-brollied one.

Armed with my faithful Baedeker guide, I took a coach to Keswick. Sitting on top of a double-decker bus, I kept imagining it was an omnibus, or, perhaps, a 'chars-a-banc [sic] – fare 6s.' (frankly, I had only a vague idea of what a 'chars a banc' would look like).

'It is needless to say that all who can spare the time should stop at various points en route,' noted Baedeker. And, needless to say, I did.

I stopped at Rydal Mount, 'the home of Wordsworth from 1817 till his death in 1850,' which 'contains no relics of the poet and is not shown' – ie, is closed to the public. The last statement was no longer true, for the house, which Wordsworth rented for thirty-seven years, is now open to the public, although it is not a museum and is still lived in by the poet's descendants, whose modern wedding photos adorn the walls.

As for the 'relics,' they included 'Wordsworth Sofa. Please Do not Use.' The sign immediately made me wonder about all imaginable uses of a sofa. But the best 'relics' of Rydal Mount were the views, the same views which inspired its tenant. You can rearrange furniture and alter the design of a country house, but you cannot change the views from its windows.

On board the lovingly restored Gondola Steam Yacht, built in 1859 and mentioned by Baedeker in 1900 ('A small steamer plies up and down the lake – 3/4 hr. each way; fare 1s., return 1s.6d.'), I crossed Coniston Lake, whose 'beautifully-wooded banks ... have a charm of their own.'

The lake was misty, deserted and, yes, extremely 'romantic.' Its water kept changing colour, as if adjusting itself to the treacherous Lake District sunlight, and nothing broke the stillness of its shores, apart from the muffled giggles of an overly 'romantic' couple canoodling in the ferns.

In Keswick, I spent the night in the former 'Keswick Hotel at the station, a large establishment with 200 beds.' One hundred years later the 'establishment' has become even larger to incorporate the station building, out of use since 1972, when the last train left Keswick station as a result of a near century-long campaign by 'The Lake District Defence Society, established ... in 1883.'

According to Baedeker, the Society provided 'a powerful and consolidated opposition to the introduction of unnecessary railways into the Lake District.' Ironically, a modern organisation calling itself 'Return to Keswick' is now tirelessly campaigning for the re-opening of the Penrith-Keswick railway as 'an appropriate way to mark the Millennium.'

I enjoyed my short stay at that lovely Victorian hotel-cum-station, whose conservatory, built in 1860 to allow guests to walk into the hotel under cover from the train, has been converted into bedrooms. These face the original canopied platform and the old station building with 'Keswick' carved under its roof, giving me the feeling that the hotel itself was ready to depart at any minute, to start chugging along the rails in lieu of the missing trains.

Shortly before dawn, I was woken up by a loud ticking noise, and my first sleepy thought was that it was the ghost of the old station clock coming to life in the middle of the night. But it was simply another heavy rainfall. It was my last morning in the Lake District, and – rain or not – it was also my last chance to climb Orrest Head.

Hiding under my umbrella, I heroically – in the best traditions of British holidaymaking – puffed up a muddy mountain path, past 'the cottage of Elleroy, the former residence of Christopher North, shaded by the splendid sycamore of which he declared it were easier to suppose two Shakespeares than such another tree.' The sycamore was no longer there. 'Labrador pups – £120 each,' said a handwritten sign on the fence. I played with the idea of buying a Labrador, but discarded the thought, having remembered that in Baedeker times one could acquire the whole cottage for £120 and still have some change left for a pup.

Halfway to the top, I bumped into a soaked, yet cheerful, American family, who asked me for directions to Orrest Head. I pointed upwards and carried on. My old Baedeker got wet, and was squeaking nervously in my breast pocket.

The moment I reached the summit, the rain stopped, and, as if by magic, the recalcitrant Lake District sun peeped out meekly from behind the clouds. What can I say? The 'View' was indeed 'fine,' 'delightful,' 'charming' and 'romantic.' It was also breath-taking. Nothing, apart from an ant-like truck crawling in the distance, was reminiscent of the end of the twentieth century.

Standing there, on top of Orrest Head, I remembered an expression of John Ruskin, who loved the Lake District and lived there for many years: 'The greatest thing a human soul ever does in this world is to see something … To see clearly is poetry, prophecy and religion – all in one.' I thought it could be used as an epigraph to my old Baedeker guidebooks.

On my way down, I noticed that the 'Labrador pups' sign was gone. They must have sold out.

Liverpool

Karl Baedeker noted in 1900 that Liverpool, 'the second city of England,' 'makes a more pleasing impression than Manchester and many other large towns.' He would have been surprised to learn that one hundred years later the population has dwindled from 740,000 to 510,000, and that a modern guidebook (*Lonely Planet*) starts its entry on the city with this uninspiring passage: 'Liverpool greets a visitor with a distinctly gap-toothed smile. The holes testify to wartime bombing and economic collapse.'

Walking around the centre with John Edwards, my knowledgeable and enthusiastic guide, I could see for myself the gruesome effects of the Luftwaffe 'Baedeker raids' (not to be confused with my own peaceful ones), of which Liverpool was one of the main targets: multiple gaps between the few remaining gold teeth have been hastily bridged with rather incongruous architectural fillings.

'This area was heavily blitzed during the war,' John would say from time to time as we trotted along the route sketched out by Baedeker 100 years ago. Despite the disappearance (read 'blitzing') of such prominent Baedeker-chosen sights as St Michael's Church ('with a good Grecian portico and the highest spire in Liverpool'), the old China Town and the Bowes Museum of Japanese Art, which boasted 'the most comprehensive and valuable collection of the kind in the world, Japan itself not excluded,' the carcass of the turn-of-the century city centre remained largely intact, and many of the war-inflicted wounds have been healed by time – a persevering and patient nurse.

'Boxers and Officials Only' said the sign at the entrance to St George's Hall, 'the finest architectural structure of Liverpool,' to which Baedeker awarded his coveted star. We were neither, but John authoritatively led me inside.

A makeshift boxing ring was set up in the middle of the Great Hall in preparation for an amateur championship. Curiously, the ring made the hall, 'erected in 1838-54 in the form of a Graeco-Roman temple,' even more Romanesque, bringing back associations with gladiatorial combat.

We climbed the stairs to 'the Small Concert Hall in elliptical form,' where Dickens, who didn't like the acoustics of the Great Hall, preferred to have his readings.

The magnificent Early Victorian creation of Charles Cockerell was now out of use, being unsuitable for the disabled (not a big worry in Baedeker times). It was also in desperate need of restoration. The graceful semi-circular auditorium smelt of generations of smokers, and the tar-saturated crystals of its multi-tiered chandelier resembled a cluster of used cigarette filters.

Smokers have a harder time today – at least in the town hall, another Baedeker-starred building. 'The practice of guests smoking in the building is prohibited,' states a peculiarly worded (Scouse affected?) memo, dated 11 February 1999. 'The oldest public building in Liverpool,' which still 'includes the official business and reception rooms of the Mayor,' can now be hired ('Large Ballroom – £1,500 a day') for any private functions, apart from discos – another wise proviso of today's city fathers.

Baedeker would still recognise Castle Street, which he described as 'the embodiment of Liverpool character and the centre of its system.' Architecturally, it is still dominated by 'a huge and heavy pile' of insurance companies and banks (the Bank of England's gold reserves were stored here during the Second World War). Signs of the city's changing character include a branch of the American-owned Starbucks coffee shop and, spilling out from neighbouring Water Street, a resigned multi-racial queue for the National Passport Office.

Baedeker would have been horrified, on the other hand, by the sight of the Metropolitan Cathedral of Christ the King, known locally as 'Paddy's Wigwam.' This monstrosity, with its leaking phallic-shaped dome and battered walls, looks like a cross between Waterloo station (pre-restoration) and the BT Tower. It was built between 1962 and 1967, and for the design we can blame Sir Frederick Gibberd. It stands over a vast crypt housing a car park – all that was completed of Sir Edwin Lutyens's plan for the cathedral, which was conceived in the Thirties and abandoned after the last war.

Lutyens's building was to have ninety-two chapels and would have been larger than St Peter's in Rome. It would have taken 250 years to build, taxing the patience as well as the pockets of Liverpudlians.

I was reminded of Stalin's plan to erect the world's largest building – the Palace of the Soviets, in Moscow, topped with the dictator's own rotating statue – on the very spot where the Cathedral of Christ the Saviour, the pearl of Russian architecture, had stood until it was blown up in the Thirties. Soon after it was started the palace was quietly abandoned, and the world's largest swimming pool was quietly built instead.

'The most characteristic and interesting of the sights of Liverpool ... consists in its Docks,' according to my trusted Baedeker 1900. 'The visitor is advised to drive from one end of the Docks to the other (6.5m.; fare 2d) on the top of an omnibus.'

In 1999, I found the last piece of advice impractical, not only because of an absence of omnibuses but also because most of the operating docks are now closed to the public.

The Landing Stage (where 'cabin passengers by the Transatlantic steamers are generally landed by tenders') is now half the length it was in 1900. The Prince's Pier, from where the SS Great Britain embarked on transatlantic journeys, had only one vessel moored to it – an Isle of Man bound Sea Cat (Sea Cat ferries always strike me as misnomers, for cats, as we know, cannot swim).

Standing there, I felt nostalgic for that golden age brilliantly summarised by the nineteenth-century English writer Samuel Laing: 'What a world of passengers on our steamer! Princes, dukes, gentlemen, ladies, tailors, milliners, people of every rank and calling, all jumbled together. The power of steam is not confined to material objects. Its influences extend over the social and moral arrangements of mankind. Steam is the great democratic power of our age, annihilating the conventional distinctions, differences and social distance between man and man, as well as natural distances between place and place.'

The only modern phenomenon that comes close to steam in its 'democratic power' is probably the Internet.

The Queen's Dock ('Russian vessels') and the King's Dock, whose warehouses used to store 'about 20,000 hogsheads of tobacco,' have both been filled in to accommodate what is said to be Britain's largest free car park. There had been plans to build Britain's largest aquarium (where does this Liverpudlian megalomania come from?), an ice-skating rink and a boxing stadium on the same spot, but they fell through.

Describing the Liverpool Docks, Baedeker mentions the Goree Piazzas, 'the scene of a commercial enterprise undertaken by Washington Irving. The experiment was disastrous, and the shock threw Irving into a lethargic condition, one of the first signs of recovery from which was the composition of Rip Van Winkle.' I made inquiries and found that Irving was once asked to keep an eye on his brother's timber company, operating from the docks. The company soon went bust. Writers seldom make successful businessmen.

I am sure a modern commercial undertaking in the old docks area will do better – and not just because its Russian owners are not writers. It is St Petersburg, Britain's only Russian restaurant outside London.

Four years ago, Sergei and Tanya, a married couple from St Petersburg, both devoted Beatles fans, came to Liverpool and bought an old warehouse on the corner of Duke and York Streets.

By coincidence, the warehouse used to belong to John Bellingham, a timber contractor who was arrested and imprisoned for debt in Russia in the early nineteenth century. Refused help by his country's ambassador, Bellingham developed a festering hatred of the British establishment.

Having served his six-year stretch, he returned to Britain and, in May 1812, shot dead the Prime Minister, Spencer Perceval, in the Lobby of the House of Commons. He fled to Liverpool, but was caught within a week and executed.

'Welcome to pre 1917 Russia!' said Sergei from behind a bar overladen with bottles of vodka and matryoshka dolls and overhung with portraits of the hapless Nicholas II. A jolly English party was under way round a table sagging under Russian food and drinks.

I thought Sergei might feel haunted by the ghost of Bellingham. Not at all. 'On the contrary, it is nice to be surrounded by history,' he said. 'We came to Liverpool as pioneers, trying to show the locals that we were not savages, that genuine pre-Revolutionary Russian cuisine was not only filling but also sophisticated. The word has spread, and now we have a lot of local patrons as well as visitors from Manchester and Leeds.'

Tastebuds die last, I concluded silently while finishing the plate of Tanya's borscht, the best I have tried since leaving Russia. The English party at the neighbouring table suddenly burst into applause. Sergei bowed to all sides before introducing Tanya, the chef, and all the waiters.

'Restaurant is theatre,' he told me afterwards with a wink.

Baedeker would have given him a star.

Cornwall and the Scillies

With the old Baedeker guidebook in my pocket, I was going to Cornwall and the Scilly Isles to retrace the footsteps of the largely disappointed worshippers of the previous month's total eclipse, which I, being on an assignment in America, totally missed.

Penzance greeted me with heavy leaden skies. The morning was dull and murky. It was if the eclipse were becoming Cornwall's more or less permanent feature. But despite these London-like skies, the scenery was different: scrawny palm trees were sticking out among dew-covered potato fields. England was definitely a big small country.

From my trusted turn-of-the-century Baedeker, I learnt that 'the climate [of Cornwall] is exceedingly mild; myrtles and certain kinds of palms thrive luxuriantly in the open air.' Baedeker must have visited the Duchy on a brighter day.

I read on: 'Cornwall is famous for its 'squab' and other pasties, made out of such heterogeneous materials that the devil, according to a local proverb, will not enter the county for fear to be put into a pie.' The pasties, recently denounced as fatty and uninspiring by a leading American daily, still 'thrived luxuriantly' in the windows of Penzance bakeries and one could put on a couple of pounds by simply staring at them for a while.

The locals were reluctant to talk about the eclipse, which, because of the weather, was not quite what they had hoped for. The proprietor of one hotel, however, assured me that his guests had all left extremely happy. Or maybe they were simply extremely happy to leave? I decided not to press the point.

On the noticeboard of the parish church of St Paul in the village of Mousehole, I came across this notice: 'Eclipse Safety Glasses. If you have no use for these, there is a total eclipse in Zimbabwe on June 21, 2001. The children there will need them. Please put your safety glasses in this box.' A capacious cardboard box underneath was empty. The eclipse-hungry residents of Mousehole, glasses in hand, were probably already on their way to Zimbabwe.

St Paul's was noted by Baedeker in 1900 as containing 'the tomb of Dolly Pentreath (died 1777), usually said to be the last person who spoke Cornish. The Rev WS Lach-Szyrma, however, in his Short History of Penzance, states that he had found two or three persons in Mousehole who could count up to 20 in old Cornish.'

The mysterious Rev WS Lach-Szyrma would have a harder time now. A helpful librarian in the Cornish Studies Library in Redruth, which stocked '30,000 Cornish books' (all in English), confessed to me that she 'tried to learn Cornish, but gave up.'

I found the grave of Dolly, whose one claim to fame was the language she spoke, in the churchyard wall. 'Dolly Pentreath who conversed in ancient Cornish,' ran the modern English epitaph, highlighting the fact that her 'ancient language akin to

Breton and Welsh' was as 'extinct' these days as it had been in Baedeker times. In short, Cornish has been fully eclipsed by English – the only total eclipse I was able to observe in Cornwall.

Baedeker was a master of understatement. I felt this peculiar skill of his during the crossing from Penzance to the Scillies on board the Scillonian III: 'This sail affords a good view of the Cornish coast, but the sea is often rough.' It was not simply rough, it was stormy, especially after we passed Logan Rock – 'a mass of granite weighing 70 tons, but so poised that it can be rocked ('logged'), although with some difficulty since Lieutenant Goldsmith's exploit. Goldsmith, a young naval officer, a nephew of the poet, had the folly to upset the rock in 1824 with the aid of a boat crew.'

Logan Rock might not be rocking any longer, but the Scillonian III certainly was, and it was not the rock but the passengers' stomachs that were upset as a result.

To cheer me up, a sympathetic purser told me that during the two world wars the German navy and Luftwaffe had instructions to spare the Scillonian from attack – as a gesture of gratitude to the islanders for looking after the mass grave of 300 German subjects, the victims of the wreckage of the German liner Schiller, which struck rocks off St Agnes island in 1875. It was good to know that we were safe from a torpedo attack by some mythical time-warped German U-boat, if not from a brush against real rocks.

The Scilly Isles, 'the Cassiterides [the tin islands] of the ancients,' were semi-eclipsed by the mist. Looking at them from the unsteady deck of the Scillonian III, I had a feeling that we were approaching Tasmania. The pines on the golden-sand beaches of Tresco reminded me of gum trees.

This impression grew stronger on St Mary's, the largest island, 'with a circumference of nine miles and a population of 1,500.' In the very centre of Hugh Town, the islands' capital, I spotted a beautiful specimen of Agave Americana, an endemic South American plant, which grows more than thirty feet a year, flowers once in a quarter of a century and serves as a base for tequila – that Mexican killer drink. It was clearly much at home and quickly approaching its annual growth quota.

Thanks to the warm Gulf Stream flowing past their shores, the Scillies have the mildest climate in Britain. The place does feel Mediterranean (if not exactly subtropical), especially of an evening, when the last flashes of sunlight linger in the dark and narrow streets of Hugh Town, like pink ribbons entangled in a brunette's shock of curly hair; when the huge soup ladle of the Great Bear hangs so low in the sky that it almost scoops water from the sea; and the flowers, of which there are more than 600 different species, fill the air with their sweet and pungent evening odours.

In Baedeker times, 'the growing of narcissi for Covent Garden, to which hundreds of thousands of this beautiful flower are sent every spring' was 'one of the most profitable occupations in the islands.' Mike Nelhams, the curator of the Tresco

Abbey Gardens, 'the finest in the British Isles (fee to gardener),' told me that daffodil-growing was now the Scillies' third-biggest industry, after tourism and a somewhat puzzling 'administration.' 'As always, we start picking up flowers in October and finish in January,' he said, sitting behind the wheel of his Lego-like gardener's buggy (cars are banned from Tresco).

'How come Baedeker says you send them to London in spring?' I asked.

'We call the flower-picking season 'spring' on the islands,' he smiled, and I realised that even Baedeker was not insured against an occasional imprecision.

In 1934, Augustus Smith, the Scillies' first Lord Proprietor, whose descendants still own Tresco, was able to lease all fifty of the islands from the Duchy of Cornwall for £20,000. For the same sum now, he could not buy a bedsit on St Mary's. The island's population and 'circumference' might not have changed since 1900, but property prices are approaching those of London. The reason: too many people from the mainland fancy having a holiday home on this warm, narcissus-growing and crime-free archipelago on England's doorstep, nicknamed the Fortunate Islands.

The Scillies had a better eclipse than Cornwall and Star Castle, 'a fortress erected in the reign of Elizabeth,' on top of a hill overlooking Hugh Town, was one of the best vantage points. On 11 August, the castle, which was converted into a hotel in 1933, was full of people. Exactly twenty-four minutes before the event was due (as one of the hotel staff assured me), the clouds parted, as if by magic, and everyone was able to see the eclipse clearly, although not half as clearly as Mike Collier, the last and only coastguard officer on the islands, who lives and works in the 165-foot Telegraph Tower.

The tower was erected in 1814 and was initially manned by a staff of ten. In 1901, Guglielmo Marconi tested his wireless from it by sending a radio signal across the sea to Cornwall. Paradoxically, the success of Marconi's experiment heralded the beginning of the end for the old-fashioned coastguard watch. 'Looking out is now a thing of the past,' said Collier with a sigh, studying the hazy horizon through a pair of old binoculars.

While on the Scillies, I experienced a total (and not entirely unwelcome) personal eclipse. At the local tourism office, they asked me whether I could read in English (I answered in the affirmative, adding that I could write, too, and had just published my seventh book) and when exactly I was going back to Germany. I thought they were misled by my accent, but the unsuspecting owner of the B&B, where I was supposed to stay overnight, made it all clear. 'It is nice to meet you, Mr Baedeker,' she smiled, opening the door. 'They have just called from the tourism office and asked me to reserve a room for you.'

As a result of a classic British cock-up, I was mistaken for the great man himself. '*Der Kutscher ist betrunken*,'[16] I replied, using the only complete German sentence that I knew by heart.

The 1886 edition of my *Baedeker's Manual of Conversation* for once proved helpful.

[16] 'The coachman is drunk.'

Isle of Man

The thing that upset me most in Liverpool, where I stayed for a couple of nights before sailing off to the Isle of Man, was that 'Bidston's, opposite Adelphi Hotel' – a mysterious establishment, from where, according to my trusty 100-year-old Baedeker guidebook, 'steamer chairs may be obtained' – was no longer there. It has been replaced by a 'Green Fish Cafe,' the sight of which caused me pangs of premature sea-sickness.

There was still a faint hope of obtaining a chair (on Baedeker's advice) 'from hawkers on board the steamers,' although my experience of modern hawkers in London's Oxford Street did not bode well for such a transaction.

My craving for a steamer chair was enhanced by the following dialogue from *Baedeker's Traveller's Manual of Conversation*, which I read on the train to the port of Heysham, from where 'slow ferries' to the Isle of Man were now operating (or plying, as Baedeker would say):

'The sea is very rough; the waves are very high; the rolling of the vessel makes me sick. – My head is very bad. The smell of the tar affects me. Smell some eau de Cologne, it will do you good. – I am very much inclined to be sick. Drink some Hollands; it will strengthen your stomach, and you will feel relieved. – I am very weak; I must lie down in my hammock …'

Instead of Hollands, I had to rely on Stugeron, 'effective prevention of travel sickness for the family.' Its listed 'unwanted side-effects' included 'drowsiness, headache and upset tummy.'

I was 'very much inclined to be sick' while still in Heysham, after a fast-food lunch at Little Chef Express – the only catering facility in the port. Most of the Isle of Man-bound passengers were burdened with dogs, motorcycles for the forthcoming TT races or obstreperous Lancashire children – all unsuitable for flying.

Ominously, stacked on a small table in my cabin on board the magnificent *Ben-my-Chree* (Manx Gaelic for Girl of My Heart) were three copious sick-bags with triskeles, the three-legged Manx emblem, printed on them. The origin of the triskeles is still being disputed by historians.

According to some, the design was derived from the spokes of a wheel or from a pagan image of the rays of the sun. Others believe that it represents stability, hence the island's motto, *Quocunque jegeris stabit*, which means 'Whichever way you throw me I stand,' or, more loosely, 'Weebles wobble but they don't fall down.'

There is no consensus as to the origin of the island's name either, but such was the brilliance of Karl Baedeker that he had managed to resolve both mysteries in just one sentence from my treasured guidebook: 'The Isle of Man, or Mann, is in the Irish Sea, between England, Scotland, and Ireland; hence its heraldic emblem (the three legs, or triune), and its Manx name, Vannin or Mannin, signifying 'middle." And although historians would certainly reject this explanation as too simplistic, no one can deny that it carries a lot of common sense.

'No foreign objects in toilet please' warned a sign in my cabin's tiny bathroom. 'How about foreign subjects?' I wondered before wandering off to use a communal toilet (just to be on the safe side) and to inspect the ship, which, almost unnoticed by me, had already been 'plying' the high seas for more than an hour. Built in Rotterdam only last year, Ben-my-Chree smelt of fresh paint, not tar. Accommodating 500 passengers and 175 cars, and run by the world's oldest Isle of Man Steam Packet Company, she felt as stable and unsinkable as the Manx triskeles itself.

It was not long before the white crescent of Port Douglas's 'fine Promenade' came into view and started crawling slowly towards the ship. I threw my unopened packet of Stugeron into the nearest bin. Modern diesel vessels might have slowed down compared to the steamers of 100 years ago (an average Isle of Man crossing was an hour shorter in Baedeker times!), but they have definitely become steadier.

Karl Baedeker seldom allowed his personal views to interfere with his guidebooks' impartiality. The Isle of Man chapter of *Baedeker's Great Britain, 1900*, however, contains the following, rather bilious outburst:

'The central part of the island is mountainous and beautifully diversified; streams, flowing through narrow leafy glens, with precipitous sides, from numberless cascades. The whole island, however, has become practically one large playground for the operatives of Lancashire and Yorkshire; and their tastes have been so extensively cared for, by the erection of dancing saloons and the like at every point of interest, as to seriously interfere with the enjoyment of the scenery for its own sake.'

Baedeker's rant was understandable, though. 'What a sight on getting berthed [in Douglas]! Thousands of visitors are above you on the Victoria Pier … and after you get up the steps it is often difficult to make your way for the porters and others anxious to get on board for the luggage, &c,' noted a Bass Brewery brochure, specially produced for its workers' 'excursion' to the island in 1904. It was in Douglas that Britain's first holiday camp was opened in 1897, next to the town's prison.

In the time-beaten 1899 guest book of the Sefton Hotel I found the following, heart-rending entry in round childish letters: 'Want to go home to my mum … ' This anonymous child must have felt lonely and confused among the crowds of playful 'operatives.'

There are no more dancing pavilions on the Isle of Man. Sunshine-hungry 'operatives' prefer to holiday in Majorca and the Costa del Sol. Or in Blackpool. The days when Douglas was Britain's premier resort, accommodating up to 600,000 holidaymakers in one season, are gone.

'We are like a funfair at the end of fun,' the Manx Chief Minister told me during my previous visit to the island, in 1993, when its decline seemed terminal, and the 'Smile of Man' logo, which used to advertise the island, had faded to such an extent that it started to look more like the scowl of a dead man.

In 1992, a £200,000 promotion campaign designed to sell the delights of the Isle of Man to tourists resulted in just eleven bookings. I remember how saddened I was by the sight of countless small B&Bs on the Promenade in Douglas ('innumerable Boarding Houses facing the sea – from 5s. per day') with either Vacancies or Closed signs in their bay-windows.

'Licensed to Sell Ale,' 'Colour TV in Most Bedrooms' and 'All Rooms with Private Baths' signs looked solitary and forlorn on their crumbling façades. I thought then that these hotels would not be able to attract many more clients even if they started selling ale in most bedrooms, installing colour TV sets in front of private baths, or indeed charging their guests 5s. per day!

To my great surprise, the place was very different in 1999: it was brighter, fresher and has even acquired a sort of a modern buzz. Spill the Beans Coffee House was doing brisk trade down town. New eating outlets included Waterfront, a classy French restaurant owned by television chef Kevin Woodward – a real breakthrough for Douglas, where in 1993 the biggest gourmet delight, offered by the town's only Italian restaurant with the unlikely Italian name of Rasputin, was 'Rasputin's Whoppa – Eat it if you dare!' (I dared not, having remembered that Rasputin himself died of poisoning.)

From the window of my Castle Mona Hotel I watched with disbelief the façade of the Savoy B&B next door being painstakingly painted – an unthinkable endeavour in 1993. All these changes were down to a belated realisation by the Manx authorities that the island could never again be the nation's favourite holiday destination. Instead, they have gone for more upmarket special-interest tourism, as well as lifting a silly regulation which banned anything, except for hotels, from Douglas Promenade. As a result a number of new shops and restaurants has appeared on the seafront.

The film industry has been another factor in the island's unexpected revival: the landscape of the Isle of Man is so unspoilt, the architecture so charming and quaint, that it has become a popular location for many a Hollywood blockbuster. Every other local will tell you with pride how he (or she) was invited to be an extra in this or that hit movie – 'Remember that barmy screaming barmaid in the saloon shooting scene? It was me!'

'A modern but very picturesque mansion on an ancient foundation' was how Baedeker described the historic Nunnery building on the outskirts of Douglas. The same description would suit my Castle Mona Hotel, 'formerly the residence of the Dukes of Athole,' which became a hotel in 1832.

The only remaining accommodation in Douglas recommended by Baedeker in 1900, it boasts a grand (if somewhat dusty) Victorian lounge with mirrored ceilings, from where the unsuspecting guests' puzzled reflections seem to dangle precariously. According to a golden plate nailed to its door, my room was the one in which 'Charles Dickens vacationed in 1866.' (I have yet to find a last-century British hotel where Charles Dickens did not 'vacation,' at least for one night.)

My gym-sized 'Dickens Suite' was dominated by a four-poster bed so enormous that sleeping in it on one's own felt like a minor offence. The four-poster was a nuisance for it blocked the dim light of the bedside reading lamp, which led me to conclude that Dickens was not in the habit of reading in bed. You live and learn.

On the way to the airport (for once, I decided to forsake the travelling restrictions forbidding the use of planes), I popped into Castle Rushen, 'formerly the palace of the Kings of Man, and until lately the prison of the island (adm. 4d.),' where I was kindly invited to wind up the 1597 Elizabethan clock ('the clock in the S tower was given by Queen Elizabeth and is still going') – a strenuous procedure that has to be performed daily.

Having completed this honorary chore, I stood for a while on the 'S tower' from where 'Snowdon, Anglesey, the Mourne Mountains, and parts of Cumberland are visible' (due to thick mist, they were not) listening to the 400-year-old clock's powerful ticking – the unstoppable heartbeat of Time.

Just like 100 years ago, when Baedeker (or one of his team) stood at the same spot on a brighter day, the clock was 'still going.'

My flight back to London was delayed indefinitely due to weather conditions. A Baedeker-recommended turn-of-the-century steamer would have been much faster …

Hereford and Hay

Armed with my 100-year-old *Baedeker's Great Britain* guidebook, I started my final 'Baedeker Raid' in Hereford, 'an episcopal city with 19,825 inhab, pleasantly situated on the left bank of the Wye.' On a dull December morning, my first priority was a good cup of espresso.

This proved harder than I had expected, not only because Hereford has grown twofold since Baedeker times and now counts about 50,000 'inhab,' but also because the tentacles of the Seattle Coffee Co have not yet spread as far as the Wye Valley.

I walked along the perimeter of its old walls, 'built to keep the Welsh in check' and now effectively protecting the charming centre from the din of the surrounding motorway. In 'Castle Green, a pleasant promenade on the river near the cathedral,' I spotted a peculiar column topped with a stone casket. A local explained that the city authorities ran out of money while erecting the monument in 1808 and thus created the world's only Nelson-less Nelson's Column.

I finally (and unexpectedly) found what I was looking for inside 'The Church of All Saints, in High St,' noted by Baedeker for 'containing fourteen oaken stalls of the fifteenth century' and for its 'lofty spire.' There were stalls there, although they dated from the late twentieth century and belonged to Café All Saints in a corner of the church. I was assured that the café did not stop trading even during church services, so that one could (at least in theory) keep saying prayers and singing hymns without interrupting one's lunch. Baedeker would have been impressed

Before departing Hereford for Hay-on-Wye, I had a quick look at the Cathedral Library, which 'contains many volumes of great interest and value, nearly all of which are chained to the shelves' – that would not have appealed to footloose Baedeker.

Old books were not chained to anything in Hay, 'an old Norman border town, with 2,000 inhab and the scanty remains of the castle,' where the 'station is in England (Herefordshire) and the town in Wales (Breconshire).' On the contrary, they were very much at large – strewn all over the town. They were generously displayed not only in numerous second-hand bookshops but also on self-service stalls, exposed to the elements and often soaked with rain. As for the station, it was no longer in England. Nor was it in Wales. The steam railway to Hereford ceased operating in 1957.

After the closure of the railway, Hay-on-Wye went into decline, until it was reborn and put on the tourist map by Richard Booth, who opened his first bookshop in the town in 1961. He started by bringing in truckloads of discarded volumes from American university libraries and even now one can see faded stamps of these libraries on many a Hay-on-Wye book. At that time, there were just two hotels and one B&B in town.

Booth was determined to turn Hay into 'a book town,' but for many years his efforts went unnoticed. The bookshops had neither appropriate light and temperature conditions nor cataloguing systems, so finding any particular title was almost impossible. Thousands of volumes, piled in cardboard boxes, were rotting in dark and humid cellars.

In 1976, publicity-desperate Booth launched a 'Home Rule for Hay' campaign. His slogans included: 'God save us from the Development Board for Rural Wales' and 'Balls to Wall's, eat Hay national ice cream.' On 1 April 1977, he proclaimed Hay-on-Wye independent with himself as the king ('Richard the Book-Hearted') and his horse, Caligula, the prime minister.

Booth achieved his objective: the village was noticed by the media and its popularity grew by the year. Some major antiquarian booksellers moved in and tourists, mostly bookworms, began trickling in, too. Soon, Hay was chosen as a venue for an annual literary festival. The number of bookshops reached thirty-nine and the number of visitors 500,000 a year. Pubs, hotels and all 108 B&Bs were thriving and the locals were singing the praises of King Richard. Thus, books and Booth changed the face of the town.

When I first met Booth in 1990, he had plans for a global book empire, with the capital in Hay-on-Wye. At that time, it was easy to dismiss them as 'haywire. Ten years on, there are more than twenty places throughout the world – from Belgium to Japan – describing themselves as book towns or villages (with another twelve in the making) – all modelled on Hay-on-Wye.

I met King Richard this time in the grim and unheated 'state rooms' of the partially restored Hay Castle, which he now owns. 'Can someone bring in the heater?' the king shouted to no one in particular from his wobbly wooden 'throne.' He sounded almost Shakespearean.

The king's brass and cotton, wool-lined crown was lying on the table next to him. His moth-eaten cotton and wool mantle was hanging on the back of a chair. The room was chilly and unkempt. It was like sitting inside an antediluvian, yet somehow still functioning, fridge.

The king's monologue lasted for almost an hour. He unveiled his plans to expand book towns to eastern Europe. He assured me that France alone will soon have at least 200 of them 'to supplement their goat cheeses.' He castigated Welsh local authorities for their neglect of small businesses (his favourite topic). He called himself a 'Huguenot in reverse.' He joked that 'every second-hand bookshop creates a museum of the unsellable.' He praised 'the democratic sunshine of Norway.' He claimed that 'no one reads books in Hay-on-Wye.'

He was simultaneously inconsistent and logical, gentle and outrageous, self-serving and selfless, brilliant and banal – but not for a second was he boring. And I was ready to believe him.

'According to the will of the people of Hay, I am reconstituting the House of Lords in Hay-on-Wye,' he confided. I wanted to ask him where he was going to get the lords from, but couldn't: my tongue was frozen stiff.

The answer, however, was obvious: if a horse could be appointed prime minister, then staid and self-important Hay-on-Wye cats could easily pass for a bunch of senile life peers …

In the backyard of Richard Booth's Bookshop, allegedly the world's largest, stood a shabby wooden barn, stuffed with Russian (or rather Soviet) books with titles such as *Socialist Realism Today*, *Scientific Communism* and *USSR-GDR Friendship Will Grow!* There was a thick layer of dust on the shelves.

It looked as though, for once, Booth had committed a blunder and hastily acquired the library of a provincial Soviet town's communist party committee. It was the proverbial junk-heap of history, and old Soviet guidebooks were there, too. One of them, *A Moscow Excursion* (1959), extolled the merits of the monument to Felix Dzerzhinsky, the founder of the Soviet secret police and the co-inventor of the Gulag: 'The monument is made of metal – the fact that has its own artistic logic, if we remember that comrade Dzerzhinsky was lovingly referred to by the people as 'Iron Felix.''

Thirty-odd years later the same people would drag their 'much-loved' Iron Felix, a sadist and a cool-blooded executioner, from his desecrated pedestal. When books, especially guidebooks, put themselves at the service of the rulers, they are bound to end up on a rubbish dump.

Unlike the anonymous author of *A Moscow Excursion*, Baedeker never got involved in political games. His only commitment was to his readers. 'I repeat that the trust which your countrymen bestow upon your books makes it your duty to undertake a really thorough revision. For the most part, we are talking about small details, but details which a hungry and thirsty man, in expectation of a good 'dinner' or 'supper,' and then disappointed, will take very badly,' he wrote to his colleague John Murray in 1858.

A dozen or so early twentieth century Baedeker guides in dark-red covers were displayed in an ancient bookcase with squeaky doors inside Booth's bookshop. To mark my last raid, I thought of putting my 100-year-old Baedeker to rest in the company of his nonagenarian brothers, but changed my mind. I still needed the old man as my travelling companion for the new Millennium.

Benvenuto Nella Bedford, la Citta di Mattoni

No, this story hasn't mistakenly stumbled into this section from Italy. It fully belongs to the Blighty part of this Bumper Book

Readers of my travel books and columns may be aware of my ever-growing collection of little-known geopolitical curiosities: enclaves, micronations, mini-states etc, all of which featured in it during nearly twelve years of its existence.

One, yet unrevealed, aspect of that collection is the world's unlikely and little-known mini-diasporas, ie small communities of migrants, stranded by fate in the far-away and remote (from their countries of origin) lands. In my global travels, I was lucky enough to stumble upon such highly peculiar and seemingly out-of-place settlements as a Swiss village in the heart of Tasmania (complete with chateaux, chalets and rosti-serving restaurants in the shadow of gum-trees), a thriving Lithuanian community in the leafy outskirts of Chicago, Russian Old Believer towns in Alaska and many more. The above-mentioned Swiss village down under, called – rather unoriginally – Grindelwald and founded by the late Dutch businessman Roelf Vos (who I used to know) was perhaps the most peculiar of all, for Swiss are generally home-bound people who do not migrate a lot, unlike, say, Greeks or – particularly – Italians, whose close-knit communities – small and large – can be found all over the globe, particularly in the USA and Australia. In the Melbourne suburbs of Carlton and Brunswick alone, there live over 200,000 Italians, whose ancestors mostly came down under to explore the Victorian goldfields in the 1850s.

To make a discovery, one doesn't have to travel to the end of the earth, for the most unlikely findings are often located right on our doorstep. Another proof of that dictum came in a phone call from an Italian engineer friend of mine several months ago. Based in Veneto, he had then just returned from a conference on cyber security at Cranfield University in the English town of Bedford, about twenty miles from another English town where I live. He told me how surprised he was to hear Italian, spoken frequently in the streets of Bedford. 'In one café, both the staff and the customers communicated in the Sicilian dialect, interspersed with English words,' he assured me. I suggested that they were perhaps Italian tourists, to which my friend objected that they all looked and behaved like locals …

My curiosity was sparked off, and I undertook several visits to Bedford, just a thirty-minute drive from where I live. I visited the excellent local history museum and an impressive Eagle second-hand bookshop. I have even downloaded on my Kindle reader a short e-book by Angie Voluti *Searching for Nonno. The adventures of an Italian grandfather in Bedford* about an old Italian man who flies all the way from Sicily 'to the unlikely haven of Bedford, England' to look after his grandchildren during their school holidays.

I walked the streets of that seemingly unremarkable (not counting its unforgettable 01234 phone code) town – past Italian churches, social clubs and even an Italian Vice-Consulate – spotting cars with UK number plates, adorned by small Italian flags. I drank espresso in the town's coffee shops (not necessarily with Italian names) full of smartly dressed brown-eyed *ragazzi* chatting away in Italian (with my more than basic command of that language, I was unable to determine which dialect it was).

After several months of such 'research,' I ended up with the following:

With the fifteen per cent of the town's population of 100,000 being Italian, Bedford was by far Britain's largest Italian town. The main distinctive feature of the Bedford Italians compared to other bits of the global Italian diaspora was that it was created and motivated not so much by poverty and despair as by the demands of technology, the so-called TMM – technology-motivated migration (my own term).

Let me explain.

In the early 1950s, Bedford's Marston Valley Brick Company found itself short of qualified workforce for the post-war reconstruction effort which, understandably, required lots of bricks. Emissaries were sent to the South of Italy, with its traditional 'insufficient employment,' to select their men. Naples was made the centre of recruitment, and soon 7,500 workers from Apulia, Campania, Sicily, Abruzzo and Calabria arrived in Bedford on lucrative four-year contracts, often to the chagrin of their wives and other family members put off by cold weather and terrible post-war rations, mostly consisting of potatoes. In many cases, rather than fleeing poverty, the recruited workers and engineers ended up in worse living conditions than in Italy. They found solace in hard work which included, among other things, the engineering of the revolutionary and then unique Fletton bricks, the 'greenest' ever produced. Those were made from the local Lower Oxford Clay, with very high inbuilt fuel content that ignites itself and brings itself up to full burning temperature without the need for using coal – the method that made the bricks much cheaper to manufacture.

Inspired by the example of the first contractors, other Italian workers started with their families. It was not long before specialist Italian shops: La Bottega Italiani and Ferretti's – opened in Bedford. Differences in work attitudes, however, led to mounting frictions with the locals. In the words of the 1960s Bedford Mayor, 'an Italian singing in the street as he goes to work at 6.30am is perhaps not appreciated by the rather staid Englishman who wants another hour in bed!' That and the shortage of accommodation for the new arrivals soon – a little over ten years after it started – brought the recruitment of Italian workers and engineers to a stop.

By then, the foundations Bedford's Italian community had been already firmly laid, and the persisting Italian subculture – all those authentic restaurants and cafés churning out the uniquely delicious pasta and the arrestingly aromatic espresso and cappuccino – now constitutes one good reason for visiting the town. That and Bedford's clean, cosy and famously quiet family pubs, which only tend to get lively when England plays Italy in soccer or in rugby …

London as a State of Mind

A nineteenth-century Russian literary critic once remarked that to write a good book about Russia, one had to leave it first.

I think this can be applied not just to Russia, but to any place one had felt attached to before having to leave it.

I have left London again – for the umpteenth time – despite my friends' advice to the contrary. Again, I have ignored Sydney Smith's pronouncement that any life led out of London is a mistake – bigger or smaller, but still a mistake. I know it is, but keep leaving London, walking out on it like on an unfaithful woman, whom I still love, only to miss it (her?) almost to tears and then – against all odds – to come back again.

Indeed, there is something distinctly feminine about London (at least, to me there definitely is). No wonder the English, while talking or writing about London, sometimes use the pronoun 'she.'

And not just the English. Didn't I myself once compare London in summer to a curvaceous bikini-clad blonde who has wandered by mistake into a drab male-only Pall Mall club?

Never before, it seems, have I missed London as much as now – after my latest 'walkout' on it (on her?). Perhaps, the time has come to do a book about it? About London as a state of mind, as a chameleon city, effortlessly adjusting to my changing moods: grieving and rejoicing with me – like no other place in the world. About the city, constantly opening up new horizons, offering hope and snatching it away the moment you succumb to its (her?) treacherous charms.

Karl Baedeker once called Paris 'the temptress of a city.' If so, London is probably the bitch of a city. An expensive and devious, yet totally irresistible, whore. A dangerous liaison for a writer …

'Having become a Westerner, better, a Londoner … ' – this is a snippet from a *Financial Times* review of one of my books. I like this ostentatious and somewhat cocky 'better, a Londoner' and tend to regard it as the highest praise I have ever received. The reviewer, whose name I cannot recall, was right, for 'Londoner' is not just a definition of residence, but rather an honorary title (like knighthood, perhaps?), bestowed on those who – whether they realise it or not – have won the main prize in the lottery of life; a title that is awarded for good and – like a 'final and unchangeable' Soviet-style court verdict – cannot be altered or annulled.

What was it that dragged him towards London with such tremendous force?

Was it London's reputation of a literary Mecca? The attraction so beautifully described by one of his favourite English writers, HV Morton, who could have been a mauvist, had mauvism been invented in his lifetime:

> 'London has always shone like a promised land in the eyes of those ambitious to make a name in English literature. Some, such as Lamb, have been Londoners; others have been drawn to London, like Shakespeare, who journeyed up from dreamy Stratford-on-Avon to try his fortunes in the great city, so typical of that hope which has, century after century, dazzled the writer or the artist with the promise that someday he might keep a tryst with Fame in the shadow of St Paul's. Some of them – as the long line of great thinkers proves – realised their ambition; some found sadness, neglect, and poverty; some harshness in this life and fame at the hands of another generation.'

Or was it something much more personal – something that, miraculously, went back to his own Soviet childhood in the dusty Ukrainian city of Kharkov?

At the age of seven, I (together with three other boys of the same age) was cajoled into learning English. The name of the private teacher hired by our persistent parents was Grigoriy Alexandrovich Polonsky. He was a tall, sturdy old man, with a loud voice and droopy Cossack-style moustache. In his youth, he studied at a pre-revolutionary grammar school, from which he graduated in the memorable year of 1917 (when the Bolshevik *coup d'état* took place), having mastered – alongside all his classmates, no doubt – three living and two dead (Latin and Ancient Greek) tongues.

Grigoriy Alexandrovich resided in the distant and obscure – like the Brahmaputra River – Kharkov suburb of Kholodnaya Gora ('Cold Mountain'). I can still see his lanky snow-covered frame (it must have snowed constantly in 'Cold Mountain'), energetically entering – almost falling into – our flat.

In his battered capacious briefcase our teacher carried – among other things – some faded postcards with coloured views of London. They came from a hard-to-obtain 'Cities of the Capitalist Inferno' (or something of that sort) postcard set, shoddily printed by our local 'Red Proletarian' publishing house. These postcards were given out to us – one at a time – as prizes for diligence in our studies of the English language. As 'moral stimuli,' so to speak … For three 'fives' (the highest mark in Russia and Ukraine) in a row we would be entitled to a bleak Piccadilly Circus postcard, for five, to the Buckingham Palace one, for ten, to something more politically significant, like, say, the grave of Karl Marx in Highgate Cemetery, featuring Marx's cartoon-like bust, with disproportionately huge head and bulging eyes, staring at the world with wild cretinous rage.

We were very proud of those postcards, gained in unfair battles with English irregular verbs. To please our parents, we even glued them into special albums. I remember a badly drawn 'British worker,' hastily printed into my Piccadilly Circus picture – probably on the orders of a vigilant postcard censor – to add a proper political balance to the otherwise rather decadent 'capitalist' view, with no tractors or red banners in sight. With a Soviet-style flat cap on his head, the 'worker' stood on the stairs next to the Eros statue holding a poster that ran simply: '1st of Mey' (the spelling mistake here is not mine, for even at the tender age of seven I already knew how to write the names of the months correctly).

This 'Mey' poster added a feline touch to the picture. At least in our still largely Russian-speaking little boys' eyes it did ('*Мяу*' in Russian equals English 'meow'). Even now, crossing Piccadilly Circus, I cannot help but look down so as not to stumble over one of the numerous cats that, as we used to imagine, must be swarming all over the square.

To earn enough 'fives' for the 'Piccadilly,' let alone 'Karl Marl,' as we irreverently nicknamed the founder of Marxism, was not easy. And not just because of the fact that at the beginning of each lesson we had to recite from memory – in English! – 'The Solemn Oath of the Young Pioneer':[17] 'I, a young pioneer of the Soviet Union, solemnly promise before my comrades to love my Soviet Motherland dearly, to live, learn and fight (*sic* – VV) as the great Lenin bequeathed to us, as the Communist party teaches us!' Not that Grigoriy Alexandrovich was so hooray-patriotic, but being a teacher, even in private, he had to play by the rules, so to speak. No, the main difficulty lay in our Pestalozzi's rather unorthodox teaching methods. These days they would have probably been branded 'forceful immersion into a foreign-language environment,' or something like that.

The whole truth was that, due to the total absence of that very 'foreign-language environment' in our industrial Ukrainian city, 'closed' for all foreigners, except for a few ever-tipsy Bulgarians, he had to invent it for us. That was why – as a way of introducing the verb 'to pinch,' for example – he would squeeze our cheeks with his stiff pre-revolutionary fingers and wouldn't let go until the victims wailed in English 'Stop pinching!'

By modern politically correct standards, he could have easily been labelled a sadist, or even a paedophile, yet in reality, he was neither. On the contrary, he was an excellent teacher, and, thanks to his learn-as-you-play approach, alien-sounding foreign words were imprinted forever in our submissive brains.

Yes, at times, on our cheeks, too ...

One day, Grigoriy Alexandrovich left his glasses behind in our flat. A couple of days later, his wife called to cancel our next lesson (and all the following ones, too), because our playful teacher had died suddenly of a heart attack.

His glasses were still lying on our table, and I remember being amazed and somewhat puzzled by their sudden and rather scary good-for-nothing-ness.

At least, he could now practise his two dead languages in peace, or so I thought.

[17] 'Young Pioneers' – a state-run communist organisation for young children (between nine and fourteen), membership in which was compulsory.

The teacher passed away, but our trophies – the postcards – remained. I looked at them for hours, and, notwithstanding the awful quality of print, could not help admiring London's unique colour pattern: red buses and red pillar boxes against the background of white Portland stone houses. That was probably how I became an Anglophile. Or rather – a Londonophile, if there's such a word at all (I don't see why there shouldn't be, by the way).

When – many, many years later – I came to London for the first time, my immediate impression was how much it resembled the fuzzy postcards of my childhood! Even the ridiculous 'worker' was still stuck near Eros, only his poster ran not '1st of Mey,' but 'The End of the World is Nigh,' which – as I already knew – was rubbish, because MY real world was only just beginning.

I realised with sudden clarity that for all those years I had resided in an alien country and had only now found my true spiritual home …

In the years to come, I would often ask myself:

Does London Actually Exist?

To anyone from, say, America or the Continent, this may seem an absurd question. It only acquires a meaning if we look at London from within. As writer Duncan Fallowell once observed, 'London doesn't have straight lines. Its space, like that of the universe, is curved. But, as with the universe, you can only be inside London. There is no way of standing outside it.'

If London does exist, then what is it: a city, a region, with not one but many centres, 'a nation, not a city' (Disraeli, 1870), 'a thousand villages' (Ian Nairn, 1966), or just 'an endless addition of littleness to littleness, extending itself over a great tract of land' (Edmund Burke, 1792)? And where are its boundaries?

To try and find an answer to all those questions, let us look at the concept of 'London identity.'

In my travel writing, I have always liked to personalise places. I once compared Venice to an ageing, yet still graceful, lady suffering from insomnia and shuffling around the house in her loose and worn-out slippers in the night. And living down under, I visualised Australia as a freckled and angular, albeit sporty, teenager. There's little doubt that towns, cities, villages and countries – just like people – clearly have identities of their own.

So what (or who) is London?

There is no consensus as to the great city's nature, character or even 'gender.' When London is depicted as a human in British literary sources, it is almost always as a woman ('she'). However, London's significant parts are often represented by male figures, as is 'Old Father Thames.'

Interestingly, in Russian, the word 'London' is masculine ('*on*' – 'he'), and a female Russian friend told me repeatedly that for her London was definitely a '*muzhchina*' ('a man') – an attitude shared, surprisingly, by renowned English travel writer HV Morton, who regarded London as 'the most masculine city in the world.'

Peter Ackroyd in his *London. The Biography* sees London as 'a human body': 'The byways of the city resemble thin veins and its parks are like lungs. In the mist and rain of an urban autumn, the shining stones and cobbles of the older thoroughfares look as if they are bleeding.' Likewise, HV Morton was convinced that London had a 'heart.' On the other hand, the late Ian Nairn, one of the most brilliant architectural commentators of modern times, once noted authoritatively that 'London as a single personality simply does not exist.'

Personality or not, London has always been able to evoke purely human emotions. TE Lawrence missed it (him? her?) so much when in Arabia that, on his return, he was ready 'to eat the pavement of the Strand.' And according to the confession of Charles Lamb in 1801, 'The wonder of these [London] sights impels me into night walks about the crowded streets, and I often shed tears in the motley Strand from fullness of joy at so much life ... ' What is it about the Strand in particular that seems to provoke such passion in writers? It would take a separate article, or a book, to muse over ...

In return, writers have always been happy to ascribe to London some purely human qualities and character traits. WS Campbell, in his book *The 'Passer By' in London* (1908) called the city 'a true democrat,' and Jan Morris has diagnosed it as 'manic depressive' – 'on top of the world one day, all despondency the next.'

One could speculate endlessly about London's qualities. I personally tend to agree with James Bone, *The London Perambulator* (1925), who observed: 'The character of London is its bulk and multitude, and the quality of London is its accidentalness. It never seems to have set out to be or to look like a capital.'

To me personally, London has always been a chameleon city – the only place in the world that is somehow capable of adjusting itself to my changing moods: bright and jolly when I am happy, dull and depressing when I am down. And I am not alone here: 'London appears beautiful or ugly, according to one's turn of mind,' AR Hope Moncrief wrote in 1910.

As you can see, London's identity (if any) is rather blurred and resides 'in the eyes of the beholder,' ie very much a question of outward appearance.

So does London actually exist?

The truth is I don't know. But I will keep searching ...

Autumn in London

A bright-yellow autumn leaf was stuck to the windscreen of my neighbour's old Volvo. It was like a parking ticket, issued by the meticulous and transparent traffic warden of late autumn, whose long droopy trousers make a soft rustling noise as he saunters around London in the middle of the night.

I read somewhere that the exact mechanism of the riot of colours displayed by nature every autumn is still unknown to the scientists. Just like the exact mechanism of human smile.

A London autumn is a wry smile in itself, a farewell grin of nature soon to be replaced with the cold impassiveness of winter. It is the time of early darkness, when lonely pedestrians hurriedly make their way home. The pale evasive moon is mooching about in the whisky-coloured sky, like a pot-bellied drunk trudging unsteadily home after a long evening in the pub. It is the season of crisp foggy mornings, when moving around London is like traveling inside a huge chilled wine-glass, and of fragile mica-like sunlight, which shrinks, crumbles and crunches under your boots …

Emily Dickinson once beautifully called November 'the Norway of the Year.' By the same token, seasons can be compared to great cities. Paris is spring. Moscow is winter. Rome is summer. And London? Autumn, of course!

Londoners are known to take perverse pride in the all-permeating drabness of their winters. Every year newspapers report with triumph that London is experiencing its dullest (darkest, coldest, lousiest) winter on record.

How do they measure dullness? In 'glums?' Or maybe in 'spleens?'

Autumn, however, is different. It cleanses thoughts and emotions. It helps trees and humans to shed the leafy baggage of their past.

By mid-November, London starts looking light and slightly barren, like the interior of a familiar house from which the excessive furniture has been removed.

Trying to uncover the secrets of London's autumn, I go for long walks in Highgate Wood, touched with a brownish seasonal rash, as if the trees are all suffering from some botanical form of measles. I trudge through piles of fallen leaves, these fading flashes of summer sunshine. I stare at well-behaved Highgate squirrels (I wouldn't be surprised to learn that they regularly pay taxes to forest authorities). I pick up round – polished and gleaming (like the handlebars of an electric chair) – chestnuts and mumble to myself some half-forgotten autumn rhymes:

> 'O dear and cheerless time, you charm the eye and tender contentment to the heart. How wondrous to behold your dying beauty is, the lush and sumptuous splendour of nature's farewell bloom; the forests clad in gold …'

Yes, on top of everything else, a London autumn is breath-takingly poetic. Its poetry affects everyone, even those who think that a trochee is a moss-like plant that grows in the desert, and a hexameter is an instrument used by joiners to measure crooked wooden surfaces.

That is why I wrote this autumn elegy – in the hope that Autumn will issue me, too, with its bright-yellow parking ticket, of which there is only handful left on a branchy maple tree behind my window.

Folkestone, Kent

While in Folkestone, Charles Dickens was suffering writer's block – a highly unusual occurrence for such a prolific author.

He came here in summer of 1855 to work on the opening chapters of 'Little Dorrit,' but … 'I walk downstairs once in every five minutes, look out of the window once in every two, and do nothing else,' he complained in a letter. The view from the window of his house at 3 Albion Villas was the main distracting factor: 'You can sit at your open window on the cliff overhanging the sea beach and have the sky and the ocean, as it were, framed before you like a beautiful picture,' he noted in another letter.

Another irresistible distraction lay in long walks across the town and along the sea-front: 'Our [Folkestone's – VV] situation is delightful, our air is delicious, and our and our breezy hills and downs, carpeted with wild thyme, and decorated with millions of wild flowers, are, on the faith of a pedestrian, perfect …'

In the intervals between walks and staring out the window, the great writer would pop in for a pint at 'The British Lion' in the Bayle[18] and would use every opportunity to give public readings of his earlier works. No wonder he had little time left for writing in this 'world of wealth, privilege, servants, carriages and bath-chairs' – as the nineteenth century Folkestone was described by an old guidebook.

I came to Folkestone in 2003. Remembering Dickens' experience, I was initially wary of being hit with writer's block too, but my worries were superfluous, for these days 'distractions' in Folkestone are few and far between. To begin with, the view from my window, 'overhanging' not the beach and 'the ocean,' but a nearby council estate, is of piles of black rubbish bags, methodically rummaged through by seagulls, approaching this task with the zest of HM Customs inspectors ransacking the luggage of a rough-looking Colombian tourist.

Torn newspapers and junk-food wrappings are flying in the wind before landing on my porch, from where I dutifully pick them up every morning.

Folkestone is still strikingly beautiful, mainly due to its unique situation among the cliffs 'overhanging' the English Channel, so vast and open that it indeed looks more like 'the ocean.'

I enjoy the town's nostalgia for its former glory, its battered Victorian beauty, its cobbled winding lanes running down the hill towards the Harbour.

On the other hand, one has to be blind not to notice the ever-growing decay. The famous Harbour, which had been bustling with ships, visitors and foreign

[18] I bet there weren't many patrons there watching football on teletext then – a common occurrence in many a Folkestone pub these days.

dignitaries since 1843, is now incongruously empty. After almost 150 years of operation, the passenger ferry link with France was stopped. For good. And shortly after that, all cargo traffic from the Harbour was terminated too. 'Folkestone will never again have a sea link with Continent,' the executives of Falcon Distribution, the port's owners, reassured the town's residents.

The only vessels to be found in the Folkestone Harbour today are small fishing boats and a huge rusty bulk of the Black Widow U475 Soviet-made Submarine. Bought from the hard-currency-starved Russian Navy several years ago, it was brought to Folkestone and turned into a floating museum under the kitschy motto 'Red Alert. Look What Has Surfaced Now That Communism Is Sunk.'

I walk along the wind-swept Marine Parade towards the Leas, 'one of the finest marine promenades in the world,' according to the 1934 *Wardlock's Red Guide*' These days bumping into a holidaymaker under sixty years old on the promenade is as unlikely as spotting an Aleut in the streets of Abu Dhabi. Rare pedestrians look sullen and flat like crude plywood mannequins in the dusty windows of a charity shop.

Of an evening, Folkestone's streets are populated almost exclusively by seagulls and flocks of idle youngsters who, irrespective of age or gender, seem to communicate among themselves with the help of one short English word and its derivatives. Businesses in the town's main streets are closing down and the owners are moving out. The most prospering establishment in the architecturally unique Old High Street is now 'Tattoo Studio. The Only Honest. Experienced and Professional Studio in the Area.'

Even the once thriving fishing industry has come to a halt (allegedly, due to the draconian EU regulations), and most of the sea-food on offer at several sea-front kiosks is 'not real' and 'made of minced fish' – as it was put by an honest saleswoman, from whom I tried to buy a fake lobster tail the other day.

The signs of decay are ubiquitous. *The Folkestone Herald* newspaper, with provincially judgmental headlines of the type 'Nasty Baker Kicks Sheep,' runs a regular photo column 'Dumped Car of the Week.' In the 'Lidl' supermarket, where I do my shopping, all portable shopping baskets have been stolen. The Leas Lift is closed down 'until further notice,' (the tiny funicular train vanished into thin air one fine night – I wouldn't be surprised to learn that it was nicked too), and the rare strollers, including myself, have to puff their way up the hill.

In a funny way, 158 years after Charles Dickens' visit, Folkestone itself has become thoroughly 'Dickensian.' I don't think the classic would have had any problems writing there these days.

True, Folkestone still has beautiful (if not very clean) beaches. Yet it is only on several warm days a year that one can safely plunge into the freezing waters of the Channel. Another challenge is not to be blown away by the unceasing icy wind, while you trudge reluctantly towards the water – in full accordance with the famous Lenin's dictum 'one step forward, two steps back.'

Masochistic by nature, I ventured to swim in the sea once or twice to the locals' open-mouthed consternation, and am now expecting my name to pop up in the next Royal Honours List.

A good old bathing machine would come handy (at least, it had walls to protect you from the wind, and an attendant was always there with a towel ready), but, alas, it is now a thing of the past.

Folkestone needs help. It desperately needs investment and government funding, and these are, sadly, not forthcoming. It also needs lots of holidaymakers willing to spend money. But crowds of 'quality' tourists are unlikely to turn up at a place which boasts one of Britain's highest per capita rate of pubs (I once saw a funeral held in a pub up my street!), but only one classy restaurant, 'Tavernetta,' whose elderly Italian owner characterised his Folkestone experience as 'twenty-five years of madness.' For me, eating out in Folkestone means a solitary dinner in my little back garden on occasional rain-less evenings.

Living in Folkestone these days is as challenging, at times as uninviting, yet always as genuine as the open sea, or, indeed, 'the ocean,' on whose steep white-cliffed shores it is so stunningly located.

A small Victorian cottage next to my house is now empty. Its former tenants – a bunch of young unemployed men – were evicted the other day for not paying their rent, and all the furniture was taken away. With its doors wide ajar, there it stands – tattered on the outside and mutilated from inside, yet still graceful.

Like Folkestone itself, it is waiting for new – CARING – tenants to move in.

I look away from the window and carry on writing …

* * *

Different Types of Rain in Folkestone:

1. Normal drizzle. Seagulls keep screaming.

2. Shower. Seagulls shut up or get outshouted by the noise of the streams of water falling down from the sky. I once unwittingly (and rather precisely) described it in one of my youthful poems, 'Shower above the Sea': The air is full of the cocktail of smells. Seagulls are piercing dark-green clouds. From heavens – a fresh-water sea is falling down into a salt-water one!

3. 'Mushroom rain' or 'blind rain' – both are Russian idioms describing rain with sunshine. Seagulls disappear from view.

4. Gale (can occur on any day of the year) – looks very much like a snowstorm, only the snow melts on touching the ground. Seagulls freeze in their flight.

5. 'Folkestone sleet' – gale plus shower (occasionally, plus thunderstorm). Seagulls get shredded to pieces …

Part Four
Travels in the Celtic World: Scotland, Ireland and Wales

Edinburgh

They were trudging down the Royal Mile hand in hand. He was smoking and munching a fried Mars bar in between puffs. His female companion – taller and much more mature than he – was swigging from a can of beer and smoking, too. In the treacherous light of a solitary street lamp, he looked no older than eight and his sister (I wanted to hope she was his sister, not a girlfriend) – about eleven.

Nightly walks up the Royal Mile to replenish the supplies of milk, duly decimated by my three young kids, were part of my daily routine during our first month in Edinburgh. 'You can never buy enough vodka,' we used to say in Russia. By the same token, you can never stock up enough milk to satisfy the burgeoning appetites of three little children.

Puffing up High Street towards the area's only open corner shop, I couldn't help thinking of how different real Edinburgh appeared to its 'cool' Festival-inspired stereotype. Irvine Welsh once claimed on BBC Radio 4 that the Scottish capital was 'a cultural desert outside the Festival,' with one of the biggest drugs and child-poverty problems in Europe. On the eve of our move from London, I chose to dismiss his words as a literary hyperbole.

The flesh-and-blood 'child-poverty problem,' multiplied by two, was now stumbling towards me – smoking, drinking beer and chewing a battered Mars bar.

Packed solid with daytime traffic, so slow that it created the impression of crawling backwards, the Royal Mile would routinely go dead after 7pm. At least, its Canongate stretch did. The Festival had just ended with a big fireworks bang into the muted Edinburgh skies. It rained twenty-five hours a day, and the evening air was thick and sticky like Haggis. One could almost scoop it by handfuls and cut it into pieces. Rare pedestrians looked sullen and flat like crude mannequins in the dusty windows of a charity shop.

On a night like that, I was wary of bumping into Deacon Brodie, the prototype of Stevenson's Dr Jekyll (alias Mr Hyde), or other ghosts from the city's eerie past. On one occasion, I thought I could discern in the distance the cocked-hatted silhouettes of Samuel Johnson and his reluctantly Scottish (like many other self-flagellating Scottish intellectuals, he 'couldn't help it,' you see) companion James Boswell emerging from Jenny Ha's Tavern to start their historic walk through the 'effluvia' of the 'odoriferous' Royal Mile. I could almost hear Dr Johnson's sardonic remark to his escort: 'I can smell you in the dark.'

* * *

'Emigration is a dress rehearsal of one's own funeral,' a Moscow friend of mine used to say. What about the second emigration then? A quick reburial after exhumation? I ask forgiveness for this moribund metaphor: too many night time walks in the Royal Mile, I presume (and I hadn't even ventured yet on one of Edinburgh's famous City of the Dead tours!). I actually argued with that pessimistic friend of mine – also a writer – saying that emigration was more likely to herald a re-birth than a funeral.

Whatever the metaphor, coming to live in Scotland after twelve years in London did make me feel a double expatriate, or an ex-expatriate, if you wish. Perhaps, it would have been easier to end up somewhere entirely diverse – in Equatorial Africa, say – with all your internal resources mobilised to cope with the culture shock. Here, in Edinburgh, many things were deceptively similar: Sainsburys and Marks & Sparks, double-deckers and fluffy old ladies – these 'God's dandelions' (a good Russian expression) and Queen Mum look-alikes, speaking to shop-attendants in a posh London accent. The street crowd, however, was different: it was considerably duller, probably due to the near-absence of African and Asian faces in it. Also, compared to London, Edinburgh felt very small. Much smaller than its thoroughly cultivated image.

As part of this cleverly engineered PR campaign, Edinburgh was promoted as the seat of the new – devolved – Scottish parliament and the site of its new – delayed – grand headquarters. Jan Morris once called Heathrow airport 'a permanently unfinished city.' The new Scottish Executive under construction struck me as a 'permanently unfinished' building. Unlike Heathrow, with its four Terminals, there was nothing terminal about it. In this respect, its constant semi-presence at Holyrood was reassuring: it was good to be reminded that not everything in this life was finite, after all.

I was amused to learn that the non-existent parliament edifice had to be 'bomb-proofed' against a terrorist attack – hence the delays and the skyrocketing costs. Allegedly, a small-scale copy of every single part of the complex had to be built and bomb-tested somewhere on the Yorkshire Moors, prior to putting together a life-size equivalent. Having examined a computer-generated image of the whole ensemble, I came to the conclusion that the new parliament's intended design was in itself the best deterrent against a terrorist attack. With its slanting, as if tipsy, roof tops, made to resemble 'upturned boats' (don't boats turn turtle before sinking?), and its irregular-shaped windows, as if bricks had been tossed through each of them, the complex gave the impression of having been bombed already. And even the most daring terrorists are unlikely to attack the same place twice.

The simple truth is that the grandness and the bomb-proofing standards of a parliament house are of no relevance to the quality of debate within its walls. If architecture is indeed music in stone, it doesn't mean that a parliament building has to be a noisy military march.

With the devolved (I nearly wrote 'devalued' – a Freudian slip) Scottish parliament controlling a meagre ten per cent of the nation's budget, no matter where they sit – in a palace or in a bomb-proofed pub, the MSPs will only be able to carry on legislating on such important matters as how to disrupt Scotland's enduring love affair with junk food. 'I intend to do everything I can to effect that change,' promised First Minister Jack McConnel.

Frankly, I cannot see how he can effectively 'effect' it, apart from occasionally opting for a fruit salad instead of a black bun for pudding.

He could perhaps introduce a bill banning sales of battered Mars bars on a par with hard drugs, but even that is unlikely to persuade Edinburghers to give up their burgers, so to speak.

One thing I learnt after thirty-six years in a totalitarian state is that one's life-style – healthy or unhealthy, honest or fraudulent – cannot be imposed from above or regulated by decree. It starts and finishes solely inside one's head. And one's heart. Just like independence, or lack of it.

* * *

I walk back home with two Pavarotti-size milk bottles weighing down my shoulder bag. Tomorrow is a new day. And although December daylight is bound to be as bleak and as brief as the final flash of a dying electric light-bulb, I know there will be a moment, when the recalcitrant Scottish sun peeps out fleetingly from behind the Castle, momentarily transforming the malt-whisky-coloured Edinburgh clouds into the sky-wide Saltire. And my scepticism will turn into hope …

From a side-lane leading to Waverley Station, I hear the whingeing whistle of a locomotive. It reminds me of the runaway engine that recently got uncoupled from its train and travelled several miles away from that very station – on its own, without a driver! The *Flying Scotsman* turned the ***Fleeing*** *Scotsman*. What, or who, was it fleeing from?

For me, that maverick engine came to symbolise modern Scotland. Having detached herself from the rusty rolling stock of the British Empire, the Fleeing Scotsman rattles along – driver-less – towards the future. The track is bumpy and in need of repair, but the signal light ahead is green.

Happy journey!

Dublin

The old chimney, with me inside, was trembling, as if swinging ever so slightly to the accompaniment of the wind's hooliganic whistles.

With some exalted American tourists, I stood on what our guide called 'the best viewing platform in Dublin' – at the very top of a former Jameson Distillery's chimney, turned into a 'viewing tower.'

There was some sad symmetry in the fact that the unsightly Dublin cityscape, dominated by concrete boxes, smoking chimneys and occasional church spires, could be best viewed from inside yet another chimney, even if disused.

From my very first day in the Irish capital, I could clearly see that Dublin in its entirety was not a beautiful place. Even so, having looked down at the capital from the top of the chimney, I found myself thoroughly unprepared for the sight 'of unparalleled charmlessness, an absence of grace so total that it was almost the thing of wonder.'

The above quote from James Cameron, incidentally, refers to Dundee – once a thriving and pretty Scottish city that had been meticulously (and successfully) destroyed and mutilated by 'city fathers' and 'developers' for over 130 years. I used it here because I had considered modern Dundee the most architecturally messed-up metropolis in the Western world. Until I saw Dublin.

If architecture is indeed a 'frozen music' (the metaphor, attributed by different sources to Goethe, Schelling and Le Corbusier), the panoramic view from the top of the chimney could be compared to an ear-grating cacophony, played by a madman. Dublin's chaotic cityscape was reminiscent of a huge sack of potatoes that had burst at the seams and was carelessly dropped onto the ground. Or of a pebbles-strewn beach after a storm.

Like pieces of amber among pebbles, however, there were occasional gems to please the eye here and there: the graceful dome of Custom House; the brown-green smidgen of Phoenix Park, skewered by the disproportionately massive phallic Monument; the pillars of the magnificent Blue Coat School in Blackhall Place straight underneath me. The latter was the only surviving eighteenth century structure in the formerly fine-looking area, disfigured by Corporation housing and the so-called 'in-fill development,' ie cramming every vacant space with as many hideous, yet profit-making, concrete apartment blocks as possible. As I could see from the top of the chimney, the frantic 'filling-in' construction was still going on.

'First we shape buildings, and then – buildings shape us,' Winston Churchill once famously remarked. And wasn't it the architectural turmoil of Dublin that had eventually 'shaped' it into a depressive and largely dysfunctional metropolis, with high crime rate, all-permeating corruption, unworkable transport system and one of

Europe's worst dressed street crowds – in short, into a city that is much less attractive than its painstakingly created PR image?

When did it all start and who is to blame for the ugly pockmarked face of one of Europe's spiritual and artistic capitals?

Unlike in Dundee, it is not just the money-grabbing developers of the not-so-distant past, for even as far back as in 1727 Jonathan Swift, himself a Dubliner, called the city 'the most disagreeable place in Europe.' And in 1937, Oliver John Gogarthy, a Dublin writer and a model for Joyce's Buck Milligan in *Ulysses*, remarked sardonically that 'Dublin has one advantage: it is easy to get out of it.'

A number of Irish historians and architectural experts throughout the years referred to 'the planning nightmare of Dublin' and the city's 'decayed physical fabric.' From Frank McDonald's book 'The Construction of Dublin,' I learned that Ireland was 'in breach of EU law relating to protection of architectural heritage.' Yet none of the pundits provided a coherent answer to one simple question: why?

In search of an explanation, I had to descend from the chimney of speculation to meet Simon Walker – an architect, a UCD tutor and a native Dubliner – for a short and strictly down-to-earth 'guided tour' of the capital.

Lunchtime Dublin traffic was so dense and slow that it gave the impression of crawling backwards. Walking to my meeting place with Simon, I had to stop (purely out of habit) at pedestrian lights, ignored by most other passers-by. And by drivers, too. A New York friend of mine once told me that freedom-loving residents of the Big Apple ignored traffic lights, because they found them 'too suggestive.' 'No one is telling me when to cross the road!' he snapped. In Dublin, the reason was more practical: most of the traffic lights seemed totally out of sync with traffic itself. As if they had some little independent minds of their own. I noticed that it was generally safer to cross the roads at red pedestrian lights than at green ones.

Looking up at Dublin facades and trying to describe each of them with just one epithet was like constantly checking with my brain's in-built thesaurus for the synonyms of 'ugly.' Most of the houses were indeed 'plain' (in the best of scenarios), 'unattractive' and 'unprepossessing.' They were also 'disagreeable' and 'distasteful,' whereas many were truly 'frightful,' 'hideous,' 'horrid,' 'monstrous,' 'repugnant,' 'repulsive,' 'shocking' and 'vile.'

Passing through two of the five remaining Georgian squares was like getting two sudden deep breaths of fresh air. I made sure I had a good eyeful of both before plunging back into ugliness ('unattractiveness,' 'unsightliness,' 'repulsiveness,' 'hideousness').

In his attitude to traffic lights, Simon was a typical Dubliner: he was resolutely pushing his bike in-between the rows of stationary traffic in total disregard of designated road crossings and angry honks. I could hardly keep up with him.

'Irish people never had a sound relationship with spaces of public appearance, and the real culture was always relocated to rear parts of houses,' he was saying as we raced along Grafton Street.

With some fiendish satisfaction, I remembered that Dublin street, where I myself resided, was designated as 'Rear.' The 'Front' bit ran parallel to it. In no other city of the globe had I come across a similar division.

'This is why,' continued Simon, 'architecture was always approached very pragmatically. If the spirit was something immaterial and not ostentatious, then appearance didn't really matter …'

He pointed at the flock of some particularly scruffy passers-by.

'The best planner Dublin ever had was James Butler, the seventeenth-century First Duke of Ormond. As for the beautiful Georgian and Victorian buildings, they were always perceived as something belonging to the enemy power – England – and therefore not worth preserving. There was even an attempt to make Dublin into a Celtic city in 1924-25 …'

'But as far as I know, Celtic Ireland was a hundred per cent rural and had no towns at all,' I interrupted. 'How could they re-create something that never existed?'

'Well, they couldn't. The Irish always enjoyed direct relationship with the land and felt alienation in towns. In any case, the people of Dublin have never been interested in preserving whatever architecture they had.'

We turned into Westmoreland Street.

'Here's a brilliant example of a typically Dublin phenomenon known as 'facadism,'' Simon pointed at the eclectic-looking building of Westin Hotel across the road. 'A row of fine houses that stood in its place were disembowelled, with only the facades kept intact, and their interior taken by just one hotel. The EBS Building Society next door underwent a similar mutilation: a Georgian mansion was destroyed, but the middle of its façade was kept and stuck to the modern building with its ridiculous mirror-like windows …'

The distorted reflections (including those of Simon and myself) in the façade of the building made the street feel even more congested and claustrophobic than it was already. I thought that 'facadism' could be traced to the infamous 'Potemkin Villages' – painted images of plenty, made of cardboard, and displayed by the inventive eighteenth-century Russian Prince Potemkin on the banks of the Dnieper to mislead Catherine the Great, when she sailed down the river to inspect her domains, and to cover up the indescribable poverty of the villages behind them.

We proceeded to the Quays of the Liffey, dominated by the new Liberty Hall that could be best described with one capacious Italian word '*casuccio*' – a huge and ugly house. The shabby concrete box of the Department of Health, looking as if it was itself in need of plastic surgery, was peeping out cheekily from behind Corn

Exchange – like an untidy primary school upstart stretching both unwashed hands into the face of a myopic teacher of History.

'Cheap and nasty ... Just money and no art ... No architecture here at all ...' such were my learned guide's comments as we moved past various concrete blocks – all in different stages of ugliness – lining what could have otherwise been a truly beautiful embankment. Old Custom House, the exquisite late-eighteenth-century creation of James Gandon, stood out like a visitor from outer space in this parade of modern architectural atrocities.

I didn't notice how we crossed from the First World into the Third (somehow bypassing the Second) and ended up in once fashionable Gardiner Street in the North of Dublin. And it WAS quite a different world: rough, run-down, shabby and unclean. Badly dressed people with sullen faces stared at us with hostility. English and Russian swear words flew in the air like sparrows. A couple of burly policemen were pushing a screaming woman into a 'Garda' van.

The architecture – or rather total lack of it – corresponded to the atmosphere (or was it the other way around?). Original Georgian houses in the lower part of the street were all 'obliterated' and replaced with five ironically named 'Custom Hall' concrete blocks of private apartments, 'façadised' with fake 'Georgian' features and imitation red bricks.

'This is what private capital would do, if allowed,' Simon said bitterly. 'The apartments are all dark and tiny: not big enough to swing a cat in. There are no gardens, trees or even courtyards ...'

Black rubbish bags were displayed on miniature balconies: there was probably no space for them inside the flats.

'No light, no space, no air,' summed up Simon. 'And the reasons are obvious: greed of speculator builders and incompetence of the conniving city authorities.'

Before rushing off to teach his students, Simon took me to Summerhill, the site of the now-defunct Luke Gardiner estate in the centre of Dublin.

'This area used to have four- or five-storey Georgian tenements, all destroyed in the 1970s and 80s. Instead, rows of standard two-storey suburban cottages were built here – in the heart of the city, whose very fabric was ruined as a result. This is a good example of how the whole of Dublin was emasculated and made into something that looks truly horrendous.'

'What is the solution, if any?' I asked.

'To begin with, there has to be a comprehensive development plan. The City has to purchase land in the centre and take it from there ...'

Simon jumped on his bike and pedalled away. I watched his receding figure for a while – until he turned the corner and disappeared behind a dilapidated Victorian chapel, now functioning as a garage.

Moscow, Scotland

'Notwithstanding the utmost efforts of the police, no trace whatever has been found of the perpetrator of the diabolical murder and robbery at Moscow …'

There's nothing like a good murder mystery to beat the boredom of the dead (pun unintended) week between Christmas and the New Year. Particularly, if the mystery is a real-life, albeit a 118-year-old, story …

Thirteen years after defecting from the Soviet Union, I was finally returning to Moscow. My brand-new British passport, however, had not been stamped with a hard-to-obtain Russian visa, for the Moscow I was heading for was in Ayrshire, Scotland – halfway between Kilmarnock and Galston. In my breast pocket, I had an unsent Christmas card to a friend in Australia whom I wanted to impress – or to be perfectly honest, to confuse – with a 'Moscow' stamp on the envelope.

This innocent chicanery was born out of necessity, or rather out of my own forgetfulness. Like one maverick tea-spoon that always ends up left in the sink after the washing up is completed, there's always one Christmas card that you forget to post in time. Getting a 'Moscow' stamp on my belated Australia-bound missive was my only chance to redeem myself in my friend's eyes by making him think it had actually been posted from Russia. I could then blame the notorious inefficiency of the Russian postal system for the otherwise unforgivable delay …

Doing my homework for this particular trip was easy: there was only one mention of Moscow, Ayrshire, that I was able to find in library books: the 1992 *Illustrated Architectural Guide to Ayrshire & Arran* described it as an 'oddly named village and telephone exchange beside the Volga Burn, for the motorist on the main road no more than two unnecessarily large signs drawing attention to the name, and a sprawling untidy garage.' My thinking was that if the village had a telephone exchange, it was bound to have a post office with a franking stamp, too … In a separate box, the *Guide* explained the origins of the village's name, which, allegedly, had no connection with Russia, but derived from the Old Scots 'Moss haw' meaning a marshy ravine. As for the Volga Burn, it was but 'a facetious nomenclature coined to strengthen the putative link,' as assured by the omniscient *Guide* or, in plain English, it was simply a joke.

I also browsed through newspaper archives. In two faded 1884 issues of the *Kilmarnock Standard* I came across a description of the mysterious Moscow murder – obviously the first, last and only village event of any distinction during the last 150 years. On the train to Glasgow and in the car, driven by Eddie, a Herald photographer, I immersed myself in its photocopied account:

> 'Mr Robert Rankin, a well-known Kilmarnock gentleman, who has lived for some years in retirement at the hamlet, had been found dead in circumstances

> which demanded enquiry. The body of Mr Rankin was found lying in a pool of blood, and even a casual glance was suggestive of foul play … In the right hand, was an ordinary nail hammer which at first was suggestive of suicide, but a closer examination showed that the hammer was not at all grasped by the hand, having evidently been placed in it after death …'

I was contemplating the sheer inconvenience of committing suicide by hitting one's own head with a hammer, when Eddie drew my attention to a road sign 'Waterside 13, Moscow 3' – the first proof that the Scottish Moscow actually existed.

It was not long before the view in our windscreen was blocked with another enormous sign, looking more like a memorable 'Lenin is Always With Us' billboard – the only sort of road advertising one was likely to see in the Soviet Union. 'Moscow. Please Do Not Stop' it ran. I am pulling your leg, of course, for in reality the sign said: 'Please Drive Carefully,' but it could have just as well been the former, for the passing cars did NOT drive carefully and made sure they roared through Moscow without slowing down. In a way, I could not blame them: 'You blink – and you've missed it,' as one Ayrshire Muscovite put it to me later.

At a first glance, modern Moscow did not differ greatly from the 1884 crime-scene description in the *Kilmarnock Standard*:

> 'Moscow, lying quite apart of any main road, consists of only a single row of small houses extending for rather less than a hundred yards. On the other side of the road … is Volga Bank Cottage, in which Mr Rankin resided … Such is the scene of the tragedy. A novelist could not choose one more fitted to excite the imagination with a sense of loneliness and awe …'

One didn't have to be a novelist to deduce that 'loneliness' was still there. The village was entirely deserted, except for a flock of sheep, grazing dispassionately next to what could indeed pass for 'an untidy garage.' As the sheep seemed to be the only living Muscovites around, I was about to try and chat them up, when a florist's van pulled over next to me. 'Do you come from Moscow?' the driver asked me. 'Yes, I do,' I replied honestly. 'Where is Dykescroft Cottage?' he then enquired to my understandable bewilderment.

Yet the very fact that flowers were to be delivered to someone in Moscow was reassuring: unless it was a funereal wreath, someone alive could still be found in the village, which I decided to keep exploring by locating first a public toilet and then a post office – in that nature-dictated order.

In both cases, I suffered a fiasco. Total absence of public 'facilities' of any kind was probably the only feature shared by the Scottish Moscow with its Soviet namesake, as I remembered it. My other negative discovery was that not only the village had no phone exchange any longer, it had never had a post office of its own, the nearest one being in Galston – the stamp that I didn't need on my long-belated Christmas card.

One positive sign though was that, unlike in the Soviet Moscow, there were no queues which could be explained by the absence of such essential queue-forming components as shops and people. The last queue in Moscow's uneventful history occurred shortly after the mysterious 1884 murder and originated from the fact that the unfortunate Mr Rankin was last seen alive at the village inn (another victim of Moscow's time-related decline), where he asked for 'a half-mutchkin of whisky, stating that a young man had come in to his house, who "thought he would be the better of a hauf-ane." ' This is how this historic event was recorded by the *Kilmarnock Standard*:

> 'On Sunday last Moscow was visited by large crowds of people from the town, attracted thither by morbid curiosity and the fineness of the weather. The village inn was literally besieged by thirsty travellers, who were admitted in relays until the entire stock of liquor was exhausted.'

Driven by the fairly benign, if pressing, curiosity of a traveller, whose state could be best described as opposite to being 'thirsty,' I simply had to find at least one living Muscovite to talk to. And fast!

I was lucky, for in the end I met and befriended not one but three: the delightful Mrs Caldwell – a widow of a local farmer; her no-less-delightful daughter Ann, and their dog – a Jack Russell called Scampi, whose bark sounded much better then both his bite (which I didn't have a chance to experience) and his height (which I did). All three lived in a Victorian croft on the bank of the vociferous – like a Russian peasant woman telling off her husband for being drunk – Volga Burn (creek).

Mrs Caldwell, a real patriot of her little Moscow, assured me she wouldn't swap it for any other place in the world. Her daughter didn't have immediate plans to move out either. The ladies lamented the gradual degradation of the village, which had recently lost its much-loved community centre. They also deplored the plight of local dairy farmers, driven out of business by supermarket chains, making sure they bulk-bought milk at ridiculously low prices

Ann told me how as a kid in the 1980s she used to play in a … nuclear bomb-shelter, built by an overcautious local farmer for his own family needs. The farmer must have been afraid that Americans would nuke the Scottish Moscow, instead of the Russian one, by mistake (I thought that had Dubya Bush been the President then, the farmer's fears could have been more than justified). This brought back memories of my own childhood on the opposite side of the Cold War fence. We had compulsory Civil Defence classes at school and state-run concrete bomb-shelters in every court-yard. Of course, as a little boy, I used to play inside them too. The Cold

War paranoia accounted for similar children's games in two Moscows on different sides of the Berlin Wall!

When I was leaving, Mrs Caldwell showed me an envelope of a letter, addressed to her, but 'missent to Russia' by the Royal Mail several years ago. With a stamp of *Moskva*'s Central Post-Sorting Office, it had finally found its addressee in Ayrshire. For once, the beleaguered Russian post proved more efficient than the Royal Mail. This reminded me of my unsent Christmas card which I posted immediately (better late than never) at Moscow's compact 'post-sorting office' in the shape of the village's only red mail box thus putting an end to the whole Christmas-card saga.

But how about the Moscow murder, you might ask? Who on earth was it that killed and burgled Mr Robert Rankin – a quiet recluse from Volga Bank Cottage? Alas, until now 'no trace whatever has been found of the perpetrator.' For all I know, it could have been a 'big cat,' similar to the one, spotted in Ayrshire last week. The only problem with this version is that a whisky-guzzling 'big cat' has yet to be identified by zoologists …

To help solve the mystery, I'd like to appeal to anyone, who might have been in the vicinity of Moscow and noticed anything suspicious on 13 March 1884, to come forward and phone Captain McHardy, Chief of the Ayrshire County Constabulary, on 'Moscow 232.'

Dundee

I could hardly keep up with Professor Charles McKean. His eyes gleaming excitedly from under the glasses, his coat-tails flapping in the wind that he himself was creating (or so it seemed), he dragged me from one stinky gateway to another to show me what remained of medieval Dundee.

We climbed some dirty winding stairs to be confronted with a miraculously preserved early seventeenth-century fireplace inside the semi-ruined former dwelling of a certain 'MacLeod, the bag-pipe maker,' as it was written on a faded door-plate.

We explored the vaulted Estonian-timber attics of merchants' houses in Gray Close. We trod on litter and broken glass in the well-shaped fifteenth-century courtyards, to which the professor respectfully referred as 'typical European spaces.'

In one of them – propped against a mouldering wall – stood an original medieval wooden hatch, with the trademark of an unknown stonemason. 'Look, this is Paris!' exclaimed the professor as we rushed along Whitehall Crescent – a brilliant example of the late nineteenth century 'environmental Gothic.'

Scotland's leading expert in the history of architecture, Professor McKean had a theory, according to which medieval Dundee was built along the same lines as Hanseatic League towns (Lubeck, Gdansk, Copenhagen, etc), where curved, crescent-like streets ran parallel to each other, with open public spaces in between.

This strict pattern was largely destroyed by the construction of the giant Overgate shopping centre in 1963. 'They didn't understand cities and ruined Dundee's medieval pattern,' he sighed, squinting at the ugly dome-shaped behemoth of a building. 'And look – as a result the whole area is still derelict.'

Professor McKean's architectural tour made me think that, alongside trials for crimes against humanity, it would be good to set up an international tribunal for crimes against towns and cities to punish those responsible for destroying their faces and souls.

A flock of sad stone penguins greeted me at the entrance to Dundee's troubled top attraction – Discovery Point – on the bank of the River Tay. They stood there, their heads down, as if refusing to absorb the mutilated cityscape – 'the facade of unparalleled charmlessness, an absence of grace so total that it was almost the thing of wonder,' as it was put by James Cameron in 1967.

With regret, I had to admit that, thirty-five years on, the view from the waterfront remained largely the same. The city's uncomplaining skyline was pierced with a couple of church spires, rivalled by high-rise Stalinist boxes of the Mecca bingo hall, the warehouse-like Hilton hotel and Tayside House – the home of Dundee City Council, with interiors reminiscent of the Stasi headquarters in East Berlin.

The next level down was criss-crossed with pedestrian walkways – an antithesis of New York's elevated railways – spanning over vast, half-empty car parks, shopping malls and underground passages – the only places where a passer-by could hide from all this aggressive ugliness.

The painful familiarity of the scene was later explained to me by Hamish Glen, artistic director of the renowned Dundee Rep theatre, according to whom Dundee was a popular 'natural' location for films set in communist Eastern Europe. Whenever there was a need for a bleak 'totalitarian' urban landscape, the ingenious British directors – rather than wasting money and nerves to obtain Soviet (or East German, or Romanian) visas, used to come to Dundee. This could not fail but enhance the city's persisting negative stereotype, which, it has to be said, was largely created by Dundonians themselves.

My new acquaintance, Professor McKean of Dundee University, referred in one of his articles to 'a certain perverse masochism in the Dundonian … designed to keep intruders, visitors and tourists at bay.'

True, cities (and even whole countries such as Scotland) can suffer from an inferiority complex – a condition often resulting in depression, which, as some psychologists assert, is but an aggression directed against oneself.

It was Dundee's city fathers who, having passed the so-called 'City Improvement Act' in 1871, started demolishing its medieval city centre – then second in its beauty to Edinburgh alone. It was they who decreed in 1952 that Dundee had only eight buildings worth keeping. It was they who, in a campaign to obliterate Dundee's industrial past, meticulously ruined and vandalised almost all remaining buildings of architectural value that still remained in the city in the 1960-70s and built car parks, walkways, ugly shopping centres and multi-storey flats (locally known as 'multis') in their stead.

Having dealt a massive blow to the city's already dwindling self-esteem, this last demolition triggered an unprecedented decline of Dundee's economy and culture.

Echoes of that old cultural masochism could be heard recently, when many Dundonians in their letters to the *Evening Telegraph* demanded that Dundee's two award-winning museums and heritage sites – RRS Discovery and Verdant Works Jute Factory – be closed down or moved elsewhere. Verdant Works, the winner of the European Museum of the Year Award in 2000, was in particular danger.

It looked as if many locals were bent on writing off the whole of Dundee's industrial past as that of poverty and despair, brought about by the satanic jute mills, and did not want to be reminded of it too often. They did not understand that one couldn't be secure in one's present unless confident of the past.

Losing Verdant Works would be a tragedy for Dundee, because the museum, with all its interactive hands-on exhibits, its fully operational Victorian jute-producing line, its numerous displays on work and leisure in Victorian times, is truly unique.

Another example of Dundee's persisting inferiority complex is the gross over-promotion of William McGonagall, the 'world's best worst poet,' whose name I saw on a Discovery Point billboard, listing three most famous Dundonians of all time, beside a Nobel Prize-winning scientist and a world athletics champion – a joke that has gone over the top.

Any inferiority complex is a two-way street, and outsiders have contributed to the negative stereotype of Dundee as much as the locals. Many of my Edinburgh contacts, on learning I was going to Dundee, would wrinkle their noses: 'But this is the armpit of Scotland. What on earth will you do there?'

Despite all this, the city's new self-confidence is on the rise.

The stretch of Nethergate next to the Queens Hotel, which was teeming with drunks and junkies several years ago, has now been 'gentrified' beyond recognition by the impressive modernistic complex of Dundee Contemporary Arts (DCA) – one of Scotland's ten top attractions. Faith Liddel, DCA director, told me that its success was not unpredictable.

'Dundee had an enormous hunger for arts and a huge potential – with all its high-tech industries and a large student population,' she said.

Architecturally, the DCA complex was an antipode of a typical 1970s Dundee structure. It was all light and openness. Everyone who entered the open-plan building was constantly confronted with art. DCA quickly became Dundee's cultural hub, from where, as Ms Liddel assured me, it was possible 'to have an intimate dialogue with all 150,000 Dundonians.'

'Do you know that the five best modern Scottish poets live in Dundee?' she asked me. I was glad she didn't mention 'best worst' poets. Many Dundee intellectuals expressed their profound dislike of McGonagall as a symbol of mediocrity and bad taste, sending a wrong message to aspiring artists and writers. They saw the future of Dundee as a centre of excellence and ideas: the new 'Ideopolis,' as opposed to the cliched 'Juteopolis' of the past.

I could see their point: the budding self-confidence of Dundee required new icons to replace McGonagall.

'Welcome! Thrice welcome to the year 1893
For it is the year that I intend to leave Dundee
Owing to the treatment I receive
Which does my heart sadly grieve,'

he lamented clumsily in one of his doggerels testifying to the fact that his relationship with Dundee was not always a happy one.

I came to love the wry gap-toothed smile of Dundee – a reflection of its tormented and well-hidden, yet beautiful, soul. I wanted to hope that one day unjustified stereotypes and complexes will leave this long-suffering city for good – in the manner of its famously talentless son, William McGonagall.

County Roscommon, Ireland

'Ireland has been mauled by the Celtic Tiger, chewed up by double-digit economic growth – and what's left is barely recognisable.'
The Guardian Weekend Magazine, 4 December 2004

Pints of Guinness were popping up on the bar in front of me like blades of flick-knives, concealed under the counter.

It was my first ever night in a 'typical' country pub ('The Corner House') of a 'typical' Irish village (Ballinagare in Co Roscommon). I was speedily approaching my personal absolute record in Guinness consumption and thinking of entering it into my own imaginary Book of Guinness Records.

Since my very days in Ireland, I wanted to write a feature on a small and seemingly unremarkable Irish village, for – from what I knew – it was there, and not amidst chaotic urban piles of Dublin, Limerick and Cork, that the 'mysterious Irish soul' was dwelling.

Indeed, Celtic Ireland was entirely rural: towns were a fairly recent Irish creation. In my imagination, it was like one huge sprawling village, populated by warriors, druids (or dreamers) and poets. My first evening in Ballinagare, to where I was invited for a weekend, did little to confirm that romantic vision. The Corner House's ambience was rather reminiscent of a scene from a book by the late Pete McCarthy: men drinking at the bar, women reclining on sofas along the wall – a timeless setting. The only reminder of the twenty-first century was a poster, advertising salsa-dancing classes in the village hall.

I felt as if I had known all the patrons for donkey's years. After the fifth (or was it the sixth?) pint, Dublin, London, elections in Ukraine and the war in Iraq – all receded, blended into distant insignificance – overshadowed by the really important issues: the previous week's closure of the village's old post-office and a new housing development project, approved by County Council …

'These thirteen new council houses will ruin the village,' a retired teacher, sitting next to me, was saying.

'That's right! Besides, what are the newcomers going to do here? There are no jobs, no childcare, no public transport and no infrastructure for them,' echoed one of the women from the sofa.

The residents of Ballinagare had been fighting the losing battle against the housing project for several years, their rationale being that one simply could not increase the village population of seventy-two almost threefold without drastically changing its way of life and its historic architectural pattern. Yet, despite numerous petitions and protests, the construction of new houses was under way: three of them were already in place – a Dublin-style 'in-fill development' in miniature …

In-between the pints that seemed to grow from the bar in front of me, I would pop out for a smoke. The tiny village outside was immersed in peaceful slumber. To a hardened city dweller like myself, it resembled a neat little old lady, who had dozed off quietly on a park bench. I thought I could even hear her snore ever so gently …

Next morning, I was woken up by the deafening silence behind the windows of my room. A pot of steaming coffee looked (and tasted) like a pint of hot Guinness.

With Pat, one of my hospitable hosts, we went for a drive around the area. We could have walked of course, but villagers all over the world love their cars, if any …

One of the two settlements of the parish of Kilcorkey, Ballinagare stood on a large Bog. For centuries, this area was the domain of the O'Conors, the famous Gaelic chieftains and landowners. The most prominent of them – historian, poet and manuscripts collector Charles O'Conor – lived in Ballinagare in the mid-eighteenth century and later retired to a secluded farmhouse called the Hermitage. After his death, the house became a 'writers' retreat' and then – a training centre for Irish Free State Army. A listed building, it was now in a deplorable state: roof and chimneys overgrown with grass, gaping eye-sockets of the windows covered with sheets of plastic. Right next to the house, stood a modern cottage, occupied by the Collins' family – descendants of Charles O'Connor's herd. A woman, who opened the door of the cottage, told us that they had been trying to maintain the Hermitage on their own money. 'It cost us a fortune. For twenty years we have been waiting for some assistance from County Council, but it claims to have no funds for the house's upkeep …'

Ballinagare's semi-ruined old church had been turned into a tip, its grounds strewn with rubbish, broken bikes and rusty washing machines. A similar fate befell the historic Old Market House in the neighbouring village of Frenchpark, the only difference being that, unlike the church, it was enclosed by a shabby fence. Once a splendid structure that, among other period features, had indoor toilets – a highly unusual detail for a seventeenth century Irish interior, it was more recently used for food storage. This brought back associations with communist Russia, where many old churches were turned into vegetable depots. 'The Temple of St George on Potatoes' – as Muscovites used to joke uneasily in the mid-1980s.

The USSR, of course, was very poor and spent almost half of its budget on 'defence' (read arms race), but how come the powerful and seemingly peaceful 'Celtic Tiger' cannot find the means to preserve the country's heritage?

We drove on to the village of Tulsk (a deceptively Russian-sounding name!) that lay in the midst of what the local tourist brochure called 'a unique sacred landscape,' dotted with Bronze Age mounds and ancient burial grounds. Indeed, there was a modern state-of-the-art Visitor Centre in Tulsk. But what did we see next to it? Bulldozers and excavators digging up that very 'sacred landscape' for all they were worth to create a modern housing estate! The same brochure obviously got it wrong when it called the people of Tulsk 'proud custodians of this unique ritual landscape.' One could see with a naked eye how greed and big business were hastily transforming Ireland from the Emerald Isle into the 'Concrete Isle.'

Perhaps, Russian associations were not that far-fetched in Tulsk.

To be fair, we did eventually find one old church that was properly, even lovingly, restored by Roscommon County Council. It was Portahard Protestant Church on the edge of Frenchpark. The reason for that was simple: the grave of Dr Douglas Hyde, the first President of Ireland, was in the churchyard, next to the Douglas Hyde 'Interpretative Centre,' no doubt. To me, however, this was but a classic case of Soviet-style window-dressing that simply underlined the neglected state of other no-less important historic buildings that could not boast of having a tomb of a prominent Irish statesman on their grounds.

The old graveyard of Ballinagare did not have any 'prominent' graves either – just those of 'ordinary' Irish village folk – all victims of the Great Famine, Black and Tans, 'Crown forces' and plain hardship of everyday life. That was probably why the present-day state of it was not just deplorable – it was disastrous. To get to the cemetery, Pat and I had to negotiate rivers of mud and hillocks of cow droppings. We had to dive under spires of torn barbed wire – the remains of the enclosure, erected by County Council instead of the promised restoration.

'Dancing' gravestones in different stages of collapse – fallen, semi-fallen and still almost upright – were hardly visible behind thick vegetation, mostly weeds. The ground under our feet was disturbingly bumpy, and every bump signified an abandoned grave. Or rather – a forgotten life. It was like trudging through the necropolis of Irish countryside itself.

It was getting dark. The winter day – bleak and short like the final flash of a dying light bulb – was coming to an end.

Despite this gruesome excursion, I did find a number of signs to support my romantic image of an Irish village in Ballinagare – the place where locals still leave their cars and houses unlocked; where wild pheasants can be seen unhurriedly crossing the 'main road'; where Tommy Connor, the oldest resident in his mid-90s and a former devoted Gaelic football player, vividly remembers 'how farmers walked their pigs a hundred miles to the nearest terminal, from where they would take them to England'; where people still believe that a child whose father died before he was born can cure thrush by blowing on the sores …

I was delighted to learn that the village – just like the whole of Ireland – had always had a disproportionate number of first-class, if somewhat surrealistic and tongue-in-cheek, amateur poets. 'Oh, Ballinagare of fame renowned, A church without a steeple, At every door there stands a whore, To laugh at decent people …' This was written by Frank Browne, a Ballinagare native, who died in 1998.

And this is how he described his experience of the 'Hill' pub in Tulsk: 'Between 'Hill' and Hell there is but one letter, And if 'Hill' was in Hell, Tulsk would be a lot better.'

A similar sparkling poetic wit could be found in the works of two other deceased locals – Bob Loftus and Seamus Dockery ('As I walked into the park one day, I could not believe my luck. I spied upon the river bank a fine bog mallard duck. I had to scheme a brilliant plan, it was all down to me, How could I catch that lovely duck to have it for my tea …')

Luckily, not all the poets-cum-eccentrics in the area were dead. Sean Browne from neighbouring Castlerea may have never written a single verse, but I was inclined to regard him as a true poet for what he had managed to achieve. A train buff from childhood, he bought a disused Irish Railways A55 locomotive and installed it INSIDE 'Hell's Kitchen' pub that he owned (and still does) in 1996. I saw this diesel-electric 'monster,' surrounded with signals, points, badges, conductors' caps and other railway paraphernalia from all over the world, and as a fellow trainspotter could not help admiring Sean's ingenuity and stamina (he had to overcome lots of bureaucratic hurdles to purchase the locomotive) in having his dream realised. 'I did it purely out of love,' he said to me proudly.

'Pub owner goes loco!' ran a headline in a 1996 Irish tabloid that also quoted one of Sean's customers as saying that his pub gave a whole new meaning to 'suppin' diesel.' As for me, I was thrilled to see in Sean's collection a badge of the Kharkov Institute of Railway Engineers from my native Ukrainian city.

Poets and dreamers (read eccentrics) were precisely the types that I had been hoping to find in my imaginary Irish village. So, in this particular respect, my short visit to Ballinagare – a microcosm of the whole of Ireland – was a success.

And although, having been born elsewhere, I wouldn't repeat after John Noone, another home-bred Ballinagare poet, who emigrated to America in 1904:

'Ah, Ballinagare I think you are
The sweetest place on earth.
My thoughts do fondly cling to you,
I've loved you from my birth …'

– my own thoughts will 'fondly cling' to this 'unremarkable' Roscommon hamlet, the first 'real' Irish village I have visited in my life.

'We all live in the present moment of the past' – I saw these words of TS Eliot on a poster inside Tulsk Visitor Centre.

Leaving Roscommon, I was hoping that one day they would be noticed and taken onboard by everyone in the old and once beautiful village called Ireland.

Fraserburgh, Scotland

The fish, joined at the fins, stood upright – balancing on their tails, as if trying to form a live shield to protect the town. But their desperate links were running loose and were about to be severed. Through the gaps between their wriggling bodies, one could see boarded shop windows and scruffily dressed rare pedestrians, scouring the streets in search of post-Christmas bargains …

'The Net' – a surrealistic bronze sculpture in Saltoun Square in the centre of Fraserburgh – a dying fishing community in the extreme North East of Scotland – was one of the most evocative works of art I had ever come across. Created by David Annand, it represented a swirling school of fish, but, in the sculptor's own words, was designed to produce a three-dimensional sensation of sea depth as viewed from the surface. With the town's ever-growing decline, triggered by drugs and the EU fishing quotas, 'The Net' has acquired a special meaning, for Fraserburgh itself was slowly sinking into the quagmire of poverty and decay, from which the fish were no longer able to protect it.

A town's demise is similar to that of a man sliding down into depression. Having lost motivation, he stops looking after himself, grows stubble and shuns sunlight. His eyes and spirit fade by the hour, he loses hope and the desire to carry on. Likewise, the depressed town's streets get covered with the stubble of refuse, and the boarded windows of insolvent businesses look like patches on the eyes of a perfectly sighted person, unwilling to face the light of the day.

Winston Churchill compared depression to a black dog. The continuing waning of Fraserburgh is more readily associated with white fish – cod and haddock, whose catching quotas were drastically cut by the recent EU directives. With over half of the town's jobs dependent on white fishing – this meant the loss of its whole *raison d'etre*. 'Each fisherman at sea supports sixty-seven jobs on land,' Alex Shand, editor of the *Fraserburgh Herald* told me. 'The latest EU quotas will be the last straw for our community when they come into effect. They will mean more drug-abuse, more unemployment, more family break-ups.'

Reams have been written about the causes of the Scottish fishing industry crisis, with heated and seemingly persuasive arguments from all sides involved. The fishermen blame the EU bureaucrats, the British and Scottish governments and the 'bogus' scientists for letting them down. They argue that Scotland has been victimised again, despite doing more for stock conservation than any other European country. They call Franz Fischler, the embattled European Fisheries Commissioner, 'Ayatollah Fischler' and publicly compare him to Adolf Hitler. The environmentalists, in their turn, are saying that the fishermen themselves are at fault, that only a complete ban on white fishing can save the North Sea wildlife from extinction, and therefore the forty-five per cent reduction of fishing quotas, with the maximum fifteen days at sea per boat per month, is the very least that can be done to prevent the disaster.

For someone like myself, whose fishing experience is largely limited to ferreting out a couple of perches from a pond at the tender age of six and who – until fairly recently – was convinced that an artichoke, an unseen delicacy in the Soviet Union of my youth, was a leafy tropical plant, taking sides in this dispute would be hardly appropriate. Yet one has to be both blind and heartless not to notice the immediate implications of the crisis for thousands of human beings, whose entire livelihood was taken away. Whatever the arguments, this should have never been allowed to happen.

Plywood seemed the only building material still in demand in Fraserburgh. In High Street, I walked past the locked and boarded 'Fraserburgh Football Social Club'; past Murray McKie Hi Fi Shop, its windows firmly shuttered; past Tech Hide Computers – the only shop, where the windows were covered not with plywood, but, in accordance with its once high-tech profile, with iron sheets; past 'Jesters Joke Factory' – a party accessories shop, boarded and 'for sale.' True, there were not many jokes (or parties) left in Fraserburgh, and the only remaining humour was rather black: 'Question: What is the similarity between the Scottish Fishing Industry and a Christmas turkey? Answer: They both get stuffed.' (*The Fraserburgh Herald*).

I moved on to Saltoun Square, once the hub of the bustling royal burgh, with its own coveted Market Cross. Three quarters of businesses in it were now closed for good. An attractive Victorian Saltoun Arms Hotel, 'commended by Scottish Tourist Board,' stood locked and abandoned; the nearby Insports and 'Sweetie' shops were shut down, and 'Furniture & Accessories' store, although still going, had a brick (or some other heavy object) thrown through its window, in which a large spider-web hole was gaping. The only outlets that seemed relatively busy were video rentals; numerous charity shops and a '99 Pence' store, doing brisk trade in cut-price children's toys, toiletries and packets of crisps. With sadness, I noted that the average value of a Fraserburgh house – as advertised in the still intact windows of real estate agents – was between £25,000, whereas flats went (if they did at all) for as little as £12,000. The town was obviously not taking part in Britain's continuing housing boom.

I stopped at the (closed) Tourist Information Bureau to read a house plate commemorating 'Thomas Blake – 'The Scottish Samurai' and a native of Fraserburgh, famed for 'his work in the development of Japan,' when I was approached by an unshaven and whisky-reeking, yet not unfriendly, character offering to find me a 'nice and cheap' B&B. I refused and questioned him about Thomas Blake, whom he claimed to have known personally ('the Scottish Samurai' died in 1911).

'It looks like Fraserburgh could do with a modern Thomas Blake,' I said to my new acquaintance

He shook his dishevelled head resolutely: 'Nah ... He was only good for Japan, but did absolutely nothing here. Nothing at all!'

He had mermaids tattooed on both wrists, and when he gesticulated, the mermaids winked and wiggled their tails playfully.

Instead of a Thomas Blake figure, I ended up finding a Joan of Arc. And not one, but three! I mean the three wives of Fraserburgh fishermen calling themselves The Cod Crusaders: Caroline Bruce, Carol MacDonald and Morag Ritchie. These ordinary down-to-earth ladies, sharing thirteen children (and one grandchild – Carol Macdonald has just become a granny at thirty-five years of age!) among them, decided to take the future of their community in their own hands.

I met them at a coffee shop in the outskirts of Fraserburgh. Only two – Carol and Morag – were able to make it: Caroline was busy with her kids. Their husbands were at sea, and I could not imagine how they coped with all the house chores (Morag being the mother of seven!) on top of running a high-profile international campaign.

'We are used to hard work,' smiled Carol. 'With our husbands constantly away, we have to be mums and dads simultaneously. We are cooks, taxi-drivers, DIY experts and decision-makers – all at the same time. In this case, we are fighting for the future of our children, and although we feel angry and let down, nothing will stop us.'

In less than two months, the ladies had achieved a lot. They brought 700 demonstrators to Edinburgh, where Jack Macdonnel refused to join their protest saying it was 'too wet outside.' In London, they handed over their Petition, with 45,000 signatures they had collected, to the MPs at Westminster and at 10, Downing Street. But the highlight of their campaign was on 9 December, when they flew to Brussels to confront Franz Fischler himself.

'He went straight past us, pretending we weren't there,' recalled Morag. 'But we accosted him in the lift and didn't let him out until we voiced all our demands.'

The Commission nevertheless decided to go ahead with the quotas. Yet Fraserburgh's Joans of Arc, with perseverance and spirit, reminiscent of the 'hope against hope' approach of Soviet political dissenters, kept fighting 'to save what little is left of our community,' as Carol poignantly put it.

In their battered four-wheel-drive, the Cod Crusaders took me to the Harbour, incongruously empty for the end of December, when most fishermen would normally be home celebrating the New Year with their families. Now, many were out at sea to take advantage of the last weeks before the quotas come into effect later this month, and the remaining few boats were rocking gently, moored to the pier.

They rubbed boards, as if trying to reassure each other, or simply – to warm themselves up.

There, in the seagull-ridden Fraserburgh Harbour, the women told me about an old local tradition, according to which fishermen's wives would carry their husbands to the boats to make sure they didn't get wet before stepping on board. This echoed a legend I once heard in Turkmenistan. When a medieval fortress was captured after a long bloody siege, the invaders' commander magnanimously decided to let all the defenders' wives walk away in peace. He declared they could take with them whatever valuables they could carry. Without hesitation, the women picked up their bearded armour-suited husbands and dragged them out of the fortress on their shoulders.

The fishermen's wives of Fraserburgh no longer practiced their ancient husband-carrying ritual. Yet, having met the Cod Crusaders, who – unlike most local males I had spoken to – have not succumbed to gloom and doom, I thought that, metaphorically speaking, this was still pretty much the case.

Looking into the women's determined eyes, I wanted to believe that their shoulders were strong enough for the burden. And also – that there was still an escape route from their common 'besieged fortress.'

Aviemore

I love snow. It has been with me all my life. I was born in Ukraine on a snowy January night, and when, five days later, my mother was carrying me in a bundle from the door of the maternity hospital to the waiting *Pobeda* taxi to take me home, several playful snowflakes sneaked under the cotton-wool blanket in which I was wrapped, and prickled my face gently, welcoming me to the world.

I learned to ski almost before I learned to walk. I would go to school on skis. They were crude and bulky, with primitive bindings – nothing like all this high-tech Western gear. But it didn't matter. On Sundays, we went skiing in a park with my father. We used to glide forgetfully along the ski-track, dividing the silent snow-ridden wintry forest into two identical glittering landscapes.

You may not believe me, but I do have 'a feeling for snow' that enables me to sense it coming many hours before the actual snowfall. To function properly, I have a pressing need to see and to touch the snow at least once every several years. This was not an easy task when I lived in Australia, but moving to England and then to Scotland facilitated it to a degree. For a snow-hungry person like myself, the timing for my journey to Aviemore could have not been better. The whole of northern Scotland was paralysed by blizzards and snowfalls, and all Highlands schools were closed 'due to severe weather conditions.'

It was my first exposure to the Highlands of Scotland in winter. How shall I describe the mountains? And should I?

'Nothing is easier to describe than scenery; nothing is more difficult and unnecessary to read,' wrote Jerome K Jerome. Perhaps, the best ever description of mountains came from Ostap Bender, a protagonist of a popular Soviet satirical novel: 'Too showy. Weird kind of beauty. An idiot's imagination.'

And yet, looking through the train window, I couldn't refrain from jotting down in my notebook that snow-capped mountain peaks, playing hide-and-seek with the train, were as taciturn, solid and serene (not to say 'senile') as a bunch of Soviet Politburo members in their identical white-topped sheep-skin hats.

The mountains were running towards the train and growing in size by the minute. They looked unreal as if made of papier-mâché. Soon they were dominating the landscape and blocking the sunlight. When their presence became totalitarian, the train came to a stop in Aviemore.

I thought I knew what to expect. My 2001 *Footprint* guidebook asserted unceremoniously that there was 'nothing of real interest in Aviemore' and explained that in the 1960s it 'was transformed into a jumble of concrete buildings, tacky gift shops and sprawling coach parks,' adding that 'the extent of the tourist tat here is so awful that it makes Fort William seem charmingly understated by comparison.' This was a stark contrast to the 1949 *Blue Guides Scotland* describing Aviemore as 'charmingly situated on the Spey,' 'convenient' and 'attracting many visitors.'

The beautifully preserved Victorian station, with its timber houses, old lanterns and cast-iron columns, did not look tacky at all. I soon learned, however, that the station was Aviemore's only historic structure, spared by the 1960s brutal development only because they were unable to pull the solid building down, no matter how hard they tried.

The legendary Aviemore Inn, where Robbie Burns once stayed (he then called the area 'a wild and romantic spot'), proved less lucky and less solid: it was bulldozed in 1969.

The intention of the developers was to create a model ski resort to overshadow the mountains. Alas, as it was demonstrated by Milton Keynes in England, Celebration in Florida, USA, and numerous other similarly ambitious projects, 'model' towns (or villages) seldom work in ordinary life. Instead of becoming a new Ischgl or St Moriz, Aviemore ended up as the Highlands' own mini-Blackpool. Showing no concern for the environment, the developers erected clusters of faceless concrete hotels (Billy Connolly once branded them 'air-raid shelters with windows'), imitation pseudo-Scandinavian 'chalets' and tasteless shopping malls, largely blocking the view of Craigellachie – the Rock of Alarm – towering above Aviemore, which means 'open space' in Gaelic.

The space was no longer 'open,' but the alarms did not sound until mid 1970s, when the 'model resort' went into terminal decay, spurred by general recession, frequent changes of ownership, corruption and most importantly by the sheer unpredictability of the capricious Highlands weather. Designed exclusively for skiers, Aviemore was unable to compete with continental ski resorts either in infrastructure or in length and quality of its snow season. As it was put by an anonymous 1920s Scottish skier, quoted by *Collins Encyclopedia of Scotland*, 'snow conditions will always prevent us from becoming really expert at home ... even on the highest hills conditions are usually bad.'

The latest example was the annual Aviemore Sled Dog Rally that took place on 25-26 January just a week before my arrival. Everything was in place: the teams, the sleds, the dexterous Siberian huskies everything, except for the snow. The sleds had to be put on wheels, and my poor canine compatriots, instead of pulling them forward smoothly, had to drag them through the mud. The same snow that was not taken into account by the adventurous 1960s planners was crunching soothingly under my feet as I trudged up the hill past rows of equally unappealing hotels, with dark windows and vacancies signs; past run-down establishments with rather more mysterious signs: 'CROFTERS B R' and 'FREEDOM NN'; past countless ski gear outlets, with enough stock to equip the whole of Scotland, but with no customers; past deserted souvenir shops trading in shortbreads, keyholders, picture postcards and all imaginable forms of 'tartan,' including 'tartan mugs.' Despite all these,

Aviemore did not feel ugly. It was actually rather pretty, 'gentrified' by the thoughtless dance of star-shaped snow-flakes, falling slowly, almost reluctantly, and melting instantly on my cheeks.

For a small town, battling the avalanche of negative publicity is like resisting a heavy snowfall: the only effective way of doing so is to wait for the snow to melt naturally. Such passive attitude, however, would have been contrary to the very spirit of the Highlanders, immortalised by Robert Burns, who would have been disappointed to see Aviemore being no longer 'wild' or 'romantic.'

Recently, a radical £30 million masterplan for Aviemore's redevelopment, masterminded by Macdonald Hotels plc, Teesloch plc and Bank of Scotland was unveiled. In the words of Dr Iain Glen, a retired local councillor, the plan will have to match Aviemore's facilities with its unique surroundings. Most of the sad 1960s architectural legacy will have to be demolished, and the new buildings will be designed to blend with the environment. This time a thorough 'landscape context analysis' was conducted and a comprehensive 'landscape masterplan' agreed upon. Another major difference with the failed 1960s project was that the town would no longer rely on skiing (read snow) alone.

'Our task is to give Aviemore an all-round destination appeal,' Sean Sullivan, one of the revamp initiators, told me. Aviemore's new lay-out will be loosely based on the 'lang toon' pattern of Granttown-on-Spey, one of the loveliest examples of Scottish eighteenth century town planning only thirteen miles away. Miraculously spared by the 1960s developers, this graceful historic town, built of local granite, is a shining example of what Aviemore could have looked like, had it not been for the unfortunate 'model ski resort' idea. Encouragingly, Mr Sullivan assured me that the same granite will be used in construction of new Aviemore. Unlike the officials, most residents of Aviemore remained sceptical. 'We'll believe it when we see it' and 'We have seen bulldozers here before, but nothing happened' were their most frequent comments.

But there was also an understanding that something needed to be done. 'This is the most beautiful place in the world, and it is dying,' Pavel Satny, the manager of Aviemore Photographic, who fled his native Prague in the aftermath of the 1968 Soviet invasion, told me in his busy office near the station. His opinion was echoed by Nando Vastano, the Naples-born owner of the award-winning La Taverna restaurant, who had lived in Aviemore for twenty-seven years. One thing was certain: despite its negative stereotype, Aviemore had always managed to attract lots of creative and entrepreneurial people from many parts of the world. Like Mr Satny, they came on short skiing visits, fell in love with the place and stayed for good.

One of them was Hans Kuwall, an Austrian-born skiing instructor, who first came to the Cairngorms in 1956. We were talking at the top of the Cairngorm Mountain, having ascended it by the brand-new funicular railway, the first of its kind in the UK. Skiers were whooshing past us throwing furtive looks at my ski-less Marks

& Spencer boots and making me feel uncomfortable and out-of-place. They stared at me as if I had no feet.

Like me, Mr Kuwall loved snow in general and the 'Scottish spring snow' in particular. 'We call the spring snow Ofiern' in Austria. In Scotland, Ofiern' is much better for skiing than on the continent: it is much more consolidated.' But the 'ordinary' winter Scottish snow seemed OK to him, too, as long as it was there of course.

'I lit the torch outside my house last night, like we do in Austria and the whole garden started sparkling,' he said.

On my last morning in Aviemore, I woke up to a rhythmic drip-drip sound behind my hotel window. The snow was melting, and it was time for me to go back. Overnight, the sparkling and crunchy pavements had turned not into Ofiern' but into brownish slush. Having heard of the proverbial 'slush-pile,' a derogatory term used by publishers to describe a backlog of uncommissioned manuscripts, I now knew what a real one felt like – wet and sticky.

But I was not particularly upset by this sudden metamorphosis of my beloved snowy world, for during my two days in the Cairngorms I had seen enough snow to keep me going for a couple of years right up to the moment when I could come back to recharge my snow batteries and to face a renovated Aviemore.

Skye

'Everybody who speaks Gaelic is a poet,' said Rob MacilleChiar, writer-in-residence at the Gaelic College in Skye and a poet himself. Brought up by English-speaking parents in Argyll, he turned to poetry as soon as he started learning Gaelic, and I thought I could understand why.

How could one not be a poet speaking the tongue, with consonants often 'aspirated,' so that the words are not pronounced, but actually breathed out? How could one's soul not be poeticised by words like 'corra-ghritheach,' denoting grey heron, but literally meaning pointed shriek? Or 'fork of wind' – for swallow; 'God's fire' – for butterfly; 'curtain of water' – for rain, and so on?

How could one stay unmoved by the fact that each of the eighteen letters in the Gaelic alphabet is associated with a tree name: Ailm (elm) stood for A, Beith (birch) – for B, Coll or Calltuinn (hazel) – for C, etc?

As Rob himself wrote in one of his poems:

'Were I to send a love letter to you,
I would send every tree in the wood …'

Rob's Portakabin on the college's old campus served not only as his writing den, but also as a literary hub of this unique educational establishment, where every other teacher, irrespective of what subject he or she taught, was a published Gaelic poet.

The college's residential quarters, equipped – among other gadgets – with the world's only Gaelic-speaking lift, became my home for three nights during my search for the Gaelic language, officially recognised as Scotland's national tongue.

It took me more than eight hours by trains and ferry to reach this 'protected Gaelic enclave' (in the words of Roy Wentworth, a college lecturer) on Sleat peninsula in south Skye, although my first exposure to Gaelic occurred while still in Glasgow: it was a 'Welcome to Queen Street' Gaelic sign at the station, where I boarded a train to Mallaig.

I was tempted to assume that the train conductor asked for my tickets in Gaelic (I couldn't understand a word of what he was saying), but it turned out that he spoke Glaswegian. Disappointingly, a group of Fort William-bound Scottish labourers, sitting opposite me, kept communicating among themselves with the help of one short English word (and its derivatives) alone. One could be forgiven for thinking that, if Gaelic was indeed Scottish national tongue, then Glasgow and even the Highlands, to say nothing of Edinburgh, were miles away from Scotland itself.

'He who loses his language loses his land,' runs an old Cornish proverb. If so, Scotland must be in real danger of shrinking to the size of Monaco or San Marino in the near future. According to the recent census, the number of Gaelic speakers fell by 7,000 during the past ten years and has reached the critical mark of 58,652.

Why critical? Because all Scottish newspapers in their coverage of the census quoted (with no source revealed) the figure of 50,000 language speakers, below which, allegedly, the tongue was considered 'officially dead.' As a multi-linguist, who wrote a lot about so-called minority languages, I had reason to doubt it.

One sign of proof was the Faroe Islands, which I visited some time ago. With just 40,000 people in total, this small semi-independent nation boasted eight daily newspapers and 150 titles of books a year in Faroese – its much-treasured indigenous language.

The purity of Faroese was fiercely defended by the committee for the protection of the language – a government-supported watchdog, making sure that every child born on the islands was given a Faroese name and that as few foreign borrowings as possible could sneak into the mother tongue. This might sound too harsh, but the Faroese had to resort to extreme measures to revive their language after five centuries of Danish domination.

Likewise, the history of Gaelic is, to a large degree, a story of its suppression, the first (successful) attempt at which was undertaken by the Romans. It was outlawed by the Crown in 1616. In the eighteenth century, Gaelic books were publicly burned in the streets of Edinburgh.

The 1872 Education Act made English compulsory in all schools, and Highland children were beaten into speaking it. This centuries-long chronicle of repression stretches as far as November 2002, when the Scottish Executive voted down the bill that would give Gaelic equal status with English in certain areas of the Highlands and Islands.

It looked almost as if it had been done deliberately – to force the number of Gaelic speakers under the 'magical' 50,000 mark, after which it would be pronounced 'officially dead' and hence not worth bothering about.

How about the occasional Gaelic signs, you might ask? How about £20 million (allegedly) spent on promoting Gaelic every year? How about regulation photos of schoolchildren, happily learning Gaelic, carried by many a Scottish newspaper? How about the college itself, after all?

I got the answer while crossing from Mallaig to Skye on a Caledonian MacBrayne ferry, whose skipper welcomed the passengers in Gaelic, only to switch over to English for the rest of his lengthy announcement concerning the ship's rules and safety procedures.

I thought it was symbolic of the executive's general attitude to Gaelic: while supporting it on a purely superficial 'window-dressing' level (signs, greetings, some public broadcasting, the 'national tongue' rhetoric, etc), very little is being done in the areas where funding is essential to stop the language from dying.

For years, the staff of the Gaelic College have been denied money for compiling and publishing a comprehensive Gaelic-English dictionary (the latest goes back to 1880s). Compared to the eight Faroese dailies for 40,000 population, there is not a single Gaelic daily or weekly newspaper left in Scotland, with its 'official' 58,652 fluent Gaelic speakers. The only literary magazine in Gaelic – the acclaimed Glasgow-based *Germ* quarterly – had to fold last year due to lack of funds. Many teachers and students at the college lamented what they called 'the death of Gaelic publishing.'

One of the college students told me bitterly: 'Gaelic has become a marketing gimmick for Scottish tourism officials promoting it as if it were a tartan.'

Outside the college, there are not many Gaelic speakers left in Sleat. Even the pupils at the local Gaelic medium school are likely to 'play in English' during the breaks. A native of Sleat himself, a Gaelic speaker (yet not a reader or a writer), told me of his shock on spotting two toddler girls 'playing in Gaelic' not far from his house.

'I haven't seen anything like this from childhood,' he said. Those two little girls were probably daughters of Lindsey Campbell, a local sculptor. She and her husband speak to the girls exclusively in Gaelic. They also had to chuck out their TV set. 'I hate it when tourists take photos of my Gaelic-speaking children, as if they were monkeys. They are like all other kids and simply play in their native language,' she said.

Sir Iain Noble, the founder of the Gaelic College and a Gaelic patriot himself, shared with me his conviction that to reverse the number of Gaelic-speakers from dwindling even further, special pockets of language-enforcement should be created on the Islands. 'In such areas, only Gaelic should be taught at schools, and all public servants should be Gaelic-speaking.'

Sadly, such enforcements, unless properly weighed up and legislated, like they were in the Faroes, seldom work in real life. Language is a living body and as such it cannot be imposed from above. But it can be helped from above to develop naturally – by carefully targeted funding and legislation. As it is, the state of Gaelic in Scotland can be compared to an old croft, with a restored and freshly painted facade, but a neglected and crumbling interior.

A language dies every week somewhere in the world. Is Gaelic destined to become one of them? 'Death is outside the language. The end of language is beyond language,' wrote Iain Crichton Smith. He was right of course. Forget about the mythical 50,000 viability mark. Even if only two people speak a language between themselves, it cannot be pronounced 'officially dead.' And Gaelic, this undisputed linguistic gem, should not be allowed to disappear in the years and centuries to come. For losing it would be like losing the very soul of Scotland.

How do people come to Gaelic? I addressed this question to many students and teachers of the Gaelic College. Only very few of them were brought up as Gaelic speakers. Some, like Rob MacilleChiar, got interested in Gaelic through its peculiar place names.

Others, like Simone Dietrich from Germany (the college has a number of students from abroad), were inspired by Celtic music. Scott MacDonald, another student, took up Gaelic after living in Holland – encouraged by the linguistic prowess of the Dutch.

'People turn to Gaelic to find a soul, a root, a ground under their feet,' Rob told me in his Portakabin, where his weekly Gaelic writing class was about to begin. Angus Macleod, a shy first-year student and a native of Skye, read his poems – in Gaelic and in English (for my sake, I presume). His verse was dynamic and full of imagery. I liked two metaphors from one of his poems: his head being 'a cluster of dreams' as he wakes up in the morning, with 'dawn scratching at the door.'

Gaelic verse was alive and well. And as long as the poetry lives, the language can never die.

Dawn was 'scratching at the door,' or rather at the window, of my room overlooking the Sound of Sleat – no more than fifty yards away.

A bright piercing light, its source still invisible, was blending the sky and the sea into a pinkish whisky of sunrise. I opened the window and heard the surf whispering something in Gaelic. It was probably saying good-bye: 'Tiaraidh an drasda!'

As the ferry was chugging further and further away from Skye, the following four-liner formed itself in my head:

Every letter – a tree,
Every sound – a sigh.
I'll be missing the sea,
Speaking Gaelic to Skye.

Newry

As I was preparing for my first foray to Northern Ireland, the advice of my omniscient Dublin friends was categorical: 'Don't poke your nose into politics, and you'll be OK!'

Well, to be honest, my poor nose was not in a condition to be poked anywhere: a respiratory infection, contracted the week before, made it swell to the size of a large Irish spud. I was only hoping that 'The Gap of the North,' another name for Newry, my destination, would be wide enough to accommodate it.

Why Newry, you may ask?

Having written a lot on borders and frontiers of all kinds, I was instinctively curious about the first town (sorry, city: the status was conferred on Newry in 2002) on the northern side of the border, separating the eurozone from the poundzone and Ireland from … er … Ireland.

My intention was to focus exclusively on mundane cross-border matters: currency, roads, healthcare, communications, prices and to stay as far away from politics as possible.

To be able to look into all those properly, I made a short 'laundry list' of the things I needed to take:

1. Some euros.
2. Some pounds sterling (I could only get hold of a £20 note, issued by the Bank of Scotland).
3. Some letters to be posted to Britain and to Southern Ireland.
4. My swollen, yet running (God knows where to – probably towards Newry) nose.
5. My British passport (I was going abroad, after all!)
6. My British NHS card.

My rationale for inclusion of the last item was simple: why should I cough up €50 to see a GP in Dublin, when I could see one for free on the British territory, ie in Newry?

A writer's life itself often becomes research …

The bus journey towards the border was smooth, not counting several road-toll booths. After Dundalk, the booths disappeared, but the road became much bumpier. I was looking in the window, blowing my nose and munching a stale sausage roll, acquired in Dublin for a staggering €3.50 the day before.

The border itself was ghostly and easy to overlook for someone who wasn't watching. But I was.

First I spotted an oblong shed with a mysterious sign 'Customs Facilitation Office' (as far as I knew, there were no customs barriers between Ireland and … Ireland, ie they had already been 'facilitated' to the extreme). Then came a row of dodgy-looking money-changing outlets. 'British Spy Post. Demilitarize Now!' ran a colourful billboard, topped with scull and crossbones. Having guessed it had something to do with 'politics,' I pretended not to have noticed it. I also tried to ignore a couple of rather 'overcrowded' cemeteries.

The road signs suddenly became green, strictly monolingual and were showing distance in miles, but it was only when I ticked off 'Give Way' instead of 'Yield' that I yielded (sorry, gave way) to the fact that we were already in the UK.

A huge juicy rainbow, with one end in Ireland and the other – in the other Ireland, was bridging two parts of the same small nation, dissected by the non-existent frontier.

Having dropped the bag at my Newry hotel, I briefly contemplated the idea of having a pint in one of the inviting little pubs in County Down across the bridge (the hotel was in County Armagh, on the opposite bank of the River Clanrye), but rejected it and decided to visit a pharmacy instead.

This could have well been a life-saving decision, but I didn't know it then …

'How do you live there, in the rip-off South?' asked a friendly pharmacist at Felix McNally's drug-store when I pretended (for purposes of research, why else?) that I only had euros in my wallet. She agreed to accept them, yet at a 'special Newry exchange rate,' whereby €10 were equal to £6.50. Even so, I paid almost twice as little for the pills as they would cost me in Dublin.

Having popped into a take-away shop next door and not feeling particularly hungry, I could not resist the temptation of buying a sausage roll, priced at an incredible 80p! Even with the shop's own 'special Newry exchange rate' of just £6 for €10, it was an unbelievable bargain compared to Dublin.

'Can it be that a third, phantom, currency – 'NEWRO' – is circulated in this town/city?' I was wondering, puzzled by the evasive exchange rates fluctuating from shop to shop.

It was 7.30pm. As I was putting my untouched €1.20 sausage roll into a bin, a gunman wearing a cheap Halloween mask stumbled into a crowded McSwiggan's pub in Newry's Water Street (a couple of hundred yards from where I was) and – paramilitary-style – shot a man and a woman sitting at the bar in the legs three times before escaping.

I only learned about the incident from the following day's papers.

The rest of the evening was spent in my hotel room, trying to work out the intricacies of cross-border phoning. It was encouraging to be able to call my friends in London and Edinburgh (both hundreds of miles away from Newry) at discount NATIONAL British rates. It was mildly intimidating to have to dial the international code (and hence to pay INTERNATIONAL rates) to get through to Dundalk – just ten miles across the border. Luckily, I didn't know anyone in Dundalk and was therefore spared the expense of calling it.

Next morning I felt lousy. My distended nose was blocked. An uninterrupted buzzing noise from the headphones I wasn't wearing resounded in my clogged ears. A faulty didgeridoo (or was it a broken Irish bagpipe?) was playing inside my brick-heavy head. I needed to see a doctor. Luckily, 'Newry Medical Village,' comprising a number of surgeries, pharmacies and a hospital, was just outside my hotel.

Meadowlands Surgery that I chose at random was full of people, mostly little old ladies, patiently waiting for their call.

'I need to see a GP,' I said to the receptionist brandishing my NHS card.

It transpired that the card was unnecessary, for residents of Southern Ireland were entitled to free treatment in the UK. I looked at the old ladies, these 'God's dandelions,' to use a nice Russian expression, and wondered whether they were all visitors from the South, too.

'What if you fell ill while in Dublin?' I tactlessly asked Dr JJ Torney, a facetious bespectacled man, as he was measuring my blood pressure.

'I would have to pay to see a GP, but could claim the money back on return. It's interesting how many people from the South suddenly feel unwell when they come here on shopping expeditions ... I don't mean you of course,' he chuckled.

The antibiotic, prescribed by Dr Torney, took its toll, and soon I was sitting inside a café perusing morning newspapers and sipping an espresso. The espresso was awful, but, on the positive side, I was able to puff away for all I was worth – an almost forgotten delight.

Everyone was smoking in Newry – as if the town (sorry, the city) itself was suffering from some collective tobacco-related NEWROSIS. Smoking seemed compulsory in most pubs, cafés and restaurants ...

Remembering my Dublin friends' advice, I rather enjoyed leafing through the totally apolitical *Armagh-Down Observer* that seemed to contain just two types of 'coverage': reports of unruly local drivers and sets of family and school photos. 'Motorist Accused of Stopping Suddenly' was one of the paper's headlines that reminded me of a heading I once saw in 'Shetland Times': 'Driver Swerves to Avoid Sheep.'

The stories carried by the Belfast-based *Irish News*, however, were different: 'Sectarian attack on youth group,' '22 children victims of shootings and attacks,' 'Man is shot in lower leg,' and next to it – 'Two hurt in pub shooting.' That was how I learned about the previous night's incident in Newry.

Staying away from politics was not that easy while in Ulster.

Newry was pretty. Enclosed by the Mourne Mountains, it combined the hustle-and-bustle of a mini-city with friendly cosiness of a small town to create a truly welcoming spirit, unspoiled by a disproportionate number of windswept (both outside and inside) shopping malls, targeting bargain-hunters from the South.

The historic Newry town hall was built in 1893 on a bridge astride the river, dividing two counties – allegedly, to settle the rivalry between the people of Armagh and Down. It stood there now as a classical red-brick memento of the all-but-forgotten, yet much-needed by modern Ulster, art of compromise.

It was hard to imagine a town more peaceful than modern Newry, where two currencies, two counties and two countries seemed to co-exist rather happily. One didn't want to think that not so long ago it was one of the world's most dangerous places.

In the local Museum I was shown an official Report, according to which '13% of all the Troubles related fatalities in Northern Ireland took place in the Newry region ... that accounted for only 5.3% of the Northern Ireland population.' It was 'the fifth most violent urban area' in Ulster.

'The attack had nothing to do with the paramilitaries – it was just a copy-cat attempt to resolve a family feud,' Rory Murphy, a young barman at 'McSwiggan's' assured me from behind the bar.

I was the only customer in the pub that early afternoon. I simply couldn't leave Newry without finding out what happened in the pub.

A strong smell of disinfectant was hanging in the air, and fruit machines were winking sinisterly in the semi-darkness.

Rory, who witnessed the attack, readily 're-enacted' it for me in situ. He then pointed to a fresh bullet scratch on the wooden bar stand, about twenty inches above the floor. I thought I could discern two dark spots under a stool next to it.

'It is so out of character with the town now,' sighed the barman.

His view was shared by Henry Reilly, the popular mayor of Newry – the first Unionist mayor in the whole history of this predominantly Catholic town – whom I met an hour later.

'We have generous and genuine people here,' he said. 'They have gone through a lot of suffering, and it will take several generations to change the violence-oriented sectarian mentality completely. It is changing already. Look at me: I served in the British Army – and still I am accepted …'

He was right about the mentality, of course. Old habits die hard, and euthanasia doesn't quite work here … Time was indeed Newry's best and only NEWROPATHOLOGIST.

'Newry has little to sustain more than a short visit, and you are unlikely to be tempted to stay,' affirms one superficial modern guidebook …

The last thing I did before leaving was post two letters – to a friend in London (it cost me 26p) and to myself in Dublin (40p), just to check which one would arrive first.

The one, sent to London, was delivered to the addressee the following day.

In Dublin, I am still waiting for my letter from Newry, the town (sorry, the city), where I was very much 'tempted to stay.'

County Meath

To begin with, 'let me make it absolutely clear' (*pace* Tony Blair) that, although in Ireland I am often confronted with the question: 'Which part of Italy do you come from, Mr Vivaldi?' I have as much Italian blood in me as Pavarotti has Ukrainian.

Interestingly, I haven't yet been taken for a Ukrainian, simply because most people in Ireland do not seem to have a clue as to what Ukraine actually is – a vegetable, a mineral, or, indeed, a country.

You won't believe it, but once in Edinburgh I was actually taken for ... an Irishman. The elderly Scottish lady, who asked me: 'You must be Irish?' was most likely not only deaf, but also blind. Yet it was the first (and so far the last) time that someone thought that I was actually Irish – not German, French, Italian or Faeroese.

My Collins dictionary defines identity as 'the individual characteristics by which a person or thing is recognised.' This effectively means that identity – like beauty – is very much in the eyes of the beholder, in how others see us rather than in how we see ourselves.

Does it imply therefore that, if the visually impaired Scottish lady with hearing problems decided I was Irish, that was what I really was?

But what does being Irish actually represent?

Intrigued by the promise of a 'Be Irish for a Day' experience at the Causey Farm near Kells (I had found the ad on the Internet), I went to County Meath in search of an answer.

'More elbow grease!' Lily, the lively mother of the Murtagh family of ten, was commanding as I was mixing flour, soda, salt, eggs and my own elbow grease in an attempt to make a loaf of Irish bread.

It was 11am, and I already felt at home at the friendly family farm. And, indeed, more 'Irish' than ever before.

My frantic bread making was followed by a short Ceili dancing lesson in the former cowshed. For someone who had always had two left feet (possibly even three), it felt like a succession of pole vaults without a pole. Then came the turn of bodhran-playing which was similar to eating a bowl of Miso soup with one chopstick (at least, that was how it felt to me – both in terms of hand movements and of the sounds I managed to extract from my uncomplaining bodhran).

Both classes were conducted by delightful Deirdre Murtagh (learning to spell Irish names – first and last – could also be a part of the 'Irish for a Day' experience), one of Lily's seven daughters.

The family's 'Irish for a Day' venture that started three years ago was booming. Bookings were coming from all over the world – from Finland to Saudi Arabia, and the feedback from the visitors was nothing short of ecstatic.

Among other typically 'Irish' activities offered by the Murtaghs were hurling, turf cutting, rope making and milking a cow. I was momentarily tempted to do the latter, but thought better of it, having remembered that while I was trying (unsuccessfully) to milk a cow for the last (and the first) time in my life in Australia, the newspaper I was then writing for was taken over by Conrad Black.

'We are trying to bring people together through Irishness,' Deirdre told me as I was munching through the freshly baked loaf of soda bread that I myself made (well, almost).

'But what *IS* Irishness?' I asked her eagerly.

Just like myself, she found this concept difficult to define.

I had to carry on searching.

'Irish timing,' Olivia Duff, the helpful manager of the Headfort Arms Hotel in Kells – the pied-a-terre of my one-day quest for Irishness – muttered sardonically looking at her watch. My next contact – Tomas O Maonaile – was running late. As it turned out, he got stuck in traffic near Kells, the only town in Ireland with nine approach roads – all of them blocked with cars from morning till night. So dense is the traffic that a bus recently hit even the famous town's Market Cross.

No one enjoys sitting in a traffic jam and breathing petrol fumes, but Tomas had reason to particularly hate this unhealthy 'Irish' experience. A native Irish speaker and an aspiring property developer, he had two passions in his life: preservation of the Irish language and protection of the environment. His hope was to try and combine both in his new project – an eco-friendly housing estate, populated exclusively by Gaeilge speakers. This might sound like a rather drastic requirement, but Tomas believed that the dire state of Ireland's long-suffering native tongue justified it.

'There are not enough Irish schools in the country, and very few text-books,' he was saying as we drove to Brugh na Mi – his prospective housing development four miles away from Kells

A solitary 'show cottage' stood on the would-be estate in the shadow of the historic Funghan Hill, but Tomas said that thirty families, willing to participate in his 'Irish for life' (as opposed to 'Irish for a day') experience, had already expressed interest in buying houses there.

'Here there will be an organic vegetable garden and an Irish language learning centre, and there – in the middle of the compound – a children's playground …'

Tomas was pointing to empty patches of land and could be easily dismissed as yet another airy-fairy Irish dreamer, but his determination was such that I knew he was going to succeed.

'He who loses his language – loses his land,' runs an old Cornish proverb. And his identity too, I could add. A language dies somewhere in the world every week, according to the UNESCO, and the ancient Irish – expressive, poetic and melodious – should not be allowed to become one of them. For with it the very concept of 'Irishness' would disappear too.

The wind was rustling through the grass, as if whispering something gently in Irish …

Tomas took me to Rath Cairn – a predominantly Irish-speaking nearby settlement, founded in 1935. Almost all signs in the town were in Gaeilge only. It was there that I learned (under duress) my first two Irish words: ***MNA*** and ***FIR*** – when looking for a toilet inside the local community centre. What can I say? There's no better way of mastering a foreign language than when confronted with everyday basic needs. To my great relief (in more than one sense), however, there was a lady's silhouette above the mysterious ***MNA*** sign (there was none above the ***FIR*** one, mind you).

I knew I would remember those short, yet meaningful, words for the rest of my life …

In Rath Cairn I met Nadya Genserovskaya – a nineteen-year-old Russian and a fluent speaker of Irish.

Moscow-born Nadya came to the town ten years ago with her Russian mother who had married an Irishman. She went to an English school, but – being linguistically alert – soon picked up Irish.

'At home we speak either Russian or Irish, but not English,' she told me with a smile. A student of German at Trinity College, this young polyglot assured me that she felt more at home in Rath Cairn than in Moscow.

'Ireland is a kind country,' she said simply when I asked her what she thought 'Irishness' was about.

Reluctant to leave Rath Cairn, I was late for my next appointment. Or was I simply getting 'Irish-ised' and, without realising it, started adjusting to 'Irish timing?'

Having missed Brian Currant, the chairman of Kells town council, in his town hall offices, I was directed to his shop called 'Shamrock.'

At the first glance, 'Shamrock' looked like an ordinary souvenir shop-cum-hardware store: kettles, irons and kitchen utensils were displayed on the shelves alongside green-clad 'Irish' dolls and 'Irish Humour' socks (the humour of the latter item was totally lost on me). A toy 'singing monkey' called Charlie greeted customers at the entrance. If touched, Charlie would start twitching and chanting in high-pitch falsetto: 'Yippy-yah-yah, yippy-yippy-yah!'

It took me a while to spot a sign above the counter, behind which the owner himself – bespectacled and redheaded – was standing in state: 'Brian Curran. Funeral Director. Personal Service. Complete Funeral Arrangements.'

Numb with surprise, I noticed a couple of funereal wreaths, discreetly tucked into a far corner, and all the regulation questions I was meaning to ask Mr Curran (about the composition of the town council, the redevelopment of Kells and so on) became irrelevant.

'Is this some sort of a joke?' was the only thing I could utter.

'Yes and no,' was the reply. 'I think every funeral director must have a gift shop as a façade …'

He took me to a side room, where half-a-dozen ready-to-use coffins were neatly stacked.

At least, they were not exhibited in the shop-window, next to the singing monkey and the mysterious 'Irish Humour' socks …

I was reminded of New Orleans, the 'live-and-let-die' city nicknamed 'Big Easy,' where they play jazz at funerals and get married at cemeteries among the graves – in short, celebrate life even after death. When I was there several years ago, my hosts took me to Bultman's Funeral Home in the plush Garden District. An undertaker, dressed in black, told me that Bultman's was often hired for parties, musical recitals and business functions. 'People come to us to have fun,' he concluded with a professional sombre grin …

From Pete McCarthy's book *McCarthy's Bar*, I knew it was not that unusual for an Irish country pub to sell bicycles as well as pints of Guinness. But I was still thoroughly unprepared for this funeral director's office, conveniently situated at one of Ireland's craziest road-crossings (of all nine Kells approach roads?) and doubling as an unpretentious and down-to-earth (forgive my unintended pun) souvenir shop.

For a reason that is hard to explain, I suddenly felt that I had come a step closer to understanding the true meaning of 'Irishness.'

'Say bye to Charlie,' suggested Mr Curran as I was leaving.

And so I did.

Irish Travellers

Little Jacinta was singing as she hopped over puddles and rubble on the way from school.

A music sheet in hand, she squeezed through a narrow gap in the concrete wall – freshly built, yet already charred, dented and covered with graffiti – separating Dunsink Lane, where she lived, from the rest of the world.

Having shaken sticky concrete dust off her school uniform, she skipped on – humming to herself.

Watching this jolly Traveller girl, I couldn't help thinking of what life had in stock for her. Was she destined to become just another 'ordinary' Traveller woman – always feeling deprived and second-rate? To give birth to ten or eleven kids, to drown in never-ending domestic chores and to pass away in her forties or fifties (a life-span of an average Traveller female is 11.9 years shorter than that of her no-less-average 'settled' sister)?

The appalling discrimination of Ireland's Traveller community has been my single biggest shock since moving to this country.

Having lived in the former USSR and in Australia and having travelled extensively in Europe, Asia and the USA, I was familiar with the plight of some of the world's oppressed minorities. Yet the last thing I expected to find in small and seemingly prosperous Ireland, a former emigrant nation that had become a country of immigrants, was the existence of yet another, hitherto unknown to me, persecuted group – Travellers.

During my first days in Dublin, I often heard the word 'traveller' on radio and TV. I also saw it in print – more often than not in a fairly negative context of petty crime, scuffles, street protests etc.

I remember feeling surprised at the sheer number of rowdy foreign visitors (for that was what I thought the 'travellers' were) who chose Ireland as a venue for their escapades.

'Who exactly are these troublesome travellers?' I kept asking my Dublin contacts.

Nine out of ten responses were along the lines: 'They are all criminals … They don't work and don't pay taxes … They live in dirt …' And so on.

I would have probably believed them, had I not heard precisely the same comments about the Romany in Russia, Slovakia and the Czech Republic about the native Americans in the USA, and the Aborigines in Australia.

On the morning of 7 October, I heard on the news that Dublin City Council had overnight erected a concrete barrier to block the only access road to one of the Travellers' halting sites. It was done under the laughable pretext of eliminating 'considerable dumping of commercial waste' which didn't make sense, for even one of the City fathers admitted that the 'illegal dumping was significantly from outsiders.'

And how on earth could a wall, erected clandestinely – under cover of darkness – prevent 'illegal dumping' – or any other illegal activity for that matter?

Walls and barriers of all sorts are useless and counterproductive by their very nature. Instead of resolving an 'issue,' they create many new ones on top of it, with the initial 'problem' remaining unsolved.

'Force breeds counterforce' – this Newton's Third Law of Motion can be applied in equal measure to social structures. The stronger the barriers – the harder people try to break through. The classic proof is the infamous Berlin Wall, the final collapse of which I was able to observe in Berlin in 1990.

'Walls are built to be pulled down,' mused a philosophically-minded Dublin taxi driver, who took me to Pavee Point, a North Dublin non-governmental organisation promoting Travellers' rights. There I learned a lot about Travellers' peculiar history, language, life-style and traditions. I was amazed by the enormous contribution to the Irish society, made by this small community, and by the amount of discrimination they had experienced through centuries.

'The depth of Travellers' exclusion is extraordinary,' said Brid O'Brien, one of Pavee Point employees. 'Particularly if we remember that there are only 24,000 of them left in Ireland.'

If discrimination has any 'constants,' one of them is that the sheer size of an oppressed minority does not matter. As long as a society feels unsure of itself, it will always find scapegoats to blame for its own imperfections. The example of modern Poland, where antisemitism is rife, with hardly any Jewish people left, speaks for itself. In the heart-felt words of Albert Einstein, had the Jews not existed, they would have had to be invented. The same can be said about Travellers.

And it is not really an issue whether they are indeed a separate ethnic unit (unlike Gypsies, they actually do not know exactly where they came from – the fact that makes them 'perfect travellers,' see the epigraph) or just a hugely underprivileged group of Irish society. Call it racism, antisemitism or anything else – the mechanism of injustice remains the same: continuous discrimination inevitably breeds resistance that, in turn, leads to more discrimination – and hence more civil disobedience from the oppressed. A vicious circle of prejudice and intolerance …

At Pavee Point, I met several Traveller women, who shared their grievances with me.

To begin with, nothing about these ladies corresponded to widely accepted stereotypes. They were all gentle (if somewhat subdued), outspoken and smartly dressed. Their first and last names – as well as their looks – were archetypally Irish. None of them wore excessive jewellery.

'They follow us around in shops – worried that we'll steal something …'

'To get a job, we have to conceal our identities. The moment they discover we are Travellers, they sack us under any pretext. This is why our kids are not keen on studying: they know they won't be able to get employment anyway …'

'There is no future for our children in Ireland …'

One of the women, sixty-year-old Biddy McDonagh, mother of twelve and grandmother of thirty-eight, kindly invited me and Derek, a Village photographer, to have a look at her Dunsink Lane caravan.

'We have to be careful: some Traveller teenagers can throw stones,' Brendan Ocaolain, another Pavee Point employee who went with us, warned as our car was approaching the Lane.

It felt like heading for a Gaza Strip in the outskirts of Dublin.

I was amazed by the thickness and solidity of the Dunsink Wall (let's call it that from now on). Did they expect the Travellers to ram through it with tanks?

Bent iron fittings were sticking out of concrete like tentacles of a giant deep-sea monster.

The pathway to St Joseph's estate was strewn with litter: tires, empty bottles, bicycle wheels. No wonder: the site was on the edge of the former Dunsink tip – as if 400 Travellers' lives themselves were dumped there by the so-called 'settled' society.

A jalopy, packed with young kids, rattled past us. The children's eyes were full of un-childish seriousness. Or was it fear?

All Traveller youngsters, whom we met on the way, were extremely civil and polite. Every single one said hello to us.

The estate itself was windswept and deserted, if you don't count numerous dogs of uncertain breed. From the hillock, next to a permanently shuttered 'community centre,' a battered statue of St Joseph, with baby Christ in his hands, was looking down at us with reproach.

The interior of Biddy's tiny caravan was neatness itself: carpets, porcelain in the cupboard, icons and family photos on the walls.

Kitchen and bathroom – both unheated – were outside, across a tiny 'backyard.' It must be freezing inside them in winter. I suddenly realised one possible reason for Traveller women's uncharacteristically short life spans …

We were invited into other Travellers' houses. All, without exception, were spotless.

James Collins, the renowned tinsmith – with the rough hands of a lifetime manual worker and an inspired face of an artist – greeted us inside his working shed. With pride, he showed an old steel measure, the so-called 'American stick' – the most precious instrument of his trade that he inherited from his father.

By then, swarms of freckled boys and girls, who had returned from school, were playing in the streets. They flocked around Derek pleading: 'Please, take my photo, mister …'

I remembered being surrounded by semi-naked Aboriginal kids with suppurating eyes on Palm Island, Queensland – an isolated ghetto-like reservation, where visitors are not welcome – several years ago. Their mantra was 'Give me a dollar, mister …'

But this was not Australia. This was Dublin. And the kids looked and behaved differently. Yet one similarity was obvious: there, the Australian government put its unwanted people on an island in the middle of the ocean; here – they dumped them onto an enclosed estate, locked them in (with a concrete padlock) and threw away the key.

It was on our way out that we met the singing Traveller girl – Jacinta.

What truly stuns me in Ireland is how quietly and matter-of-factly the ongoing oppression of Travellers is taken by many of those regarding themselves as liberals and intellectuals.

'We in Ireland know … about the traveller problem,' Kevin Myers claimed in his 'I'm Irish, I know about the gipsy problem' (!) column in London's *Daily Telegraph* on 8 October.

In it, he branded Travellers 'a socially-dysfunctional minority who believe that they should be allowed to do as they want' and characterised 'traveller life' (yes, conspicuously – with a small 't') as 'patriarchal, caste-based, dirty (*sic* – VV), diseased, alcoholic, illiterate, violent, misogynistic, low-achieving … and, most of all, short' (as if the Travellers' untimely deaths were their own fault, too!). 'Only multicultural mumbo-jumbo at its most fatuous crowns this dismal tribal phenomenon with the title 'culture,' he concluded tautologically ('multicultural' – 'culture').

Let me tell you straight away: I hate political correctness, invented by mediocrities in an attempt to paint the whole of our colourful world grey. I think that, in its worst forms, PC represents the greatest danger to human civilisation since communism. There's only one thing worse than PC: total INDIFFERENCE to human suffering, exacerbated by patronising 'upper-class' ARROGANCE – of which the above-quoted clumsily-worded rant is a shining example.

There's one meaningful Russian borrowing in the English language – a tongue-breaking word 'intelligentsia.' It denotes a hard-to-define concept that has little, if anything, to do with intellect, intellectuals and/or erudition. The best (to my mind) definition of it was coined by Chekhov, who described members of 'intelligentsia' as the people who feel personal guilt for every single injustice in world.

Kevin Myers is certainly not one of them.

The Berlin Wall officially ceased to exist on 3 October 1990, when Germany, forcibly dissected into two, finally got reunited. I will never forget that date.

On a par with it, I will always remember the crack of dawn on 14 October 2004, when – from under an umbrella – I was watching the collapse of the Dunsink Wall. It was the second major human divide to crumble apart in front of my eyes.

Derek and I were the only members of the media witnessing this truly historic event.

The philosophising taxi-driver was right: barriers are only built to be demolished.

In contrast to the stealthy construction of the ill-fated wall in the middle of the night, its demolition was conducted in the open. Only there was hardly anyone to see it: a nasty drizzle must have deterred Irish 'watchdogs of democracy,' read journalists, from turning up *en masse*. Pity, for it was democracy as such that was at the centre of the Dunsink Lane confrontation.

Diggers, bulldozers and pneumatic drills were painstakingly tearing through the wall that – in the treacherous light of dawn – was coming to resemble a black rotten tooth. I was thinking of all the wasted effort that had gone into erecting it in the first place and was now going into pulling it down.

In Berlin, they decided to keep a graffiti-covered chunk of the Berlin Wall intact as a memorial. Perhaps it would make sense to preserve a slab or two of reinforced concrete from the Dunsink Wall and to put them on display in the centre of Dublin as a monumental reminder of human prejudice, cruelty and outright foolishness.

The time was approaching 9am, and soaked Traveller kids were trickling through the growing gap in the wall on their way to school.

From where I stood, I could not see whether little Jacinta was among them …

'Are you a Traveller?' a dust-covered foreman in charge of the demolition asked me worriedly.

'Yes, I am a traveller,' I replied.

A Mini-Guidebook to Corkonia

'We are constantly open to surprise. As a matter of principle we are always open to the unexpected – after all, that is why we live in Cork.'
From 'Cork 2005 European Capital of Culture' brochure

General Information

Corkonia (or – for brevity – 'Cork') is a semi-independent country to the South West of Dublinia, sometimes referred to as 'Ireland.'

The natives are a fiercely patriotic lot, defining themselves as non-Dubliners first and only then – as Corkonians. The capital is Cork City, also known as Festival City, City of Making (no one knows exactly of what), Rebel City (no relation to Fallujah) and – more recently as 'ECOC' which stands for 'European Capital of Culture,' or, according to other sources, for 'Extraordinary Capital of Corkonia.'

There is no consensus as to either the size of the city's population (the estimates vary from thirty-three to 250,000) or the exact number of bridges across the River Lee (from none to twenty-eight).

Cork's national colours are red and white, also known as 'blood-and-bandages' (see 'hurling' in 'Sports and Pastimes' below). The national symbol is an eleven-foot salmon, also known as 'Goldy Fish' (see 'Food'). The Corkonian pro-independence movement is represented by a People's Republic of Corkonia dedicated website and by the name of the official national broadsheet 'The Corkman.'

History

The most formative event in Corkonian history, the so-called 'Cork Gunpowder Explosion,' took place on 3 November 1810, when twenty-two people were killed and more than forty injured as a result of carelessness of a drunken gunpowder factory worker, who tried to dry stolen gunpowder (before selling it to some powder-hungry quarrymen) by holding a burning candle to it. Since then, Cork became the hub of the initially successful Temperance Movement, led by Father Theobald Matthew, that resulted in somewhat lower production of whiskey in the 1840s, yet failed to affect the natives' ongoing love for their own brews of stout – Murphy's and Beamish (see 'Where to Drink,' or simply drink without looking). The next significant event occurred in 2004, when Cork won the World Cup in hurling (see 'Sports and Pastimes').

Geography

The country's flood-prone capital lies on an island, formed by the River Lee, and is connected to the rest of the nation – the deprived North and the more affluent South – by bridges (for the exact number of the bridges see 'General Information'). At the moment of writing, the locals are campaigning to name one of the bridges 'Roy Keane Bridge' in memory of the famous Corkonian warrior and national hero.

The access to Corkonia by land is largely blocked by the insurmountable Kinsale Street Roundabout, which Corkonians lovingly call 'The Magic Roundabout' for its pivotal role in the country's relative isolation from the rest of the world.

On 8 November 2004 – to Corkonians' considerable dismay – the Monasteverin By-Pass, cutting the journey between Dublin and Cork by thirty minutes, was opened. 'Dublin Has Moved Closer to Cork,' as it was put by Cork's main broadsheet *De Paper* (at times incorrectly referred to as *The Irish Examiner*) on the same day.

Local Time

Unspecified and variable – as reflected in the nickname of the country's best-known clock, 'The Four-Faced Liar.'

Language

'To understand the people of Cork, one must know their language,' noted Sean Beecher in the Introduction to his hard-to-obtain (outside Cork) *Dictionary* of Corkonian.

Corkonians speak 'Gammin' – their unique language – with inimitable singsong drawl, swallowing vowels (of which there are twenty-six in the Corkonian alphabet) and consonants (of which there are two), too. A first-time foreign visitor may be led to believe that they all have little church spires inside their mouths which – on inspection – usually proves untrue.

Below are some useful words and expressions:

'Dead man' – empty glass
'Gauzer' – good-looking girl
'Gowl' – fool
'Hack' – fun
'Magalorim' – drunk
'Mombolised' – very drunk
'Gawked up' – drunk out of one's mind
'Langer' – a multisemantic term with no exact equivalent in English
'Langers' – a plural of 'Langer' (see above); also – drunk.

'Belt away' – carry on with what you are doing
'Fair Dues' – well done
'Over there la' – over there
'Great Tack' – great stuff
'Alright boy' – hi, langer (see)

Apart from the above-mentioned *Dictionary*, another highly recommended manual of Corkonian is *Dowtcha Boy* by Morty McCarthy – a native linguist, who recently emigrated from Cork to Stockholm to teach English (!). The country is now bracing itself for the invasion of Corkonian-speaking Swedes.

Getting There

Visitors from Ireland normally do not require a Corkonian visa. Unlike those from Dublinia, who do not need visas either.

Aer Arann has daily flights between Dublinia and Cork International Airport. Do not be surprised by the following onboard announcement before landing: 'Cork airport authority requires all mobile phones to be switched off until you are well inside the terminal.' The reason is that, on top of the smoking ban, Cork airport has recently introduced a talking ban (Corkonians have a reputation of one of the world's most garrulous people). Make sure you do not speak to anyone (including yourself) until you leave the terminal building.

Getting Around

Unless you want to spend the whole of your visit admiring the Magic Roundabout (see 'Geography'), do not use buses or cars while in Cork. Do not ask local bus or taxi drivers for directions: their sense of time and distance is distorted by being permanently stuck in traffic jams. When walking around, watch your step: in preparation for the forthcoming ECOC season (see 'General Info'), the country is in the throes of frantic road works. Before leaving your hotel, consult the popular 'Pothole of the Week' section the People's Republic of Corkonia website for the latest road re-developments.

Sports and Pastimes

Corkonia's most popular national sports are 'pickey' (a street version of hopscotch), 'up against the wall' (a street version of soccer, normally played at the National Football Stadium), go-carting or 'steerning' (usually inside a supermarket), taxi racing (use of blinkers and honking are not allowed), street boating (at the time of floods), hurling (balls, stones, bottles etc), road bowling (see above for 'Pothole of the Week') and road crossing – the latter being the most dangerous of all (see 'Getting Around').

The favourite Corkonian pastimes, apart from the one mentioned below (see 'Where to Drink'), are 'slocking (stealing apples) and 'Doing pana,' ie wandering up and down Patrick Street without any purpose.

Food

Corkonian mouth-watering culinary specialities include: *tripe* (animal stomach), *crubeens* (pigs' feet) and *drisheen* (blood sausage – see 'blood and bandages' in 'General Info'). A more recent one is *Kalina Jagerspeck* – a German-manufactured Russian specialism: pure lard with tiny insets of smoked pork. The latter can only be acquired at *Staraya Rus* (Old Russia) Russian/Lithuanian shop in North Main Street.

NB. Do not ask for 'Russian boots' – a Corkonian term for 'Wellingtons' – at *Staraya Rus*. Also, not to upset the natives, do not try to consume 'Goldy Fish' (see 'General Info') – one of the country's symbols, even if you manage to remove it from the spire of St Anne's church in Shandon.

Where to Eat

Anywhere, except for the places listed below (see 'Where Not to Eat').

Where Not to Eat

- 'A Taste of Thailand' restaurant in Bridge Street where 'Thai' food has an unmistakable flavour of Cork (and of cork)
- *Staraya Rus* (see 'Food,' and this includes seafood!)
- 'Kylemore' restaurant at Cork International Airport, where they charge international prices for nationally and locally sized portions

Where to Drink

At 'Preachers,' 'Thirsty Scholar' and pretty much anywhere else – as the natives do.

Where to Stay

At 'Cork City Gaol' that, according to www.cork-guide.ie, has 'cells, furnished with life-size figures, souvenir and refreshment areas, friendly staff and good facilities …'

Where to Shop

For the European Capital of Culture 2005 souvenirs and memorabilia (badges, pamphlets, wines, notebooks etc) try the ECOC Headquarters (50 Pope's Quay), where they are all stocked in a little side room next to the Reception. Make sure you don't confuse ECOC brochures with paperback copies of *The Da Vinci Code* (Waterstone's bookstore, 69 Patrick Street) – the best-selling thriller by Dan Brown (not a native of Cork), for they have almost identical black-amber colour schemes on their covers.

What to Do

See 'Getting Around,' 'Where to Eat,' 'Where Not to Eat,' 'Where to Drink,' 'Where to Shop,' 'Where to Stay' and 'Sports and Pastimes.'

What Not to Do

Do not run the risk of trying to track down the people behind the People's Republic of Corkonia website – a highly conspiratorial underground organisation of 'People's Republicanism' striving for Corkonia's complete independence. The exact strength, composition and whereabouts of the organisation are closely guarded secrets – to everyone, including its own members (if any). Among their revolutionary activities are: campaigning for the relocation of the Government from Dublin to Cork, cleaning road signs and secret patrolling of the country's border – to search cars for such subversive (from the People's Republicans' point of view) foreign goods as Dubliner CDs, Brennan's bread, cans of 'Guinness' etc – and to confiscate them. To be on the safe side, do not bring these goods to Corkonia.

Some experts believe that the organisation is funded by the proceeds from selling 'Peoples' Republic of Cork' t-shirts that are safe to buy and to wear outside Corkonia.

Sense of Humour

Corkonians are renowned for their peculiar self-deprecating wit (no wonder that Cork City is about to be twinned with Shanghai!). A good example of it is the sign in the windows of some of the country's newsagents: 'Sober or Blotto – Remember the Lotto' (Corkonian National Lotto has a prize-fund of 40 billion shandons. **NB**: Shandon – '$n' – is a local currency unit. €1 buys $n10 billion at the current exchange rate).

On a More Serious Note

Cork is unlike any other place in the world (see 'Mini Guidebook to Corkonia' above). If Culture indeed needs a capital, the Rebel City is bound to be a great success as ECOC.

As they say in Corkonia, 'fair dues' and 'belt away!'

Greenock, Scotland

'Greenock? You'll need a bodyguard there,' an Edinburgh friend chuckled on hearing of last week's destination. He was right: I did need to guard my body while in Greenock, although not in the sense he meant.

If modern Scotland has won itself the dubious title of 'the sick man (and woman) of Europe,' then Greenock and the whole of Inverclyde could be safely described as the dying man (and woman, no doubt) of Scotland.

Statistically, the average life expectancy of an Inverclyde man is five to seven years less than that of a Scottish male in general. Women do slightly better, with an average Inverclyde female living 'only' one to three years fewer than her no-less-average Scottish sister. No wonder Inverclyde has shown a 'negative population growth' in recent years. In plain words, the area is dying out, the main cause of death being obesity-related coronary heart disease.

These gruesome figures have one common denominator – healthy diet, or rather total lack of it. Before setting off to Greenock to look at the locals' eating habits, I decided that, to get under their skin, it would be fair to try to survive on fast food alone for the duration of the trip.

Here is the diary of that pioneering (for me, at least) experiment in the fields of social medicine and self-mutilation.

Tuesday 7.30am Having forsaken my normal breakfast of cereals and espresso, opted for a peanut butter sandwich and a German sausage – an elongated chunk of consolidated fat, reminiscent of 'salo' (pure lard), the main component of a Ukrainian peasant's menu, with each slice carrying more calories than all the dishes from Delia Smith's *Complete Cookery Course* combined.

9.30am Departed by train from Edinburgh Waverley to Glasgow Queen Street. With the most eye-catching feature of both being Burger King joints, thought it would make sense to rename the stations Burger King, Edinburgh, and Burger King, Glasgow, respectively. Had a burger at each.

10.30am On the train from Glasgow Central to Greenock. Feeling peckish. Who said junk food was addictive? It is not. It is simply moreish … A girl in her late teens across the aisle kept munching crisps while talking about chocolate on her mobile, her exposed midriff flowing over her jeans belt like a generous portion of vanilla ice-cream over the cone.

11.30am On the way to my hotel, discovered three things about Greenock:

1. Every other pedestrian was nibbling at something as he (or she) walked.
2. Newsagents in town doubled as 'tuck shops' and/or fast food outlets, with newspapers and magazines barely visible behind mountains of crisps, hillocks of chocolate bars, piles of boiled lollies, and batteries of Coke and Irn-Bru.
3. West Greenock had (probably) the world's highest density of dental surgeries per square mile: I counted three within a 200-yard stretch of one street. Made a mental note to talk to the dentists.

12.30pm Fiasco. Two dentists, one private health clinic administrator, and a deputy head teacher of a primary school all refused to discuss Greenockians' eating habits. The moment I mentioned 'fast food' they would become defensive and uncomfortable. 'We don't talk about such sensitive issues,' they would mutter. I was half-expecting them to roll their eyes up to the ceiling, like we did in the Soviet Union to let the interlocutor know that Big Brother was, if not necessarily watching, then definitely listening.

1.30pm Had lunch at the canteen of James Watt College, whose grey high-rise concrete box dominated the townscape. The timing was not good, as most of the students had already had their lunches and were now puffing away happily in the ground-floor no-smoking lobby. As I was passing through it, one girl gave out a loud burp. At the counter, I was shocked to see that all hot fast food (including the healthy option: pork and pineapple curry) had been consumed already and the only thing left was ... salad – obviously the least popular dish among the students. Had a white cotton wool-tasting roll with five slices of pale sausage of indefinite origin. In the meantime, students started popping in for after-lunch snacks. The girls would routinely go for a chocolate bar and a Coke, the boys for crisps and Irn-Bru.

3pm Finally, a stroke of luck with the dentist, who agreed to talk to me on condition that neither his/her name nor even gender would be revealed. I had to comply. Having worked in other parts of Britain, he/she said that he/she had never seen anything as bad as Greenock. In terms of 'dental decay' that is. He/she assumed that he/she had probably not seen the worst, for forty per cent of adult locals and seventy per cent of children had never attended a dentist.

'The main problem here is not fast food, but fizzy drinks,' he/she asserted. I thought he/she would always have his/her hands full in Greenock – this dentists' paradise on earth. A capacious truck was unloading crates of 'fizzy drinks' in front of his/her surgery – for the benefit of a fast-food newsagent next door.

5pm Spent the rest of the afternoon exploring Oakmall shopping centre. A massive sale was under way in its Holland & Barrett health-food outlet, totally devoid of customers. The busiest shop in the Mall was Leo's – a fast-food café, selling irresistible black puddings for 30p each. One could easily put on a couple of kilos by simply staring at all those yummies. Bought a huge packet of doughnuts for dinner.

9pm Fat oozed from every pore of my body after a huge takeaway meal in my hotel room. With doughnuts coming out of my ears, I felt greasy, unclean, unable to move or to think. The only thing I could do was watch TV.

Wednesday 8am Having gone to sleep on my own, woke up with severe heartburn. Together we (I and my heartburn) shared a full Scottish breakfast. It took us half an hour to climb two flights of stairs back to our room.

10am Explored two of Greenock's 'fitness centres' and discovered that both had chocolates, lollies and 'fizzy drinks' on sale in their lobbies. I noticed a while ago that 'fitness centres' all over the world offered fast food in their buffets and/or lobbies, thus creating a vicious circle, whereby a famished patron was bound to restore every single calorie shed painstakingly in the gym (and to gain many more on top of that) at the in-house snack-bar.

The extreme form of such health cynicism I once saw in a private cardiological hospital in Australia, which had a busy fast-food outlet straight in its lobby, so that it could successfully clog human arteries and thus supply potential customers for expensive bypasses from its own territory.

11am Popped into the McLean Museum and found out that Greenockians' love-affair with fatty and sugary foods had a historical background: in the eighteenth and nineteen centuries it was Britain's primary destination for West Indian sugar. At one point, twenty-four sugar refineries operated in Greenock, which became known as Sugaropolis.

It was also the place where Scotland's first Italian immigrants opened their famous ice-cream cafés. 'Sugar was an easy way to make money and, apart from the refineries, Greenock always had lots of sweet shops selling lollies from their windows,' said Vincent Gillen, the museum's assistant curator – a brave man, not afraid of the 'sensitive' issue.

Noon Found another courageous person – Andrina Reid, a public health practitioner at the local health centre. She was quick to acknowledge that Greenockians' eating habits were 'bad' – largely due to 'limited access to healthy food.' She added: 'It's all about availability. If you are surrounded by fish-and-chip shops, that's where you go.'

I wanted to show her the following passage from the latest issue of Inverclyde Visitor and Clyde Coast Advertiser, which I had picked up at the town library – 'The 'fish supper' must be drenched in vinegar and loads of salt should be added. Inverclyde is awash with good 'chippies' so make a point of sampling this excellent dish. Oh! remember to wash it down with large amounts of Iron Bru! (*sic*) – Our other national drink' – but thought better of it.

Mrs Reid told me about the ready-to-be-launched Joint Health Improvement Plan for Inverclyde – a complex of co-ordinated measures in the fields of housing, education, employment, etc aimed at 'revamping' the town's perilous, self-destructive trends.

'It won't happen overnight, but you have to start somewhere. I am sure we can change things, if we all pull together,' she smiled. I wished her luck, thinking that her job was probably one of the most challenging in modern Scotland.

1pm Had farewell lunch at West Station Cafe, founded by A Biondi, an Italian immigrant. With its pleasant 1950s interior and decent espresso – my first in Greenock – it was the first tentative step towards the town's budding 'café culture,' which Andrina Reid was trying to create. Although I was unable to finish the ice-cream (to be honest, I was hardly able to start it, so full I was after my thirty-hour-long fast-food indulgence), I left the café with a good feeling.

'Come back in five years' time and you might see the difference,' said Mrs Reid earlier. I thought that five years would probably be enough for me to detox after my 'experiment' and promised that I would.

3pm Trying to extinguish my heartburn, kept guzzling Vittel mineral water on the train from Burger King, Glasgow, to Burger King, Edinburgh. What a treat it was to feel like a normal person – not a faceless consumer, targeted by money-grabbing fast-food manufacturers – again.

County Tipperary

'Made familiar to many by the World War I marching song It's a Long Way to Tipperary, the county was actually picked simply for the rhythmic beat of its name. In fact, Tipperary isn't particular far from anywhere …'
The Rough Guide to Ireland, 2004

I visited Tipperary (both the county and the town) on the way to the Aran Islands. It was a filming trip, initiated by my good friend Jerry O'Callaghan – a veteran Irish film director and TV presenter, who wanted to make my impressions of Ireland into a TV series for RTE. To have the series commissioned, RTE needed a pilot, and that was precisely what Jerry and I were trying to put together during the journey.

I was lucky to have Jerry as my travel companion and guide: his knowledge of Ireland was second to none. Besides, he was still widely (and fondly) remembered from numerous TV programmes he had presented for RTE and was often recognised by strangers – a fact that helped us overcome a number of (metaphorical) road hurdles and allowed me to bask in the shadow of his fame.

We left Dublin on a drab October morning, both properly armed: Jerry – with his ultra-modern state-of-the-art digital camera and recording equipment; I – with a small portable collection of mostly very very old books and gazetteers, of which *Murray's Ireland 1912* was a gem.

Our first coffee stop was in Kildare, 'a neat little town' (Murray) and the capital of its namesake county. Or was it the other way around: the town was the county's namesake? A Dublin friend told me once that all Irish towns, sharing their names with those of the county they were in, were horrible. If true, then Kildare was definitely an exception: the town looked solid, leafy and still very 'neat.' 'A Tidy Town' a road sign at its entrance announced proudly.

Whereas Murray wouldn't have had a problem recognising Kildare's general appearance, he would have been stunned by the new Celtic Tiger noises in its streets: English language was hard to overhear, and most passers-by spoke a peculiar tongue that I initially took for Gaelic.

'No, it is not Gaelic,' Jerry told me authoritatively.

I pricked up my linguist's ears. Of course! I should have guessed: it was Lithuanian, occasionally interspersed with Polish – a direct result of the 2004 EU enlargement.

A Polish waitress at Macani's Diner spilled coffee onto my freshly washed jeans (I regularly become a receptacle for waitresses' and air hostesses' spillages) and apologised. In Polish, of course. The much-publicised EU enlargement had so far cost me a would-be visit to the dry-cleaners.

A Bank of Ireland money dispenser in the main square offered a choice of 'English' and 'Gaelige' on its screen, but no Lithuanian or Polish. Not yet …

Every rubbish bin in Kildare was decorated with a spidery (somewhat swastika-like) cross of St Brigit which made me wonder whether religion in Ireland was slowly but surely relegated to litter. Our next stop – Roscrea, Co Tipperary – was supposed to throw some light on the issue.

As we were entering Co Tipperary (the *Rough Guide* was right: it was NOT a long journey from Dublin – see epigraph), I was reading the 'Holy Ireland' chapter of Filson Young's outstanding 1903 monograph *Ireland at the Cross Roads*:

'The great unfading inheritance of Ireland is her religion. It has outlived her war-like traditions, it has stifled her romantic spirit, it has smothered her worldly ambitions; and to-day [I am keeping Filson Young's antiquated orthography here – VV], the narrowest and least advanced form of Catholicism, it burns with a great nervous and wasting vitality in the frail body of the country …'

Living and working in Ireland, I was able to witness a tremendous popular backlash against religious totalitarianism that had governed the country for centuries. In a small newsroom of the Dublin magazine, where I worked, my colleagues would start swearing and spitting every time the sound of church bells was broadcast over the radio.

'I hate the church so much for what it has done to our country,' one of them told me.

'Aren't you a Catholic?' I asked.

'Yes, of course,' she replied. 'But I don't believe in God …'

I had visited Roscrea once before when I stopped there to have a look at St Cronan's Roman Catholic church and to have a drink of water.

On the outside wall of a public toilet shed right behind the church, there were two signs: 'Drinking Water,' with no tap underneath, and 'Holy Water,' with a tap firmly in place – a classic example of Hobson's choice.

The 'Holy Water' had a distinct after-taste of rust.

I thought then that those two signs, with just one tap, could serve as a good metaphor for the state of religion in modern Ireland: the alternative was there, but only on paper. In reality, people had to use the only 'tap,' made available to them by those in power and by their own prejudice – historically motivated and therefore deeply rooted in their psyche. The spiritual alternative for Ireland's declining religious zeal was yet to be found.

It was those two signs above the only available water tap that we wanted to film in Roscrea.

It was pouring. Driving through the outskirts of Roscrea, we saw half a dozen excavators and bulldozers, their headlights flashing, digging through an old street, next to the ruins of St Cronan's Augustinian Priory. As we were passing by, the metallic Celtic Tiger beasts were biting through a lovely old pub, overgrown with ivy and already half-ruined, as if mauled by their insatiable jaws, to make space for some modern 'cottages' or bungalows, no doubt. Those non-descript structures were springing up all over Ireland like mushrooms after rain in an unprecedented 'bungalow blight' disfiguring the country's fragile landscape. Ireland was in the throes of an unseen property boom. Only days before, I had read with disbelief that a decrepit garden shed somewhere in the Irish Midlands had been snapped up for a quarter of a million euros …

Had avarice and Mammon come to replace religion inside Ireland's tormented soul?

A discarded excavator's digging bucket was lying in the mud – like a skull of a dead (yet not extinct) sable-toothed Celtic Tiger …

There is nothing as drab as an Irish small town on a rainy and dull autumn afternoon. We drove up the hill and made sure that both signs and the only tap were still there. Yet filming was out of the question due to a big funeral liturgy taking place inside the Church. The black-clad congregation was spilling out onto the Church grounds, and we decided the mourners wouldn't quite approve of two strangers filming the wall of a public toilet. So we drove off for a cup of coffee.

When we returned a couple of hours later, the funeral that we had witnessed was over, but another one – even bigger and plusher than the previous – was in full swing.

'Let's go and film the bulldozers near the Priory,' suggested I without realising that the town's cemetery was on the Priory's grounds. By the time we reached the spot, the first funeral had relocated there, and two grave-looking grave-diggers in dirty pom-pom hats were gravely finishing their grave job.

As I had noticed, the Irish loved funerals and did them with gusto. During my two years in Ireland, there was rarely a morning, when going to work in Dublin and later in Sandycove, I wouldn't bump into a long and lavish funereal procession – complete with limo-hearses and solemn stone-faced undertakers. In Russia and Ukraine, bumping into a funeral procession first thing in the morning is thought to be a good omen for the day. Yet in all my years there I had seen such processions only three or four times (not that people did not die there – they did like flies, it was just that the funerals were normally private and low-key). That was probably why my Russian/Ukrainian days (and years) were not particularly lucky …

It was getting dark and clear that we were not destined to do any filming that afternoon. And although we had been literally pursued by funerals, it was obvious that Russian superstitions did not apply to Ireland. We had to stay overnight in Roscrea and hope that the following morning would be relatively less mournful.

According to its own glossy brochure, Rocket Country House Hotel in the outskirts of Roscrea was the eighteenth century 'Olde Worlde Country House exquisitely refurbished in keeping with its true character.' In reality, that meant 'mutilated, disembowelled and painted bright-yellow in keeping with the peculiar Celtic Tiger Ireland taste, or rather total lack of it.' Several bits of the original eighteenth century façade, spared by the jaws of the voracious beast, did well to highlight the atrocity. Inside, it was all cheap 'luxury': imitation pillars and lots of plastic.

The same brochure assured that 'each guest room overlooks one of the many spectacular views surrounding this prestigious Victorian dwelling.' We couldn't verify that last bit, for our rooms only 'overlooked the views' of heavy rain and cotton-wool-thick mist.

Racket Country House was surrounded by golf courses (at least, that was what the brochure asserted), all thoroughly hidden by the fog, and was doubled 'Golf & Conference Hotel.' I knew that golf had become a big industry in Celtic Tiger Ireland – the process that must have started a long time ago, for, according to *Murray's Ireland 1912*, 'the game has taken a firm root in Ireland in recent years, and the interest is daily increasing.' The guidebook went on to explain that golf was played in Ireland 'probably as far back as 1855, having been introduced by the officers of Highland regiments stationed there, but … was little known until 1881, when the Royal Belfast Club was founded.'

I had always been a bit suspicious of golf and, particularly, of golf-players. The reason was that, although the game did not exist and was never played in the Soviet Union where I grew up, it had a very negative connotation there. In Soviet films about the West, the 'baddies' – and those were invariably 'decaying' yet cheerful 'capitalists' plotting against the USSR – were always playing golf. Playing and plotting … Plotting and playing … Pok-pok … Plot-plot … One could be forgiven for thinking that in the West golf was only played by spies and spymasters. That was probably why when I had to attend (on a newspaper assignment) the Australian Masters Golf Tournament in 1990, I could not help the spying associations. 'Plotting entry to the game of spymasters' – was the title of my one of my *Melbourne Age* columns.

Watching the would-be golfers, driven inside by rain, in the lobby of the Racket Country House, was enough to change that Australian misconception of mine. From the look and sound of them, it was obvious that golf in Ireland was played exclusively by old and fat Americans. The democratic nature of the game (ignoring the costs of the gear) must have laid in the fact that it could be enjoyed by grossly overweight people (remember Chris Patton?) as well as slim ones. Looking at the Americans in the lobby, I decided I was not old and fat enough to become a golf-player. Not quite …

There was one bright spot about the hotel though. It was in the shape of a blue-eyed open-faced girl behind the reception desk. I thought she might be Russian and, possibly, from Siberia – only Siberian girls, to my knowledge, had such aquamarine eyes, reflecting the waters of the world's largest lake, the Baikal (I had a Siberian girlfriend many many years before).

My guess proved right: Masha, the receptionist, was indeed from Siberia, and what's more – from Irkutsk, the nearest city to Lake Baikal! She had come to Ireland a year before and had already acquired an Irish boyfriend, a student at the nearby Garda School.

To salvage the day's shoot, we decided to film an interview with both of them. Masha proved eloquent and knowledgeable, if somewhat camera-shy: she admired Ireland and Oscar Wilde. Her Irish boyfriend was a bit disappointing: he had no idea who Oscar Wilde was. It was obvious that Wilde's writings were not on the Garda School curriculum …

In the evening, we drove back to the town centre to check our emails.

Roscrea's only Internet café was on the top floor of a shop selling cheap Irish souvenirs and Barbie dolls. I could not believe my ears when they told me that the price of Internet access was €5 per hour – the highest I had ever come across. They also claimed to have broadband, whereas in fact they didn't: the computers were extremely slow, and it took me minutes to download a small attachment! To cap it all, their Microsoft Word was exclusively in … Hungarian, one of the most obscure European tongues (to make working on your PC as difficult and as slow – and hence as pricey – as possible, no doubt). Despite several European languages at my finger-tips, while in Hungary I routinely ended up with an unreadable (ie Hungarian) newspaper, having asked for a bottle of mineral water from a street kiosk. The Hungarian Microsoft experience was even worse than the one I once had at a hotel in the Swiss town of Schaffhausen where the only PC available to the guests was stubbornly printing 'Z' instead of 'Y,' and 'Y' instead of 'Z.' A friend of mine was rather puzzled to receive my message that ended with some Turkic-sounding interjection 'Bze-bze!'

There were fewer funerals at St Cronan's Church the following morning, and we managed to successfully film both signs above the one and only water tap. I even had enough time to record in my notebook a great epitaph, spotted on a tombstone in the neat and picturesque Church cemetery:

'In loving memory of Paddy O'Connor

Born into Time, May 22 1900
Born into Eternity, December 30 1980.'

The Irish, it appeared, not only loved funerals, but were rather fond of cemeteries, too.

We drove through the town of 'Parsonstown or Birr in the centre of Ireland,' according to Murray. He also referred to a certain Sir William Petty, who 'in his 'Survey of Ireland' calls it 'Umbilicus Hiberniae' ' and explained that in 1642 it 'was successfully defended by William Parsons against the Irish' (!), hence its outdated English name Parsonstown not to be found on any modern Irish maps. It was interesting to see that Birr still advertised itself as the 'geographical centre of Ireland.'

We didn't have time to properly explore Cashel, 'though a city, but a poor place' (Murray). From the distance – the stunning Rock reminded me of a ruined Moscow Kremlin (if one can imagine a thing like that). The resemblance got stronger when we came closer and saw clusters of ugly modern bungalows around the Rock. The aggressively omnipresent Celtic Tiger cottages blocked the view of Ireland's prime historic and architectural gem.

'The Cashel Rock' gift shop had the tackiest collection of 'souvenirs' I had ever come across – worse even than the souvenir kiosk in Dallas's Seventh-Floor Museum. Most of the Cashel 'gifts' had anal connotations: postcards with bare bums, towels with 'Bumming Ahead Ireland' printed on them in large letters. A number of 'items' had 'Kiss my ass' in Irish (as kindly translated by Jeremy) written on them, too.

Who were all those multiple bottoms targeting? Paedophile priests? Or some unsuspecting 'ordinary' tourists?

'The tourist is at the mercy of every kind of ruffian ... he is always looked upon as a low fellow, an inquisitive vulgar beggar, a loud-mouthed trot-about, a coarse eater, a foreigner,' Liam O'Flaherty wrote in his highly ironic *Tourist's Guide to Ireland* that came out in 1929. His words sounded extremely apt and up-to-date nearly eighty years later – in 2005 Cashel.

I thought that WG Blackie's 1855 description of Cashel as the city of '*mean and poverty-stricken appearance*' was still of relevance, if only partly, without the '*poverty-stricken*' bit. Whatever economic developments and other welcome changes the Celtic Tiger might have brought to Ireland, refined (or plain good) taste was definitely not one of them. We found another proof of that in the outskirts of Cashel as we pulled over next to an ornate country cottage, introducing itself on the road sign as 'Blue River Villa.'

In the 1910 Ireland, if we believe the idiotic *Near Home or Europe Described* guide for dumb (possibly, even mentally retarded) English brats, 'In many places the [Irish] cottages' had 'gardens in front, as pretty as English gardens' (*sic* – VV). There was 'generally a little patch of potato-ground near the cottage, and a cow or some goats grazing about, and the pigsties are outside at the back …' This pastoral description finishes with a rather stunning statement of the anonymous author: 'I have heard of a family who kept a horse in their room!'

Well, for better or for worse, the reality of the 2005 rural Ireland was strikingly different. The cottage (sorry the 'villa') itself was hardly visible behind countless garden gnomes, gazebos and pseudo-antique statues in its front garden. Further 'decorated' with imitation 'classical' pillars at the entrance, it was an epitome of unadulterated kitsch that testified not only to its owners' appalling taste, but also to the fact that they (the owners) were awash with money and weren't quite sure what do with their sudden wealth.

There were unlikely to be any horses kept inside 'Blue River Villa,' but I could bet it had plenty of skeletons (and not just those of horses) hidden it its cupboards …

We had spotted a number of similar dwellings before finally reaching Tipperary Town.

'Tipperary town is much less important than it sounds. If you've already visited Clonmell, it will come as something of a shock – compared to Clonmell's yuppy prosperity, Tipperary feels somewhat down at heel,' asserted my no-nonsense 2004 *Rough Guide to Ireland.* As for older sources, there seemed to be no consensus. Whereas WG Blackie (1855) was rather scathing to Tipperary (as he was to most places in the world, except perhaps for London and Glasgow – he was a Glaswegian) dismissing it as 'all dirty and ill kept; houses of stone, but with few exceptions badly built and incommodious,' 1912 Murray called it 'pleasantly built and laid out.'

Faced with those contradicting opinions, I was left to make my own judgement, and initially was in full agreement with Blackie and the *Rough Guide* (notwithstanding a century's gap between them) – not with Murray.

The town that seemingly consisted of just one long main street, from which nearby fields could be clearly seen, looked grim and run-down. And so did its inhabitants. I noticed that, for some obscure reason, most of male Tipperarians were subdued, scruffy and unshaven, albeit all unexpectedly gentle, polite and friendly when approached for directions. The only two buildings of note were St Mary's Church, with its 'conspicuous tower and spire' (Murray) and the incongruous modernistic Excel Centre, right next to it. The Disney-like Centre was taller than the church suppressing and dominating it to the extent that the latter's 'tower and spire' were now much less 'conspicuous' than in 1912.

As the centre of Ireland's most 'demoralised' (Blackie) and 'disgraced' (Ibid) county, Tipperary town – or rather its only significant street, with disproportionate number of pubs – was dotted with 'bold' (*Rough Guide*) statues of republican fighters and one of Charles Kickham, 'Poet, Novelist but above all Patriot.'

In accordance with some peculiar Irish tradition of monumentalism, Charles Kickham was not standing on the pedestal, but sitting in state on it.

Perhaps in no other country had I seen so many 'sitting monuments.' In Ennis, Co Clare, there were several sitting statues, and one of them was just of a huge stone chair, onto which passers-by were encouraged to plop down. In the end, I had to conclude that – on a par with numerous Bronze Age standing stones – Ireland was also resplendent in 'sitting stones,' ie statues made to sit on their pedestals – the tradition, triggered not so much by compassion for the sculptures (just imagine: standing straight and still under the elements and pigeons' droppings for hundreds of years!), but by the simple fact that sitting figures required a bit less sculpting material than their upright counterparts. Or so I thought …

As for the 'above all Patriot' bit, there was something vaguely American in it. To me, at least, there was … It brought back memories of a blue plate I once spotted in Cambridge, Massachusetts, while looking for the house of HW Longfellow, my favourite American poet: 'Tony George Ruggles – Patriot, lived in this house in 1764-1774' it said. I thought then that 'Patriot' was obviously regarded as an occupation, a life-time achievement, or an honorary title – on a par with knighthood in Britain – in the USA.

It was the same in Ireland, and I began to understand why 'patriotism' as the main cause of one's life was OK both here and in the USA, but not quite kosher in Britain, the country that – at different times and by different means – tried to stifle both Irish and American aspirations for freedom and independence.

It was getting dark, and we had to find accommodation for the night. None of the Murray-recommended hotels were any longer in place. As for the *Rough Guide*, it did not recommend we stay in Tipperary at all, advising just a 'brief stop over' to have a quick look at 'the small and intriguing museum hidden away in the foyer of the town swimming pool.'

We were already too soaked and too tired to be either tempted or intrigued by the museum-cum-swimming pool. And here my many years in Britain led me into a trap: I was mislead (if not seduced) by the large sign 'The Royal Hotel' and forgot for a moment that I was not in the UK, where 'royal' was a synonym for 'quality' and 'grand,' but in the Republic of Ireland, where it was much more likely to stand for 'poorly' and 'horrible.'

'What? You want to stay here?' The unshaven and scruffy, yet perfectly civil, young receptionist looked genuinely astounded, as if we had asked him not for two rooms in his hotel, but for directions to Puerto Rico.

The hotel that could easily pass for an Irish equivalent of 'Fawlty Towers' was not just smelly and shoddy. It was clearly 'suicidal' (the adjective one Russian writer of the 1920s applied to Swiss hotels). The 1960s hits, played in the dark foyer, added to this sombre ambience. My room had holes in the floor and a huge bottle-shaped gap in the wall. The tiny bedside table was a real health hazard, so dirty and slimy it appeared. Everything in the room was soiled, battered, broken and/or falling apart. Except, of course, for a brand-new copy of the Bible.

Yet, whereas one could theoretically survive a night in my room, the one allocated to Jerry was not just 'suicidal' but outright murderous: the frames of both windows in it were smashed and could not be shut which, incidentally, did not matter, because there was no glass in either of them!

'Broken windows? They should have been fixed two weeks ago,' shrugged the receptionist when we complained. His confession made us realise that we were the first paying guests at the Royal Hotel for a fortnight, and most probably – for much longer …

'Tipperary is a very republican, very IRA town,' Jerry told me pensively from behind his pint of Guinness, as we sat in The Tony Lowry pub across the road half an hour later. Unlike our hotel, the pub was warm and cosy, its doors and windows decorated with stained glass, its walls overhung with hurling trophies and pictures of horses. Three sad-looking men and one woman were sitting at the mahogany bar silently staring at their pints. A bald publican behind the counter was watching Sky Sports. The scene was pristine and proverbial, almost home-like … I soon arrived to the Guinness-induced conclusion that Tipperary not only had 'bold' statues, but bald landlords, too.

'GAA began here,' continued Jerry. 'It was here that the first Independence War engagements took place …'

I quoted to him WG Blackie's dismissive characterisation of Tipperary (see epigraph).

'Yes, it is a rebellious place,' he said. 'But also – the Gaelic and Catholic heart of Ireland …'

Young and stocky local women in tracksuits were power-walking behind the windows of my hotel room next morning – just like they did on the promenade in Sandycove, Co. Dublin, where I lived.

We had breakfast at the brand-new (like the Bible in my room) downstairs restaurant of our hotel.

'They neglect rooms for the benefit of restaurants in Irish hotels,' Jerry noted hopefully as we were sitting down at our table.

As we soon discovered, that questionable Irish tradition – like almost everything else at the Royal Hotel – had been broken.

I solemnly promised myself never again to come close to anything that was called 'Royal' while in Ireland.

Our progress along the town's main (and pretty much the only) street was disrupted by yet another money-delivery drama. Just like in Rathdrum (see co Wicklow Chapter), a black armoured van suddenly breeched to a halt next to the local Bank of Ireland branch. A platoon of gun-wielding soldiers (some of whom looked as young as fifteen), headed by a fat red-bereted corporal, fell out of it – like peas out of a lunch box – and encircled the building, aiming their weapons at several unsuspecting pedestrians, including Jerry and myself. The only creature visibly affected by this fairly pointless (from my point of view) demonstration of military prowess was a tiny stray doggy, who kept barking at the soldiers for all it was worth during the whole of the five-minute siege. Eventually, the doggy had its way: the soldiers jumped back into the van and drove away, and the little mongrel, having struck a satisfied 'mission accomplished' look, followed Jerry and myself all the way to the Excel Centre.

The incongruity of the tall and turreted Excel building was striking. It was squeezed between a row of old Victorian cottages and a historic tower with a grassy roof. And next to Excel, the ubiquitous Celtic Tiger bulldozers were already clearing space for another 'Substantial Development Site. Proposals Invited' (as announced on the billboard).

'At least, there's going to be something substantial in Tipperary,' I remarked to Jerry. 'Up to now, I have been unable to spot anything of the sort, except perhaps for the town's rebellious spirit ...'

The Centre housed an exhibition gallery and a café. On one of the tables, I spotted a brochure with an intriguing title *The Excel Guide to Tipperary Heritage* which probably listed all the town's historic sites yet to be 'developed' (read destroyed).

'They should have called it *The Excel Guide to Getting Rid of Tipperary Heritage*, I thought.

Outside, Jerry, having filmed enough of the remains of once historic and 'pleasantly built' town centre, was dismantling his camera's tripod.

It was time to move on.

Part Five
Travels Down Under (1990-92)

Melbourne

First impressions are usually misleading; that's what they say.

Curiously, Melbourne reminds me of Odessa, the city on the Black Sea, the home town of poets, romantics and seafarers.

I felt this similarity acutely on my first day in Melbourne when I went to the Queen Victoria market. Certainly for choice it was far superior to the famous Privoz market in Odessa, but the spirit, the general atmosphere of the place, was pretty much the same: the hubbub of bargaining voices, the cheerful faces of all colours, all merging into a colourful palette of life. It was not just a place for buying food, but rather a cross-section of the country, a very peculiar social happening.

As to the food, it was unbelievable. I will spare myself the trouble of describing this horn of plenty; you know it only too well.

Before 1917 Odessa was world famous for its seafood, but if you go to Privoz market now you won't find a single fish for sale. Though the Black Sea is still there. Where did it all go? It all went down the drain, together with meat, fruit and clothes. It went down the black hole of so-called socialism, which for many years has been methodically killing any initiative to grow, to fish and to live. Anyone who grew, fished and lived above the average was automatically branded as an exploiter and either shot or sent to a labour camp.

'Oh, Odessa, the pearl on the sea coast. Oh, Odessa, you have known too many woes,' the popular Russian song goes (the free translation is mine). Indeed, Odessa knew many woes and its main one was communism, or Stalinism, to be more exact.

Melbourne beaches with miles of sand and patches of wild grass are also reminiscent of Odessa. Despite the popular joke to the effect that if they had socialism in the Sahara Desert it would quickly result in shortages of sand, communists have not succeeded in reducing the amount of sand on Odessa beaches. What they did succeed in doing was polluting the sea to the extreme and infecting it with bacteria. You cannot swim in the Black Sea unless you are determined to commit suicide.

I always liked sea ports. When giant ships approach the harbour they hoot good-naturedly and the window glass in the neighbouring seamen's houses starts trembling in anticipation: the man of the house is coming back.

More than 100 years ago the steamship *Great Britain* was going from Liverpool to Melbourne bringing early settlers to Victoria. Some of them were hoping to find gold, the others were hoping for a new life. Victoria – what a beautiful name! There is so much hope in it.

The journey from Liverpool to Melbourne took several months; babies were born and some of the older passengers died. It was like a floating piece of prosaic nineteenth-century life that has rebelled against this very prose and set out on a long and difficult trip to find poetry.

Standing on the embankment near the Melbourne port and staring intently at the flat and empty surface of the ocean, I could almost discern the outlines of the *Great Britain*'s wind-bitten sails on the hazy horizon. Who is it carrying this time? I could almost see myself standing on its deck dressed in tails and a bowler hat. I was looking into my own eyes from the distance.

Russian football was born in Odessa. That's probably why Odessites are soccer crazy. The players of the local Chernomorets team are god-like creatures in Odessa. No matter whether they win or lose, they remain heroes.

Sitting on the terraces of the main stadium in Melbourne and watching the Demons play Carlton, I could not stop the flow of Odessa associations. Aussie rules was too unusual for me to follow all the intricacies of the game, and after a while I started watching the fans instead. What amazed me was the number of single elderly women sitting on the terraces with thermoses of coffee clutched in their hands. They were sipping coffee and shouting, 'Go, Demons, go!' – sip, sip – and again at the top of their lungs, 'Go, Demons.' Towards the end of the game, their voices went hoarse and coffee didn't help any longer. But they kept whispering, crackling and squeaking 'Go, Demons, go.' No wonder the Demons won, having such powerful support.

Do you know what the main transport in Odessa is? Trams, just as in Melbourne. I prefer trams to buses or trains. I think they are much more human; the rattling of their wheels is soothing and they do not stink.

Despite these wonderful trams, Melburnians, like Odessites, like to walk around the city in the evening. I fell in love with Melbourne after my first evening walk in the centre. Street performers, musicians and bands were everywhere. There were even street ballerinas, street magicians and street karate fighters (luckily no street walkers this time). The yellow leaves were tumbling from the trees, the people were watching and smiling and trams were passing nonchalantly to and fro. It was a movable feast, the feast of freedom.

Do you know what they call small juicy melons in Odessa? *Kantalupki!* Does it ring a bell for you? Yes, yes, cantaloupes! *Kantalupki* is purely an Odessa word – it is absolutely unknown outside the city. Sometimes young Odessa girls – buxom and suntanned – are lovingly called *kantalupki* by the locals. I see here a romantic story of an Australian ship from Melbourne with a load of cantaloupes coming to Odessa port many years ago. 'What is this?' Odessites must have asked pointing to mountains of nice looking melons on the deck. 'Cantaloupes' the Australian sailors would answer. That's where *kantalupki* must have come from! Another Kangaroo tale.

Odessa is the place where I wanted to be born. Melbourne is the city where I want to live. They are not so far from each other.

But they are still very, very different. The other day, walking along a Melbourne street, I saw a workers' picket. Do you know what they were demanding?

Among other things, they were demanding free beer from their employers. It was then that I felt very strongly that I was not in Odessa.

First impressions are usually misleading; that's what they say.

Who knows? Let's wait and see.

Canberra

'So, where is the city?'

'Which city?'

'Why, Canberra, of course.'

'What do you mean, 'where?' We are smack downtown!'

Canberra is a cross between Kiev, Washington and Leongatha. It resembles Anaheim with Parliament instead of Disneyland. There is something soporific about the air here; it makes you sleepy and you feel like yawning all the time. That's probably why the MPs like to nod on the terraces of Parliament. I sympathise with them.

Canberra is like no other town in the world. It is simultaneously distinctive and faceless, beautiful and ugly, effervescent and dull, full of life and lifeless. It's the toy town capital of a toy town country.

There's something artificial about it. Normally, towns are built on river banks and around harbours, on the intersections of trade routes and in other lucrative places. Unlike them, Canberra was created mechanically, in the middle of nowhere, just to appease the notorious hostility between Melburnians and Sydney-siders. It was truly a Solomon's judgment, but judgments, unlike harbours and river banks, are not the best things on which to build cities. This lack of proper foundation must have prompted the remark by the English satirist Alan Coren, who called Canberra a suburb without an 'urb,'

'Hullo, can I speak to Mr Green?'

'Sorry, he is at the meeting.'

'What about Mr Brown? Is he available?'

'He is at the conference.'

'Mr Black?'

'He is at lunch. We have flexible lunch hours, you know.'

Canberra is the town of bureaucrats who are impossible to get hold of. In fact, it was probably not such a bad idea to try to send all the country's Government servants to one place where they could happily stew in their own juice, giving instructions to each other. The biggest problem with bureaucrats, though, as observed by Northcote Parkinson, is that each of them generates two more of the same. They multiply like rabbits and constantly demand new offices, new secretaries, new telephones and new deputies. So, in the near future Canberra is likely to be congested.

It is a town of bosses without underlings, leaders without followers, slave drivers without slaves. Can it be that this very social perversion is behind the fact that Canberra has one of the highest suicide rates in Australia?

'What are your plans for tonight?'

'I am invited to the reception at the Burlandia embassy to bid farewell to the first deputy of the second secretary. And you?'

'I have an invitation to the cocktail at Pythonia's high commission. They will serve smoked pythons there.'

Diplomats are bureaucrats of international standing. I am sure they feel very well in Canberra, which used to be a hardship post many years ago (no restaurants, no mistresses, no conversation, according to a French ambassador), but now it is a luxury one.

The embassies in Canberra stand in clusters, like mushrooms in a forest. The sizes and shapes of these mushrooms differ. The correlation is simple: the poorer a country, the bigger and grander the embassy. Britain, France and Japan are satisfied with modest, undecorated houses, whereas Mayalsia, Indonesia and Mauritius maintain plush mansions. The embassies of some tiny states are almost as big as the countries themselves. The Chinese mission – a huge complex of temple-like buildings, with tennis courts and a swimming pool – stands empty. The Chinese construction workers who built it defected, and the diplomats haven't moved in yet. I understand the builders; it's difficult not to be led astray by the grandeur they themselves created.

Diplomatic life in Canberra must be very tedious; no terrorists (fingers crossed), very few demonstrations of protest, nothing much to spy for. That's why the embassy part of the town is full of tennis courts, golf courses and jogging grounds. The diplomats must treasure their quiet existence and probably take care not to make a faux pas so as not to be faced with the gloomy prospect of being transferred to somewhere like Lebanon or Moscow. The best way to avoid this is to do nothing but play golf and tennis and throw receptions for each other.

'What do you think the flagpole on Parliament House symbolises?'

'I don't know. It reminds me of a big spider.'

'Silly! It's a bonfire, a symbol of life in the bush!'

'You mean that the national flag is being symbolically burnt all the time?'

If architecture is music in stone, then Parliament House in Canberra is a noisy military march. It is the stone incarnation of an illusion of grandeur. For me, the main principles of Australian life are modesty and comfort. The new Parliament House has neither.

After three days of running through its endless, dimly lit corridors, my new English shoes fell apart. The ceilings in the building are low; they press upon you and make you feel small and helpless. The building is also very clearly segregated; the routes of the MPs and parliamentary clerks never cross those of the public (unlike in the Capitol or even Westminster).

Standing high on the hill, Parliament House dominates the town. Getting there is like climbing a mountain, to the Peak of Power. I don't see much of the Australian spirit in this. The old Parliament House, apart from being beautiful, is quite normal. The public and politicians used to mix with each other there. Someone probably thought it was too small and modest for the great Australian leaders but, for me, this elegant house is the embodiment of my perception of Australia as a country that is proud but not conceited.

Canberra, too, has lots of things to be proud of. The air, which is crisp and clean, the mountains on the horizon, the wattle trees in their golden bloom, the people (not all of them are bureaucrats), who constitute the intellectual elite of the country, who in the evenings are involved in lively discussions in restaurants and cafés, and the amazingly bright stars in the sky at night. Even the fact that it is small and quiet compared with most capitals has its own attraction: it allows you to stop and look around, which is just what I did on my first visit to this very unusual place.

Victoria

Sometimes you feel like getting away from the humdrum of everyday life, from office routine and news of the world. You feel like fleeing to the country for a whiff of fresh air, or to drink a glass of air, as they say in Odessa. In Victoria, as far as I know, there's no better place for that than Gippsland – with its green grass and transparent air. Fresh air inspires the appetite, and if you like good views and good food, go to Gourmet Deli Tourism and take one of its delicious trails, as I did with my wife and son one Saturday morning.

It was like watching a movie with us both actors and viewers.

Sometimes we felt as though we were sitting in our tiny Moscow flat watching a Soviet-made film about our own adventures in Australia. That's why, in my memory, this wonderful day still exists in a make-believe form of a Soviet film script. And that's how I want you to see this day too. So get your popcorn ready. Here starts the show …

Title sequence: the Drouin West Fruit and Berry Farm.

Video: hot summer day. Neat farmhouse under the gum tree. Swarms of flies. Swarms of tourists-with plastic buckets picking raspberries, blueberries, strawberries, apples, nectarines, tangerines, submarines and whatnots … Most of the goodies. end up not in the buckets, but in the bellies (you have to pay for the ones in the bucket – this is capitalism, not communism yet). **Close-up:** the face of a tourist trying to swallow two pears, three apples and a handful of strawberries simultaneously. **Sound effects:** buzzing of flies. Clinking of buckets. Smacking of lips. **Audio:** (solemn voice): this is a so-called pick-your-own farm. It means that the lazy farmers decided to save themselves the trouble of harvesting, and are using poor tourists as living fruit and berry combines. This is the ugly face of Australian capitalism (to coincide with the face of the tourist choking on fruit – see above). But the working masses managed to outwit the capitalist exploiters: they eat much more than they can carry. And although the place does look like the fictitious Garden of Eden we, dear comrades, know only too well that neither Edens nor gardens exist in real life, so everything you can see on your screens, except for the flies, is just a clever set-up

Title sequence: the Jindivick Smokehouse.

Video: the interior of the smokehouse shop. The owners, Sid Mrasek and his wife, are behind the counter. Salamis and sausages are hanging from the ceiling like stalactites. The van with the inscription 'Sid's Meats' is parked outside. The tourists are coming out of the van with garlands of sausages around their necks. **Audio:** (very solemn voice): what a horrible smell! I've never sniffed anything as anti-Soviet as this before. As our poet Andrei Voznesenski wrote: '... and in the shop windows in the West they have sausages and ham and other anti-Soviet things ... 'Yes, my dear comrades, socialism and food are incompatible.

Title sequence: Gippsland Blue Cheese Factory.

Video: The factory's storage rooms look like Aladdin's cave, with pyramids of round cheeses slowly but surely maturing on the shelves. The tourists are dressed in white gowns, white plastic caps and rubber boots. Robert Johnson, the cheese-maker, is taking them around the factory. This unusual apparel makes the tourists look like doctors and patients of a psychiatric hospital. Before entering the storage room they rinse their boots in special tubs with brown disinfecting liquid. **Sound effects:** splashing of disinfecting liquid. Shuffling of rubber-booted feet. Muffled moans of maturing cheeses. **Audio** (extremely solemn voice): blue cheese ... The idea of such a thing! I will never make myself eat something which is blue ... Now, let's proceed to the factory's restaurant. Look at the menu: cheese for the starter, cheese for the main course, cheese for the dessert. Cheese for drinks too! Ha-ha! That's what they call prosperity in the West! And look how these poor people are dressed (close-up of the tourists in white gowns). You may think they are the workers at an atomic power station.

Title sequence: Victoria's Farm Shed at Tynong.

Video: the angry-looking shearer, dressed in dirty singlet, with huge scissors in his hands, is struggling with a wriggling sheep. He is not shearing the sheep, he is virtually peeling it. What emerges looks not like a sheep, but rather like a big pink frog. The ceremony is commented upon by a young smiling MC who says 'Thank you!' after every other word. Who is he thanking: the sheep, the shearer or the tourists, mainly Japanese, who watch the whole procedure with poker faces? In the courtyard a small black sheepdog with a high sense of responsibility is driving the frightened naked sheep from one corner to another. **Sound effects:** bleating of the sheep. Clanking of scissors. Clinking of cameras. Barking of the dog. **Audio** (desperately solemn voice): here you have the decaying West at its best. As you see, the living standards in Australia are so low that even the sheep have to participate in strip shows to earn some grass-money for their lambs. Look how desperately the poor creature is writhing in the hands of this pimp, the shearer. It's disgusting, isn't it? So you'd better stop looking.

Tasmania

'Megan Wallace loves to dance but unless she finds a like-minded young man she may have to dance alone. Anyone interested can call Megan on … ' (From the front page of Tasmania's main newspaper, 9 April.)

I've just come back from a trip. I've been to England and Italy, Norway and Switzerland, Germany and America. I visited Frankfurt and Hastings, Copenhagen and Zurich, Naples and San Francisco. All these venues are within a one-hour flight from Melbourne. They are all in one place – Hobart, the capital of Tasmania.

As the plane came in to land, I looked through the window and held my breath; the view was literally breath-taking: a sparkling harbour lined with gracious green hills.

My first thought was that my Tasmania-bound plane had been kidnapped and redirected to Italy. I have never been to Italy; but that was exactly how I imagined it must look. I held my breath, I opened my mouth – and for the whole week in Tasmania I was breathless with my mouth agape. I regained my breath and shut my mouth only on the plane back to Melbourne, as outlines of the 'holiday island' disappeared behind the clouds.

'Look out for a chirpy young conman who took a second-hand motorbike for a test ride at Bridgewater on Sunday afternoon and never came back. Police suspect the bike already has been reduced to a pile of parts.' (From the front page of Tasmania's main newspaper, 9 April.)

No, it was not Italy. The building that first attracted my attention at the airport was a white-washed one-storey shed the size of an ice-cream van. It stood at the end of the tarmac, proudly marked 'HOBART INTERNATIONAL.' A local resident told me later that this international terminal was Tasmania'a gateway to the world, with only one flight to New Zealand operating from it.

The main shipping terminal in Hobart is Constitution Dock. Here the tired bulks of ice-breakers from the Antarctic come to rest. There is no other town, not even a piece of land, anywhere between Hobart and the South Pole. The distance from Hobart to the Pole is a wee bit longer than from Hobart to Darwin. The end of the earth – that's what it is.

Hobart's port is spotlessly clean and cosy, and smells of sea and adventures. If you look down at the water, you will feel as if you are looking up into the sky at night: myriads of sea stars are visible through many metres of aquamarine water.

Hobart comes straight out of my childhood dreams. Neat houses under red-tiled roofs, quiet streets running down the hill to the harbour, the hunched back of the Tasman Bridge, Battery Point – a toy-sized English town – tiny antique shops in Salamanca Market.

'To dear Colin with love from Auntie Margaret. Xmas 1925.' (the dedication on *The Australian Boys Annual* on sale in Hobart Antique Centre in Salamanca Market.)

The fishermen on the pier ferreted out huge squid one by one. The squid wriggled desperately on the asphalt, swelling and quickly changing the colour of their jelly-like bodies from brownish to light grey. At dusk the silhouettes of yachts stood out against the fading sky. And the day itself, similar to the dying squids on the asphalt, was in the process of change, turning quickly from blue into black.

'Deckhand's bonus' (the name of a dessert in the Drunken Admiral restaurant in Hobart).

Hobart had the American battleship *Missouri* in the harbour at the beginning of April. This 58,000-tonne colossus was on its way home from the Gulf war. Several Hobart girls were waving to it from the shore.

For three days Hobart was swarming with crew-cut American sailors. They were drunk and were walking the streets carefully, swinging and stumbling with every step as if treading a rolling deck in storm.

'Cash vanishes from police safe' (front-page headline of Tasmania's main newspaper, 9 April).

Hobart is largely a toy town. It is almost unreal in its European beauty and cleanliness. In a small park smack downtown the locals play chess with man-sized pieces, the type of entertainment to be found in every Soviet holiday home. Holiday town in 'holiday state.'

'In real estate terms Hobart can be schizophrenic.' (From *Australian Adventure.*)

Hobart is not only schizophrenic, it is also very nostalgic. The first English settlers fell over themselves to recreate in Tasmania their good old England which, as they knew, most of them would never see again. These English judges, doctors and prison warders just copied the designs of their former households.

Walking through Richmond, outside Hobart, and Battery Point, just up from the dock, you cannot help feeling you are in Ledbury, Trenton-on-Trent, Hay-on-Wye, Wye-on-Hay or Abbotsfield. The streets are called Cheltenham Place, Waterloo Crescent and the like. And Arthur Circus in Battery Point is a miniature copy of London's Barnsbury Square. Just like a model railway: true to life, but still tiny, still a copy, still a toy.

In fact, the Jenni family, who came to Hobart from Switzerland, did construct a 350-metre model railway recreating the views of the Bernese Alps in minute detail. They demonstrate the railway to tourists at their Hobart home. Another case of homesickness.

Nostalgia for England seems to be felt all over Tasmania. Telephones purr with feline English intonations, the chimes on the GPO building in Hobart repeat the musical signals of Big Ben, Devonshire teas are served everywhere, and pubs have not only English interiors, but also English names – the Fox and Hounds, the Richmond Arms.

Tasmanians, as real islanders, constantly ask English questions: 'How long have you been here? Are you enjoying Tasmania?' I was confronted with the last question twenty minutes after arrival. 'Yes, the airport was very impressive,' I said.

It is also a predominantly white society. The last Aborigine was shooed out to Flinders Island in 1876, and the chance to see a non-white native Tassie resident now is almost as slim as running into an extinct Tasmanian tiger.

'The Tasmanian devil (*Sarcophilus harrisi*) is mild of manner and clean. It even washes its face.' (From *Berlitz Australia.*)

I think Berlitz has confused the creature with the koala. The Tasmanian devil stinks. (You feel like washing your hands even after watching the animal from a distance.) It is also irascible, or was when I watched it in Bonorong Park, a wildlife centre near Hobart. The Tasmanian Devil reminds me of a koala exiled to Tasmania from the mainland and kept off eucalyptus as a punishment.

In the Royal Botanical Gardens in Hobart you look not so much at the plants as at the views. All is in harmony there: Tasmanian views, African cacti, Australian cedars, Japanese sacuras and Russian birch trees – the most cosmopolitan place on this beautiful but rather xenophobic island.

The thing that attracted me most at the Botanical Gardens was the so-called Easy Access Garden. This featured plants in big bowls lifted to about one metre above the ground. It was intended for people in wheelchairs and should enable handicapped people to do some gardening of their own without having to bend down.

A small garden for the disabled, a beautiful toy with a serious meaning and warm human touch.

Tasmania. From now on, you will be like an easy access garden for me. Indeed, you are easily accessible: only a one-hour flight from Melbourne.

'A report in yesterday's paper … led to about twenty hopefuls phoning Megan to offer their services … Mark, a carpet salesman from Kettering, said his previous partner did not want to go on to competition dancing but he did … Megan and Mark took their few tentative steps, and confidently agreed they will make a good team.' (From the front page of Tasmania's main newspaper, 10 April.)

Hobart

Wrest Point Hotel Casino is the loudest architectural statement in Hobart. It is a piercing scream in the placid symphony of the city. The building, dominating the local harbour, resembles a big candlestick without a candle.

Gambling, in my mind, has always been associated with topcoats, evening dresses, burning candles and an exposed card shark being hit on the head with a heavy brass candlestick.

On the Soviet scale of moral values, a casino has always occupied the last-but-one place, followed only by a bordello. Casino-style gambling is still illegal in the USSR, apart from the best hotels for foreigners, who are usually exempt from the moral code of the builders of communism.

It's interesting, though, that in the new casino of the Savoy Hotel in Moscow you can't win money – just a receipt that you can only cash outside the country.

Reading Russian literary classics, I had a notion of bubbling passions, strokes of wild luck and terrible blows of fortune connected with gambling. 'A three, a seven and an ace' from Pushkin's *The Queen of Spades*, Dostoevsky's Prince Mishkin and things like that.

If gambling was able to inspire so many writers, there must be something about it, I was thinking. But for many years I was sure one had to be at least a millionaire to be allowed into a casino.

Wrest Point kept dragging me like a magnet, especially during the night, when it was brightly lit from inside. I felt like a night-time moth attracted by a street lamp, but still scared to approach it in case its wings were burnt. On my last night in Hobart I decided to risk my hypothetical wings and visit this den of passions.

The first revelation was that eighteen storeys of the finger-like building had only seventeen floors. Floor number thirteen was missing, and in the lifts the twelve button was followed by the fourteen.

At the casino's main floor entrance was a curious banking machine with only one function – cash withdrawal. It accepted all types of credit cards.

Next to the machine stood a burly guard (or rather a bouncer) who also performed only one operation – removing drunks and people in jeans from the crowd and blocking their entry.

The dimly lit room was full of winking screens of poker machines. People crouched around them were all smoking like chimneys, so one could be excused for thinking that non-smokers were not allowed to gamble, like drunks and people in jeans.

The players' faces were very serious. The machines were emitting short squeaking sounds like rubber toys when squeezed tightly. From time to time the clinking of coins falling out of the machines' bellies could be heard. The sound was excessively loud.

In the corner the game of keno was in progress. The jackpot was $149,637.61. The 61 cents, for some reason, looked impressive.

But the main gambling was taking place in another big room, where more chain-smoking fortune seekers were playing cards with croupiers. With quick and smooth movements the croupiers shoved banknotes down the narrow slits of the green tables. The money disappeared down the slits like greased lightning, never to be seen again.

I started watching the players. A middle-aged, bespectacled man was counting tokens, paying no heed to the smoking cigarette stub protruding from his mouth. The filter was burning already, but he remained unperturbed, totally engrossed in his important business. Another man was mumbling to himself with his eyes fixed on the table. He wore a black collarless shirt under his jacket and looked like a praying bishop. .

A woman with darting eyes and her pregnant daughter, both smoking, were pulling alternately at their wine glasses and at stacks of tokens on the table.

The most distinctive feature of the room's atmosphere, apart from clouds of smoke, was a complete lack of joy, grief or any other emotion that gambling should theoretically inspire. The gamblers reacted with equal nonchalance to wins and losses. Poker face – now I know exactly what it means.

The croupiers acted automatically, like machines. A casino official whose position was 'pit boss' explained that the croupiers, like doctors or lawyers, must have a licence. ('A Licence to Gamble' – a good name for a thriller.)

I couldn't leave my first casino without an attempt at gambling. The only game that was vaguely familiar was blackjack. I climbed onto a stool opposite the croupier and handed him a $10 note. Before I could say 'Jack Robinson' or even 'Blackjack,' the money disappeared down the slit.

I was cautious and tried to put on the cloth no more than two $2 tokens at a time. Twenty!' announced the croupier, giving me the third card. 'Enough!' I said, rubbing my hands (mentally, of course). The croupier started making his bid. In a flash, he threw three cards on the table. I couldn't believe my eyes: he had twenty-one!

Next time I had twenty-one and was already triumphant. You won't believe it, but the croupier drew a ten and an ace – the blackjack! for himself. He definitely had all the cards, that croupier.

I slid down the stool and started towards the exit. Strangely, I didn't feel sorry for the lost money. I did have a good time and temporarily forgot about all my big and small problems. I discovered that gambling (within reasonable limits, of course) was fun.

I went out. The waves were rustling against the sand like a croupier's fingers against the cloth. The half-moon was hanging above the casino like an ace of hearts on the black card of night. The evening lights of Hobart were blinking like a ten of spades.

The blackjack! At last!' I cried out into the darkness.

Health Farm

Brisbane vampire Tracy Wiggington could not stand mirrors. Vampires do not reflect in mirrors, you know … I am not a vampire and I do have a reflection. But I used to hate mirrors, because it's not much fun to see one's own ageing sallow face with dark shadows under the eyes and the yellow teeth of a chain-smoker.

Some time ago I finally got rid of my old phobia of mirrors.

What do I see in the looking glass now? The rosy, cheeky face of a youngish man, the face of a non-smoker! That's what happened to me after only four days in East Gippsland at the Ontos health farm – or, more correctly, Ontos Natural Health Retreat. For me it was a retreat indeed …

To make myself go there was the most difficult thing. My friends who had been to Ontos told stories that were a cross between a Hitchcock horror movie and a set of rules for Soviet labour camp inmates – they don't allow you to smoke or drink (not only alcohol but also tea and coffee), they have no newspapers or TV, don't let you wear shoes indoors, the food is strictly vegetarian …

I could not imagine what could be particularly great about eating grass and running barefoot in the middle of nowhere. I also kept thinking how they could possibly prevent someone drinking, smoking or reading a newspaper. What do they do? Shoot him? Pictures of exquisite vegetarian repressions were haunting my nightmare dreams. As a product of a totalitarian system, I could not imagine an effective means of persuasion other than torture or a gun.

At the same time I did realise that this was my last chance. My health had been practically ruined by smoking, lack of exercise and the continuous stresses of thirty-six years in the Soviet Union where you don't really care whether you'll drag on for ten more years of incessant queueing or you won't. Anyway, it's only four bloody days, I was telling myself. So I will go to this cosy retreat and do my best to prevent it becoming my last abode. It would be a shame if my obituary started with the sentence: 'He died on a health farm.'

In such a cheerful mood I left Melbourne one fine morning in March to find the new me.

Day one

The drive to the farm takes five hours. On the way we stop at every single McDonald's and stuff ourselves with junk food to bursting point. We also smoke like chimneys. In short we do everything to minimise the destructive effect of the forthcoming four days of healthy life.

At the last junk food joint before Ontos we have three hot dogs each and smoke half a packet of Benson & Hedges between the two of us. My son, meanwhile, is giving grass to a horse grazing on the lawn nearby. The horse consumes the grass with doomed obedience. 'Look,' I say to my friend, 'we'll all soon be like this horse.'

Before starting the last part of our journey we solemnly throw all our remaining cigarettes into a rubbish bin and photograph each other with the last (?) smoking stubs in our mouths – as a reminder of our past (?) bad habits. Well, as they say in Russia, 'The sooner you go to prison, the sooner you come out.'

And here we are. 'Welcome to your home away from home!' the sign at the gates read. The place does look strikingly beautiful standing among the hills overgrown with thick forest. But I hardly notice all this beauty; I can think only of cigarettes. I haven't had one for more than an hour! But there are no cigarettes flying around – only rosellas and kookaburras. Our cigarettes are lying in a bin eighty kilometres from Ontos with no towns or shops in between. We could go back for them, but we are too tired for that after the long journey. So we go into dinner instead.

It is a real gourmet's delight (if this gourmet were a horse or a sheep). Pumpkin soup, beetroot, some grass and vegetables and a little pasta (at least something familiar!). I find salt and pepper, my old trusted friends, tucked away in a dark corner, and use them profusely. A big teapot is boiling on a small table. But the tea is only herbal. And the coffee is decaffeinated. Decaffeinated coffee! It is like a four-angled triangle! In a glass canister on the table is something that looks and smells like tea. I grab the canister. The label says Madura – a good name for a Turkish beauty, but an awful one for a drink.

Despite all this I rather enjoy the dinner and don't feel hungry afterwards.

The people spending their weekend at Ontos are a curious lot. There are about 100 of them. With me and my cholesterol it makes 102. In the dining room they talk exclusively about food and health. Do they know what real suffering means? Do they know what it is like to spend three hours a day trying to buy a kilo of sugar? No, they don't eat sugar, preferring Hermesetas instead. Again, what can pass for a good name for a Paris harlot in a Guy de Maupassant novel – Hermeseta – becomes an ugly mocking term for ersatz sugar!

The essence of holiday-making in Russia is to break as many taboos as possible in the shortest possible time – eat, drink, be merry and forget about the gloomy everyday life. In Russian rest homes teetotallers temporarily become dipsomaniacs, vegetarians grow into trenchermen, blue stockings and family men are miraculously transformed into harlots and Don Juans. Here it is the other way round – everyone tries to pretend that he (or she) is as good as gold. What for? To procrastinate for several additional years of grass-eating?

Curiously, I don't feel like having a cigarette any longer. The air is so crisp and clean that smoking is starting to look like a perversion or a sacrilege. What I really can't endure is the lack of news from the outside world. With so many things happening in the Soviet Union it would be unthinkable to be detached from the news. To tell you the truth, I have something up my sleeve – a small transistor radio smuggled into Ontos at my peril. I don't know what exactly the peril entailed, but there was the peril all right.

So, after dinner, I run away to the bush and switch on the radio, imbibing the news from our turbulent Ontos-free world. What will they do to me if they discover this small ruse of mine, I wonder? They will probably make me eat another vegetarian dinner as punishment.

Before falling asleep, I read *When the Going was Good*, by Evelyn Waugh. Yes, the going was good only yesterday.

Day two

'He died on a health farm.' This sentence keeps ringing in my poor de-nicotined brain.

Guess what is for breakfast. Bran! Branfast instead of breakfast! I think I'll start neighing soon.

After breakfast I go to the tiny farm library, full of health magazines and English-Sanskrit dictionaries. Real cliff-hangers! Find a gripping book, *How to Train Your Donkey*, and read it until lunch.

Then it's time for a tour of the farm, conducted by the farmer. His name is Krishna and the van on which we are touring his 280-hectare property has the numberplate YOGA. Never before have I seen such beautiful scenery. Angora goats are bleating, birds singing, kiwifruit, lemons and mandarins growing bountifully. We pick them up and eat. Heaps of mohair is piled in the farm shed. Back in the USSR, mohair was very much in short supply, a sort of 'soft currency' that every traveller thought a must to bring from abroad. Here in the shed there is enough mohair to make a shipload of Soviet tourists jump with joy and sink the ship. And I see my first wild kangaroos! Krishna disappoints me a little by saying they are actually wallabies, but they do seem very kangarooish to me. Krishna himself looks like an organic part of nature – like a tree or a flower. Everything here is so placid and primaeval that you forget all your mundane worries. (Ontos means 'being' in Greek, by the way.)

I am coming to grips with the place gradually and, surprise, surprise, with the food as well. I am also getting used to taking off my shoes whenever I enter a building – just like a Muslim entering a mosque.

After lunch we have a course of deep relaxation in the temple. The temple dominates the farm grounds and is multi-denominational. Relaxation is conducted by a young man called Neal who lives on the farm with his wife. We lie in a circle on mats and Neal's quiet pleasant voice carries us away, somewhere to the beach where the ocean waves rustle gently, making us forget everything, everything, everything ... I must have fallen asleep because when I open my eyes many people around me are snoring gently.

In the evening, instead of running away to the bush with my clandestine radio, I decide to attend a discussion at the temple about the meaning of life. This must be reflectory, but I fall asleep soon after the discussion starts. That's probably how the temple affects me. When I wake up though, I have a feeling I knew more about the meaning of life than I did before. It suddenly dawns on me that the sense of life is not in smoking, drinking or other means of self-destruction. So far, so good. Or rather – in for a penny, in for a pound!

Day three

In the morning I borrow a *Being Healthy* magazine from the shelf in the dining room. 'Stress must be avoided.' I read. 'Stress is induced by allowing the thoughts to rampage into the future or wallow in the past … Focusing on either the future or the past, other than for constructive planning or positive lesson achievement detracts from the importance of the ever present now … the only moment in which we can achieve positivity, joy and happiness …'

'What about arts and literature which are nothing but 'rampaging into the future' or 'wallowing in the past,'' I am thinking. 'Are they useless? No, I really prefer *How to Train Your Donkey*. It's much more positive and constructive!'

Carla, Neal's wife, is cooking lunch to the accompaniment of soft pleasant music. 'You must be in a good mood when you cook,' she says. 'It affects the food.' Judging by the quality of lunch, her mood is good indeed.

In the evening I go for a walk with my radio. Large velvety stars hang over my head. The bright full moon rocks in the sky like a big street lamp in the wind. 'Supreme as Empress of the Night …' That's what Longfellow called the moon. Cicadas are screaming. 'I heard the trailing garments of the night sweep through her marble halls …' Longfellow again. The radio announcer's voice sounds irrelevant and alien in this serene harmony. I switch off and listen to the music of the night.

Day four

Finish *How to Train Your Donkey* and start reading an article called 'Guilt and Worry – Needless Emotions.' After three days here I am ready to agree with the title.

Shall I buy a donkey when I get back to Melbourne? I could ride it to and from the office, which would be cheaper and quicker than public transport.

After lunch I have a long talk with Krishna. Here's a summary of what he had to say:

'I was born in America, and my original name was Fred Koch. My father was a very wealthy person, a real tycoon, and he wanted me to follow him. I studied business administration at the university and after that worked as a stockbroker. But business never attracted me, so after a while I gave it up and went to work as a primary schoolteacher in a black ghetto of Chicago.

'My pupils adored me and used to flock around my car every morning when I arrived. But I had no qualifications as a teacher and was dismissed after a while. Having spent some time roaming the world as a hippy, I bought a farm in Arkansas from money I had saved when selling stocks. Soon I developed a serious case of hepatitis, and the doctors didn't know what to do. They were sure I was going to die. But then I met a girl who was a vegetarian. She put me on a diet without meat, fish, eggs and so on. Three weeks later I had a blood test, which showed that my illness had completely disappeared.

'This prompted me to start growing organic food on my farm. One day a young man came to work on the farm. He was an ardent follower of yoga. He ate nothing but yoghurt and practically did not sleep, spending days and nights in meditation. He converted me. I gave up smoking marijuana and took up yoga instead. It was in the mid-1970s and there was lots of pollution in America. I suddenly felt that I could not go on living in such an atmosphere and decided to move to Australia. Why Australia? I was interested in it from childhood. I came to Sydney, spent the whole day in the library studying maps and found this neglected farm in East Gippsland which was on sale. I came here, and as soon as I entered the gates, I had a feeling – it was like an electric shock – that this was the place. I spent the night in the sleeping bag out of doors, and next day I bought the farm.

'The first seven years here we spent cleaning the place. It was in an awful state. Then my spiritual teacher, Swami Satchidananba, came here from India. He gave me my new name, Krishna Yogi. At the moment there are four adults living and working at the farm full time. But lots of volunteers come here to work for food and accommodation. Several years ago we started running the health retreat. Many people gave up smoking here, and six former heroin addicts parted with their addiction. Our basic motto is serving people. Ontos, as you know, means "being." And "being" for me is "doing." As long as we are doing we must do useful things. Our three basic principles are: be peaceful, be easeful, be useful. These three principles are interconnected: you can't be useful, say, without being peaceful and easeful.

'If you don't cure your own sins, you can't cure the sins of the world. Yoga is not selfish. By doing good to himself, one does good to the people. Giving is one of the greatest actions in the world. What is easeful? My father said, "Never worry about anything you can do nothing about." That's why I am not interested in the world news. We don't have newspapers. We found out that President Ford had been shot only three weeks after it had happened. Or was it Reagan? I don't care. Television? We don't have it. I think television is an evil force, a typical case of a good invention being abused. My kids watch videos occasionally at their friends' houses, and their whole being changes for the worse after this … No, I never get lonely, because I am everything: I am a horse in the field, I am an elephant in Africa, I am Vitali Vitaliev, I am a prostitute in St Kilda, My energy is everywhere, and it won't disappear even after my death. Yes, I think I am very lucky being able to do what I want.'

Krishna's house stands on top of the hill from where a breath-taking view of the farm opens. The interior of the house is truly spartan. They all sleep in one bedroom:

Krishna, his wife Clare-Lisa, and his five kids. Each of the kids is allocated his own part of the organic garden to look after.

When we finally leave Ontos, they all stand near the temple and wave goodbye to us. I suddenly feel pity for this tiny bunch of people living here alone for days and months. 'Here you lose track of the days,' Krishna told me. 'You lose track of the years, too. Sometimes, I feel as if I came here only yesterday.'

Yes, it's true, you lose track of time at Ontos. But you also lose something else – harmful habits, cheap ambitions, excessive vanity. And you find your new ego, new awareness of your body and soul.

Goodbye, Ontos. I will be back!

PS: If when walking past the *Age* building in Spencer Street one day you see a donkey grazing near the entrance and a pair of shoes at the front door, don't be surprised. They'll be mine.

Adelaide

'I went to Adelaide once, but it was closed.' I heard this joke on the train.

I was lucky: Adelaide was open. In fact it was one of the most open places I've seen so far in Australia. It does not try to hide behind the skyscrapers. It does not suffer from delusions of grandeur. The city gives an unparalleled feeling of freedom. That is probably because, unlike other Australian capitals, Adelaide was founded not by convicts but by free settlers.

Lots of space, wide streets and very few people around – that's how I saw Adelaide.

'Where are the people?' I kept asking my hostess from Tourism South Australia on the way from the station to the Terrace Hotel. 'It's Sunday today, you know,' she shrugged apologetically.

But on weekdays the streets remained deserted. Even Hindley Street, with its reputation as a local Kings Cross, was empty when I walked along it one evening. That's if you do not count a homeless man sitting on the porch of a restaurant and a small gang of teenagers crowding near the discotheque. Shops, cafés, strip clubs looked totally abandoned. It was probably too cold for South Australians to go out.

The only place where life could be felt was Adelaide Casino, a huge, ornate building with the interior of both a stock exchange and a railway terminal. Indeed, it used to house the railway station.

Adelaide, this half-empty city, has lots of charm. The locals sometimes call it a half-an-hour town, since it takes exactly thirty minutes to get from one place to another.

I don't know whether it is true. I would call Adelaide not a half-an-hour town but a city of halves. Half Melbourne and half Canberra, half European and half Australian, it lies halfway between Sydney and Perth. North Terrace, its main street, is half Swanston Street and half St Kilda Road. Adelaide is half modern and half old, half progressive and half conservative, half well-planned and half eclectic.

Adelaide has the contradictory character of a woman who is well aware of her beauty, so she can afford to be whimsical and not very punctual.

It is the only place in the world with a half-hour time difference from the country's capital, creating lots of problems for the locals and the rest of Australia. Adelaide is half-heartedly sticking to the difference.

Adelaide is the venue for unending festivities. It is the festive capital of the festival state. When I was there, the 'Come Out 91 Festival' was launched. This is the festival for children, a little brother to the Adelaide Art Festival.

The motto of 'Come Out 91' is the famous Paul Keating expression, 'Shut up and listen and you might learn something.' In the context, it means that we adults must temporarily shut up and listen to whatever children have to say about us. For that, a special speakers' corner was set up in Adelaide's Old Parliament House.

One hopes that this children's festival will provide a good distraction for local graffiti artists. Adelaide is the world champion in graffiti. Nowhere else have I seen so many street drawings. The ubiquitous graffiti covers even one of the local landmarks, Flinders Lighthouse on Mount Lofty, which is luckily out of operation, otherwise this would lead to shipwrecks.

It is not surprising that at the Museum of Political History in Old Parliament House one stand is reserved solely for graffiti. But this stand remains blank. Young vandals do not like to desecrate designated places. They like to draw wherever they want and nowhere else.

Coming back to the city of halves, one may assume that Adelaide is home to half of Australia's best restaurants. Statistics indicate that the locals support more restaurants per mouth than any other Australian city. At Flannigan's Riverfront Restaurant, I ate the best oysters Kilpatrick in my life. Only for some local reason, on the menu they were called Oyster Tompatrick. The main thing was that the oysters were not half, but totally, delicious.

I can say that I felt almost at home (that is, in Melbourne) in Adelaide. Half at home, to be more exact. I enjoyed this city of halves where I spent two-and-a-half days and of which· I have seen only half. But I feel like coming here again to see the second half.

Barossa

The church bells are ringing at dusk in Bethany. The chimes float in the air above the Barossa Valley, and after a while they start sounding not like bells but like human voices, moaning and laughing, groaning and singing.

What language do Bethany bells speak? They speak German. Not the authentic Prussian or Silesian dialects but a very special one called Barossa Deutsch, the one in which *schluck* means a glass of wine.

In the soft sounds of the bells one can clearly hear the musical names of the first German settlers in Australia. 'Jo-hann Sonn-tag, Wil-helm Kla-u, Hein-drich Me-yer,' the bells are tolling. But no one answers their calls: Johann Frantz Sonntag, with all his twenty-three children, and Poznan-born Wilhelm Klau, and Pastor Heindrich Meyer are all lying in Bethany's pioneer cemetery.

'In memory of our pioneering forefathers who left Germany in search of religious freedom and who first settled in Bethany in 1842,' reads the plaque at the cemetery's entrance.

This tiny cemetery in Bethany is one of the most moving places I have seen in Australia. The existence of a sizeable German colony in the Barossa Valley, fifty kilometres from Adelaide, came as a complete surprise.

Driving through the valley, I was puzzled by names like Seppeltsfield and Lyndoch, by the sign Die Weins tube above the wineries, by the fact that even the hill dominating the predominantly flat landscape was called Kaiser Stuhl, by the gracious Lutheran churches standing in the shadow of gum trees.

What vicissitudes of life drove these people from the banks of the Rhine to this remote land? Why did they have to flee their Silesian homes and settle in Australia? 'In search of religious freedom.' Is it not strange, that – people looking for freedom in Australia, the land of convicts? There must have been some magnetism about this place.

The first settlers, escaping the ferocious rule of King Friedrich Wilhelm III of Prussia, arrived in 1842. There could be no return. Life was tough, but the Germans were stubborn and sinewy. In Bethany's cemetery the graves are mostly those of little children and octogenarians. This shows eloquently how hard it was to stay alive. If you did, it seems you had good prospects of living to an old age.

Hoffnunstahl – the Valley of Hope – that is what they called their new homeland. Hope is a powerful state of mind, and it quickly bore fruit. In 1843, the *Southern Australian* called the German colonists 'industrious, sober and persevering people.' In 1892, the *London Gazette* referred to some of the German wineries in the Barossa Valley as 'the most modern in the world.'

During World War I, however, the German settlers had to withstand another wave of persecution – this time in Australia. Their Germanness was suddenly a liability, and many Teutonic names turned Australian. The village of Gnadenfrei ('freed by the grace of God') became Marananga, an Aboriginal name. The village of Siegersdorf ('conquerors' village') was transformed. Schmidts became Smiths.

This attempt to destroy the German spirit was doomed to failure. Strangely, it reminds me of the epidemic of renaming places in Soviet Russia after 1917. Petrograd became Leningrad, Tver was Kalinin, and Tverskaya Street in Moscow became Gorkovo Street to commemorate 'the great proletarian writer.'

Now the original names are being gradually returned to all the hastily renamed cities, towns and streets. Gorkovo became Tverskaya again, Kalinin turned back into Tver, and even the big city of Gorky has regained its original name of Nizhni Novgorod.

'What's in a name? That which we call a rose by any other word would smell as sweet.' Shakespeare, as usual, was right. It is a hopeless business to try to erase national feeling by forced assimilation. By trial and error, Australia has learnt this lesson. In 1975 the name Siegersdorf was revived.

Yes, the German spirit is alive and well in the Barossa Valley. In the village of Seppeltsfield, I visited the old winery long owned by the Seppelr family. I was eating smoked ham with sauerkraut, drinking Riesling and talking to Joyleen Seppelt, an attractive middle-aged woman with blue eyes and German features.' She was telling me the story of her ancestor, Joseph Seppelt, who arrived with his family in 1851. The wine was cool, astringent and clean as a tear.

Indian Pacific

I am writing these lines on board the Indian Pacific Express, joining two great oceans of the world in one trans-Australian train ride. We are in 'the long straight,' the longest stretch of straight railway track in the world, which, if you believe the *Guinness Book of Records*, extends for 478 kilometres.

The window of my tiny compartment is like a television screen showing an endless landscape. For three hours already this screen has featured nothing but red desert, flat as a dining table, with thickset, grey shrubs growing here and there. The landscape is both depressing and invigorating. It reminds me of a red ocean with neither waves, nor ship masts on the horizon. Eternal calm, immeasurable vastness, spartan severity ...

A tiny whistle stop flashes by. It is just a faded signpost and a dozen empty petrol barrels scattered around it. A farmer in a wide-brimmed hat is standing near the truck with his freckled daughter. They both wave to the train and smile.

Cook Station. 'If you are crook come to Cook,' the sign on the platform says. And here is another one: 'Help our hospital, get sick.' Very welcoming ... Thanks, Cook.

My trans-Australian train journey started several days ago at 9prn. This was my first experience of Australian long-distance trains. 'Will you have coffee in your room or go to the club?' the conductor asked me as soon as I boarded the Overland Express in Melbourne. I was irritated by such a blatant invasion of my privacy and politely advised the nosy attendant to mind his own business.

The Overland Express was standing in Spencer Street Station, a stone's throw from the *Age* building. I was looking at the three familiar neon letters AGE from my window when the letters suddenly jerked and started sliding away from me slowly. The depot-like building of the *Age* was receding.

In ten minutes though, the frisky building stopped with a squeak. I could see it very clearly from a distance, since all the lights in our train went off. We waited for more than three hours in dead silence and pitch darkness. 'Electric problem,' the conductor announced cheerfully, peeping into my compartment. There were clear notes of fiendish pleasure in his voice – his revenge for my earlier outburst. That was the start of my first Australian train journey.

After a while, I groped my way to the club car; there was a handful of passengers drinking their frustration away in the darkness. 'What would you like?' the voice of a waitress was somewhere in front of me. 'Some light for the starter and a bit of movement for the main course,' an invisible passenger answered.

When I was about to grab my suitcase and go home, the lights reappeared and the train rushed forward at a snail's pace. I had plenty of time to examine my first-class compartment. It was a masterpiece of practicality: everything bent and folded.

The washing tub, the sleeping berth and even the john were all collapsible. After spacious Russian travel compartments, this one looked and smelled like a medium-sized snuff box without tobacco. I could hardly squeeze myself inside with my suitcase. And what if I was slightly bigger? I'd have to sleep in the corridor.

Instead of tobacco, my snuff box was filled with ominous- sounding signs, warnings and instructions on how to flush the toilet and what to do in case of fire. (Point one: tell the conductor and other people.) Gripping reading.

Next to the door there were two plaques saying respectively 'shoes' and 'towels.' I started looking for one more saying 'Vitali' but failed to find it.

Trying to lower the sleeping berth, I faced a dilemma. The compartment could accommodate the berth or myself, but there wasn't enough space for both. I eventually went out into the corridor, lowered the berth through the open door of my compartment and quickly jumped onto it, slamming the door shut in my flight.

I switched off the light and immediately the compartment was brimming with the sounds of vibrating objects. Each vibrated with its own peculiar pitch and tone. The glass was clinking in its metallic holder, the coke was splashing in the can, the door hinges were squealing, the spoon in the glass was jingling. Even my shoes, stuck according to instruction in the dark tiny closet in the wall, were rubbing against each other and making a muffled, clattering sound as if they were either dancing or shivering with cold. A real railway symphony. Towards the coda, it was joined by some snoring sounds, I presume.

We arrived in Adelaide four hours behind schedule.

The Indian Pacific has just crossed the border into Western Australia. Just imagine – this state is bigger than Texas and Alaska combined, and more than ten times the area of Great Britain. The landscape though hasn't changed a bit: same desert, same empty barrels scattered near the track. Steel bands in the Caribbean use such barrels as percussion instruments. It would be good for musicians from Jamaica and Guyana to come here and pick up the barrels one day.

The train is now standing at Rawlinna. The engine drivers went shopping. And I remembered how once on a train in Siberia I shared a bottle of vodka with the engine driver in my compartment. The train by the way kept moving forward at neck-breaking speed all the while. Railway journeys are like that; they always have lots of surprises waiting for you on the track.

Kalgoorlie

The Indian Pacific Express has been groping through the pitch darkness of the Nullarbor for several hours.

Looking through the window, I felt I had been locked in a pitching and rolling cellar on wheels, with neither windows nor doors. Australian darkness is much thicker than in Europe.

Travelling by overnight train in Europe, you can always see, if not the lights of a city or of a station, then at least a glow of lights on the horizon. This Australian darkness was solid and impenetrable, almost like that seen from a trans-Siberian train. But in Siberia the landscape is slightly brightened by the snow.

The darkness of the Australian desert is like an ocean at night. A sailor who falls overboard cannot swim: he is paralysed by the darkness and quickly drowns.

The conversation at dinner that evening was about the coming stop at Kalgoorlie, where the train was to arrive at 9pm. It was announced that during a forty-minute stop there would be a guided bus tour of the town.

The males in the restaurant car were winking at each other and rubbing their hands in anticipation.

'What's so special about Kalgoorlie?' I asked a middle-aged man at my table. He squinted at his wife sitting next to him and seemingly preoccupied with her cup of tea, then hissed in conspiratorial whisper: 'There is a terrific red-light district there, mate. Just like in Amsterdam or like the Reeperbahn in Hamburg.'

'Not a chance,' my neighbour's wife snapped. 'You won't leave the bus for a single moment.'

I was certainly intrigued by this enigmatic town. As soon as the darkness behind the window was broken by distant lights, I dressed and hurried towards the exit.

The platform in Kalgoorlie was brightly lit and empty, not counting some drunken young men in jeans jokingly chasing a young woman with a bare midriff. She was running away from them. They were all laughing.

'Miners playing with a local prostitute,' my knowledgeable table companion remarked. His wife gave him a push in the ribs. She also decided to go on tour just to keep an eye on her playful husband, I suppose.

An old, tattered bus was waiting behind the station building. In no time it was filled with Indian Pacific passengers, mostly men.

Suddenly I found myself in a Hollywood western. Saloons, bars and pubs with verandas were on every corner. The guide said there were several hundred. Just to make sure that nothing much is left of a miner's salary, I thought.

The architecture of the town is colonial; even the shops look like settings from a nineteenth-century play. In the central town square stands a small monument to an

Irish chap called Patrick Hannan, whose only claim to fame was that he had once stumbled over a huge gold nugget and thus signalled the start of the gold rush.

The pragmatic locals have turned the monument into a drinking fountain. Very ingenious. Water has always been scarce in Kalgoorlie. It was first brought here by another Irishman, C Y O'Connor, who stretched a pipeline from Perth. But ironically he is not commemorated by any monument In Kalgoorlie.

The message is clear: gold is more important than water.

We passed the goldmines. The garlands of lights made them resemble big Christmas trees. Trucks and tiny rail-carts were moving hither and thither. Excavators were folding and unfolding their metallic trunks.

The gold rush was in full swing. The guide said that from time to time one could still find a big chunk of gold. The passengers chuckled sceptically.

We saw only one living being in the streets: a stumbling man in a wide-brimmed hat, pressing a bottle of whisky to his chest. Our bus nearly ran over him.

With ten minutes remaining before our train's departure, our bus crawled into notorious Hay Street, which is quite narrow.

'Well, this is what you all have been waiting for, our red light district,' our guide announced ruefully.

All the males on the bus were glued to the windows. Three low, oblong houses were lit by red lamps from inside, and in their open windows topless girls with bored faces sat in state.

They stared at our bus with complete indifference. Only one waved lazily, and all the men on the bus (me included) waved back frantically. What for? I don't know.

In less than a minute it was all over and we were riding towards the station.

'The girls undergo weekly checks,' the guide announced, as if it could now matter, and added apologetically: 'We have a big single male population in Kalgoorlie, you know.'

This last remark caused a cackle. My neighbour's wife was laughing in her handkerchief. She was watching her disappointed husband triumphantly from the comer of her eye.

The tour lasted about twenty-five minutes and cost $6. One passenger commented that this was the world's most expensive guide tour. No wonder: we had just had a touch of gold rush.

Another passenger remarked that a visit to one of the three Hay Street establishments would have cost him less. This sounded like a gross exaggeration.

The train rattled away from Kalgoorlie and in no time was again enveloped in darkness. Only the crackling sounds of Kalgoorlie's 6KG radio station were heard from the radio in my compartment. Soon they too disappeared without trace.

Perth

I like arriving in a new city early in the morning when, not yet fully awake, it lazily stretches the muscles of its streets and thoroughfares, just like a human after a good night's sleep. In the morning you can see the city in its real light, without gloss, with all its night-time warts.

The Indian Pacific was moving through the outskirts of Perth.

It was a fine sunny morning, and the city looked like a sunlit Eldorado after the long journey across the Nullarbor. The onion dome of a gracious Russian Orthodox church swam past my window. Then, on the wall of a hotel, I saw a printed sign: 'Authentic Melbourne Strippers.'

The streets were spotlessly, almost lifelessly, clean. There were no 'night-time warts' to be seen. A resident told me later that each morning between four and five o'clock special washing cars splash the streets clean with water. It was 7am already, and the cars were nowhere to be seen.

Perth has several nicknames: the city of lights, the sunshine city, the city of the America's Cup, the most isolated city in Australia. The locals, for some reason, like to call themselves sandgropers. But for me, from the beginning, Perth acquired the charm of a bright and cheerful teenage boy, smiling at the rest of Australia from across the Nullarbor.

How can I call someone who is 162 years old a teenager? To prove my point, let me take you for a short walk around the city.

The city looks like a boy's big toy, a working model of Manhattan, only many times smaller and cleaner. The similarity will become even more evident if you look at the city from the Swan River, a sparkling Western Australian Hudson.

And where is the Statue of Liberty, you may ask? Here it is. Only, for some reason, Perth's Liberty is chained to the wall of a house. She is made of wax and waves her electric torch tirelessly and mechanically. The lamp inside the torch is blinking temptingly.

We are now in Northbridge, a Perth suburb, a cosmopolitan melting-pot of restaurants and nightclubs, a sort of a local Soho. The chained Statue of Liberty guards the entrance of an American restaurant with the frightening name Trains, Planes and Automobiles. Here you can have a peaceful dinner facing a train engine, built into a wall, with an old Mercedes hanging from the ceiling above your table. During the meal you will be blinded repeatedly by rotating flashlights.

What? You don't like the idea? Teenagers do. They fill this motorised restaurant to the brim every evening. Even the theoretical probability of getting petrol instead of sauce with the main course one day would not drive them away.

Northbridge, the teenage suburb, is the heart of Perth, the teenage city. Teenagers like hot food, clowns and loud music, and Northbridge abounds with all these. Street musicians, jesters and open-air eateries with deafening sounds of rock music coming out – this is the portrait of night-time in Northbridge.

Apart from entertainment, teenagers have a fascination with someone else's wealth. This explains the poorly hidden pride with which the people in Perth speak of Alan Bond.

'This is the house where Bond lived ... This is the yacht which he built ... When Alan Bond won the America's Cup ...' they keep saying with obvious pleasure. 'Bond is in real trouble now,' they sometimes add with genuine sympathy.

It is quite possible, though, that the teenage city is on the way to having a new hero, or rather anti-hero – Brian Burke. I would not be surprised: teenagers are not capable of strong affiliations. They cannot be faithful to the same idol for a long time, being constantly in need of fresh ones.

Here is the so-called Millionaires' Row, the object of unceasing local admiration. It comprises incredibly expensive palaces and mansions facing the Swan River. The first thing you will see here is the house of Alan Bond, which resembles a large Pizza Hut with its curved oriental roof.

With genuine pride, the youthful locals will show you the six-week-a-year holiday retreat of a Malaysian millionaire, a shack with five bathrooms and a couple of swimming pools.

They will point out the $32 million Lang Hancock house, the most expensive piece of private property in Australia, and will certainly add that countless bathrooms of this house are equipped with electric backscratchers.

Teenagers are not allowed to gamble, but they like the idea. In Perth you will hear lots of stories about millions of dollars lost or won at the local Burswood casino with the largest gambling pit in the Southern Hemisphere where, among other things, people play such an utterly childish game as two-up.

I liked the story of an old woman who spent forty-eight hours on end at the casino without realising it: Australia's largest pit has neither clocks nor windows. She was found by police, alerted by relatives who had reported her missing.

Tired? Then we can take Daryl Crosby's old Perth tram, which is in fact not a tram, but a bus, disguised as a tram – a very boyish thing to do. Driving this unusual tram-bus, Daryl Crosby, in a vivacious boyish manner, will tell you many more gripping stories about Perth, this eternally young, effervescent city on the shores of the Indian Ocean. The city which became for me one of the living incarnations of the Australian spirit.

Kangaroo Island

'Blue and green waves are running into the shore, changing their colours in the wind like millions of chameleons ... Somewhere, very far away, there must be the land of Dolphinia and Kangaroo Island.'

These are words from a popular song, 'Dolphinia,' by Novella Matveyeva, a well-known Moscow romantic poet and composer. In her search for a romantic image she could probably never imagine that there might be a genuine Kangaroo Island somewhere on our guilty earth.

For an average Muscovite or a Leningrader, Kangaroo Island sounds like a fairy tale name, too exotic to exist. Something like Ali Baba's Cave.

I was lucky to visit this fairy tale, to plunge into Matveyeva's romantic song and spend the whole day there.

My plunge into the fairy tale started on a rainy Adelaide morning with the flight of a tiny Cessna 402. I was one of four passengers on this Air Kangaroo Island (no kidding, there's such a local airline in Adelaide) flight. There were no security checks for the passengers, which put me on the alert. 'First stop American River,' the pilot announced, putting on his earphones. My first thought was that he was a disguised terrorist who, instead of flying us to Kangaroo Island, wanted to hijack our Cessna to some obscure river in the United States. And I didn't want to go to America ...

Sitting next to the pilot in a tiny cabin I kept imagining myself in the role of West German youngster Matthias Rust, who landed his Cessna in Red Square in Moscow in 1987. Not that I particularly wanted to land in Red Square either. I simply could not help the associations ...

Never before have I flown on a plane as small as that. To make things worse, it was raining heavily. Streams of water were hitting us from all sides, and at times it was not clear whether our Cessna was a two-engined plane floating in the sky above the sea or a little submarine submerged into that very sea under the grey rain-soaked sky.

'When landing on the water, you may be required to remove shoes,' I read in the safety instructions and quickly removed my shoes – just in case we were already in the water. 'What's the reason for taking off one's shoes after a sea landing?' I was thinking. 'If you have to dive underwater, you wouldn't care about keeping your shoes dry, would you?'

Finally the pilot, who no longer looked like a terrorist, began slowly pulling the joy-stick towards his chest as if trying to hug it, and the plane started landing. I looked down, and to my horror did not see either an airfield or even an airstrip. The waves were pounding the rocky coast of the quickly approaching island and breaking into heaps of bubbling foam.

We were landing straight on a dirt track. I closed my eyes getting ready for a crash, but instead of sounds of crumbling glass and metal, I heard a man's voice: 'Who is Vitali here?'

I was met by a lanky sun-tanned young man. His name was Craig Wickham, and he was to be my host for the day.

In his new four-wheel-drive vehicle, we roamed the island far and wide. Craig Wickham can be called a full-blooded Kangaroo Islander: he has spent most of his life there. On graduating from Adelaide University, he worked as a ranger and then opened his own business taking tourists around the island. He knows the place like the back of his hand and has a purely domestic attitude towards it. He will stop his car to pick up the smallest piece of paper lying on the road; he greets every islander with a wave, be it an animal or a human being.

Mr Wickham feels at home here, and the last time he left the place was twelve months ago. Even his girlfriend works for Air Kangaroo Island.

The island is 145 kilometres long and thirty kilometres wide.

The population is 4,000. The island has four airports (with only three airstrips, as far as I could see), eighteen national parks, 243 species of birds, thirty-five species of eucalyptus, 400 farms, three schools, four doctors, three policemen, two local councils and only one Craig Wickham.

Some of the birds come from as far as Siberia to spend winter on Kangaroo Island and then fly back home. I envy these birds: their life is much simpler than ours.

As to the island's three guardians of law and order, they probably have the quietest police job in the world: crime is non-existent on Kangaroo Island, where everyone knows everyone else by his first name. There's nothing much for them to do, except try to stop koalas consuming too many eucalyptus leaves and getting intoxicated enough to present a threat to public order.

The last serious accident here occurred several months ago when the little son of a local farmer was playing with his father's lighter and accidentally started a fire that destroyed 250 hectares of forest. The little arsonist got away scot-free: the three policemen only shook their index fingers at him in reproof.

As to the two local councils for just 4,000 islanders, I think it's a sure sign of Australian bureaucracy successfully competing with its Soviet counterpart, at least in numbers.

Whenever someone in Australia writes about Kangaroo Island, they write about the seals that have become the main moving landmark of the place. There's nothing much I can add here. I was not particularly impressed by the seals. For me they were just a cross between a garden slug and a cow (creeping like slugs and mooing like cows).

As to kangaroos, emus and koalas, just the same, I can hardly say anything new. There are lots of them on the island and they are all lovely; that's all.

I have always had a taste for unusual detail that can tell you more about a place than heaps of guidebooks. While driving across the island, I was fascinated by old refrigerators standing here and there along the country roads next to mailboxes.

Craig Wickham explained that the island postmen, apart from bringing mail, also deliver food to remote villages. They put the food in an old fridge, used simply as a closet, to protect the food from feral cats and other naughty animals.

One more curious detail of islander life. One of the island's lighthouses is served by two families living in two houses next to the lighthouse. There are no more people for dozens of miles around. Once the two families quarrelled and didn't speak to each other for eight months.

I'll never forget our lunch in Flinders Chase National Park. In no time Craig Wickham prepared a barbecue out of nothing (this is a peculiarly Australian skill that I still have to master). We were eating in the open air, inside a little metallic enclosure that looked like a cage. And outside, watching as we ate, were emus, kangaroos, brush turkeys, peacocks, white pelicans and black cockatoos.

It was the closest thing to a human zoo, in which we, two adult *Homo sapiens*, were the exhibits.

Chewing a barbecue lunch in the cage surrounded by native animals, I felt acutely as never before that I was indeed in Australia, and this fairy tale was for real.

Flying back in a slightly bigger plane and looking down at the receding island, I was humming Novella Matveyeva's song: 'Somewhere, very far away, there must be the land of Dolphinia and Kangaroo Island … ' Now I knew exactly how right she was. Only the poet has never been to her fancy land. And I have.

Craig Wickham assured me that I was the first ever Russian visitor to Kangaroo Island.

Rottness Island

Travelling in south and Western Australia, I tried all kinds of transport: long-distance trains and buses, planes and boats, cars and hovercraft. While on Rottnest Island, I added two more to this list: bicycle and submarine.

Yes, the first thing I did on arrival at this earthly paradise (one-and-a-half hours by boat from Perth) was plunge under the surface of the Indian Ocean on board the *Underwater Explorer*, a little fancy submarine.

It was stormy, and the water beyond the submarine's windows was murky and opaque. That is why we were unable to see the shipwrecks and the coral reefs and had to be satisfied with only one item on the program, advertised as 'fish school.'

Suddenly our submarine was surrounded by hundreds of fish, and it was difficult to say who were students and who were teachers in this school.

It was rough indeed, and the sea looked sombre and uninviting. I had to give up the idea of having a swim in the Indian Ocean, which sounded great but was a little bit too ambitious in weather like that. So I straddled a bike and went for a ride around the island instead.

On my way, I kept bumping into whole families on bicycles, making their way to the beach or to the shopping centre. Bikes are the only private means of transport on the island. Even toddlers were riding bicycles, which made me think that the children must first learn to ride a bike and then to walk.

At one curve in the road, I nearly ran over a very strange little creature – a cross between an oversized rat and an undersized wallaby.

This was the famous quokka, thanks to which the island got its name. When Commodore Willem de Vlaming, a Dutch captain, landed on the island in 1696, he was greeted by hundreds of fluffy and friendly quokkas, which he understandably mistook for rats because of their tiny black eyes and ratty tails. Hence the island's name, Rottnest, which in Dutch means 'rat's nest.'

Quokkas are wonderful – lively, cuddly and tame. I gave one a lollipop, it took it into its tiny 'arms,' jumped aside and started crunching like a child.

Quokkas are endemic, which in plain English means you will not find them anywhere else, only on Rottnest Island.

Although I solemnly promised myself before the trip not to buy any mass-market souvenirs (plastic boomerangs, koala key-holders and fridge magnets with the inscription 'It's hot as hell in Cook, SA'), I could not resist the temptation and bought myself a toy quokka in a souvenir shop.

At some point I saw several dozen people crowding on a cliff in Thomson Bay. They were looking down at the beach, where three young men were fishing. Three tourist buses with their engines idling were standing nearby. As it turned out, the young men were the drivers of these buses, and tourist guides, too.

'They have been fishing here for fifty minutes already,' one elderly man complained, 'and we have to wait and watch.' After a while, the drivers climbed up the cliff. They were in a bad mood, since they had not caught anything. The tourists hurried to their buses, the engines snorted angrily and the tour resumed. 'What a wonderful way for the driver-guides to spend their working time!' I thought and remembered Chekhov's words to the effect that the time you spend fishing is not included in your lifespan.

Could it be so that the drivers were Chekhov fans? But what about the tourists, for whom the time spent waiting and watching was definitely included in their tour?

It is interesting that this holiday island started many years ago as a prison. Most of the buildings were designed by one man, Henry Vincent, the superintendent of Rottnest Prison from 1839 to 1855.

Apart from convicts, obnoxious boys from Europe were sent for up to six months to be re-educated. The former boys' reformatory building is one of the island's landmarks.

I can imagine how English mothers of the last century kept scaring their disobedient scions: 'If you don't behave, they'll send you to Rottnest Island!' For a modern Australian child, Rottnest Island is a reward, a bonanza, not a bugaboo. Well, punishments change and mischievous children remain.

I did not notice how I terminated my round-the-island journey and returned to the pier. With a sigh (who knows when I'll be able to ride again?), I climbed off the bike and boarded the boat.

I was very anxious not to reveal my souvenir quokka, being sure that other passengers would start making fun of me for having bought such a down-market thing. But my fears proved superfluous: every other tourist, boarding the boat, was holding a green plastic bag with a plastic quokka in it. The tourists were waving their bags going up the gangplank; the toy quokkas were jumping inside as if they were alive.

This souvenir animal is now standing on a bookshelf in my study. It is watching me steadily when I write my articles. From time to time I stand up from my desk and give it a lollipop.

Fremantle

From Barrack Street Jetty in Perth I took a Captain Cook Cruise boat, ingeniously named *Captain Cook*, to Fremantle.

In my imagination, the name Captain Cook has always been associated with rough seas, unpopulated islands, geographic discoveries and incredible adventures, including the possibility of being eaten by hungry savages.

On board the *Captain Cook* there was no danger of ending up in someone else's tummy, but there was a wonderful opportunity to stuff your own with a good lunch and a glass of wine served in the saloon. The discoveries were limited to locating the best piece of chicken on the plate. As to the adventures, the most exciting thing that could theoretically happen to you was getting a chicken bone stuck in your throat, if you were not careful.

So I was carefully munching my chicken and sipping wine while the boat was sliding softly down the Swan River, past the notorious Millionaires' Row, to the harbour of Fremantle.

Twenty-five years ago Fremantle was one of the biggest passenger ports in the world. Long and exhausting sea voyages of many migrants from Europe used to terminate here. Thus Fremantle provided the first glimpse of Australia for the country's future citizens. It was like Australia's visiting card, and in this capacity it must have been quite impressive. This wasn't a tattered, bleak visiting card of a journalist or a taxi driver, printed on rough, flimsy paper. This was rather a glossy gold-framed card of a prosperous businessman. The place was bursting with life and was growing quickly.

With the reopening of the Suez Canal, Fremantle's importance started dwindling, and soon it turned into just a tourist place, almost a ghost town, still beautiful and full of charm, but living solely in the past. The town started to resemble a retired captain of an ocean liner, smoking his pipe and telling colourful stories of his past adventures over a glass of beer in a pub.

The main passengers in Fremantle port now are sheep. A huge sheep ship, the *Fernanda F*, was moored in the harbour. It looked like a floating block of Khrushchev flats – notoriously cramped and uncomfortable pre-fab units built in the Soviet Union in millions on Khrushchev's orders – or a beehive. It was a sheep-hive, to be more exact.

Fremantle, formerly (again formerly!) a home of the America's Cup, is now a home to several hundred crocodiles, accommodated in the local Crocodile Park. I was quite surprised to read the crocodiles' feeding schedule above the park's front entrance. According to this schedule, the large adult crocodiles are fed at 2pm, whereas the subadults (!) are fed at 11am. So there are subs even among crocodiles.

Inside, the atmosphere was close to that of crocodile buffoonery, if you can imagine such a thing. The large-toothed buffoons' names were Bismarck, Nelson and even Rasputin.

Instead of speaking Russian, though, the reptile Rasputin spoke an Aussie TV-commercial version of English. 'Hi, I am mean, spiteful and cranky!' the plate on his cage ran. His mate Bismarck was no better: 'Hi, I am Bismarck, and I am top crocodile here. I am seventy years old, but feel forty …'

This kind of style is probably contagious. It has definitely affected the park's administrators, who composed the following big-lettered warning for the visitors: 'Beware!! This fearsome crocodile can kill you, your wife and your children and come back for your dog!' Ha ha.

I must say that crocodiles and their minders are not the only beings in Fremantle with a dry sense of kindergarten black humour. Lunching in the Oyster Beds restaurant above the Swan River, I was taken aback by the following sign, displayed in the main eating hall: 'Persons falling in the river do so on their own risk. No responsibility is taken for any personal property.'

Fed up with puzzling signs and inscriptions, I remained sceptical when in the port I saw a tent with a sign reading 'Huge White Shark Is On Display Here.' I thought it was another subadults' subjoke, but it was not. Inside, Paul Cornley, a naturalist and a shark hunter, had arranged a small but informative exhibition that could be called 'Everything You Want to Know About Sharks.' Among other instructive exhibits, it contained a surfboard with a huge chunk bitten off by someone with very sharp teeth, possibly a shark. At the same time, Paul Comley assured me that sharks could be very domestic and could even miss their owners. He said that he had kept two sharks in an aquarium at his house for a while, and when he was out they refused to eat, but as soon as he appeared on the threshold they would gobble everything around them in an obvious manifestation of joy.

What about Fremantle itself, you may ask? Well, I can say that it's quiet and moody, and that the beauty of its port is equalled only by Constitution Dock in Hobart, although Fremantle is many times bigger.

But my main impressions of the place consist of sailing sheep, domestic sharks and witty crocodiles. These may certainly seem rather skin-deep, but they don't pretend to finality. I simply had a quiet day aimlessly walking around Fremantle, the former visiting card of Australia.

Part Six
Islands and Islets

The Channel Islands

Swastika badges and swastika bookmarks. Key rings, made of war-time German bullets. Pencil-sharpeners in the shape of Nazi fighter planes and warships. Audio tapes of 'Hitler's Radio Addresses to the Third Reich' (a set of two) and 'Music of the Third Reich.' Facsimile copies of the war-time German newspapers, occupation maps and orders of the German military commandants. Occupation postcards (sets of eight) featuring German troops marching in the streets of a small English town.

This is a random sample of souvenirs an inquisitive tourist can now obtain on the Channel Islands, the only part of British territory occupied during the second world war. And books, of course. The book section of De Gruchy supermarket in St Helier alone offers over twenty-five 'occupation titles' including *A Child's War* by Molly Bihet, *Recollections Of Two Blind Boys In Wartime Guernsey* by Neville Tostevin and *A Collection Of Occupation Recipe*s by Lillie Aubin Morris.

Significantly, it is impossible to buy these books outside the Channel Islands. Likewise, on the islands themselves you cannot get a copy of *Island Of Dread*, a heart-turning memoir by Georgi Kondakov, one of the hundreds of Russian prisoners-of-war who ended up as German 'slave labourers' on the island of Alderney.

There seems to be a peculiar pride in the islands about the fact that they were occupied by the Nazis. This is slightly disconcerting for the rest of the world, which has been brought up to regard them with nothing but horror and hurt. Indeed, Jersey has more occupation museums than anywhere in the world. In St Helier – a small town with a population of under 50,000 – there are at least five 'occupation sites.' Many more are scattered around Jersey, whose total area is just forty-five square miles. There is even an organisation dedicated to remembering the war.

'Not all the Germans were Nazis,' says Michael G, secretary of the Channel Islands Occupation Society, an organisation created in the 1960s with the aim of collecting and preserving German war-time relics.

According to G, the members of the society promote 'reconciliation between former enemies.' But whereas there is nothing wrong with reconciliation between Britain and Germany, there can never be any 'reconciliation' with the ideology of Nazism, the elements of which most of the 'occupation sites' unwillingly promote. In modern Germany, by the way, any public display of Nazi symbols is deemed illegal.

Apart from collecting Nazi relics, the Occupation Society publishes a glossy annual *Channel Islands Occupation Review*, which invariably spells the word 'Occupation' with a capital 'O.'

A good deal of space in its latest issues was devoted to attacking Madeleine Bunting, who has written a book about the occupation, for exaggerating German atrocities and the degree of local collaboration with the enemy.

'Such journalism is merely following a tradition of propagandistic reporting about the horrors of Nazi occupation,' fumes the journal's 1997 issue.

G insists that 'Bunting wrote her book to the agenda' and that she 'co-operated with David Cesarani,' a respected British professor of Jewish history, in trying to blame the locals for the fate of the Channel Islands Jews. 'There was no SS or Gestapo on the Channel Islands, but too many British journalists came here looking for muck after the war,' he says.

'Of course the Gestapo blokes were here,' objects Marguerite Syvret, who lived on Jersey throughout the occupation, working for the St John Ambulance and was herself denounced to the Gestapo for helping foreign 'slave labourers' by one of her neighbours (the names of local informers are still classified).

The beleaguered tourist boards of both Jersey and Guernsey are falling over themselves to stop the decline of the tourist industry. The number of visitors to the islands in August that year was eight per cent lower than in August 1997, which may explain some of the enthusiasm for these museums.

'Our attitude is hands-on tourism,' explains a Jersey tourism official. What could be more 'hands-on' than wandering around a real German bunker, following the 'jackboot marks' on the concrete floor to the sounds of Horst Wessel? Alderney is the only place on the Channel Islands that has not been turned into an occupation theme-park. Three crumbling stone pillars are the only visible remains of the horrific Sylt concentration camp. In a sad irony, the territory of Norderney labour camp is now occupied by the island's official campsite. There is no trace of the cemetery where foreign 'slave workers' were buried.

'The States (Alderney's governing body) decline to commemorate the sites,' says Colin Partridge, a local historian. In his opinion, this may be due to the locals' desire to dissociate themselves from the accusations of collaboration. A faded memorial plate, tucked away behind the island's parish church, vaguely mentions '45 Soviet citizens who died on Alderney in 1940-45,' without saying how they died and why.

Partridge is convinced that a decent memorial must be built on Alderney. He and a group of enthusiasts have managed to establish the names of all 460 people who perished in the island's four camps. They are planning to unveil a memorial plate with 460 names on it. If they succeed, this is going to be the first real 'occupation site' on Channel Islands – the site commemorating the victims of Nazism's heinous crimes, not their perpetrators.

Note: For the Isle of Man Story, go to Part Three

Tiree

At a time of uncertainty and anxiety, it is good to know that there is still a place in the world where a policeman walks his dogs through the stars.

This is also the place where a postman enters unlocked houses without knocking and leaves the mail on kitchen tables;

- where people sing psalms to seals resting on the rocks;
- where low-built thatched cottages squint at you playfully with their deep-set little windows;
- where a local remedy for blisters is cotton dipped in whisky;
- where in the morning you wake up not from noises, but from silence so deep and deafening that it almost makes your teeth ache …

I am talking about Tiree, the outermost island of the Inner Hebrides archipelago, where I spent several relaxing days in the wake of the horrendous 11 September events in the USA, when the whole world held its breath in grief and fear.

Not that the terrorist attacks didn't have any effect on the islands. On Mull, the most populous and the closest to the mainland, the already high real-estate prices began to rocket. On Tiree, the carriage of mail by the service plane has been suspended, and the locals who normally receive morning newspapers in early afternoon had to wait for the arrival of a late-evening ferry. A local guest-house owner, who had gone on a Transatlantic cruise, got stranded in Boston. And John Brady, the editor of *An Tirisdeach*, the island's fortnightly newsletter, has been showered with questions about the well-being of his North Carolina-based son.

'I cannot look at these planes now,' Charles MacLeash, a pensioner, told me pointing to a silvery dot of a Boeing flying high over the island: Tiree lies on the path of Transatlantic flights to and from the UK, and a mosque-shaped white dome of the radar station, locally known as 'golf-ball,' is its main man-made landmark.

And yet my time on the Hebrides could be best compared to a three-day-long exposure to the 'relaxation tape' which I bought shortly after the tragic September events. While still in London, I tried to beat the stress by listening to a deep-voiced shrink (ironically, he had an American accent) urging me to imagine myself in an idyllic place – lying supine in the tall grass and staring into the blue sky, or walking along an empty beach towards the surf. The Hebrides in autumn were a 'relaxation tape' that came to life. Mull's checked forest-covered mountains, touched by contrasting shades of yellow, red and brown, made me think of Scottish Tartan, the very pattern of which had probably been prompted by the Highlands in autumn.

Autumn in the Hebrides is the time when quiet and stillness reign supreme, when most tourists are gone and the strong winter gales that are known to have lifted school-kids off the ground have not yet arrived. It is the season of crisp sunny mornings, of vast all-embracing skies mixing with granite-coloured sea, of stunning schizophrenic sunsets – exorbitant and over-the-top for a solitary viewer having no one to share them with, and of cool whisky-tinted nights, when a lonely island policeman walks his dogs through the pimple-like stars.

The dog-walking policeman is neither a metaphor nor a figment of my writer's imagination. He is a real person whose name is PC Daniel Apsley – the only guardian of law and order for the islands of Coll and Tiree. He took charge of me the moment I stepped onto Tiree soil after the almost four-hour-long ferry crossing from Oban. Because of a Scottish Bank Holiday, all my local contacts were out of reach and their phones were dead. I stood in a red public phone cabin on the pier listening to long dispassionate tones until a uniformed policeman knocked at the glass and asked whether he could help.

'Don't you have answer-phones on Tiree?' I asked him sardonically.

'No, we don't,' he replied. 'There's no need. People are likely to bump into each other the moment they leave their houses.'

He offered me a lift to my guest-house, about eight miles away.

All roads on Tiree, an island ten miles long and one to six miles wide, were single-track, and the rare passing vehicles waited patiently in special road pockets for our police van to go by. Daniel waved to each of the drivers, and they waved back. It looked as if he knew all 720 residents of the island personally – and, in actual fact, he did. As we rode, he would often roll down his window to enquire about their health and families. At some point, a boy in his late teens caught up with us on a bike. On his way to take his driving test, he wanted Daniel to certify his photo. The formality was completed in the nearest road pocket.

'Bicycle is the best means of transport for Tiree,' the policeman remarked as we continued our unhurried progress. 'If you wish, you can hire one from Mr McLane who lives in the croft over there …' Two minutes later, my freshly hired bike was rattling amicably in the back of the police van, where drunks and offenders are routinely carried on the mainland – the observation which I shared with Daniel.

'Crime on the island is virtually non-existent, and houses and cars are normally left unlocked,' he said.

I thought that his job was probably the world's second best police sinecure, the first best being on the Maltese island of Comino, with two policemen for the population of three.

My guest-house, the Glassary, stood in an open field overlooking a rocky bay. As soon as Daniel left to continue his leisurely island beat, I jumped onto the saddle and cycled off 'to where my eyes looked,' as we used to say in Russia, along Tiree's only paved road.

The day was surprisingly warm and sunny, and I was ready to believe that, due to the proximity of the Gulf Stream, Tiree indeed held the UK's sunshine record, although I had heard the same claim in several other places.

Coincidentally, my previous bike ride was in Amsterdam, where I had to veer among cars, trams and absent-minded tourists. Cycling on Tiree was very different. I rode past grazing sheep and stern-looking cows, who gave me (or was it my red sweater?) heavy disapproving stares. Tiree's answer to Amsterdam canals were numerous little lochs, from where flocks of wild geese would take off noisily on my approach. And instead of gable-topped Amsterdam houses, I was whooshing past Tiree's traditional thatch-covered cottages, their neatly combed roofs held down by large round pebbles on ropes – the detail that gave the huts a slightly hip-hop modern look, as if they were wearing bandannas. With their chimneys canted outwards and away from the roof – to minimise any collapse in a storm and to divert sparks from thatch – they also looked like some dare-devil Russian Cossacks in their sheepskin hats.

I dismounted near a detached parish church, built of local pink granite. On its gate, there was a plaque commemorating a Tiree family who emigrated to Canada in 1893 – the time when the population of the island was in the region of 7,000. It has been declining ever since …

'There is not a single tree
On the island of Tiree.'

I was humming this unsophisticated doggerel of my own making (variant: 'Life is totally stress-free, on the island of Tiree'), to the accompaniment of the wind whistling in my ears like a hooligan, all the way back to the guest-house. Indeed, if you don't count three smallish hillocks, Tiree was flat and totally treeless, due to the tireless winter winds ranging between point 8 ('Fresh gale') and point 12 ('Hurricane') on the Beaufort Scale. 'Tiree,' 'treeless,' 'tireless' – I was savouring the melodious alliterations of Tiree which in Gaelic, a nice-sounding and laconic tongue with just eighteen letters in the alphabet, means 'Land of Corn.'

Agitated seagulls were screaming something in Gaelic that evening as I sat at the conservatory of the Glassary's small restaurant. The last tinges of red were lingering in the dark sky like the taste of malt whisky on my palate. On the plate in front of me, one could observe the fourth 'natural' landmark of Tiree – a hillock of haggis, topped with a sharp-edged carrot rash.

The whisky was excellent, and I came to understand why many islanders had flush faces. 'Whisky helps us to beat the wind,' a local woman told me. So the fact that their faces, particularly noses, often resembled badly printed maps of the

London Underground was probably the result of combined effects of whisky and the winds it was supposed to beat.

'It takes time to adjust to the slow pace of the island's life,' Daniel, the policeman, was saying to me next morning from behind the wheel of his private 'civilian' car (it was his day off). A compulsive traveller spending every holiday overseas, he was on the verge of leaving Tiree several times. But each time he eventually changed his mind. 'As I exercise my two dogs on the beach every night I look at the stars – so bright and near you feel you can walk through them. How can one leave a place like this?'

Instead of moving to the mainland, Daniel bought himself a 'summer cottage' on Tiree – a semi-ruin in a secluded part of the island on the very edge of the ocean.

At Daniel's 'main' Tiree house doubling as … the police station, we were eating a sumptuous lunch, cooked by his wife Liz. The tiny police office, complete with a standard detention cell, was next to the family kitchen. 'When Daniel locks someone up, I cook for the detainee too,' Liz said with a smile. 'Luckily, this doesn't happen often.'

I asked Daniel if he had a weapon. 'I do have a truncheon, but I never used it and never will. If I use it even once on Tiree – it will mean I have lost the battle.'

He told me that the island's elderly, who live alone, trust him with spare keys to their houses in case something happens to them. 'If a single person has a stroke, there is no danger that it will go undetected and he or she will die as is often the case on the mainland. Within minutes the alarm will be raised.'

I thought that was probably why the residents of Tiree routinely lived well into their nineties.

I spent the whole of my return journey on the ferry deck watching yet another glorious sunset. I knew what I would do first thing on returning to London – chuck out my 'relaxation tape.' There was no longer a need to imagine an idyllic place where all my worries will disappear as if by magic. Instead, I could simply remember my thirty stress-free hours on the real-life island of Tiree.

When darkness fell and the piercingly bright stars popped out above the sea, I looked up: there, between the Great Bear and the blinking little light of the international space station, was my new friend, the Tiree policeman, walking his dogs along the Milky Way.

The Falklands

I am often asked at public talks and parties what my favourite place in the world is. The answer to that is obvious – London.

No, they say: we mean what place you enjoyed most of all during your travels?

Answering that is not easy. I love all mini-states of Europe, Tasmania, the Channel Islands, the Faroes, Norway, Amsterdam, Perth, Alaska, Salzburg, the Hebrides – both Outer and Inner – and so on and so on …

Yet, my most memorable journey was probably that to the Falklands.

It started with a peculiar RAF flight to Port Stanley.

A civilian to the core of my bones, I have always been puzzled by the military. The only bad mark I got at my Soviet University was in Military Tactics – a compulsory discipline for every high-school student in the jingoistic and paranoid USSR. I remember that among the things we studied were composition and equipment of NATO armies – our potential enemies, the British Army being one of them. Not even in my wildest dreams could I imagine that twenty-odd years later I would be given a chance not only to mix with British servicemen – and women, as political correctness requires us to say these days – better known as squaddies, but also to fly onboard a real RAF jet.

It was the most curious journey in my entire, highly peripatetic, life.

The adventure started in Swindon, Wiltshire, where I was waiting for a bus to take me to RAF Brize Norton airport for a Tristar military flight to Mount Pleasant – the quickest, the cheapest and the only (after the scrapping – or, should I say 'Pinocheting?' – of the only commercial flight from London via Chile) way to get to the Falklands. The bus was late, and I realised with horror that I would be unable to 'report for check-in' by 'the latest reporting time,' specified in strict 'Reporting Instructions JSTC/R2/30,' attached to my ticket. Shifting from one foot to the other, I was nervously, for the umpteenth time, checking the availability of an overnight bag in my cabin luggage: the same Reporting Instructions demanded that every passenger had an overnight bag handy – in case our Tristar gets suddenly diverted to bomb Iraq, or so I thought.

The overnighter was there, but the bus wasn't.

The delay did not seem to worry my fellow-travellers – a large group of vociferous crew-cut youngsters communicating with each other with the help of one f-word only, probably the servicemen (sorry, but there were no women among them), and a handful of confused and dishevelled civilians like myself.

Having finally received my RAF boarding pass: 'rank – none,' I wandered aimlessly around the airport lounge, where only two outlets were open – a tiny newsagent, with an impressive choice of soft-porn magazines, and a note-exchange machine – 'Insert £20 Queen's face up and last.' They were calling out passengers by names in alphabetical order, and for the first time in my life I rejoiced at having a name starting with 'V' which allowed me to have three additional fags before a strictly non-smoking flight.

Twenty minutes after the take-off, plastic cups of 'RAF Fruit Juice' were served, or rather 'distributed,' by muscular stone-faced stewards, who all seemed to stick assiduously to some mysterious no-smiling-under-any-circumstances military regulations. Just like the stewards' faces, the drink was frozen stiff. It melted and became drinkable by next morning, when, to my great relief, I discovered in a seat-pocket in front of me an indispensable 'NATO Stock Number 8105-99-130-2180' air sickness bag.

Next to this thoroughly encoded bag, there was a copy of the RAF in-flight monthly, ingeniously entitled *Inflight*. Compared to it, a glossy safety leaflet in the same seat-pocket read – and looked – like *Hello* magazine.

Soon, we started our descent on Ascension Island, a barren volcanic rock in the middle of the Atlantic, for a refuelling stop and were duly instructed 'on de-planing procedures' over the intercom.

On RAF Ascension, I hesitated in front of a plywood shed with a scary sign 'Terminal Drinks Kiosk' before plunging into Tom Clancy's 'Executive Orders,' a 1,374-page-thick brick of a paperback, which could itself easily prove terminal, if dropped onto your head from a ground-floor window, or in the more unlikely case of being read to end.

The second leg of the flight was not that different from the first one. Same juice, chips and stale rolls with unidentifiable (probably classified) filling were served – sorry, 'distributed' – by a different, yet equally unsmiling, cabin crew. Same peremptory announcements forbidding any movement around the cabin during meal times were made at regular intervals. Same choice of four old videos camouflaged as 'flight entertainment' was offered.

It was hard to believe that the cost of an average ticket to the Falklands was almost twice as high as that of a Qantas flight from London to Melbourne.

'Didn't you know that in their flight documents, the military refer to civilian passengers as SLF – self-loading freight?' a facetious Falkland Islands official, who met me at Mount Pleasant, said as we were waiting for my luggage to arrive.

'You must be joking,' I wanted to say, but choked on my words as I looked at the moving conveyer and spotted my long-awaited weather-beaten backpack. The word 'Civilian' was printed in large letters on a cardboard tag, tied to its handle.

At RAF Mount Pleasant, the Falkland Islands' 'international airport,' the passengers of our Ministry of Defence flight RR3200 were welcomed by blazing summer sunlight and by two unemotional bomb-disposal experts, a Sergeant and a Corporal. In the Arrivals lounge, they showed us the dummies of Argentine land-mines, the sad relics of the 1982 conflict, of which 26,000 still sit unexploded in the Falklands' scarred terrain, and warned that venturing onto a minefield constituted an offence punishable by a £1,000 fine.

I thought that to collect this fine, they would have to collect and put back together all 1,000 pieces of the trespasser first.

The minefields, clearly marked with 'Danger: Mines' and 'Slow: Minefield' signs, lay on both sides of the road to Stanley, the Islands' tiny capital of 2,000 people. In the seventeen years since the conflict, the locals have learnt to live with the mines. On the island of West Falkland, I saw a golf course next to a minefield, and one of the houses in Stanley is adorned with a mock skull-and-crossbones sign: 'Danger: Karl.'

Despite, or maybe because of the minefields surrounding it, there was an immediate charm about Stanley, with its multi-coloured roofs, with its quiet streets running down the hill towards the harbour, with its several little pubs, where some ancient ABBA hits were still played, and all conversation stopped the moment you walked in.

Complete strangers said 'Good morning!' to you in the streets, and soon you started greeting them too. If you forgot about the newly opened Internet Café, this was what a typical British village of yesteryear must have been like. Only this wayward 'village' had split up from its motherland and ended up 8,000 miles away, near the South Pole.

The smallest capital city in the world, Stanley had a life of its own. Shortly before my arrival, the Islands' first zebra crossing appeared in Ross Road – Stanley's main street, outside the Post Office. *Penguin News*, a lively local newsletter, wrote that: 'police are now looking at ways to educate the public in how to use it.'

The residents of Stanley might be still unsure of how to cross the roads, but they did love driving their Land Rovers. Or, maybe, they simply did not like walking. I was constantly offered lifts from Upland Goose Hotel opposite the Post Office, where I stayed, to Malvina House Hotel opposite the Post Office, where I went for lunches and dinners, despite the fact that the hotels were no more than a hundred metres apart.

This puzzling reluctance to walk might lie behind a sudden proliferation of taxis in Stanley, where several years earlier the only cab was the Governor's car, which doubled as a taxi when His Excellency was away or asleep in his stately residence.

Taxis and cars as well as houses were routinely left unlocked in Stanley.

'Familiarity makes crime difficult,' Ken Greenland, the Falkland Islands' police chief, told me in his headquarters, opposite the Post Office. Murder is practically unknown here. When the corpses of two Chinese fishermen were fished out of the sea in the Falklands' territorial waters several months before my arrival, a forensic pathologist had to be flown in from London.

The local Community School was the pride of Stanley, and its oblong modernistic building on top of a hill was the loudest architectural statement in town.

Its state-of-the art classrooms and laboratories were among the best I had ever seen.

But the school's main assets were its 150 pupils – all neat, polite and well behaved. Probably because there were few distractions for them in the Falklands.

'Kids are such a joy here: out of 150, I haven't met a single nasty one. They are such a pleasure to teach,' one of the teachers confided in me.

By 9pm Stanley goes dead. At this time, it is nice to walk along its deserted sea-front, under strange unknown stars, breathing in the amazingly clean and crisp air, listening to splashes of water in the bay and to the gentle rustling of the fern and Diddle-Dee – an indigenous plant similar to heather. During one such walk, when I was ready to believe that I was in Zurbagan, a fictitious town of poets and seafarers created by Russian romantic writer Alexander Grin, I suddenly heard the theme tune of 'The Archers' from a house nearby …

After a couple of days in Stanley, I set out to explore the Camp. A derivative of the Spanish word 'Campo' meaning 'countryside,' the Camp denoted 'everything outside Stanley.'

The area of the Camp, 4,700 square miles, was roughly equal to that of Northern Ireland. These vast expenses of windswept and tree-less land, comprising hundreds of big and small islands, were populated by 800,000 sheep and less than 200 people. With the near absence of roads, the only effective means of communication between the settlements was a small fleet of miniature Islander aircraft, whose pilots also acted as couriers carrying food, letters, money and gossip from one settlement to another.

The Islander that took me from Stanley to Port Howard was also carrying beer, ice-cream, burger-buns and a teenage schoolgirl travelling to her settlement for holidays.

Embarrassingly, not only my backpack, but also its owner had to be weighed up before the boarding, and, naturally, I had to pay for the excess baggage which was myself, no doubt. I suddenly felt like 'a self-loading cargo,' probably even ballast.

Our four-seater was hovering low above the ground, narrowly avoiding hilltops and sharp toothbrush-like rocks. I was rummaging through my pockets in search of airsickness pills and looking down at the barren brownish plane, only occasionally dissected with dirt tracks.

Wherever there was a hut, it meant settlement.

The pilot would then pull the joystick towards his chest, as if trying to bear-hug it, and the Islander would promptly land on a bumpy turf-covered air-strip to be met by two locals in a dusty Land Rover, to which a cart with regulation fire-extinguisher would be dutifully and rather unnecessarily attached. The Islanders were safe, and the only recorded accident happened several years ago, when the plane's chassis got stuck in a penguin burrow on an airstrip during a take-off.

Luckily, the penguin was not at home …

'Port Howard is pretty large,' I was told in Stanley.

What can I say? Einstein was right: everything is relative. In the Camp, where most settlements have the population between two and ten, Port Howard, which numbered over thirty and boasted a store, a school with three pupils and even a tiny War Museum, could be regarded as a huge metropolis and a cultural centre, on a par with Birmingham in Britain, perhaps.

My host was Robin Lee, a farmer and a fifth-generation Falklander, whose great-grandfather came to the Islands as a shepherd in the 1870s. His farm had an area of 200,000 acres – enough to accommodate several European mini-states.

Well-mannered and softly spoken, Robin toiled non-stop from morning 'till night.

His farm's main produce was wool, but with the world wool prices going down, he was desperate to expand and to diversify his sphere of activities. He also helped his partner Hattie, a sophisticated cook from Cumbria, to run the Lodge – a warm and cosy B&B, with by far the best food in the Falklands.

'The most unpopular person here is the one who is not prepared to help others,' he said from behind the wheel of his Land Rover at the start of our quick – only half-a-day-long – drive around his farm.

To illustrate his point, he showed me an abandoned hut that used to belong to Mrs McCuskie, who lived there on her own in the 1980s. Coincidentally, it was straight above her house – the only dwelling for miles around – that the antediluvian telephone wires used to – literally – cross, and Mrs McCuskie volunteered to act as a telephone exchange operator answering phone calls at any hour of day and night and putting the callers through to their destinations. Only God knows how many lives she has helped to save and how many problems to solve. Mrs McCuskie had been dead for several years, and with the Cable & Wireless now operating in the Falklands, people could communicate without intermediaries, but the selfless lady was still fondly remembered in the Islands, and the bay of the Charters River, where Robin and I went fishing, was named after her.

And what wonderful fishing it was! Having hardly learnt to cast, I was able to catch five large spangled sea trout within just forty minutes. The fish could not wait to swallow my Silver Toby spoon-bait.

'Time you spend fishing is not included into your life span,' Chekhov once wrote. Indeed …

On the way back to the lodge, Robin showed me the wreck of an Argentine Mirage plane, with the paint on its twisted fuselage still untainted – a reminder of how relatively recent the Conflict was. A small crater nearby was filled with rainwater, and two silvery Steamer ducks were floating happily on the surface of this man-made mini-pond – a triumph of Nature's common sense over the cruel irrationality of war.

Having spent some time on Sea Lion Island, I started having difficulty with the term 'wildlife.'

The abundance of birds and animals on this tiny – five miles long and one-and-a-half miles wide – islet was such that after a while you start perceiving them as the main – and only – legitimate form of life, and a handful of visiting humans as a superfluous and largely unnecessary link in the chain of evolution.

It was our hectic life in overcrowded smoky cities that suddenly seemed wild to me.

Wandering on my own along the beaches, I did not feel alone for a second, for I was rubbing shoulders with thousands of red-nosed Gentoo penguins walking to and fro past me in their black-and white business outfits like leisurely lunch-time shoppers in Oxford Street, bumping into each other and into myself and moving on without apologies. They were demonstratively ignoring me, and I was ignoring them until I inadvertently stepped into a puddle of their droppings – the stinkiest stuff I have ever come across, let alone stepped in.

It took me a good half-hour of rubbing my trainers with 'Travelwash' back at Sea Lion Lodge to get rid of the all-permeating stench.

And the elephant seals – these huge (up to four tons each) tubs of fat with smallish by comparison feline faces – lying supine on the sand and snoring like drunken octogenarians in a nursing home. They were all males – enjoying themselves while females – each male had up to 120 in his harem – were busy procuring food and bringing up pups. What a life!

The seals did seem clumsy, lethargic and too heavy to move – a cross between a garden slug and a cow.

One feels tempted to pat a seal on his oily belly or even to carve some graffiti on his uncomplaining back. But this impression is deceiving. The seals can be extremely agile, when in danger or hurt. Some time ago, a man from Stanley stumbled accidentally across one and had a buttock bitten off as a result.

I heard he had problems maintaining his balance when sitting ever since.

While on Sea Lion Island, I seriously wished I were a birdwatcher.

But even the absence of a spy-glass, a silly Panama hat and other essential birdwatcher's equipment could not stop me from actually **watching** all these Rock Cormorants, Black-Necked Swans, Red-Beaked Oystercatchers, Striated Caracaras, Turkey Vultures, whom I came to call Cookie Monsters – they did look pretty monstrous: the head of turkey and the body of an eagle – their names alone could make any aspiring British birdwatcher cringe.

As for a spyglass, one actually didn't need it, for most of the birds were totally unafraid of humans and were easily approachable.

I got quite used to tiny black Tussock birds pecking matter-of-factly at my shoes.

But the bird that I truly fell in love with was the famous Upland Goose. There are only about 300 of them left in South America, but in the Falklands they are still present in their thousands. You can see them everywhere: crossing the main street in Stanley, mingling with sheep in the Camp, or bravely waddling across a minefield.

The thing that attracted me about Upland Geese was not just their natural grace and beauty – they have long necks, shapely bodies and lovely striped feathers – but their devotion to their families. Upland Geese mate for life and always walk and fly either in couples, or in extended families of four or five. They are very protective of each other, and males always hurry to the rescue of their partners, when the latter are in danger – what a difference to the blatant male chauvinism of elephant seals (and of some of the humans)!

I couldn't help admiring these wonderful birds and thinking that by creating them Nature was trying to teach us humans a lesson.

In the Falklands' Government Archives in Stanley, I was shown a bulky folder of hand-written dispatches to London from Richard Moody, the Islands' first British Governor. In Dispatch 13 of 1842, he writes: 'The settlers best adapted to colonise these Islands would be from among the industrious population of the Orkneys and the Shetlands, accustomed to a hardy life and as much seamen as landmen ...'

This observation stood true over a century-and-half later: the Falklanders remained a special breed.

Torn away from their historic motherland, they nevertheless were tirelessly clinging to their roots defying the notorious 'tyranny of distance.' They were flexible, hard working, extremely adaptable and always happy to help each other.

Just like in the days of Governor Moody, when people in isolated settlements did not see any fellow humans for months on end, they still greeted their guests with substantial 'smoko' – tea with mountains of home made cookies. Just like in the past, they were always happy to provide shelter for their fellow outcasts from all over the world – that was probably why I felt almost at home in the Falklands.

And the country itself has the hardy resilient character of its first settlers: in a matter of years, despite the war and the continuing intimidation, it had travelled a long way – from a semi-forgotten impoverished outpost of the shrunk British Empire to the prosperous and self-sufficient state, with one of the world's highest gross domestic product.

Interestingly, among 250 or so 'land-based' visitors coming to the Islands each year there were a number of escapists. Travelling in the Camp, I came across recent divorcees, who had come to the Islands 'to recover'; the bereaved, grieving over the loss of a loved one; and simply dreamers fleeing the suffocating reality of modern Europe and America.

Remember Oscar Wilde: 'Society can forgive a murderer, but it never forgives a dreamer?'

The Falklands forgive dreamers. This distant country, whose soil is stuffed with unexploded landmines, gives them a warm welcome, a hearty smoko and coveted peace of mind.

Is it because, in their heart of hearts, the hardy Falklanders are themselves all dreamers?

One has to be one to be playing golf next to a minefield …[19]

[19] In November 2020 – nearly 40 years after the conflict – it was reported that the Falklands had been cleared of nearly all the landmines.

The Faroes

It is not easy to find a more football-crazy nation than the Faroe Islands, a tiny Nordic country of 50,000 people and 80,000 sheep.

The tiny archipelago of eighteen barren volcanic islands in the North Atlantic has over 400 men's and twenty-five women's football teams. All of them – including the country's national squad – are amateurs, playing football after (and sometimes before, but never instead of) work.

A sand or an artificial turf football pitch can be found in every single village, no matter how small. To build such a space in the Faroes, where the only natural patch of flat surface is reserved for the country's only airport (with the world's shortest runway, by the way) is not an easy task. In many cases, nearby mountains had to be excavated by the determined villagers.

By far the biggest day of fame in the history of Faroese football, if not in the whole of the country's history, was 12 September 1990, when the Faroese national team of amateurs defeated Austria 1:0 in their first European Championship qualifying game.

The victory, which was later labelled one of the biggest shocks in international soccer records, was achieved on a neutral field in Landskrona, Sweden, although officially it was the Faroes' home game: the other three members of the qualifying group refused point-blank to play in the Faroes, despite the fact that the first REAL grass pitch (it cost the country one more mountain) was built specifically for the tournament in the village of Toftir. The excuses varied from difficulties of travel to the unpredictable weather, with changeable wind making the players kick the ball in one direction and run in another (something Ireland's players should bear in mind when confronting the Faroese on their territory next June).

The reverberations of the sixty-third minute victorious shot were heard throughout the world.

For the Austrians, it was perhaps the biggest humiliation since the *Anschluss*. 'Resign, Waldheim!' the headlines in all eight (!) Faroese daily newspapers yelled. Indeed, it was hard to imagine that one of the world's best professional football teams could be defeated by a bunch of part-timers from the top of a cliff in the middle of the Atlantic Ocean

Eventually, it was not Chancellor Kurt Waldheim, but Josef Hickberger, the Austrian manager, who had to resign (Waldheim followed in his footsteps later – after his murky Nazi past was revealed).

In the Faroes, a national holiday was declared. 5,000 chain-dancers[20] came to meet their heroes at Vagar airport. 'Now it's the turn of the Danes!' the triumphant and belligerent Pal Gudlaugsson, the winning team's manager, announced to the cheering crowds, having in mind their next qualifier with Denmark.

But miracles do not happen twice (otherwise they wouldn't be called miracles): the Faroese team didn't make it into the finals.

Once, however, was certainly enough for the game's two protagonists: a timber-office clerk, Torkil Nielsen, who scored the winning goal, and a lorry driver and part-time goalkeeper, Jens Martin Knudsen, who prevented the Austrians from scoring a good dozen of theirs. Overnight, they became the country's most popular celebrities, and Knudsen's bobble hat, worn during the match, was elevated into a national symbol, no less – on a par with the Canadian maple leaf, Scottish thistle, Irish shamrock and England's laxative pill.

That bobble (or pom-pom, of you wish) hat had acquired a history of its own. It was knitted by the future hero's granny at the suggestion of a doctor, to protect the fourteen-year-old Jens Martin's poor head from being kicked by his junior soccer teammates, who must have been repeatedly mistaking it for a football. Since then, Knudsen was seldom seen on a football pitch without it (I mean his bobble hat of course). 'Once, early on, I forgot to wear it and had a bad match,' he confessed in one of his interviews.

A couple of months after that historic game with Austria, two visiting Norwegians stole the pom-pom mascot from Knudsen's unlocked house (they don't have locks on the houses in the Faroes – on some heads, yes, but not on houses).

Luckily, the thieves were promptly apprehended at Vagar airport (the country's only point of fast escape), and the hat was duly returned onto the locks of its legitimate owner.

This was the third recorded robbery in the whole of the Faroese history.

* * *

In Tórshavn, the picturesque Faroese capital, I had a chance to sit in the Speaker's chair in the Løgting, the Faroese ancient parliament (which was not in session of course), the origins of which can be traced back more than 1,000 years, when a shipload of Vikings stumbled upon the umbrella-shaped Faroese archipelago on their way to Iceland. According to some sources, they were simply too seasick to continue their journey, and chose to settle on the islands, driving out the wandering Irish monks who had lived there since the seventh century AD.

[20] Chain dance is a long and monotonous Faroese folk bop, in which the dancers gradually whip themselves up into a trance.

The Løgting, where, in line with the Home Rule Act of 1948, only Faroese internal matters are supposed to be debated by thirty-two local MPs (foreign policy and executive power are in the hands of the Danish crown), sits in a black log cabin with a turf roof in the centre of Tórshavn. All procedures in it are conducted in the Faroese language – a derivative from old Norse and West Norwegian, now recognised as the main language of the Faroe islands (until 1938, it was forbidden to teach it at schools: Danish had been the only official tongue in the Faroes since 1400).

The Danes treated Faroese language as a small regional dialect. For centuries, it remained just a popular spoken tongue, and there was no literature in it until 1890.

This is no longer the case. One of the most amazing sides of modern Faroese culture is the number of books (150 titles a year!) written and published in the native language. Shakespeare, Dostoyevsky and even Homer's hexameters have been translated into Faroese by local enthusiasts. The mini-state of 50,000 also publishes eight (!) daily newspapers in Faroese.

The biggest problem the Faroese faced when trying to recreate their old tongue and turn it into a written language was the absence of words for such modern notions as 'television,' 'video,' 'computer,' 'compact disc' and so on. Instead of using foreign borrowings, they decided to come up with some genuine Faroese neologisms. Thus a computer became *telda* – from *tal* (number); a computer screen – *skiggi*, from the sheep's stomach stretched across the smoke-holes in the rook of traditional Faroese houses to keep out the rain and let in light (predecessors of windows). And

the now-defunct compact disc was baptised *flöga* – from round wooden pancakes put under haystacks!

The Shetlands

The painfully familiar Cyrillic letters were crabbed and uneven – as if battered by gales. A Russian sign was the last thing I had expected to see in Lerwick – the wind-swept 'capital' of the Shetland Islands. Yet there it was: '**DOM NADEZHDI**,' and underneath – the English translation: 'The House of Hope.'

The house in Mounthooly Street used to belong to the Norwegian Seamen's Mission – a religious charity looking after the crews of Norwegian fishing vessels during their visits to Lerwick Port. In the late 1980s-early 1990s, flotillas of Soviet (then Russian) *klondykers* – floating fish-processing factories – came to Lerwick to buy mackerel from Shetland fishermen. This was when 'The House of Hope' became also **'DOM NADEZHDI'** offering a cup of tea and a bible to every Russian who would venture inside.

Russian fishermen stopped coming to Lerwick in 1996, and the only Russian visitors to Shetland these days are migratory birds (I don't count myself among them) and the bitter northern wind, which, as the locals assured me more than once in a mildly accusatory sort of way, always blew from Russia – the fact that invariably (and for no clear reason) made me cringe a little.

The Russian house-sign was one of many unexpected discoveries I made in Shetland, Scotland's northernmost archipelago. They started long before I boarded a miniature two-engine plane to Sumburgh, the islands' main airport, with a breath-takingly short runway at the very edge of the North Sea surf. On most maps, the Shetlands were plonked in a box somewhere near Aberdeen. Only after looking at my son's globe, I got a proper perspective: the tiny specks of land were closer to Bergen than to Edinburgh, and, in proportion to the size of their Scottish mainland, a journey there was an equivalent of a trip from Moscow to Vladivostok in Russia, or from Melbourne to Darwin in Australia. What better place to start my exploration of Scotland from?

The fresh issue of *The Shetland Times*, the islands' weekly tabloid, which I had bought in Edinburgh, was gruesome reading. The Shetlands had just been hit by a succession of disasters: their two major industries, oil and fishing, were in deep trouble – the former due to massive job cuts at the Sullom Voe Oil Terminal, the latter – because of the draconian cod and white fish catching quotas imposed by Brussels. Almost simultaneously, a major local construction firm collapsed with the loss of many jobs, and the islands' council was pressing ahead with the proposed school closures. This negative build-up brought to mind a joke about the Russian Pessimist, who said that life was so bad that it couldn't possibly get worse, to which the Russian Optimist retorted cheerfully that it could, it certainly could!!!

The stories on just one page of the same paper were: 'Tanks stolen from boats,' 'Light vandalised,' 'Man arrested,' 'Man injured,' 'Laundry stolen.' Against this sombre background, the headline 'Driver swerved to avoid sheep' on the same page stood out like a beacon of positivity – if only for the sheep and not for the driver, who hit a fence.

The first thing I did on hitting the twenty-five-mile-long stretch of road from Sumburgh airport to Lerwick was ... Yes, you got it right: I swerved to avoid sheep!

I couldn't wait to see the next issue of *The Shetland Times*, with this momentous event properly highlighted.

I drove through the grey rainy dusk of an early Sunday afternoon, with scanty daylight clinging to hilltops desperately before being swallowed by darkness. It was not yet 3pm. The landscape was barren, brown and totally tree-less. It reminded me of the Faroe Islands, where, as they told me, 'flowers did not grow because of the wind, and trees because of the sheep.'

I didn't need to swerve to avoid Shetland ponies – these vertically challenged endemic horses, whose faces, framed with long shaggy manes, had a shy 'girlish' look. Martin Martin, a seventeenth century Skye-based explorer and a Scottish namesake of Vitali Vitaliev (or so I wanted to think) described 'shelties' as 'hardy' and 'sprightly, though the least of their kind to be seen anywhere.' Conscious of their importance as part of official Shetland Heritage, the ponies kept to the grass patches alongside the road and never played Anna Karenina with passing cars. Unlike the unruly sheep – those fluffy felons of the Shetlands pastures – they were so orderly and law-abiding that I wouldn't be particularly surprised if they duly paid council tax to the islands' authorities.

First impressions are often misleading. Next morning, I noticed that the belated December dawn was emerging not from the sky but from the voe (the local Norse name for a sea-bay) in front of my hotel. The water was slowly oozing out a soft and transparent light it must have accumulated the day before (or, more likely, during the last summer). For the first time in my life, I was watching an upside-down sunrise!

It was not long before the sun found its legitimate place up in the sky – and its first timid rays got entangled in the narrow winding lanes ('closses') of Lerwick – like bright-yellow ribbons in a Victorian beauty's elaborate hairstyle, dishevelled by the wind. The tiny 'capital' of Shetland turned out to be one of the loveliest towns I had ever seen. It resembled a cosy bedsit with sea-views and 'many Victorian period features,' to use the peculiar jargon of real-estate agents.

My subsequent conversations with Brian Smith, a Lerwick archivist and historian, and several other locals, helped to deconstruct the following persisting stereotypes of the Shetlands:

1. Shetlanders were more Scandinavian than British.

Apart from place names, ruins and the *Up Helly Aa* Fire Festival, there was not much Scandinavian culture left in Shetland, which stopped being a province of Norway in 1472, when it was given to Scotland as the dowry for a Norwegian princess. In the run-up to the last World Football Cup England-Denmark game, a Scottish tabloid sent a pack of hacks to Lerwick in the hope of finding thousands of Denmark supporters. Not a single one could be identified: everybody in Shetland supported England. They should have tried Glasgow instead …

2. Shetlanders were fiercely pro-independence.

A small Movement for Independent Shetland, which ceased to exist in the late 1980s, had never stood for complete independence – just for a bigger autonomy within the UK. True, at times the islanders still called Shetland 'a country' and said 'I am going to Scotland next week,' but there were no independence undertones in those statements, coined purely by the islands' geographic remoteness. At the same time, there was definitely such a thing as a 'Shetland identity' which – like any other cultural character – was fairly hard to define.

3. Shetlanders spoke a variation of Old Norse, like their Faroese or Icelandic neighbours.

Norse, as spoken by the Vikings, died in Shetland in the eighteenth century. Modern Shetland dialect, taught at the islands' schools, was closer to Lowlands Scots, and the number of Scandinavian borrowings in it was constantly decreasing (incidentally, I also noticed that the islanders spoke the best English I had heard anywhere in Scotland so far).

Brian Smith translated for me a randomly chosen passage from a story in *The New Shetlander* magazine: '*Noo bairns. My peerie kist is aa tied up. I'm ready to geng.*' – 'Now, children. My little chest is all tied up. I am ready to go.'

I liked both the sound and the message of these three short sentences in the living 'Shetlandic language.'

The only visible 'Scandinavian' feature of modern Lerwick was its extreme cleanliness. The ubiquitous rubbish bins had special (and very un-British) receptacles marked 'gum.' While Glasgow and Edinburgh were conducting propaganda wars against this sticky bane of city streets, little Lerwick had solved the problem by simply providing sufficient quantity of clearly marked 'specialised' bins. As a good Russian writer once noted, rather than struggling for cleanliness, it is much better to sweep the floor. '*Dunna chuck bruck*!' as they say in Shetland.

Another tell-tale detail was that black rubbish bags, left for collection in Lerwick's streets, were covered with ... pieces of disused fishing nets. It was tempting to conclude that, in view of the looming collapse of the islands' fishing industry, it was the only remaining use for the nets. But the truth was much more prosaic: the nets, provided by the council, offered the best possible protection from seagulls, these flying pests of Lerwick, who used to rummage through the contents of unprotected rubbish bags with the zest of Her Majesty's Customs inspectors ransacking the luggage of a suspected Colombian drug baron.

In a BBC Radio Shetland evening program, I heard the islanders coming up with possible solutions to the seagull problem – from destroying the birds' eggs to persuading them to fly over Lerwick upside down! What could I say? Thank God, Shetland ponies cannot fly!

Lerwick, bustling with traffic and agitated Christmas shoppers, showed few signs of gloom and doom. 'Times are changing and we must change with them,' Tavish Scott, a youngish local MSP, told me in his Lerwick office. 'Fishing and oil industries are indeed in crises, but we are trying to find alternatives.'

I saw what he meant, when I went to the island of Unst, Scotland's most northerly point, connected to Mainland (I mean the Shetland largest island, where Lerwick is located) by excellent roads and frequent ferries. In Haroldswick, its northernmost settlement, I was saddened to learn that its 'UK's most northerly post-office' had closed down a couple of years before, and its coveted franking stamp was now used by the post-office in Baltasound, the island's 'capital.'

Driving back to Baltasound, past a cluster of historic ruins, resembling some obscure Cyrillic letter, I nearly missed the world's most amazing bus shelter – complete with a sofa, a microwave oven, a floor rug, an old Amstrad computer and a telephone with a 'hot line to the Palace.' A local schoolboy, Bobby Macaulay, started this charming joke several years ago, when he got fed up waiting for a school bus in the old shabby and leaking bus shelter. With the help of his family and friends, he transformed it into the island's most popular tourist attraction. The quirky bus shelter now attracts thousands of tourists. It even has its own website, designed and maintained by Bobby himself.

I thought that Edinburgh and Glasgow bus stops would never look the same to me again, and, waiting for a bus, I would always be on the lookout, if not for an in-shelter PC, then definitely for a sofa!

Initiative must be running in the Macaulay family. I met Bobby's father, Sandy, Manager of Unst Regeneration Project – the position that spoke for itself. Windmills rotated merrily behind the window of his little office. 'This is part of our renewable energy project,' he said pointing at the windmills. 'We have to think strategically. The power of the wind is never going to run out – not in Shetland.'

Unst, this remotest bit of Britain, was also home to an IT and training company, a learning centre, a modern brewery and a number of other 'un-traditional' modern businesses. It even had a filmmaking unit – Unst Animation Studio, to where I popped only to make sure that, with its state-of-the art equipment and hairy (Shetland-pony-like?) filmmakers, it looked like a twin of its many a counterpart in London's Soho.

It took me just one step out to be confronted with piercing wind and the black hostile waves of the North Sea a mere hundred yards away.

Lighting up a cigarette was like stopping a low-flying skua with bare hands.

Before leaving, I went to have the last look at 'The House of Hope.' Hope was what I found on this trip to the Shetlands, with all their voes and woes. It was Hope not just for the islands, but also – for the whole of Scotland, my new country-size '**DOM NADEZHDI**.'

'Now, children. My little chest is all tied up. I am ready to go.'

But I know I will be back.

Comino, Malta

The boat to Comino leaves from Mgarr Harbour. It is a traditional Maltese fishing boat – small, narrow and snub-nosed. The island's only link with the world, it carries a couple of crates of beer and a carton of Nescafé for Comino's shop. We are the only passengers.

Comino is the smallest of the three Maltese islands. About two and a half square kilometres in size, it has a permanent population of five – three humans and two donkeys. There are no roads on the island, which nevertheless boasts its own priest and ... police station.

The first thing we see as we approach Comino is the seventeenth-century tower, built by the Grand Master Alof de Wignacourt (there's nowhere you can hide from the Knights of St John in Malta). The second thing we see is the modern oblong building of Comino Hotel, overlooking the lagoon. There is nothing else on the island to attract the eye.

Gordon Muscat, the assistant manager of Comino Hotel, greets us on the pier. 'Welcome to Comino, Europe's smallest populated island!' he chants.

Comino Hotel is a perfect hideaway. It was built ten years ago, when the island still had a population of fifty – an impressive figure. The hotel was expected to attract more people to live on Comino, but the effect was polarly opposite: Comino's population kept dwindling, from fifty to fourteen, then to eight, and finally to three. The locals were probably afraid that the four-star hotel would bring hordes of noisy holidaymakers to their quiet haven. It didn't.

'Our goal is to keep Comino as it is,' says Gordon Muscat as we sit on the hotel's terrace. 'Our staff do not live here, they come and go. We don't disturb the locals or make any noise, and our only two vehicles are a service truck and a Land Rover.'

We have to hurry to meet the remaining islanders before they all leave Comino for good, so we board the Land Rover and drive towards the village, scaring away lizards from under the wheels.

After about three minutes of a rough cross-country ride, we see a windowless clay hut with the sign 'Comino Police Station' above the door.

Inside, the police station looks as if it has just been raided by pirates. Or by the Knights of St John. Pens, walkie-talkies, details of police uniform, registers and a kettle are scattered all over the duty room. What's going on? Where are the policemen? Have they all been killed and dumped in the sea?

From the adjoining room we hear sounds of commotion. A scantily dressed and red-faced man emerges in the doorway. 'I am the policeman,' he says, pulling on his trousers. He is all creased, rumpled and sweaty, as if he has spent an hour inside a washing machine. 'Sorry, I was asleep,' he yawns. It is 2pm. They seem to have late mornings in Comino.

We enter the room from which the policeman has just emerged. It smells of army barracks. A couple of blankets are spread on the floor.

'We sleep here,' the policeman explains.

'And what is in there?' I ask, pointing to a little door in the corner. With unexpected dexterity, the policeman jumps in front of me, blocking my view. 'It is a bathroom,' he says. Too late. I notice a frightened human shadow hiding in the bathroom, before the policeman slams the door shut. I have no time to establish whether it was a man or a woman.

'Have you got loads of work here?' I ask the clearly embarrassed guardian of Comino's law and order. 'We have some accidents in summer,' he mumbles, throwing furtive looks at the bathroom door. 'How about crime?' 'Only speeding boats,' he mutters. 'Have you got a police boat to chase them?' 'No, we haven't.' I find further conversation meaningless.

'We've got a mobile telephone!' the policeman exclaims suddenly. He takes a battered old Motorola out of his pocket and scrutinises it with the joy of a child who has just spotted a new colourful fish in his home aquarium.

We find two thirds of Comino's permanent population repairing a motorboat in the village. They are Father Hili, the priest, and a man called Salvu. The remaining one third, whom they call 'ante Maria,' is nowhere to be seen. Maybe it was she who was hiding in the police station bathroom?

Father Hili reeks of home-made wine. Dressed in a threadbare sweater, turned inside out, he giggles and chain-smokes, fumbling two packets of Rothmans in his hand like rosaries.

'I have been living here for twenty-three years, ha-ha-ha,' he sniggers, puffing at his cigarette. 'My parish is small, hi-hi-hi … I will probably go to Gozo soon. They have twenty-six priests in Gozo. More fun, uh-hu-hu!'

It is sad to realize that Comino is about to lose a further one third of its population.

'And I will never leave Comino,' says Salvu. 'I like it.' He has rough, crab-like hands and sports an 'Admiral' baseball cap.

Father Hili forces me to smoke one of his Rothmans. 'Smoking is pleasing to God, ho-ho-ho …'

On the way back to the pier, we pass by the toy-size parish church where Father Hili conducts his Sunday liturgies. The door of the police station is wide open: the policeman is probably out on the beat – chasing lizards and keeping an eye on 'ante Maria,' Salvu and the priest, in case they decide to commit an offence …

Heymaey, Iceland

'Flowers are immortal, you cut them in autumn and they grow again in spring – somewhere.'

Halldor Laxness, Icelandic writer, winner of the Nobel Prize for Literature

Due to never-ceasing winds, flowers do not grow on Heymaey, the main island of the rocky Westmans archipelago off the southern coast of Iceland.

Winds whistle like bullies at the top of the *Stórhöfði* mountain, towering above the town of Vestmannaeyjar, the Westman Islands' capital and only settlement, with the reputation of Europe's windiest place. Indeed, lighting up a match anywhere in its wind-swept hilly streets is harder than catching a puffin with bare hands ... Puffins of which the island has the world's biggest colony, are also affected by the winds. With their short wings and relatively large bodies, they do not float in the sky like other birds, but flutter – balancing in the air like some reckless wave-riding surfers. The wind often takes over, and the birds' fledglings get blown off the cliffs and thrown down into the gleaming black waves, tirelessly pounding the island's ragged shore.

Winds were a blessing for Heymaey in January-February 1973 – during and after a huge volcanic eruption which nearly destroyed Vestmannaeyjar and eventually made the entire population set sail to the mainland. In the words of a witness, 'When I pulled back the curtains in my bedroom, I could see a huge pillar of fire and then saw a long gaping fissure no more than 400 metres away. It was as though the earth had been zipped open ...'

The lava flow was advancing slowly, and the wind kept blowing the burning ashes away from the town which helped to avoid major fires and gave the locals ample time to evacuate. Coincidentally, the same strong wind prevented the whole of the town's fishing fleet from leaving the port on the days when the 160 metre-high flow of lava, tephra and tuff, having enveloped thousands of homes, was crawling towards the harbour. The stranded fishing boats were used to rescue all of Heymaey's 5,300 residents.

From my impromptu vantage point, I can see the green patch of an eighteen-hole golf course at the foot of the mountain down below. Considering the strength and persistence of the winds, the small treeless island is an unlikely spot for the slow and fairly static game of green continental valleys. Yet, to me, the very presence of a golf course on Vestmannaeyjar symbolizes the unbending spirit of the islanders – and of Icelanders in general too. Watching the unhurried wind-defying twitches of the golf players, I couldn't help remembering a similar golf course near Port Stanley, the tiny capital of another remote archipelago – the Falklands. That pitch was next to a minefield, stuffed with thousands of unexploded Argentinian mines, and was separated from it only by a row of barbed wire, with skull-and-bones 'DANGER MINES' signs.

It takes a good deal of optimism and strength of spirit to be playing golf among minefields, or else, like on Heymaey – on top of a natural powder barrel (read active volcano), with a smouldering detonation cord attached.

A Gateway to Hell

In his 1864 novel *A Journey to the Centre of the World*, Jules Verne described Iceland as a gateway to the Earth's interior. Indeed, for millions of years, Europe's second largest island has been sitting on top of the highly seismic Mid-Atlantic Ridge, separating North American and Eurasian tectonic plates. Every year, over 20,000 earthquakes and tremors of different strength are registered in the country, whose territory straddles four volcanic zones, thirty-two volcanic systems and 130 volcanic mountains. Thirty of those 130 volcanos are active, and many have erupted mightily and repeatedly throughout the years, having changed not just the shape of Iceland, but the whole of the world's history.

Laki mountain's fissure eruption of 1783 was perhaps the most 'ground-breaking' – both literally and figuratively – of all. It had been happening for over eight months: from early June 1783 to February 1784, and ended up producing the largest ever lava flow on Earth – 2.9 cubic miles (!) which covered 218 square miles of Iceland's territory. Much of the country's livestock and the quarter of its human population died during the famine that ensued due to massive emissions of poisonous gases into the atmosphere.

The far-ranging impact of that natural disaster was not limited to Iceland. The huge cloud of volcanic dust, mixed with sulfur particles, was carried over much of Europe reaching as far as Egypt and North America. Due to the resulting thick fog, ships were unable to leave many a European port. Crops were also affected. According to Benjamin Franklin, a 'constant fog' hung over 'all Europe and a great part of North America.'

The winter that followed was therefore particularly harsh, with lots of floods and famine in Egypt and in Europe, where, according to some historians, it played a decisive role in the build-up to the French Revolution of 1789! If I remember it correctly from my Soviet school's sketchy history course, 100 or so years later, Lenin called the aftermaths of wars and natural disasters, with the resulting impoverishment of the 'masses,' ideal breeding grounds for revolutions. Thus a volcanic eruption on a small island in the Atlantic may have changed the course of history.

That history-altering scenario came close to repeating itself as recently as in April 2010, when a powerful volcano erupted from the Eyjafjallajökull mountain in South West Iceland. The effects of this eruption, also felt all over Europe and as far as Beijing, were amplified significantly by the interaction of magma with the ice of the adjoining glacier, and most of us can still remember clouds of sticky brown dust that had brought many European airports to a stand-still. For over a week, the skies of Britain were free of any traffic. People would wake up in the morning to the eerie silence – so unusual and intense that it felt deafening. In an amazing case of synchronicity, my father-in-law, a Lancaster bomber pilot during World War II, who was then dying of cancer at a hospital in the North East of England, passed away hours after all the UK air traffic was stopped, as if having waited for the skies to be cleared for his final 'take off.' . .

Filming and Not Fleeing

On the way to Landelackyahofn – a small mainland port, from where ferries depart for Heymaey – we stopped at a small roadside 'Visitors' Centre' at the very foot of the troublesome Eyjafjallajökull. Never before had I seen a mountain so sinister – a black finger-shaped peak piercing grey satin skies dagger-like. It looked as if the Polyphemus' cave, or the mythical workshop of Hephaestus, Mount Olympus' 'in-house' blacksmith and the ancient Greek god of volcanoes, could be hiding inside it.

The Visitors' Centre, staffed by the entrepreneurial family of farmer Olafur Eggertsson, attracts dozens of tourists, who are offered a guided tour of a small, yet very visual, exhibition telling the story of the April 2010 eruption, which the farmer's family had lived through. At the end of the tour, normally conducted by Grudny Valberg, Mr Eggertsson's wife, visitors are shown a twenty-minute video about the eruption and its impact on the lives' of the local farming community. The movie, shot as the disaster was unveiling, is professionally photographed and edited.

'When the eruption began on 20 March, we were told to evacuate,' Grudny Valberg told me. 'But how could we abandon our whole lifestyle? We chose to stay and invited a filmmaker from Reykjavik to chronicle the event.'

So, instead of fleeing, they were filming – heroism, driven by practicality!

Since then, the natural catastrophe, which brought half of Europe to a stop (with 107,000 flights cancelled for over a week), has become a substantial article of the farm's income, alongside rapeseed, wheat, barley and dairy products.

Practicality is an archetypal Icelandic trait. One has to be pragmatic to survive on these barren volcanic islands. Not only have the Icelanders learned to live on top of the proverbial powder barrel, but they have managed to turn this daily threat into an income-bringing attraction. Some tour operators even invite tourists to venture inside volcanoes. 'For the first time in history, travellers have the opportunity to see what a volcano looks like on the inside. Descend 120 metres into a 4,000-year-old magma chamber and experience a new underground world,' promises a daring PR brochure. In the Hrifunes guest-house near the town of Vik, where I stayed overnight on the way from the Westman Islands, the shower-room floor was made of compressed tuff – small volcanic rocks, pleasantly massaging one's foot soles. And on Heymaey itself, they found the way of heating the whole town with the energy of the cooling down lava shortly after the 1973 earthquake!

This brings us back to Vestmannaeyjar. Unlike the memorable 2010 Eyjafjallajökull disaster, whose aftermaths were felt all over Europe and beyond, the 1973 eruption of Eldfell was much more localised, but it had changed the face of Heymaey and its small community forever.

When the Fire Mountain Erupted

To get to Heymaey from Landeyahofn, we boarded a small, yet clean and comfortable, ferry boat called 'Herjolfur.' Apart from a dozen or so cars and several empty refrigerator trucks (they will get loaded on the islands which provide one third of the overall fish catch of Iceland), she was carrying islanders returning from the mainland and a flock of American tourists.

The crossing took under one hour. We chugged past an archipelago of barren meteorite-like rocks, skerries and islets, one of which – Surtsey – was a fairly recent addition to Iceland's global territory, having emerged from the ocean as recently as in 1963 as a result of an underwater eruption. It took nature (or was it Hephaestus?) five days to create, and by 15 November 1963, the baby island was born. By the following January, it was 174 metres high – rocks grow faster than people. Unlike some other – smaller – islets that appeared briefly in the subsequent years only to get submerged by the ocean again shortly afterwards, Surtsey, named after a mythical giant Surtur, who – according to a Nordic saga – wanted to set the world on fire, was there to stay. It is closed to visitors, and only scientists are allowed to step ashore that newly formed national nature reserve.

The sight of Vestmannaeyjar, the islands' 'capital,' comes almost as a surprise after the boat circumvents an umpteenth craggy rock. An unexpectedly large, neat and modern-looking harbour, reputedly the best in the south of Iceland, nestles at the foot of the Helgafell mountain, officially renamed Eldfell – the Fire Mountain – by the Icelandic Place Names Committee after the 1973 eruption. It looks as if the harbour had been there forever, whereas in fact a large chunk of it is ten years younger than even Surtsey and was added to the island's territory as a direct result of the eruption, when about 300 million cubic yards of lava and 26 million cubic yards of tephra were generously deposited on Heymaey.

The old harbour was then saved by the innovative procedure of spraying cold seawater (by forty-three powerful pumps through nineteen miles of plastic pipes) directly onto the hot lava. The water increased its viscosity and thus created internal barriers in the flow causing it to thicken and ride up over itself. That hugely successful experiment was later described as human history's most ambitious attempt to control volcanic activity.

The eruption stopped in early July 1973. And shortly afterwards people started returning home to Heymaey, which – fittingly – means 'home island' in Icelandic. What they faced was total devastation. A number of houses were literally wiped off the face of the earth, and to reach the remaining ones, buried by tephra or set alight by glowing lava bombs, hundreds of thousands of tons of ash had to be cleared. Ironically, the rebuilding of Vestmannaeyjar was helped considerably by the additional eruption-delivered landfill material, of which there were shortages before. Plus, as I have noted already, for the first several years after the disaster, the thermal energy of the lava was harnessed and used to heat the houses – new and old. As you see, just like winds, volcanoes can occasionally be helpful …

Not the Pompei of the North

The house at Gerðistraut 10 had been buried under ash and lava for over forty years before being excavated and turned into a museum, called – rather bluntly – 'Eldheimar,' the House of Fire. It was built over the carcass of the destroyed dwelling which used to belong to Gerður Sigurðadóttir. 'Seeing my old home after all this time filled me with conflicting emotions … I miss my late husband, with whom we used to live there, but am happy that the excavation is now complete and the house is still standing,' she said.

The Eldheimar Museum is modern, revealing and interactive. At times, perhaps over-interactive. 'You can follow the destruction with joystick,' reads a sign above one of the highly digitalized displays. Modern technology is, above all, an indicator of well-being. And there's no hiding the fact: Vestmannaeyjar is booming. It is now larger and much more prosperous than before the devastating eruption, which – rather ironically – was also a stimulus for renovation, helped by the thriving off-shore fishing industry. The town's high-street has a cluster of 'posh' designer shops and boutiques of the kind that wouldn't be out of place in London, Paris or Stockholm. The prices are hefty, but one has to remember that every item had to be brought from the mainland. There's also a handful of excellent restaurants and bars.

According to Kristin Jóhansdóttir, Vestmannaeyjar's director of marketing, the town centre's reconstruction cost over €5.6 million. 'Ever since the excavation began, we have put a lot of energy into rebuilding, and people all over the world have shown a keen interest in our volcanic history.'

That was how she put it – 'volcanic history.' And in Vestmannaeyjar's case, it is not a metaphor.

'Aren't you worried that Eldfell, the Fire Mountain, will fire up again?' I addressed this question to the locals repeatedly while in Heymaey. And the answer was always the same: 'We think we are ok for the next 200 years or so …' I heard that particular estimate – 200 years or so – from almost everyone. It sounded random, but having thought about it, I realized that it wasn't: 200 years spans over three-four generations:

children, grand-and great-grandchildren etc – as far ahead as the present-day islanders could allow their worries to stretch. It is easy to connect this kind of thinking with a selfish '*après nous – le déluge*' attitude, but it struck me as yet another manifestation of the all-permeating pragmatism of Icelandic life and psyche.

On the ferry back to the mainland, my VW was squeezed into the far corner of the car deck by an enormous refrigerator truck – the biggest I had ever seen. Loaded to the brim with Heymaey's main produce – fresh seafood, it was reeking of fish and dripping sea water.

My personal baggage, however, was not at all heavy. I was bringing back memories of the resilient island community – a taciturn, yet tough and proud, lot whom neither winds nor volcanoes could bend. Just like the 'immortal' flowers of Halldor Laxness (see the epigraph), these people had to leave their island in spring of 1973 and started returning the following autumn. By then, the ever-so-helpful winds of Heymaey which had been blowing ash and the evacuees' boats away from the island, had changed direction. Until now, the islanders keep coming back to their long-suffering 'home island,' whose population is approaching 5,000, only 300 short of what it was before the eruption forty-three years ago.

In PR brochures, Heymaey is sometimes called 'the Pompei of the North.' I find this cliché not just incorrect, but inappropriate and even insulting. The difference between Pompei and Heymaey is striking in its simplicity: the former, after all, is dead, and the latter – very much alive.

Aurora Borealis

According to the July 2015 issue of *Iceland Magazine*, the Northern Lights occur in Iceland all year round.

Before I recount my (partially) successful attempt at Aurora watching – which, I believe, should be at the top of every human being's things-to-do-in-this-life list – let us remember what the Aurora actually is. My trusted *Wordsworth Dictionary of Science and Technology* defines it as 'luminous curtains or streamers of light seen in the night sky at high latitudes, caused when electrically charged particles from the sun are guided by the Earth's magnetic fields to the polar regions, there colliding with atoms in the upper atmosphere.' Of course, this definition, precise and solid as it is, pays as little poetic tribute to those magnificently divine lights in the night sky as the breaking down of chlorophyll and other chemical processes do to the riot of autumn colours in the forests of New England.

Poetry or not, in Iceland one is never far away, if not from the Northern Lights as such, then definitely from 'Northern Lights' – a moniker as common for local restaurants, shops and hotels as 'Sea View' is in Britain. Only in Britain, a 'Sea View' B&B can be miles away from the actual sea and face a smoky factory or a rubbish dump, but the Northern Lights in Iceland are always there, above you. The question is whether you can see them or not.

Well, there are numerous science and technology aids to help you spot the evasive Aurora – from Celeston SkyMaster binoculars to Aurora Forecast apps for iPhones. In many Icelandic hotels, they ask you at check-in whether you'd like a wake-up call if the Aurora starts 'dancing' during the night (I don't think anyone has ever refused such an offer). And in case you are lucky enough to be there when it actually happens, there exist numerous tips on how to see, film or photograph it better. These include advice on lenses, film, ISO settings, exposures and all kinds of star-gazing optical devices.

My first chance to see Aurora arose on the second night of my holidays at a ranch-style Ranga hotel in South Iceland. Nature's 'show' started at about 10pm, and I hurried to the hotel's own retractable roof observatory, with computerised telescopes manned by students from Reykjavik University. They explained that the display was not at its best – grade 3 (low) out of 10 on Aurora's activity scale – but I was still mesmerised by the moving pale lights, which, I have to confess, looked more impressive when viewed with a naked eye than through a telescope's viewfinder.

Not being entirely happy with my grade 3 experience, I could not wait for another Aurora opportunity. Sadly, it rained non-stop for the next few days, and the Lights, if any, were firmly concealed behind a thick curtain of clouds, which no telescope could penetrate. 'Would you like a wake- up call, in case Aurora starts playing?' a hotel receptionist inquired matter-of-factly. It was the last night of my holiday, and I was staying at the Northern Lights Inn next to Keflavik airport, from where I was to fly back home the following morning. 'No, don't you dare!' I responded. Only kidding ... Of course I shouted: 'Yes!!' (at least ten times).

The inn did not incorporate an observatory, but had a dedicated balcony on which some German Aurora hunters were already installing their telescopes. When nothing happened for a couple of hours, I went to my room for a quick nap ...

Do I need to tell you that the 8-grade display (as the triumphant Germans informed me at breakfast) started the moment I shut my eyes? The receptionist called me twice, but I was dead to the world. To torment me even further, the Germans told me that the skies were so crystal-clear on that night that they didn't need to use their telescopes.

But at least I did manage to get a glimpse of Aurora at Ranga and could now repeat after one respected travel website: 'To look at the auroras, you don't really need any equipment – the night sky in Iceland is beautiful to the unaided eye.'

Now you will understand, why on clear starry nights at home in England I find it hard to go to sleep, hoping against hope for a sudden Aurora wake-up call.

Sark

It is not common knowledge that until recently Britain had the world's last fully-functioning feudal state right on its doorstep. I am talking about the Island of Sark, which – like all other Channel Islands and the Isle of Man – constitutes a part of Great Britain outside the United Kingdom.

Not part of the UK, the Island of Sark, population 500, is the Commonwealth's smallest semi-independent nation. It makes its own laws and manages its own money. Administered by the Seigneur, a hereditary ruler who held the island for the British crown, Sark was the last remaining feudal community in the Western world until 2008 when the islanders voted for democracy and the Seigneur's powers were significantly curtailed. The Seigneur, however, still pays an inflation-free tax to the Queen of £1.79 a year – obviously a fortune five hundred years ago when it first came into force and constituted 'one twentieth part of a knight's fee.'

Cars are banned from Sark, and planes are not allowed to land there, or to fly over the Island under two thousand feet. The place is engulfed by a strange quiet, broken only by the wailing of wind.

The island still abides by medieval laws, one of which says that 'unspayed bitches are not allowed to be kept on the Island, except by the Seigneur.' This law was adopted in the seventeenth century, when Chief Pleas (the island's parliament) decided that too many dogs could cause problems with sheep farming.

'Yes, our island is bitch-free,' Michael Beaumont, the facetious previous Seigneur and the father of the incumbent one (Christopher Beaumont), who inherited his estate from the Dame of Sark, told me with a smile during my first visit to Sark in 1996.

Another law states that forty local family heads, including the Seigneur, are obliged to keep muskets to protect the island from invaders.

A modest-looking brochure, *Constitution of Sark*, is one of the undisputed gems of my esoteric book collection.

One of its articles states that, under Norman custom, a person can obtain immediate cessation of any action he thinks is an infringement of his rights. At the scene, he must, in front of witnesses, recite the Lord's Prayer in French and cry out in *patois*: '*Haro, Haro, Haro! À mon aide, mon Prince, on me fait tort!*' At which point, all actions must cease until the matter is heard by the Court.

The Haro cry didn't help the islanders, and the forty muskets of Sark remained silent during World War II, when Sark was occupied by a garrison of three hundred Germans. Not a single shot was fired from either side, and the locals still refer to that period as a 'model occupation.' One of them told me how the German commandant of Sark refused to take any action against those local residents who defied the occupation authorities by keeping short-wave radios at their houses – an offence punishable by death anywhere else in occupied Europe.

In 1989, the island experienced another foreign invasion, albeit on a much smaller scale. It was taken over – single-handedly – by a drunken Frenchman, André Gards, who landed on Sark with a rifle and a small load of explosives. In a 'manifesto,' written in broken English and pinned on the village noticeboard, he announced that he was taking control of the island. Having stated his intentions, he retired for a refill to a village pub, where he was apprehended and disarmed by the part-time Constable (head of Sark's part-time police force) and frogmarched to the island's miniature prison, consisting of one small windowless cell.

The Constable soon came to regret his bravery, for another island law made him responsible for feeding prison inmates, and the Frenchman proved to be extremely voracious. Luckily, two days is the maximum jail term in Sark, and in due course the gluttonous invader was deported to his motherland.

Exempt from the UK's ailing social security and health schemes, the island takes good care of itself. Special community funds help young people through schools and universities, pay medical bills for the sick, and provide pensions for the old.

While in Sark, I noticed that many of its residents had a peculiar twinkle in their eyes. 'What is it?' I asked Jennifer Cochrane, a local writer. 'It is contentment,' she replied. 'We Sarkese are a fairly fortunate lot!'

Soay

My feet got soaked the moment I stepped on board the moored powerboat, tossed about by the waves, as if we were already at sea. Through the thick curtain of unceasing rain, I could discern the dark, forbidding presence of the Cuillins across the bay.

I was about to join the cheerful crowd of 1,200 or so Scottish lairds, who jointly owned two-thirds of the country's territory. True, I could not afford the Cuillin mountains, put up for sale for £10m, and even if I could – what would I do with them? They were a bit too bulky for a paper press on my desk … I was after something more affordable – an island, to where I was about to cross.

It all started several days earlier with a short newspaper report announcing the sale of 'the three-mile-long island of Soay off the coast of Skye,' with 'no roads or shops,' but with a nineteenth century two-bedroom 'mission house' and several other buildings thrown in. As a writer, I always dreamed of having an island of my own, where I could pen the most important book of my life.

I contacted Inverness-based Macleod & MacCallum estate agents for an advertising brochure. To my surprise, it referred to 'Soay House & the Owner/Occupancy of South Soay Croft & Common Grazings' rather than to a straightforward romantic island. 'Common Grazings' did not sound very romantic, yet even my rudimentary knowledge of farming was sufficient to deduce a direct link between 'grazings,' which featured in the brochure, and 'droppings,' which, for obvious reasons, didn't. The encouraging thing, however, was that, between 1945 and 1951, Soay was owned by Gavin Maxwell – one of the last century's most interesting Scottish writers, who used it as a base for his ill-fated shark-fishing enterprise, described in one of his books, *Harpoon at a Venture*. Gavin Maxwell always struck me as an underrated genius. Best remembered for *Ring of Bright Water* – an internationally acclaimed book about otters – he was not just a naturalist turned writer, but also an artist, a racing driver, an army officer, a secret agent, a fisherman, a traveller and a poet.

Maxwell once complained that he could not write a novel, because he was unable to structure it properly. His own life, resplendent with dramas – financial and personal – was itself like a badly structured, yet gripping, work of fiction. 'Rabbits, have two habits, breeding, and feeding (the purpose of the second, is just to keep them fecund),' he wrote several hours before his agonising death of lung cancer (he was a chain-smoker, too) in 1969 at the age of fifty-five. What an iron-cast spirit he must have had to crack jokes from the very 'jaws of death!'

Whatever the dramas, Maxwell had lived his short life to the full, and Soay, to which he often referred as 'my Island Valley of Avalon,' played a huge role in it. The writer bought it in 1945 for £900, borrowed from his mother, and sold it in 1951 –

two years before all thirty islanders were evacuated to Mull, except for one family – that of Joseph 'Tex' Geddes, Maxwell's wartime friend and his shark-fishery's harpooner. It was Tex Geddes's Orkney-based son Duncan, who was now selling the vacant island croft for 'over £280,000' – the price of an average two or three-bedroom flat in London or Edinburgh.

My crossing to Soay could be best compared to a rollercoaster ride under a cold shower. In my borrowed wetsuit, I felt like a U-boat captain who gave an order to submerge and only then realised that he had left his submarine at home.

The weather forecast for once proved right: 'gale-force wind,' mixed with rain, was targeting me with what felt like handfuls of prickly deep-frozen shrimps, some of which would stick (and then thaw reluctantly) in my ears and nostrils. Grabbing my seat handle with both hands, I was sinking and flying up in the air – all at the same time ...

'I had not dared to cross to Soay myself, lest I might be stuck there for an indefinite time,' Gavin Maxwell once wrote. I realised what he meant by the end of the crossing. The powerboat could not approach the shore, and we (Chris, a *Herald* photographer, and myself) had to be 'evacuated' from it by a fisherman, Oliver Davies, one of Soay's two remaining permanent residents (his wife Donita was the second) in his multi-purpose inflatable dinghy.

Despite wind and rain, the island felt beautiful, although, with my eyes full of water, I could not be quite sure what it looked like and kept conjuring up photos from the real-estate brochure and lines from Maxwell's poems about Soay (.' . . and the waves crept over the lonely beach ... ' and so on) – in my rain-soaked imagination. I thought that Maxwell's quick decision to buy the island could largely be explained by the fact that he first visited it on a hot summer day in 1944. We 'inspected' the mission house, which was blissfully dry and felt very much alive – as if the residents had just popped out for a ... whatever one could pop out for in Soay. Books were everywhere. In one room, I saw a faded complete set of *National Geographic* magazine for 1984. We went inside Soay's one-room primary school, now serving as a 'community centre' (rather bizarre, with no community left), with a brand-new and seemingly untouched pool table and a box of library books under a not-too-promising hand-written note: 'Next delivery date 10 October 2002.'

Oliver told me how all the current and former islanders got together to protect the school building from being sold as a holiday cottage several years ago.

'If this house is kept as a school, there is a chance that one day the island community can be revived,' he said.

'Do you seriously believe in this revival?' I asked him.

'Why not? It's a great place to live and to bring up children. Here you don't have to put up a show – you can be yourself, and life itself becomes your only challenge.'

I asked him how he saw a potential buyer.

'We need an active person. Preferably, a writer. He will also have to be a fisherman, for fishing is the only way of making some money here.'

I wanted to tell him that they had found such a person: I was a writer, still fairly active (as proved by the crossing) and once managed to ferret out a couple of perches from a pond at the tender age of six. But at that very moment, Donita, Oliver's wife, ran into the room and said that we had to dash back to the shore: the weather was getting worse (could it?), and the skipper of our boat radioed her to say that we had to sail off immediately.

'Life is precious, and there are enough beds in my house,' said Oliver somewhat mysteriously. I thought he simply didn't want us to go.

Although vetted (well, almost) as a potential new laird by half of Soay's population (I mean Oliver), I still wanted to clarify the crofting and (particularly) the 'grazing' issues. In Inverness, I was lucky to get an appointment with Derek Flyn, one of Scotland's leading experts in crofting law.

'Can I buy Soay?' I asked.

'First, you'll be advised to finalise your plans as to residency on the island,' Mr Flyn replied in legal-speak. In plain words, it meant that I had to decide whether I was going to live there or not. That came as a shock, for like many present-day Scottish lairds, I would be quite happy to spend a couple of weeks on my croft, and to cruise the globe for the rest of the year (using the change left from my would-be National Lottery jackpot).

Mr Flyn proceeded to tell me that the main purpose of crofting legislation was to protect the land against such absentee landlords. 'You will either have to live on the island, or to find a tenant,' he said sounding as weighty and authoritative as the three-volume *Encyclopedia of Value Added Tax* on a bookshelf above his head (I thought that compulsory reading of all three could be a good punishment for absentee landlords – like myself). He explained that not only would such a tenant have to be approved by the Crofters' Commission, but, in accordance with the new Scotland's Land Reform Act, he (or they) would have an immediate right to buy the croft from me, whether I wanted it or not.

'Buying a croft involves responsibilities, and you'll have to demonstrate your commitment to the land,' he concluded gravely and added: 'Soay is a special place for a special person.' I was obviously not special enough. Besides, I always had a problem with commitments. But I could now understand Gavin Maxwell, who wrote on leaving Soay: 'I remember it on those glorious summer days when a smooth blue sea lapped the red rock of the island shore and the cuckoos called continuously from the birch-woods; or on bright winter mornings when the Cuillins were snow-covered, hard, intricate and brittle as carved ivory; I remember it with nostalgia for something beautiful and lost, the Island Valley of Avalon.'

The Hebridean Avalon – Soay – is waiting for its new King Arthur.

Note: The story about the island of Skye is in Part Four of this Bumper Book

Stornoway

'Only he who is familiar with the din of battle can fully appreciate quiet,' said Volodya Grishpun, the favourite Russian poet of my youth.

There are different types of silence: A hush-hush conspiratorial whisper, a pause in a conversation, a lull before a storm, or a minute of silence in mourning or commemoration.

In Russia, all broadcasts would stop for three minutes at midnight to allow any SOS signals to be heard – three minutes of anxious, listening silence. Also, a silence à la my friend Bill Bryson: 'It was so quiet in the pub one could hear a fly fart.'

Compare any of those with: 'Wailing air raid sirens were drowned out as laser bombs homed in on military installations and Republican Guard strongholds' – a newspaper account of the first days of the second Gulf war.

What would you rather listen to? Silence is becoming an increasingly coveted and hard-to-get commodity in our noise-ridden war-torn world.

Sh-sh … Close your eyes, shut out all noises and listen to silence …

On Sunday morning, I awoke in my Stornoway hotel to the shattering, deafening stillness behind the window. All habitual noises that constitute part of a quiet Sunday morning in any small town – the sounds of passing cars and human footsteps – were missing. Even dogs did not bark.

The silence was such that it almost made my teeth ache. With awe, I remembered that had I indeed had a sore tooth, there would be no chance of buying a pain-killer: all pharmacies and shops (as well as pretty much everything else) on Lewis were firmly shut down for the sabbath.

The best description of this most silent of all silences ('the mother of all silences,' as Saddam Hussein would put it) can be found in HV Morton's *In Search of Scotland*:

'It is the sabbath. I lie in bed for a time listening to it. You can feel the sabbath in the Highlands of Scotland just as in cities you can feel a fall of snow: the world is wrapped in a kind of soft hush; normal early morning noises are muffled or absent.'

Morton wrote this in 1929, when the sabbath was strictly observed in many rural areas of Scotland. Seventy-five years later, the Outer Hebrides were among its very last strongholds.

Thank God, water in my bathroom taps was not affected by the sabbath and kept running, as it must have done for HV Morton in 1929:

'I sing in my bath; then, remembering with shock that I am breaking the sabbath, stop, and feel criminal.'

I took the previous day's newspaper to breakfast. Until a couple of months earlier, when the first Sunday flight from Inverness landed in Stornoway to a fairly low-key protest at the airport, the only Sunday paper you could read there was a Saturday one.

Even now, after Jock Murray, the entrepreneurial landlord of The Whalers' Rest Hotel, has arranged for a stack of Sunday papers to be flown in (he has to pay for the freight out of his own pocket), the earliest you can get them is at 2pm – if the plane is on time, that is.

This shunning of Sunday newspapers (the sabbatarians are not supposed to use anything produced on Sundays) did not make a lot of sense, for they were all printed on a Saturday, whereas Monday newspapers were put together on a Sunday. Paradoxically, from what I knew, there was no stigma attached to reading Monday newspapers on Lewis – a pleasing realisation for a writer of a Monday column.

At breakfast, the rising air-bubbles in the glass of mineral water on my table were the only things that moved in the whole of Stornoway.

I made sure my car had a full tank of petrol: all filling stations on the islands were closed (well, except for one pump, as it turned out later). Unlike a hapless visitor of several years ago who didn't bother to stock up with the basics, I was not in danger of starving: a small handful of pubs, restaurants and takeaways were now open for Sunday custom.

After a couple of days on Lewis and Harris, I was pleased to discover that the general situation around the sabbath was much more peaceful and relaxed than its portrayals in the mainland media and the gossip.

After a generous dose of both, I had expected a mini-Belfast scenario, with sabbatarians and anti-sabbatarians at each other's throats. Nothing could be further from truth. The issue did split the island community down the middle, but this split was largely in people's minds and not at all bellicose or aggressive. 'It is the clash between the head and the heart,' a local journalist told me.

Having spoken to a number of islanders, I came up with the following spectrum of opinions (most of my interlocutors asked not to be named – not out of fear, but purely out of reluctance 'to upset the neighbours'):

Radical supporters of the strict sabbath observance (among them, significantly, Western Islands Council and the local tourism board) would argue that the fourth commandment left no space for middle ground and/or compromise and were therefore strongly opposed to Sunday flights and ferries as well as any commercial activity on 'God's day.'

They maintained that they didn't need to prove anything to anyone, for 'God knew best what was good for us,' and snubbed the latest opinion polls – heavily in favour of livelier Sundays. 'When in Rome, do as Romans do' was their favourite mantra. (What if some Romans did certain things differently, I was wondering.)

They feared that even slight deviations from God's rule (like three existing Sunday flights and a couple of open pubs) would open the floodgates for total secularisation of the islands. Yet even they stopped short of any sort of violence and/or force to make themselves heard and restricted themselves to 'praying and writing letters.'

Moderate sabbath supporters, like the Rev Dr Iain Campbell, believed they had to accept the changing reality, but should keep making their point and 'showing a different example.' They thought that, rather than putting would-be visitors off, the islands' Sundays could be turned into a tourist attraction for those who wanted to get away from it all and indulge in quiet contemplation.

Radical supporters of change, like Donald MacSween, a local councillor, stood for a referendum that would give a green light to Sunday ferry services and referred to the day of the first Sunday flight as 'the day of liberation.'

They argued that increased industrial activity on Sundays was the only way to reverse the islands' stagnating economy and declining population.

'Tourism and jobs will come to an end, and the Free Church will be the last one out,' an angry Stornoway youngster told me. They recounted horror stories of unsuspecting Sunday visitors trapped on Lewis and Harris without food or petrol.

Moderate supporters of change, like Eileen Macdonald, the proprietor of Doune Braes Hotel – the first fully licensed hotel on the islands – thought that the changes, although welcome, should not go too far the other way and that some 'mysticism' of the sabbath should be preserved and kept intact.

Out of countless local opinion poll results, shown to me by Mr MacSween, I was most impressed by one: fifty-nine per cent of all islanders 'did not feel restricted' by the beliefs and attitudes of others. Unbeknownst to most, the residents of Scotland's last truly Sabbatarian islands taught the country – and the rest of our conflict-ridden world – a quiet lesson of tolerance and democracy.

I enjoyed walking the empty streets of Stornoway on Sunday, between 11am and midday, when ninety-nine per cent of the locals were attending their Sunday services. Being the only pedestrian in town at this hour of prayer did feel, if not exactly 'criminal,' then definitely like a minor breach of public order.

Muffled, yet strangely synchronised, singing could be heard from numerous churches. Dozens of cars, parked bumper-to-bumper near the islands' largest Free Church in Kenneth Street, were patiently waiting for their owners. It was another sign of change: even the strictest of sabbatarians thought it was now acceptable to drive to church on Sundays.

If one so wished, one could have a pint or three at The Whalers' Rest or at HS 1 – a 'cool' modern bar with a Sunday 'table licence.' Sundays were getting unstoppably 'normal' on Lewis, and I was not sure whether to rejoice at this or to grieve.

I drove twenty-five miles west to see two of the island's landmarks: the five-thousand-year-old standing stones of Callanish and a couple-of-years-old 'historic' petrol pump at Doune Braes Hotel – the first and only one open on Sundays.

The stones' visitor centre was closed, but the mysterious phallic rocks, thoroughly arranged by hard-working Neolithic farmers, stood there silently as they did on any weekday. Unbreakable and refusing to budge, yet gradually and inevitably worn out by time and elements, they were the living metaphor of the enduring sabbath tradition.

One day – many years from now – it will crumble away completely, and petrol pumps will spring up all over the place, like obelisks on the mass grave of some of the islands' unique ways and beliefs.

I did fill up my already nearly full tank in the end: how could I beat the temptation of using the islands' only sabbath-less petrol pump? It was only a five-minute drive from the equally sabbath-less standing stones of Callanish.

All the way back to Stornoway, the road was empty.

Sherkin Island

'Sherkin Island is 3m. long and 1,5 m. wide, the E.coast of which is bold and rocky, but has a safe landing-place; it has a pop. of about 400 … Fuel is scarce and has to be imported from the mainland. The inhabitants are brave and expert fishermen and pilots.'
Murray's Ireland, 1912

'Tiny Sherkin Island is a delightfully pretty place …'
Rough Guide to Ireland, 2004

I was about to visit Sherkin – another island in my peripatetic life. Having not been to a *proper* isle since the Arrans (forgetting for a moment that Ireland itself was an island too), I was craving for an island and couldn't wait to get there.

My island-craving had to be kept in check, for the next ferry was not due for another hour or so.

A gregarious Harbour Newsagents' owner was duly puzzled by my accent.

'We have all sorts of people in Baltimore: Poles, Russians … In fact, two Russian girls from Turkmenistan work in a local restaurant …'

'Calling Turkmenistan Russia is like calling Ireland England,' I remarked dryly while browsing through the shelves. Among the items displayed were several Sherkin Island colouring books for kids and a magazine-like *Sherkin Island Community Newsletter.*

'This Newsletter is published by an English dentist who lives next door,' explained the loquacious shop owner. 'It sells like hot pies. I've already disposed of twenty-five copies today …'

I coughed up £2, opened the *Newsletter* and was pleasantly surprised by the relatively high quality of its contents and design – not bad for the 'community' that had shrunk five-fold since 1912 (see the epigraph) – to fewer than eighty people.

In the 'Sincere sympathy' column of the 'Announcements' section, I spotted a distinctive Russian name – 'Alenka Dunaeva' (the sympathy was expressed to her family and friends). The name puzzled me somewhat: firstly, one wouldn't expect to find a Russian on the Sherkin Island (well, at least, I wouldn't); secondly, diminutive suffix 'nk' in Russian personal names was normally reserved for little girls (the full lady's name in that case would have been 'Alena'). There was little doubt that some sort of a tragedy had occurred.

The punters of the only harbour pub were drinking their pints outside, their backs towards the strikingly beautiful bay, to which Murray referred as 'fine.' It was obvious they were all locals.

The ferry finally docked at the pier. She was called *The Black Point*. When I was already on the deck, I saw a man run out of the harbour pub and jump on board. He was the skipper.

The ten-minute crossing cost €7 one way – the fact that put *The Black Point* on a par with Heathrow Express, the world's most expensive train.

A boy of about twelve, probably the pub-loving skipper's son, was selling tickets on board. The boat carried just a handful of passengers, among whom was a man with a camera tripod going to Sherkin to take some scenic shots.

It was a bright sunny day, and the island itself was clearly visible all through the journey. Sitting on top of a rock was a phallic white lighthouse. Here I cannot deny myself the pleasure of quoting Murray's splendid description of the structure:

> 'The new Lighthouse (1889 – 1904) is one of the most important off the W. coast of Europe. It consists of a granite tower, 147 ft. high, with the focal plane of light 160 ft above high-water mark. It rises from foundations which stand at 11 ft. above low-water mark. The tower is a magnificent specimen of masonry; it was erected in sections in the contractor's yards in Cornwall to test the fittings before shipment. The dioptric apparatus is supplied with an incandescent petroleum burner, and the brass is a five-second flashlight, with a 750,000 candle-power. It was designed by the late Wm. Douglas, Engineer to the Board of Irish Lights, and erected at a cost of 90,000 pounds. The coast peasantry have a superstition that the rock sails a mile to the westward at daybreak, on the 1st of May every year.'

Incorporating history and technical details and providing a nice human touch in the end, it was one the finest descriptions in the whole of *Murray's Ireland*. It made me feel sorry for the global demise of lighthouses, these magnificent poetic structures that had helped our ancestors to find right directions in their lives ...

Although it was not 1 May, the rock, with the Lighthouse on its top, had indeed been moving closer and closer to me. In reality, of course (ignoring the *'superstition'*), it was actually *The Black Point* that was approaching it. I could already see the pier, to which we were about to moor, and next to it – a pile of picturesque ruins. Those were most likely the remains of the fifteenth century '*Friary for Franciscans*' (Murray), founded by the O'Driscolls. Destroyed in 1537 'in an attack by Waterford citizens,' in 1912, according to Murray, they were 'in a fair state of preservation.' By 2005, as I could clearly see from the boat, their 'state of preservation' had deteriorated, and several island cows were grazing peacefully amongst a cluster of moss-covered 'standing stones,' made of crumbling red bricks.

Dozens of cars were parked near the island's pier. Remembering that Sherkin was just 3.5 square miles large, it was surprising and could serve as another proof of my observation that the Celtic Tiger Irish could not (or rather didn't want to) walk and would soon mutate into Americans, about whom Ilya Ilf, a Soviet satirist, noted as far back as in 1935: 'Americans' legs will atrophy soon and will be replaced with special gadgets for pressing pedals.'

Among the parked cars, was even one Sherkin taxi!

On the same-sized Isle of Sark, from where all forms of transport, except for bikes and a handful of tractors, had been banned, they seemed to be coping without cars beautifully – as I could see for myself during my visit there several years before.

I resisted the urge to book that very island taxi for a 100-metre ride up the hill …

Followed the island's only paved road, I soon reached an isolated hut with a sign 'O'Neill's Shop.' The shop was shut. Rolls of toilet paper were prominently displayed in its dusty windows. Such a display would have been a huge hit in the pre-perestroika USSR, with its chronic shortages of toilet paper.

The shop also doubled as a post-office which, in its turn, doubled as a library. All three important island establishments seemed to be closed forever. Not a single living soul was in sight, and the silence was so intense that it made my teeth ache.

A dishevelled cat came out of the shop and rubbed against my leg. I was glad to have some company on the island that felt as if it had been unpopulated since the bellicose 'citizens of Waterford' ravaged it in 1537.

On the shop's locked doors there were several notices. One was for 'Cinderella Wants a Fella' – a play at the island's community hall. Next to it, there was a rather mysterious sign 'Toilets available at the Islander's Rest.' From the map I had picked up on the boat, I knew that Sherkin had two pubs: The Islander's Rest and The Jolly Roger. Having in mind the island's minuscule size, the establishments must have been in fierce competition. The kind invitation to the toilets was probably a clever marketing gimmick in that rivalry, and I wondered whether it meant that The Jolly Roger did not have toilets at all?

At least, there was something to investigate. There also appeared an urgent need to check the state of the publicised facilities, and not just for the purposes of research.

The publican was smoking outside The Islander's Rest in the company of a patron (until my arrival – the only one). They were the first two living creatures I had come across on Sherkin, if you don't count the friendly cat, of course. I could overhear snippets of their conversation: 'It was like a fecking Siberia in fecking Russia,' the landlord was saying. He was probably referring to the previous day's weather which had been truly awful indeed. At least, geographically he was more advanced than the Baltimore Harbour newsagent.

Inside, the pub was empty. The only seafood dish on the blackboard menu above the bar was tuna steak – a sure sign that the island's glorious fishing traditions were no more.

I picked up the pub's leaflet from the bar stand: 'The newly renovated bar is one of the island's informal meeting places. Here you can enjoy panoramic views in comfortable surrounds (*sic* – VV). The feeling is 'Just sit back, take it easy and enjoy yourself." Well, it was all true (including the 'surrounds'), apart perhaps from the 'enjoy yourself' bit …

The toilets, however, were in place and functioned properly.

The Jolly Roger, Sherkin's second 'informal meeting place' was about a hundred yards away. My footsteps were echoing in the air as I walked towards it. Halfway between the competing pubs, I stumbled upon a roadside map, with arrows pointing to local landmarks:

- Abbey
- Castle
- Lighthouse
- Church
- Post Office
- Beach
- School
- Community Hall
- Wildlife nature Reserve
- Library
- Accommodation
- Telephone

It was like a graphic imprint of the island's life.

The map made me realise that, having walked no more than 300 yards around the island, I had 'covered' most of Sherkin's 'sites,' with the exception of the 'Wild nature Reserve' and the 'Telephone.' The latter was ten yards away, and it worked! I ticked off yet another island's attraction in my notebook.

The Jolly Roger was twice as busy as The Islander's Rest: not one patron, but two – a young local couple. Yet it was still was anything but 'Jolly.'

I sat outside and had a snack and a cigarette (Ireland's smoking ban was in force on Sherkin, too!). A friendly little robin landed on my table, and I shared the sandwich with it.

Having looked around, I realised why The Jolly Roger did not advertise its toilets: they were outside and not particularly fragrant. On closer inspection, they were also very basic: just a hole in the ground. I hadn't seen 'facilities' like those since my visit to Romania in 1996. In the Australian Outback, they would call such a toilet a 'dunny' ('as lonely as a brick dunny in the desert' was my favourite Australian simile).

'It was so quiet in the pub that one hear a fly fart,' my good friend Bill Bryson wrote famously in one of his books.

I was reminded of his profound, if grossly down-to-earth, observation, when the young couple at the bar took turns to use the outside 'dunny.' It was so quiet that I could hear ... Well, I am not Bill Bryson and won't get away with describing the accompanying noises.

Before leaving The Roger, I asked the landlady about 'Alenka Dunaeva.'

'She was a toddler daughter of the Russian doctor, who came to the island with his family three years ago. Once she was playing near the school's swimming pool, fell into it and drowned. The whole island was in a shock for weeks. The doctor and his wife were normally very careful and watched their two children like eagles. It was only once they overlooked her ... Since then, no one has seen much of them, although sometimes they do come to the church choir rehearsals. There's one tonight and you can meet them, if you wish ...'

It was the second offer (the first being to join William on a fishing trip) I had to refuse on that day. Only for entirely different reasons.

Like every other populated bit of our planet, the tiny island of Sherkin did have a life, with its own joys and dramas.

It was time to retrace my (few) steps to the pier to catch the day's last ferry to the mainland. On the way to the harbour, I passed by another locked and abandoned plywood hut, with the sign 'Josephine Jeffries Art Gallery.' One of the works, displayed in the window, was called 'Brave Naivety.' I rather liked the title and thought it would have been a good name for the chapter about life on Sherkin. It also nicely summed up the very act of opening an 'Art Gallery' on a tiny wind-swept island. I felt affection for Josephine Jeffries and for her dry and self-deprecating sense of humour.

The cold winter sun was setting behind the ruins of the Abbey as I stood alone on the pier waiting for 'The Black Point.' The last rays of the ungenerous winter sun were being dissolved in the sea, like drops of milk in a tea cup. With every soft splash of the surf, the sky above my head grew a little bit darker, and the sea – a little bit lighter. Soon the sun vanished on the horizon, and the sea began emanating the fading translucent 'sunrays' of its own, as if slowly releasing the light it had accumulated during the day. A curious seal poked his rodent-like head out of the water, had a quick look at the sunset (and at me) and disappeared.

I was alone on the pier, surrounded by the islanders' rusty jalopies that seemed to have been parked there for ages. Most of them had no road tax stickers on the windscreens, and some didn't even carry number plates. 'Brave naivety,' indeed!

The ferry was nowhere to be seen, and I was suddenly hit by a mild fit of panic. What if the last boat of the day had been cancelled for lack of passengers and I would have to spend the night here, on the pretty, yet comatose, Sherkin? For all my love of islands, the thought did not feel very appealing. It made me realise with sudden clarity that islands were only perfect for brief getaways. Having spent the first three years of my life inside the impenetrable compound of a Soviet 'secret town,' which was itself embedded in a much larger cage of the former USSR, I had experienced a certain 'dark' nostalgia for enclosed spaces. Yet it was massively outweighed by the innate desire to break out of them.

'No man is an island, entire of itself; every man is a piece of the Continent, a part of the main,' wrote John Donne.

I was grateful to Sherkin for that revelation.

As my worries about the ferry grew, a woman and a boy – both wearing parkas – stepped onto the pier. Seeing them meant that I was no longer on my own, no longer 'an island' on the island.

Across the bay, I could discern the tiny black dot of *The Black Point* leaving Baltimore Harbour and heading towards us.

Having thrown the last glance at Sherkin from the ferry's deck, I had the impression that the rock, crowned with Murray's favourite 'Lighthouse,' which had become just a smudge of white on the darkening canvas of dusk, had moved again. Only this time, it had sailed not 'to the westward,' but away from me – to the East.

* * *

'Did you enjoy your trip?' The Harbour newsagent was waiting for me on the pier in Baltimore. His shop had been closed for the day, but he had been lingering on the pier to greet me back to the mainland.

He had probably felt a bit guilty for referring to Turkmenistan as a part of Russia.

But I had already forgiven him.

The Aran Islands

I knew we had entered Connemara when all road signs in English suddenly disappeared to be replaced by those in Gaelic. 'Connemara is country you visit for its scenery rather than its history,' claimed my 2004 *Rough Guide to Ireland.* Well, the part between Galway City and Rossaveel, from where we were to take a ferry to the Aran Islands, was rather barren and had very little 'scenery,' except for brown rocks and construction cranes, towering above them here and there. Looking at the cranes – the new milestones of the Celtic Tiger Ireland landscape – I was asking myself an old sacramental question: 'If to assemble a crane you need another crane, then how did the first ever crane get put together?' No one was ever able to come up with a plausible answer. Even Jerry O'Callaghan, my omniscient friend and travel companion, only shrugged when I confronted him with this daunting mystery of our existence.

A lot of digging was going on in the Rossaveel Harbour: excavators, bulldozers and heavy trucks were busily (and rather pointlessly) shifting piles of pebbles and sea rocks from one place to another. Loud blasts could be heard from the grounds of a nearby fish-processing plant. With every explosion, a cloud of shrieking seagulls would take off the rocks only to return several minutes later and to be met by yet another bang.

'Blasting activities!' – warned a serious sign on the pier.

'Why couldn't they just write 'blasts?' I wondered. ' Or has Ireland adopted the American politically correct style of signposting, according to which 'Food Center' was preferable to 'Restaurant' and 'Cremation Center' – to good old 'Crematorium?'

'What's all the shooting?' I asked a facetious pier-master.

'They must have heard you were coming – ha-ha-ha!'

In reality, as it transpired, the sounds of the blasts were broadcast at regular intervals by the fish-processing plant's loudspeakers to keep seagulls away from the fish tanks.

My friend and companion Jerry was very much in his own element speaking Irish to everyone. The replies he was getting were more often in English than in Gaelic.

On top of all other noises, a small, yet powerful, radio was blasting away in the pier-master's shed broadcasting the news of another hostage crisis in Russia. I had noticed that the world was much more prone to all sorts of wars and crises while I was away from home which made me think that had I stayed permanently put, our planet would have become a much quieter place.

In the café near the pier, I saw an elderly couple who had just returned from the Islands. They both had ruddy, wind-beaten faces of travellers and explorers. Or, possibly, heavy drinkers.

'We first went to the Arans forty years ago and then we learned one Irish word,' the man was saying. I was unable to find out which word they had learned as our ferry was already hooting angrily at the pier …

I always loved islands, and in the last fifteen to twenty years of my travel writing career had visited dozens of them, including the Faroes, the Falklands, the Ascension Island in the Pacific, the Hebrides (both Inner and Outer), the Channel Islands (all of them) and a number of islands and islets off the coast of Australia and Tasmania, including the obscure Three Hummock Island. The latter was then populated by hundreds of giant red kangaroos, thousands of poisonous snakes and one elderly English couple, who had their food and mail dropped from a plane once a week. Separated during Word War II, they vowed never to leave each other again and lived on the island until their deaths (within a month of each other) several years ago.

The islands' relative isolation from the rest of the world had always had a calming effect on me, and made me feel at home on almost any of them.

As the ferry was approaching Inishmore, 'the most tourist-oriented and least authentic of the Aran Islands' (*Rough Guide*, 2004), the first thing we saw was the neon sign of a Spar supermarket blinking above the harbour, like a lighthouse that had stranded ashore. Next to it, we saw another neon sign – 'Supermacs.' The latter was a fraction too small to pass for a lighthouse, yet large enough to be mistaken for a beacon.

We left our bags at an empty guest house on the pier, where we were greeted by a young receptionist – an Irish-speaking dark-eyed brunette of about eighteen. In pitch windy darkness, full of thick aromas of fish and sea, we climbed up the hill to the village. On the way, I shared with Jerry my puzzlement as to the guest house receptionist's swarthy and seemingly 'un-Irish' appearance.

'She must be a descendant of the Spaniards from the Armada who came ashore and settled here over four hundred years ago,' my knowledgeable companion explained.

Bracing myself for an evening in the company of Irish speakers, I asked him to teach me a couple of common forms of greeting in Gaelic.

The Inishmore Spar supermarket was the largest of all its namesakes I had seen anywhere in Ireland. Brightly lit and modernistic in style, it looked like a UFO that had crash-landed on the island. As I found out later, it was the ONLY shop left on Inishmore.

Inside, the supermarket was empty, not counting several salesgirls in bright-red aprons behind the tills and some of the counters.

Thinking it was a good opportunity to practise my non-existent Irish, I approached a plump and visibly bored young girl in the 'Deli' section.

'Dia is Muire Dhuiz!'[21] I greeted her amicably.

She looked at me strangely, yet with some distant recognition on her round face.

'Vi govorite po-russk?'i'[22] she asked me all of a sudden.

I would have been less surprised had she addressed me in Amharic.

Her name was Iovita, and she was a Russian-speaking Lithuanian from Vilnius!

'Most of the girls in the shop are Polish,' she told me (in Russian!) with a smile. 'Except for the one at the till who is from Estonia …'

We agreed to catch up with her the following day for possible filming (a Lithuanian living and working on the Aran Islands sounded like an interesting sequence). I had to restrain myself from practising on Iovita the second Irish phrase that Jerry had taught me: *'Slan Agus Brannaucht!'*[23]

We trudged through the dark and deserted village in search of any of the two Inishmore pubs. At some point we were overtaken by a lonely cyclist wearing traditional Sikh headgear. Then a couple of Aussies materialised out of darkness and asked us where they could get some 'tucker.' . . Authentic or not, the Celtic Tiger Inishmore was ethnically mixed, or 'ethnically filthy,' as my late friend Peter Ustinov used to jokingly refer to himself. In the course of a couple of hours, we had encountered many more foreigners than native islanders.

We finally installed ourselves inside the 'American Bar' – another 'unauthentic' reality of the islands, where we were surrounded by a small crowd of Irish-speaking local youngsters (the swarthy young receptionist from our guest house was among them, too). The interesting thing about their verbal exchanges was that their Irish conversation was heavily interspersed with **English** four-letter words. The melodious and poetic Irish tongue must not have had swear words as colourful and expressive as the language of Shakespeare and Gordon Ramsay …

I was hastily writing down that last profound observation, when Jerry interrupted me with a warning:

'You should be careful making notes here, for the patrons may take you for a government inspector checking whether they speak enough Irish …'

'What?' I muttered in disbelief.

21 Irish for 'God and Mary be with you!'
22 Russian for 'Do you speak Russian?'
23 Irish for 'Go with blessings,' or simply 'Goodbye!'

'The Irish speakers get special allowances for conversing in their indigenous language, but only provided they use it in everyday life …'

Despite my genuine interest in Irish and other European minority tongues, I was shocked by such a blatant case of politically correct linguistic tokenism. It suddenly because clear why on Ryanair flights from Dublin the attendants stumble through a couple of regulation Irish sentences before switching into English while making in-flight announcements. I also understood why at the opening of a session at the Dail the Speaker has to go through the same meaningless rigmarole … Tokenism does little to revive a dying language (or anything else, for that matter). On the contrary, it is the surest way of killing all remaining passion for it.

Had I indeed been a government 'language inspector,' I would have failed the youths in the pub: you cannot claim to speak your language 'enough' until you actually start swearing in it!

On the way back to our pier guest house, we popped into 'Supermacs' for a take-away meal. I normally wouldn't come close to a burger joint, but 'Supermacs – 100% Irish' was the only catering outlet on Inishmore still open on that late November evening.

The burger joint was staffed by one person – its manager, a short middle-aged man, with bushy 1970s-style whiskers that gave him a cockroachy look. He kept sniffing constantly – probably suffering from a cold.

For lack of customers, he was bored out his mind and, having put together our greasy fat-oozing packages, went outside to see us off.

'I am from Galway, but have lived on the island for twenty years,' he sniffed out.

'Do you miss Galway?' I asked him

'Not really. You see, I love the smell of rotten seaweed and miss it terribly every time I leave Inishmore.' He greedily sniffed in the cold island air which was indeed abundant with the stench of rotten seaweed.

The manager was the first Irish person with whom we had spoken on the Aran Islands so far. He was also the first rotten-seaweed addict I had ever come across …

There was only one TV channel available in our guest house – TG4, the Irish station based in Connemara. All its output was in Irish, except for commercials that were all in English! All but one – of TG4 itself! Another example of language tokenism?

To me, watching one of TG4 programmes (I think it was some sort of a literary debate in Irish) was – if nothing else – a great night cap: I was fast asleep ten minutes into it.

* * *

On the way to the village the following morning, I spotted a strict 'No Dumping!' sign in the harbour. Underneath the sign, there were two smaller-print inscriptions: one in Irish (translated with Jerry's help) threatening would-be 'dumpers' with a fine of €1,900; the other – in English promising a … €1,904.61 fine for the same offense! Using simple arithmetic, it was easy to calculate the price of being an English speaker on the Aran islands: €4.61 – not too harsh a penalty by any standards.

Next to the sign, there was a shop with the no-nonsense name 'Out of Aran' (only the missing exclamation mark stopped it from sounding rude and peremptory). It was selling locally knitted woollen sweaters, and one of its windows was adorned with another forbidding sign in five European languages (but not in Irish!) saying: 'Only five students at a time allowed into shop!' Obviously, it was not just English-speakers, but also 'students' who were not particularly welcome on the islands.

I was always of the opinion that the best starting point for exploring a city, a town or an island, for that matter, was a local coffee shop, and we were lucky to find a 'Lios Aengus Coffee House' right next to the above-mentioned Spar superstore.

Despite the café's obviously Irish name, it was owned and run by a … Norwegian lady, who was serving customers from behind the counter. The coffee shop was also doubling as a 'book exchange' (due to the recent closure of the island's library, as I was told) and that was probably why its menu, on a par with a 'Soup of the Day' was offering a 'Saying of the Day' which, on that particular morning was by Arnold Bennet: 'A cause is like champagne and high heels – you must be prepared to suffer for it.' I thought it was rather tasty …

'Lios Aengus Coffee House' was without doubt a focal point of the island's community. Inside, an old lady was busy dipping slices of bread in her coffee mug before consuming them slowly at one the tables. Jerry said he had not seen that peculiar way of Irish coffee-drinking since his mother did it ages ago.

Due to the smoking ban, most patrons were sitting outside. We shared a table with a twinkle-eyed local woman, whose hands were trembling as she was rolling up a fag. She looked and behaved as if she were either tipsy or on drugs. Or possibly both.

Having stared at me intently for some time, she declared: 'You used to be a priest in your previous life!' She then added that there was something Gaelic in me, too, and that I resembled Peter Ustinov (albeit, as far as I knew, the latter, having had an extremely mixed background that included some Ethiopian genes, did not have a drop of Gaelic blood in him). I was not sure whether to take her last remark as a criticism or a compliment. Peter Ustinov once wrote the following dedication on one of his books presented to me: 'To Vitali – brother, nephew, son – in spirit, in laughter, in rotundity, and in the tranquil earnestness of purpose.'

I think it was the 'rotundity' bit – more than anything else – that accounted for our slight 'resemblance.'

The woman then went back inside the coffee house and emerged with a scratch card that, as it turned out, had won her €10.

'See: I am in direct contact with the Lord,' she commented.

The only other obvious local (not counting two kittens playing happily on the road) in – or rather outside – the café was an old man in a 'peculiar costume': a black woollen hat and a matching black knitted sweater. He had the same twinkly sparkle (or was it a sparkly twinkle?) in his eyes. I had noticed a similar twinkle in islanders' eyes on numerous occasions on different small islands of the world. Was in because their eyes constantly had to reflect the water? Or, maybe, they simply felt more grounded and secure – and therefore happier – than most mainland dwellers?

A young man at a neighbouring table was sporting a sweater with 'Ventspils' (a town in Latvia) written across his chest.

'This is Dmitri, a Russian from Latvia,' the clairvoyant woman explained. 'He does minibus tours of the island.'

Having finished our drinks, we left the cosmopolitan coffee house and went for a walk along the island's main (and only) road – past the new primary school, the shed of the Bank of Ireland branch ('Open Wednesdays Between 1.30 and 3.30pm') and the weather-beaten road sign 'Next Cafe 4 Miles.' From time to time, we were overtaken by horse-drawn carts, or 'traps' as they called them on Inishmore, probably heading for the 'next cafe.' The road soon led us to the coast, where several bulldozers and excavators were digging up the beach to clear space for more Celtic Tiger bungalows with a sea view, next to a cluster of those constructed already.

The Celtic Tiger had definitely made it across the sea to the Aran Islands. The beast COULD swim, after all. Yet, its presence on Inishmore did not feel as oppressive and out of place as on the mainland. Maybe, it was due to the fact that, despite all the mess it created, the overall view from here was still stunningly beautiful. Even if the legendary 'island of O'Brazil, or Hy Brasail, the blessed paradise of the pagan Irish' *(pace* Murray) was nowhere to be seen.

Our interview with Iovita, the Lithuanian girl, in the island's second pub that evening was a disaster. Outside the Spar store, she was a shadow of her cheerful and smiling self. She complained of being lonely and kept downing one drink after another – to the point when her speech became slurred and no longer 'filmable.'

'There's n … nothing else to do here but d … drink,' she muttered shortly before we had to call the island's only taxi to take her home.

'It is like the plight of so many Irish workers abroad in the past,' Jerry sighed while packing up his camera. 'What an amazing turnaround!'

A Japanese couple, resident on the island, were our only travel companions onboard the ferry back to the mainland the following morning. They were taking an old radio receiver for repairs to Connemara.

I went out onto the deck. The blinking neon beacon of the 'Spar' sign was the only thing I was able to discern on the quickly receding cosmopolitan island of Inishmore.

Rathlin Island

A handful of sleepy morning commuters and a black retriever dog are the only passengers on the tiny Caledonian MacBrayne ferry called *Canna*, taking me to Rathlin – Northern Ireland's only populated off-shore island, six miles across the sea from Ballycastle.

One young man's luggage consists of several dozen toilet rolls and a baby car seat – a load that makes him look like a Soviet train passenger returning from a shopping trip to Moscow (toilet paper was always in short supply in the USSR, and triumphant pedestrians carrying dozens of toilet rolls on crude ropes, wound around their bodies like bands of machine-gun bullets, was a common sight on Moscow streets). Supplies must be not that brilliant on the island …

'Listen carefully to the safety announcement,' crackles the ferry's intercom, yet no announcement is forthcoming.

I come out onto the deck, from where I can see the whole of Ballycastle harbour, enclosed by a fence with barbed wire on top – a detail I was unable to spot from the shore. This makes me wonder whether I am going to find any barbed wire on Rathlin. From my printed travel companions (old and modern guidebooks), I know that the island's population has been going down steadily – from 753 in 1855 (Blackie), 350 in 1912 (Murray) to 'around seventy' now (Caledonian MacBrayne *Sail Away to Rathlin Island* brochure). Such steady decrease is due not just to 'traditional' Irish reasons: poverty and the Famine (in fact, during the Great Famine, the islanders may have fared better than most, with the abundant harvest from the sea around them) – but also due to centuries of ravaging clashes over the island between the English and the Scots.

There is one vehicle travelling on the ferry's car deck – an old battered jalopy without number plates. The skipper tells me that cars on the island are only allowed by special permission and can only be driven by islanders themselves. I wonder who may need a car on six-mile-long and one-mile wide Rathlin? Is it, like Sherkin Island with its abundance of cars to travel three miles, just a reflection of a new, Celtic-Tiger-inspired, reluctance to walk or cycle that I have observed all over Ireland, particularly in the South?

The small ferry is rocking violently, and I get worried that the car will end up overboard. Looking at it makes me dizzy: I must be experiencing the onset of sea-sickness. Luckily, there's not enough time for it to get worse, for one of Rathlin's lighthouses is already coming into view.

A red Royal Mail van is waiting for the ferry on the pier. The few passengers disembark and walk or drive away. Completely alone, I walk along the shore, past a children's playground under the sign: ADULTS ARE NOT WELCOME UNLESS ACCOMPANIED BY A RESPONSIBLE CHILD, and come to the oblong barn-like building that is the Richard Branson Activity Centre. Branson crash-landed on the island (or rather *splash-landed* in the sea few miles away from it) in his hot-air balloon thirty-one hours into his trans-Atlantic flight in July 1987. The islanders ferreted him out. Several months later, Branson returned to Rathlin to donate £25,000 to the restoration of the Manor House – the same building that now houses his own Activity Centre. I wonder what sort of 'activities' the Centre is involved in, but there's no one inside (or around) to ask.

Richard Branson was not the only famous island's visitor to drop by (in his case – almost literally). In 1898, Guglielmo Marconi and his assistants, Kemp and Glanville, set up the world's first radio transmission across the water from Rathlin to Ballycastle.

I pass by the island's only red phone box. As a mobile-phone *refusnik*, I find it hard not to use a public phone (there are not many of them left – in Ireland or in Britain) whenever I see one. I drop a coin into the slot, and – to my amazement (I am always surprised by a public phone that actually works) hear a loud buzzer. I call my best friend Sasha, who lives near Bratislava in Slovakia, and tell him I am calling from a tiny island in the Atlantic. There's nothing much else to say, so I put the phone down, but hearing my friend's voice – as clearly as if he were standing in the booth next to me – makes me feel less lonely.

I soon wander into Craig's Bar, on the sea front. The only other patron is a grey-haired old woman silently sipping coffee and periodically nodding off in her chair. A podgy ruddy-faced man, an archetypal little-island pub owner, is behind the bar. I think this must be Craig himself, but the publican says his name is Bertie.

I introduce myself and ask him to tell me about life on Rathlin. Bertie grabs this unexpected opportunity to talk.

'I grew up on the island. When I went to school in the 1960s, there were 250 people here. Lighthouses then had to be manned, you see … We had fifty or sixty pupils at the school, and now they have only three …'

With a distinct Northern accent, he recalls Rathlin's biggest moment of fame – Richard Branson's splash-landing.

'After rescuing Richard, boys from the island went in a boat to pick up the balloon, but failed – it was too big, massive – like an elephant …'

I ask him whether Rathlin was ever affected by the Troubles.

'Nah. We're too far away. The closest the Troubles came to us were a couple of little bombs in Ballycastle – that was all …'

The pub is getting busier: three sullen men with beefy wind-beaten faces come in and install themselves at the bar. It is obvious they will not be leaving soon. The coffee-sipping granny is sleepily pulling the handle of a fruit machine in the corner.

On the walls are old photos of island life and maritime paraphernalia: bits and pieces from the ships that crashed near Rathlin. Also – the stuffed head of a bull.

The head looks ragged, with tufts of brown hair peeling off here and there. He doesn't look very happy.

'Yeah, it does look a bit tired,' Bertie cackles. He has just finished serving the grim newcomers. 'The Lord of the Manor once got cross with the bull and shot him. Then he repented and had his head stuffed …'

A poster for Famous Grouse whisky hangs on the wall next to one for Guinness, and the TV is tuned to BBC1, which is broadcasting the Remembrance Day parade from Westminster.

Outside stands a marble sculpture of a chair facing the sea. THE WRITER'S CHAIR.UNDERTAKEN BY BALLYCASTLE WRITERS, says the faded plate on it that also carries a poem by Seamus Heaney:

'When you sat
Far-eyed and cold
In that basalt throne,
The small of your back
Made very solid sense.'

The poem brings about a pang of remorse at wandering on a wind-swept little island, instead of sitting in my 'writer's chair' and penning a great Russian (English? Irish? Australian?) novel. Most writers are familiar with this feeling: missing the process of writing when you are not writing and hating it when you are. Just like the proverbial seaman's nostalgia for *terra firma* when at sea, and for the sea when on land.

The more I explore Rathlin, the more I like it. I have a solitary picnic outside Richard Branson's manor house, munching away synchronically with the cows grazing behind barbed wire twenty metres away. It is soothing to realise that, unlike elsewhere in Northern Ireland, the only barbed wire on Rathlin is to stop the cows from escaping their pastures.

The already familiar Royal Mail van pulls over next to me, and the postman peeps out of the window. 'You must be the writer researching a travel book on Ireland,' he smiles. 'Welcome to Rathlin!'

He must have been tipped off by Bertie. Rumours travel fast on the island.

'Do you always work on Sundays?' I ask him.

'Unofficially,' he winks and drives away.

Further down the road, I come across a small general store called Island Treasures. Behind the counter is a young woman who was among my fellow passengers on the ferry this morning. She recognises me too. 'You must be the travel writer,' she says, and I am again amazed by the speed of Rathlin's wireless verbal telegraph. The heritage of Marconi?

Her name is Katrina. Born on Rathlin, she now lives in Ballycastle, but comes here daily during the season and on Sundays in winter to run the shop.

The stock of her 'treasures' is small, yet versatile – from socks to picture postcards. There are also British tabloids, which Katrina herself brings from the mainland, and amateur photos of Rathlin (£1 each) which, she assures me, are rather popular with visitors.

Katrina seems to share my love of islands: 'I don't like places where you can't see the sea,' she smiles while wrapping a loaf of bread for a little girl, squeezing coins into her tiny tanned fist.

'There's now only one teacher on Rathlin,' she continues. 'He commutes from the mainland and so does the island's only policeman and the Protestant priest.'

Katrina and her husband left the island several years ago, because he couldn't find a job here, but she always brings her ten-year old son to Rathlin with her. When he is not at school, of course.

Through the shop window, I see a little boy playing with the black retriever from the ferry. After a couple of hours on the island, I can recognise not just people, but animals, too!

The pair is playing next to another shop – a tiny grocery across the road. Its windows are boarded up, and the doors are locked, yet the hand-written sign above the entrance reads OPEN.

'The owner of that shop died last year,' Katrina sighs, 'and her son can't be bothered.'

I ask her about the man who was carrying the toilet rolls onto the ferry. 'He moved here with his girlfriend several years ago. They only recently got married. His wife is an artist, and he works from home too.'

Katrina seems to know everything about the island. In this little world, every minuscule detail suddenly acquires considerable importance, and the mainland, with all its conflicts, worries, troubles and The Troubles, fades away and appears increasingly insignificant. A very calming sensation. Like meditation that becomes life itself.

Before leaving Island's Treasures, I buy a pair of warm woollen socks, perhaps attempting (subconsciously, no doubt) to smuggle out some of the human warmth that I feel so strongly on Rathlin. As on every island that I visit, a fleeting thought of making it my home crosses my mind, but quickly vanishes – like a seagull dashing past the shop's dusty window with its piercing, almost human-like, scream.

As I walk back to the harbour, I am overtaken by a shabby island jalopy without number plates. The toilet-roll carrier from the ferry and his wife are inside. They wave to me like to an old acquaintance.

The last ferry of the day is chugging away from Rathlin as I approach. It turns out she was just changing piers – like a steam engine on a turntable – before mooring again.

This time the *Canna* is full of kids on their way to secondary school in Ballycastle for the start of a new week. Among them is a plump teenage boy on crutches who looks like a smaller copy of Bertie, the publican – most likely, his son (or grandson?).

Katrina is also on board, with her boy and the sad-looking dog. 'He doesn't like the noise of the engine,' she says stroking the retriever gently.

The almost familiar island is receding as the ferry makes her way through the burning sunset. I stand on the deck thinking of the rather clichéd story of Robert the Bruce's short exile on Rathlin. Having been defeated in battle, he (allegedly) fled to the island and hid in a cave where he took to watching a spider trying to climb up his thread. The spider kept falling down, yet persevered in its attempts until finally – on the seventh try – it succeeded. The sight of the stubborn spider (again, allegedly) inspired the beleaguered king 'to try, try and try again' – to the extent that he returned to Scotland and won his next battle with the enemy.

It occurs to me that, naff as it may be, the story serves as a good example of the spirit of Rathlin itself: ravaged, devastated, abandoned by so many islanders, it nevertheless maintains its own slow and laid-back life.

'Faith is the refusal to give up,' this quote from Jonathan Sachs, Britain's Chief Rabbi, hangs above my writing desk. I've been trying to follow it all my life.

Despite the presence of two churches – Protestant and Catholic – on Rathlin, it is 'the refusal to give up' that seems to be the islanders' main faith. This is probably why I feel almost at home here …

I take out my notebook and re-read the notices copied from the island's notice board:

RATHLIN FILM CLUB – EVERY WEDNESDAY.
COTTAGES TO RENT … (I wrote down the phone number – just in case).

And the most evocative one:

HAVE YOUR VHS OR VIDEO TAPES CONVERTED TO DVD. CONTACT DAVE.

No contact details follow …

St Kitts

My undying wanderlust was, most likely, first triggered by the four kilometre-long narrow-gauge Children's Railway in the outskirts of my native Soviet city of Kharkov. It was run and staffed almost exclusively by kids, who carried out all the duties (apart from the driving) for two under-sized yet gleaming and fully functioning locomotives – a diesel and a steam engine – pulling a dozen or so mini-carriages between the two stations: Park and Lesopark (Forest Park).

All Kharkov children wanted to be part of that toy railway and the number of small, yet fiercely incorruptible, conductors and ticket inspectors, all in smart uniforms, would at times reach twenty per carriage.

Unlike those kids, however, I never wanted to work on the trains. I wanted to travel on them, to be a passenger, to sit near the window with my eyes shut and, inhaling the inimitable railway aromas of tar and hot steam, imagine myself on board the Orient Express or the Trans-Siberian Railway. That was the start of my ongoing passion for railways, which later, having got mixed up with a passion for islands, resulted in my persisting fascination with island railways.

Since coming to the West nearly thirty years ago, I have experienced the Victorian ambience of still-thriving steam passenger trains on the Isle of Man, the squeaky electrical Soller trains and trams of Majorca, the freight-only narrow-gauge trains of Tasmania – where I was once lucky enough to take a ride in an engine-driver's cab – and many more. There's some inexplicable charm in those few remaining railways, confined to relatively small pieces of land and stubbornly refusing to be pushed out by other much more practical, yet much less romantic, means of transport.

Now, stuck at home as I am, recovering from major surgery and still in pain, I often meditate by looking back at the blissful sun-drenched day I spent last November on the island of St Kitts, which used to be England's very first settlement in the Caribbean – the so-called 'Mother Colony' – and is now part of the western hemisphere's smallest (and the world's seventh smallest) independent nation of St Kitts and Nevis. It is not common knowledge that this tiny island, with a population of under 40,000, boasts the 'last and only' railway in the West Indies (if we ignore private freight lines).

'Welcome to paradise!' smiled the skipper of the motor boat, taking me across the Narrows – a three mile-long stretch of the sea separating Nevis (where I stayed) from St Kitts, past the cone-shaped Booby Island, home to the magnificent brown pelicans, locally known as 'boobies.' The name of the boat was *Point Taken*, by the way.

Talking about the peculiar toponyms of St Kitts, I cannot help mentioning Mount Misery, renamed Mount Fertile in 1983, an extinct volcano dominating the island, and the station called Needsmust, from where my train journey 'needed' to start.

The eighteen-mile, thirty-inch-gauge railway was built between 1912 and 1926 to deliver sugar cane from the fields to the main sugar-processing factory in Baseterre, St Kitts' capital. With over 200 plantations and estates, the sugar industry of St Kitts and Nevis was the most advanced in the Caribbean. It was the first to move on from wind to steam power in 1870 and – unable to cope with growing international competition – the last to close at the end of 2005. Between those dates, sugar had been the undisputed king of the island's economy, with the railway as its main and only transport artery.

I had (needed?) to wait at Needsmust for nearly twenty minutes until a flock of coaches delivered several hundred tourists, mostly elderly Americans, from the huge Norwegian cruise ship, moored in the harbour and dominating the island like a new movable Mount Misery. The railway now functions only for the benefit of cruise liners' passengers and I was lucky to be there on that day.

Then, the so-far empty train arrived. It was like nothing I had seen before. Its double decker island series WR & YR coaches, with six-foot vaulted windows in the spacious air-conditioned parlours and open-air observation platforms, looked very much like a set of paddle steamers on wheels. Filled to the brim with obstreperous American tourists, brandishing pina coladas from the upper decks, it soon started to resemble a peculiar dry-land cruise ship.

Off we rattled, led by a small hand-car travelling about fifty yards in front of the little 0-6-0 Lyd2 hydraulic-power diesel locomotive (which was, as I later discovered, built in Romania and originally sold to the Polish State Railways – here we go: Eastern Europe comes to the Caribbean!) and testing the track to make sure it was safe for the train.

That brought back another, this time rather sinister, East European association: during night time feasts at his out-of-Moscow dacha in the early 1950s, the dying and utterly paranoid Stalin used to ask his factotums to taste food first to make sure it was not poisoned. 'Comrade Molotov, would you care to try that nice-looking herring?' he would say. That may seem irrelevant to the Caribbean, but for me, frequent flashbacks to history and to my own past have always been part of the magic of train travel.

The whole two-hour journey was like a slow levitation above the spectacular tropical landscape, as our eccentric ten-mile-per-hour train puffed unhurriedly past abandoned sugar plantations, with their crumbling chimneys and sail-less windmills.

To the accompaniment of the railway's own vocal trio, we rattled over twenty-three tall steel bridges spanning deep 'ghuts' (canyons), past small farms and villages, where cute local schoolchildren in their colourful and surprisingly neat uniforms were waving to the train for all they were worth. From their faces, it was obvious that each of them dreamed of becoming an engine driver, or at least a train conductor, and looking at them I couldn't help remembering Kharkov's Children's Railway, from where – many years ago – my global wanderings began.

Note: A story on the St Kitts' sister island of Nevis is in Part Twelve of this Bumper Book

Kefalonia and Ithaca

Never a keen beachgoer, I very much prefer exploring my holiday destinations' history and culture to being slowly barbecued on a beach bed. It was no different during my recent short break on the marvellous Greek island of Kefalonia, stuffed with history like your typical Greek dolmades are with rice.

Indeed, at different moments in the past, the island was ruled by the Romans, the Venetians, the Turks, the Turks together with the Russians, the French, the British, the Italians and the Germans. Yes, and occasionally by the Greeks, too (as it is now).

To me, the most amazing feature of the island was its Venetian baroque architecture (Kefalonia was ruled by The Serenissima for nearly 300 years) – all those graceful palazzi, with distinctive Venetian shutters, some of which even survived the massive 1953 earthquake, when ninety per cent of the island's buildings were destroyed.

As for the local technologies, on an island with just two working traffic lights, a handful of roundabouts and no new building allowed to have more than three floors, they initially looked disappointing. With time, however, I found that modern-day Kefalonians are technologically savvy, particularly the motorists on the precarious mountain roads (they have to be!) and the goat and sheep farmers, who routinely use drones and special GPS apps on their smartphones to keep track of their peripatetic herds, while still not discarding the back-up of good old jingle bells on the goats' and the sheep's submissive necks. The muffled sound of the bells, mixing with the chirping of cicadas, the trills of tireless nightingales and the gentle breathing of the Ionian Sea, merged in my ears into one harmonious Kefalonian symphony.

I soon discovered the Katavothres Sea Mills near Argostoli, the island's capital. An imitation water wheel now stands on the spot where a unique natural phenomenon was harnessed – sea water entering sink holes and creating a flow sufficient to power the mill. The people, who used the mills for centuries, were always wondering where the sea water ended up after going through the sink holes. In 1963, hydrogeologists proved (by adding 140 kilograms of fluorescent dye to the flow) that the water, having travelled many miles under the surface, re-emerged at the other side of the island, in the Melissani Cave – one of Kefalonia's main tourist attractions.

Inside the cave, visitors tour the underground lake in gondola-shaped boats, steered by Charon-like guides fond of cracking horrible jokes of the type 'this stalagmite was made in China.' I was put on the alert, however, when in between the quips, our guide claimed matter-of-factly that the cave we were in was also known at the Cave of the Nymphs – one of the unmistakable landmarks of Ithaca as described in Homer's *Odyssey*.

'Wait a moment!' I said. 'We are in Kefalonia, not on Ithaca, which was the home of Odysseus, according to Homer.'

'Ha!' our omniscient Charon chuckled. 'Don't you know that scientists have proved that the real home of Odysseus was here, in Kefalonia, and not on Ithaca?'

I was ready to dismiss the guide's words as another 'stalagmite-made-in-China'-type joke, for how could I forget our university's eccentric Foreign Literature lecturer, Professor Limonov (he had a terrible habit of wiping his nose with an Uzbek skullcap he used as a hanky and occasionally wore on his head, too) introducing Homer's notion of Ithaca (not Kefalonia!) as a powerful long-lasting metaphor for 'home' and 'homecoming?' Yet, having done some research later on, I came to the conclusion that our grimly facetious Charon might have had a point.

Indeed, when describing Odysseus's ten-year-long journey home from the Trojan War, Homer portrayed Ithaca as a low-lying westernmost island of four, which doesn't fit the actual mountainous Ithaca to the east of Kefalonia. There's a huge mismatch in other geographical details too. A British amateur scholar, Robert Bittlestone, having studied numerous ancient accounts, recently came to the conclusion that *Odyssey* could have been set not on Ithaca, but on the Paliki Peninsula (in western Kefalonia). He argues that the isthmus now connecting it to the rest of Kefalonia was submerged in Homer's day, making Paliki an island at that time.

This brazen point of view was shared by a number of experts, including Professor Anthony Snodgrass of Cambridge University, Harvard's Gregory Nagy and – significantly – Greek historian Nikolas Livadas, who in his book *Odysseus' Ithaca: The Riddle Solved* claimed to prove that the real-life site of Odysseus's Palace, to which the hero had been craving to return and where his faithful wife Penelope waited patiently, was indeed not on Ithaca, but near Livadi on the Paliki Peninsula.

Livadas's approach was highly scientific: to establish the exact location of the palace, he used (among other techniques) the pioneering radiocarbon method, based on measuring the radioactivity of archaeological samples. Thus science came to undermine the historical veracity of Homer's beautiful reality-based legend,

Does it really matter? On Ithaca itself, just a short ferry ride from Kefalonia, they think that it does, and I don't blame them: who would wish to let go of the world-famous historical concept that attracts visitors in their thousands? A local tourism brochure *Welcome to the Island of Ulysses* (another name for Odysseus) tries to explain the now obvious discrepancies between the real Ithaca and Homer's version by 'Homer's lack of knowledge' or by his 'poetic licence.' But during my brief visit to Ithaca, I had a feeling that the locals were themselves no longer sure – which explains the proliferation on Ithaca of 'Odyssey Studios' and 'Odyssey Apartments.'

Yet, if you ask me, they do not need to worry: Ithaca is still stunningly beautiful. As such, it will always be associated with Homer's immortal poem and with the idea of homecoming, too.

After all, it does not much matter where travellers have to return to – Ithaca, Kefalonia, Manchester or Timbuktu – as long as they call it 'home.' The ultimate distinction between a traveller and a tramp remains unchanged since the times of Odysseus: unlike the latter, travellers do come back.

Part Seven
My Europe

Venice

'When I went to Venice – my dream became my address,' Marcel Proust wrote famously in one of his letters.

To write about Venice is banal. But it is even more banal *not* to write about it.

After my many visits to this amazing city, I came to regard it as an ageing, yet still graceful, woman suffering from insomnia and dragging restlessly around the house in her worn-out, loose-fitting slippers in the night. Soft splashes of water against the ancient Venetian stones are like shuffling of slippers across the floor …

Yes, let's face it: Venice is geriatric and slowly dying. This 800-year-old town-sized toy was never intended to last that long. Its founders, the spice-trading Venetian merchants, lived by the principle, later formulated by Madame de Pompadour, '*après nous le déluge*' – 'after us the deluge,' and were successful in translating it into reality (or rather into unreality, for Venice is so thoroughly *unreal*). They built this baroque equivalent of Disneyland for their own delight and hedonism, without giving much thought to the future.

Unable to withstand the pressure of time, Venice is now crumbling apart. Its underwater supports, made of Siberian cedar, can no longer resist the rot. The walls of the palaces on the banks of the Grand Canal are covered with cracks and moss. Priceless paintings inside are being eaten by moisture.

Fastidious and down-to-earth American visitors are right: Venice stinks. Who wouldn't after 800 years of slow decay?

And yet, Venice is like no other place in the world.

At sunset, when the opaque, mica-like water in the canals begins gleaming suddenly with a magical translucent glow of its own, as if slowly, almost reluctantly, discharging the sunlight it has accumulated during the day; when blinds fall like thick black eye-lids of an Italian beauty on the gaping eye-sockets of tired old houses; when gentle tolling of distant church bells mingles with the soft sucking chorus of lovers' kisses – there suddenly comes a whiff of fresh sea breeze, a reminder of the days when Venice signified ships, exotic ports and new trade routes to be explored.

On a par with moisture and rot, the walls of modern Venice are being eaten methodically by the voracious eyes of tourists, mainly couples, coming here from all over the world in search of romance. Venice is romance guaranteed. No one knows how many families have been ruined and how many love affairs moulded by this tender Venetian sea breeze, full of lust and libido.

To come to Venice as a loner – as I have done on numerous occasions – is a torture and should probably be made punishable as a minor breach of public

(Venetian) order. The place is so overwhelmingly 'romantic' that you feel an irresistible urge to share it with someone you love.

However, it's not all romance for the locals, whose number keeps dwindling unstoppably: between 20,000 and 30,000 native Venetians leave their city every year in search of a more mundane existence …

What is happening behind these tightly shut blinds, which make Venetian houses look so lifeless and aloof after dark?

The truth is that everyday life in Venice is agony. The city's sewage system is in a deplorable state. Antediluvian rubbish-collecting boats are not coping with the tons of waste that keep floating in the canals like little drifting archipelagos of empty Coke cans, potato peelings, shreds of paper and other refuse of slovenly modern civilisation.

One of the main reasons for the locals' exodus is that in Venice one cannot drive a car, and a car-less Italian is as unsustainable as a beer-less German, a Vodaphone-less Finn, or a camcorder-less Japanese.

True, some young Venetian males do try to impress their dark-eyed girlfriends by tearing along the canals in their motorboats at breakneck speed, with a roaring ghetto blaster astern. But even this popular way of local courting is growing increasingly difficult with tightening of water-traffic regulations. After a hapless American tourist drowned in the Grand Canal, when her gondola was overturned by a wave raised by a passing motorboat several years ago, the Venetian water police clamped down on reckless drivers, or rather sailors. Speed limits were introduced. Special parking havens for boats were established. Boat parking tickets were being issued.

In short, life is tough for the resident Venetians; that is why they are leaving – and no town, not even Venice, can survive without locals.

The only natives who still seem to be prospering are luggage porters and gondoliers (as of last year, the latter require official licences). An unwary tourist is always at risk of having his shoulder bag snatched from him by an overzealous and uncalled-for porter the moment he steps of the airport shuttle boat on to Venetian soil. The bag would then be mounted onto a huge (and empty) luggage trolley, capable of carrying a ship container, and taken a couple of hundred yards to a hotel – for the price close to that of a business-class plane ticket from London.

As to the gondoliers, I came to realise why they are were all so cheerful and always ready to burst into a song, despite the fact that most of them had clearly had both of their ears trodden on by a bear (a Russian idiom to describe the people with no ear for music). Prices of gondola trips are so exorbitant that only reckless honeymooners and rich wastrels seem to be able to afford them. Stone-faced and uncomfortable, off they float along the canals to the accompaniment of squeaky 'Santa Lucia-a!'

Like every reasonably large city, Venice has its morning and afternoon rush hours, flotillas of multipurpose boats chugging up and down the Grand Canal: taxi boats, fruit and vegetable boats, fireboats, bread delivery boats, even black-and-red hearse boats. On board the *vaporettos,* locals can be easily identified by not looking around themselves like troubled hens, but talking on their mobile phones, or burying their faces in a fresh issue of *Il Messaggero* or *Il Gazzettino* (Venetians – like most Italians – are very politically astute). They are likely to be catching up on a yet another corruption scandal in the highest echelons of Italy's power.[24]

I remember seeing obituaries for Bertino Graxi, a former Italian prime minister, implicated with Mafia connections, put out on display in the cobbled streets of the colourful and almost tourist-free Venice's Old Jewish Ghetto, next to some medieval stone sign-plates warning against the use of foul language, about ten years ago. Underneath the posters – ageless hook-nosed women were chatting loudly on the benches and boys were forgetfully kicking the ball against a synagogue wall, with imminent collateral damage to the windows of the neighbouring houses.

The curious thing was that Graxi was then still alive, and the obituaries were but a sign of the Venetians' contempt for the disgraced politician who had let them all down. The natives of Venice have always been known as somewhat 'picturesque' and demonstrative ('In Venice one never loses the sense that life is being staged for the onlooker,' as noted by Jonathan Raban), but also – straightforward and uncompromising.

Even if Venice – as environmentalists assert – will be submerged by the sea in the next 200-300 years, that peculiar Venetian spirit is not going to die. You can feel it now on the ever deserted and overgrown with wild grass island of St Georgio Maggiore, just a three-minute *vaporetto* ride from St Marco Square, teaming with flocks of tourists and pigeons. You can sense it in the Giardini area, the venue of the famous Biennale, where incongruous avant-garde sculptures from all over the globe stand in the park, scaring away fussy Venetian sparrows. You can feast on it in an ordinary *al fresco* trattoria, off tourist tracks, where you will expose yourself to the obstreperous exhibitionism of Venetian street life (when Venetians shout at each other, it's normal; when they start whispering, it means anger). You can savour it in the old Armenian monastery on the island of San Lazzaro, where Lord Byron once

[24] For a number of years, I entertained a tongue-in-cheek 'theory' of the possible origins of the seemingly ineradicable Italian sleaze: the country, after all, had almost sixty governments since the end of World War II – each next more corrupt than the previous. My observations showed that the level of fraud in this or that part of the world was in direct proportion to its climate: the higher the average temperature – the more scam-ridden the country. Indeed, Italy was Europe's warmest place and by far the most corrupt. The same was true about Queensland in Australia, Brazil in South America, India in Asia and the Central Asian and Caucasian republics of the former Soviet Union. On the other hand, I had never come across a major corruption case in Finland, Sweden or Norway. To say nothing of Greenland …

lived in a monastic cell, studying the beautifully intricate Armenian language, with all its guttural gurgling sounds and twelve noun cases.

'The visitor [to the monastery] will be convinced that there are other and better things even in this life,' he wrote there.

There are few better things in this life than Venice – this unique old city on 117 islands in the Adriatic Sea.

At the peril of sounding banal, I have to conclude: if we are given the doubtful happiness of being born, we must at least see Venice.

Amsterdam

I don't know why, but Amsterdam always evokes in me childhood associations, not just the memories of my own early years, but rather the joyful feeling of being a child again similar to the one experienced by adults in Disneyland and in Venice, this medieval playground of doges and spice merchants.

Is it the characteristic smell of canal water mixed with odours of tar and tulips? Or, maybe, it is the soothing shuffle of bicycle tyres against the cobbles? Or the sight of Amsterdam's old ladies – these 'God's dandelions' (a good Russian expression) and Queen Mum look-alikes, with the mischievous twinkle of past indiscretions in their fading eyes? Or clusters of narrow-facade gabled houses (in the Middle Ages, Amsterdam landlords were taxed per square inch of their house façades' area), huddling around the canals and looking like tower-chambers from a Russian fairy tale?

But most likely, it is the trams – these moving wrinkles on Amsterdam's face that, curiously, make it look younger. Trams were the main (and pretty much the only) vehicles of the city of my childhood, and no noise is more familiar to me than the sound of an old tram, squeakingly turning the corner. As a little boy, I used to wake up to it every morning ...

For me, Amsterdam begins and ends with tram number one, from the Central Station to Overtoom, where my elder son Mitya now lives. Chatty, smiley, multilingual and multi-racial, this tram is a microcosm of the Dutch capital itself. It is a stark contrast to a taciturn and stuck up London bus, or to a Tube train carriage, with its strict mind-the-gap attitude.

The people on Amsterdam's tram number one make a lot of noise. They laugh out loud; they read Kafka and Umberto Eco as the tram freezes for what feels like an eternity at the permanently red Amsterdam traffic lights. Its progress along the congested narrow streets is so slow that at times it gives the impression of sliding backwards in space and in time – towards the melting pot of medieval Amsterdam, and its passengers get miraculously transformed into diamond-cutters from Antwerp, Jews fleeing the Spanish Inquisition, Huguenots from France and dissenters from England, all of whom found refuge in this most tolerant and accommodating city in the world, the 'people's' capital of Europe.

Amsterdam's main distinctive feature is (and always was) that – unlike London – it never pigeonholes people according to their origins, occupations and addictions. It accepts them as humans first and only then – as politicians, junkies, academics, beggars, plumbers or prostitutes. It embraces humans in all their complexity: with their merits and sins, peculiarities and idiosyncrasies, passions and peccadilloes. It invites them all, without exception, to the never-ending party celebrating tolerance, if not temperance: the twenty-four-hour-a-day bash called Amsterdam.

Overtaken by cars, cyclists and some disabled pedestrians in wheelchairs, tram number one is crawling towards the city centre – past canals and across bridges – a seemingly endless journey. On this bridge over Keizergraht, bike-junkies – the addicts maintaining their habit by stealing and quick-selling bicycles – congregate. In pre-euro times (BE – Before Euro) one could acquire a stolen bike from them for as little as 20 guilders (£7). It is not common knowledge though that the bike-junkies have their own website, where a potential buyer can view a stolen bicycle before agreeing a pickup point. Old bikes and those that do not sell fast enough are routinely dumped into the canals, from where a special city council dredger fishes them out once a month.

From the tram window, I spot a smallish Die Port Van Kleve Hotel in a street off Dam Square, where I stayed during my first ever visit to Amsterdam in August 1991. My KLM flight Melbourne-London (I was flying to London from Australia, where I then lived) included a free stopover in Amsterdam which I decided to use walking off my jetlag and preparing for a week of interviews and public talks in the UK. For the first two days, I was staggering along the canals as if drunk, overwhelmed by the half-forgotten smells of European summer. Of course, I committed a common boo-boo of a first-time visitor to Amsterdam by asking for a cup of espresso (and nothing else!) in a seedy coffeeshop next to my hotel, and the barman eyed me with scornful disbelief, as if I had ordered a cup of sulphuric acid. On the second night, I went – alone! – on a candle-lit dinner cruise along the canals. Surrounded by snogging homo- and hetero-couples, I wouldn't have been surprised to discover that going on such a 'romantic' cruise on one's own constituted a minor offence in Holland. But I didn't mind my loneliness in the least. The boat was sliding noiselessly under the bridges, and the reflections of burning candles were wriggling in the water like some restless fiery serpents.

I remember feeling such indescribable happiness at being back in Europe after many months down under, at being re-united with the smells and sounds of my childhood that I couldn't help thinking this simply cannot last. From experience, I knew that one could only feel such bliss on the eve of a disaster.

The following morning, the military coup took place in Moscow, where my mother was still living. Barred from returning to the Soviet Union as a recent defector, I spent the next several days trying – in vain – to get through to her by phone, from Amsterdam, from Brussels and then from London. Persistent crackles at the other end of malfunctioning lines were like muffled screeches of tank caterpillars against the old stones of the Red Square. I was only able to speak to her after the putsch was defeated. Having given up smoking six months earlier, I lit up again on the first day of the coup and have been unable to quit ever since.

Yes, Amsterdam has a somewhat sinister touch for me too. It was there that I learnt about the 9/11 terrorist attacks on America. The night before, Mitya and a bunch of his cosmopolitan Amsterdam mates dragged me into a disco – the first disco experience in my entire life. I tried to resist, saying I was too old for it, but they persevered, and, fuelled by a couple of Amstels, I soon found myself twitching and shaking next to my son in the middle of a crowded hall. Contrary to my expectations, I was enjoying it all: the music, the open and civilised faces of my fellow-dancers of whom – I was pleased to note – I was by far not the oldest. Everyone in the disco was bouncing strictly within his or her imaginary little square never trespassing into someone else's space. At some point, a young Dutch woman came up to Mitya and whispered something in his ear pointing at me. 'What did she say?' I yelled trying to outcry the deafening techno beat. 'Have I done something wrong?' 'No!' my son screamed back. 'She told me that looking at the two of us she had guessed we were father and son and that it was very nice to see us dancing together …' In short, the experience was profoundly *gezellig*, to use a popular Dutch colloquialism.[25]

It was early morning of 11 September 2001 – Mitya's 21st birthday.

Past my favourite café 'Chaos,' with its wonderfully eclectic interior and friendly informality of service (patrons are encouraged to dump pistachio-nut shells on the floor which makes it easier to sweep), tram number one enters the fringes of the Red Light District which I always found not much raunchier than London's Carnaby Street. If you overlook occasional drug-peddlers, the tax-paying law-abiding women in the windows (the District police brochures warn repeatedly – and somewhat intriguingly – that 'they are not always women') and confused British louts haggling with bouncers over the price of those women (or whoever they may be)[26], it can be a very interesting place. Where else in Europe can you see establishments like 'Cannabis Connoisseurs Club?' Or a thought-provoking exhibition of conceptual 'Media Art' under the motto 'Are You Experienced?' (one of the exhibits – 'Disinformation' – allows visitors to inscribe a huge painting with images created by their own shadows)? Where else tourists desperate for a pee are officially invited to relieve themselves at the district police station? But the thing that strikes me most about this little 'enclave' of super-tolerance in the midst of tolerant Amsterdam is how strict its boundaries are: three metres away there's no sign of it whatsoever. You can literally brush past it without spotting anything unusual. Like the Cheshire Cat's smile, the Red Light District is noticeable only to those who want to see it.

[25] The closest English word to *gezellig* (pronounced heh-ZEL-ick) I can think about is 'cool,' although its meaning is much broader. A *gezellig* environment is one that allows good times to happen. It is almost like a vibe, and it is contagious. As a Dutch friend once explained, a *gezellig* place is cosy and inviting and full of *gezellig* things that make it so *gezellig*. A two-hour leisurely meal with friends is *gezellig*, whereas gobbling up a Big Mac on your lap in the car is not. He said that the constant pursuit of *gezellig*-ness is the key to the Dutch psyche.

[26] I once overheard a bouncer trying to extract a payment for two consecutive visits to a 'window woman' from a British man of a soccer-hooligan appearance. The latter was only prepared to pay for one visit only, his argument being: 'I was on my way out, but she just pushed me back in!'

The tram screeches to a long, seemingly endless, stop in Laidseplein – a small square in the hub of Amsterdam. Here, after 11pm each night, one can watch an amazing street performer – a slightly built teenage-like young man, with a sad Mediterranean face. Dressed in a soiled tracksuit, ridden with holes, he attracts crowds by climbing lampposts and trees while kicking a football in the air and never dropping it onto the ground. His technique being second to none, I think that the only reason this 'feet juggler' (as I came to call him) hasn't yet been recruited by Ajax, Eindhoven or some other Dutch premier-league football club is a worry that he would start climbing goal-posts in the middle of a match. Also, I often wonder what he does during the day: sleeps in some dodgy vermin-infested room pressing the ball to his chest like a piece of his sultry childhood somewhere in Turkey or in Macedonia?

In a lane off Laidseplein, there's a small cinema showing obscure foreign movies that never hit the big screen. I once went there with Mitya. They were running an American film, with Dutch subtitles. At some point, a protagonist said: 'I don't like wogs' which was subtitled 'I don't like Italians' in Dutch. 'They don't have derogatory words for Italians or any other nations in Dutch,' explained Mitya, who had just come back from a live-in crash-course in Dutch in a suburban … convent paid for by the Amsterdam company for which he worked. A player for an Amsterdam amateur soccer team, he also assured me that the worst curse he had ever heard on a Dutch football pitch was 'Goddamn!'

What a gentle nation, I thought then.

Gentleness and tolerance of the Dutch have their limits though. They will be quite happy to chat to a visitor in colloquial English, or in a number of other European languages which most of them can speak after secondary school. But if you have lived in Holland for a year and still do not make an effort to learn Dutch, they are likely to start ostracising you. I don't blame them.

The tram turns into Overtoom, a long traffic artery connecting the city centre with the melodiously alliterated suburb of Lelyllaan. Halfway along it, hidden from idle tourist eyes by massive wooden gates, is an establishment, which for me represents the spirit of Amsterdam better than anything else. It is the city's oldest and the most prestigious (*sic*) squat yes, a 'wrongfully and unlawfully' (by both British and Dutch legal standards) tenanted premises, known to Amsterdam police and happily tolerated by them, despite its obvious illegality. Getting a place in The Squat is almost as hard as finding a reasonably priced apartment in London's Mayfair. Only in The Squat accommodation is free. Its residents: tramps, buskers, travellers, recovering drug-addicts and impoverished students, often with small children, also enjoy free Internet access, free charity-supplied meals, free in-house concerts of leading Amsterdam pop groups, and so on. In its basement, The Squat houses Radio Patapoe – Amsterdam's oldest pirate radio station, also illegal, yet tolerated, because, as my son explained, its signal is rather week and does not reach outside central Amsterdam.

Mitya certainly knew what he was talking about, for on top of his other Amsterdam incarnations, he was also a DJ for Radio Patapoe, the world's only radio station whose casually vetted (by squatters) 'anchors' were not just unpaid but had themselves to contribute €5 a month towards the equipment maintenance to be allowed on air. He once invited me to his basement 'studio' to take part in his Saturday program on music in poetry, or poetry in music – we couldn't quite sort that out. As a regular visitor to The Squat he was entrusted with a coveted key to the wooden gates.

I felt at ease in the tiny cubicle of a 'studio,' lit by an antique lamp in the shape of Patapoe the dog, in whose memory the station was named. Sitting on a battered leather sofa, so deep and soft that it negatively affected one's self-esteem, I spoke with relish into an old-fashioned, heavy (and, no doubt, extremely 'tolerant') microphone and read out poems in English and in Russian, whereas Mitya was introducing musical pieces with a peculiar estranged and almost robotic radio DJ's voice.

The basement studio reminded me of my writing closet in Moscow. When Mitya was a baby, we occupied a single room in a communal flat, and I had to type away in an extended wall cupboard not to wake him up. By ironic coincidence, the room's previous occupant had been a radio pirate, using the cupboard for illegal broadcasts at considerable risk to himself: the word 'tolerance' was not in the police lexicon in Brezhnev's USSR. So, in way, I was an old timer in radio pirates' dens …

Meanwhile, The Squat was living its normal life. Children were playing with crude self-made toys in a small walled courtyard. A dishevelled man in ragged clothes was browsing the Internet. An invisible young woman's voice, with a good London accent, was loudly complaining of 'cold turkey': 'I can hardly walk, and the headache is splitting …'

On shutting the wooden gates behind me, I suddenly realised that I had fallen head over heels in love with Amsterdam.

I hop off the tram at Overtoomsesluis, and pop into Ter Brugge – a pub, where Mitya always leaves a set of house keys for me, our family key-drop, so to speak. The staff know me and fish out the keys from under the cash register. Before moving on, I drink a cup of tepid wishy-washy Amsterdam espresso tasting and smelling of unclean canal water, with 'Sally,' my obnoxious Salisbury suitcase, parked at my feet. It is late afternoon, and the city canals start slowly releasing the sunlight they have accumulated during the day, but many patrons are still having their breakfasts. Amsterdam wakes up late. At midday, it often feels like London at 6am, and in late afternoon, like London at 9 o'clock in the morning. This peculiar Amsterdam time-loop makes lunch there feel like breakfast, and dinner like lunch. Sometimes, it is hard to believe that anyone works in this permanently partying city. But some people do, and my son is one of them.

I wait for a drawbridge across the canal to join together after letting a barge called *Marianne* and a flock of carefree Amsterdam ducks pass through a small lock. The skipper waves to me from the cockpit. From here, it's just a hundred yards to my son's flat. In a couple of minutes, I am looking up at a handwritten plate underneath the doorbell – 'M de Boer; R Wilson; D Vitaliev.'

I could stare at it for hours rejoicing at the lucky fortune of my Moscow-born and Melbourne-educated boy, for there are few better things in this life than being young and living in Amsterdam.

Vienna

Similar to the alcoholic protagonist of V Yerofeev's famous *Moscow-Petushki* (*Moscow Stations* in English) novella who, having wandered around central Moscow for years, could never find the Kremlin, I had been unable – no matter how hard I tried – to spot the Danube while in Vienna last December.

Mind you: unlike the hapless Yerofeev's anti-hero, I was perfectly sober!

Was the Danube, Europe's main water artery, avoiding me? I don't think so. The real reason for my failure was that the wide and spotlessly clean streets of the Austrian capital contained too many distractions to leave an inquisitive pedestrian much river-spotting time.

I was in Vienna for a couple of days to take part in the Future of Transportation World Conference. There could be no better venue for that kind of gathering – and by that I do not mean the spectacular Vienna Messe Conference Center, the world's best and biggest, but the Austrian capital itself, recognised by several well-reputed surveys as the world's most liveable city, with excellent public transport as one of the main 'liveability' criteria, at the end of 2019.

I take interest in those surveys, probably because I had myself lived in the city that repeatedly came on top of them – Melbourne, Australia. In all the surveys' history, Melbourne was by far the most frequent winner of the world's most liveable city title, with Vancouver and Seattle as runners up. Yet in recent years, much to everyone's surprise, Vienna overtook them all.

To better understand the technology of the cities' 'liveability,' let's have a quick survey of some of those annual surveys (tautology intentional).

The most prestigious of them is probably the one conducted by the Economist Intelligence Unit (EIU) which routinely assesses 140 cities for their stability (safety), healthcare, culture, environment, education and infrastructure, including transport. Between 2011 and 2015, Vienna was ranked second behind Melbourne, but in both 2018 and 2019 the Austrian capital came first.

For the sake of comparison, let us note that in the last year's survey Paris took twenty-fifth place, London forty-eighth, and Damascus, the capital of war-torn Syria which has been getting the world's lowest ranking for the past seven years, came last.

American HR and financial services firm Mercer releases its own highly regarded annual city ranking (with the main criteria being safety, education, healthcare, culture, environment, public transport, access to goods and services, hygiene, economic stability, etc) – the Mercer Quality of Living Survey, which ranked Vienna first for ten consecutive years – from 2009 to 2019!

The other two notable rankings – by the Monocle's Quality of Life (one of the main criteria – international connectivity) and Deutsche Bank Liveability (pollution, affordability etc) surveys – had also listed Vienna among their top five during the last several years.

How do you know that you reside in the world's most liveable city? The Viennese would probably have their own answers, but looking back at my own Melbourne experience, I could name the following: clean air, broad streets, plentiful shops, affordable and comfortable housing, excellent healthcare, no traffic jams, no visible poverty, little crime, no slums, no homeless people. Indeed, in all my years in Melbourne, I saw rough-sleepers only once or twice, and they were – quite obviously – just sleeping off a boozy night …

How about heat waves, you may ask in the aftermath of the recent Australian bushfires?

Well, unfortunately (or, maybe, fortunately for some) climate was not a defining criterium in any of the above-mentioned surveys …

Surely, to spot such long-lasting indicators as well-being and crime levels, one has to reside in a city more or less permanently. Therefore, there wasn't a lot of boxes that I was able to tick off while in Vienna, with most of most my time spent inside the spacious auditoriums and endless corridors of the Messe Conference Center. But I did manage to take some short walks – not in the tourist-ridden city centre but in the residential parts of Vienna Prater, not far from my hotel. And if inside the Messe, the talk was mostly about the future of transport, about autonomous, electric and vertical-fight vehicles, it was all quiet and down-to-earth in the clean and quiet baroque-style streets and lanes, with names like Hillerstrasse and Schonngasse. To me, the area, with its merrily chirping sparrows and bleak satin skies reminiscent of my Ukrainian childhood, felt nostalgically East European.

Strolling unhurriedly under a timid, almost reluctant, snowfall, I saw groups of local council workers in green uniforms mulching and wrapping up trees for winter, then sweeping the already thoroughly swept-up ground spotless. Trams and buses, mostly electric, were silently rolling past – frequent, dispassionate and half-empty. Near the entrance to the Metro station there stood a capacious wooden crate with 'Lost Property' written on it in English. It was obviously intended for the visitors, for it was highly unlikely for the punctual and meticulous locals to lose anything in their beautiful Vienna, which has changed so much since 1980, when Alan Whicker labelled it 'a … city with a streak of gentle hopelessness.'

Having failed to find the Danube, I nevertheless discovered (at the Conference and beyond) that the medium-sized city's public transport network ('Wiener Linen') operated five underground, twenty-nine tram and 127 bus lines; that the tickets could be bought everywhere, including tobacconists (until 1 January 2020, Vienna was the last European capital that allowed smoking in public places), and by smartphones, which made it possible to buy a ticket for another person (as a Vienna friend kindly did for me) in the online ticket shop. Well, if there's a motto for a highly liveable city anywhere in the world, it should probably read 'No Hassle!'

Speaking of hassles and how to overcome them, the accessibility of the 'Wiener Linien' is one of the world's highest. As for the blind and visually impaired people, they can get help from the special machines at stations and tram stops that offer tactile maps and voice output ...

At the Conference, I also learned about PTV Optima's real-time traffic management software offering detailed forecasts for the entire 'Wiener Linen' up to one hour and thus helping operators and advance planners to save time and to reduce carbon emissions. To quote the PTV Optima's promotional brochure, 'Vienna's citizens benefit from a high quality of life. They spend less time stuck in traffic or searching for less congested route to reach their destination ... ' But what I actually liked most about the brochure was the expression 'Vienna's citizens' (as opposed to 'Vienna residents'), as if Vienna were indeed a separate country issuing its own highly coveted passports.

I would've loved to have one!

Montreuil-sur-Mer

Nothing about Montreuil-sur-Mer is what you expect. To begin with, it's not quite 'sur mer,' but is built on a silted-up river estuary, about twenty miles away from the actual sea.

First-time visitors tend to be swept off their feet by the unexpected charm and beauty of that seemingly unremarkable small town in the north of France, a mere forty-five-minute drive from the Port of Calais. It happened to me about twenty years ago when I first stepped on the town's ancient cobbles, still remembering the touch of the wheels of the cart in Victor Hugo's *Les Miserables* that ran down the old man Fauchelevent, only for him to be saved when reformed convict Jean Valjean famously lifted up the cart with his bare hands.

Yes, Hugo adored Montreuil, visited it often and used the town's ancient streets as real-life settings for his best-known novel. Hugo's creative time in the town is commemorated each summer by a special *son et lumière* festival when the best-known scenes from the novel and its numerous stage and movie adaptations are re-enacted by the locals with the help of specially engineered light and sound effects.

Montreuil has always encouraged creativity and innovation – artistic, literary and technological. The town's amazing engineering heritage began in the year 987 with the construction of the first fortifications on the promontory above the Canche river valley. Over the next thousand years, they were constantly improved and modernised to keep up with technological progress. With the advent of artillery, for example, the medieval defence system was adapted to suit new attack techniques and the archers on top of the towers were replaced with cannons. By 1567, military engineers had made the town a French border stronghold against Spanish forces – which had captured Calais and Amiens – with bastions, earthworks and new fortifications in one weak point, which had a gentle slope to the river.

In the seventeenth century, the town's ramparts were improved first by Jean Errard, engineer for King Henri IV, and later by the noted military engineer Sébastien Le Prestre de Vauban, who added to the Citadel its distinctive '*demi-lune*' (half-moon-shaped) entrance, the arsenal and in line with his own famous 'more powder, less blood' doctrine – a large powder house.

The pillboxes, added to the bastions in 1845, came to good use during the First World War when they housed a telephone exchange for the British Army General Headquarters (GHQ).

Yes, it is not widely known that the British GHQ was based in Montreuil from 1916. According to a rare book *G.H.Q. Montreuil-sur-Mer*, penned by an anonymous author under the nom-de-plume 'GSO' (General Staff Officer), and published in London in 1920 (I own a copy): 'Military convenience alone dictated the choice of Montreuil as the site of the General Headquarters of the British Expeditionary Force in France as soon as that Force reached to such a strength as to take a full share of the campaign.'

Undoubtedly, the fact that the town had already been heavily fortified played a role, too. To quote the same mysterious GSO again: 'Had it not been for those Rampart walks, the toilsome life of GHQ at Montreuil would have been hardly possible. The road from anywhere to anywhere, if time allowed, was by the Ramparts and most went by the Ramparts unless work was hideously pressing.'

GSO goes on to say that the already existing fortifications of an old fosse were converted into 'hard tennis courts,' which were not used a lot, because 'really there was not time to follow tennis or any other sport.'

Walking along the same ramparts today is a fascinating experience for those who do not suffer from acrophobia, for looking down at the valley deep underneath, with birds floating above the tree tops well below your feet level, can easily take your breath away. Not a big fan of heights myself, I looked up and was delighted to see some local lads kicking a ball inside the same enclosed 'old fosse' that used to house the tennis courts.

Field Marshal Douglas Haig, the British Commander-in-Chief, resided with his entourage at Beaurepaire, a country house on the outskirts of Montreuil. A keen horseman, he could often be seen riding through the town and the countryside in the company of his aide-de-camp. When in 1928 the question of erecting a statue in his memory was raised by friendly Montreuil townsfolk, an equestrian version was opted for. The Nazis, who occupied the town in 1940 (they turned the Citadel into military barracks), removed the statue and melted it down. After the war, the people of Montreuil recovered the original mould from the sculptor Paul Landowski and cast a new one.

Thus, Field Marshal Haig can still be seen on horseback in the middle of the Market Square. In summer, the famed Commander-in-Chief becomes hardly visible in the 'camouflage' of plane trees and flowers surrounding his statue and filling the whole town. Montreuil is an official 'ville fleurie,' the second most beautiful (according to the latest competition) in the whole of France, with overabundance of wisteria-covered balconies and window boxes, bursting with petunias and geraniums.

On 14 July, Bastille Day, all the natural 'guardians' of Field Marshal Haig's statue are joined by countless stalls and makeshift tents of the annual brocante – one of northern France's largest flea markets, specialising in antiques and bric-a-brac.

From 6am, the town turns, Cinderella-like, into one flowery market place, with stalls filling all of its streets and squares – a cross between a somewhat chaotic open-air art fair and a history-of-technology museum. Or a proverbial scrapheap of history that came to life.

Among the goodies on sale at the 2019 brocante, I ticked off: old motorbikes and spinning yarns; tobacco-flattening machines and coffee-grinders; antediluvian Nikon cameras and electric salt grinders, as well as knives, swords, saxophones, bath tubs, sewing machines and an early twentieth-century American 'Warbler' phonograph ('Worm-driven governor, can be wound while laying') that could easily be mistaken for a modern analogue record player.

Yes, the 'phonograph' was genuine and in good working order. Just like Montreuil-sur-Mer, my favourite French town.

And This is One of my Favourite Hotels in Europe, also in France:

Like any proper detective story, this one starts with a corpse in a hotel room. Or rather with the coffin containing the dead body of a hotel guest, who – after a thorough investigation by hotel detectives – turns out to be alive, albeit asleep, and even snoring loudly!

In my travel writings, I have repeatedly touched upon the subject of techno hotels – a growing brand of guest houses presenting themselves as technologically savvy and astute. I spoke of the HI techno hotel in Nice, Colour Hotel in Paris, Krakow's Metropolis Design Hotel, Wilde Aparthotels and many more. At the recent Business Travel Show in London, I learned about the brand-new 'music hotels,' 'fashion hotels,' 'movie hotels,' and even 'the world's first ice-cream hotel,' with 'vintage furnishings, Nordic design' and state-of-art ice-cream-filled freezers in each room, in Helsinki, Finland, where it's freezing most of the time anyway ... To woo customers in the ever-so-competitive hospitality market, enterprising hoteliers more and more often resort to extremes, including technological ones. A couple of other examples:

If you are obsessively fond of flying and can't have enough of long-haul flights (I still have to meet such an individual), in Tokyo's Akasaka Hotel, you can prolong the pleasure by staying in the firmly grounded first-class cabin of a jumbo jet. For those equally obsessed with trains, the Washington Hotel in Tokyo's Akihabara neighbourhood offers a room stuffed with functioning model trains travelling day and night along ninety-eight feet of the in-room track. If that's not enough, guests are encouraged to bring their own model trains (imagine a peripatetic businessman who always carries a couple of those in his suitcase) and play with them for all he is worth, only occasionally stopping to look out of the hotel window facing ... yes, Akinabara station, with the full-size and very real Shinkansen (bullet trains) passing through it.

And at Berlin's Propeller Island City Lodge, which can be safely described as the quirkiest techno hotel in Europe, you can literally sleep on the ceiling – without first turning into a fly, Jeff Goldblum-style (in a special box suspended from the floorboards), if you stay in the 'upside-down room,' where even the windows, with the help of special optical effects, have upside-down views. You can also opt for a frighteningly convincing prison cell, or indeed a 'coffin suite,' mentioned at the very beginning of this piece. In short, as it was put in a review of that very hotel in a British tabloid: 'If you want a good night's sleep, you may not want to stay there.'

But what if you actually like themed and techno hotels (for you always learn something new while staying in them) and still crave 'a good night's sleep,' meaning all the habitual good hotel's comforts? I've been searching for a perfect themed hotel for many long years and am happy to report that I have finally found one: Detective Hotel in Etretat, Normandy, France – where I stayed for one night last January.

Let me assure you first of all that my stay there was not a freebie. Like the notoriously incorruptible Karl Baedeker's hotel inspectors of yesteryear, I paid the full fare for my Inspector Clouseau room. Yes, each room in that amazing hotel is named and themed after a famous fictional detective: Sherlock Holmes, Miss Marple, Tintin, Maigret and so on. One of the featuring sleuths – Arsene Lupin, often called 'the French Holmes' (in one of the stories, he helps Britain's royals to find some stolen family jewellery), has a local association as the creation of writer Maurice Leblanc, who had his holiday home, Le Clos Lupin, in Etretat.

Unlike all the fictional characters the rooms were named after, the hotel's founder and owner, Noel Chambellan, was a real-life detective, albeit retired. Most of his professional life, he worked as a forensic scientist and graphology expert at the French National Institute of Crime Research. His scientific skills have helped to solve a number of 'big' crimes, including the 'famous' 1990s robbery of a money-transporting armoured van, shot at with an armour-piercing projectile by the robbers. By analysing the shell's make and trajectory, Mr Chambellan was able to establish its origins which lead to the criminals' arrest. A fragment of the van's pierced armour plate now adorns one of the walls in the hotel's spacious lobby, which can be easily mistaken for a spy technology museum, its closets and cupboards brimming with such long-outdated, yet intrinsically charming, gadgets as voice-recording pens, rear-vision glasses, tiny spy cameras, UV torches to read the notes made in invisible ink, antediluvian radio transmitters, and so on, all selected and displayed with expert knowledge and good taste.

Unlike in many other techno hotels, technology there was not the main attraction, but a welcome addition to cosiness, hospitality and good service.

What made the hotel particularly attractive was not just its owner's taste and professionalism, but also his irrepressible sense of humour. 'This whole detective make up is but a good joke,' Mr Chambellan told me. And rightly so, for despite the a *priori* gruesome contents of corpses and murders, rightly associated with the detective theme, most guests leave the hotel with a smile. And the rooms' quirky, yet tasteful and not overloaded, interiors play a role in that too. My Inspector Clouseau room, for example, had only a handful of the relevant objects and gadgets, but each of them was both meaningful and spot-on: the authentic-looking inspector's (or Peter Sellers'?) beige rain coat on the hook behind the door; Clouseau's nunchaku, a Japanese martial arts weapon of two sticks on a chain, for the training fights with his assistant Cato; the bespoke flowery curtains familiar from the movies, and the famous pink – reminiscent of the Pink Panther – telephone apparatus, with a peculiar ear-phone (also pink) extension. The illusion of Clouseau's presence in the room was almost complete, and all through my short stay in it I could not stop smiling.

I bet I kept smiling in my sleep too, but no one can confirm that. Except perhaps for Inspector Clouseau ...

Marseille

'Shock! Horror!' These words sum up my first impression of architect Le Corbusier's famous Radiant City (Ville Radieuse) on the outskirts of Marseille.

Exhausted after a prolonged train journey, I arrived on a scorching July afternoon. The moment I stepped out of the cab, the enormous fifty-six-metre-high fortress-like building fell on top of me. Well, it actually didn't, but it felt indeed as if I was about to be squashed by its oppressive raw-concrete Brutalism.

The moment I walked through the rows of piloti, concrete columns that prop up the structure like stilts, and entered the semi-dark lobby, I was inundated with memories of similar high-rise concrete dwellings in the Soviet Union. The only thing missing was the all-permeating cabbage-soup stench that used to dominate the doorways, the stairs and other communal spaces of Moscow apartment blocks in the 1960s and 70s.

Unlike in the latter, however, the lifts in the Radiant City were all in good order and appeared not to be used as public toilets. I got out on the third floor and checked into my room – one of Le Corbusier's renowned cellules ('cells'), modelled on a monastic cell of Galluzo, a Carthusian monastery in Tuscany visited by the architect in 1907. To reach my cell, I had to walk along a long, dimly lit corridor, lined on both sides with flats and occasional offices.

The cell was tiny and ascetic: a bunk, with a capacious storage compartment underneath, a bedside table that doubled as a cupboard, a small balcony and a minuscule walk-in shower cabin of the type you find on board overnight ferry boats. The outside toilet was to be shared with the dwellers of neighbouring units – again, a familiar feature of a Soviet communal apartment, where multiple wooden toilet seats, one for each of the sharing families, used to hang in the corridors like oversized and totally luckless horseshoes.

Notwithstanding the shared toilet, the room was surprisingly cosy, pleasantly cool and perfectly functional. Having shoved my few luggage items into the abundant wall closets and storage boxes ('as little furniture as possible' was one of the main principles of Charlotte Perriand, Le Corbusier's interior designer), I installed myself in one of the iconic LC04 steel chairs to look through my notes on Le Corbusier, the most famous and controversial twentieth-century architect, and his equally famous and controversial creation – the Radiant City.

The vertical garden city

The design of the Ville Radieuse was largely inspired by the shared utilities inside the Constructivist Narkomfin building, which Le Corbusier spotted in Moscow while working on a blueprint for the House of the Soviets in the 1920s (his project was eventually rejected by Stalin). The young architect was then under a huge influence of Ebenezer Howard, the founder of the world's first Garden City (Letchworth in the UK) and his book *Garden Cities of Tomorrow*.

If Howard's ultimate aim was to take London workers out of the late-Victorian slums and resettle them in the countryside, Le Corbusier, who hated the very concept of a conventional urban dwelling ('Let's kill the street!' was one of his favourite mottoes), aspired to build 'a garden city in the sky' to provide affordable accommodation for those who had lost their homes in the First World War. His dream was to create 'a calm and powerful architecture,' which, in his view, necessitated (among other things) the use of reinforced concrete. His vertical city was supposed to be a truly 'brutalist' structure (nothing to do with 'brutality,' but from the French betonbru, meaning 'raw concrete') – unappealing and even shocking (as it was initially for me) from the outside, for, to me, Brutalist architecture cared little about appearances, but practical and comfortable for the residents. The building's dimensions were to be calculated using Le Corbusier's own 'Modulor' system, based on the proportions of a human body.

The Marseille Project, commissioned by Raoul Dautry, then France's Minister of City Planning, took many years to mature and over five years to complete. It was initially pooh-poohed by the locals, who christened it '*La Maison du Fada*' ('the nutter's house' in the Provencal dialect). When the building finally took shape in 1952, it was astounding: a 50,000-tonne tower block sitting on thirty-four pillars of bare reinforced concrete. The structure had 337 apartments of fifteen different kinds, yet each of them, irrespective of the style, had a large balcony and a bay window.

Most of the Radiant City's public spaces, lifted high above the ground, were situated in fully functioning but traffic-free 'mid-air streets' on every third floor, including the main 'high street' on floor 3, with several shops (a bakery, a café, a supermarket – now closed and turned into a disco) and later a hotel. In the long and straight 'streets' (corridors) on other levels, one could find a primary school, a kindergarten, doctors' surgeries and small workshops.

The main communal area, with its Narkomfin-style shared utilities, was on the vast roof terrace. It consisted of a running track, a playground, a paddling pool and a gym. In Le Corbusier's eyes, the roof, with its 180-degree sea views, was supposed to represent the upper deck of an ocean liner, moored in the Marseille cityscape.

Not very popular in the beginning, the Radiant City eventually became one of the most desired residential properties in Marseille. Its Corbusian duplexes (two-level apartments) now attract affluent upper-middle-class professionals.

In for a walk

After a much-needed nap, I went for an evening Radiant City walk – all inside the one-building 'Machine for Living' – Le Corbusier's vision for urban dwellings.

Having left my room on the fourth floor, I walked past Dr Herve Aubin's surgery, then descended to the 3rd floor 'high street' from where muffled sounds of music could be heard. The bakery, the café and the bookshop were closed, but in a small public square near the lifts a party was in full swing: several dozen youngsters were dancing obliviously to music played by a DJ.

I took the lift to the top floor and found myself on a spacious roof terrace. Large and bright southern stars mingled with the distant lights of the off-shore Frioul Islands.

Despite the late hour, the roof was full of people. As in many southern cities, where siesta is observed during the hottest hours of the day, the residents were out for a stroll. Families paced the perimeter of the roof leisurely. Occasionally, they were overtaken by joggers running around the circular racing track. Children splashed in a paddling pool, lit up with blue lights, while their mothers practised Pilates nearby. Older residents, with coffee cups in their hands, sat on benches between a funnel-shaped ventilation shaft and a windbreak protecting the now-empty outdoor theatre stage. They sipped coffee and looked up at the stars.

I was pleased to see that despite the off-putting Brutalist exterior, the community inside the Radiant City was thriving. The 'Machine for Living' was very much alive.

I also came to realise why the building appeared so painfully familiar to me. Le Corbusier's far-reaching plans were picked up by urban developers all over the world, but were never implemented in their entirety. And whereas the Corbusian concepts of high-rise high-density buildings were put into practice almost everywhere, the architect's 'quality of space' principle (both inside and outside the tower blocks) was mostly forgotten. Hence all those drab residential 'estates' of Sheffield, Glasgow, East Berlin and East London, the 'new development suburbs' of Moscow and other Soviet cities: all poor imitations of Le Corbusier's radical, yet fully functional (as shown by the Radiant City) projects.

A frozen dream

In the morning, the corridors of the Radiant City swarmed with dog-walkers returning to their flats with their pets in tow.

I had breakfast in a superb in-house restaurant, Le Ventre de l'Architecte ('The Architect's Belly'), on the terrace overlooking the sea. The restaurant, just like the hotel, the bookshop and the estate agency specialising in 'unusual living spaces,' were not part of Le Corbusier's original plan. In fact, he would have probably been unnerved by the fact that a hotel named after him was now part of the Radiant City, intended for permanent dwellers, not tourists. But tourists these days are a daily reality of the Ville Radieuse.

'Inside the building, there used to be lots of unused and abandoned spaces,' says Alban Gerardin, who bought the would-be hotel in 2003. 'We were passionate about architecture and tried to restore the rooms, corridors and terraces to the original Le Corbusier design. We scoured antique shops and flea markets in search of Charlotte Perriand's furniture pieces and placed them in the hotel rooms. The idea was to reproduce the soul of the place without too much glitz.'

I had a chance to look at a number of other cells and duplexes where Le Corbusier's esprit nouveau ('new spirit') is lovingly preserved, including the legendary apartment number 50, which used to belong to Lillete Ripert, the Radiant City's in-house nursery school teacher and Le Corbusier's friend. Yet perhaps the most convincing example of how well vintage Corbusian spaces could be adapted for modern use was, again, on the building's multi-purpose roof. In 2010, Marseille-based artist Ora Ito discovered that the old 1960s gym was up for sale. With the support of the Le Corbusier Foundation, he bought the space, restored it to its original design and, in line with the Radiant City philosophy of a 'place for all to share,' opened MAMO Gallery, an arts centre to which all residents of the building have free access. When I was there, it hosted an exhibition of Dan Graham's breath-taking large-scale steel-and-glass pavilions. They fitted beautifully in the uncomplaining roof terrace, next to the children's playground.

So, what is the Radiant City? A radical architectural statement? A masterpiece of modern design and construction engineering? A village in the sky? It is all those and many more. If Schelling described architecture as 'frozen music,' I would rather call the Ville Radieuse Le Corbusier's 'frozen dream' – his concrete, in both senses, vision of what modern public housing was supposed to be like.

Lyon

'When you can see Mont Blanc from the city centre, it is going to rain soon,' they say in Lyon. Rain was obviously not on nature's agenda on the morning of my arrival: Europe's highest mountain peak was firmly out of sight. Instead of Mont Blanc, however, I was about to see something much more spectacular. That 'something' was called 'the future.' Far from being just a soundbite, the future was both visible and palpable. Some of it was also liveable and lived-in. It was located on the isthmus between the rivers Rhone and Saone, to which old guidebooks unanimously refer as 'a tongue of land' – the site of the old Port of Lyon plus seventy-odd hectares of industrial wasteland right in the city centre. Dubbed 'La Confluence,' or the Confluence Project, it was a major part of Lyon's redevelopment within its historic confines – a kind of regeneration which did not and will not spill out to surrounding suburban green belts and the countryside, as is the case with most similar projects almost anywhere in the world, the latest UK example being the recently endorsed housing development in the green zone outside Cambridge.

La Confluence, on the other hand, will double the population of Lyon's historic downtown without expanding its territory, thus bringing the original hub, with its rivers, wildlife and the new residential infrastructure, back to the city while making it modern, sustainable and eco-friendly: emitting no more greenhouse gases in 2020, the expected year of the project's completion, than it did at its inception in 2000. In short, La Confluence is all about developing the city in the middle of … the City!

City of the Future

In the words of Lyon's mayor, Gerard Collomb, 'Confluence will give us a clear vision of the city of the future that we are seeking to build – here and now. This smart city will combine economic growth with a smaller impact on the environment.'

The project is now in its second phase. The first phase was completed last summer, when the Lyon-based Euronews TV Channel and all its 400 journalists moved into its new headquarters in Jakob MacFarlane's Orange Cube Building, a spectacular red rectangle, with a designer gap in the façade and multiple patio atriums – virtual wells of light – on each level.

La Confluence is Europe's largest urban development scheme – an architectural Mont Blanc it its own right. So I did manage to see a 'peak' after all.

The environment I was exposed to that morning was in stark contrast to the ugly claustrophobia of an enormous, yet architecturally suffocating, 1970s hotel near Gatwick airport where I had spent the previous (sleepless) night before boarding an early flight to France's third most populated city and its second (after Paris) most important cultural metropolis.

Nestling in a valley and surrounded by hills, Lyon immediately makes a visitor feel cosy and almost at home, as if you have finally arrived at your chosen destination. Unlike London, which was allowed to grow higgledy-piggledy throughout the years, Lyon has always tried to control its expansion, and that historical trend was taken into account by La Confluence's main developers – the international architectural firm Herzog & de Meuron in cooperation with the landscaper Michel Desvigne.

Nothing compares to actually being there and seeing with your own eyes the harmonious and highly innovative architectural structures, parks, roof gardens, e-bikes (traffic is very pedestrian-friendly, for the area advocates shared parking and shared electric car schemes) and the rivers adding a special water-colour-ish tint to its natural light. It does look rather like a vision of the utopian future that came to life. But, unlike most urban utopias, La Confluence is for real.

Tradition

Developing a city 'within itself' is not unique to Lyon or to France, although French cities have the reputation of being historically less static than elsewhere in Europe and more open to transformation, remodelling and restructuring.

One simple architectural or engineering solution is often capable of changing the face of a neighbourhood anywhere in the world. In Rio de Janeiro, a cable-car line has altered a formerly unremarkable part of the city beyond recognition. In Barcelona, the removal of an old port from the Old Town has opened up the sea front and made the city centre much more spacious. In Melbourne (I was told that La Confluence's developers had learned a lot from that Australian city), the construction of the Southbank Quarter on the banks of the once grossly neglected Yarra river had added an entirely new 'suburban' dimension to the otherwise highly urbanised environment. In Ljubljana, the pretty Ljubljanica river has been made the main architectural and cultural artery and a focal point of the Old Town, uniting it into one new social entity (I was always of the opinion that rivers connect rather than separate, whereas seas and oceans divide). Yet in Lyon, they went farther than all the above – not so much in the method of urban redevelopment, but in its sheer scope.

The statistics behind La Confluence are impressive, to say the least. The project covers an area of 150 hectares of which seventy hectares are reclaimed land. Over €750 million have so far been invested in the project's business real estate. On its completion in 2020, the area will incorporate 140,000 square metres of housing space divided among 4,000 apartments; 230,000 square metres of service and business premises; 15,000 square metres of shops, hotels and other consumer services, and 35,000 square metres of public amenities. The number of new homes will reach 4,000, and the area's population is expected to be 16,000, compared with 7,000 in 2000.

The district, sometimes referred to as the first fully sustainable neighbourhood in France, will also generate 25,000 jobs, compared with 6,000 available there in 2000.

Behind these seemingly dry figures lies a new identity of the old city centre – aquatic, green and eco-friendly, with 3,280 planted tall trees, clean water, clean air and thirty-two species of wild birds nestling in its unpolluted parks and forests, certified by the World Wide Fund for Nature (WWF).

'The environmental policy for Lyon Confluence is continuously raising the bar and constantly fuelling the quest for further innovation,' says Jean Pierre Gallet, managing director of SLP Lyon Confluence. 'Recognised as a WWF "sustainable neighbourhood," this urban planning project is now aiming to become carbon-neutral.'

Partnership of Light

Speaking metaphorically, La Confluence district is being created by the confluence of two 'rivers' – Creativity and Technology. The undisputed flagship on the waters of both is known as Hikari.

'Hikari' means 'light' in Japanese. It is also the name of the partnership between property developer Bouygues Immobilier/SLC and the renowned Japanese architect and engineer Kengo Kuma. Hikari's aim is to reach an architectural balance between nature and human needs.

Kengo Kuma's company is one of the Confluence Project's main players, overseeing the construction of the complex of three highly innovative buildings: Higashi (East), Minami (South) and Nishi (West). Together, they will comprise Europe's first positive-energy development (PED), meaning that on completion the buildings will produce more energy than they consume.

Due to their box-like shapes, with large triangular notches and extensive glazing helping to minimise the borders between 'inside' and 'outside,' the buildings will be literally full of light, or, in architect-speak, will have 'exceptional luminosity.' Made of materials that limit energy loss through their surfaces, they will all accommodate internal gardens, shops and offices, as well as residential premises. The entire complex, which will be finished in 2015, will give the impression of lightness and movement, consistent with Kuma's vision of nature-inspired architecture. Its main distinctive feature, however, will be not architecture, but energy efficiency.

Each of the three buildings will have three sources of renewable energy production: photovoltaic elements on the roofs and facades, a geothermal energy system, and a co-generation power plant fuelled by locally produced rapeseed oil.

The energy production and consumption will be pooled through a power communication network. A battery storage system will cover the risk of power failure and over-consumption at peak times. It is expected that the complex will consume 1,400MWh per year, ie fifty to sixty per cent less energy than required by the existing thermal design code, and will produce about 0.2 per cent more than that. With the help of the special in-built monitors, the buildings themselves will be able to adapt to changing environmental conditions and reduce or increase their energy input and output accordingly.

Who said that houses were dead? The Hikari complex – like the whole of the new Lyon city centre district – is definitely going to be very much alive. And full of light too.

As it was put by Kuma himself, 'Lighting is one of the most energy-hungry aspects of office environments, in particular. As such, light has been both the starting point and the common thread in this project. We started out with the various technical, thermal and energy constraints and sought to find the ideal form. The architectural line we adopted led us to make deep openings in the facades in order to provide as much natural light as possible, cutting down the need for artificial lighting and improving visual comfort.'

Factory of Light

'Light' – or '*lumière*' in French – is one of the most frequently used words in modern Lyon, which, among its many other claims to fame, is the birthplace of the modern cinematograph – a machine that records and projects moving images. It was created here – coincidentally – by the Lumière brothers, whose last name (rather symbolically) means 'light,' and whose first ever film, released here in 1894, was the forty-six-second-long *Sortie de l'Usine de Lumière a Lyon – Workers Leaving the Lumière Factory in Lyon*, which a not-too-experienced translator could render as 'Workers Leaving the Factory of Light in Lyon.'

I would like to stick to that last version, even if it is not one hundred per cent correct, for modern Lyon, and particularly its emerging 'new' old city centre, can be best described as the Factory of Light, where 'light' stands for energy, architecture and lifestyle.

Calais

A couple of years ago, a group of Anglophile Calais youngsters, frustrated by the persistent negative stereotyping of their city by the British media, chipped in and published a richly illustrated and highly unorthodox *Calais Free Map For Young Travellers Made by Locals* which also contained a lively *Guide*, listing multiple attractions of that ancient French city.

'In the past few years, you've probably heard of Calais in a negative way because of the refugee crisis. Calais ... has been depicted as unwelcoming, even dangerous, place. But you are reading these lines which means that you are curious enough ... and ready to discover what Calais truly is: a town full of unexpected beauty, generosity, hopeful youth, funny people, poetry and creativity (and also seagulls, masses of seagulls),' they wrote in the tongue-in-cheek, yet warm and sincere, Introduction to the *Guide*, which – like a couple of other, mostly self-published, Calais guidebooks and maps – quickly became a bibliographic rarity.

Indeed, the Hatchards bookshop in the concourse of St Pancras Station, next to the Eurostar terminal, stocked multiple guidebooks to most sizeable French cities and towns, including Calais' neighbours Amiens, Arras and Boulogne, but absolutely nothing on the region's largest metropolis and Europe's closest city to London (just one hour by Eurostar), which at different times was described by the famous British visitors John Evelyn (in 1643) and Mary Shelley (in 1814) as 'extraordinary' and 'very pleasing' (respectively). Dickens had a love-hate attitude to Calais (one of the reasons for the 'hate' bit could have been his proneness to sea sickness: in his own words, he once arrived in Calais after a particularly rough English Channel crossing 'a mere bilious torso, with a mislaid headache somewhere in its stomach'), but wrote in 1861 that he was 'always so very glad to see it.'

And of course, the most famous (if somewhat over-dramatic) 'endorsement' came from Mary Tudor, who, lamenting the return of Calais from British back French rule in 1558, said (reportedly): 'When I am dead and opened, you shall find Calais lying on my heart.'

The Power of Stereotype

Researching this feature, I stayed in Calais for several nights – unlike the overwhelming majority of the 10 million annual statistical visitors, who simply step or drive off the boat and then speed on through the city without stopping, as if pursued by hordes of some mythical illegal migrants – as I myself have done repeatedly. Stereotypes are contagious. As the locals would be happy to tell you, after the closure of the notorious 'Calais Jungle' camp in the neighbouring Sangatte in

2016, potential asylum seekers heading for Britain are now harder to find here than perhaps in any other city in Europe.

Throughout its tempestuous history, the city has been both a beneficiary and a victim of its proximity to Britain, with the White Cliffs of Dover clearly visible from the city's beaches in good weather. As Benoit Deval, a devoted local historian, working for the Pas-de-Calais Tourism, told me, 'The geographical situation of Calais has brought the town the best opportunities as well as the most challenging ordeals.'

Just like some social media users, towns, cities and even countries can be bullied, or 'trolled,' and of that Calais remains an example being almost invariably portrayed by the (mostly British) media as drab, uninteresting and crime-ridden, all of which, I am happy to assert, are simply not true. It is certainly not 'drab' but often basking in bright sunlight, best enjoyed when walking along the endless surfing beaches, with a strong Mediterranean feel in the outskirts, just several minutes away from the Port.

As for 'uninteresting,' you cannot possibly say that about a relatively small city which boasts the best collection of Rodin's works after Paris; a trend-setting International Centre for Lace and Fashion; the country's most beautiful historic neo-Flemish Town Hall, with a spectacular seventy-five-metre belfry; and France's only church (La Notre Dame de Calais), built in the style of English Gothic, same as Westminster Cathedral, in which the legendary President Charles de Gaulle married his wife Yvonne (nee Vendroux), a native of Calais, in 1921. De Gaulle himself was a frequent visitor, and now one can see the lanky Charles and his miniature wife (known locally as 'Auntie Yvonne') walking together in perpetuity across Calais' vast Market Square, where they have just done their morning shopping – an extremely vivacious sculpture by NE Gibot.

To that we can safely (and Calais is, incidentally, very safe indeed!) add a thriving restaurant scene, numerous parks, the plane-tree-lined Paris-style boulevards of St Pierre, one of Calais's two main *arrondissements* (I had to pinch myself to believe that I was not in the French capital); some interesting modern architecture, art galleries, one of France most spectacular theatre buildings, and many more …

The Federal Republic of Calais

All my writer's life, I've been collecting unusual and little-known bits of history and geography. Calais is a real treasure-trove of those. See for yourselves:

– It is one of only five French cities to be allowed by an old royal decree to have its own flag. The flag is white-and-blue and resembles the Scottish Saltire. The other four cities are Dunkirk, Boulogne, Le Havre and Saint Malo.

– It is not widely known that the Mayor of Calais (at present, the outspoken and rather well-known in the UK from her numerous media interviews on how to control the flow of illegal migrants, Mme Natacha Bouchart) is simultaneously the president, or in the case of Ms Bouchart, '*la presidente,*' of the so-called '*Grand Calais Terre et Mere,' or Le Communaute d'agglomeration du Calaisis* – a government structure, created in December 2000 inside the Pas-de-Calais department and consisting of ten smaller communes. 'The mayors of the Grand Calais agglomeration develop a collective programme to be put in action after the municipal elections,' ran a headline (translation is mine) in the local *La Voix du Nord* newspaper on 6 February 2020. That and its own flag make Calais sound more like a mini-state than just a small city …

– Present-day Calais itself has a somewhat 'federal' structure and is the result of the 1885 merger of two neighbouring towns: the largely working-class old Calais, incorporating the Port, and the unexpectedly 'posh' St Pierre – a 'little Paris,' with its Baron Haussmann-style boulevards and Art Deco facades.

– To enhance the persisting impression of 'mini-statehood,' Calais has its own ports of entry – the Eurotunnel, and the sea port, France's largest for passenger traffic (and fourth-largest for cargo), now undergoing a major extension and reconstruction.

– Last but not least – as is customary for a city state, the people of Calais have their own … well, if not a language, then definitely a dialect, in which '*so vo?*' stands for 'how are you?' and the popular polysemantic exclamations '*fiu*' and '*min*' can mean almost anything depending on the situation. The closest English equivalent to either would probably be 'wow!' – the sound I made frequently during my short stay in Calais.

A Part of England that is Forever France

Above the bed in my hotel room in Calais were two electric plugs: a round-faced UK's, and a 'noseless' European. Together, they could pass for an adequate symbol of the city's ongoing dichotomy: Calais' chequered history gives us a good reason to call it the most British of the French cities, or the most French of the British!

It all started ages ago when teams of Mesolithic fishermen and hunters were able to walk (*sic*) the twenty-two miles from Dover to Calais on dry land. After the appearance of the English Channel about 10,000 years ago, such raids became more difficult, but the twenty-two-mile-wide stretch of water did not stop Julius Caesar from dispatching his legions and centurions on the first of the three invasions of Britain in year 56 BC. A couple of centuries (and centurions) later, Richard the Lionheart arrived in Calais from the opposite white-cliff side of the Channel to start his crusade against the Turks.

In 1346, Edward III of England, unnerved by the French corsairs harassing English merchant ships in the Calais Harbour, besieged and eventually conquered the town, which remained in British hands for 211 years. Calais was then often referred to as the 'brightest jewel in the English crown.' It was sending its MPs to Westminster, and, at some point, Dick Whittington, the legendary cat lover and the Mayor of London (named, as some unreliable sources assert, after a well-known North London hospital) was also the Mayor of the staple of Calais.

The British left Calais rather reluctantly in 1558 (it was that unwilling departure – read military defeat by the French – that prompted Mary Tudor's remark about Calais 'lying on her heart'). They, however, keep returning in increasing numbers ever since.

In 1816, Nottingham lace-makers smuggled their machinery across the Channel to Calais and set up what later became the world's largest centre for machine-made lace, with dozens of British-owned lace factories, which at some point were the area's largest employer.

Calais of course served as a British military base at different points of World War I and World War II, yet the latest attempt to rebrand the city as part of Britain happened in the peaceful 2012, the year of the London Olympics, when some of the region's councillors – in an attempt to boost the area by sponging off other countries' generous Olympic budgets – invited foreign teams to conduct their pre-Olympics training across the Channel.

That failed attempt at rebranding was largely unnecessary, for – to paraphrase Rupert Brooke – Calais remains in many ways a part of Britain which is forever France. I came to that conclusion while finishing a typical '*fameux*' called *Welsh Coyote Girl* inside the Welsh-owned Calais restaurant *L'Hovercraft*.

The Hero City

In the USSR of my childhood and youth, it was customary to bestow an official 'Hero' title not just on individuals, who distinguished themselves in battles or in 'communist labour,' but also onto cities and towns (Brest, Volgograd, Kursk, Odessa etc) And if the 'hero' people would automatically be entitled to some peculiar Soviet perks, like, say, 'the right to jump the queues in cinemas and shops,' the 'hero' towns got nothing.

Had Calais been located in that part of the world (God forbid), it would have certainly qualified for a 'Hero City' title.

Throughout its tempestuous eleven-century-long history, Calais has survived three major occupations (not to count the initial Roman invasion), including 211 years of British rule and the near-forgotten invasion of the Spanish Armada and the subsequent Spanish rule of 1596-1598. In 1940, the city was literally raised to the ground by the advancing Germans, and whatever was left to stand was finished off by the RAF bombers, who mistook the already liberated Calais for Dunkirk in February 1945!

In addition to the military disasters, the city had gone through a number of industrial crises: the crash of the lace industry, which used to employ over 20,000 locals in 133 (mostly British-owned) factories and workshops after World War I, and the virtual loss of its fishing port and fishing markets in the second half of the twentieth century.

Then of course, the notorious migration issues of the early twenty-first century, when illegal migrants and would-be asylum seekers from the third-world countries started arriving in large numbers, lured by Calais' proximity to Britain which most of them naively perceived as the promised land of milk and honey – a dangerous stereotype that, in its turn, led to the distorted image of Calais itself.

Each time – faced with the above-mentioned crises and disasters, the city had to mobilise its innate fighter spirit and reinvent itself. And each time it eventually succeeded.

The latest self-reinvention came with the completion of the Channel Tunnel, when the long-suffering city became the main gateway to Britain from Europe and vice versa. These days Calais is inseparable from the Eurotunnel, one of the seven engineering wonders of the world (according to the American Society of Civil Engineers) processing 1.6 million trucks, 2.6 million cars and 22 million passengers a year.

In the words of Benoit Deval, 'The busiest cross-Channel port town has been coveted for centuries, and has recovered from the Pale of Calais, the Napoleonic and two world wars. The twenty-first century challenges will make no exception. Resilience and adaptability are part of the DNA of the town and its people.'

'How does Calais see its future?' I asked Pascal Pestre, the city's Vice Mayor. 'I think in a few years Calais will become the best place on the north coast of France, a popular seaside destination for families and for those who like nature, culture and gastronomy,' he said.

I would very much like to believe that Monsieur Pestre proves right: that the city will eventually become not just the gateway, but also the hub!

Then all those writers and journalists who had kept undeservedly maligning Calais for years, will be able to repeat after Dickens: 'Calais *en gros*, and Calais *en detail,* forgive one who has deeply wronged you. – I was not fully aware of the other side … ' (*The Calais Night Mail*, 1861)

* * *

I am walking along a sandy Cap Gris Nez beach near Calais, just centimetres from the softly murmuring surf. It is an uncharacteristically bright sunny morning in early

February, and looking across the English Channel I can clearly see the White Cliffs of Dover twenty-two miles away.

These few miles of white-capped sea can safely be called one of the most emotionally charged and fought-for stretches of water in human history. For centuries, it has been the ultimate Rubicon for desperate refugees, idealistic travellers, peripatetic dreamers and failed invaders. Staring at the hazy outlines of the White Cliffs of Dover from Calais is like taking a vicarious journey back in time.

It was here that Napoleon stopped in 1803 to contemplate the invasion of Britain. It was from here that Louis Bleriot started his historic cross-Channel flight in 1909. And on Christmas Eve 1940, Adolf Hitler came here to inspect the emerging fortifications of what he liked to refer to as 'Fortress Europe.'

What is it about the English Channel that makes its crossing a matter of prime significance for many? For decades, people have been travelling across it on all kinds of vessels – from state-of-the art ferry boats to surfing boards and bath tubs. During the last hundred or so years, they have also flown across the Channel in all kinds of flying machines, propelled by steam, petrol, solar energy, or just pedals, with the latest attempt by the French inventor Franky Zapata, who – after a couple of failed attempts – carried out a thirty-five kilometre-long cross-Channel hop in a bespoke jet-powered hoverboard in August 2019.

My own countless Channel crossings were mostly by ferries starting from the very first one in October 1988, when I chose train and ferry for my first ever trip to the UK (and to the West). When defecting with my family a couple of years later, we chose train and then ferry crossing again, for fear of being stopped by the Soviet airport emigration controls which were much stricter than those on land-base transport. It is for good reason therefore that I always step on board a cross-Channel ferry with trepidation, for each time it feels like crossing the watershed (both metaphorical and real) between my present life and my Soviet past. Flying over or rattling along underneath it on board a Eurostar train does not feel quite the same …

I have to confess that I have also managed to WALK along the Chunnel – twice!

The first time was in 2012, when – after endless security clearances – I was indeed allowed inside the Eurotunnel (though only the service tunnel, on account of not being a train – a point I found hard to dispute) with several other UK journalists. So powerful was the impression that I had dreamed of repeating it ever since.

The second time, in early 2020, security formalities took even longer: I had to post a copy of my passport to the Tunnel offices weeks in advance. The Chunnel surroundings were so full of barriers, fences, barbed wire and CCTV cameras (600 of those, as I was told) that they reminded me simultaneously of the Berlin Wall and a Belfast police station from the time of the Troubles. Probably to make me feel more at home, my official escort John Keefe, director of public affairs for the tunnel operator, Getlink, assured me that all the barriers had been made in the UK by a company called Jacksons Fencing.

It was nice to know we were still manufacturing something.

And here we were – on the Calais side of the service tunnel, looking into 31.4 miles of winding dimly lit corridor that ended in Folkestone, Kent.

Accompanied by two security guards (to stop us if we suddenly decided to run all the way to Folkestone?) we walked along the tunnel, with John pointing out a cable monorail snaking above our heads, countless fire hydrants, one of the thirty-five fire-fighting stations, and ventilation shafts – parts of the sophisticated air-circulation system that could blow dust and fog out of the main tunnel. Having lived in Folkestone for several years, I didn't feel like running away towards it, and neither, it seemed, did John.

My only regret was that this time we didn't see a lizard-like yellow STTS (Service Tunnel Transport System) vehicle – a specially engineered rubber-tyred techno-reptile used for maintenance and for carrying workers from one end of the Tunnel to the other, always travelling on the right (even when in UK territory).

Back in the daylight, we stood for some time on a small observation platform right outside the Tunnel's French portal. Every couple of minutes a Shuttle, a Eurostar or a freight train whooshed past us. I asked John what Brexit would mean for the cross-Channel traffic.

'Brexit is not a barrier,' he said. 'It simply means a different approach to the same issues – in short, it's not a change, but rather a challenge!'

I looked at the gaping black hole of the Tunnel entrance less than fifty metres away. Another Eurostar train was just sliding into it slowly, as if being sucked inside by some invisible and utterly unstoppable force.

Perigord, France

Let's start on a familiar Hans-Christian-Andersen note:

'It was lovely summer weather in the country, and the golden corn, the green oats, and the haystacks piled up in the meadows looked beautiful ...'

It was on that very lovely morning in Dordogne, France, that Mother Duck decided to sit a bit longer on an unusually large egg she had just laid. The egg was refusing to hatch and when it finally did ... 'a young one crept forth crying, 'Peep, peep.' It was very large and ugly ... ' and everyone in the farmyard hated him for being different, as animals – as well as people – often do. Other ducks laughed at their new sibling, and no one wanted to play with him. No one, except for the Farmer.

'Look at you, poor thing,' the Farmer said to the Ugly Duckling one day. 'You are so large and bulky, so you must be constantly hungry ...'

'Merci beaucoup, Monsieur,' the Duckling answered in French, for despite being Ugly, he was still a French duckling. 'Thank you for asking, sir, but I am not hungry at all ...'

'Come on, don't be shy: I can see you are starving!' asserted the Farmer, throwing handfuls of maize grains at the Duckling, who – in full accordance with his name – kept ducking clumsily to avoid direct hits ...

The Duckling's refusal seemed to irritate the Farmer.

'You silly bird!' he exclaimed. 'I'll force you to eat! Look at how big your oesophagus is! Your liver must be big too and I will make it even bigger!'

From his pocket, the Farmer took out a long metallic tube, its end dripping engine oil. Having grabbed the Ugly Duckling by the neck, he began shoving the tube forcefully down the bird's throat. While doing so, he kept repeating sinisterly: '*Foie gras ... foie gras ...*' And also: '*Gavage ... gavage*!'

The Ugly Duckling nearly choked to death. 'Help me ... help me, Mummy!' he was croaking. But Mother Duck was nowhere near, and all other birds and animals in the farmyard were laughing at him: 'Serves you right, you Ugly monster!' they were saying. In French, no doubt ...

After that, the Ugly Duckling's life became one long nightmare. The tube kept being inserted into his uncomplaining throat several times a day. In-between the tortures, he was offered lots of fresh maize and sweet golden corn, but couldn't even look at them after being force-fed repeatedly.

And so the Ugly Duckling lived in the farmyard for many weeks getting bigger and bigger until one rainy autumn morning his liver exploded with a loud pop ...

'Pop, pop,' echoed far and wide in the distance, and whole flocks of wild geese rose up from the bushes.

Unlike the domesticated ducks from the farmyard, the geese were wild and therefore not in danger of blowing up from overeating …

I hope Hans Christian Andersen will forgive me for such a blunt distortion of his famously humane fairy tale, which came to my mind often during my recent visit to the French region of Perigord Noir, famed – among other things – for its *foie gras.* For those readers who may not know, it is a thoroughly delicious (as I think) pâté-like food product, made of the liver of a duck or goose that has been specially fattened. Some gourmets refer to it as 'the slice of haven.' The French officially define *foie gras* as the liver of a duck or goose fattened by force-feeding – a process also known as *gavage.*

The technology of the *gavage* is simple: a long tube is inserted into the bird's mouth and throat up to three times a day for three to ten days in a row.

French rural code L654-27-1 states that '*Foie gras* belongs to the protected cultural and gastronomical heritage of France.' At the same time, production of *foie gras* using the *gavage* technology has been banned on humanistic ground in twenty-two out of the twenty-eight (or twenty-seven if we do not count Britain) EU nations as well as in California, and from last November – in the state of New York too …

The beautiful ancient town of Sarlat in the Perigord Noir region is often called the home of *foie gras* which is on sale everywhere, and the sculpture of a flock of happy (obviously, 'pre-*gavaged*') ducks decorates one its main squares. On the third Sunday in February each year, a special Foie Gras Festival – *Sarlat Fest'oie* – is held there. Naturally, the Perigord *foie gras* makers are very protective of their famous brand. They assert that all their ducks and geese lead very happy organic lives – prior to being 'gavaged' that is. They also try their best to make the procedure itself as fast as possible: if formerly the standard *gavage* time per duck was forty-five to sixty seconds, modern technological advances, with pneumatic pumps used to accelerate the process, reduce the operation to two to three seconds.

Some *foie gras* apologists insist that certain bird species, including ducks and geese, are capable of eating prey that is much wider than the diameter of their oesophagus and hence, in plain language, their tracheas (throats) are both larger and more flexible than in mammals which, in turn, makes the whole *gavage* procedure less intrusive and, possibly, less painful. Whether that is true or not, only birds themselves can confirm. And birds, except for those featuring in Andersen's fairy tales, unfortunately (or perhaps fortunately for us), cannot speak …

Another common *foie gras* folly is that is being made exclusively in France. Not so. It is also produced in the USA, Hungary, Spain and many other countries. Recently, the *Independent* newspaper claimed to be in possession of secret footage taken on a farm in Ukraine, where post-gavage birds were being violently thrown into their cages leaving them injured and disoriented.

And closer to home, here's the title of a thoroughly scientific article, recently published by Oxford University Press on behalf of the British Poultry Science Association: *Evolution of liver fattening and foie gras technological yield during the overfeeding period in mule duck*.

Well, what can I say? I (like so many of my readers, I am sure) absolutely adore *foie gras* for its unique taste and its soft velvety texture. Like many of you, I cannot afford to buy it too often, but would still try and procure it for the Christmas and New Year feasts. At the same time, I do find the existing *gavage* procedure not simply cruel and deplorable, but also largely unnecessary. Yes, the no-less-yummy *foie gras* can (and must be) produced by much more humane methods, and such alternatives are in existence already.

Look again at the title of the article, quoted above: *Evolution of liver fattening and foie gras technological yield during the overfeeding period in mule duck*. With *gavage* banned in the UK, it must be talking about natural feeding, or natural overfeeding, to be more exact and more honest – the method widely practised, among other countries, in Spain (in the region of Extremadura), where birds are provided with unlimited amounts of high-quality foods at pre-migration periods (when they are bound to be particularly hungry), without force-feeding and are allowed and encouraged to eat *ad libitum*, ie freely. If the migration time is still a long way away, the bird's body clocks get artificially (chemically) adjusted to dupe them into believing that it is nigh …

There also exist different *foie gras* substitutes, including the vegan-friendly mixture of the Michelin-starred chef Alexis Gaithier made from olive oil, shallots, salt, garlic, button mushrooms, rosemary, thyme, sage, cognac, cooked lentils, toasted walnuts, soy sauce and beetroot purée – no less! Not too appetising? Perhaps … But perfectly edible. And a hundred per cent ethical too, for one cannot force-feed beetroots or mushrooms!

Another alternative *foie gras* that is quickly gaining popularity is the so-called *Foie Royale*. It is made from the normal, not grossly enlarged, livers of geese and ducks reared for meat production. Those birds normally enjoy much greater freedom than their egg-laying counterparts and aren't subject to wing or beak clipping. The R&D department of the Institute of Food Technology in Quakenbruck, Germany, has developed a method whereby the liver cells of those birds are broken down and then fused back together in exactly the same composition as in *foie gras*.

So, thanks to technology, there may be now some light in the end of tunnel for Andersen's tortured and embittered Ugly Duckling, who has a chance to grow into a beautiful foie-gras-resistant swan!

Then, in full accordance with the ending of Andersen's beautiful fairy tale, its world-famous poultry protagonist will be able to say one day: 'I never dreamed of such happiness as this, while I was an ugly duckling.'

Vennbahn

Vennbahn is a recently decommissioned Belgian railway, which used to form several small pockets (exclaves/enclaves) of Germany inside Belgium. It is a historic railway that is simply no more. In fact, the very last section of its former track between Auel and Oudler is being asphalted at the moment of writing. On completion, all 128 kilometres of Vennbahn will become one of Europe's longest public cycling paths, which, however, won't affect its unique enclave-forming capacity.

Here it is important to note that, by the old and still existing international regulations, not just the track, but five metres of land on both sides of it, with all the buildings and installations, belong to the country that owns the railway.

Built in 1889 as a fully German railroad, Vennbahn was given to Belgium by the Treaty of Versailles in the aftermath of the World War I. A special international commission agreed – after several years of deliberation – that part of Vennbahn, namely 'the trackbed, with its buildings between Raeren and Kalterherbert,' was to be ceded to Belgium, whereas the resulting five enclaves were to 'remain part of Germany.' The German names of all five stations on the stretch were retained, freight charges and fares could be paid in either German or Belgian currency, and countless strict German regulations about ticket-offices, waiting rooms, notice boards, left luggage, etc were all accepted by the Belgians. Both countries ran customs controls for both German and Belgian passengers at both ends of the section. And whereas conductors, pointsmen and other 'minor' railway workers could be either Belgian or German, the train drivers had to be exclusively Belgian nationals!

On 18 May 1940, Adolf Hitler ordered that Belgium's *cantons de l'Est* be re-annexed, and Vennbahn was triumphantly returned to service as a fully German railway line. During World War II, it was in much use supplying the German army until it was all but destroyed by the Allied offensive in the winter of 1944-45. Scarcely a viaduct was spared, and it was not until 1947 that Vennbahn was partially reopened under its previous – Belgian – ownership. By 1990, the railway had become commercially unviable, and the local community was trying to raise money to transform it into a tourist attraction – a kind of a would-be 'happy end' for the world's first and only railway that belonged to one country and ran across another. That unique status has been preserved until now, despite the complete cessation of all railway activities in 2008, due to a special bilateral agreement, according to which the former trackbed, even if no longer in use, will stay Belgian, and that, in turn, means, that the enclaves will remain intact too.

I last visited Vennbahn in 2003, when it was still operating as a railway, if only just. The only trains at Raeren station that were actually moving were those on the screen-saver of an old computer in the office of Edgar Hungs, the Vennbahn's acting manager.

'The phone cables at the station are so old that we cannot even have an Internet connection,' he complained, sucking on a charred and stinky cigar butt, which must have been lit for the last time in the middle of the previous century, when Vennbahn was still up and running.

Herr Hungs was then Vennbahn's only employee (and employer). His German company, with the tongue-breaking name Eisenbahn-Bau Betriebs-Satisfizierung AG, had just taken over the troubled historic railway. A couple of months prior to my visit, Vennbahn, then a state-run Belgian enterprise, had gone bust, and its entire staff – both German and Belgian – had been made redundant. Herr Hung was now facing the difficult task of turning the railway around by hiring a new workforce, finding new investors and changing Vennbahn's whole image.

We left the station building, which, although on Belgian territory, was typically Prussian in its design and architecture – a reminder of Vennbahn's 'enclave-forming' nature. A couple of trains without locomotives were 'parked' on rusty tracks, overgrown with brown railway weeds. It was clear they had been stationary for many months.

'Our trains consist mostly of 1935 Belgian carriages and Mitropa cars, built in East Germany,' Herr Hungs said without much enthusiasm.

I noticed a faded chalk inscription on one of the cargo trucks, which was tucked away in a sideline: 'Not in common use: Return to Harwich.'

Just like the forgotten Harwich-bound cargo truck, Vennbahn itself was no longer 'in common use.'

My escort pointed out other signs of dichotomy in Vennbahn, like a grey Deutsche Telecom cabin in front of the Belgian station building. The railway used German signals, but with Belgian colours. Despite being German, the signals were situated on the right side of the track – Belgian-style – whereas in Germany they would belong strictly on the left.

We passed by a deserted pointsman's hut next to what Herr Hungs called 'the last manual-change point in Germany.' I wanted to point out that, since the point was actually part of the track, he should have called it 'the last manual-change point in Belgium,' but I didn't, having noticed that the hut itself stood several metres away from the rails – in what could be Germany.

Before leaving Raeren station, we popped into the engine shed, where disused Belgian and German-made diesels and steam locomotives – looking equally tired and forlorn – stood next to each other, like exhibits in a deserted transport museum …

Well, even if no longer a railway, Vennbahn has not disappeared entirely as a unique geopolitical phenomenon. I do hope that at least some of the carefree German and Belgian bikers, whooshing forgetfully along the new asphalted cycle path, which used to be Vennbahn, are aware of the uniqueness of the very ground they are riding on …

Berlin

My first introduction to one of Berlin's lesser-known Cold War relics, the so-called 'ghost stations,' or Geisterbahnhoffe, was spontaneous and totally unexpected. Having just landed in Berlin's Schoenefeld Airport, we took an S-Bahn (overground) train to Friedrichstrasse Station, where we changed to a U-Bahn (underground) U6 line to get to our hotel. As the train was leaving Franzosische Strasse Station, only two stops away from our destination, I had a quick vision of a dimly-lit and deserted platform sliding past the train window. There was enough time to spot some scaffolding on the walls and a solitary concrete mixer in the corner.

'Can you pinch me, please?' I said to my wife. 'I think I've just seen a ghost …'

Well, my suspected hallucination was not that far from reality. As I discovered later, what I had witnessed from the train window was one of the fifteen former 'ghost stations' of East Berlin, or rather what was left of it. What I saw was actually the island platform, which the trains of the West Berlin BVG used to pass slowly, yet without stopping. During our several days in Berlin, I was able to tick off similar abandoned 'ghost platforms' at two other U-Bahn stations: Potsdamer Platz and Oraniennburgerstrasse, as well as at the S-Bahn's Nordbahhof.

We stayed at a brand-new super-comfortable Staycity's Wilde Aparthotel, next to the former Checkpoint Charlie and right across the road from the Museum of the Trabants (or 'Trabbies') – the iconic East-German tin-shaped car, designed to the principle 'the fewer parts – the better' (it did have wheels!). My own past was facing me everywhere, and there was no escape from Berlin's gruesome Cold War history either above or below the ground …

Ghost train stations of Berlin had a special attraction to me for a couple of reasons. Firstly, as a devoted train buff I was automatically drawn to anything railway-related. Secondly, I had my first glimpse of the West just there, in Berlin, then still divided by the Wall, from the window of the Moscow-Hook of Holland train carriage in which I decided (uncharacteristically) to travel to Britain (and to the West) for the first time in my life in October 1988.

In the middle of the night, having just cleared the Wall and the paranoid East German passport controls, our train stopped briefly at the West Berlin's Berlin Zoologischer Garten Station. It was there that I saw (from the train window) the first ever Westerners –a man and a woman – I had a chance to observe in their natural habitat, so to speak. They were probably just a couple of middle-aged burghers returning to their suburb after a late-night party. And yet to me, they looked like creatures from a different planet. Their faces were totally devoid of the habitual Soviet 'seal of oppression' – that haunted look, moulded by years of queuing and humiliation, by the daily struggle for survival and repressed emotions, as if constantly expecting a blow from behind – the look that made my firmer compatriots so easily recognisable in any Western crowd.

It seemed to me that the small white poodle the woman was cradling under her parka had the same satisfied 'Western' look too …

But prior to that, there was a long stop at Friedrichstrasse, then firmly and fully in East Berlin. It was there that a dozen or so East German border guards, with portable ladders and dogs straining at their leads, boarded our carriage for a grand search for God knows what …

Little did I know that (as I have found out during my last Berlin trip) Friedrichstrasse Station – now just a busy commuter hub – used to be known then as the Palace of Tears. The Berlin Wall, albeit invisible, ran between platforms, with a metal partition dividing the area with the S-Bahn trains to the West from the 'Eastern' platforms. It was the place of sad farewells with relatives and other visitors from the West returning home. East Germans were not allowed to step onto that 'Western' platform which they could only watch from the distance, from behind the dispassionate backs of the Stasi-controlled border guards.

As an official crossing point from East to West, however, the Mother of All Cold War Stations, as I am tempted to call Friedriechstrasse, was not a 'ghost station' by definition. 'Ghost stations' appeared as a direct result of the construction of the Berlin Wall in 1961. And although the actual dividing Wall was entirely above the ground, its dark shadow reached down to the U-Bahn train tracks, with some stations, still served by West Berlin trains, finding themselves on the East Berlin territory. Those stations were firmly closed to East Berliners: all entrances shut, bricked up and barred with iron railings.

The armed Stasi guards kept patrolling the empty stations, through which the 'Western' trains were passing slowly but not stopping. The soldiers were able to watch the mysterious creatures from the free world moving past them inside the brightly-lit train carriages. The 'Western' passengers must have felt uneasy under their stares …

Later, the soldiers were all hidden from the Westerners' view inside the special bunkers. The main reason for that was the fear that the East German border guards could easily jump onto a slowly moving train and flee!

In the words of a former senior officer of the GDR Grenzpolizei (Border Troops), '… our guards were actually walled-in on some stations. They stood inside walls with observation slits … so that they wouldn't desert … But that was in the eighties when things had been tightened up. At the beginning, the guards were allowed to walk up and down the platform …'

The cruel hypocrisy of such 'arrangements,' when even the most trusted guardians of the regime were not actually trusted, defies belief and the norms of human behaviour.

With the collapse of the Wall and the reunification of Germany, the divided stations and railway lines of Berlin were 'reunited' too. The last 'ghost station' was reopened to all passengers in 1992, and the very term – 'ghost station' – has come to denote any disused platform remaining from the divide, like the ones I was able to see in Berlin earlier this year. They are all being restored now, although I would keep one or two of the platforms intact as silent witnesses of the not-so-distant time when not just countries, cities and human souls, but also rail tracks and train stations, were dissected by the ruthless, ridiculous and entirely meaningless borders.

Italy
Cattivo Ricordo. Around Italy in Search of a Bad Meal

(a previously unpublished extract from an unfinished book)

Aperitivo (introduction)

'You will love the restaurants in Italy. Most are small, family-run places. Almost every meal is the best meal of your life. It would be easier to list the places where you had a bad meal, than to list where you had good meals.'
From *Dining Out in Italy* section of a popular website

'Italy is Holland in reverse. There it's hard to find a bad restaurant.'
David Dale, *The Obsessive Traveller*

'I treasure my bad teeth as souvenirs of all the good food I have eaten …'
Ostap Bender, protagonist of *The Twelve Chairs* by Ilf and Petrov

An age-long proponent of the Italian CULTURE of dining – as opposed to the French CULT of food – I have always wanted to write a funny, educational and instructive book about Italy as reflected in its magnificent, versatile and profoundly democratic cuisine.

Having travelled extensively around the country researching some of my previous books, having taught for a short while at the University of Bologna, I had NEVER come across a thoroughly bad meal. Pasta at the students' canteen at the University's medieval Bertinaro campus was always top-notch – as well as unlimited 'free' wine which the students, incidentally, didn't touch (it would only take a day or so to bring down any British university campus by making wine freely available at its canteen!). Even a hurried plate of spaghetti, swallowed once in haste near Palermo's hectic railway station, had some redeeming features about it and could compete in quality with any of its namesakes from Britain's ever-growing chains of 'Italian' restaurants: Prezzo, Ask, Pizza Express etc. No wonder Italian government has recently unleashed its dynamic, secretive and (allegedly) incorruptible assault squad of food inspectors upon the numerous pseudo-Italian restaurants of the globe with the aim of uncovering those who abuse the sacred and immaculate concept (if not the conception) of Italian cuisine and mercilessly closing down the impostors.

Eating out in Italy is like dining at an Indian restaurant in London. Or like drinking Russian vodka … You cannot really make a mistake, for all of the above appear in only two varieties: good and very good. Well, an Italian meal – more often than not – exists in a third category too: excellent!

If great restaurants are so well-spread, they must have become routine, whereas the bad ones should be rare and therefore interesting – this was the tongue-in-cheek 'rationale' behind my quest …

Is it actually possible to have a bad meal in Italy outside the ubiquitous McDonalds and other fast food joints (some Italian provinces – like, say, Le Marche – boast of not having a single one of those) or the tourist traps of Venice, Florence and Rome?

Some of my friends assure me that it is. But finding one is not easy. Probably harder than discovering all the restaurants of the acclaimed 'Unione dei Ristoranti del Buon Ricordo' of which there are only 102 in the whole of Italy. David Dale, an Australian travel writer and a good acquaintance of mine, once tried to visit them all, to dine at each and to collect all the coveted Buon Ricordo plates awarded exclusively to their diners and loved by collectors all over the world.

I am going to set myself a much harder task: to celebrate the Italian cuisine and the Italian way of life (the same David Dale conducts a workshop called 'Why Italians have found the secret of human happiness and how to become Italian' in Sydney) using the rule of contraries, so to speak: by criss-crossing Italy incognito – in the manner of an old *Baedeker Guide* morally upright inspector – in search of a bad meal and perhaps, not dissimilar to restaurateur Dino Villani, who founded the Buon Ricordo Association in 1964, laying foundations for the 'Unione del Cattivo Ricordo' (or 'Unione del Brutto Risotto') and – for the first time in the history of Chianti and Mozzarella – compiling the list (short as it may be) of the country's worst eating places. IF ANY …

And, on top of it all (or, if you wish, for the dessert), coming up with a design and a concept of the Cattivo Ricordo (or 'Brutto Risotto') souvenir plates too. Would they feature a pile of turds and the words 'Unione Ristoranti del Cattivo Ricordo' along the rim?

But let us ask ourselves: is 'bad' necessarily 'horrible' and 'awful?'

It depends …

On the bookshelf in my garden office there stands a fascinating volume *The Joy of Bad Verse* by Nicholas Parsons, and next to it – a monograph, *The Art of Writing Badly* by Richard C Borden. The title of the first is fairly self-explanatory: it takes the reader on a fascinating tour of the poetry that is 'bad' from literary connoisseurs' point of view, yet can be charming and delightful and in its sheer clumsiness and genuine naivety – like the works of William McGonagal, officially 'the world's best worst poet,' from Dundee. The second is about 'mauvism' (from the French 'mauvais' meaning 'bad') – a post-modernist poetic and thoroughly un-chronological literary style invented by Valentin Kataev, an acclaimed Soviet/Russian writer, who once decided to deviate from the USSR's only officially accepted literary doctrine – socialist realism[27] – and cleverly declared that, unlike all other Soviet writers who write brilliantly, he was going to be different and will write 'badly.' He got away with this simple ruse and had managed to publish a number of beautiful novels and stories in the beautiful 'bad-writing' style of his own!

'Badness' – just like goodness, beauty, virtue etc – is a very subjective concept and what appears (or tastes) bad to one person, can be charming and delicious to another. This is probably why teenagers, those eternal rebels, use the words 'wicked' and 'awesome' when they mean 'good,' 'great' and 'cool' (with the latter actually meaning 'hot,' ie 'great').

Apart from uncovering some little-known intricacies of the Italian cuisine and life-style, this book will usher in a NEW INTERNATIONAL BRAND OF 'BADNESS': 'bad' eating, 'bad' meals and 'bad' restaurants which – at a closer inspection – turn out not so bad at all!

I will end with the first ever Recipe Book of Bad Italian Meals and the pioneering DIY mini-manual on How to Open and Run a Bad Italian Restaurant – both in the Appendix.

Yes, alongside travelling in Italy, I'll be cooking 'bad' Italian meals as I go, so that by the end of the journey I become a self-proclaimed master chef of 'Brutto Risotto' and 'Cattiva Cucina Italiana' and will be able to share my 'bad' recipes with the readers.

And then perhaps a list of 'NOT-SO-BAD Italian Restaurants' which may end up as nothing much else but a CLEAN SHEET OF PAPER – who knows? The latter scenario would account for an even more eventful journey …

For the purposes of comparison, I will partly focus on some Italian restaurants in the UK, the areas of France bordering on Italy and will at times fluctuate between the two countries, two cuisines and two polarly different attitudes to eating. Remember: 'cult' and snobbery in France (where a famous chef recently committed suicide when his restaurant lost a Michelin star – soothing utterly unimaginable in Italy) as opposed to 'culture' and democracy in Italy, where even the best Buon Ricordo and Le Soste (a new exclusive restaurant club) restaurants are not in a hurry

27 The best definition of socialist realism as applied to fine arts can be found in an old Soviet joke: as opposed to an expressionist artist who draws what he feels, or an impressionist artist who paints what he sees, the socialist realist painter depicts only what he hears …

to publicise themselves and culinary excellence is a matter of pride rather than of money and fame.

I will also track down and interview the elusive (possibly even undercover!) members of Italy's little-known Food Police – the growing breed of fearless food detectives tracking down and exposing makers of fake Italian foods, like, say, cheese impostors producing Lithuanian (!) *Parmigiano*, as well as the staff of DNV – a government organisation which certifies Italian restaurants outside Italy (out of all the countries in the world, only Italy and Thailand have such government bodies).

I will ask them too to recommend the absolutely worst Italian restaurants they have visited or just to describe the latter in case they had closed them down!

So, not just a 'search' but also an 'investigation!' With all the twists and turns of a thriller (albeit an ironic one of course).

A formidable task. An adventurous and risk-ridden journey to tackle – first and foremost – not so much the bad meals, but the stale foreign stereotypes of Italy – and tourist stereotypes in general. An anti-tourist voyage into the unknown which will make it into a proper travelogue, for, as Lin Utang once noted, 'A good traveller doesn't know where he is going to, and a perfect traveller doesn't know where he comes from.'

It is only a tourist who knows exactly what he is heading for, when and from where he will leave and when exactly he will arrive. How horribly boring!

Welcome to the first ever 'BAD,' ie ANTI-TOURIST GUIDE TO ITALY!

Antipasti (warming up before the journey)

'Best restaurant lists are idiotic and misleading'
Francois Simon, Le Figaro

La Bella Vita, 3 Sun Street, Hitchin, Hertfordshire, UK

Once in Paris, I came across an article by Francois Simon, the food critic of *Le Figaro,* criticising the list of the world's fifty best restaurants published by a British trade magazine. The wrath of the respected French foodie was most likely triggered by the fact that not a single French restaurant had made it to the top ten, and the first spot was taken by some obscure Danish (!) eatery with a 'minimalist' menu based on roots and herbs. The famous Parisian Le Chateaubriand, with its three Michelin stars, scooped just eleventh place – a fact which, in Simon's highly refined (if only in the culinary sense) opinion was 'hilariously surreal,' no less. 'How, tell me, is it possible to come to a decision that an excellent creperie is better than a delicious couscous restaurant, a Japanese sushi bar or an Italian trattoria?' he fumed and proceeded to brand the whole list 'idiotic.' 'There's no such thing as the best restaurant in the world,' he concluded.

He might be right here (albeit I somehow think that had the list had been compiled by a French source, not by some miserable *Les Anglais*, with shepherd pie as their biggest gastronomic achievement, and had it been consequently topped by French restaurants, the respected food critic wouldn't have been that categorical in his appraisal): with taste – like beauty – being a hugely subjective experience very much in the mouth (if not the eye) of the beholder, the world's best restaurant is rather hard to define.

It is easier with the world's worst restaurant, and I know exactly which one it is – Restaurant 'Mari,' attached to the eponymous ('Mari') hotel in the no-less-eponymous Turkmenistan town of Mari on the Afghan border.

I had the misfortune to stay at that hotel once – many years ago.

I remember a bearded Turkmen woman solemnly giving me the key to the hotel's only 'luxury suite.' The room was filthy, semi-dark and smelled like a mortuary. It was forty-two degrees of heat, but the air-conditioner did not work. Nor did the shower. The biggest surprise, however, was that I was supposed to share the room and the only medium-sized bed with a male Communist party official from Ashkhabad. He was snoring and fretting on his side of the bed all night, and I when I finally managed to nod off, I dreamt of an earthquake …

As for the hotel's restaurant, it was swarming with fat Central Asian flies, and only had eggs and cucumbers on the menu (not counting the flies which often fell onto the patrons' plates and were matter-of-factly consumed by some as the only bits of 'meat' they could ever hope to taste) – but that proved enough: after just one meal of fried eggs with cucumbers and flies, I got severe food poisoning and nearly died.

Now, unlike some pseudo-omniscient ramblings of French and/or British restaurant critics, food poisoning and the resulting NDE (near death experience, thoroughly investigated by Dr Raymond Moody in his bestselling book *Life After Life*), are very powerful qualifying criteria which cannot be disputed. So rest assured, if you happen to kick the bucket after a meal at a restaurant, you (or rather your grieving relatives and friends) can easily and without fear of repercussions brand that particular catering establishment the worst restaurant in your life ….

Let's, however, try to forget about extremes and define what an ordinary 'bad' restaurant should be like.

Here I have to refer again to my fellow Italomaniac, Australian writer David Dale, who in his book, with the long and somewhat pretentious title *The Obsessive Traveller Or why I don't steal towels from great hotels any more* (meaning that he still does from the not-so-great ones?), came up with some 'rules of thumb' to help travellers in avoiding bad restaurants:

1. Never eat in a restaurant that revolves or floats.
2. Never eat in a restaurant that is more than ten metres above the ground.
3. Never eat in your hotel dining room.

4. A restaurant that has a pepper grinder on every table is likely to be good (to me, a huge pepper grinder on every table would rather symbolise a powerful, yet repressed, masculinity of the owner – VV).
5. A restaurant that offers 'thousand island dressing' as an option for your salad is likely to be bad (no comment – VV).
6. Greek food is always better outside Greece than inside it (hm … disputable – VV).
7. There is no such thing as a bad Thai restaurant (? – V).
8. There is no such thing as a good Dutch restaurant (?? – VV).
9. There is no such thing as a good restaurant in Las Vegas.
10. Oolichan grease is not for the White Man (??? – VVV).

Dale also quotes 'the great American food writer Calvin Trillin who urged to beware places with names like 'La Maison de la Casa House Continental Cuisine' to which I could add that one should also stay away from restaurants with flags and/or banners above the entrance …

Having summed it all up and having discarded the irrelevant bits, we may safely conclude that, according to David Dale, your archetypal bad eatery would be a revolving Dutch restaurant on the top floor of a Las Vegas hotel. I can add that, in line with ever growing and all permeating political correctness in the USA, it would probably be known not as restaurant, but as a 'food center,' with the waiters calling themselves 'servers': 'Hi, my name is Jack/Gill and I will be your server today..' Those genderless 'servers' would repeatedly interrupt your meal with questions like 'Is everything ok?' and 'Are you still working on your steak, Sir?'

Eating in such a restaurant is indeed like carrying out a boring and joyless chore …

Before starting my quest for a bad Italian meal, I needed some more objective signs of a clearly bad restaurant. In our electronic age, I didn't need to subject myself to many more life-threatening Mari-style near-death experiments, but simply did a 'signs of a bad restaurant' Google search. The results exceeded all expectations. The subject of bad restaurants was obviously close to the heart of the broad Internet-browsing masses and was routinely raised in a number of virtual discussions. The participants of a lively 'digital spy' UK forum on food and drink were able to add the following important bad-restaurant signs to the list:

1. Menu with pictures.
2. Huge menu.
3. Laminated menu.
4. Lots of 'ready-meal packaging, or rats (*sic* – or rather quite sickening – VV)' in the bins area.

5. A Brake Bros (UK's cheap wholesale food delivery company – VV) lorry in the restaurant car park.
6. Chavs (a UK slang for 'rough youths,' from Romani 'chav' – child' – VV) in the kitchen; one participant has narrowed it down to 'spotty-faced teenagers who can't speak a word of English, even though born, raised and taught in the UK, serving you.'
7. Empty dining area.
8. Flies.
9. Caterpillars in the salad, as discovered by one captious lady.
10. Dirty toilets.
11. Stink.
12. Food served in cardboard boxes (I only experienced this once onboard an RAF flight to the Falklands – VV).
13. A squashed cockroach on the stairs …

And so on. The participants of the forum could be forgiven for being at times somewhat maximalist and extremist. If I tried to collate their meaningful signs with those of David Dale and myself, the extended description of a typical bad restaurant would probably read roughly like this:

A totally empty and stinking revolving Dutch 'food center,' with huge laminated and colourful menus, filthy toilets, rats in the backyard, cockroaches on steps, flies on walls, caterpillars in salads, pimpled deaf-and-mute, or – in the best of scenarios – dyslexic youngsters as both cooks and waiters (sorry, servers) on the top floor of a dodgy hotel in Las Vegas.

Pretty definitive, isn't it?

I was about to travel to Italy and check whether I could successfully apply this pattern in my quest for a bad Italian meal, but, on reflection, decided to try it first closer to home (purely as a warming up exercise of sorts) – in Hertfordshire, or to be more exact, in the old market town of Hitchin. Why Hitchin? Simply because, encouraged by my successful Google search for the signs of a bad restaurant (see above), I narrowed it down to 'Bad Italian restaurants in Hertfordshire' – and Bella Vita, Hitchin popped up second. The first was The Globe in Letchworth Garden City, conveniently situated in the very street where I live, just a couple of block away from our cottage. The Globe was bad indeed. Yet starting my search with having a meal in it was problematic for a couple of reasons:

- It was not Italian.
- It was not a restaurant.
- It didn't exist any more having gone bust several months earlier.

True, I once had my life's worst spaghetti bolognese in that ill-fated local. The dish was obviously acquired in bulk, prefab and frozen, and was hastily and insufficiently warmed up in a microwave before being put in front of me. But 'horrible Italian food' it seemed was not on my list of bad restaurant signs. And besides, The Globe was no more – a pitfall of the dispassionate Internet search!

> 'I went to the la Bella Vita for the first and last time on Saturday and had a terrible experience. We had booked a table for 8.45 and when we arrived we were not greeted and had to hang about in the doorway for a good five minutes. A waitress eventually told us to go through to the bar at the back where the barman took our drinks order and brought us the menu. We asked if we could have some olives or bread with our wine and were told no …'

> '**Bella Vita, Hitchin**, has an extensive menu with fantastic fish dishes – top class cuisine. friendly staff and unusually large character rooms … Superb. We will return. What a great place …'

These two rather controversial Internet reviews were next to each other on the same page of the same hotel-and-restaurants reviews site. So different they were in tone and conclusion that I started wondering whether the first one was supplied by a nit-picking competitive restaurateur from across the road (big deal: had to wait for five min; and you don't normally have 'bread and olives' with an aperitivo!) and the second – by Giorgio, La Bella Vita's owner and manager of more than thirty years standing (according to the restaurant's website) himself.

I had to go and see for myself.

So, with my lovely partner Christine who had agreed to play a role of my incognito research assistant, off we drove to Bella Vita, which promised on its website 'the true charm of Italy.' Even more promisingly (for my purposes), the restaurant was part of the eponymous hotel – a firmly established (see above) good sign of a bad restaurant.

The 'true charm of Italy' was only three miles away …

Giorgio himself meets us at the door and leads us to the bar in the far corner of the restaurant. It is a very old building, the ceilings are low and pierced – as if skewered – with Tudor beams, on one of which I spot a 'Mind Your Head' sign. Indeed, what are we trying to find here? Are we mad? Should we turn back?

The moment we sit down at the bar, a young waiter starts fluttering above our heads, brilliantly corresponding to the colloquial Czech word for 'waiter' – '*Pan Vrchny*' ('Mr Upper'), repeatedly urging us to have a drink. We refuse and say we'll have some wine with our meal. The set menu for £16.95 consists of two courses, with neither antipasti nor primi piatti – not very Italian.

The room has no windows and feels airless – where is the promised 'charm of Italy?'

In the corner, two bespectacled men are leafing through piles of documents while drinking Pelegrino mineral water. My hope is they are hotel (or perhaps restaurant) inspectors whose presence would encourage the staff to do their best to please the customers even if just to throw some dust into the 'inspectors' incorruptible and clear Pelegrino-washed eyes … On my penultimate day in the USSR before defection, I was lucky to have had a great slap-up meal in a normally horrible restaurant due to the presence of some sort of 'government controllers' …

Giorgio soon returns and takes us to our table which turns out to be beautifully set: flowers, snow-white napkins, polished silver cutlery. The sight of a bottle of Fiorile, Sicilian house wine which we have ordered, cheers me up even further.

'I leave the wine to breathe for three hours,' says Giorgio filling our glasses.

I suppress a laugh: having done some research on the subject, I know that leaving wine to 'breathe' does absolutely nothing for its taste and is a good example of the so-called wine snobbery … But, of course, I don't say this aloud …

'Do you have a large pepper grinder?' I enquire remembering one of D Dale's signs of a good restaurant. And immediately blush in fear of being misunderstood ('pepper grinder' is sometimes used as a conversational euphemism for 'penis' – you can't ignore its obvious phallic shape!)

But Giorgio doesn't get offended: 'They don't have them in classy Italian restaurants, like ours; only in some cheaper trattorias …'

And I recall with sudden clarity that indeed I have never seen those massive priapic utensils in Italy … It is only in Britain that they offer to spray your food with ground pepper from a grinder. In Italy, they just bring you some grated Parmigiano!

At a table next to ours is a group of posh elderly gentlemen, 'the old boys.' I sit with my back to them, but can hear from their accents that they are stuck-up. When I gain some courage and turn back I see that I was right: they do look like retired British Expeditionary Force officers, or like some well-bred and puffed up British bulldogs – all wearing tweed jackets and ridiculous regimental ties. One of them is so aristocratic that he can hardly speak, only blows up his cheeks and guffaws semi-audibly.

'My duck is tough …' he burbles to the waiter. I wonder whether he said 'duck' or 'dick'– cannot quite discern from his guffaw … At his age, however, the latter scenario seems much less likely than the former …

'It is tough and tasteless,' he carries on. 'I am really disappointed …' He pronounces 'disappointed' with a deliberate lisp and hardly opens his mouth, so that it sounds like 'disjointed' …

It suddenly occurs to me that 'Tough Duck' could be a good name for a Chinese take-away in Hitchin …

As our order arrives, I gasp: presentation and service are both perfect. My veal is tender and nearly melts in my mouth. Christine's fish is nice and fresh too … And the wine tastes fresh and fruity. Could it be that leaving it to 'breathe' was indeed beneficial? In any case, it didn't seem to do it any harm …

'It's like being on holiday,' says my hard-working daily-commuter partner Christine using one of her biggest forms of praise. 'They have a nice English-Italian ambience here,' she adds.

True: probably every country in the world has its own Italian ambience …

Giorgio comes up to our table and tells us he travels to Billingsgate Market in London Docklands twice a week to get fresh fish. Billingsgate is a wholesale seafood market on the Isle of Dogs. It opens up at 4am, wraps up by 7am and is about fifty miles away from Hitchin – quite a journey …

Listening to Giorgio, I recall a small Italian restaurant, La Tavernetta, in Folkestone, Kent, the place of my protracted 'exile' in 2002-2004. It was run and owned by an elderly Italian man called Giancarmine who liked to describe his Folkestone experience as 'thirty-five years of madness,' but in his heart of hearts loved the town and made sure his restaurant stayed open and offered good Italian food every single day of the year. Like Giorgio, he was a member of that brave cohort of Italian restaurateurs, the fearless ambassadors of pasta and lasagne, who came to Britain in the 1950s-60s and started the so-called 'Trattoria Revolution,' when many people in the UK seriously believed that spaghetti indeed grew on trees. They opened their restaurants against all odds offering the British new food and drinks, new style and new attitudes to life. La Trattoria Terrazza in Romily Street, Soho, started by Marco Cassandro and Franco Lagatolla in the late 1950s, soon became the most famous and influential restaurant in London, ushering in a true revolution in Britain's social culture and having the likes of Peter Sellers and Spike Milligan among its regular customers. It was followed by Alvaros' in Chelsea in the early 1960s and by many many more …

What drove and still drives these members of the Italian restaurant Diaspora? Not just the money, I assume … 'thirty-five years of madness' indeed … Their efforts, it has to be said, were not in vain: according to a recent survey, forty-seven per cent of the British respondents named Italian food as their absolute favourite, well above Chinese, French and even 'English' (if there's such a thing).

Our dinner at La Bella Vita did in a way contain 'the true Magic of Italy,' as promised by the restaurant's website, despite, or possibly, also because of the 'old boys' tough duck experience, for who on earth orders duck in an Italian seafood restaurant?

What an excellent start to my quest! Italy, it seems, can be found anywhere – in Hitchin, Folkestone, London … It is a category of the soul, rather then just a country; a state of mind, not just of geography, and much much more than simply food …

Giorgio is holding my jacket for me: 'Now that you've paid the bill, I can look after you properly,' he chuckles. 'Next time – bring your wife!' He winks at Christine …

I say that I will … And wink at Christine too …

How come La Bella Vita popped up in my search for 'bad Italian restaurants,' you may ask? I found the explanation later, having repeated the search. The entry on another Italian restaurant, L'Artista, in Letchworth was on the same page and started with the sentence: 'Been there many times, never had a bad meal.'

Search engines pick up the programmed words – in this case 'restaurant' and 'bad' – without thinking … They may have dexterity and speed, but no intellect and no taste …

I then decided I would not search for bad (or good for that matter) restaurants on the Internet ever again …

Driving back to Letchworth from Hitchin that evening, I suddenly realised why the duck could have tasted tough: 'the old boy' must have had no teeth!

* * *

I Primi Piatti in Tuscany

'Italian dishes are messages of love from cook to guest.'
Douglas Harper and Patrizia Faccioli, *The Italian Way*

Ristorante Maiori di Pastore Andrea, Piazza Archivescovado, 3, Pisa, Toscana

I tend to attract topics and events even before I start researching them. One example is coming to Bratislava to interview Slovakia's President Alexander Dubcek for *The European* newspaper (where I then worked) in 1993. On the next day after my arrival, the President, sadly, died, so I had to do a report from his funeral instead … The same happened when much later – in December 1999 – the *Telegraph* sent me to New York to do a feature on Joseph Heller's Coney Island, with Joseph Heller himself as an escort. One day before the pre-planned tour, I learned from an evening newspaper on a subway train that the great man of letters had sadly just passed on …

Some of my friends, who know this peculiar quality of mine, do not always welcome me to their homes, towns and countries, and I don't blame them …

I have to add immediately that nothing as dramatic has happened during my search for a bad Italian meal. At least not as yet … But some small and innocent signs of having been subconsciously immersed into the subject while still hundreds of miles away from Italy could not be ignored.

At a WH Smith outlet in Stansted airport where I was to board my flight to Pisa, they were selling (among other books, no doubt) a paperback *The Gourmet* by an

Italian-sounding French female writer Muriel Barberi. From the book's back cover, I deduced that the plot was as follows: a celebrated French food critic (not Francois Simon, I was hoping) is dying and remembering all the best meals he's ever eaten. To quote the blurb, 'he ransacks his memory for the best culinary moment of his life.' How very French!

I immediately wondered what would a dying Italian foodie be likely to remember? Conversations at the table? Views from the restaurants' windows?

My own best 'culinary moment' (unlike the worst Mari one) is hard to establish (finding my favourite gourmet delight, Russian 'Napoleon' cake, in a small bakery in Melbourne? Tasting poor man's caviar, the most common comfort food of my Soviet childhood, in Ireland?) and, besides, I am not dying yet, so it may still lie ahead of me. In fact, I am sure it is, for according to a favourite proverb of mine (which I have just invented): 'Tastebuds die last.' By that I mean that craving for your childhood comfort foods abandons you many years after nostalgia and even some weeks after hope itself …

On the same WH Smith counter, I spotted another flimsy (£4.99) Penguin paperback – this time written by an American:' by Michael Pollan.

I opened the book on the Contents page and silently (in square brackets, for the author has monopolised the normal round ones – see below) commented on its own rather unusual contents, as if the author was asking his would-be readers the questions only he himself was able to answer (or so he thought – in round brackets!):

1. What should I eat? (Food). – [how highly unusual, I thought the answer would be 'telescopes and hadron colliders']
2. What kind of food should I eat? (Mostly plants) [including KGB plants?]
3. How should I eat? (Not too much) [stylistically incorrect. It is the same as answering the question 'How much should I eat?' with 'Slowly!']
4. Acknowledgements.

Who would need to actually buy the book with such an in-depth, even if totally inane, Contents page?

The Food Rules (or rather its Contents page) has cheered me up a bit and I tried to imagine what a Soviet Eater's Manual could have looked like. Possibly, approximately like this:

The Soviet Eater's Manual

What should I eat? Anything that doesn't kill me …
What kind of food? Whatever I can lay my hands upon …
How should I eat? Quickly (lest the meal should be taken away from me) and silently (not to attract attention and thus cause the above scenario).'

'Does food pursue me on this journey before it even started, or do I simply take more notice of it now?' I was musing as relaxed brown-eyed Italian children were playing around my Ryanair flight boarding queue …

My mental food assault continued as I crouched in my famously uncomfortable Ryanair seat, with everything, except for the seat itself, removed for the purposes of economy, and that included a seat pocket where formerly one could put a book or reading glasses (or such like) and forget both there on disembarking, as I myself did repeatedly.

With the seat pocket missing, one had to nurse a book (or a sandwich) on one's lap as I was doing with William Boyd's *Ordinary Thunderstorms*, freshly acquired at the airport. I opted for it, having snubbed both *The Gourmet* and *The Eater's Manual*, in the hope to have a short break from food and eating – if not as pastimes (feeling hungry, I had to choke hastily on a stale Ryanair sandwich), then definitely as topics, themes and subjects of research. And what did I see, having reached page two of I? 'He conjured up a vision of a plate of Parma ham and halved fresh figs …' And further on:

'A sudden need for Italian food: Italian food of a simple, honest, basic sort – *insalata tricolore, pasta alla vongole, scallopine al limone, torta di nonna*. That would do nicely …'

Having consulted my portable Italian menu reader, I came to the conclusion that none of the above listed dishes actually existed, the closest to reality being '*torta della nonna*' … Instead of having a break from research, I plunged (or rather was pushed) into it head (and mouth) first!

The book's protagonist – a young American academic looking for a job in London – was walking across Chelsea Bridge and craving Italian food. He then popped into the nearest Italian restaurant – and it was from there that all his subsequent nightmares started …

A hidden warning to myself?

* * *

Gentle breeze from the sea brings faint aromas of garlic and pesto floating above the Tower and the whole of the Miracle Square – and pleasantly titillating my nostrils …

I am standing on the top tier of the leaning side of the Leaning Tower of Pisa grabbing the banisters with both hands while looking down … The smell of the pasta sauce and the angle at which I can observe the Square underneath, make me feel a bit dizzy …

I have climbed the Tower is search of a vantage point in the company of fat puffing Yanks, stubbornly squeezing themselves up the narrow steep corridor, with stairs shaped and worn out by generations of climbers. I was worried the Americans could get stuck forever between the walls – like Winnie the Pooh in the door of Rabbit's hole – any moment …

From the top, the Tower appears taller than from the ground …

At least I now know that on the highest tier of the Leaning Tower of Pisa one can smell Italian food!

I had been leaning towards the Leaning Tower for one simple reason: the area around it was one of the world's biggest tourist attractions (read traps) and therefore an obvious spot for finding a bad, hopefully even very bad, Italian restaurant. The quick Internet search for 'bad restaurants near the Tower of Pisa,' conducted well before my eye-opening La Bella Vita experience in Hitchin, came up with La Torre Pizza restaurant, which was pretty horrible, if you believe the reviews. The only problem was it was in Milan! Another downside of the Internet piling all the key words up without any order and mixing them up – like ingredients in *insalata mista*!

What a blow!

My simple rationale was: the closer the restaurant is to the Tower, the more likely it is to be bad.

And here I am.

I heroically let go of the banisters and take out my late Mum's old theatre binoculars to look down at the magnificent square and beyond. I then make a mental note about two restaurant terraces that seem to be the closest to the Tower …

The wind soon changes direction: no more smells of food – time to get down to *terra firma* and taste the pizza, so to speak – or rather to continue my search on a different, more down-to-earth (I mean literally), level …

Ristorante Antonietta Antica Trattoria, in an old building with peeling stucco and Venetian blinds behind the Duomo, which I had spotted from above, looks like it could be the one. A group of Somali leather-belt sellers, looking like some record-breaking snake charmers with their leather goodies winding around their necks, and some angry-faced street musicians – either Turkish or Albanian by appearance – are vying for the patrons' attention near its entrance …

My second choice is a restaurant round the corner. It may be several metres further away from the Tower than Antonietta and is surrounded with souvenir stalls, loaded with mini-Pisa Towers of all sizes and colours. Also, it appears to be part of a Villa Kinzica hotel – a promising sign (as we have established earlier) of a bad restaurant. Another good bad sign is rather literal – a Menu Turistico sign in front of it: Pizza Margherita + Patates Frites – €8.80.

The decision is made: the hotel restaurant wins (loses?) by points – if not by distance!

I enter the restaurant's terrace, empty (it is well past lunch time) not counting a group of hugely overweight American girls in baseball caps, with pink and orange knickers bursting out of their shorts, eating, or rather stuffing their faces, at a long table in the corner. To my sheer delight, I see that the menus on tables are all large, coloured and laminated and mentally tick off three more boxes in my no-less-mental bad-restaurant chart …

A waiter in a black shirt finally emerges from the building. I say to him: 'Buon Giorno!,' but he doesn't reply and waves me away like an importunate fly …

Good choice!

A rubbish truck is turning noisily next to the terrace: it looks like there may be a mini-landfill somewhere near – in a side street. Somali belt and watch sellers wander in and out of the terrace freely … The place looks worse, sorry better, I mean badder, with every passing moment … As they say in Italy, *perfetto!*

Uninvited, I sit down at an empty table, covered with a not-too-clean oil cloth, and start making notes.

From where I sit, I can peep inside the hotel lobby: a fly-stained cheap reproduction above the reception, chandelier with half of the bulbs dead (the bleak light is on despite the blazing sunshine outside, yet the lobby is still immersed in semi-darkness), keys with large brass knobs in the wall niches …

I can clearly see four clocks above the reception desk showing time in different parts of the world:

According to them, it is now:

- 7.40 in New York
- 8.20 in Moscow
- 9.45 in Tokyo
- 8.55 in Rome

The time on my fairly accurate watch (in Pisa), incidentally, is 2.32pm!

A peculiar multiple time loop in which anything can happen!

Another waiter – in a red shirt – soon comes out to take my order: *Minestra di verdure* (vegetable soup); *Cotoletta alla milanese* and *bira* (beer) to beat the heat.

Fat pigeons are waddling slowly among the tables; too lazy even to pick up the crumbs … From the corner of my eye and without leaning or turning, I can see the upper half of the Leaning Tower and a bit of the Duomo.

The Red Waiter brings my minestra, followed by the whole plate of grated Parmigiano, leaves both on my table and winks at me (meaning what? Hopefully, meaning: 'Here you are, mate: sitting at your table and not realising you are about to have the worst meal of your entire life …')

Will be calling the waiters: Red Waiter (RW) and Black Waiter (BW) from now on – the latter not out loud of course, due to the danger of being overheard, attacked and subsequently squashed to death by the enormous and, no doubt, politically correct to the core of their deeply hidden bones American girls …I know only too well that the word 'black' is strictly banned in the USA and cannot be used in a conversation in any context.

Minestra turns out unexpectedly excellent, with fresh home-made countryside-ish taste; like a granny's soup of my childhood. Mint leaves and carrots floating in my plate make it resemble a small easel of a tyro artist …

BW then brings bread: warm, rustic, freshly baked …

I order half-a-litre of vino rosso locale, feeling shamed by the sheer decadence of drinking wine at lunchtime – something I never do in the UK or anywhere else. Except for Italy … The wine is young, aromatic, with a pleasant tingle to the palate …

RW promptly delivers some olive oil and balsamic vinegar for my *insalata mista* …

'In another life, I'd like to be a restaurant critic,' I scribble down unexpectedly in my notebook. Am I getting tipsy?

An accordion and a small Spanish guitar, topped with two sullen faces, float past my table and disappear inside the hotel. Remembering one of the basic rules of dealing with street beggars, I try not to make eye contact with the musicians, fearing that the moment I do so, banknotes will get sucked out of my wallet by the sheer power of their hypnotic, possibly even magnetic, stares …

A sad-looking donkey (don't all donkeys look sad?) meekly drags a cart with a canoodling tourist couple. Two police women cycle past. They wave to Somali watch-sellers from their bikes …

A Latino-looking youngster is sipping mineral water and reading a book at the table next to mine …

A lovely gentle sea breeze – like that on the top of the Tower – is blowing in my face …

After a frantic search, I do find a speck of a bad meal in my lunch – a not-too-fresh, possibly even pickled, tomato in my salad! Only later I read in a cook book that for some salads it is best to use pickled tomatoes due to the coagulating nature of their juices helping to keep the ingredients together … Not sure that the 'un-fresh' tomato though was put in the salad deliberately.

In the proximity of the Americans, I have to be careful not to refer to the tomato as 'rotten.' Some time ago, the proponents of political correctness tried to ban this word in reference to vegetable and fruit 'not to offend the plants' dignity' (I swear I am not fibbing). That trend ('vegecide?') was a logical continuation of the still thriving 'petocide' whereby you cannot say 'I have a cat,' but have to say instead: 'the cat who agrees to share my house with me.' Petocide reached its absolute extreme several years ago, when some of its supporters claimed that by feeding pets you were insulting them and that they should be left to their own devices while looking for food. Luckily, that last trend had never caught on, otherwise there wouldn't have been any cats or dogs left in America by now …

So how should one refer to a rotten tomato then? 'Un-fresh?' 'Hyper-ripe' perhaps? For some reason, these lazy lunch-time musings bring back to mind a joke once told me in Moscow by the now deceased Labour MP John Smith:

> Maggie Thatcher is having lunch with her Cabinet ministers. A waiter comes up to take her order.
> 'I'll have soup,' Mrs Thatcher says.
> 'And how about vegetables?' asks the waiter.
> 'They will have soup too,' she replies.

With that sort of animated 'vegetables' one has to be careful indeed …

My *Cotoletta* arrives. It is very tender, with pleasant, slightly lemony, aftertaste …

Meanwhile, the time on the New York clock inside the hotel lobby has changed to 8.20; the Moscow clock now shows: 4.25, the Tokyo one – 10.40 and the Rome one – 9.35. My very precise watch, bought years ago for £2.99 from the Folkestone branch of Lidl, insists it is 3.12pm!

The gross American girls have left, and some round-bellied (and rather American-looking – as if also wearing tiny baseball caps on their scalps) Pisa pigeons have taken their place …

But where are the street musicians? They haven't come out of the building yet! What are they up to in the hotel's mysterious dark recesses? Fast asleep? Sharing the day's profits? Or having gay sex?

It eventually turns out, however, that the restaurant is separate from the hotel, albeit located in the same building.

RW looks impressed by my '*macchiato doppio*' request – uttered with my best Ukrainian/Hertfordshire Italian accent … I ask for some '*aqua*' too and he brings a small jug of boiling hot water (I may have actually said '*aqua calda*' by association with 'cold water,' I have to confess), but he should have known better.

It is not only in English and Italian that two similarly-sounding words can denote polarly opposite concepts. Russian and Czech are even worse, for exactly the same word which in Russian means 'fruit' means 'vegetable' in Czech, and the word '*chiorstviy*,' which in Russian means 'stale,' means 'fresh!'

Without realising it, I once popped into a Prague bakery and asked for a loaf of stale bread!

Back in Pisa, I mark in my notebook three brutto ricordo points in what was otherwise a very good meal:

1. Poor welcome (it could have been dictated by RW's shyness rather then rudeness).
2. Not too fresh a tomato in the salad (although that could have been deliberate – see above).

3. Hot water with espresso (albeit that could have been my own fault).

I am now alone on the terrace, not counting the pigeons. A coach pulls up next to the hotel. Some ancient Americans fall out and start pushing their suitcases on wheels towards the hotel entrance.

BW pours out the remains of the mineral water from the bottles left on tables onto the floor to freshen it up …

'Ristorante Maiori di Pastore Andrea' says my bill.

'My father,' notes BW proudly. I wonder whether his father was/is a priest or is it just his family name, but stop short of asking BW.

Last test. The bill amounts to €.31.55 (a rather suspicious sum). I give BW €40 … Will the change turn up? (In a similar situation in Como a couple of years earlier, a waiter 'forgot' to give me €15 change referring somewhat enigmatically to his '*mamma malata'*).

It does – to the last eurocent, and I gladly leave BW (he can now be renamed BMW – Black Meticulous Waiter!) a fiver in tips for reinstalling my faith in Italians' honesty!

His Mum must be ok then …

BW then takes me inside the restaurant and shows a faded photo of Alfonso Pastore (mystery solved!), a couple of even more faded diplomas of uncertain origin and merit and a framed pass to a 'No Frills' travel industry exhibition in the name of 'Alfonso Pastore' on the wall – as if it were a diploma too (it is like framing a London One Day Travel Card – well, almost).

If it were up to me, I would have had the 'No Frills' pass enlarged and put above that lovely small restaurant's entrance …

* * *

On the way back to Viareggio where I was staying at the Principe Di Piemonte Hotel, I had a shocking encounter. Outside Pisa train station, I saw a group of Italian tramps – '*bomzhi*' in Russian: unshaven, yet neatly dressed, men and some young ruddy-faced girls (also neatly dressed) were swigging cheap cider from large plastic bottles on a grass patch in the middle of the station square. I walked past them several times to make sure they spoke Italian and were not East Europeans …

Another Italy … Not that concerned about the quality of their meals and of their lives too …

Still having several minutes to kill before my train, I popped into a Chef Express fast food outlet inside Pisa station. Its menu sounded like an index page of a non-existent *Encyclopaedia of Great Italians – Real and Fictional*:

– Panini

- Ulisse
- Captain Nemo
- Marco Polo (made me wonder what sort of a discovery may be hiding inside it)
- Atilla
- Vasco de Gama (with prosciutto, mozzarella)
- Colombo
- Scilla
- Vespucci (basilico, mozzarella) – all at about €3 each

I thought that sandwiches with such beautiful names were simply bound to be tastier and healthier than Big Macs …

Stereotypes kept crumbling during my first Italian trip in search of a bad meal … As another proof of that, I discovered a balcony and a sea view in my Principe di Piemonte hotel room which I thought had no windows yesterday when I checked in – knackered – at about midnight. The huge window was simply covered with thick curtains! Now, looking at the beach and the aquamarine horizon behind it, I thought it was another apt metaphor for my peculiar quest: discovering a sea view in what you thought was a thick stone wall!

Also – timely: after a great 'bad meal' in a 'tourist trap' of a very nice restaurant!

* * *

Ristorante Romano, Via Mazzini, 120, Viareggio, Toscana

Having eaten in two Italian supposedly bad restaurants that turned out very nice, I thought it would be worth applying the rule of contraries and reverse the equation: if one has problems finding a bad meal in 'bad' restaurants, maybe one should try a 'good' one instead?

With that in mind, I asked my hotel's guest relations clerk –a young Byelorussian brunette called Kristina who, incidentally, looked more Italian than most Italian girls I had ever met, to book me a table at Romano's, Viareggio's only Buon Ricordo restaurant.

Founded in 1964 by Dino Villani, I Ristoranti di Buon Ricordo, which loosely translates as 'Restaurants worth remembering fondly,' is an exclusive club promoting regional Italian cuisine, with about 120 members all over the world, but mostly in Italy. Each of the restaurant-members has its signature dish, and any customer who orders it is entitled to a souvenir plate. If previously one had to guess which dish to order to receive the plate, now it is usually clearly stated in the menu which makes the plate collectors' task easier, yet destroys the element of surprise turning what was supposed to be a culinary adventure into a rather predictable procedure, like paying one's bill …

Buon Ricordo plates have indeed become very collectable over the years, there's even a special international collectors society/club, although I've never heard of anyone who had managed to accumulate more than twenty. David Dale himself has 'only' nineteen. Partly, this is because many of Buon Ricordo restaurants are in unlikely locations. A small town somewhere in Sicily or Sardinia can have several, but there are none in the whole of Torino!

As for me, I did own a Buon Ricordo plate once, having received it after a nice lunch at a villa-cum-restaurant near Como the name of which I cannot recall. I had no idea of what Buon Ricordo stood for then and was rather surprised to receive what looked like a cheap-ish plate with the restaurant's name around the rim and a primitive drawing of the signature dish in the middle, hastily painted by either a talentless amateur or a child. No need to say, I didn't treasure it at all and might have even left it behind in my hotel room or had it cracked and broken in my backpack – can't remember …

Apart from the plate, a Buon Ricordo customer used to receive the coveted (even more than the plate!) list of all existing member restaurants. Connoisseurs were prepared to pay a fortune for this list which is now available for free on the Internet – what a shame!

Romano's restaurant in Viareggio was very popular, for apart from being a member of Buon Ricordo for nearly forty years, it also belonged to the new and, according to some experts, even more prestigious, restaurant club 'Le Soste.' On top of all those, it had a Michelin star!

Needless to say, Kristina failed to get me a seat. 'They are completely booked,' she shrugged apologetically. Our conversation was overheard by the hotel's press and media relations manager called Francesco, an intelligent (he spoke fluent Russian) young man with velvety brown eyes and a no-less-velvety voice. 'Let me try,' suggested he.

When I returned to his desk two minutes later, it was all fixed. 'Romano himself looks forward to welcoming you tonight,' said Francesco and added: 'You'll have a whole table for yourself …'

'What did you tell them?' I asked.

'Nothing much. Just that you are the world's best journalist …'

I was relieved he said 'best,' not 'richest' …

Italy was still a male-dominated society, or so it seemed …

My biggest concern was the cost of that dinner. One was unlikely to be able to dine at a Michelin-starred restaurant for a tenner … Taking a shower in my room before the long-awaited Buon Ricordo experience, I suddenly thought that Francesco had probably introduced me as a Russian oligarch, a Roman Abramovich type, and was now worried that they would want to rip me off accordingly. On reflection, however, I decided that if they indeed took me for Abramovich, they were likely to charge me nothing at all!

And I calmed down a little bit …

After a long, nearly endless, walk along the Promenade and Via Mazzini, I finally arrived at Romano's. The restaurant was hard to miss due to a huge 'Romano's' sign above its entrance.

Inside, it was cool – in more than one sense. I mean not just properly air-conditioned, although on that scorching evening it was a relief that it was – but also, in teenage-speak, classy. The interior décor was simple, almost minimalist. Light-brown walls and curtains with hues of yellow. Yellow roses on tables. A scarily plain and not-too-long black-and-white menu (no pictures!) without prices.

I had only seen a price-less menu once before – at a peculiar London restaurant Just Round the Corner in Finchley Road. The principle of its owners was seemingly altruistic and simple: customers pay as much as they think appropriate. That was an extremely clever move. Whereas, of course, there's always a danger that someone may decide to pay nothing at all, those who have truly appreciated the cooking, the service and the (again, seemingly) generous 'pay-as-much-or-as-little-as-you-want' arrangement, would be tempted to pay the very top dollar as a matter of their pride and prestige. A psychologically impeccable calculation which had quickly made 'Just Round the Corner' extremely profitable …

Yet, under normal circumstances, few things can appear as unsettling to a person of average means as a restaurant menu without prices …

I was served by Roberto, Romano's son, who, unlike his father, spoke some English. Elderly waiters, in black suits and with the noble faces of musicians or academics, were fluttering to and fro with youthful dexterity and grace …

Worried about the costs (no wonder: with no prices in the menu!), I refused champagne and asked for the wine list. It had prices in it. But I immediately wished it didn't! They made me nearly fall off my chair: it was clear I couldn't afford any … What to do? Salvation came in the shape of a bottle of '*Il Pageiano Romano Franceskini*' produced by Romano's own small family winery. I found it in some obscure corner of the wine list, and it was several times cheaper than the cheapest of the rest (yet still expensive by my standards!). 'I can claim I want to try the wine made by the famous Romano,' I was thinking frantically. 'That would make me appear curious and even graceful without looking too poor or greedy …'

The wine proved excellent: fruity, utterly drinkable … But it took me some time to discover all its merits: Roberto opened the bottle, showed it to me and then rather cruelly took it away! To breathe! … Or maybe he was simply punishing me for something I had done wrong? For having refused the champagne perhaps?

The signature dish for which I would get a Buon Ricordo plate (or so I hoped) was easy to find in the menu, for it said '*Piatto Buon Ricordo*' in brackets next to its name – '*Minestra di farro con verdure e pesce.*' My second minestra verdure of the day! If Roberto only knew where I had my first one (in the shadow of the Leaning Tower and next to a mini-landfill)!

Eventually, he brought my still breathing (if only just) bottle of wine back. I took a sip: 'Beautiful!' to which Roberto reacted strictly, almost angrily: 'Not beautiful. But very nice …' And repeated even more sternly: 'Not beautiful!' A strange way to promote his own family wine …

I put on my reading glasses and squinted at the label: the wine was fourteen per cent. I would have never have guessed – so stunningly light and drinkable it appeared.

Another 'judgement of Solomon': I chose half of each of the two starters suggested by Roberto: *Calamaretti ripieni di verdure e crostacei* and *Insalata di crostacei i moluschi* – again, my verbal reasoning was wanting to try as many dishes as possible, whereas the real reason was money, or rather lack of it, of course.

In the end, my glasses proved useful, for these were the tiniest squid I had ever seen …

I was forgetfully cracking the poor crustaceans, struggling with a reluctant langoustine – or whatever that curiously shaped sea creature was called – and again mopping all the sauce up with bread in an uncouth peasant-like manner! Then came a frightening thought: here's an empty side plate – was I supposed to drop all the shells onto it?

I was half expecting all the patrons to jump off their seats and shame me …

At times, I felt almost paranoid. The waiters kept picking up my bag from the floor and putting it back on the chair next to me … 'Am I breaking some obscure Italian law by putting my bag on the floor under my feet?' I was thinking …

In the meantime, the meal was getting better and better – like a prelude to an opera: the music gets louder and louder, as if in anticipation of the main act, sorry course …

I suddenly realised that Romano's was in effect but a FOOD THEATRE – nothing more, nothing less!

Out of six chairs at my table, only two are taken – by me and by my bag. But now – with some help from '*Il Pageiano Romano Franceskini*' – I can easily imagine my whole family there: Dad, Mum, grandparents – all around that table, all smiling, looking at me, and feeling proud … No matter what the real reason is, but anyone dining at a Buon Ricordo restaurant in Italy must have done something right in this life …

When my granny was dying of cancer, her last wish was to try beluga caviar. In the USSR, that ultimate Russian delicacy was only available to foreigners and party apparatchiks, so my Mum had to use all her resourcefulness to gain entrance to our city's only Intourist hotel, and – past a Cerberus-like doorman – to that hotel's restaurant, where she begged the manager to sell her some 'black caviar' as an 'exception to the rules' to pacify her dying mother … She did manage to acquire a small amount in the end, but it was too late: my granny passed away on the same day without ever tasting the treat …

I recall standing in an endless queue for butter as a little boy in the Soviet Ukraine of the early 1960s – with my granny and granddad. Khrushchev's idiotic strategy of planting maize everywhere had led to near-starvation in Ukraine, with such staples as white bread and milk disappearing almost completely …

Butter, that precious product, was rationed per capita, that was why my grandparents, having wrapped me up in several layers of warm togs, took me to the queue with them.

We were standing in the snow for over five hours before our turn came.

We were then let inside the Tempo food store where a fat artificial blonde of a saleswoman in once-white overalls dispensed our three carefully weighed butter slices: two larger and one smaller. I remember burying my little capita – mouth first – into the cold moon-like slice I was entrusted to carry the moment we were back in the street, in full view of the still endless queue snaking along the snow.

'Look at this boy – he likes his butter so much,' the people, who were themselves about to enter the shop, were saying amicably, whereas those farther away from the entrance only tut-tutted.

An aspiring little glutton, I couldn't care less about gluten. To be honest, I had no idea it existed then.

Scratches left by my sharp little teeth on the yellow surface of the butter slice were like faint outlines of the craters on the face of the Moon I was able to spot in my toy plastic telescope – a birthday present from Dad …

On one of the book shelves in my Pegasus Cottage in Letchworth stands a large light-brown folio of *Kniga o vkusnoi I zdorovoi pishche – The Book of Tasty and Wholesome Cuisine*, published in Moscow in 1952. As a child I enjoyed leafing through its pages with coloured pictures of alluring and not necessarily 'wholesome' Russian foods (never seen in reality and therefore exotic). The 'subversive' book of recipes (with all but imaginary ingredients) which had miraculously withstood all my life's wanderings (Kharkov-Moscow-Melbourne-London-Melbourne-Edinburgh-Folkestone-Dublin-London-Letchworth etc) began with a huge-lettered quote from Stalin on a special flap preceding the title page:

> 'One of the peculiarities of our revolution lied in the fact that it gave the Soviet people not just freedom but also material well-being and a possibility of a plentiful and cultured life.'

I recalled that insipid quote many years later – in the late 1970s, when working as a translator for the Institute of Some Obscure Research in Moscow. The best thing about that Institute was that it was located next to another one – the Soviet Academy of Sciences Institute of Nutrition, and we were allowed to have lunches in the latter's coveted staff canteen. The Institute of Nutrition used to award Doctorates in Nutrition Studies, with the subjects of the theses prominently displayed on the Institute's notice board in the lobby. I remember one: *Necessity of proper nutrition for the female weavers of Ivanovo region.*

Not belonging to the cheerful (and well-fed) ranks of the Ivanovo weavers, we, the staff of the Obscure Research Institute, were obviously not in need of proper nutrition and not entitled to it, despite being allowed into the holy of holies of the Nutrition Institute canteen. The canteen, by the way, was crap …

As you see, my childhood and youth were not particularly hedonistic. Food was a commodity that was always in short supply and therefore one had to be happy with whatever one could get … Many years later, I ended up in one of the world's most hedonistic countries – Australia – where I quickly became a well-known columnist for the nation's largest newspaper, *The Melbourne Age.* Initially, I was finding it hard to believe that the paper had a special sixteen-page weekly section on nothing but food and restaurants which employed a whole squad of grim, yet rosy-cheeked, critics writing on nothing else but food. 'What a horrible waste of precious newspaper space – when there is still so much suffering and injustice in the world,' I was thinking then (fresh from the USSR) while swearing silently never to write about food myself …

Well, only a year or so later, the all-permeating Australian hedonism started taking its toll. I was eating out several times a week, I had put on a lot of weight … Missing Europe and being bored with the slow pace and insularity of Australian life, I began to think that perhaps the most exciting thing around was indeed food … In one of my columns, I mentioned a couple of my favourite restaurants and was pleasantly surprised to see that both of them had prominently displayed my article in their windows. By then, my column was already very popular and when we habitually went out for dinner to our local Chinese one evening, a long queue to its entrance was snaking all over the street. We were unable to get a table! 'Daddy, please do not write about this nice restaurant or we wouldn't be able to get in next time,' my eleven-year-old son Mitya would say routinely when we were enjoying a meal out in Melbourne …

Contrary to all my beliefs and promises, a little over a year after coming to Australia, I started writing about food … Among many other things of course …

Years later while researching my columns on the USA for London's *Daily Telegraph*, I met and befriended the omnipotent *New York Times* food critic William Grimes, nicknamed Biff. William was a sombre-looking and extremely thin intellectual, who hated his job. A polymath and a polyglot (he spoke fluent Russian), he would routinely tell me on the phone: 'Sorry, Vitali, I can't see you tonight. I have to eat … Again … To eat …' There was so much pain and suffering in his voice when he uttered the verb 'to eat' that one could be forgiven for thinking that, in William's perception, 'eating' and' waterboarding' (or another form of sophisticated torture) were synonyms.

Charged with the ability to close down restaurants (or to propel them to fame and prosperity) with a single twist of his food critic's pen, William often had to work (meaning to eat) undercover. He once showed me half-a-dozen credit cards in different names which he used to pay for his 'working' meals.

'How can you claim to be unrecognized when there's your head shot to accompany each of your columns in the paper?' I would ask him.

'Well, it's an old photo and it is deliberately blurred …' he would respond …

One day William invited me to keep him company during one of his 'working' lunches in a new posh restaurant in Park Avenue.

'Don't forget: the table is booked in the name of Mr Smith,' he told me. 'Surely, they could have come up with something more original at the *New York Times*,' I was thinking on my way …

The moment I crossed the threshold of the Park Avenue restaurant and mentioned the name of Mr Smith … they picked me up and carried me to the table, at which habitually sour-faced William was already 'working' on his starter …

There was little doubt they knew who he was. And he knew that they knew …He also knew that I knew that he knew that they knew, but none of us voiced it either during or after the rather schizophrenic meal, which combined the elements of Italian, Jewish, Japanese and French cuisine. 'Frankly, my favourite gourmet experience in New York is a street cart,' said William as we were being carried out of the restaurant by the staff …

Immersed in reverie, I didn't notice how a rather interesting amorous couple appeared at the table next to mine: he was about seventy – bald, short and in a pink tracksuit; she – a typical specimen of what Italians call *'la bionda'* – of about twenty-five. Soon they were joined by another similar couple: he – in his mid-seventies, a smug Berlusconi look-alike (or maybe Berlusconi HIMSELF?), she – about nineteen (Berlusconi's notorious teenage girlfriend?), this time a brunette. Looking at her, he was openly salivating … I mean literally: you could see opaque old man's saliva dripping off his lips down his chin and onto the table cloth … No, he couldn't possibly be Berlusconi who had just been hit with a statuette on the face by a madman, so should still be wearing bandages and/or scars, I was musing …

La bionda in the meantime kept running her hand up and down her pink-suited companion's back in mock passion …

All four were drinking, snogging and taking photos of each other for all they were worth, but not eating much. One thing was clear: they were not loving daughters (or granddaughters) on a family outing with their respective (if not quite respectful) daddies or granddads. Sugar daddies, perhaps?

At some point, they all suddenly stood up and marched out of the restaurant, having left some of their belongings and clothes items (like bras and knickers – only joking) behind … About twenty minutes later they returned – all red-faced and excited … What were they doing? Having a foursome in the car? Or – more likely – simply smoking outside?

Watching the Berlusconi couples nearly killed my appetite.

Back to the Romano's signature dish though … The thick fish soup-cum-risotto tasted familiar, like an old fairy tale, although I had never tried anything similar: soothing, almost kindergarten-ish …

The girls at the next table were getting raunchy – they were now all over their saliva-dribbling 'granddads'; I wondered how much they charged for their services (I mean the girls, not the granddads, of course). The sight was fairly disgusting and made me feel like kicking all four of them – not a nice feeling …Everyone – including families and children of whom they were still a lot in the restaurant – were now staring at them as they were making all those nasty noises until they finally stood up and left – probably to f … or – more likely – to fumble …

I had a cup of perfect macchiato …

The amorous age-gap couples suddenly reappeared again – that must have been a real quickie (one sugar daddy has a large '3' on his t-shirt which probably meant a three-minute-long performance; or perhaps it stood for 'a third rate lover') which meant I had to go: I couldn't stand the sight of them any longer. The rubbish truck circling around the Pisa restaurant where I had lunch had felt aesthetically much much better … And, I guess, smelled better too …

Roberto brought in my first Buon Ricordo plate, without much pomp … It featured the name of my main course – '*Minestra di farro, verdure e pesce*' – and a couple of happy langoustines, or whatever they were, canoodling underneath it. I then wanted to see Romano himself to thank him for the meal, and he turned out to be one of the elderly waiters serving the tables next to mine … He said (in Italian, while Roberto was translating) that he had been running this restaurant for twenty-eight years and since then had only changed his plate thrice … The restaurant also had a Michelin star ('You have to apply for Buon Ricordo, but Michelin finds you – that's the difference') and belonged to a new molecular gastronomy club Le Soste, too;

He sweetly addressed me as '*Caro Signore*' and said that he chose his fresh fish three times a day and that women only were responsible for the 'back of the house' which reminded me of a banner I once spotted above a rather mediocre Italian restaurant in Melbourne: 'European women in the kitchen!'

I was walking back to the hotel along the promenade pressing my first Buon Ricordo plate to my chest like a bit of a semi-forgotten childhood dream … It was midnight; crowds were everywhere; children were playing under the palm trees while their parents were having coffees and ice-cream in *al fresco* bars on the embankment. It was a highly energised crowd – as only the Italian seaside crowd can be. I was then literally swept off my feet by 'Maestro Tony D'Amico' performing Tom Jones' songs in one of the open-air cafés – Bar-Pizzeria Contemporanea – better than Jones himself …

I dialled Christine in Letchworth on my mobile – and here we were: sitting together on the promenade under the velvety Tuscany stars – listening to Tom Jones …

I thought that David Dale was right: Italians did somehow manage to discover the secret of happiness …

In my exhausted mind I was hastily compiling the brand-new 'Italian rule of food contraries': looking for a bad meal in Italy – you find a good one; looking for a good one – you find … er … no, no, not a bad one, not in Italy … you find an excellent one!

From the author

It is largely my fault that you are unable to read this book to the end … To assuage my feeling of guilt, I offer you a small 'consolation bonus' 'on the house,' as they say in restaurants. Please see next page.

NB: This short article won me a GOLD TABPI AWARD in the USA in 2016. VV

Railway Dining

'Rail passengers eat a lot!' noted Ilf and Petrov, celebrated Soviet/Russian satirists of the 1920s-30s, and they were spot on. I don't know about you, but I start experiencing pangs of hunger the moment I board a train. The duration of the trip does not matter: it can be a ten-minute ride to work, a five-hour journey to Edinburgh, or a three-day escapade from Sydney to Perth on board the Indian-Pacific Express – as long as the train is chugging along, I feel hungry. Perhaps some obscure hunger centres in my brain get stimulated by the gentle rocking of the carriage and the repetitive clickety-clack of its wheels ...

If I were to write a personal history of my own railway dining, I would start with the traditional 'railway chicken,' wrapped in a month-old copy of Pravda, and frozen at the point when it was covered with goose-pimples (or shall I say 'chicken-pimples?') and was almost shivering with cold. On seemingly endless Russian train journeys of my childhood, even that pitiful anorexic creature tasted divine.

Then comes my journalistic adulthood, characterised by with ubiquitous and unchangeable borscht and cutlet menus of Soviet restaurant cars. The meetings, the romances, the fights I've experienced in those carriages (over the same cutlets and borscht, which, incidentally, were always yummy, or appeared as such washed down with generous helpings of vodka).

Once in the early 1980s, I was sent on a seemingly 'dream' assignment by *The Whistle*, the Soviet national railway daily. My mission was to travel across the USSR in as many restaurant cars as possible and to write reports from the road. The overall title of the series was '*Appetit ukhodit vo vremia yezdi*' ('Appetite disappears as you ride') to echo a popular Russian proverb '*Appetit prikhodit vo vremia yedi*' ('Appetite appears as you eat'). As you may have deduced, I was lucky to have survived the ordeal with just a severe food poisoning ... but I still loved the experience and look back on it as one of my best assignments ever.

In my post-Soviet railway eating history, two memories stand out. The first of these is of the Indian Pacific Express in Australia, onboard which I experienced several truly astounding five-course dinners – my only regret was to have been assigned to the second sitting, which meant I had to wait until the lucky first-sitting diners had finished their meals.

The second 'outstanding' memory was that of a rotten sandwich, recklessly consumed on a train to Blackpool, to where I was sent by *Spectator* magazine in the mid-1990s to write an objective critique of the town's (in)famous tourist attractions. I was fortunate on this occasion, because the restless sandwich literally jumped out of my stomach before getting digested as I was on the famous Pleasure Beach roller-coaster ...

All of the above is but an appetiser for the very best railway dining experience of my life, which took place a couple of weeks ago in my own living room. Let me explain. At the beginning of this year, I went to Canada to visit my son. While there, I discovered the stunning Canadian Railway Museum on the outskirts of Montreal. We all know that Canada is one of the world's vastest countries and hence one of the greatest railway nations, with over 50,000 kilometres of track. Just like its neighbour, the USA, it was railways that made Canada into one of the world's leading industrial nations. Railway fever hit Canada in the 1830s, and less than a century later the rails joined together the country's Atlantic and Pacific coasts. Just like in Russia, it was not unusual for railway journeys to last for three or four days; these days of course most people facing a long-distance journey would rather fly. The fact remains that long trips, however you choose to travel, mean hungry passengers.

The first passenger car to provide lodging and meals in the USA and Canada was engineered and patented by Isaac Knight of Baltimore in 1829. It incorporated 'a dining table, and other accommodations, such as stoves and a kitchen …' By the end of the nineteenth century, over 100 dining cars were plying the length and breadth of the country. Most of them were truly luxurious and offered fine dining to rival stationary restaurants. The cars' vibration used to be a problem, but it was eventually resolved by George Mortimer Pullman, an engineer and an entrepreneur, who invented and installed rubber shock absorbers on his famous Palace Cars in the 1860s.

From then on, passengers could enjoy their soups without spilling them all over their attire. The challenge for the railway chefs, however, has always been to maintain the high quality of the dishes with the smallest possible number of ingredients (trains could only carry limited supplies), cooked with as few kitchen utensils and pieces of equipment as possible. With those aims in mind, they started developing special simplified recipes for their 'meals on wheels.'

In the Museum gift shop I was thrilled to spot the first ever collection of such recipes in the form of a beautifully printed cookbook *100 Years of Canadian Railway Recipes*, compiled by Marie-Paul Partikian and Jean-Paul Viaud, who put together ninety of the best culinary creations from the three largest Canadian railway companies: CN, CPR and VIA Rail Canada. The recipes' simplicity and practicality make them ideal for an amateur chef like myself, and I have already rewarded myself and my wife (or so I hope) with an authentic Canadian railway dinner in our Hertfordshire cottage.

For a starter, I made 'Fried Potato Western' patties, using the 1934 recipe by the dining car chef Fred Conway; and for the main course – a mouth-watering 'Chicken Sauté Chasseur' by chef Philippe Vignal of Canadian Pacific Railway (1936). Both were easy to cook and absolutely delicious.

Besides, they made me feel as if I was visiting Canada again and absorbing the view of an endless row of snow-covered trees floating past the window of a famous

Canadian railway dining car, of which – sadly – only thirteen are still in operation now …

'Midva' – the Two of Us. Life on the Slovene-Italian Border

The story of a unique Italo-Slovenian community which came to be united by the same border that used to divide it (first published in *Geograpical* magazine)

One of the saddest sights is that of an Italian town in lockdown …

It is an early Saturday afternoon in March 2020, and I am the only pedestrian in a sun-lit cobbled street in the centre of Gorizia, an ancient border town in north-eastern Italy, a former provincial capital, now paired with the Slovenian town of Nova Gorica on the other side of the state frontier to create a peculiar bi-national metropolis – a jointly administered trans-border conurbation Gorizia/Nova Gorica.

Via Roma, normally resonating with the loud, yet peaceful and amicable, buzz of an Italian crowd, feels gagged, and my solitary footsteps echo bluntly in the silent, as if comatose, Art Nouveau facades …

In Gorizia/Nova Gorica, the normally invisible state border runs across roads and lanes. It dissects the railway station plaza, now called Europe Square, from where both Italian and Slovenian streets radiate. It is habitual therefore for the Gorizia dwellers to dash 'across the street' for a drink of a cheaper Slovenian beer, and for the Slovenes to pop over to Italy for a cuppa of a hugely superior espresso.

I visited Gorizia/Nova Gorica early last March – at the truly unique historical moment, when the border – totally open and all but imaginary since December 2007, when Slovenia joined the Schengen Area – became real and visible again, for the first time in thirteen years!

With Italy already deep in lockdown, Slovenia was still practically unaffected by the Covid-19 pandemic, with zero Coronavirus-related deaths and just a few positive tests in Ljubljana, the capital, about fifty miles away. It was a bizarre and sinister sight: the Slovenian part of the town lively and full of people, and its Italian half – semi-deserted. And just a week after my departure, due to the quickly spreading pandemic, the Slovenian-Italian border inside the town had to be closed entirely – with fences, concrete blocks and barbed wire reappearing overnight at all designated crossings for the first time since the 1970s – a gruesome throwback to the times of the Cold War, when they were separating Marshal Tito's Communist Yugoslavia (of which Slovenia was a federal part) from the Western world.

My Nova Gorica contacts, who still remembered the Cold War era, reported watching in disbelief the return of the guarded checkpoints, through which only the key workers were allowed to pass, in the town's streets and squares.

The global pandemic was probably the only force in the world capable of restoring the Cold War borders, even if for a relatively short while, thus temporarily re-introducing the divide between Gorizia and Nova Gorica, which by then had merged to the point of running together for the title of the European Capital of Culture 2025 – the first and so far only case in history when two urban communities from two different countries strived to become one-and-the-same cross-border 'capital'!

Smuggling Across the Square

With my Slovenian escort David Kozuh, a local historian and the curator of the regional museum, we are standing next to each other in the middle of Europe Square – a living symbol of the town's present-day unity. We are both on the Slovenian side, where social distancing is not yet in force. I make a small step to the right – and bingo: I am in Italy, and Mr Kozuhnow has to keep two metres away from me …

On the Slovenian side, the Square is dominated by the Nova Gorica railway station, built in 1906 as the Gorizia station of the Bohinj railway, crucial for the Austro-Hungarian Empire, of which Gorizia was then a part. Yes, local history here can be complicated, and that is why is it great to have a knowledgeable historian as my guide.

Mr Kozuh explains that the station building became part of Yugoslavia in September 1947, when the Square was divided in two parts in accordance with the February 1947 Paris Peace Treaty. The station entrance was just thirty-eight metres away from the border. Until 1954, the square had been dissected along the frontier line by several barbed wire rows, later supplemented with a concrete fence. All those barriers were partially removed in 2004 and taken away completely in 2011.

The history of that Italian-Slovenian divide was far less sinister than that of the Berlin Wall, and yet hundreds of people, mostly from the Yugoslavian side, were killed and injured trying to cross over the border illegally, particularly in the first several years of its existence, between 1947 and 1950.

Then of course there were smugglers.

Here it is important to note that Tito's Yugoslavia, or the Yugoslav Federal People's Republic (FLRJ), as it was officially known, was much better off in terms of material well-being that any other country of the former communist block (in the Soviet Union, where I grew up, it was as hard to get a permission to travel to Yugoslavia as to the USA, or other 'capitalist' countries). And yet, the gap in the living standards with neighbouring Italy was striking – to the point when the few lucky Slovenes, officially allowed to travel across the border, made sure they carried substantial amounts of the locally made produce: meat, honey, wine etc. – and brought back manufactured goods: cameras, radios, household items and later, electronics.

'Smuggling was a way of life here, with no stigma attached to it,' explains Kozuh. So widespread it was that at some point the Belgrade government had to make provisions for the Gorizia border to be guarded exclusively by the supposedly incorruptible soldiers from Serbia, another Yugoslavian republic, who had no connections with the locals and were therefore harder to bribe! Kozuh's own granny used to smuggle out rabbit meat, tied to her body, and bring back such coveted Italian goods as chocolate, coffee and brooms.

'Brooms?' I ask him in disbelief.

'Yes, indeed, ordinary sorghum brooms, which were in short supply in the communist Yugoslavia, like many other basic household goods,' he smiles.

Those hard-to-obtain brooms swept their way into history when in August 1950 a crowd of nearly 5,000 Slovenes illegally crossed the border in protest against the checkpoint's temporary closure which left them unable to stock up on some basic necessities they had run out of. The crowds stopped short of trespassing, but staged a peaceful demonstration on the neutral land between the two check-points – Slovenian and Italian – and many of them were waving their old worn-out brooms. That impromptu gathering became known as The March of the Brooms, or The Brooms Sunday.

Those times are firmly in the past. With both Italy and Slovenia (which declared independence from Yugoslavia in 1991) being EU members, there are no more shortages of foods and consumer goods in either country (even if such basics as petrol or beer remain cheaper in Slovenia). And yet, some people on both sides of the non-existent fence still tend to slightly romanticise the old way of life, of which smuggling was an important part.

'Border mentality has always been in our psyche,' Anja Medved, Slovenian writer and filmmaker, told me in a Nova Gorica bar. 'We always looked at the West with a longing, and when the border went, its disappearance reverberated in my soul which used to thrive on the uncertainty. At times, I have a feeling that it is still there, that it is the world that has changed, but the border remains. To me, it is not a geopolitical concept, but a category of the mind. And wasn't it great to be twelve and on a bike and on your own – riding to a different world?'

Anja grew up in the 1980s when the borders between the 'socialist' Yugoslavia and the West were all but open (unlike his Soviet counterparts, Marshal Tito decided to grant the right to travel to all his politically oppressed subjects in exchange for loyalty), and the Yugoslav citizens, including Slovenians, were free to live and work anywhere in the world. For someone like myself, however, who had felt tremendously claustrophobic and entrapped in the world's largest cage of the former USSR, it was hard to share Anja's nostalgia for the borders …

The Town With Two Faces

I visited the HQ of EGTC-GO, the Gorizia branch of the European Grouping of Territorial Co-Operation, literally hours before it too succumbed to lockdown. Unlike some other EU-supported organisations, designed to 'facilitate cross-border co-operation', but in reality bureaucratising it even further, EGTC-GO was established in 2009 by both municipalities as a tool to overcome the numerous bureaucratic obstacles to joint projects and initiatives.

EGTC-GO staff do not waste their time and budgets on parades, festivals and other public manifestations of cross-border solidarity. Its director, Dr Ivan Curzolo, spoke to me about the importance of such down-to-earth issues as joint waste collection and cross-border ambulance services serving both communities equally rather than being disrupted by all sorts of bureaucratic regulations. One of the organisation's significant achievements was that women from the Slovenian community could now give birth in Italy, the country with higher midwifery standards, if they so wished. I found that particular fact reassuring: it was like building a firm foundation for the area's borderless future.

Not everything in the cross-border relations is good and bright, and Dr Curzolo claimed that his organisation's initiatives have yet to find support in the respective national capitals, refusing to put up with diversity.

I could not help overhearing notes of dissatisfaction when speaking with Aldo Rudel, a Gorizia-based Slovenian writer, translator and former teacher, who volunteered to show me around his Italian town, described in my vintage *1905 Baedeker's Austria-Hungary* as 'the capital of a province, charmingly situated on the Isonzo [River] and frequented as a winter resort.'

We started in the central square, known as Travnik (Meadow) in Slovenian and Piazza della Vittoria (Victory Square) in Italian, where Mussolini spoke twice – in 1938 and 1942.

Rudel pointed at a billboard with the town map and the legend in both Italian and Slovenian. The Slovenian part of the legend was sprayed with black ink to the point of being unreadable.

'Someone keeps stubbornly desecrating this map,' complained Rudel. 'We clean it up – and overnight they do it again!'

He lamented some anti-Slovenian attitudes in Gorizia which, in his words, have resulted in ethnic Slovenes being underrepresented in the local government bodies. His other complaint was of the lack of Slovenian street signs. Here I have to say that I hadn't spotted many Italian signs in the town's Slovenian part – Nova Gorica – either.

Of course, not everything looks and feels the same in Gorizia and in Nova Gorica, and, frankly, my hope is that they will forever remain parts of one-and-the-same border town, with two distinctly different faces.

When Le Corbusier Went to the Casino

My very first impression of Nova Gorica, the modernistic Slovenian part of the Gorizia conurbation, was that I had been there before, even though I certainly hadn't.

Architecturally, that 'planned community', built after World War II on the orders of Marshal Josip Broz Tito (1892-1980), Yugoslavia's communist leader, struck me as a cross between Minsk and Stevenage, with a touch of Le Corbusier's brutalist 'Living Machine', inside which I once stayed in Marseilles. The latter association was actually quite relevant, for Nova Gorica was designed and built under the supervision of the Slovenian architect Edo Ravnikar – Le Corbusier's disciple and keen follower.

A special committee to organise the construction of a new Slovenian town on the Italian border was set up in April 1947 following the signing of the Paris Peace Treaty, and the first groups of workers started arriving to the site shortly after that – in October 1947. They were followed by the so-called 'youth work brigades' – volunteers from all over Yugoslavia.

Alas, orders from the top, combined with compulsive 'socialist planning' and a touch of enthusiasm, were not sufficient for the project's success. Ten years after the town's foundation, Slovenian geographer Igor Vriser wrote: 'Despite huge efforts, Nova Gorica is still only a half-built town paralysed by territorial division, deficient in economic resources, with a housing problem, unfinished municipal services etc.'

It was not until 1980 that, according to a survey, the town 'has taken a significant step forward'. That was largely due to the decision – in stark contradiction to the 'communist principles' – to open several large casinos, in which the locals were not allowed to gamble. According to a 1988 Yugoslavian guide to Nova Gorica, 'The proximity of the border is stimulating the growth of business in the hotel industry, and the Casino is now one of the features available to visitors from abroad (*sic* – VV).'

Indeed, the large Soviet-style hotel, where I stayed, was part of an even larger casino, semi-empty because of Covid-19. The locals were no longer banned from gambling, but not too many seemed interested. The remaining punters were mostly confused and uncharacteristically taciturn Italians, caught unawares by the pandemic and either unable or unwilling to return to their country.

With David Kozuh, we took a stroll around the town, which, just like most of the 1970s-80s urban developments in the Soviet Union, had no obvious 'centre', but just rows of high-rise housing blocks, hastily constructed from grey prefab panels, with standard-shaped balconies. I was pleasantly surprised, however, by the proliferation of small green spaces, with fountains, flowerbeds and tasteful modern sculptures, nestling casually among all those concrete monoliths – a welcome post-communist addition to the otherwise unimpressive and drab 'socialist' townscape, so different from that of its much older sister town across the Italian border.

* * *

As a keen linguist, I was happy to find out that among the various cross-border initiatives overseen by the Gorizia-based EGTC-GO was 'mutual language learning', i.e. helping Slovenians to study Italian, and Italians – to come to grips with Slovenian. And here's a small lesson of the latter: unlike most of other Slavic tongues, Slovenian possesses the so-called 'dual grammatical form', or 'the dual number'. Whereas most languages are happy with just a singular and a plural, Slovenian has a special way of saying 'just the two of us' – '*midva*'. It is often used in relation to newly married couples – two individuals, joined together to create one new entity.

That nicely-sounding pronoun – '*midva*', 'the two of us' – alone can pass for an adequate, if super-laconic, description of Gorizia/Nova Gorica – two border towns that have merged together to form one new identity of their own.

Part Eight
Travels in a Perfect Country – Switzerland

PostBuses

The legibility of my scribbles has always left much to be desired. From primary school, my handwriting could best be described with a Russian idiom *kak kuritsa lapoi* – literally, 'he writes like a hen with her paw (*sic*).' More often than not, I have little problem deciphering my own notes. This time, however, the scrawls in my notebooks were particularly bouncy and uneven, reflecting the curves and gradients of the steep and winding Swiss mountain roads on which they were written. They resembled an ECG of a person on the brink of a heart attack.

My aim was to criss-cross a chunk of Switzerland, using nothing but the yellow PostBuses – or 'post autos' – the country's iconic public transport vehicles. While in Switzerland, so attached did I become to those agile and ubiquitous vehicles that I started personalising them in the same way travellers personalise countries and cities. It was hard not to, for the PostBuses' role in the life of Swiss towns and villages has always been much more significant than merely being a reliable means of taking citizens from one place to another.

Transport Links

The Swiss PostBus Limited is the largest of the country's seventy-eight coach companies. Administered by the Motor Services Department of the Post Office, it carries over 120 million passengers each year and is carefully integrated with other public transport services: trains, boats and mountain cableways. According to Fritz Jenni, a former operations manager for the PostBuses, the Swiss transportation system resembles a tree, with the larger branches representing federal and private railways, smaller branches being the coaches, and the twigs being the urban transit operators running trams, city buses, boats, chairlifts and so on. But the trunk that holds the tree together is the vast post auto network which also operates in Liechtenstein and the South of France.

There isn't an inhabited place in Switzerland that cannot be reached by some sort of public transport. The federal law and the Swiss Constitution stipulate that every village with a population greater than forty is entitled to regular bus services. The frequency of these services is in direct proportion to the population density. Timetables are put together four years in advance. They tend to be rather conservative and seldom change. If a new route is to be introduced, the population of the area affected is invited to have a referendum.

At times, PostBuses are the main – sometimes the only – links between settlements. Bright yellow coaches, often with a small mail van in tow (for post autos still carry post), are a common sight in high-altitude regions and their signature sound – the first movement of Rossini's *William Tell Overture*, played by the drivers on three-tone post horns with electrical compressors at every road turn, is perhaps one of most familiar Swiss 'voices' – melodious, if somewhat ear-grating.

A little-known – and fairly 'human' – fact of the three-note horns is that they can still be used to 'talk' to post offices (and each other) from a distance. By altering the combination of the tones, a driver can announce 'departure of post,' 'arrival of post,' 'arrival of special post,' 'bus swerving out' and so on – so much more romantic and often more reliable than radio or mobile phones. This musical 'language' started in the mid-nineteenth century, when the coach drivers could also blow their horns a certain number of times on approaching the station to indicate the quantity of horses needing to be fed, giving the station master time to prepare the fodder.

The PostBus history goes back to 1849 when the Swiss postal service was made a monopoly of the young Confederation. The role of today's modern yellow buses was, back then, played by horse-drawn carriages (or in winter by sleighs), also coloured yellow. By the First World War, well after the first motor coaches were introduced on the eleven-mile stretch between Bern and Detlingen in 1906 (a line still in operation today), there were 2,500 horses, 2,231 coaches (or carriages) and 1,059 sleighs in service.

After the war, Swiss Post bought a fleet of decommissioned military trucks which were converted into PostBuses, but it was not until 1961 that the last horse-drawn coach was replaced with a motorised version on the high-altitude route from Cresta to Juf.

Today, the Swiss Post Office boasts one of the world's most advanced coach fleets, including fuel-cell models and the world's first driverless bus, launched in 2015 in the town of Sion, the capital of the canton of Valais.

History Lesson

Mountain tourism in Switzerland began in the early nineteenth century, when the first British mountaineers climbed two main peaks of the Bernese Alps: Jungfrau in 1811 and Finsteraarhorn in 1812. It was not long before the horse-drawn postal coaches started climbing the mountains too, yet it took motorised buses to conquer some truly serious heights.

Having stocked up on altitude sickness pills, I travelled up the steepest bus route in Europe (average gradient twenty-eight per cent) – from Reichenbach to Pochtenalp, at 3,660 metres above sea level, along the Kiental-Griesalp line. The pills remained unused, for despite countless sharp turns, with a nearly uninterrupted post horn symphony played by Manfred Mettier, the driver of our compact Mercedes-Benz PostBus, the journey was surprisingly smooth. At times, the bus would come to a sharp halt to give way to a descending lorry (descending traffic gets priority in the Alps). The driver would change gears, and the passengers would gasp involuntarily as the vehicle slipped back several inches. Our bus had a mail trailer in tow and, looking back, I could often see it folding into a particularly sharp turn of the narrow road, like a dagger in a sheath, and getting almost parallel to the bus itself.

This climb to Griesalp was first completed in 1860 by British mountaineer and historian Leslie Stephen (1832-1904), father of Virginia Woolf , who branded the Swiss Alps 'the playground of Europe.' Twelve years later, the first postal diligences (the name given in French to a solidly-built coach with four or more horses) were introduced to parts of the route.

The Tour Guide

PostBuses often go to places that other means of transport cannot reach. Most of the drivers therefore see themselves as educators and tour guides. Although it's not their direct duty, they never miss a chance to point out the sights – waterfalls, gorges, peculiar bridges – and are always ready to pull over for a photo opportunity (such 'unofficial' scenic stops are tentatively included on the timetables). 'Without them [post autos], the Alps would have remained an unknown land to thousands of travellers,' John Withers, President of the English Alpine Club, wrote to the Swiss Postmaster General in 1932.

I realised the validity of these words while on Switzerland's longest (and one of the highest) PostBus journeys: across four Central Alpine mountain passes on the Grimsel-Nufenen-Gotthard-Susten Pass route – an eight-hour trip undertaken by a single Setra 415H PostBus. The journey took me through several cantons; two languages (German and Italian); all four seasons – from burning sunshine to showers and heavy snowfalls; and countless 'places of interest.'

Ostap Bender, the protagonist of *The Twelve Chairs*, a satirical novel by Soviet writers Ilf and Petrov, dismissed mountains as 'useless thing[s] ... too much luxury ... idiot's imagination ... ' I was ready to agree with him after the first several hours of the journey, when the mountain views behind the windows of our PostBus became overwhelming and somewhat oppressive, with swollen rivers and mountain streams in the gorges resembling muscled sinewy torsos of giant bodybuilders.

At 2,120m, altitude sickness kicked in making my head feel heavy and alien. It was then that Adolf von Bergen, our driver, announced a scenic stop. As the passengers were admiring the views, he told the story of the Gotthard Pass, often described as 'the People's Road,' probably because it connected the German-speaking canton of Uri with Italian-speaking Ticino. In June 2016, the Gotthard Base Tunnel, the world's deepest and longest, at a length of over fifty-seven kilometres, was completed under the pass. The tunnel opened on 11 December 2016 slashing by a good hour the journey time between Zurich and Milan.

One word in the driver's monologue was particularly familiar. 'Suvorov,' he kept repeating, pointing at a distant mountain peak. I recalled my Soviet school history manual which featured the painting by Surikov, a late-nineteenth-century Russian artist, *Suvorov Crossing the Alps.* It was a scene from Russia's successful military campaign to expel the French from Italy (Russia was then part of the anti-French coalition) led by a renowned military commander, Count Alexander Vassilyevich Suvorov, in 1799. Upon reaching central Switzerland, Suvorov's army was all but surrounded by the French. After ferocious fighting across 'St Gotthard Pass,' Suvorov managed to escape the entrapment by leading his army of 18,000 exhausted and hungry soldiers over three Alpine passes in just ten days. The painting showed Suvorov's troops sliding down a snow-covered mountain on their bottoms, laughing. Looking at the peak, semi-hidden under a fluffy fur hat of clouds, I could almost discern the spectres of bearded Russian soldiers, their long Cossack-style tunics being used as sledges to whoosh themselves down the mountain. There were neither trains nor PostBuses to catch here in 1799.

Tongue Twisting

Shortly after a 2,150-metre altitude marker had flashed past, we crossed into the canton of Ticino – and the automated intercom announcements, all in German only minutes ago, switched over to Italian. Like Switzerland itself, PostBuses 'speak' all four state languages: German, French, Italian and Romansh (in the canton of Grisons) – and, by law, each bus starts 'speaking' the language of whichever canton it is currently passing through.

Ticino is like a different country within Switzerland. Its Alpine areas were much less densely populated than those of the German-speaking canton of Uri. The driver announced (in Italian) that the villages we had driven past had only seventy-five residents across all three of them.

We had an hour-long lunch stop in the village of Airolo where I sat next to our driver. Adolf is sixty-one and has worked as a driver for forty-one years without a single accident. Prior to being hired by PostBus, he was in the army driving heavy lorries. 'Being a PostBus driver is like belonging to the elite,' he said and explained that, irrespective of his vast previous experience, he had to undergo lots of training. During the first year, he was not allowed to drive post autos on his own, only under supervision of a more experienced driver. It was only after two years of safe driving in the valleys that he was pronounced 'ready' for a mountain bus.

The training of PostBus drivers includes psychology and communication skills. 'A city bus driver can stay inside his cabin, but a PostBus driver has to be among the passengers,' smiled Adolf, dipping his fork deep into a hillock of spaghetti strings.

Valley Life

The village of Saxeten in the canton of Bern has a population of ninety-six, and its only connection to the world is a Mercedes 'mini' PostBus, which shuttles between the village and the town of Wilderswil six times a day.

Apart from being the scene of the Saxetenbach Gorge flooding disaster, in which twenty-one people, mostly tourists from Australia, New Zealand, England, South Africa and Switzerland, perished in July 1999, the village is unremarkable. It lies at the entrance to the nearby mountain valleys that containing the Lütschine river. The route is not at all busy, with the bus often carrying just two or three passengers at a time. But for people of Saxeten, still living off cattle-breeding and farming, it is of the utmost importance.

The small PostBus not only carries the villagers to town and back, it takes village kids to and from school, delivers mail, transports milk from the village farm down to the valley, collects rubbish from the village taking it down for recycling (Swiss laws do not allow dumping anywhere in the mountains), and brings building materials to households. It takes elderly villagers to Wilderswil shops and helps them 'carry' the shopping up the hill to their homes. More a friend than just a means of transportation, for the dwellers of Saxeten the PostBus epitomises their constitutional right to freedom of movement.

It was on the morning PostBus service that I met Erika Seemater on her fortnightly trip to bring food to her ninety-two-year-old father Gotlib, who lives in the village on his own. Saxeten-born Erika, who had herself moved to the valley a while ago, told me how her life in the village had been inseparable from PostBuses, which used to take her to shops, hairdressers and cooking classes in the valley. Gotlib was waiting on the porch of his large wooden chalet as the bus drove up. He looked much younger than his age, as many highlanders do.

I had a couple of hours to spare before the return trip – ample time to talk to Carolyn Lansdell, the driver of the Saxeten service, over a cup of coffee in the village restaurant. Married to an Englishman, Carolyn has been a PostBus driver for just a couple of years. She was also a well-known paraglider pilot, a member of the Swiss national paragliding team, and only drives the Saxeten bus when there is 'not a lot of flying or snow-boarding on offer.' Carolyn lives in the valley, and drives her own car to Saxeten every morning to re-join the PostBus, which she leaves in the village overnight.

'I know all the villagers by name, and most of them are heavily dependent on my PostBus,' she said. 'One couple in their eighties sometimes ask me to pick them up from their house, and I do, although the rules do not allow it. My bosses know and do not mind.' Always being on time is not obligatory here, for there is just the one bus line and no train connections to make.

'There are mostly older folks left in the village – and at times I feel more like a community liaison officer than a bus driver,' she confessed. 'Once I was asked to bring up the tiles to repair the roof of an old couple's house. There is a ninety-year-old lady suffering from dementia who always tells the same story while on the bus, and I always pretend I hear it for the first time.'

Eventually it was time to head back down to the valley. Apart from me, there were no passengers waiting at the village bus stop. Carolyn sat behind the wheel and started the engine. Before driving off, she backed down, attached a neat rubbish container left behind the shelter to the back of her vehicle, and all three of us – Carolyn, myself and the PostBus – began our slow descent to Wilderswil.

Swiss Trains

I have a confession to make. Despite my promises (after thirty-five years in the totalitarian USSR) never to join any membership-driven organization, I have just become a member of one – The Swiss Railways Society (SRS). What drew me to it was the logo in the Society's promotional leaflet: 'Join 1,100 other members and discover the paradise that is the Swiss Transport System.' 'Paradise,' no less! To me as a champion of Swiss technology and life-style, however, it didn't sound excessive.

Where else in the world can you pre-order sushi and fondue on some of the trains; travel in 'family carriages,' equipped with mini-playgrounds; use a request stop button at some small stations; have train schedules and route maps printed (!) on the surface of the tables in your carriage, as I myself saw recently on board a BOR (Bernese Oberland Railways) train from Grindenwald to Interlaken? Where else can you hear the announcement: 'The train at platform four is ten minutes late due to an incident in another country,' as I did at the Swiss station of Spiez?

If all of the above strikes you as the emotional ramblings of a 'Helvetifile,' here's a bit of official statistics: The Swiss Federal railways (SBB) network has the world's highest frequency of daily train services – 148 trains per kilometre of track per day, compared with 136 in the Netherlands, 103 in Japan, ninety-one in the UK, eleven for the USA and six for Canada. Each day an average of 123 passenger trains per kilometre run at ten-minute headways from 5am to 1am the following morning. As for the overall punctuality, it has reached the staggering ninety-six per cent (by a five-minute standard) mark. No 'leaves slippage' or 'wrong kind of graffiti' (a real-life recent 'excuse' for a Thameslink service cancellation) here ...

Swiss train timetables, of which I am a passionate fan and collector, play a huge role in this modern paradise on wheels. First put together four years in advance, they undergo repeated checks and tests before acquiring the power of law and seldom get altered after that. They are also unique in the amount of information they contain – not just train times and platform numbers, but how many minutes you should allow to change trains, or to walk from your train to a connecting bus, boat or cable car – all integrated into the super-efficient Swiss Public Transport Network.

To catch my flight back to the UK last July, I took the 5.21am SBB train from Interlaken West to Basel. The integrated timetable featured a three-minute walk between the train and the airport bus outside Basel train station. It took me precisely two minutes and forty-five seconds to reach the waiting bus number 50 which started for the airport three minutes later ...

* * *

Among all the big and small demises of 2017, there was one hardly noticed by anyone, except perhaps for the shrinking breed of train timetable collectors and compilers, as well as by a few technologically backward travellers who still prefer printed copy to the online version. I am talking about the super-comprehensive and reassuringly trilingual Swiss Official Timetable, also known as the *Offizielles Kursbuch* (in German), *Indicateur Officiel* (in French) and *Orario Officiale* (in Italian), or simply the *Kursbuch* – a bulky, over 2,000 pages each, three-volume set covering railroads, cableways and boats (Volume 1), buses in Western Switzerland (Volume 2) and buses in Eastern Switzerland (Volume 3).

This unique publication, the Mother of All Timetables, so to speak, was until last year readily available at all Swiss station ticket offices for around £12. The real problem was how to carry and where to keep those 'three door-stoppers,' in the words of my friend Fritz Jenni, the former operations manager for Swiss PostBus, the largest of the country's seventy-eight coach companies, who was kind enough to post me the very last edition of the *Kursbuch* in a parcel that, by the size and weight of it, could have easily contained a small locomotion unit.

Yes, after 112 yearly editions (the first in 1905), *Kursbuch*, this weighty Swiss institution, has come to an end, or rather moved entirely online – to the sheer dismay of the USA's National Association of Timetable Collectors and a handful of enthusiasts like Fritz Jenni and yours truly.

My friendship with Fritz, a sprightly and dynamic eighty-year-old who I met several years ago when he was assisting me in my research into Swiss PostBuses, has so far resulted (among other things) in several precious additions to my ever-expanding collection of timetables. But before sharing a couple of those little (and not-so-little) treasures with you, let me ask again: what on earth is the use and value of the faded and no-longer-valid timetables? How do I benefit from knowing that, according to the 1947-48 Winter Edition of the *Kursbuch*, the 6.51 train from Basel SBB was due to arrive at Geneve-Cornavin at 10.04?

Or let's take a fresher example, from last year, of an InterCity train 872 from Milano Centrale due to leave Lugano, having first cleared the Italian border station of Chiasso, at 11.10 to arrive in Luzern at 13.21. What's the point?

It all depends on how you read the timetable. As I look at the seemingly dispassionate numbers, I can clearly see the red-bereted Italian frontier guards boarding the train in Chiasso to check the passengers' passports, as they did on my train from Basel to Como in 2002. They then ransacked the possessions of my neighbour – a thoroughly decent if somewhat hapless Dutch youth, who complained that he always got searched just because he was a Dutch youth and so, stereotype dictated, could be carrying cannabis or other drugs.

I then see the train stopping at Lugano, from where one could take a boat to Campione D'Italia – a peculiar Italian enclave inside Switzerland. It was at that station that I once hurriedly (had to urgently open a bottle of wine, you see) bought a Swiss

Army knife at a platform kiosk, and when back on the moving train realised that I had been charged (mistakenly, no doubt) twice for it. And then Lucerne – a majestic old city on the eponymous lake with my favourite hotel Schweizerhof on its shore. With the timetable in hand (or in the case of the massive Kursbuch, in both hands), I am in for endless vicarious – and entirely free – travels and adventures.

My older timetables, however, sometimes contain destinations that I wouldn't have wanted to revisit, even if I had been alive then. Take the gem of my collection: *Tachenfahrplan fur die Ostliche Ukraine* (*Pocket Timetable for Eastern Ukraine*), published in August 1942 – yes, during the Nazi occupation – in German of course. The most striking feature of this extremely rare brochure is how 'normal' it looks at first glance: a neat folding map at the front, impeccable tables of times and distances, etc. It takes another good look to notice that the map shows uninterrupted by any borders a through route from Berlin Zoo to my native city of Kharkiv, referred to as Charkow Hauptbahnhof (Hbf). You can trace the 4.00 3356 train ('Zug Nr 3356') from Charkow to Slawjansk in Donbass, to where the trains from today's Kharkiv (the city's Ukrainian name) do not go, due to the ongoing proxy war with Russia.

At 4.40, that Zug used to stop for two minutes at Komarowka – a suburban village where I used to be taken for holidays as a kid. For some reason, looking at its name rendered in German made me realise the horrible reality of the Nazi occupation of my native land better than ever before.

My more recent and much less sinister 'gem' is the *2014 Service Timetable for Engine Drivers* for Ukraine's Yuzhnaya (Southern) Railway. Inserted in the book is a note in Russian, probably written by an engine driver: 'Kharkiv – 23.33; Northern Post – 23.43,' and also the printed timetable of all train departures from Kharkiv passenger terminal.

A fascinating insight can be found on pages 67-69, chronicling the route of train 56 from Sumi (via Kharkiv) to Simferopol in the Crimea. The timetable was published in 2014, but clearly prior to Russia's annexation of the Crimean peninsula in March that year, after which all direct train connections to the Crimea from Ukraine were terminated. Another case of painful political reality made crystal-clear by a seemingly useless four-year-old timetable.

I'd like to finish on a positive note though. Fritz Jenni has just informed me that the printed edition of the Swiss *Kursbuch* has been salvaged from demise, if only partially, and one of its three volumes, covering trains, boats and cable-cars, has been printed and is in the post to me. Hopefully, it will continue well beyond 2018. I can't wait to get hold of it.

* * *

Today, I want to focus again (for I have done it repeatedly in the past) on the unique Swiss organisation called SBB – Swiss Federal Railways.

I have written a lot on the Swiss Railways' unbeatable punctuality, with precision and frequency of trains made into one of the Swiss citizens' constitutional rights. I have also mentioned SBB's state-of-the-art train-timetable brochures (as well as the massive – and now, sadly, defunct – three-volume *Kursbuch*, incorporating the schedules for all of the country's thoroughly integrated trains, buses, post-autos, boats and chairlifts). The brochures' circulation, it has to be said, has gone down somewhat with the advent of online timetables, but the former are still readily available at all Swiss train stations. As a passionate timetable collector, I always pick one up whenever I see it, as I did this time shortly after we landed in Geneva Airport and were wheeling our suitcases towards the eponymous train station only a five-minute walk away. At the aquarium-like SBB station office, I helped myself to two super-compact timetable booklets – for 'Region Geneve-Lausanne' (in French) and for 'Geneva Airport' (in both French and English).

Little did I know how indispensable those two tiny brochures were going to prove on the very last day of my trip, when – after a long hike in the Alps, followed by a prolonged tasting of a dozen or so wines and consummated with a plentiful lunch (which included the local speciality '*Malakoff*' – fried cheese balls, originating, allegedly, from the time of the Crimean War), I boarded an SBB train in Morges for the final forty-one-minute-long (according to the timetable) ride to Geneva airport.

I was tired and soon started dozing off in the comfort of the dimly lit air-conditioned first-class carriage, gliding smoothly, almost imperceptibly, along the tracks. I could relax in the knowledge that no matter what happened on our guilty planet during the next forty-one minutes, with the exception perhaps of the Earth's head-on collision with an asteroid, or a sudden outbreak of World War III, the train was going to arrive at the airport forty-one minutes later. Not forty or forty-two, but exactly forty-one minutes later! From my many visits to Switzerland, I knew that arriving ahead of schedule was deemed as reprehensible there (for people as well as trains) as arriving late. It had to be neither earlier, nor later, but precisely on the dot. I will never forget an intercom announcement, once overheard at a large Swiss train station (I think it was Basel): 'The train on Platform Three is running ten minutes late, due to an incident in another country.'

After a busy morning of hiking and wine-tasting, I thought I could do with a forty-one-minute-long quiet meditation. But before shutting my eyes, I spotted an electric socket above my seat and decided to charge my Android smartphone. I stuck the charger into the socket (via an adaptor), put the phone on the armrest and went deeply into my favourite *metta bhavana* – the love-and-kindness Buddhist mediation whereby you wish wellness, happiness and freedom from suffering to the whole universe, including yourself, your friends and loved ones, as well as complete strangers and even your sworn enemies (if any).

Meditation after wine-tasting is never a good idea. Of course, I promptly fell fast asleep. And because I was on a train, and not in a Rinzai Zen Buddhist monastery, where a duty monk is routinely instructed to hit any other monk who falls asleep during meditation on his back with a stick, no one woke me up until the train stopped and a loud intercom announcement in four languages brutally intervened in my *metta bhavana*, or, to be totally honest, just a deep sleep.

I woke up with a jerk, grabbed my suitcase and dashed out onto the platform.

The check-in queue took no more than five minutes. When my turn came, I opened the side pocket of my travel bag to grab the phone and show my e-ticket, emailed by the airline that very morning. The phone was not there. Cold covered my forehead as the realisation hit me: I had left my phone behind on the train!

To lose one's phone these days is nothing short of a tragedy – not quite like the loss of a loved one or a relative, of course, but close to a major personal disaster, with your whole life disrupted and put on hold. It is twice as devastating if it happens abroad.

I looked at my watch: about fifteen minutes had lapsed since our train arrived at Geneva Airport station, which was its final destination.

Perhaps, I still had a chance …

Having asked one of our party to look after my suitcase, I ran back to the train station, where several red-and-white SBB trains, each looking exactly like the one that had brought me there, were parked. I boarded one and ran towards the first-class carriages, chased by a uniformed platform attendant, or whoever he was, shouting in French that the train was due to depart in one minute.

It was hopeless. I jumped off and promptly tried to board another waiting train, but was stopped by the same platform attendant who said he would check it for me himself. Two minutes later, he returned with a … charger, which was not mine, and with no telephone.

'The only thing I could find,' he shrugged and added reassuringly: 'Your train must have departed already!'

He then suggested that I checked with the left-luggage office upstairs. 'If someone found your phone, they would be likely to take it there,' he said.

I ran upstairs only to make sure that no one had deposited anything – except for some bags and suitcases, no doubt – to the left-luggage office either.

Remembering that my flight back to London was due to start boarding any moment and I hadn't even checked in yet, I jogged back to the airport where I persuaded an agreeable Swiss Air check-in lady to register me for the flight without a ticket, on the basis of my passport alone (at least, I still had my passport and therefore was not quite persona non grata).

About to proceed to the Immigration, I looked at my watch and decided that if ran with the speed close to that of sound, I would still have enough time for a final check at the station. In my heart of hearts, of course, I no longer had any hope of finding the irretrievably lost (or so I thought) phone, for which I had already started grieving …

Back inside the station, I was approached by a uniformed SBB official with a crackling walkie-talkie in his hand.

'Is everything all right, sir?' he asked me worriedly, probably alerted by my crestfallen facial expression.

I told him.

'Do you remember exactly which train you were on?' he asked.

'Does it matter? It was ages ago …'

'Please, try to remember,' he insisted.

I suddenly recalled the tiny Geneva Airport timetable booklet, picked up on arrival three days earlier. Miraculously, it was still resting in the back pocket of my jeans.

'Let me see,' I opened the booklet. 'Our train left Morges very close to 3pm … Here it is: 14.58, train number 90!'

My interlocutor already had the same timetable on the screen of his portable computer that I had initially mistaken for a walkie-talkie.

'Your train arrived at the airport at 15.39 and then departed again back towards Geneva at 16.02. It was scheduled to stop at Geneva Central for three minutes before proceeding to Morges and then to Lausanne at 16.15 … What's the time now?'

I looked at my watch: '16.12!'

'Wait here and don't move! I'll be back shortly!' barked out the official. He ran down the escalator towards the platform speaking excitedly in French to his walkie-talkie-cum-PC.

I was sure I'd never see him again. Fifteen minutes was the longest I could wait for him without missing my flight. And it was exactly fifteen minutes later that the SBB official reappeared. His face was beaming, and in his hand he was holding … goodness gracious! … my good old smartphone, complete with the charger and even the adaptor!

'Is it yours?' he asked rhetorically and handed it over to me.

'But how … how … did you …?'

'No time to tell you … it's a long story. Now you must run to catch your flight!'

I tried to give him a tenner, but he refused point-blank: 'This is what we are here for!'

I jogged back to the airport (for the third time within less than an hour) pressing the phone to my chest – like a father reunited with his long-lost child, and thinking that at times being in Switzerland makes you feel immensely proud of belonging to human race …

So, how did he they do it?

It was only much later that, with the help of the above-mentioned timetables, I managed to recreate the most likely scenario of what had happened.

The official, with whom I had spoken, must have called the attendant on board my recently departed (after about twenty minutes in the station) number 90 train, which was then approaching Geneva Central, and asked him to check the first-class carriages. The attendant must have found the phone and during the train's three-minute stop at Geneva passed it on to his counterpart on board the Intercity 1 train at the opposite platform which departed Geneva Central at 16.20 and arrived at Geneva Airport at 16.27 to be met by my (and my phone's) saviour, whose name I did manage to find out in the end.

Merci beaucoup, Monsieur Blendi Berisha, passenger assistance team manager at Geneva Airport station!

It will be to you that I will devote the whole of my next *metta bhavana* meditation wishing you wellness, happiness and freedom from suffering.

I will also make sure that I do it at home, not on the train, and taste no wines prior to it.

Wines, Cheese and E-Bikes

For someone like me, still recovering after open-heart surgery, the official promotional logo of the Swiss canton of Valais – 'Engraved on Your Heart' – was bound to sound a tad too punchy (if not to say scary) in the beginning. The fact that I had – perhaps rather foolhardily – volunteered to tour the canton and the surrounding Alps on an electric bicycle made my patched-up heart, with a new, bovine, aortal valve sewn on to it, beat even faster. 'Do I fancy any more 'engravings' on my ticker?' I was thinking ruefully.

The dilemma was resolved by my cardiologist. 'Your main foes are immobility and stress!' he declared sternly, and added: 'A bit of e-biking therapy should do you a lot of good.' He went on to say that mountain biking had been proved to protect the heart muscle and to lower blood pressure. 'Besides, as far as I know, travelling and learning about the places' history and technology makes you happy, so go for it!' he concluded.

To me, the most impressive feature of Valais was a carefully maintained balance of tradition and innovation, with adherence to traditional technologies of cheese- and wine-making, say, going hand-in-hand with cutting-edge robotics, AI, ICT, life sciences and AVs (Europe's first driverless shuttle bus was trialled in the canton's capital, Sion, a couple of years ago).

The first living metaphor of that amazing fusion of old and new was to be found right at my first – rather traditional (if only in its lack of air-conditioning) – hotel in the town of Martigny, which shared the building and the reception area with the Idiap Research Institute, a body whose specialisations include 'artificial intelligence for society.'

Waiting for my e-bike to be delivered to reception, I had ample time to study Idiap's annual report, highlighting some of its engineering innovations, including SIIP (Speaker Identification Integrated Project), which aims to identify criminals by their voices in 'lawfully intercepted phone calls.' Interpol is a partner.

Well, if someone tried to identify me by my voice during my first e-bike ride in the streets of Martigny, they would have definitely failed, for my speech consisted of some untranslatable Russian expletives as well as loud squeaks and squeals, emitted while trying to negotiate a roundabout in the wrong direction (I was still getting to grips with the right-hand traffic), or when the automatically adjustable saddle would suddenly pop up and hit me … you know where, at times making me fall off the bike. The town's rush-hour drivers must have had fun watching my progress that afternoon.

Luckily, my first ride was to the local 120-year-old Morand Distillery, which uses traditional technologies alongside super-modern bottling lines to produce some yummy syrups and liqueurs from locally-grown fruit. It must be due to the intensive tasting of the syrups and (particularly) the liqueurs that my cycling back to the hotel was much more confident, if somewhat less straight-line.

But it is not for the syrups or the liqueurs that Valais is best known. One of the most popular activities offered by the local tourism authority is cycling (or, in my case, e-cycling) through the Valais vineyards in the Rhone valley.

Vineyards? Yes! Unbeknown to many, vines have been cultivated for over 2,000 years on the territory of modern Switzerland. As John C Sloan notes in his rare book *The Surprising Wines of Switzerland*, 'fine Swiss wines remain among the country's best and undiscovered secrets.' Well, I was in strong mind to discover them for myself, for as my trusted cardiologist assured me, a bit of red wine is almost as good for the ailing heart as cycling.

Valais, bordering on France, has both ideal terrain and perfect climate (with over 300 days of sunshine and just 600 millimetres of rainfall a year) for viticulture, hugely helped by the warm '*foehn*' winds blowing from the mountains and drying the grapes, helping them to ripen.

So, off I rode – along the ancient '*bisses*' (historic irrigation channels) and across the much-less-ancient hanging bridges, one of which, the Charles Kuonen bridge, is at 494 metres the longest of its kind in the world – to visit the local vineyards. Due to the testing (and tasting) nature of this endeavour, I cannot clearly recall all of them, though the wines that I drank (sorry, tasted) everywhere were superb, so I will mention just two.

Mathilde Roux – a young viticulturist who greeted me at La Cave de l'Orlaya, took over the eight-hectare vineyard in 2016 and has already achieved prominence in the local wine-making circles. Indeed, her original Petite-Arvine white wine, which she offered me to taste, had the distinctive aroma of citrus fruit and the smell of mountain flowers. Her success is due in part to new technologies, such as temperature control during fermentation with the help of a hot or cold glycol solution circulated around the tanks. With her in-depth knowledge and sheer passion for viticulture, Mathilde could probably make even glycol drinkable, or so I thought as I finished my second glass of Petite-Arvine.

To my deep regret, I was not offered anything to drink, or even to taste, at the second vineyard I want to mention. Why? Because the Farinet vineyard in the medieval village of Saillon consists of only … three vines! No, it's neither a typo, nor the result of too many tastings – just three (3) vines.

The world's officially smallest vineyard was started in 1980 by the Swiss journalist Pascal Thurre as a joke – a joke that gradually evolved into a serious and important charity to help children. Hundreds of celebrity volunteers, including stars of Hollywood, have been taking turns looking after the three vines, whose humble harvest is mixed with grapes from another vineyard to produce 1,000 bottles of very special wine that get auctioned for about $35,000 every year. All the money goes to charities, with the process being supervised by the vineyard's honorary owner, the Dalai Lama.

Looking at the three fragile young vines, stirred gently by the wind, I couldn't help feeling a touch of warmth and love for this beautiful land being 'engraved' on my slowly but surely recuperating heart.

* * *

'Do not cut corners' and 'do not overestimate your abilities,' advised my *E-Bikers' Guide*, picked up in the Alpine village of Verbier where I ended up on the second day of my recent e-cycling tour across the Swiss canton of Valais. While being OK with the first dictum (cutting corners on narrow high-altitude cycling paths could lead to a hapless cyclist's fall down the precipice – wheels first), I repeatedly breached the second one, which resulted in multiple scratches and bruises all over my body.

Undertaking this trip, only several months after major open-heart surgery, was one of my life's biggest challenges – an attempt to prove to the world (yet primarily to myself) that there was still some gunpowder left in my powder bag – a softer Russian equivalent of 'there's life in the old dog yet.'

The latter metaphor was perhaps more relevant to Valais – home of the famous St Bernard breed of fluffy and good-natured rescue dogs. Originating from the ancient Great St Bernard Hospice, a sanctuary for wandering monks and pilgrims, the dogs have been used to rescue travellers lost in the snow and fog since 1707. The wellbeing of this endemic-to-Valais breed is now in the hands of the Barry Foundation (named after Barry, the legendary avalanche rescue dog), where about twenty pedigree puppies are born each year.

No St Bernards were needed to rescue me – not because I didn't get lost, for I did, and more than once (albeit mostly in villages and towns), but rather due to the nice summer weather, with no fog or snow, and also because I tried not to deviate too much from the well-beaten mountain paths. Unfortunately, the famous road over the Simplon pass, built by Napoleon to connect France and Italy in 1805 (it was then the best in Europe – a true masterpiece of engineering) was not on my route, which took me higher and higher into the Alps.

At an altitude of 2,000m, I had to stop due to a loud mooing-and-jingling ('moongling?') , which I initially ascribed to a headache caused by oxygen deficiency, coming seemingly out of nowhere. But I was wrong.

On a vast Alpine meadow, multiple duos of compact black cows of the canton's endemic Hérens breed were engaged in locked-horn embraces. The animals, watched by dozens of excited onlookers, pushed each other with slow and stubborn force, like horned and somewhat slimmed-down Sumo wrestlers in black kimonos. They mooed, or rather 'moongled,' for all they were worth, with large copper bells on their necks jingling melodiously.

Since having had my aortal heart valve replaced with a bovine (ie taken from a cow) one last year, I regard all cows with affection, not unlike my non-existent second cousins, so my first reaction was outrage. 'Why are you tormenting these beautiful animals?' I asked a local farmer among the spectators. 'Tormenting? Nothing of the kind!' he smiled. 'It is this breed's instinct that prompts such clashes. Our Hérens breed are unique in their strong hierarchic nature – the world's only fighting cows.' He told me that each year the canton's dairy farmers organise fights to determine a regional and cantonal 'queen.' It was one such event that I was witnessing.

Allegedly, the cows' pugnacious character has no adverse effect on the quality of their milk and dairy products, particularly cheeses, as I was assured by Carmen Bateson, an Aussie who worked at the nearby 'Alpage de Mille' cheese factory. With her partner Christophe Prodanu, they produce the famous raclette – literally meaning 'scraper.' To make it, they first go through the basic cheese-making process: coagulating the milk, cutting the curds, moulding, pressing, finishing, and then leaving the cheese to ripen while washing and turning it daily. At the final stage, the matured cheese is sliced and placed in front of an open fire. As the cheese melts, it is scraped (that's where the 'scraper' name comes from) onto a dish and gobbled up immediately with potatoes, gherkins and pickled onions.

Savouring the richness of raclette, I couldn't help thinking that cheeses – like wines – have memory. They 'remember' the aromas of fresh grass and alpine flowers, the rough tongues of cows and the caring touch of the cheesemaker's hands. In Valais's Val d'Anniviere valley, that cheese's 'memory' reaches sinister proportions: according to an old custom, when a couple gets married, a large cheese is set aside to be eaten by relatives on the day(s) of their funerals, by which time it can get so hard that a chisel ('cheesel?') may be needed to 'scrape' it! They call it 'death's cheese.'

That gruesome ancient custom was, of course, triggered by practicality and extreme poverty: the newlyweds wanted to make sure that their loved ones had something to eat on the day of their demise. In contrast to that, modern Valais, like the rest of Switzerland, is overabundant with food and food manufacturers, including the country's only producer of saffron – an ancient spice made out of rare crocus sativus flowers, cultivated on a beautiful sunny plateau according to centuries-old traditions – and the makers of the real beluga caviar. This is not a typo – the real Russian-style Kasperskian (the name is a play on 'Caspian Sea') caviar from locally bred sturgeons, which is not just sustainable but also ethical.

In Russia (and elsewhere), the fish are normally killed to retrieve the precious eggs, whereas in Valais they came up with an innovative method whereby the roe is retrieved from female sturgeons without harming them – by gently 'massaging' their tummies until the eggs are released. That is why the Kasperskian caviar has been nicknamed 'caviar with life.'

Indeed, this small Swiss canton seemed to excel in ingenuity, which could be felt in everything it produced – from cutting-edge robots to Hermesetas sweeteners; from Alpine cheeses and locally cultivated bananas (!) to the 'caviar with life.'

And, let me tell you the secret: musing over the canton's official motto, 'Engraved On My Heart,' I think that maybe, just maybe, my new heart valve has come from one of the battling cows of the Hérens breed.

Myself a fighter, I would welcome that, for sure.

* * *

Swiss wines' is an unlikely combination for British (and most other) ears, let alone palates. No wonder: only one per cent of Swiss-made wine gets exported outside Switzerland. The wisely practical and self-respecting Swiss, having made their watches, chocolates and Swiss Army knives worn, eaten and coveted all over the world, still prefer to drink their wines themselves. And I don't blame them.

Wine is an extremely image-driven product. Its popularity is closely linked to the general perception of the producing country. Indeed, it took enormous social changes in Bulgaria, Chile and South Africa for their wines to become successful on the competitive international market. But how about Switzerland's persisting image of a 'perfect country,' where everything works like a proverbial Omega clock and where the astounding 97.2 per cent of all trains (according to the latest statistics) depart and arrive on the dot? Are precision and punctuality always good for such a highly creative endeavour as wine-making?

Having visited several of the country's wine-growing regions and drunk (sorry, tasted) dozens of locally made reds, whites and rosés, I can – firmly and responsibly – answer 'yes' to that question. I have even come up with my own 'oenological' term for them – 'precision wines.' By that I mean that most wines in Switzerland are not simply made, but rather 'precision- engineered' – grape-growing, harvesting, bottling and wine-making as such – subject to strict technological rules and procedures.

Take, for example, the Italian-speaking canton Ticino on the border with Italy. A frequent visitor to the canton, I've been a long-time admirer of the Ticino-made Pinot Noir, Cabernet Sauvignon, Gamaret and, particularly, the unique White Merlot! No, it's not a typo: I mean the Merlo Bianco, an elegant white wine from the Merlot grape, which originally came to Ticino from the Bordeaux region of France and soon became the main variety there. The canton's acid and limestone soils are great for cultivating all kinds of grapes, and its viticulture technology, traditionally combining Italian creativity with Swiss precision, is one of the best in Europe.

Here's an amazing figure for you: with a population of just over 350,000, there are 3,869 vineyards in Ticino – a vineyard for every 100 people, including babies, children and those old enough to be past their drinking age (120 years and over), no less!

My latest foray into the wonderful world of Swiss wines was a couple of months ago, when I was invited to visit the canton of Vaud – the second-largest wine-producing region of Switzerland, on the shores of Lake Geneva, known primarily for its fresh and fruity whites from the Chasselat grape and for its distinctive well-structured reds: Gamais and Pinot Noir.

Almost all vineyards in Vaud have a biodynamic approach, which means they use organic farming methods – compost as a fertiliser, no pesticides or insecticides etc, in both cultivating the grapes and processing the harvest. Some also use special soil supplements, following a vine-planting calendar which depends on strict astronomical configurations. That is where 'precision' comes into the picture … the grapes are harvested manually, then pressed gently (maximum pressure two kilograms) with pneumatic wine-presses and naturally fermented, with the yeasts coming from the berries themselves. The result is that local wines are fresh-tasting and full-bodied.

On top of my tasting list was Les Freres Dutruy winery in the village of Founez. Started in 1918 by Gustave Dutruy, it has been in the same family ever since. Re-equipped in 1983 by Jean-Jacques Dutruy, the father of the present-day owners, the wine-producing estate, covering over forty hectares, has always been open to technologies – old and new: from the well-tested *methode champenoise* to the pioneering and environmentally friendly gravity-flow winemaking, when the harvest is transported to the presses in a tank resembling an alien mini-spacecraft and propelled by gravitational force, which allows the grapes to preserve their wholeness, or, in plain English, stops them from being prematurely squashed.

We turned up at the Frères Dutruy winery ten minutes early. From my many visits to Switzerland, I knew that arriving ahead of schedule was deemed as reprehensible (for people as well as trains) as being late. Until the exact time of our appointment, no one came out to meet us …

'Sorry, it's chaos: the harvesting has just begun,' apologised Julien Dutruy.

The insides of the winery were far from chaotic, however: impeccable cleanliness, neat rows of wooden barrels and sparklingly polished fermentation vats.

'Chaos and Switzerland are incompatible,' I was thinking while tasting Frères Dutruy's spectacular Chasselat Cuvée Speciale and Rosé de Pinot Noir.

The brothers' 'precision winemaking' seemed to work very well, for just like the country on whose soil they were produced, the wines were not simply good – they were perfect!

Horns and Knives

Our agile yellow PostBus was approaching Habkern, a Swiss village at the foot of the Austmatthorn Mountain in Canton Bern. In line with an age-long tradition, at every turn of a winding mountain road, the bus driver blew a three-note post-horn playing the first movement of Rossini's William Tell overture. As we were getting closer to the village, however, the wistful wailings of the post-horn were gradually muffled by much stronger and much more melodious sounds, as if some crystal-clear mountain springs of music were running through the skies. 'These are our alphorn players practicing for the forthcoming music festival,' a fellow passenger explained.

Mesmerised by the sound, I wanted to know more about these amazing musical instruments. Luckily, Habkern, the village I was heading for, was home to Switzerland's best known alphorn factory, 'Bernatone Alphornbau.'

Well, 'factory' was a bit of an overstatement to describe a spacious workshop on the first floor of a vast wooden chalet next to the village hall (almost everything else in Habkern was next to the village hall, too). It was Saturday, but due to the approaching festival, Heinz Tschiemer, the factory's thirty-three-year-old owner, manager and the only full-time worker (his wife would sometimes comes down to help) was there to meet me.

The workshop smelled of varnish and freshly cut wood. In the centre stood a massive joiner's bench, the size of a railway platform, and on it rested a couple of unfinished alpine horns looking like giant tropical flowers, with long stalks but yet no buds. Several finished alphorns were hanging under the ceiling. This traditional joiner's shop atmosphere was somewhat disrupted by a modern Emcoturn E25 turning lathe, winking its LED monitor from the shop's corner.

'This is my masterpiece-making machine,' Heinz smiled.

He went on to explain that alphorns are still made by hand, but can now be designed on a computer. 'An average alphorn takes about 3,600 frames,' he said.

Normally, Heinz churns out one 3.5-metre-long alphorn each week. The wood he uses comes from local pines growing at an altitude of 1,500 metres. These trees are often curved at the base by snow and therefore are handy for making the tailpipe – one of the alphorn's main parts (other parts include mouthpiece, hand tube, central tube and bell). The technology of alphorn-making remains largely unchanged from 500 years ago: individual parts are bonded together and then carved into shape. Then comes gouging of the walls until they are four to seven millimetres wide, the so-called hallowing. The hallowed pieces are joined together with rings, then wrapped in wicker and – bingo – the alphorn is ready to be played.

Unlike other brass or wind instruments, alphorns do not have valves or finger holes, so the twelve individual tones they are capable of can only be generated by altering lip tension which is much easier said than done, or blown. I did blow it (not the alphorn itself, but playing the alphorn) in a big way when Heinz invited me to test one of his recent creations. No matter how hard I strained my lips, the only sounds that came out of the instrument's uncomplaining bell 3.4 metres away from my mouth could be described as fairly timid, yet ear-grating, cracklings, comparable to the mysterious intercom announcements on some British trains.

Apart from being an Alpine shepherds' favourite means of communication for hundreds of years, an alphorn is of course a musical instrument in its own right featured in works by Mozart, Brahms and other composers – the fact that could explain (partially at least) my complete failure at playing it. My complicated relationship with music started at the tender age of seven when I, like many Soviet kids from 'good families,' was coerced into learning piano playing. Not that I had been innately averse to music, or, as they say in Russia, didn't have a bear step on my ear, but my general attitude to it could be summarised by the words of Samuel Johnson who thought that of all existing noises music was probably the least disagreeable.

My teacher's name was Nadezhda Adolfovna, the patronymic which implied that her father was called 'Adolf.' I had little doubt that she was a clandestine daughter of Adolf Hitler himself, for she had a nasty habit of hitting me on my fingertips with a ruler whenever I pressed a wrong key. No wonder that after a couple of such one-to-one classes, I started running away and hiding in the park for the duration of a lesson – the ruse that was soon uncovered by my parents, who disrupted the torture. That was the end of my musical education, yet even now the sound of badly played piano at times triggers dull pain in my fingertips.

My pathetic alphorn playing in Habkern must have been causing Heinz heart-ache, for he hurried to distract me by coming up to his Emcoturn E25 and quickly turning up an alphorn mouthpiece, which he gave me as a gift. The obvious advantage of the mouthpiece over an alphorn (in Heinz's eyes, or rather ears, no doubt) was that no matter how hard I tried I could not extract any sound (except perhaps for some semi-audible hissing) from it.

Heinz is one of the twenty or so remaining alphorn makers in Switzerland – a disappearing breed. Yet the popularity of this amazing musical instrument keeps growing and he manages to sell dozens of them locally and to foreign buyers, mostly from Japan. Unique as it is, the Swiss alphorn has a number of prototypes in other countries – from Australian didgeridoo to Polish Ligawka, Romanian Bucium, Argentinian Erke and Ukrainian Trembita – all manufactured to the same principle, yet using different technologies.

* * *

'I was installing my new invention for sewage at Seneca Falls, NY,' Gilbert A Levin, an engineer from the US, wrote to me in 2014.

'One morning, as I was crossing the bridge over the aeration tank of the treatment plant, I saw that the setting on one of the instruments was incorrect. I took out my Swiss Army Knife to make the necessary adjustment.

'The knife slipped out of my hand and fell into the aeration tank whose function is to oxidise organic waste – the oxidising environment which is extremely corrosive to metals. Four years later, I received a small parcel with a note from Al Hawk, the supervisor of the Seneca Falls plant. They had emptied the aeration tank and found my knife at the bottom. The parcel contained the knife which was in astonishingly good condition. The plastic casing and cover had only suffered very minor damage …

'I can assure you that very few products could have survived treatment like this, the components would have dissolved or simply disappeared …'

I used to regard my multi-function Swiss Army Knife, bought in Lucerne in 1991, as one of my most treasured possessions. For many years the knife had been my faithful travel companion. It had opened innumerable wine bottles. It had cut through countless chunks of cheese and sausage. At home, it had helped me carry out multiple domestic chores. That is why I am still reeling from the shock of having my precious knife confiscated in Edinburgh airport several years ago – in the wake of 9/11 – when I absent-mindedly forgot to put it in my suitcase and was carrying it in my cabin luggage.

It was like losing a trusted friend. It didn't take long to buy a replacement, of course, and I never travel without a new Swiss Army Knife, making sure (once bitten, twice shy) I take it out of my shoulder bag before heading for the airport.

The blow of losing my little knife appears insignificant, however, compared to the post-9/11 upset experienced by its makers – the famous Victorinox factory in the small Swiss town of Ibach, Canton Schwyz, and particularly by Carl Elsener, the factory's CEO and the great-grandson of its founder Karl Elsener, the Swiss Army Knife inventor.

'Our sales plummeted almost overnight,' he says. 'All airport shops were suddenly banned from selling knives and we lost thirty per cent of our income that came from the so-called spontaneous airport purchases.'

What would an ordinary company do in this situation? Most likely, it would shut down some of its production lines and get rid of a considerable chunk of its workforce to cut costs. Not Victorinox. In all 125 years of its existence, the factory hasn't fired a single person (906 people are currently employed there) for economic reasons.

The Victorinox solution was to develop and manufacture new products: laser-fronted ballpoint pens, bladeless 'inflight' knives, Swiss Memory and Swiss Flash foldable USB drives with up to 16GB storage capacity, Swiss Card tool kits, My First Victorinox for children, and so on – and to explore new markets. In the true Swiss spirit of survival, instead of succumbing to the disaster, they chose to regard it as an opportunity.

Among the factory's new products is the Victorinox Rescue Tool, developed in co-operation with Swiss emergency and rescue services. With its one-thumb-opening blade, a disc glass saw and a glass breaker, it can be opened and made ready for use in seconds. If trapped in a car, the rounded belt cutter can be used to cut through seatbelts. The blades and the six-millimetre screwdriver are fixed in position when open, thanks to the liner lock mechanism. The very outward look of the Rescue Tool is eye-catching due to its luminescent yellow grips. Indispensable for mountain climbers, firemen and rescue workers, it can also come in handy for any motorist or biker. The first customers' feedback shows that the Rescue Tool is already saving lives.

In the neat office of Urs Wyss, Victorinox's head of PR, I was shown the first ever knife produced in 1891. The Soldier's Knife, as it was then called, has a wood-coated handle. Its single blade and the can opener are both made of iron (stainless steel appeared thirty years later, in 1921), but it opens and closes with the same characteristic loud click as my relatively new knife. The mechanism feels as tight as if the knife was made yesterday.

'It is our main secret – the indestructible spring,' explains Wyss. 'Precision and attention to small detail that no imitators were able to reproduce. We call the distinctive clicking sound it makes "walk-and-talk" '

From one of his office drawers he takes out a large box with dozens of fake 'Swiss Army' knives, made mostly in China. Many of them look similar to the original; they even have the familiar Swiss cross on the handle. I open one at random. The blade feels loose and limp, like a handshake of a dying octogenarian, and there's no walk-and-talk. The low quality spring is an immediate give-away.

'We have exhausted all legal means for the brand protection of our popular products,' says Carl Elsener. 'Our best means of protection is quality which remains unsurpassed and speaks louder than words …' As loud as the genuine walk-and-talk, I am tempted to add.

It all started in 1884, when Switzerland was one of the poorest countries in Europe. Many unemployed Swiss were forced to emigrate to the USA, Australia and Tasmania (the latter still has a sizeable community of Swiss migrants). It was then that young cutlery maker Elsener, supported by his mother Victoria, founded the factory with the aim of producing knives for the soldiers of the famously non-belligerent Swiss Army.

The first knives were delivered in 1891. They were robust and heavy and that was why Karl went on to develop a lighter and more elegant one, with two springs and six tools, which he called 'Officer's and Sports Knife.' The brand was officially registered in 1897 and was a great success. The company was soon able to pay off its creditors and made its first profit. The name Officer's Knife, however, never took off – perhaps it sounded too elitist – and in the 1930s the product was renamed Swiss Army Knife.

After the death of his mother, Elsener chose her first name as the company's brand name, and when stainless steel came to Ibach in 1923, the suffix 'inox' – the international designation for stainless steel – was added to it. That was how Victorinox, one of Europe's most recognisable trademarks, came into existence.

The real breakthrough in the company's sales occurred after World War II when American GIs bought the Swiss knives in Europe and took them to the US where they quickly became a very strong brand.

Today, the Victorinox factory in Ibach assembles 27,000 knives a day, plus nearly 100,000 other items. They come in over 100 different variations, with the flagship being the so-called SwissChamp with thirty-three features. More than 450 steps are required in its manufacture.

Both the New York Museum of Modern Art and the State Museum of Applied Art in Munich have included it in their permanent collections for excellence in design. All American Presidents starting with Lyndon Johnson, the Pope and all NASA astronauts carry their personalised Swiss Army Knives (the latter had often found them handy and indispensable during space missions). With Victorinox's agreement, over 250 different companies all over the globe have used the Swiss Army Knife image as a symbol of their products' quality.

At present, knives are only forty per cent of the company's output (twenty years ago it was one hundred per cent!) which now includes lots of other products: tools, kitchen utensils, watches, cosmetics, perfumes, luggage items and casual clothes, of which two collections a year are unveiled in the US and Japan. Last autumn, Victorinox opened a new store in London – its largest in Europe – where all its merchandise, not just knives, can be bought.

'I was on board the space shuttle Atlantis,' wrote NASA astronaut Chris Hadfield. 'Our task was to dock with the Russian space station. It was my job to open the hatch of the shuttle so that we could enter the station. I had to undo a lot of little screws, cut through cables and re-position the camera. My only tools were three small keys that the Russians sent to us. These sufficed for undoing some of the screws, but were not capable of doing all that I had to do. I was about to go back to the middle deck of the shuttle to fetch my big tool kit, but then I said to myself: why not use the knife? Thanks to the Swiss Army Knife, I was able to open the hatch …'

The location of Victorinox factory is near-idyllic. Most of the oblong building's vast windows overlook the permanently snow-capped Alpine peaks. Urs Wyss took me on a short tour of the production line so that I could observe every step of the knife-making: from hardening martensitic stainless steel at temperatures between 1,010 and 1,060°C (to make the blades flexible and edge-retaining) to tempering, annealing, grinding, polishing and sharpening.

And the quality control, of course, which is particularly strict at Victorinox and during which every single blade of the finished knives is opened and checked. An interesting detail: only women work at the quality-control stretch of the assembly line. Why? 'Because their fine motor skills are generally more distinctive,' explains Wyss.

Among the workers I see a number of young people in their teens. Victorinox runs a comprehensive two-year apprenticeship scheme. Having completed it, the youngsters become part of the factory's highly paid and well looked after workforce.

As we were walking through light and spacious factory premises, the workers were having one of their seven-per-shift Alexander technique exercise breaks.

'I started my work in a hospital of a small town called Tororo in Uganda two years ago,' wrote Dr John Ross from Canada. 'For my work I brought a wide range of surgical instruments, one of which was a surgical saw for amputations. Shortly after my arrival here, the surgical saw was stolen. So my Swiss Army Knife was sterilised in boiling water and its saw used for amputations. It worked very well. It took an entire six months to get a new surgical saw. During this time I carried out at least six amputations using the saw on the knife. Although the knife lost its lovely red plastic cover due to being repeatedly boiled in water, the instruments otherwise worked faultlessly ...'

'What's the secret of your continuing success?' I ask Elsener before leaving Victorinox.

'Pride, modesty and family values,' he replies and explains: 'We are proud of our product and its history. It has become a global icon, but we stay modest about it and concentrate solely on improving it. Nor a revolution, but a continuous evolution of range and quality.

'Having grown manifold, we still remain a family-run company where family values are of utmost importance.'

The Elsener family remains the factory's main shareholder, although it now controls only ten per cent of them. Two of the family's fifth generation – Carl's children – are already working at Victorinox: one in the IT department, the other in book keeping.

Family values or not, one thing is certain: during its 125 years of operation, Victorinox has succeeded in creating a product which is not simply popular, but also loved. I certainly love my Victorinox 'Cyber Tool' – the replacement for my previous, confiscated, one bought in 1991 – and will try never to lose it again.

Part Nine
Travels in North America

Introduction: The Land of Plastic Fossils

In the year 2000, I celebrated the onset of the new millennium by taking a long Trans-American journey following in the footsteps of my own personal Columbuses – Ilya Ilf and Evgeny Petrov, the famous tandem of witty and insightful Soviet satirists who visited the USA in 1935-36 and wrote a book *One-storied America* (or *Little Golden America* to echo the title of their internationally bestselling adventure novel *Little Golden Calf* – a sequel to *The Twelve Chairs*). Dispatched to the states by the *Daily Telegraph* newspaper, I was filing my features and columns from the road, having visited thirty-nine states of the Union in less than ten months. In my columns and reports, I introduced the turn-of-the millennium British readers to the writers' 'one-storied' America – the country of FD Roosevelt and George Gershwin, of 'yellow journalism' and the New Deal, of the first 'air-conditioned refrigerators' and the superb WPA guides – as well as to mine and much more modern, Vitali's America. And although many American (and Russian) realities have changed dramatically in the course of sixty-five years, I tried to stick to the main principle of Ilf and Petrov, who, according to the 1937 *New York Times* review of *Little Golden America*, were 'never guilty of sacrificing the facts as they saw them for the sake of a quip' – a huge compliment for the writers who had managed to retain their wit and integrity against all odds.

Having returned to Britain, I started working on a travel book about that trip. *The Land of Plastic Fossils* was its title. Then 9/11 happened – and the book remained unfinished.

Below I will reproduce the hitherto unpublished first chapter of that book as well as a handful of my columns written – literally – on the road.

Fireworks Over Waterfall

Driving across the Arizona desert in 1935, Ilf and Petrov entered a reservation of petrified forest. 'It is an astounding spectacle to find in the midst of the great silence of the desert prone trunks of petrified trees which have preserved the outward appearance of the most ordinary reddish-brown wooden trunks,' they note and continue: 'The process of altering the wood of the trees into salt, lime and iron had gone on for millions of years. These trees have acquired the hardness of marble.'

The reservation had a small museum, where, as they would say in modern America, the 'interpretation' of petrified wood processing (cutting, polishing, etc) was conducted. Having left the 'carefully guarded' (to stop tourists from stealing pieces of precious wood, no doubt) reservation, the writers stopped at a gasoline station, 'surrounded by a fence made up helter-skelter out of the petrified trees.' What they saw there, largely spoiled their mood for the day: 'Here was carried on a lively trade in pieces of wood at fifteen cents and up. A handicraft man with a motor that roared throughout the desert feverishly manufactured souvenirs in the form of brooches and bracelets … Was it worthwhile to lie for so many millions of years in order to be transformed into an unprepossessing brooch with the inscription "Souvenir of …"?'

Without realising it, the writers pinpointed a very important trend characterising the prevailing American attitude to their natural environment – the ever-growing phenomenon, which Todd Gitlin, a modern American social scientist calls 'Domestication of nature.' Still in the bud in 1935, this attitude has been growing ever since and had reached truly alarming proportions by the beginning of the twenty-first century.

In the course of my travels across America in year 2000, I came to the conclusion that 'domestication' of wild nature involves two main trends: plasticising (ie making it look and feel plastic) and packaging. Let me give you some examples.

I arrived in Badlands National Park by the end of my American travels being so tired that I didn't feel like getting off the bus. It was scorching outside and, having visited several canyons and national parks within the previous couple of weeks, I thought I could hardly get excited by the sight of yet another moose or a curiously shaped rock The numerous 'Scenic Turn Off' highway signs had suddenly acquired a negative second meaning. To my exhausted self, American canyons were like lap dancers: no matter how stunning, if you've seen one – you've seen them all.

The ground in the Badlands was barren, bumpy and hard to walk upon which led me to understand why the Dacota Indians referred to the area as *mako sica*, meaning 'land bad,' and early French-Canadian trappers termed it *les mauvaises terres a traverser* – 'bad lands to travel across.'

In the end, I was glad to have made the effort. Thanks to a couple of knowledgeable and straightforward rangers, I learnt a lot about this ancient natural reserve, which used to be the bottom of a giant sea and later – a breeding ground for such pre-historic creatures as three-toed horses, sabre-toothed cats and ruminating pigs (!), whose politically correct scientific name was Oreodonts. These (and other) animals' remains gradually turned into millions of fossils that – due to the unique nature of the soil – stood a good chance of remaining in the Badlands forever, had it not been for fossil-hunters who started carrying away wagonloads of petrified remains to be sold to museums, scientists and private collectors, or just for souvenirs.

With such methodical embezzlement of fossils going on for over a hundred years (since the late nineteenth century), no wonder that by the end of the twentieth century there were none of them left in the Badlands. What could be done about it? Anywhere else, but in America, probably nothing. But the Badlands – for better or for the worse – WERE in America.

In the early 1990s, it was decided to make a number of replica fossils out of … plastic and scatter them around the park. This done, the pseudo-fossils kept disappearing even faster than the real ones, probably because they did look exactly like the real ones, who knows. There is no such force that can stop an average American from pocketing a nice natural 'souvenir,' particularly if it is free, for his general hands-on approach to nature can be best characterised by the notorious quote from Ivan Michurin, a Stalinist Soviet biologist and Ilf and Petrov's contemporary: 'We must not expect gifts from mother nature – we must forcibly take them away from her!'

In the end, it was decided to collect all remaining plastic fossils and to put them under glass cases displayed along the footpaths. This is where they are now, and I had a chance to stare at them for as long as I wanted (about ten seconds at a time). They did look authentic, even slightly dusty (with the carefully replicated dust of history?) – but the fact remained: unbeknownst to most visitors, the Badlands fossils were made of plastic! Their real place was not under museum-style glass domes but on the shelves of the nearby Wall Drug shopping mall specialising in kitsch of all shapes and sizes under a dubious logo 'A Blast From the Past.'

This is how the title of this book was born.

I was told that the Badlands were all about erosion, and they were – in more than one way: to me, the plastic fossils of the Badlands became symbols of the on-going erosion of human values in the world's only remaining superpower – the United States of America.

'This claw is an authentic replica from a grizzly bear,' ran a price tag which I spotted in the gift shop of Kodiak Museum in Alaska. The 'authentic replica' (what an oxymoron!) was obviously made of plastic. The thriving American tradition of plasticising nature can be traced back to 1887, when Professor George Lincoln

Goodale, founder of the Harvard University Botanical Museum, ordered life-size copies of plants and flowers to be made of glass to facilitate teaching botany. Over 300 glass flowers, produced by German artisans Leopold and Rudolph Blaschka between 1887 and 1936, are now on display at the Harvard Museum of Natural History, where guides describe them as 'unique works of art.' It so happened that I was touring Harvard in the company of a loquacious art historian from Brazil. 'Art?!' he exclaimed in disbelief looking at a model bee (also made of glass!) hovering above a model water lily. 'These glass flowers have nothing to do with art – it is simply superior craftsmanship closer to jewellery than art!'

I couldn't help thinking that the whole flower-production exercise was triggered by the sheer laziness of the respected Professor and his students reluctant to go on field trips and to explore living, not model, nature. Or could it be that as far back as in 1887 – long before the age of the motorcar – they already had an aversion to walking? 'Americans' legs will atrophy soon and will be replaced with special gadgets for pressing pedals,' remarked Ilya Ilf in his 1935 American notebooks. Sixty-five years later, I remember causing outrage by announcing to the owners of a small B&B near Woodstock, Vermont that I was going out for an evening walk. 'What?!' they yelled in chorus. 'A walk?! Tell us where you want to go, and we'll give you a lift.' 'No, thanks, I want to walk,' I insisted. 'But where are you going to walk to? No one walks anywhere here. It's dangerous …' They were right: the B&B stood near a roaring highway with no sidewalks in sight. Blinded by headlights every five seconds, I had to trudge along a slippery grassy track during that bizarre evening stroll which I still undertook – if only out of principle.

Staying with friends in Pennsylvania in late May, 2001, I was puzzled to see them loading cross-country skis onto the roof of their car one warm sunny morning. 'Isn't this year's skiing season over?' I asked. 'Not at all,' they replied and explained that for $40 per person per day one could ski all year round on the carpet of artificial plastic snow, brought to their area by truckloads. After that I was not particularly surprised to learn from a guide that the ice in New York's Madison Square Garden arena is painted white before important hockey matches, just to make it appear 'more presentable' – the logic similar to that of a Soviet Army officer routinely ordering his men to paint the grass around the marching square green before a senior commander's inspection.

For all the futility and exorbitant costs of modelling and making up the living nature, they are still preferable to its packaging – in the true sense of this word. In August 2001, some British newspapers ran a story on a growing USA fad for using live butterflies as an exciting alternative to confetti at weddings. A minimum mail or internet order of fifty live butterflies, packaged (!) and shipped in a special envelope, costs $200. The envelopes are handed to wedding guests to open above the heads of newlyweds at the climactic moment. The Florida Monarch Butterfly Farm, one of the live-confetti distributors, advised customers to store butterflies 'in a cool, dark place to keep them calm.'

Despite some muffled protests of butterfly experts that the packaging of live insects was cruel and environmentally damaging, the Butterfly Farm and its parent company Insect Lore were quick to offer a new kind of service asserting that 'butterflies released at funerals can be very therapeutic to the mourning process.' They didn't specify whose funerals they were talking about – deceased humans,' butterflies' themselves, or (most likely) those of common sense.

When two ten-foot pythons were packaged and mailed to an animal shelter in Virginia by an anonymous sender (who probably decided he'd rather got fed up with the pets before they got fed up with him) in year 2000, it created a mild outcry in the USA. 'I would call it cruelty if nothing else,' Sylvia Smith, an animal control officer, said to the Associated Press. 'You just don't wrap up a couple of snakes and mail them.' But it is obviously OK to wrap up and mail hundreds, if not thousands, of butterflies, who unlike snakes, cannot even bite ...

It has to be said, however, that occasionally wild nature does bite back. Quite literally I mean. In the hot summer of 1999, New Yorkers experienced multiple bites by locally bred mosquitoes (some of them were carriers of malaria and encephalitis), who invaded the Big Apple in unprecedented numbers as a result of global warming, to which the USA themselves were the world's main contributor. The US is responsible for twenty-five per cent of the world's production of carbon dioxide, yet the American government, leaned on by the coal, oil and automobile industries, has shown little will to cut that figure – the reluctance which leads to much more painful bites than those of mosquitoes. I am talking about tornadoes, floods, bush fires and droughts causing havoc to the economy and costing thousands of human lives.

At roughly the same time (July 1999), when New Yorkers were frantically scratching their multiple mosquito bites, Challenger, a bald eagle, bit President Clinton on the White House Lawn in Washington, DC. The incident took place during the ceremony to mark taking the bird, whose image appears on the Great Seal of the United States and on the dollar bill, off the list of endangered species. The bite of the First Executive's left hand came shortly after Clinton referred to the eagle as 'the living symbol of our democracy.'

As he left the ceremony, the President told his aides that Challenger 'was not the only creature in Washington who would like to have a go on him' and that 'he had never had sexual relationship with that bird' (I have made up the second part of the quote). But, seriously, I think that Clinton was deservedly bitten not only by the symbol of American democracy, but also by the over-exploited American wild nature, endangered by plasticising and domestication.

* * *

Travelling in America is like being constantly exposed to one and the same familiar cliché. The only part of the country that beats all Hollywood-coined stereotypes is Alaska. And although Ilf and Petrov had never made it to the 'the forty-ninth state' (which was not even officially a state in 1935), during my hectic two weeks there I was often reminded the words of Ostap Bender, the main protagonist of their satirical novels, who once ironically characterised the breath-takingly beautiful mountains of the Great Caucasus as 'Too showy. Weird kind of beauty. Idiot's imagination.'

Being so obviously 'un-American,' Alaska nevertheless fits America well. In quantity and variety of natural wonders, it resembles a huge shopping mall of beauty: there's so much of it that it becomes almost routine, and more often than not a traveller finds himself at a loss as to where to look – left, right, straight ahead or up in the sky. I would normally opt for the latter: nowhere else in the world, not even in Australia, have I seen such vast, all-embracing skies which are always alive with some sort of movement and drama. Staring at the skies was my favourite pastime in Alaska that never failed to distract me from more mundane things underneath.

Alas (a derivative of 'Alas-ka?'), nature does get exploited and plasticised here too. Saying this, I don't just mean such notorious human 'exploits' as the Exxon Valdez tanker running aground in Prince William sound and polluting 1,500 miles of Alaska's coastline with eleven million gallons of crude oil in 1989; nor the routine dumping of toxic waste into Alaska waters and of millions of unscrupulous day-tourists into its fragile historic towns and villages by hundreds of giant cruise liners; nor even President Bush's ambitious (if barbarous) plan to drill for oil and gas in Alaska's wildlife reserves approved by the US House of Representatives in August 2001. While in Alaska, I was able to observe (when not staring up at the skies, that is) numerous smaller-scale and trivial, yet no less annoying, attempts at 'domesticating' nature to make it palatable, tame and 'presentable' for the American eye.

One of the first billboards I spotted on the way from Anchorage airport advertised 'Aurora Borealis Presentation' – an electronic recreation of the elusive Northern Lights, probably having as much likeness to the real thing as a roast-beef has to a cow. The next billboard – '26 Glacier Cruise in One Day! No Motion Sickness – Money Back Guarantee! All-You-Can-Eat Buffet!' – sounded more tempting, and not because of the buffet. At least, the glaciers in the Prince William Sound were bound to be real, not recreated. Although in America one never knew for certain. To find out, I signed up for a cruise the following morning.

The starting point was Whittier, a peculiar town, all 300-odd inhabitants of which dwelled in one fourteen-storeyed tower. It took me two hours to get there from Anchorage by a special Alaska Railroad shuttle. The cruise vessel – a medium-size catamaran – was called *Klondike Express*.

'Welcome aboard! My name is Tracy!' a young blonde in white sailor's uniform announced through the microphone the moment we sailed off. 'You won't hurt our feelings if you don't listen to our commentaries on history and places …' She carried on to say that the vessel had 'co-educational heads' and that the captain would try to come as close to the glaciers as possible. 'Whatever is legal, we'll do for you!' she concluded cheerfully. To my considerable surprise, her introductory comments were followed by a protracted round of applause from the passengers. I was trying to determine whether the applause was their reaction to what she had said, or the expression of joy over the fact that she had actually finished speaking.

It took me a while to realise that Americans simply loved applauding, as if eager to check whether both their hands were still in place and could be slammed together every five minutes or so. The passengers would applaud the views of the white-capped, as if gift-wrapped in snow, mountains on the horizon. They would clap their hands at the sight of each of the promised twenty-six (I didn't count them, but a number of my fellow-travellers did!) glaciers which made me remember how I once witnessed in Paris a busload of American tourists bursting into applause at the sight of the Eiffel Tower – as if expecting the famous structure to curtsy in return. The intermittent applause grew into an ovation when, half-way through the journey, three large photo vignettes were brought up to V-deck by the crew. 'Merry Christmas!,' 'Happy Holiday!' and 'Happy Chanukah!' was written on them. A cheerful queue of the passengers willing to be photographed with Cascade Glacier in the background (and under a relevant inscription) immediately formed, and a specially delegated member of the crew kept snapping right and left with other people's cameras. I came to understand the origins of the taciturn glacier's emerald colour: like the long-suffering 'Mona Lisa' in Le Louvre, it must have been affected by camera flashes. Or just turned green with embarrassment.

The main paradox of the situation lay in the fact that the three-million-year-old Cascade Glacier represented eternity, while most people aboard the catamaran did not have this word in their lexicon and were only preoccupied with the given photographic moment under a silly 'Happy Holiday' vignette.

'Classifieds' and 'Personals' are by far the best reads in Alaskan newspapers. Where else in the world can you see hundreds of ads offering to buy (or to sell) second-hand snowmobiles and hydroplanes and/or spare parts to them? Alaskans are a prosperous lot (they are exempt from federal taxes, but receive a $1,000 per person per year from the US government as a special allowance), and there are thousands of hydroplane owners in Anchorage alone, and parking spots for the planes are as common there as supermarkets and fast-food outlets. There is also a growing problem of night-time drink-flying, when tipsy plane-owner locals whiz back home after a rowdy evening in the bar.

As for 'Personals' (or 'Lonely Hearts') ads, they beat anything of the kind in their sheer desperation. I mean the ones coming from men seeking women. The reason for that is that men outnumber women five- to sevenfold in Alaska. Here are a couple of examples from 'Pressonals' – the 'Personals' section of *Anchorage Press*: 'Need a F right now! Let's have hot monkey love in public places!'; 'Need a woman! Age and race open. You will not be disappointed!' The last 'cry in the women-less Alaskan wilderness' might be just a bit too optimistic, for Alaskan women do get 'disappointed' fairly often. They have even come up with a saying to describe their chances of finding a 'quality' partner: 'The odds are good, but the goods are odd.'

The only other regular features of Alaskan newspapers that can compete with the ads in their idiosyncrasy are stories of encounters with wildlife. The headlines of such reports are usually self-explanatory: 'Bears Sighted in Town' (*Homer News*) 'Bear Attacks Second Dog in Sitka' (*South East Empire*), 'Jogger Chased by Bear' (*Anchorage Daily News*), and so on. They show that Alaskan wildlife is generally alive and well, with the exception perhaps of some unfortunate Sitka dogs who do not count as wildlife anyway. Every resident of Alaska has his (or her) own wildlife encounter story to tell. A woman from an Anchorage suburb assured me that elks routinely wandered into her back garden of an evening. She also told me how she was pursued by a brown bear while jogging (jogging seems to be a risky occupation in Alaska unless you can run faster than a bear). But the story that I read in *Homer News* one day was so utterly incredible that I could be forgiven for taking it not with a grain, but with a good handful of salt. Here it is:

> Orca Takes the Hali-Bait
> *('Orca' is another name for killer whale – VV)*
>
> Clients aboard a Flat Fun Charters boat last week got their money's worth when an unexpected guest paid a visit. A deckhand on the *Sea Hawk* was pulling in what he thought was a fair-sized halibut when a bull Orca surfaced with the fish in his mouth. The crew and the passengers spotted the killer whale about 50 feet from the boat, which was in open water near the Kachemak Bay. 'He rolled and looked at us and chomped it then kind of spit it out,' said Martin Reid, the skipper. The Orca crushed some bones in the halibut but didn't eat it … Then it came for a closer look, dodging under the boat and swimming next to it. 'You could have stepped off the boat onto his back,' said Reid. 'It was kind of freaking everyone out.'

The story was substantiated by photos (made by the skipper) on which one could clearly see a hapless angler trying to pull out a torpedo-shaped submarine-sized whale, or at least pretending to do so.

I ran to the harbour and promptly booked myself on a halibut fishing charter the following morning. 'Remember all the fish you caught can be packaged and sent anywhere in the world,' a 'fish controller' girl told me from the window of her shabby wooden booth on the pier. I said that I didn't want my whale to be sent 'anywhere the world': I wanted it to go straight to London, even if they had to charter a special cargo flight for that. 'Sure!' the girl replied with a smile and proceeded to compliment me on my 'lovely British accent' (it is only in Alaska and, possibly, also in Tasmania that I can occasionally pass for a Brit).

But instead of hooking a whale, or even a halibut, I caught a severe bout of sea-sickness and spent all my time on board the *Sea Witch* lying supine in the boat's tiny cabin. My only consolation was that, with my environmentally friendly fishing (ie fishing with no catch), I played no part in the packaging of Alaska's burgeoning wildlife.

The boat's owners were called 'Sorry Charlie Charters,' by the way. I wish I knew it before embarking.

Having failed to catch, or even to glimpse, a whale, I was determined to make up for it on the Kodiak Island, famous for its 'watchable wildlife' – as it was put by a local tourist brochure, particularly its brown Kodiak bears. The same brochure contained some 'Common Sense in Bear Country' tips which included:

- Avoid surprising bears and make plenty of noise
- Avoid crowding bears; respect their personal space
- Plan ahead, stay calm, identify yourself, don't run

I was quite happy not to 'crowd' the bears, albeit not quite sure how that could be combined with 'identifying myself' and not running away immediately afterwards. Should I just say: 'Hi, my name is Vitali, and I came here just to watch you!?' But what if the bear mistakes this tirade for an intrusion of his 'personal space?'

With all these questions on my mind, I boarded a four-seat Cessna 206 hydroplane for a forty-minute flight to the shores of Fraser Lake in the depth of Alaskan wilderness. Apart from Dan, the pilot, there were two more passengers on board: a young honeymooning couple from Philadelphia.

'Can your hydroplane land on the ground?' the husband asked Dan shortly after we took off.

'Yes, it can. But only once,' the taciturn pilot replied.

It was the best joke I had heard during all my travels in America.

We landed ('watered?') on the lake and, having put on anti-mosquito nets, kindly provided by Dan, walked through the dense forest for about ten minutes until we saw a happy family of brown bears trout-fishing in a stream. I was about to identify myself, but Dan pressed a finger to his lips. So preoccupied were the bears that they paid no attention to us for the whole duration of our one-and-a-half hour watch. I was particularly taken by a fluffy bear-cub, being taught how to fish by his daddy (or was it mummy – I couldn't be sure). The cub was a quick learner, and soon he started ferreting out a wriggling fish each time he dipped his little paws into the water. He was a much better fisherman than I.

When we were hiking back to the plane, I felt an urge to go to the loo. 'Can I quickly hide behind the bushes?' I asked Dan. 'There's no need to,' he said. 'There's a nice lavatory on your right.' He pointed to a little clearing in the forest. There, half-hidden by lush foliage, stood a gleaming stainless-steel hut. Inside, it was spotless – with hot water, hand-drier, general supply of paper towels and paper toilet seats. In the corner, there was a special tap for washing one's feet!

If you asked me what impressed me most in America, I would probably say: 'A state-of-the-art public toilet in the midst of Alaska's Bear Country – a pristine and untouched wilderness, with no roads and no humans for hundreds of miles around.'

I must have looked ridiculous emerging from that air-conditioned loo into clouds of mosquitoes in the middle of nowhere. What's more, it made me feel ridiculous too. Suddenly my bear-watching experience was no longer an adventure, but a virtual-reality 'presentation' in a museum auditorium, with soft comfy seats and 'Exit' signs glowing soothingly in the dark.

* * *

'After a visit to Alaska, you never quite go home' – or so they say. And I didn't. Instead I went straight back to … America, for Alaska, as I had heard so many times while exploring 'The Last Frontier,' had nothing to do with it.

At the end of their first month in the USA, Ilf and Petrov were invited to address the prestigious Dutch Treat Club at the New York Hotel Ambassador. They prepared a brief speech, which was translated into English, and one of them, 'in no way embarrassed by the fact that he found himself in such a large gathering of experts of the English language, read it from a sheet of paper:

> 'Mr Chairman, Gentlemen:
> We have come on a great journey from Moscow to see America. Besides New York we have had time to be in Washington and in Hartford. After living a month in New York we felt the pangs of love for your great and purely American city. Suddenly we were doused with cold water. "New York is not America," we were told by our New York friends. "New York is only the bridge between Europe and America. You are still on the bridge." Then we went to Washington, District of Columbia, the capital of the United States, assuming thoughtlessly that surely this city was America. By the evening of

> the second day we felt with satisfaction that we were beginning to discriminate a little in matters American. "Washington is not America," we were told. "It is a city of government officials. If you really want to see America, you are wasting your time here." We dutifully put our scratched suitcases into an automobile and went to Hartford, in the state of Connecticut, where the great American writer, Mark Twain, spent his mature years. Here we were again honestly warned: "Bear in mind that Hartford is not yet America." When we began to ask about the location of America, the Hartfordites pointed vaguely to the side. Now we have come to you, Mr Chairman and gentlemen, and ask you to show us where America really is located, because we have come here in order to learn as much as we can about it.'

'The speech was a great success. The members of the Dutch Treat Club applauded it a long time,' Ilf and Petrov remark in *Little Golden America*. 'Only much later we learned that most of the members of the club did not understand a single word of this speech, because the strange Russo-English accent of the orator drowned out completely the profound thoughts concealed in it.'

I kept recalling the writers' 'speech' often while travelling around New England during the so-called Fall Foliage season, normally occurring between mid-September and mid-October. On a bus from Boston airport to Concord, New Hampshire, I was glued to the window. With my mouth agape, I was trying to absorb the wild riot of colour displayed by the trees lining the highway. It was simply beyond description: I never knew so many shades of purple, red and brown existed in nature. I felt myself dissolved and drowning in this incredible natural palette.

The moment I arrived in Concord, however, I was 'doused with cold water.' 'You have come too late,' a young woman from the local Chamber of Commerce who met me at the bus station commented. 'The leaves are just behind peak. Not half as good as ten days ago …'

I tried to object meekly that they were still good enough for me, but she didn't listen. 'Leaf-peeping is a big business here,' she said while driving me to my hotel and explained that the season is 'officially' (*sic*) divided into four 'official' (*sic* again!) stages:

1. Just beginning
2. Well-established
3. Peak and
4. Just behind peak.

With my Jewish luck, I obviously hit the last – and the least interesting ('officially,' no doubt) stage.

The Notting Hill Carnival of maples, aspens and birches was whooshing past the windows of our car. Having suppressed a sudden yawn, I had the impression that the screaming brightness of their leaves had indeed faded in the past several minutes.

In his *United States, 1893* guidebook, Karl Baedeker remarked that 'the colour of autumn leaves is an additional attraction' of New England. 107 years later it has become the main attraction and a 'big business' indeed. True, one can still admire autumn leaves for free, but, as I was told in Vermont (after they dutifully assured me that my arrival was 'belated': what I saw was not the 'real fall' and the leaves were not as good as the week before), the visiting leaf-peepers add over a billion dollars to the state coffers each autumn. No wonder leaf-peeping is often referred to as 'a cornerstone of New England tourist industry.'

Like every big (and small) business, New England autumn has to be properly managed. In New Hampshire, they designate twenty 'official leaf-peepers' whose no-less 'official' duties include observing the leaves, compiling twice-weekly reports and suggesting the best 'leaf-peeping routes.' There were not many of those on offer by the time I arrived in Connecticut, where I was immediately informed that 'the oaks had turned' (meaning became brown and no longer gold) and the prime fall-foliage was over. They nevertheless kindly offered to take me to a 'primary foliage viewing area,' where, allegedly, I could still catch some last 'truly golden' leaves, but I refused.

I couldn't, however, refuse a copy of *Leaf-Peeper's Guide* which I studied in the quiet of my hotel room. I had read somewhere that the exact mechanism of the spectacular displays of autumn leaves' colours was a mystery to scientists. Whether it was true or not, I preferred it to remain a fairy tale – like that of Santa Claus. But a 'big business' New England autumn had become in America had no place for fairy tales. My brand-new *Leaf-Peeper's Guide* left no stone (or leaf) unturned to shatter the mystery to smithereens: 'In fall, partly because of shorter periods of daylight and the cooler temperatures, the leaves stop making food (*sic* – VV). The chlorophyll breaks down and the green color disappears. Yellow and orange, previously masked by the green (? – VV), appear. The vibrant reds, purples and bronzes come from other chemical processes …' Nice and clear.

A brilliant book *Vinyl Leaves. Walt Disney World and America* by Stephen M Fjellman, a leading American anthropologist, starts with the following description:

'There is a tree in Central Florida. It is maybe ninety feet high and huge around the base and has a crown that stretches across almost as many yards as the tree is tall. From the top of this tree, when the wind is still, you can see almost to the Caribbean. The trunk looks about as much like that of a live oak as one might wish. The bark is deeply grained and covered with that pea-soup green colored stuff you see on the trees in hot, wet places. It's a big nice tree, a good place for the treehouse that adorns it. But it's not made of wood. The trunk and the branches are formed out of pressed concrete wrapped around a steel-mesh frame. The bark and green stuff that cover much of it are painted on. ***The leaves, all 800,000 of them are made of vinyl.*** (italics are mine – VV).'

Stephen Fjellmam proceeds to explain that the tree, 'Disneyodendron eximus ("out-of-ordinary Disney tree")' is in the Adventureland part of Walt Disney's World Magic Kingdom. For him, it became a symbol of 'commodification' (just another word for 'plasticising,' I presume) of modern American culture.

The widow of my hotel room in Concord, NH, overlooked a vast courtyard of a Victorian lunatic asylum, now – a 'psychiatric hospital.' In the treacherous semi-light of the early dusk, the 'past-peak' autumn leaves in it were aglow and blending with the headlights of the cars behind the hospital fence. What 'chemical processes' had made them look so desperately gorgeous? Or was it because they preferred burning alive to being plasticised?

The trees were offering no answers. Only the falling leaves slowly pirouetted in the air, as if trying to delay the ultimate moment of dying. And the snow-white trunks of birches were bursting through the red-brown setting – like piercing screams of discord through the harmonious symphony of autumn …

* * *

'At any time of day, at any time of year, in the worst possible weather, passenger autobuses race across America. When at night you see a heavy and threatening machine flying across the waste spaces and the deserts, you involuntarily remember the post diligences of Bret Harte run by desperate drivers … America is located on a large automobile highway.'

Travelling across America by buses in the year 2000, I often recalled these words by Ilf and Petrov. Sixty-five years on, America still stood at the roadside of a hypnotically endless and surprisingly empty (outside big metropolises) highway.

Having crossed New Mexico, our hard-working 'autobus' rolled into Texas, America's second largest state after Alaska.

For the first hundred miles or so, the landscape remained unchanged: same arid, sun-burnt prairie; same brown mountains on the horizon; same ranch fences along the highway, which was getting more and more forlorn and deserted. As Ilf and Petrov observed driving through the area sixty-five years ago, 'the gasoline stations became less and less frequent, but to make up for that, the hats of the rare residents became broader and broader.'

The 'gasoline stations' where we stopped were selling only local newspapers, carrying little apart from school lunch menus and 'Lonely Hearts' ads, with head-shots of people in different stages of obesity. They also offered fly-stained collections of bearded 'cowboy jokes,' appalling machine cappuccino and cans of mysterious

'Meat Food Product.' The customers were beefy, ruddy-faced farmers in 'broad' Mexican hats and leather belts, with buckles so huge that they covered their groins.

'Don't Mess With Texas' warned a sticker on the windscreen of a passing farmer's truck, carrying a sad, cockroach-like (black and compact) longhorn cow in its back. To be frank, there was nothing much to mess with, for after this brusque encounter other vehicles disappeared, and the only moving things in sight were oil pump-jacks, nodding tirelessly, like praying Orthodox Jews. We were in the Chihuanuan Desert, whose sandy, cactus-thorned fingers reach into Texas from Mexico, across the Rio Grande, to blend with the southern extremes of the Rocky Mountains.

'One can hardly find anything more grandiose and more beautiful in the world than an American desert ... the beauty created by nature is supplemented by the beauty created by the deft hands of men,' wrote Ilf and Petrov. Coming from the hastily 'industrialised,' yet still distinctly third-world-ish, USSR of the 1930s, the writers could not help admiring 'the even highway with its silvery bridges, its neatly placed water mains, its mounds and dips.' They even concluded that 'the automobile in the desert seemed twice as beautiful than in the city!' Could it be partly due to the fact that the speed limit in Texas was then just forty-five miles per hour?

Riding along the semi-dried Rio Grande, marking the border with Mexico, sixty-five years later, I was ready to share the Russians' enthralment with the natural beauty of the desert – its piercing silence and quiet loneliness echoing the official logo of Texas – 'the Lone Star State'; its resilient Dead Man's Fingers – a breed of red-blossomed cacti, stubbornly sticking out of dry earth; with its carpets of blue bonnets (tiny azure flowers), making parts of it aquamarine and almost sea-like; its 'dust devils' – gentle puffs of sand and dust lifting above its surface here and there, as if the desert itself was breathing them out, while mischievously indulging in the most subversive of all anti-American activities – smoking.

As for the 'man-made beauty,' I was not so sure. It was nice to see (and to feel) that the desert highway was indeed as smooth as the Beltway around Washington DC, that plumbing in the abundant and spotlessly clean road-side 'rest-rooms' in the middle of nowhere was as perfect as at a Marriott Hotel in Manhattan. On the other hand, I was rather taken aback by the eyesore of a huge hot-house, which, in the permanently red-hot desert, looked as appropriate as a fridge on top of an iceberg; or by a handful of useless picnic gazebos, made of iron and offering no protection from the scorching desert sun. The only good thing about these gazebos was that burgers and sausages would fry spontaneously (together with the unlikely picknickers) inside them.

Unlike Ilf and Petrov, who stayed for several days in El Paso, I stopped in the little border town of Lajitas, claiming to be 'the remotest settlement in the USA.' Local tourist brochures assert that more people have spent the night at the bottom of the

Grand Canyon than in Lajitas, boasting 'the most breath-taking sunrises and sunsets in Texas' – the fact that is probably meant to make the gullible Grand Canyon revellers green with envy. According to the brochures, Lajitas was also the home of the 'famous beer drinking goat' (one resident wit confided in me that he was actually the town's Mayor).

Built in 1915 as a cavalry post to protect the area from the Mexican 'hot-eyed bandit' Pancho Villa, Lajitas had gone into decay by 1977, when it was bought by the Mischer Corporation, with the aim of turning it into a popular health spa. A couple of hotels and a small touristy shopping mall were constructed, but potential holidaymakers were not in hurry to visit this natural sauna, especially in summer, when the temperature in Lajitas seldom drops below 100 degrees Fahrenheit.

As for the 300 local residents, their plight remained almost as pitiful as in the times of Pancho Villa, although much less exciting.

An ageless local woman – dried-out and sinewy, like a desert plant – told me that to buy basic groceries they still had to travel 160 miles, and that children had to be driven to school to the town of Terlingua – a two-hour-long daily journey.

'Parents of schoolkids get partly reimbursed by the state government, but, in actual fact, we spend this money – 25 cents per mile – on other things,' the woman chuckled.

Listening to her, it was hard to believe that she was talking about the twenty-first century USA.

The breakthrough came last February, by which time the Mischer Corporation had all but given up on Lajitas and put the town up for auction. The bids were lazy and half-hearted, like the biting of bream in April, until – one hour before the closure – the auctioneer heard the characteristic rattle of chopper blades above his head. Like in a good ancient Greek tragedy (or in a bad Hollywood movie), the sound signified the arrival of *deus ex machina* (a god routinely introduced into an ancient drama to resolve the intricacies of the plot), or, in this case, the highest bidder, who – quite literally – descended onto Lajitas from the heavens, in his personal French Astar 350 B3 helicopter. Having barely touched the ground, Steve Smith, an Austin property developer and a co-founder of Excel telephone company, snapped up Lajitas for $3,950,000 ($4.2 million with the auctioneer's fees).

'The sale ends an era. Begins another,' commented the *Lajitas Sun*, the town's monthly rag, in its usual laconic fashion, imitating the locals' habit of speaking curtly and through clenched teeth to prevent ubiquitous flies from entering their mouths.

I was lucky: Steve Smith was in town and agreed to a quick interview. A tall, thick-set man in a navy polo-shirt, he had a radiant smile and oozed with the famous Texan can-do attitude.

'I love the desert. I came here to realise my dream and to express my creativity. The place was stale when I bought it, and I'm gonna change it,' he said.

He shared his plans to build a jet strip, a golf course and a swimming pool in Lajitas 'to attract families in winter.'

I asked about the locals, and he promised 'to improve utilities and to supply school buses and medical facilities' – a perfect rhyme, which, as I hoped, would not end up as just another abstract example of the never-ending poetry of the desert – the poetry, only slightly marred by the fact that some bits of it could now be bought and sold.

'The word 'desert' is frequently used as a symbol of monotony. The American desert, however, is unprecedentedly varied,' noted Ilf and Petrov. Indeed, the last thing I expected to find in Lajitas, the remotest and the most 'un-American' place in the USA, was an archetypal 'American' story of the sale of a modern, even if God-forsaken, town – with all its long-suffering inhabitants.

The Russian writers were right: the American desert was anything but boring.

Brighton Beach

In the course of their Trans-American travels in 1935-36, only once did Ilf and Petrov bump into their émigré compatriot – a Ukrainian from Volhynia selling popcorn in Schenectady.

These days, they would have had many more similar encounters. In the New York area alone, there now live over a million Russian speakers – the people, washed up on American shores by the latest waves of Soviet (and later Russian) emigration.

The Russian network of modern New York is as thick and branchy as a Siberian fir-tree. It incorporates more than fifty newspapers in American-accented Russian (for those who haven't quite learnt English yet) and one – in Russian-accented English (for those who have all but forgotten their Russian); countless Russian restaurants, where – in full accordance with Soviet culinary traditions – one can get borscht, caviar, vodka and, occasionally, food poisoning; Russian book-shops, bath-houses, surgeries and funeral homes. People concluding business deals, arguing or swearing into their mobile phones in a curious mixture of Russian and English have become common sight in the streets of Manhattan, Brooklyn, Queens and the Bronx, to which the Russians jokingly refer as Bronsk.

Had Ilf and Petrov come to New York in the year 2000, they would have definitely visited Brighton Beach – the area in south-east Brooklyn bordering Coney Island – also known as 'Little Odessa.' 150,000 Soviet emigrants, mostly former inhabitants of Odessa, settled there in the last twenty-five years, having radically altered the face of that 'old world' New York neighbourhood, once nicknamed 'a retired poor man's Miami Beach.'

Not worth a visit in the 1930s, when, according to the 1939 WPA Guide to New York, Brighton Beach was but 'a densely populated year-round residential area, with closely packed apartment houses,' or even in the early 1970s, when it was a rapidly declining and crime-ridden ghost town, it is now one of the most idiosyncratic places in New York, if not in the whole of the USA. Going there is not just stepping twenty or thirty years back in time; it is a unique opportunity to visit the country that doesn't exist any more – the Union of Soviet Socialist Republics.

Spiritually, linguistically and psychologically, Brighton Beach is not part of the USA. 'We don't go to America. We have nothing to do there,' its residents like to say. An American, arriving there by accident, stands out and gets stared at – like an Eskimo in the streets of Abu Dhabi.

On a wet winter morning, when Manhattan resembled a post-modernist version of Venice and the shoe-cleaners near the Grand Central Station were earning more in one hour then during the whole of July, I left the United States and boarded a B-line Subway train to Brighton Beach.

My wobbly and unkempt carriage resembled an Aeroflot plane of the 1980s. Having crawled through China Town, covered with spider-like hieroglyphic graffiti, the train rattled across Manhattan Bridge and entered Brooklyn, whose ugly littered streets and battered red-brick houses were full of unspeakable Soviet-style despair. Having heard a lot about the dangerous types, riding the Subway during the day, I looked around nervously and kept my hands in my pockets (which were empty anyway).

Soon, I concluded that I was the most dangerous type on the train, simply because for most of the trip I was alone in my carriage: no one in his right mind – not even beggars or muggers – would think of going to the Soviet Union by New York Subway in the middle of a working day.

Nearly two hours later, I got off the train in Coney Island Avenue – Brighton Beach's own 'Broadway.' It was raining, and the strong wind from the ocean immediately grabbed my umbrella, like a street bully, trying to break it in two. Nestling in the shadow of the Elevated, the whole neighbourhood looked like the interior of a huge neglected house with leaking roof.

Suddenly I was surrounded by semi-forgotten and painfully familiar smells and sounds. The air reeked of borsht and fried '*pirozhki*' (meat pies). In front of me, a fat angry-faced lady was telling off a young woman with a pram: 'Button up your baby, mother, or you will freeze it to death!'

Almost all signs were in Russian: 'Michael Kozhin – American Dentist,' 'Footwear from Italy,' 'Best Goods' (it was a one-dollar shop selling hats, toys, suit-cases and tacky post-cards), 'Cheap Goods from Russia' (this shop was Chinese-owned), 'We Accept Foodstamps' and 'Bella Works Here.'

Having resisted the temptation to see the mysterious (and obviously famous) Bella at work, I wandered off to the nearest Gastronom (food shop). Inside, there was a queue for cut-price concentrated orange juice. Just like in the Soviet Union, one had to queue to the cash desk first, and then – to the counter, behind which a busty peroxide blonde in a grubby apron was unhurriedly handing over the coveted cartons of juice to the customers. 'Are you buying it or not, woman?' she shouted at a little old lady, whose decrepit shopping trolley squeaked like a Moscow tram turning the corner. The queue was regularly jumped by rough-looking men buying packets of Marlboro – without a whisper of protest from the queuers.

The whole scene struck me as utterly un-American, for in the USA, according to *The Americans. A Study in National Character* by Geoffrey Gorer, even 'the smallest purchase should be accompanied by a smile, and the implied assurance that the vendor is delighted and privileged to serve you ...' The people did not smile in the Gastronom, where the facial expressions fluctuated between the uncomplaining indifference of the customers and 'the implied assurance' of the vendor that she had a personal vendetta against everyone in the queue …

I couldn't tear my gaze from the display of '*vatrushki*' cheese pies – like the ones I used to have for my school lunches; from fat-oozing '*salo*' – a pure pork lard that can be sliced and eaten with bread, with each slice containing more kilojoules that all the dishes from Delia Smith's *Complete Cookery Course* put together; from dusty bottles of '*Troika' kvas*' – a mildly alcoholic drink, made of yeast and rye bread, and from other culinary delights of my previous Soviet life.

'Can I have a cabbage pie, please?' I asked the salesgirl politely, when my turn came.

'Are you flirting with me, or what?' she snarled back. She must not have heard the word 'please' since childhood.

There were no self-service food stores in Brighton Beach, where, despite the over-abundance of food, shopping for it remained a masochistic Soviet experience, featuring totally superfluous cash-desks, rude salesgirls and queues to be jumped.

Not so in numerous music stores, where I was allowed to browse on my own, having deposited my shoulder-bag with a blue-faced attendant in exchange for a '*nomerok*' – a soiled piece of cardboard with a number. For some reason, the biggest sections in many of these stores were reserved for '*Blatnaya Muzika*,' or 'Thieves' Cant.' 'We've got plenty of Russian criminal folklore,' an attendant told me proudly inviting me to look at the stand with hundreds of tapes and CDs. 'Do I look like an underworld type?' I was wondering.

I ventured into 'Parikmakherskaya,' a barber's shop run by Syoma, an old Jew from Minsk and a former 'Soviet activist' (in his own words). Cutting my hair and squinting to ensure he didn't chop off my ears, he complained of his life in Brighton Beach: 'We are besieged by home-grown gangsters here. The other day they killed a jeweller round the corner. Burst into his shop and shot him in broad daylight. And took the jewellery. Shame our Jews …'

'The Mafia? Which Mafia?' Liova, a leading Brighton Beach businessman raised his bushy eye-brows in response to my question. 'All this Russian Mafia bull was invented by New York City fathers, who hate us for being so entrepreneurial and successful …'

He proceeded to tell me how they were slowly but surely pushing out Africans and Puerto Ricans from the area, and I suddenly realised why music of the underworld was in such great demand in Brighton Beach. The people, who – for generations – had to cheat the Soviet system to survive, were finding it hard, if not impossible, to change their way of thinking in the West. Some of the scams, originating from Brighton Beach, like the one which involved selling water-dissolved petrol to hundreds of gas stations across America, stunned the whole country by their crafty simplicity. Talking of the so-called Russian Mafia, a NYPD spokesman once noted: 'It is much easier to deal with a criminal who breaks the law than with a person who doesn't know that the law exists.'

By mid-afternoon, the rain stopped, and couples of elderly immigrants, carrying the indelible 'I-am-waiting-to-be-hurt' expression on their faces, could be seen strolling along the wet wood-paved boardwalk. From time to time, they would stop and stare at the ocean, as if trying to discern the outlines of their native Odessa on the horizon.

Some of them would later flock to 'Odessa' Restaurant, where local bard Willie Tokarev performs his poignant nostalgic songs. In one, he calls Brighton Beach 'a gypsy encampment.' True, its residents were as rootless and as homeless as gypsies, only, unlike gypsies, they have stopped wandering …

It was with relief that I boarded the train back to America. Half a day in a country, which no longer existed, was more than enough for me.

To while away the journey, I leafed through a thick Russian rag that I had bought in Brighton Beach. My attention was captured by the following ad: 'Never!!! The Weiner Brothers' funeral parlour will **never** refuse service to Russian Jews!' I remembered that in 'the regional centre of N,' a fictitious provincial Russian town, described by Ilf and Petrov in their brilliant satirical novel *The Twelve Chairs*, there was a 'Do Us the Honour' Funeral Home.

Had the writers not been dead for sixty years, I would have thought they had indeed visited modern Brighton Beach.

New York

'New York … thunders and gleams much more thoroughly than any storm. It is an excruciating city. It constantly rivets all attention to itself. It makes your eyes ache. Yet it is impossible not to look upon it.'
from *One-Storied America* by Ilya Ilf & Evgeny Petrov, 1935-36

Ilf and Petrov spent several months in the Big Apple, the starting point of their Trans-American journey. They wandered the streets of Manhattan, saw a boxing match at the Madison Square Garden, had a drink with Ernest Hemingway. It was in New York that they bought a 'sedate, mouse-coloured Ford' to take them across America and met the bubbly Mr Adams, their would-be travel companion and guide. It was there that they pledged 'to find out as soon as possible how these people [the Americans – VV] work, how they amuse themselves, what they dream of, what they hope for, what they eat …'

Among the first things the writers discovered in New York was that – of all American culinary delights – a glass of mundane tomato juice, which they would pepper heavily before drinking, was 'best suited for their South Russian stomachs' (they were both born in Odessa). 'Americans eat a blindingly white but utterly tasteless bread, frozen meat, salty butter, unripe tomatoes [evidently, only good for the juice – VV], and canned foods,' they concluded after a meal in a newly emerged self-service 'Cafeteria' in 42nd Street – the experience they described in the chapter with a self-explanatory title 'Appetite Departs While Eating.'

How has New York's food scene changed in sixty-five years? To find the answer, I tried to contact William Grimes, the acclaimed *New York Times* restaurant critic, who, as I was assured, could close down restaurants by the sheer power of his pen.

In no time, I got through to a pre-recorded message of the *New York Times* switchboard: 'If you want to advertise with us – press one. If you don't want to advertise with us – press two. If you don't want anything at all – press three. If you want to go to hell – press four …' Or something like that. In the end, when I was offered to 'enter the first four letters' of my contact's last name, I slammed down the phone and appealed for help to a technically-minded contact of mine with two PhDs under his belt. 'It doesn't take a rocket scientist,' he mumbled, having completed the task in just thirty minutes (he was a nuclear physicist, by the way).

Here it must be said that, despite (or, maybe, because of) modern electronic gadgets aimed at easing up communication, contacting a person in New York has become much harder than sixty-five years ago, when New York friends of Ilf and Petrov promptly threw an impromptu reception, to which their contacts, admirers and pen-friends were invited. These days it would take several months to organise such a soiree. The writers' friends would first have to leave messages with answering machines, voicemail boxes, pagers, computers, etc and to wait for them to reply, which could take anything from several minutes to eternity. It is becoming increasingly hard to hear a genuine (as opposed to pre-recorded or computer-modulated) human voice in New York, where everyone – from the powerful NYPD to a street fortune-teller – is already on the Internet. 'Visit our website, if you want to know the recipe of our beautiful knishes,' I read in the window of a small Jewish bakery in Brooklyn. Soon, they will discover how to send pizzas by fax – and that will be the end of all human communication ...

William Grimes did call back several days later and had a lovely conversation with my own answering machine. He invited me (or was it the machine?) for a 'working lunch' in a fashionable Park Avenue restaurant, having warned the machine (or myself?) that the table was booked in an assumed name.

'Are you still working at it, sir?' a waiter asked me two hours into the somewhat schizophrenic meal, which combined the elements of Italian, Jewish, Japanese and French cuisine. I was tempted to say that it was not me but William who was actually working, but restrained myself.

'Austrian cuisine is now the biggest thing in New York,' William said over dessert, while fastidiously assessing the qualities of a crispy Napoleon cake (or was it matzos?). 'But, frankly, my favourite gourmet experience in New York is a street cart.'

I asked him about the Hollywood restaurant, where Ilf and Petrov watched a burlesque show with Dos Passos. Several days later, he (William, not Dos Passos) faxed me a photo-copied page from *Dining in New York* by Rian James, published in 1930, according to which the restaurant 'in Broadway at 48th Street' offered 'the most beautiful girls in the world, dancing, and a no cover policy, with a minimum food charge of $1.50.' Ilf and Petrov were duly impressed by the exorbitant cost of their dinners – 'about two dollars per person'[28] (I wonder whether Dos Passos picked up the bill?), but were rather disgusted by their 'uninteresting and in no way inspiring American soup' and by the 'weary' 'half-naked, three-quarters naked and nine-tenth naked' girls, who danced 'zealously on their floor space, their feathers dipping occasionally into plates of soup or jars of mustard.'

To find out what else was happening in New York in 1935, I visited the 'New York Century' exhibition in the rather drab-looking Museum of the City of New York in Harlem. Unfortunately, the 1935 section, listing the year's main highlights, was blocked by a pillar, and the only events still visible were: 'Harlem riots,' 'First public

[28] By comparison, a gallon of petrol cost 10 cents in 1935, and a loaf of bread – 8 cents.

housing project,' 'Works Progress Administration' and 'the Depression.' Interestingly, the last was not mentioned by Ilf and Petrov in their book – probably due to the fact that, compared to the gloomy 1930s USSR, the Great American Depression looked like a huge economic boom.

There could have been a different reason for the omission though. In 'Strand' second-hand bookstore in Broadway, boasting of having 'eight miles of books' (never before have I heard of books measured in miles), I bought a mere dog-eared inch of Jay Franklin's 1937 biography of Fiorello H La Guardia, who was the Mayor of New York in 1935. On the book's flap-jacket, there was a miraculously preserved sticker: 'The publishers call to your attention that, owing to objections made by Mayor La Guardia, a portion of the text on pages 58 and 74 has been excised.' I opened the book and saw that several offending paragraphs on the indicated pages were neatly **cut out with scissors !** No wonder *One-Storied America* became the innocuous *Little Golden America* in the 1937 USA translation.

The difference with Stalin's Soviet Union, however, was that the Soviets wouldn't bother attaching an explanatory sticker to a shredded book (my mother told me that, from time to time, all subscribers of the *Big Soviet Encyclopedia* would receive specially printed new pages to be inserted in place of politically incorrect ones, which the subscribers were ordered to remove[29]). Also, the biographer himself would stand a good chance of being 'censored,' ie arrested and shot.

Such blatant intrusion is hard to imagine nowadays, when an average New Yorker is so obsessed with freedom of expression that he (or she) consciously ignores the red 'Don't Walk' signs at street crossings. 'They are too suggestive,' a New York friend explained while happily jaywalking across Madison Avenue. This is probably why many New Yorkers dislike their present-day Mayor, Rudolf Giuliani, who proved no less radical than his 1930s predecessor. Not only did Rudy (as he is popularly known here) ban the notorious British elephant-dung exhibition in the Brooklyn Museum of Fine Arts, he also pledged to banish all 23,000 New York homeless. 'Streets do not exist for the purpose of people sleeping there. Bedrooms are for sleeping,' he declared.

Walking in Manhattan, where the traffic is so slow that it gives the impression of crawling backwards, I spotted an elderly woman asleep inside a capacious shopping trolley, her bare feet sticking out like two freshly bought overbaked baguettes. She must have somehow slipped through Giuliani's 'zero tolerance' net … Luckily for her, the weather in New York was mild, and one could be forgiven for thinking that

[29] (eg) When Lavrentiy Beria, a one-time chief of Stalin's secret police, was officially branded an 'enemy of the people' and a British spy, a biographical article on him in the *Big Soviet Encyclopedia* was replaced with an unusually lengthy entry on the Bering Strait.

the ebullient Giuliani, alongside the homeless and the pickpockets, has inadvertently outlawed winter …

On my last evening in New York, I took the elevator to the 27th floor of the Marriott East Side (formerly the Shelton Towers) Hotel, where Ilf and Petrov stayed sixty-five years ago. The design of the hotel hasn't changed much, except for a 'tobacco stand' in the vestibule which disappeared without a trace. Indeed, these days a New York hotel is more likely to have a coffin store in the lobby than an un-PC 'tobacco stand.' Erected in 1924 by Arthur Loomis Harmon, the acclaimed architect of the Empire State Building, the Shelton was originally designed as a 'bachelor residence,' but by 1935 it began accepting female guests and married men, like Ilf and Petrov.

In 1935, in their 'little rooms' on the 27th floor Ilf and Petrov could feel 'the warm wind,' which 'wafted from the Atlantic Ocean.' They saw 'several skyscrapers' which seemed so close that 'one could touch them with his hand' and 'their lighted windows could be counted.' And further away, behind a 'dark unlighted swath (the Hudson? Or was it the East River?),' there 'gleamed a sheer gold dust of tiny lights.'

Despite the presence of a several new high-rise stalagmites, the 1935 view remained largely unchanged. Down below, New York was steaming, bubbling and heaving like a giant jacuzzi bath, left running overnight by a forgetful owner. A warm waft of eternity gently ruffled my hair as I looked at the 'sheer gold dust of tiny lights,' still dancing tirelessly in the distance, behind the black ribbon of the Hudson.

Or was it indeed the East River?

Chicago

In their book *Little Golden America*, Russian satirists Ilya Ilf and Evgeny Petrov drew a surprisingly balanced portrait of 1930s USA. Only a couple of times they allowed their emotions to intervene with their judgement. One example is the chapter 'That Horrible Town Chicago,' the very title of which testifies to the writers' disgust of the Windy City, characterised by them as 'heavy, clumsy and uncomfortable' and compared to 'a huge, ugly, poisonous fungus.' During their brief visit to Chicago in 1935, they were angered by its yawning gap between wealth and poverty, between the gleaming facades of Michigan Avenue, 'the most beautiful street on earth,' and the adjoining 'narrow, dark, dirty lanes ... real dives with the blackened brick walls of shoddy houses, fire escapes, and garbage cans.' The contrast led Ilf and Petrov to conclude that 'scarcely anywhere else in the world have heaven and hell intertwined so intimately as in Chicago.'

It has to be said that Ilf and Petrov were not the only foreigners to have been annoyed by the great divide of 1930's Chicago. 'There are two separate and distinct parts of Chicago. One is Michigan Boulevard, and the other is all the rest. The Boulevard is a truly magnificent street. The rest of Chicago is hideous,' noted AG Macdonnel, a talented Scottish journalist, who visited the city in the same year, 1935 ('Boulevard' was probably the 1930s Scottish equivalent of 'Avenue').

The Russians were even more enraged by Chicago's thriving gangster culture. 'In this city shooting goes on. It would be surprising if people did not shoot here,' they remarked after mocking the typical shouts of Chicago's vociferous 'news vendors': 'Policeman Murdered!' 'Bank Robbery!' 'Gangster Filos, Alias "Little Angel," Killed Instead of Detective Patterson!' 'Racketeer "Baby" James Arrested!' 'Kidnapping on Michigan Avenue!'

In this case, Ilf and Petrov's bitterness is understandable: the streets of Stalin's 1930s Moscow, where both writers lived, were relatively safe (totalitarian rulers tend to monopolise everything, including crime, of which they themselves become the main perpetrators), and the sounds of 'shooting' from distant gulag, where thousands of innocent people were executed daily, could not be heard there.

1930's Chicago was indeed a chaotic and crime-ridden place, the conurbation of underground brothels, drug dens and speakeasies, run by infamous Al Capone, branded 'America's public enemy number one,' and his brother Ralph 'Bottles' Capone. It was there that the word 'racket' first came into use in 1927. According to some historians, at the time of Ilf and Petrov's visit, there were at least sixty active rackets flourishing in the city, where crime was the second biggest 'industry' bringing the gangsters six million dollars a week ('Everybody calls me a racketeer. I call myself a businessman,' bragged Al Capone). In 1935, a Chicagoan who wanted his trousers pressed had to pay fifty cents to the racket, since crooks fully controlled the cleaners' and dyers trade. Bakers, barbers, electricians, garage men, shoe repairers, plumbers, rubbish collectors, window cleaners, milkmen, confectioners and undertakers were all under the heel of the Mob.

And yet, having re-read 'That Horrible Town Chicago,' I couldn't help wondering about the reasons behind Ilf and Petrov's uncharacteristic negativity and the almost total lack of humour in their portrayal of the city. Could it be that their editors from Pravda Publishers had ordered them to use Chicago as an epitome of American capitalism?

To find an answer in 2007, I had to immerse myself in the street life of 1930's Chicago. For that, I couldn't have a better guide than Richard Lindberg – a lifelong Chicagoan, an author, a historian and a member of the Chicago Crime Commission, who took me on a walking tour of the South Side, also known as the 'Levee,' one evening.

'This door used to lead to bordellos and gambling joints ... Over there, where the Hyatt Hotel is now, there used to be a famous drug den, and on that street corner Tony Lombardo, a famous gangster, was gunned down in broad daylight in 1928,' Richard was saying with a tinge of nostalgia in his voice (or so I thought). He led me up a little lane nicknamed Whisky Row during the Prohibition. Adventure-seekers who ventured there in search of bootleg liquor were likely to end up swallowing a 'Mickey Finn Special' – a mixture of booze and drugs that made you pass out and consequently get robbed.

The building of the former Central Library was a silent witness to one of the most controversial tragedies in Chicago's history. On 9 June 1930, Alfred 'Jake' Lingle, *The Chicago Tribune*'s celebrated police reporter, was murdered in front of it by mobsters. It was only after his death that his mob connections and lush life-style came to the surface. For many years, Lingle was on the gangsters' payroll and was friendly with Al Capone, who eventually decided to dispose of the double-crossing hack. The news-stand, at which Lingle stopped moments before his death to buy a paper, was still there. Its irregular twisted shadow on the pavement looked like a spot of dried blood in the treacherous light of a lonely street lantern. For a fleeting moment, it felt as if we were surrounded by ghosts of Chicago mobsters – in white gaiters and wide-brimmed straw hats – still dwelling in the dark deserted streets of the Levee.

Seventy-two years later, downtown Chicago feels perfectly, almost disappointingly, safe. The 'dives' have disappeared, and the whole of the formerly vice-ridden South Side is being gentrified and turned into a prestigious residential area., where a modern 'condominium' in a converted warehouse costs around $500,000 – a sort of real-estate 'racket' of 2000.

How about crime? Having perused 'Police Log' and 'Police Blotters' pages of several local newspapers, I decided that if the city's 'news vendors' returned to their shouting practice of the 1930s, in 2000 their piercing screams would sound approximately like this: 'Pokémon Cards Stolen!' 'Nintendo Game Taken from Apartment!' 'Flashlight, Radio and Baseball Cap Taken from a Garage!' 'Robber Flees Empty-Handed after Victim Attacks Him with Umbrella!' and so on. An archetypal crime of modern Chicago was reported by a small newspaper, with an unfortunate and somewhat disturbing name *The North Loop News*: a woman went into a dressing room in department store on the 700 block of North Michigan Avenue and, having put $553 in merchandise – a purse, dress and bathing suit – into her bag, left without paying. She was arrested and told police: 'I am under pressure to dress nice for my job.' Like the whole of the United States, Chicago is living through a period of unparalleled prosperity which, among other things, has brought about a certain 'trivialisation' of its crime scene.

The city centre is now clean, spacious and architecturally attractive. Similar to the hapless woman-shoplifter, Chicago must have succumbed to the pressure to look 'nice' at the time of unprecedented economic boom. This metaphor acquires a more direct meaning when one looks at the Chicago Tribune Tower, its façade decorated with pieces of Taj Mahal, the Leaning Tower of Pisa and other famous foreign attractions nicked and brought home (without paying, no doubt) by some peripatetic *Chicago Tribune* journalists. No wonder the Tower of Pisa keeps leaning …

The shoplifting analogy came to my mind again when I saw a photo of the Wrigley Building, 'boasting a clock tower design borrowed from Seville, Spain' (according to the caption) in the glossy *Where: Chicago* magazine. 'How can one boast something that is "borrowed?" ' I thought. 'And isn't "borrowed" just a nice-sounding euphemism for "plagiarised," "stolen" or "shoplifted?" After all, it can be said that the poor North Loop woman simply wanted "to borrow" a dress or two from the store …' Semantics aside, one could be forgiven for thinking that the vivacious gene of chicanery (if not of full-scale crime), inherited from the troublesome 1930s, was still affecting the appearance of Chicago's ever-changing city-scape.

Among other imaginary shouts of Chicago's 'news vendors' of today could be: 'Twelve Customers Gunned Down In Convenience Store Clerk's Imagination!' 'Woman On TV Gives Birth To Four-Month-Old Baby!' 'Earliest Known T-Shirt Found!' and 'US No Longer Responsible For Lost Or Stolen Items!' All these are front-page headlines from just one issue of *The Onion* – a spoof weekly newspaper with offices in Chicago. *The Onion* made its name across the USA by brilliantly lampooning American politics and mass media. It is laid out as a normal newspaper, with lead stories, comics, weather forecasts and even horoscopes. But nothing in it, except for ads and some reviews, is serious. My horoscope in the same issue of *The*

Onion said: 'Your plan to put on a fun dance show to raise money will save your financially threatened strip club.'

It is a shame *The Onion* was not in existence in 1935 (it was founded in 1988), for it could have brightened up Ilf and Petrov's sombre view of Chicago.

So, what happened to Chicago's notorious gangsters – all these 'Babies,' 'Bottles' and 'Little Angels' – with guns, not wings, under the armpits? Have they disappeared together with the downtown 'dives' which so shocked Ilf and Petrov?

'The gangsters are still here,' Richard Lindberg reassured me. 'Only the mob in Chicago is not traditional 'Mafia' as it is commonly understood. It is one single entity numbering about 300 members, predominantly Italian, but with a number of Jews, Poles, Irish, Germans and other ethnic groups included. In Chicago, we simply call it the "Outfit." There is no "five families" structure like in New York. There is no initiation ceremony. It is a crime confederation without the trappings of old world Sicilian custom, because so many members are not Italian. There is less murder and violence today, but the Outfit is still influential and penetrating legitimate businesses.'

Well, it was good to know that modern Chicago's ethnic diversity has been reflected in the composition of the Outfit, which, for all its unseemly sides, appears to be totally free of national prejudice. The culture of political correctness has turned the once-feared Chicago Mob into a model equal opportunities employer. Not a bad story for *The Onion* …

Sing Sing

While in New York in late 1935, Ilf and Petrov, the Russian satirists in whose footsteps I was travelling across America, met Ernest Hemingway, who had come to the Big Apple for a week from Florida, where he lived. 'He proved to be a large man with moustaches and a peeling sunburnt nose. He wore flannel trousers, a woollen vest which did not come together on his mighty chest, and his bare feet were in house slippers.'

At some point in the conversation, the Russians mentioned Sing Sing, the famous American prison, of which they 'had heard from childhood, having been then ardently interested in the adventures of Nat Pinkerton and Nick Carter.' By coincidence, Hemingway had come to New York with his father-in-law, 'a neat little old man whose thin neck was encased in a very high and old-fashioned starched collar,' who happened to be a friend of Mr Lewis E Lawes, the Sing Sing Warden. On Hemingway's request, the starchy 'little old man' agreed to arrange for the writers to visit the prison. The permission was granted the following day.

Ilf and Petrov were lucky, although I suspect that, in reality, their interest in Sing Sing was prompted not so much by their childhood passion for Nick Carter as by the mounting 'great terror' in their motherland: they were probably curious as to what to expect in the very likely case of their own arrest.

Without the backing of Hemingway and his frail, yet powerful, father in-law, I had to rely solely on myself to arrange a visit to Sing Sing, still functioning as a maximum-security 'correctional facility' in the village of Ossining in Westchester County – thirty miles north of New York. Having received no reply to my numerous faxes, emails and phone calls, I had to take a Metro-North train to Ossining hoping that my luck would prove stronger than my pull.

I have been to many prisons – not as an inmate, mind you, but as a journalist – from the overcrowded and de-humanising 'strict regime colonies' of the Soviet Union to the relaxed and often over-lenient jails of Australia (looking more like the Gold Coast holiday resorts) and Holland (where, among other perks, the inmates were allowed to make wine and to keep pets in their cells). I knew that America's founding fathers sincerely believed that jails would never be necessary in this cradle of democratic freedoms, and it was sadly ironic that the modern USA boasted the highest incarceration rate in the world, with over one million people behind bars.

'There is something unmistakably American about the prison system we have created,' assures the 1996 edition of *Encyclopedia of American Prisons*. If so, 'Sing Sing Correctional Facility,' the country's oldest and most notorious penitentiary, where 614 inmates were put to death in the electric chair between 1891 and 1963, could be called an archetypal American institution. I doubted I would see any pets there ...

On the way from New York to Ossining, Ilf and Petrov got lost. They 'were obliged to stop' and to ask a man, 'unloading some neat little boxes at the edge of the road' for directions to Sing Sing. 'Having finished his explanation, the workman smiled and said: "Hurrying to the electric chair? Wish you luck!" At the time of their visit, the famous Sing Sing 'sparky,' constructed in 1891 by the inmates themselves (!), was still working full steam: sixteen prisoners were electrocuted in it in 1935 and twenty-three (including one female) – in 1936.

'How do I get to Sing Sing?' I asked a solitary well-dressed lady waiting for a taxi at Ossining station.

'You have just escaped from it,' she smiled and explained that all trains from New York passed through the middle of the 'facility' before arriving at the station. I cursed myself for being unobservant.

'If I had more time, I would have driven you there,' the woman continued amicably, pointing at an oblong grim bulk of a building overlooking the Hudson, about a mile away. Through morning mist, I could discern the blurred silhouettes of watch-towers. 'But don't even try to get inside: due to some disturbances this morning, the inmates are all confined to their cells, and all visits have been cancelled.'

I soon discovered that whatever happened inside Sing Sing immediately became the talk of the village, where many of the 1,000-strong prison staff lived.

To deter curious onlookers (like myself) from visiting the prison, a special 'exhibit' was operating inside the Ossining Community Centre. It was a mini-Sing Sing, complete with three authentic prison cells, sound-effects, the smell of burnt prison gruel (they had a kitchen for senior citizens in the Community Centre basement) and ... the life-size replica of the electric chair, 'made by the Building Maintenance Vocational Class in Sing Sing prison in 1992,' according to a plate on the wall. And although it was obvious that the chair was not the one that Ilf and Petrov saw in 1935 (the original 'sparky' was moved to Greenhaven penitentiary in 1971), I couldn't tear my gaze from it:

'This is a yellow wooden chair with a high back and arm rests. At first glance it seems innocuous, and if it were not for the leather bracelets with which the hands and feet of the condemned are tied, it could very well stand in some highly moral family home. A deafish grandfather might well be sitting in it to read his newspapers there. But an instant later the chair was very repellent to us, and especially depressing were its polished arm rests. Better not to think about those who had polished them with their elbows ...'

The inmates of the Sing Sing Building Maintenance Vocational Class did a good job replicating the chair, for I could still see my own puzzled reflection in its cold, sinisterly polished arm rests.

The death penalty was abolished in the State of New York in 1968, only to be voted back into law in 1995. I thought I wouldn't be surprised if one day the hard-working old 'sparky' returned to Sing Sing's dreaded 'Death House,' which so far has been converted to a 'Vocational Education Centre' for the inmates.

In a last desperate attempt, I dialled Sing Sing's switchboard number from Ossining's only Italian Deli, which, among other things, had a mysterious 'Mafia Wedge' on its lunch menu. For twenty minutes or so, I had to listen to snippets of Moonlight Sonata as my phone call was bouncing off thick prison walls like a squash ball in one of Sing Sing's exercise yards. In the end, I was put through to a certain Lieutenant Gibson, who staunchly refused to let me see the prison, because, as he put it, all Sing Sing executives were 'very occupied.' The rumours of 'disturbances' inside the prison might have been true, after all.

When I was about to hang up, Lieutenant Gibson said he would leave something for me at the 'front entrance' to Sing Sing. I jumped into a cab.

'Two rows of automobiles stood at a prison gate. Our heart contracted at once when we saw that out of the machine which had driven up simultaneously with us came a stooped, pleasant old man with two large paper bags in his hand … The old man went to the entrance carrying the "outside bundle." What kinsman of his could be sitting there? Probably a son, whom most likely the old man though a well-behaved splendid boy, yet he was a bandit, or maybe even a murderer. Old men have a hard time of it.'

Sixty-five years later, the scene was exactly the same. Except for the old man, of course. As I paced towards the entrance, I nearly bumped into a lanky black youngster, with faded expressionless eyes, coming out of the massive iron gates. In his right hand, he was holding a black rubbish bag with his possessions. He had just been released from Sing Sing.

I always wondered why in prisons all over the world they pack the inmates' scanty belongings in rubbish bags? To humiliate a prisoner for the last time before release?

Had I visited Sing Sing forty or fifty years earlier, I could have assumed that the man, who emerged from the gates with a rubbish bag in his hand, was the son of Ilf and Petrov's 'old man.' In the year 2000, however, he was too young to pass even for a grandson. But I was somehow sure that the old man's hapless offspring had the same expression (or rather lack of it) in his hollow eyes when he was leaving Sing Sing.

This is what prisons, even the most lenient and 'comfortable,' do to people: they drain their eyes and their souls.

And although I didn't make it inside Sing Sing, I suddenly felt I had seen enough.

The parcel, left at the 'front entrance' (like sixty-five years ago, it was still 'fenced off by a grille as large as a lion cage' and guarded by three 'policemen,' each of whom 'weighed no less than two hundred pounds … not of fat but of muscle, pounds used for suppression, for subjugation') contained a brochure on the colourful history of Sing Sing, put together by prison staff with the help of several 'inmate assistants.' The flimsy and badly printed booklet ended with the following statement: 'This document is one of the many prides the employees of Sing Sing (that are ever so giving) hold close to their heart, Thank You. May our paths cross many times again!'

I sincerely hoped this heart-felt wish of the 'ever so giving' Sing Sing employees would never come true.

Santa-Fe

Only four out of forty-eight chapters of *Little Golden America* – a witty and insightful book by two Russian satirists Ilya Ilf and Evgeny Petrov, who criss-crossed the United States in an 'automobile' in 1935 – are each fully devoted to one particular city or town: 'Dearborn,' 'San Francisco,' 'That Horrible Town, Chicago' and 'Santa Fe.' These were obviously the places that had left the most profound (if not always favourable – *pace* Chicago) impression on the tireless tandem of Russian writers. Following in their footsteps sixty-five years later, I could not possibly miss Santa Fe – the historic capital of New Mexico, where Ilf and Petrov spent a couple of days halfway through their eleven-month-long Trans-American journey.

My first impression of Santa Fe was that it looked distinctly un-American. Instead of the habitual brick and wood structures of the American Southwest, it had lots of low-built Spanish-mission-style houses of clay or brown adobe (a clay-like Santa Fe dirt mixed with water and straw and baked in the sun). The main square, the Plaza, was brimming with souvenir stalls, manned by impassive Indians and offering all sorts of 'authentic' Indian decorations and housewares, the bulk of which, I suspected, was made in Malaysia or Taiwan.

In the lobby of the Indian Arts Museum, they were selling *Indian Killer*, a paperback thriller by Sherman Alexie. According to the blurb, the book described the escapades of a 'serial Indian killer' terrorising and murdering the white people of Seattle (which was probably perceived by the Museum curators as a form of Indian art).

Crowds of tourists were milling in the cobbled winding lanes, surrounding the square. These streets were so spotlessly, even lifelessly, clean that they felt plastic. The good old 'Santa Fe dirt' was nowhere to be seen, and I had to (reluctantly) agree with Ilf and Petrov, who wrote in 1935: 'The city as a whole seems somehow artificial, as if it were made for American tourists.'

'The Oldest House in the USA' was now home of 'Upper Crust Pizza' . The two signs were hanging next to each other under the ceiling beams of a solid, heavily buttressed house, next to which an old Indian woman, her face resembling a sun-dried peach, was selling rugs, beads, clay pots and red chillies. And whereas the Pizza sign was most likely true to reality, I had good reasons to doubt the authenticity of the first one: in the course of my American travels I had so far come across at least three state capitals claiming to have America's oldest Capitol building, as least three 'America's oldest' public libraries and a couple of 'America's oldest' synagogues, let alone half-a-dozen newspapers, proudly naming themselves 'America's first' in their mastheads.

America's obsession with old things, natural for a relatively young country, hasn't changed since 1935, when, on their way to Santa Fe, Ilf and Petrov stopped at an old well, advertised as 'the first in America.' It was adorned with a peremptory notice: 'Your grandfather drank water here on his way to California for gold.' Your grandfather might have never been to America and might have spent all his life selling bagels in Odessa, but the poster accepted no objections: it simply knew better.

'Beside the historical well a man sat in his little booth and sold coloured postcards of the same well,' the writers noted with amusement.

While in Santa Fe, Ilf and Petrov stayed at the Hotel Montezuma. Their Spartan room had 'two beds with good springs, several blankets and pillows as flat as a dollar.' They chose 'Montezuma' at random, their only principle of hotel selection being that 'modest travellers should not stop in hotels called "Mayflower".'

It didn't take me long to find out that Hotel Montezuma did not exist any longer. Similar to its namesake, the medieval Aztek emperor of Mexico, overthrown and killed by the Spanish conquistador Cortes, the hotel was blown up (overthrown) and raised to the ground (killed) in the 1960s to clear the space for a more modern structure.

To be fair, there were plenty of hotels still standing in Santa Fe. I wandered into the air-conditioned lobby of the 'historically charming Hotel St Francis' only to discover from its glossy brochure that it was 'handicap accessible' and offered 'basic alerting and phone amplification equipment for the hearing-disabled' and wondered what Ilf and Petrov would have thought of the linguistically handicapped and emotionally disabled modern PC-speak, which seems to have penetrated all spheres of American life.

At another hotel, a 'Bead Expo – International Symposium on Beads' was in progress. Americans adore symposiums and conventions which they regard as a coveted opportunity to get away from it all, preferably at their company's expense. In the lobbies of different hotels around the country, I would periodically bump into happy, wine-glass-fondling participants of a Texas Safety Association Symposium, or of a California Convention of Users (probably on how to use useless conventions to one's own advantage), or of other, no-less mysterious, official get-togethers.

Among dozens of addresses, presentations and workshops of the Bead Symposium, as featured in its lengthy program, there were: a report 'Bead Revolutions: The Role of Beads in Technological Change' by Peter Francis, Jr, 'the director of the Center for Bead Research,' a lecture 'Technology of Bead and Female Amulet Production in Ice Age Europe: Social and Cosmological Implications,' and a workshop 'Fusing Beads, Buttons & Pendants.' I instinctively unbuttoned my shirt-collar (to make sure the buttons were not fused) and went out for lunch.

Here it must be said that after more than five months on the road, the Russians got so fed-up (in the true sense of this word) with 'Anglo-American cooking that has brought forth such hybrids as sweet and sour pickles, bacon fried to the consistency of plywood, or blindingly white and utterly tasteless (no, having the taste of cotton!)

bread,' that they felt exhilarated when they spotted the sign 'Original Mexican Restaurant' in one of Santa Fe's streets. Having observed that the waiters inside the restaurant 'wore orange silk blouses and satin neckties the colour of a drunkard's liver,' they ordered a soup and 'something else called "enchilada". The name of the soup was forgotten because the very first spoon knocked everything out of our heads except the desire to seize a fire extinguisher and to put out the bonfire that broke out in the mouth. As for the enchilada, they proved to be long, appetising blintzes filled with red pepper and gunpowder, thinly cut, and covered with nitro-glycerine.'

To use a PJ O'Rourke expression, after a meal like that, they could probably clean ovens with their breath.

Certain things (like the thermo-nuclear power of Mexican chilli sauces) do not change with time. I found another proof of this truism in the Church of St Miguel, allegedly, the oldest in the USA. Here's what Ilf and Petrov saw there in 1935:

'The abbot ... proved to be a Frenchman and a Franciscan monk. His enterprise was on a commercial footing. In the first place, he took seventy-five cents from us for looking around. The building of the church itself was old, but all the sculptures were new German factory work. But the greedy abbot liked them and assiduously urged us to admire. This led us to conclude that the venerable Franciscan did not know anything at all about art.'

An old black-robed monk, sitting at his desk in the semi-dark ante-room of the church sixty-five years later, was immersed in *The Reader's Digest.* A outsized plastic name-tag on his chest (of the type worn by the FBI agents and the delegates of the Bead Symposia) identified him as 'Brother Regis.' He looked up to take my admission fee of £1 – not too bad considering the inflation. 'Proceed to the church, and they will give you a nice explanation,' he said.

The 'nice explanation' was provided by a short audio tape, which sounded as if it was recorded by a control freak: 'Stand in the middle of the church ... Now you may look back ... Now step back and watch the main door ... Step up the altar and you'll be able to see ...' And so on. I returned to the ante-room, which contained (apart from Brother Regis) a gift shop, dominated by a huge 'Clearance Sale' banner.

I looked in disbelief at the tacky (and grossly overpriced) goodies: puffy angels, crude statuettes of Christ, crucifixes made of straw, Mexican dolls with blank shameless faces, tequila (or vodka?) tumblers with tastelessly painted crosses. A flimsy *One Page History of the Church* cost $1.50. I thought it should have been called 'A Dollar-Fifty History of the Church.'

In one of the shop's corners, I saw a big church bell under the plate 'Jose Bell – Oldest in the USA,' but couldn't find a price tag. 'This bell is not for sale,' Brother Regis declared gravely.

It was good to know that at least something was NOT for sale in this supermarket of human faith.

Tourists kept coming in and out of the church, and Brother Regis, would say to them 'Have a nice day!,' but only to those who had bought something in his Holy Emporium.

The monk's hard-working cash-register was clicking cynically as I was leaving – without a purchase and hence without his cordial American farewell. An exact replica of Ilf and Petrov's 'greedy abbot' of sixty-five years ago, he continued to keep his 'enterprise' on a firm 'commercial footing.'

As for the 'German sculptures,' I found them, covered in dust, in one of the church's alcoves. Only Brother Regis assured me that they came from Italy ...

Ilf and Petrov spent their last evening in Santa Fe in the company of Witter Bynner, 'the famous American poet,' who came to the city in the early 1920s, when Georgia O'Keefe founded an arts colony there. The poet told the Russians that Santa Fe, lying in the centre of three ancient civilisations – Indian, Spanish and Mexican – was home for many writers, artists and poets, who 'fled there from contemporary America.'

'But America fled after them,' he continued. 'Following the poets and the artists, millionaires rushed into Santa Fe. They built villas and likewise breathed the atmosphere of ancient civilisations, having previously stocked up on contemporary dollars.'

Apart from Ted Turner, one of whose ubiquitous villas was pointed to me by a local, there might not be many 'millionaires' left in Santa Fe. But the spirit of blatant commercialism, brought to the city by the money-grabbing entrepreneurs and industrialists of the 1930s and picked up by Ilf and Petrov, still permeates its ancient streets.

Seattle

'The American sits in his office with his coat off and works. He works quietly, unobtrusively, without making any fuss. He is never late anywhere. He has only one telephone ... Should an American say in the course of a conversation, even incidentally, 'I'll do that,' it is not necessary to remind him of anything at all in the future. Everything will be done ...'

from *One-Storied America* by Ilya Ilf and Evgeny Petrov, 1935-36

While in the USA, Ilf and Petrov had a chance to visit two American industrial giants of the 1930s – the factories of General Electric in Schenectady, NY and the automobile plants of Henry Ford in Dearborn, a suburb of Detroit. Despite coming from a hostile country and travelling as correspondents of the *Pravda* newspaper – the main mouthpiece of communist propaganda – they had no problems obtaining all necessary permissions for the visits. 'Our permit was granted very quickly,' they wrote afterwards.

America must have changed a lot since then, for when I tried to obtain permission to visit the same General Electric factories (the process took several weeks and dozens of faxes, emails and frantic phone calls), I got a blunt and unsubstantiated refusal in response. The factory gates that were wide open for *Pravda* correspondents in 1935 were firmly shut for a *Daily Telegraph* writer in the year 2000. And whereas Ilf and Petrov carried away from Schenectady 'an impression of high technical wisdom and organisation,' my only impression of General Electric, even without visiting it, was that of red tape and overcautiousness bordering on paranoia.

Such a setback could lead anyone to believe that the American business world has become less open and more restrictive since the 1930s, but I decided not to jump to conclusions. Banned from seeing modern American industrial culture in action in the East, I decided to try my luck on the country's West Coast and flew to Seattle, the city known as one of the main engine rooms of the computer age.

With Jeff Wright, a leading Seattle property developer, we climbed to the very top of the Space Needle, the city's main landmark, using a steep service ladder. Soon we found ourselves on a small landing, well above the public viewing area. By doing so, we didn't break any rules, for Jeff Wright was the owner of the Space Needle as well as the Chairman of its Board of Directors.

Originally owned by Jeff's father, Howard S Wright, the 605-feet-high tower played a role in the US-Russian space race and was officially opened by President Kennedy in April 1962 – shortly after the Russians unveiled their own Space Obelisk in Moscow. Instead of appearing in person, JFK had to declare the rocket-shaped

Space Needle open by telephone, for he was stuck in Washington, DC trying to deal with the Missile Crisis brewing in Cuba. Since then, the Needle became the official symbol of Seattle, the monument to its unfading entrepreneurial spirit.

'I remember my Dad bringing me up here, when I was three and the Needle was still under construction,' Jeff reminisced. 'He then held me by the ankles and let me peep down …'

I tried to visualise toddler Jeff dangling in the air 600 feet above Seattle. The image was enough to make me dizzy.

'What's your favourite thing about Seattle?' I asked him, looking down at the unknown city, sprawled underneath me like a hastily put together giant jigsaw puzzle.

'It is a home town. People are honest, friendly and outgoing, and the weather allows spending a lot of time out of doors which helps to come up with new ideas and inventions …'

Jeff had a point. My press kit contained a long list of Seattle inventions which included gas station, monorail, water skis, chain saw, hydroplane, colour television, electric guitar, heart defibrillator, desktop publishing, sexless oysters and 'first airplane hijack for money.' Take these innovations away – and the world would become a duller, even if a somewhat quieter, place.

Seattle is now home to some of the world's best known and most successful companies: Microsoft, Boeing, Amazon.com, Cosco and Starbucks to name just a few.

The secret of the city's long-lasting prosperity lies in its relatively short history (it was founded in 1851), dominated by two momentous events: the great fire of 1889 and the Gold Rush. After the whole of the city's business centre burnt down (as a result of a shop apprentice carelessly heating up a plate of glue), it was promptly rebuilt in a much more substantial manner. When gold was discovered in Klondike Valley in 1896, Seattle as the gateway to Alaska became the place where adventurers would stock up on food and equipment before going north. All sorts of businesses flourished. A special 'publicity committee' was formed to spread the stories of Klondike's unspeakable wealth all over the world.

In all the years of the Gold Rush, the diggers discovered $10 million worth of gold. In the meantime, the merchants of Seattle made $20 million without ever setting foot on Alaskan soil. The real Klondike therefore was in Seattle.

This amazing ability to make money out of thin air has become a distinguishing feature of Seattle's business community since then.

A cup of steaming espresso is a new consumerist idol of America, where only several years ago most people from outside New York and Washington, DC did not have a clue as to what it stood for. This coffee revolution was masterminded by one Seattle-based company – Starbucks.

'Starbucks Support Center' said a huge sigh above the entrance to the company's headquarters in Utah Avenue where I turned up one day agonising over not wearing a suit and tie (I didn't take any on this trip). Mr Soon Beng Yeap, the company's PR manager, who greeted me in reception, put me at ease: 'We wouldn't have let you in in a suit,' he smiled. He himself was in his shirt-sleeves, whereas the only person in the office who was wearing a suit was Mr Howard Schultz, the Chief Executive and the founder of Starbucks, but only because he had a business meeting with some Japanese visitors later in the day, as Mr Soon Beng Yeap explained apologetically. He told me that Mr Schultz did not have an office of his own, but kept walking around the building all day long. This reminded me of Ilf and Petrov's meeting with Henry Ford, who, as they wrote 'did not lock himself in, but was constantly on the go through the plant.' 'Mr Ford circulates,' his employees used to say.

Well, I saw Mr Schultz 'circulating' around the office Henry-Ford-like, his suit and tie standing out among t-shirts and cardigans like a birch tree in a forest of conifers. The office itself was a curious hybrid of an exhibition hall (paintings on the walls, lots of flowers), a coffee shop (everyone seemed to be drinking coffee all the time) and a nursery (little kids were running in between desks).

'Why do you call yourselves Support Center?' I asked Dave Olsen, Starbuck's Senior Vice-President (he was sporting a beige polo shirt, by the way).

'It means that we executives are not the most important people in the company. Our most important people are there, with our customers.'

Sipping an espresso, he proceeded to tell me that, for the first time in American history, Starbucks offered medical benefits, profit shares and share options to its part-time staff; that their success was due to the concept of 'the 3d Place' (a coffee-shop – between work and home) which they had developed; that their plan was to expand to … Italy. 'Coffee is a democratic drink and it was not popular in America, dominated by the soft-drink market, until recently. We have created another resource for the Americans to lead their lives …'

Dave volunteered to see me to the lift. 'You know, my ex-wife hated the informality of this building,' he said as we shook hands.

'Whoever his ex-wife was, she wasn't a coffee drinker,' I thought on my way down.

Ilf and Petrov had little problem arranging a meeting with Henry Ford in 1935. My in-advance request for an interview with Bill Gates, the Henry Ford of computer-age America, was denied by Microsoft for the simple reason that 'to see Bill is as hard as getting an audience with the Pope.' I said that I actually had an audience with the Pope in 1991, but it didn't help. It was already in Seattle that I read a column by Emmet Watson in *Seattle Times* – all about his failed attempts to fix a short meeting with Bill Gates, who was evidently much busier (if not much holier) than the Pope. At least I wasn't the only one whose request was turned down. And although the gates to Gates were firmly shut for me, I was nevertheless invited to visit Microsoft's Main Campus (that was what they called it!) in Redmond – about thirty miles east of Seattle.

'Where is everybody?' I asked Mark Thomas, Microsoft's International PR Manager, who met me on the steps of 'Building 19' of the compound, which looked indeed like an upmarket university campus in the middle of summer holidays. On that ordinary working afternoon, the grounds of the world's most successful company, with over 30,000 employees worldwide, were deserted, not counting occasional joggers and a group of youngsters playing volleyball on a green lawn behind a fountain. The only vehicle in sight was a 'Microsoft Copyright Security' van, slowly cruising around the Campus.

'They can be anywhere,' he replied with a smile. 'At home, at a library, or on a beach. We don't have office hours and can move around freely. For example, I have five things to do this year. If I did them the old way, I'd be here twenty-four hours a day. But, although we all have offices, it doesn't matter where I am, for I can tap into my computer from anywhere. We are successful because we have rejected a starched-shirt office environment.'

True, I saw no starched shirts in the brightly lit corridors of Microsoft. To be honest, I haven't seen many t-shirts either. Like the rest of the Campus, the offices were semi-deserted, and it was almost a surprise to find David Pritchard, the company's HR Director and one of Bill Gates' closest mates, bent over his desk, overhung with photos of rock stars.

'What are you doing here?' I asked him. 'I am having fun,' he said seriously.

'But you are supposed to be in charge of the employment for the whole of Microsoft,' I objected meekly.

'This is what I mean! It is great fun to be working here trying to employ the people who are capable of change, who do not sit on laurels but have a flexible long-term view. And although I am proud of my impact on the company, my main goal is to hire people better than I am …'

The volley-ball players were still jumping on the lawn when I was leaving Building 19. None of them looked hippyish or nerdish – the image many wrongly associate with Microsoft employees (or 'Microsofties' as they call them in Seattle). They all had young, open faces and neat hair-cuts. A bunch of smart guys playing a serious game, they were – quite literally – falling over themselves to do it right.

A blonde bespectacled lad picked up the ball. Bill Gates (or was it his mid-1970s self look-alike) was ready to serve …

New Orleans

A life-long admirer of Ilya Ilf and Evgeny Petrov, two Russian satirists, who travelled in the USA in 1935-36 and recorded their impressions in the book *Little Golden America*, I was rather disappointed by their sketchy and half-hearted description of New Orleans, the country's most idiosyncratic city, which they visited towards the end of their eleven-month-long trans-American journey. The reasons for such aloofness were explained by the writers themselves: 'New Orleans is a beautiful city ... But the feeling of indifference and boredom, which overcame our automobile group after New Year's Eve, like a never-ceasing rain pouring constantly from an ever-cloudy sky, did not even think of leaving us. We have skimmed the cream of the journey. Man is not equipped to enjoy himself eternally. Therefore, all the beauty of New Orleans was appreciated only with our minds. The heart was speechless.'

What a pity! According to the 1938 WPA guide to the 1930s New Orleans, at the time of the Russians' visit, the city was still a half-European, half-American melange, a sultry meeting ground for 'the imps, the pimps, and the shrimps,' with a characteristic 'live-and-let-live' liberal attitude toward human frailties. It was the place where a thriving voodoo cult could still be found in Congo Square; where sixty cents could buy you lunch at the famous Galatoire's; where a seven-cent streetcar ride took you past banana wharves and molasses sheds, and the French Quarter still rang each morning with the calls of the coal peddler and the blackberry woman – while at night ghostly denizens walked the upper stories of grand mansions and humble cottages alike ... One had to be deaf and blind, or else extremely tired (which was obviously the case with Ilf and Petrov), to skim through a city like that.

Retracing the writers' footsteps sixty-five years later, I couldn't help being influenced by their attitude to New Orleans. At least, initially.

My first couple of hours in the city substantiated Ilf and Petrov's feeling of detachment: I liked the un-American smells of tobacco and chicory permeating Le Vieux Carre – the city's French Quarter – but otherwise its shabbiness, its eclectic colonial architecture, its ostentatious (and somewhat threatening) hustle-and-bustle left my heart 'speechless.' The French street names sounded pretentious, and the whole place looked a mess – a bad imitation of Europe, uncertain of its past, present and future.

This initial impression gradually transformed as I was dining at Arnaud's, the much-celebrated Creole restaurant in Rue Bienville, where the waiters were so friendly and intelligent that I felt like inviting all of them to my next birthday party. Creole dishes struck me as coarse and spicy – a bit like New Orleans itself. And the cocktails ... The indigenous Sazerac was an unlikely mixture of Bourbon whisky, vermouth, absinthe, sugar and orange bitters, whereas Ramos Gin Fizz was a concoction of gin, egg whites(!), sugar and lemon-and-lime. They both tasted great.

'In New Orleans, we take something simply delicious and make it into something decadent,' one of the waiters commented in response to my protracted: M…mmm.'

I also noticed that, unlike in many other American restaurants, women were still invited to place their orders first at Arnaud's.

'We don't embrace all this PC garbage in New Orleans,' another waiter explained.

After dinner, the French Quarter's cheerful raucousness was no longer irritating. 'New Orleans is a Sazerac of cultures,' I scribbled hastily in my notebook while elbowing my way along bustling Bourbon Street – the hub of New Orleans' never-ending fun. It was the first of the many metaphors that kept haunting me in the Big Easy (one of the city's numerous nicknames). Never before had my uncomplaining memo pad registered so many comparisons and similes – my futile attempts to catch the evasive spirit of New Orleans. Never before had they come off the tip of my pen so easily. Never before had my shaky scribbles been so hard to decipher the following morning, as if they had somehow recorded the erratic cardiogram of New Orleans – the city's jumpy heartbeat.

I ended my first night in New Orleans dancing in the plywood shed of Preservation Hall, home of one of the city's best-known jazz bands. For lack of a dancing partner, I was pressing my faithful notebook closely to my chest.

A lonely saxophonist was playing *It's a Wonderful World* all night long behind the windows of my Monteleone Hotel in the heart of the French Quarter. The music didn't stop me from sleeping and seeing wonderful Technicolor dreams. When I woke up, I knew I was head-over-heels in love with the 'wonderful world' of New Orleans.

The macabre mood in which Ilf and Petrov arrived in New Orleans, explains their gruesome fascination with 'above-ground' cemeteries – the only detailed description in their woolly portrait of The City That Care Forgot (another New Orleans' nickname). But even there they largely missed the plot. Having noted that 'no matter where they try to dig the ground' in New Orleans, 'they find water' and hence 'people always bury their dead in the manner of the ancient Egyptians, in sarcophagi, above the earth,' they concluded that this 'two-storied brick dullness makes the cemetery reminiscent of a small American town.'

To me, the cemeteries of New Orleans were anything but dull. I was quite taken by the way a caretaker (or a 'director of operations' – her modern PC job title) of St Louis Cemetery No 1 greeted a funeral procession at the cemetery gates – with a broad smile on her face. Like everything else, they seemed to take death easy in the Big Easy, where it is not unusual to have jazz played or a cocktail party held among the double-decker tombs.

'New Orleans is a rough place, but my cemetery is safe,' the same caretaker told me with pride which reminded me of the dubious Soviet-style poster I once saw in the office of a Moscow graveyard – 'Let Us Turn Our Cemetery into Muscovites' Favourite Resting Place.'

The plush Bultman's Funeral Home in the prestigious Garden District of New Orleans is often hired out for fun gatherings, musical recitals and business functions. Having a company's board meeting at a funeral home would be bizarre anywhere else, but not in the Big Easy which constantly celebrates life – even after death. 'People come to us to have fun,' a black-clad Bultman's official assured me with a professional sombre grin.

In 1980 a businessman from Houston, Texas chose New Orleans' Lafayette Cemetery as the site for his wedding. The ceremony was held in one of the cemetery isles, while a lone trumpet played *Summertime*. The bride and groom, both married previously, told the graveyard superintendent (executive director of operations?) that they had come to New Orleans to bury their past.

While in New Orleans, I was tempted to compare it to:

- A joyful scream.
- A gentle shock.
- A sophisticated mess – like a Cajun dish or an Arnaud's cocktail.
- A cup of strong black coffee that cheers you up and keeps you awake throughout the night.
- A friendly blow in the solar plexus that leaves you bent over and gasping for breath, yet with a blissful smile on your face.
- The Blue Dog from the paintings of George Rodrigue, a local Cajun artist, who places a pale-blue icon of his late dog, Tiffany, on all his canvases, irrespective of their theme. The canine image seems irrelevant at a first glance, but the longer you look at a painting, the more mesmerising and eye-catching it becomes.
- A glass of wine to go. New Orleans is the only American city outside Las Vegas with no closing law which means that alcohol is on sale twenty-four hours a day; it is the city where you can ask for a 'to-go' plastic cup of wine at a bar and drink it behind the wheel of your car. It is the city where one often bumps into pedestrians with glasses of champagne in their hands. In a broader sense, New Orleans is a 'movable feast,' a flask of good wine that you carry with you wherever you are.
- A *trompe l'oeil*, similar to the one of a huge clarinet on the wall of the Holiday Inn Hotel, built on the spot where – out of a sophisticated cacophony of numerous street bands – modern jazz was born in 1890. Understanding New

> Orleans takes some adjustment of vision, for it is never quite like what it looks from a distance.

Whatever the metaphor, there's no better place to re-charge yourself with hope, optimism and joie de vivre than New Orleans. 'Laissez Les Bons Temps Rouler' ('Let the good times roll') is an old Cajun expression which remains the city's main (and only) rule of life. On my last night in the Big Easy, as I was lying wide awake in my bed listening to the muffled sounds of street jazz, mixed with distant nostalgic whistles of South Pacific trains, I suddenly visualised New Orleans as a deviant vintage rail car that had come uncoupled from the gleaming express train of modern America. Derailed and rudderless, it keeps rolling ahead on its own – jingling, clattering and opening its squeaky doors only to those who board it with singing, not 'speechless,' hearts.

Small Town America

Eleven years after my defection from the Soviet Union I was finally returning to Moscow. I was travelling without a Russian visa, for the Moscow I was heading for was in America, just a two-hour drive from New York.

I consciously chose Moscow, Pennsylvania (population 1,500), as the final point of my long journey in the footsteps of Ilf and Petrov, Soviet satirists who drove across the USA in 1935 and summarised their impressions in the book *Little Golden America.* The writers saw America as 'preponderantly a country of one-story and two-story houses,' ie the land of villages and small towns, the perception which – sixty-five years later – I was ready to share.

Just like the Russians, I passed through countless little American towns and came to the conclusion that they reflected the country's character much better than its big and smoky metropolises.

'Everlasting is the automobile and gasoline tedium of small cities,' remarked Ilf and Petrov before observing that, to beat the 'tedium,' some of them 'make heroic efforts to distinguish themselves from their brethren of the same type.' They illustrated their point by quoting the road signs, 'hung at the entrance to the town, quite, let us say, like signs over the entrance to a store, so that the customer may know what is being sold there. "Redwood City." And under it in verse is written: "Climate best by government test!" ' The writers also mentioned another town's entrance sign: 'The Biggest Small Town In The United States.'

I can testify to the fact that the sixty-five years that ensued did little to diminish small-town America's megalomania and its childish passion for clumsy doggerels.

'To select the ideal vegetation
For our city curbside decoration
Required some botanical discrimination
And horticultural education.'

This is the opening verse of the poem 'Petunias' by Ruth Hopkins which I found in *River Life* – a newspaper published in Pierre, the capital of South Dakota. With its incongruous Capitol building, open to the public twenty-four hours a day, Pierre (population 12,000) is a rather charming small town, where strangers say 'Hi!' to you in the street and, if you ask for directions, there is a good chance you will be offered a lift. Despite being designated a state capital, in its heart Pierre remains an archetypal 'cowtown' – friendly and sheepish in equal measure.

'What sort of beer are you drinking, buddy?' a local man in a blue singlet asked me as I was sitting on the bank of the Missouri, with a glass of Chardonnay in my hand. Having learnt that I was from London, the man inquired if it was very hot there and whether I knew Steve.

Pierre, whose only claim to fame is that 'Dances with Wolves' was filmed there, seems to be in the grip of two obsessions: petunias in the streets ('To make our hometown famous and pretty, Pierre will become The Petunia City' – *pace* unforgettable Ruth Hopkins) and guns.

'Sorry, we are closed, please come again!' ran a polite sign on the door of 'River Traders Gun Shop' – one of many similar stores in Pierre, where the only forthcoming 'events,' advertised in a local newsletter, were marathon shoots, gun club sitter shoots, handgunners pin matches, bowling pin shoots, Dacota Territory Muzzleloaders meetings, and even a 'Ladies and Juniors .22 Pistol Shoot.'

I couldn't help the uneasy feeling that it was one of those towns where friendly locals periodically go berserk and, for no obvious reason, start spraying everything around them (including the ubiquitous petunias) with bullets.

Unlike Pierre, the Vermont town of Cavendish had a real opportunity to 'distinguish itself from its brethren of the same type': Alexander Solzhenitsyn, the great Russian writer and the Nobel Prize winner, had spent seventeen years of his exile there. Yet, its residents chose to forsake Solzhenitsyn in favour of their compatriot Phineas Gage, a nineteenth century railway foreman, who once had his tamping iron accidentally blown through his skull and out of the top of his head – and survived. I could hardly believe my eyes, when I saw a granite memorial to the vivacious foreman in the middle of the town square.

While in Cavendish, I also learnt that the Phineas Gage Historic Festival and Anniversary Commemoration to mark 150 years from the day when poor Phineas' head underwent its historic piercing was held there in 1998. The events of this Rod-Through-the-Head Commemoration Festival included a 'BBQ chicken lunch, hosted by American Legion Post!' The sheer mockery of commemorating the piercing of Phineas Gage with a barbecue was lost on the proud natives of Cavendish, who now want to make the Festival (and the barbecue, no doubt) an annual occasion.

But by far the most peculiar American town that I have visited during my travels was Whittier in Alaska. This 'city' (as it insists on being referred to) on the shores of Prince William Sound could easily market itself as the world's only one-house municipality, for all its 334 residents live in one fourteen-storeyed Begich Tower – until recently, Alaska's tallest building. To be precise, only 333 people reside in the skyscraper: one maverick chose to escape the high-rise hustle-and-bustle by settling down in an abandoned bus, terminally parked in the harbour.

The Tower, built by the US military during World War II, has all necessary conveniences: shops, restaurants, a laundromat, a post office, a museum (down the hall from the post office), a beauty salon, and even a church. There used to be a small jail there too, but it had to close down for lack of offenders. One floor is occupied by the 'city government,' headed by Carrie Williams, the outgoing and chain-smoking 'City Manager.' The Tower also accommodates two rival newspapers – the mild-mannered *Whittier Sentinel* and the censorious *Turnagain Times*, but has only one public 'restroom.'

The initial decision to house all the town's residents in one building was an attempt to minimise clearing away of snow, of which there's no shortage in Whittier in winter. When the military left in 1963, the town, sorry the city, went into hibernation, only occasionally interrupted by the Alaska Railroad trains from Anchorage bringing tourists for Glacier Cruises in the Sound.

The railroad had been the mini-city's only link to the outside world (not counting a tiny airstrip, left by the military and locally known as 'Whittier International Airport') until the Whittier-bound extension of the Alaska Marine Highway was completed. The town is now preparing for a boom and the average price of a Begich Tower condominium has already skyrocketed from $15,000 to $30,000.

Alas, prosperity doesn't come cheap these days: with the number of annual visitors expected to jump twelvefold, Whittier's 'city government' will most probably have to invest in a second public restroom.

* * *

'The machine flies down the road. Little cities flash by. What pretentious names! Siracuse, Pompeii, Batavia, Warsaw, Caledonia, Waterloo, Geneva, Moscow – a little Moscow, where you can get lunch Number 2 in a drug-store, griddle cakes with maple syrup, and where for dinner you are entitled to sweet-salty pickles, where in the motion-picture theatre a film of bandit life is unreeled – a purely American Moscow,' wrote Ilf and Petrov in 1935.

There are about a dozen little Moscows all over America, and Moscow, Pennsylvania, where I decided to terminate my journey, was no different from many other small American towns. Cars were passing through it without slowing down. It didn't even have a 'motion-picture theatre.' A short town profile, kindly emailed to me by Lackawanna County CVB, mentioned 'three playgrounds offering recreation for children of all ages' and the annual Moscow Country Fair.

I failed to locate a single playground, but spotted a row of rusty tracks and a half-ruined wooden shed of a long-deserted railway station, with the word 'Moscow' still clearly visible on its battered façade. I also ticked off a 'China Delight' takeaway, a 'Synergy' hair salon, a 'Moscow Vol Fire & Hose Company' and, encouragingly, a 'Vital Link Chiropractic Center.' It was good to know that I still had some sort of a link to Moscow.

The only building of note was a colonial-revival mansion on the hill. 'This building was given by Joseph Loveland to the men of Moscow to be used as YMCA,' ran a memorial plate above the porch. Well, Joseph Loveland would have been upset to learn that, contrary to his wishes, the mansion now housed Moscow Borough Police Department and – aptly – 'Women's Self-Defence Courses,' too.

'Ask Why We Are Successful' invited a poster above a dingy car-wash outlet. I wanted to ask but there was no one inside. Behind the car wash, the town ended.

I sat down on the grass, opened a copy of *Moscow Villager*, which I had picked up in the general store, and read the lead story: 'On the first day of this fine month, Moscow's Borough Council conducted the first of its two regular monthly meetings … Council offered its congratulations to fellow Council member, solicitor Zero (*sic* – VV), who recently became the father of a bouncing baby boy … Zero now has enough members in his household to warrant two recyclable (*sic* – VV) bins …'

'We can say honestly, with hand on heart, that we wouldn't like to live in America,' Ilf and Petrov wrote in the end of their book. As for me, I was not sure about the rest of America, but I knew for certain that I did not want to live in Moscow, Pennsylvania, even if they offered me all the *recyclable* bins in the world.

Having looked up from the paper, I noticed a 'Moscow Borough Police' van cruising nearby. A patrolman inside was staring at me suspiciously. Reading a newspaper on the grass was probably an offence in this town.

I walked back to my car, started the engine and, for the second time in my life, **defected** from Moscow – never to return.

A Day in Mexico

'A Day in Mexico' is one of my favourite chapters in *Little Golden America* – a quirky and insightful travel book by Ilya Ilf and Evgeny Petrov, two Russian scribes who criss-crossed the USA in 1935-36. As it transpires from the chapter's title, they made a brief foray into Mexico while staying in the Texan city of El Paso. They only had to walk across 'a bridge over the Rio Grande … and there it was Mexico – the city of Juarez.'

The seeming ease of their walkabout was complicated by the writers' fear of borders: they were wary of – literally – making a *faux pas*, which for them, citizens of the Stalinist USSR, could prove – no less literally – fatal. 'We were afraid to go to Mexico,' they wrote and explained: 'On our passports was a one-year visa for staying in the United States … But every visa ends automatically as soon as you leave the country … Horror possessed us at the very thought that the remainder of our days we should have to pass in the city of Juarez, located in the Mexican state of Chihuahua. On the other hand, we wanted very much to be in Mexico.'

In the end, the Russians must have recalled one of the unwritten rules of Soviet life: 'If something is forbidden, but very much desired – then it is allowed' – and ventured onto the bridge. A cigar-smoking (it was 1935, don't forget!) American immigration official, having carefully scrutinised their passports, kindly escorted them over to the Mexican 'border station.' 'There, true enough, near a booth stood a saffron-faced man with a dirtyish neck, dressed in a dazzling uniform of dark-coloured khaki, with gold pipings. But on the face of the Mexican border official was utter contempt for the duties imposed upon him. On his face was sketched: "Yes, a sad fate has obliged me to wear this beautiful uniform, but I will not soil my graceful hands by looking over nasty scraps of paper. No! You will never live to see that done by the honourable Juan Ferdinand Cristobal Collbajos!" We … were very glad that we had come across such an honourable hidalgo, and quickly walked down the main street of Juarez.'

Ilf and Petrov had a full day in Juarez: they tasted Mexican food, visited a church, witnessed a street rally and attended a bullfight. On their way back to the States, they walked past 'Juan Ferdinand Cristobal Collbajos,' who as before, paid no attention to them …

Although I tried to follow in Ilf and Petrov's footsteps as closely as possible in my trans-American journey sixty-five years on, certain deviations from their itinerary were inevitable. Unlike the Russians, who stopped in El Paso, I spent several days in Lajitas, a border town priding itself in being 'the remotest settlement in the USA.' A small Mexican hamlet of Paso Lajitas was a stone's throw away, across the Rio Grande. Similar to my predecessors, I was very keen on the idea of venturing across the border and adding Mexico to the list of fifty-odd countries which I had visited in the last ten years.

My indisputable advantage over Ilf and Petrov was that I had a multiple-entry US visa in my passport, and with the Cold War firmly in the past I did not expect any complications resulting from my distinctly Russian-sounding name in the unlikely, as I hoped, event of my detention by frontier-guards.

I knew that the 2,000 mile US-Mexican border was guarded, even if sporadically. On the way to Lajitas, our bus was stopped a couple of times by heavily armed (and heavily sweating) US border guards, dressed in dark-green battle fatigues and cowboy hats, for perfunctory checks. They were looking for drugs, which smugglers, as they explained, often hid inside *pinatas*, traditional Mexican toys. Having made sure that none of the passengers was carrying *pinatas*, they wished us a nice day and waved the bus through. Border-patrolling, like almost everything else in Texas, seemed to be taken easy. No wonder a leading American Mexico specialist recently compared the US-Mexico border to 'a sieve blasted by buckshot.'

The residents of Lajitas assured me that they routinely went to Paso Lajitas for a cheapish Mexican lunch – and thus encouraged, I eventually decided to follow their lead.

With my dog-eared Australian passport in my breast pocket (and with a good deal of trepidation underneath), I walked down to the Rio Grande one scorching afternoon. I nearly turned back, having spotted an empty 'Waco Christian School' van parked on the river bank, next to a strict 'Permits Required' signpost: anything coming from Waco, Texas, could be safely regarded as a bad omen.

A battered leaking boat, paddled by a bearded Charon look-alike, materialised from nowhere. I jumped in without thinking. The dark-green waters of the Rio Grande (or was it indeed the Styx?) were opaque and uninviting. My grim Mexican ferryman didn't utter a word throughout the crossing. 'Permits' were obviously *not* required. Nor was conversation.

Having barely stepped onto the Mexican soil, I saw two Mexican soldiers, their tunics unbuttoned, having a siesta in the shade of a tree. 'Border guards,' I thought with awe, bracing myself for an unpleasant encounter. But, being probably the descendants of the honourable Juan Ferdinand Cristobal Collbajos, they didn't pay the slightest attention to me.

Another unshaven type appeared and offered me a lift to the village, only several hundred yards away, in his jalopy of a pick-up truck. Just like 'Charon,' he was taciturn and seemingly altruistic (he adamantly rejected payment). I wondered whether they both received commissions from one of the village's restaurants.

The first thing that struck Ilf and Petrov in Juarez 'were smells of fried food, burned oil, garlic, red pepper,' so different from 'the odour of gasoline, which reigns in the United States.' When I got off the pick-up truck in the centre of Paso Lajitas, I was hardly able to smell (or to see) anything at all. A dust storm was raging above the village. Rags, empty plastic bags and torn newspapers were flying in the air. The wind, like a bored village bully, was tugging aimlessly at the permanently unlocked doors of lop-sided clay bungalows, trying to tear them off their rusty hinges.

When clouds of dust somewhat dispersed, I started along the unpaved main (and only) street of the village. Escorted by a couple of sorry-looking dogs with dust-ridden tearful eyes, I went past skeletons of ruined cars, past an empty water tank, past an unexpectedly clean and freshly painted basketball pitch (the only bit of the village that seemed to be properly maintained). A lonely satellite dish on a holey house roof, hastily patched up with rubber-foam, looked alien and out-of-place – like a stranded UFO, which had landed here by mistake. Further down the street, I stumbled over a toy truck, abandoned in the dirt and no-less-decrepit than its full-size counterparts lining the road. Everything in Paso Lajitas spoke poverty and despair of the proportions I had only seen in the most deprived parts of Romania and on some East London council estates.

A man in a greasy singlet sat on the steps of *Tienda Rural*, the village general store, swigging beer from a can. Inside, a sad-faced and dark-eyed teenage girl of about fifteen was rocking a baby behind the counter. The stock was limited to rolls of toilet paper, cans of chillies, several packets of cornflakes, one (!) bottle of *Kahlua* – a strong Mexican liquor – and a couple of crude wooden eagles.

'Where did he buy the beer?' I asked the girl pointing at the man outside, barely visible through a grimy shop window. 'In America,' she replied with a clear-cut Texan accent. ' I went to school there,' she explained, having registered my surprise. 'All village children do, although it is kinda illegal …' Her lips parted in a radiant half-smile that momentarily lit up the shop's gloomy interior.

She told me that she was born in America, since village women always preferred giving birth across the border. 'There's little choice: the nearest Mexican town is two hours away …'

'Why aren't you at school now?' I asked.

'I kinda dropped out,' she shrugged, squinting at the baby in her arms.

In the shop's tiny 'front garden,' all plants were dead, except for one fading red rose, its few remaining petals covered with thick layer of dust. It was obvious that the miraculously surviving flower wouldn't last here for much longer …

I had a late and solitary lunch of *Platillo Mexicano* – a plentiful Mexican food platter – at *Los Amigos*, the village's only functioning restaurant (which made the choice easy), and washed it down with a bottle of local *Carta Blanca* lager. The meal was prepared by a fat Mexican woman, who lived next door. When she saw me approaching, she waddled out of her hut and into the restaurant and, without saying a word, started cooking. The dining area was Spartan, yet clean, and the menu was in English. The place was obviously targeting clients from across the border. Behind the window, ostriches were grazing among rusty carcasses of smashed cars. The woman's son, a little boy called Orlando, was running in and out of the kitchen munching a *burrito* …

My return journey to the USA passed without incident, and soon I was back in my air-conditioned hotel room in Lajitas watching CNN. Larry King was grilling his guest, but, staring at the screen, I could only see the eyes of the Mexican girl from the store – the eyes full of quiet resignation to all the injustices of fate.

I switched off the TV, opened my copy of *Little Golden America* and reread the last paragraph of the 'A Day in Mexico' chapter: 'Having travelled considerably in the United States, we had become so accustomed to good roads, to good service, to cleanliness and comfort that we stopped taking any note of it. But after one day in Mexico we began to appreciate once again … all the material achievements of the United States. It is useful at times, in order to know a country the better, to leave it for a day.'

With sadness, I had to conclude that the last sixty-five years did little to bridge the gap between the First and the Third Worlds, still securely separated by the narrow and virtually unguarded stretch of the Rio Grande.

Part Ten
My Mini-Discoveries

The Enclaves of Europe

'Perchance on your penknife you'll find
A speck of dust from lands afar,
The world will once again arise
Mysterious, wrapped in veil bizarre …'
Alexander Blok

At moments of sadness and indecision, I often wander off to Ely Place – a seemingly unremarkable cul-de-sac off Holborn Circus in the centre of London. Passing through the ornate iron gates, separating this quiet little street from the hustle-and-bustle of Holborn, is like entering a mysterious 'fourth dimension,' the name of which is dislocation.

This straight tree-less lane, the former residence of the Bishops of Ely, is not officially part of London. It is a little corner of Cambridgeshire, still enjoying freedom from entry by the London Police, except by the invitation of the Commissioners of Ely Place – its own elected governing body. The results of the latest elections, duly dated and certified by 'J Franks, Esq, Clerk to the Commissioners,' are displayed on the notice-board of the magnificent St Etheldreda Chapel – the oldest Roman Catholic church in Britain – halfway up the street.

One of London's best-kept secrets, Ely Place is a living anachronism from medieval times when the influential Bishops were determined to remain in their Cambridgeshire diocese even while on ministerial missions in the capital. In the local pub, one can view a stack of recent letters addressed to 'Ye Olde Mitre Tavern, Ely Place, Holborn Circus, Cambridgeshire.'

Why does this place agree with me so well? Why does it evoke in me the peculiar feeling of being elsewhere – the sensation both calming and disturbing? Is it due to the fact that as a Ukrainian-born Russian with an Australian passport and British residence I am a thoroughly 'dislocated' person myself?

Whatever it is, Ely Place never fails to charge my batteries with the high-octane energy of discovery. Making a discovery is like writing a poem, for which, if we believe Boris Pasternak, one doesn't have to look up in the sky (or to board a long-haul flight – to paraphrase and to 'update' the classic slightly), since there is plenty of it scattered in the grass underneath our feet. One only has to go to the trouble of spotting it, bending down and picking it up. The very existence of Ely Place is proof of the fact that the most wonderful discoveries can be made right on our doorstep – in Europe, in Britain, or even in London which we think we know so well, whereas in actual fact we don't.

Ely Place can be also regarded as a fully operational model of one of the most obscure features of modern Europe – the existence on its map of a handful of the so-called enclaves (also known as 'exclaves' or 'outliers') – parts of one country totally surrounded and landlocked by the territory of another. Many of them appeared in the Middle Ages – after the Treaties of Madrid (1526) and of Westphalia (1648), the latter ending the Thirty Years War and creating diverse and independent principalities which made the map of Europe resemble a sloppily manufactured patchwork quilt. Others resulted from landownership disputes, or plain mistakes. With the advent of capitalism, Napoleonic wars, creation of German and Italian states and the Swiss confederation, most of the enclaves were eventually reattached to their mother-countries or swallowed up by host-states. Verenahof, a German village in Switzerland, was the last European enclave to lose its status as recently as in 1964, when it was happily absorbed by the Swiss.

Not counting Vennbahn, a Belgian railway cutting into Germany south of Aachen to form several Belgian 'pockets' (see Part Seven of this book), and three Alpine Austrian villages that can only be accessed from Switzerland or Germany (so-called 'pene-enclaves'), only four 'proper' enclaves can now be found in Europe. They are: Campione d'Italia – an Italian town in Switzerland; Llivia – a Spanish (or rather Catalan) town in the French Pyrenees; Busingen – a German village in Switzerland; and Baarle-Nassau/Baarle-Hertog – a unique Dutch/Belgian municipality comprising twenty-two patches of Belgium and eight of Holland.

It took me months to locate and to visit all four. The enclaves' near-obscurity is a shame, for their ambivalent and often ambiguous status makes them ideal for studying the increasingly cross-cultural and cross-national character of Europe. There are no better places for exploring the growing interdependency of European nations, further boosted by the introduction of the euro, as well as their struggle to preserve their ethnic, cultural and linguistic peculiarities. Politics aside, each of them is resplendent with fascinating (often schizophrenic) idiosyncrasies of everyday life making these geographical and historical anomalies into perfect destinations for an inquisitive, knowledge-hungry traveller.

Having come to explore Campione d'Italia, I was put up at a hotel in Como, about twenty kilometres away, and had to cross the Swiss-Italian border several times a day. This was irritating due to long tailbacks and the unpredictability of the customs officers who would occasionally wave my car aside for inspection. Being part of Italy, Campione is nevertheless not part of the EU (it is excluded from membership by a special Protocol), although its residents as Italian passport holders have the right to live and work in any EU member country – but not in Switzerland, on whose territory Campione is located. What a mess! No wonder Kristina, a local journalist, confided in me that she didn't know who she was: 'In Switzerland, they take me for an Italian, whereas in Italy, they dismiss me as a Swiss.'

To add (Swiss?) apples to (Italian?) oranges, I soon discovered that although the residents of Campione slipped Italian voting papers into Italian ballot boxes choosing from the competing parties in the Peninsula, they received their salaries in Swiss francs, to suit the prices that were Swiss. The safeguarding of law and order was entrusted to the Como-based Italian police unit, and every time a policeman went home after the beat, he had to leave his weapons in Campione, in accordance with a Swiss law forbidding foreigners to carry arms across Switzerland.

The Campionese drove around in cars with TI number plates for Ticino, the neighbouring Swiss canton, and carried Swiss driving licences, but mailed their letters with stamps of the Italian Republic. Paradoxically, they were not expected to show their Italian passports when going to Switzerland, but were routinely checked when travelling to their native Italy. 'I always have my passport with me, just in case,' said Fedra, my Campione-based guide.

It all started in the year 777, when Totone, a local landowner, tried to buy an indulgence for his sins by donating his holdings, including the fishing village of Campione, to the Basilica of St Ambrose in Milan. As a result, Campione fell under the rule of the Milanese ecclesiastical authorities, and not those of nearby Como, as would have been more logical. Miraculously, this illogical bond survived all the ups and downs of history, including Napoleonic wars and numerous attempts by the Swiss to reclaim the village for themselves.

Campione's modern townscape is stunning: narrow streets winding up and down the hill; mountains, spotted with red-roofed houses, as if suffering from measles; the mirror-like surface of the Lugano lake. This Italian town looks and feels distinctly un-Italian – in its tidiness, in the absence of washing on the balconies, in the quiet demeanour of the locals who seldom gesticulate and/or raise their voices. Its spotlessly clean Italian coffee-shops sell inimitable Italian espresso, for which you have to pay in Swiss francs. Two seemingly incompatible life-styles packed into one square kilometre of the town, once poetically compared by Giovanni Cenzato to 'a little Italian boy wearing a Swiss costume.'

In his *1891 Handbook to Southern France*, Karl Baedeker – somewhat disdainfully – referred to Llivia as 'a dirty village of ancient origin with some ruins remaining.' It is a pity that the great guidebook writer overlooked the most interesting feature of Llivia – the only Spanish enclave in Europe.

Founded by ancient Romans, Llivia had been a pawn in Franco-Spanish struggles up until 1659, when the Peace of the Pyrenees Treaty gave thirty-three 'villages' (*sic*) in the Cerdagne Plain to Louis XIV of France. The French thought that Llivia was included in the transfer, but the Spanish regarded the territory not as a village (*pueblo*), but as a town (*villa*). Having spotted the discrepancy, the patriotic residents of Llivia, who wanted to remain Spanish, claimed that the Treaty had nothing to do with them, and the French had to agree. So we may assume that the enclave status of Llivia was the result of a simple historical boo-boo.

Today's Llivia is much less 'dirty' than it, allegedly, was in 1891, and its per capita rate of recycling bins must be one of the highest in both France and Spain. Yet the hooray-patriotism of its 1,000 inhabitants remains unchanged. Modern Llivia is fiercely Catalan, with very few people willing to speak French to a visitor – an unusual scenario for a village, sorry … a 'town,' totally surrounded by France.

A huge red-and-yellow *Senyera* – Catalonia's national flag – stood in the corner of the modest office of Josep Alcalde, Llivia's thirty-six-year-old Mayor, a member of the United Catalonia Party, which he himself described as 'moderately nationalistic.' He told me of a letter he received the day before from a nearby French village a couple of miles away. The letter took fifteen days to arrive, for according to EC regulations, all inter-EU mail has to go though a sorting office in Amsterdam. 'I could have walked there myself in half an hour and picked it up,' he shrugged. The Mayor also complained that to call the same French village from Llivia he would have to dial an international code – the irritating discrepancy that I had experienced myself when my France Telecom phone card was rejected by a local public phone.

Unlike in Campione, which is not going to benefit from the introduction of the euro in February 2002 (Switzerland is not an EU member), they can't wait for the euro in Llivia hoping it would help clear at least some of the financial mess in the town, where both French francs and Spanish pesetas are freely circulated. 'Our prices are much lower than those in France, and a glass of the same French wine that will cost one euro there will only cost half a euro here, so we are bracing ourselves for the French invasion,' smiled the Mayor.

As the owner of the town's biggest hotel, 'Llivia,' he certainly knew what he was talking about, although his French wine analogy wouldn't have gone down well with the Mayor's own brother – the proprietor of Llivia's oldest restaurant *Can Ventura*. Only five out of a hundred wines on his impressive wine list were French.

At noon, Llivia goes dead. Its narrow cobbled streets become deserted, and elaborately carved wooden shutters fall upon the windows of rustic stone cottages, as if the houses themselves shut their eyes for a *siesta* – a Spanish tradition, not observed in the nearby French towns. A warm stateless breeze brings a faint duty-free fragrance of wild flowers from the French Pyrenees across the border.

Busingen – a small German enclave in Switzerland – cannot be found on any maps. This must be due to the fact that it is actually a suburb of the Swiss town of Schaffhausen, where the residents of Busingen routinely do their shopping. Few of them, however, would choose to go shopping in their native Germany. Firstly, because they would have to show their passports or ID cards at the German border – the procedure they are spared when going to 'foreign' Switzerland. Secondly, there are very strict quotas on the amount of German goods these German subjects can bring back to Germany(!): no more than half a kilo of meat, 125 grams of butter or a kilo of sausages. The quotas are imposed by numerous Swiss and German customs posts scattered along the erratic Swiss-German border that goes totally haywire in the Busingen-Schaffhausen area. In one instance, it runs across the beer garden of a Busingen pub, so that the tables are in Switzerland, and the bar – in Germany. Luckily, the customs posts are only open (or shall we say 'closed?') from 8am to 5pm, except for weekends and public holidays, when they stay closed (which – obviously – means 'open!').

The reason for this frontier madness is that – not dissimilar to Campione – economically Busingen is Swiss, whereas politically it is German, albeit not part of the EU. Busingers get their salaries in Swiss francs – the only currency allowed to circulate in this one-street German village but, being German citizens, they have to pay German income taxes, which, as I was assured by delightful Ursula Barner, Busingen's Deputy Mayor, was the bane of the villagers' existence. True, Swiss prices are high, but the taxes are relatively low, whereas in Germany it is the other way around: lower prices and very high taxes. In Busingen therefore they have the worst of both worlds, so to speak. 'If the situation doesn't change soon, all villagers will end up in Switzerland,' Frau Barner remarked sarcastically.

Alas, realistically speaking, this is rather unlikely. Indeed, Busingers are free to shop in Switzerland, but those willing to work (let alone to live) there need a hard-to-obtain permit, normally granted after many years of residence. A classic Catch-22 situation. And a possible nightmare scenario for a unified, yet thoroughly 'dis-united,' Europe of the future ...

German inventiveness and practicality help Busingers ease the burden of their duality, if only slightly. The village has its own car number plates – 'BUS,' but two different post codes: Swiss and German – to avoid the missives from neighbouring Swiss settlements going to Amsterdam, no doubt. In the village centre, next to modernistic *Burgerhaus*, two differently coloured public phone boxes – Swisscom's and Deutsche Telecom's – stand next to each other, sparing the locals the expense of international phone calls when phoning the nearest cinema or supermarket.

In their daily trials, the residents of modern Busingen are reaping the consequences of their own ancestors' unforgiving pride, better known as stubbornness. In April 1693, Eberhard Im Thurn, a popular ruler of then Austrian Busingen, was kidnapped and put in prison in Schaffhausen for a religious offence – to the villagers' considerable dismay. He was released in 1699, but Busingers had a long memory, and when Schaffhausen tried to incorporate the village into the Swiss federation in 1723, they came out adamantly against it. Eventually, Busingen fell under German control where it still remains as a living reproach to Schaffhausen for the mistreatment of its leading citizen. The fact that Swiss flags in the windows of sturdy Busingen houses by far outnumber German ones, however, can be seen as a sign of the villagers' belated readiness to swallow their pride after all.

If Busingen strikes a visitor arriving by accident as eccentric and 'wrapped in veil bizarre,' then Baarle-Nassau/Baarle-Hertog – a cluster of Belgian and Dutch enclaves to the south of Breda – can be safely described as insane. The border here resembles an ECG of a patient on the brink of a heart attack. Like a hank of wool thread, chased by a playful kitten, it thoughtlessly leaps across streets and squares cutting through houses, offices and shops. The confusion is such that every single building in town has to be marked not just with a number, but also with a tiny Dutch or Belgian flag underneath it. Out of three houses, standing next to each other on the same side of the same street, one can be in Belgium, one in Holland, and the third one – split between the two.

'If the border runs through a house, it is better for a baby to be born on the Belgian side, because child benefits are higher in Belgium,' Anne-Miek Smit-Rygersberg, a local Dutch artist with appropriately double-barrelled first and last names, explained without a shade of irony. In rural Baarle, it is still common to give birth at home with the help of a midwife.

Anne-Miek, who, according to her own words, was born in the house on the edge of Baarle where smugglers often popped in 'for a cup of tea,' and went to a Belgian school 'because it was closer,' showed me her two purses – one with Dutch guilders, the other with Belgian francs. 'I buy medicines at the Belgian pharmacy where they are less strict with prescriptions, but flowers, cheese and spirits – at Dutch shops, where they are cheaper,' she said.

The most thriving trade in the Belgian parts of Baarle is in … fireworks (I counted half a dozen fireworks shops in the town centre), which can be legitimately sold all year round in Belgium, but only on Christmas eve in Holland. The Dutch bits of the town respond with numerous sex shops, not allowed anywhere near public buildings in Belgium, but thriving on the Dutch territory, next door to (and across the road from) the Belgian town council in Baarle.

There is literally no end to the duplicity of life in Baarle – the town with two Mayors (Belgian and Dutch), two sets of political parties, two town councils, two fire brigades trying to beat each other to conflagration sites, two post offices, two refuse collection services, and so on. It is the only town in the world where police forces of two different countries share not only the same police station building, but also same rooms, with respective filing cabinets painted in the colours of Dutch or Belgian national flags.

The existing twenty-two Belgian and eight Dutch enclaves that constitute modern Baarle are a huge improvement to 1843, when, in the aftermath of the Treaty of Maastricht, 5,732 parcels of land between just two border posts: 214 and 215 – had their nationalities laid down separately! This 'duplicate' 214/215 border post now stands in the town centre as evidence of Baarle's persisting split personality crisis, started in 1203 by the Duke of Brabant, who – in a gesture of gratitude and appeasement – lent a chunk of his territory to Godfrid of Schoten, the powerful Lord of Breda, but kept all inhabited – and hence tax-paying – bits (houses, farms, etc) for himself. In the course of centuries most dwellings disappeared, but the patches of land on which they stood retained their original 'nationhood.'

It is not just people that go crazy in Baarle – this natural testing area of 'unified Europe.' I came there in the company of two friends, armed with mobile phones, one of which showed 'Belgium,' the other Holland on their mini-screens, whereas the operator's messages in both switched into French! And yet, some of the town's features gave me hope that united Europe and the euro might eventually work. Here's an example. Several years ago, Belgium and Holland had different licensing hours which the landlord of one of Baarle's pubs, dissected by the frontier, blatantly exploited by installing a set of doors on each side of the border. When they stopped selling alcohol in Belgium, the patrons hastily left through the Belgian door only to re-enter immediately through the Dutch one and to carry on boozing. The situation was so ridiculous that eventually both states had to harmonise their licensing laws. More often than not, an absurdity has to reach its apogee to trigger authorities into action.

My visits to the enclaves, these tiny specks of historical dust on the face of modern Europe, made me think that the only way for the 'common European home' to work was economic harmonisation without cultural interference. And Baarle's graceful **Dutch** Church of St Mary (the town has two separate Roman Catholic parishes – Belgian and Dutch), built by **Belgian** architects with **Belgian** red bricks could pass for the best symbol of European unity I had come across so far.

At the end of my journey, I was pleased to conclude that with all its hassles, life in modern European enclaves is a good example of the triumph of human spirit and ingenuity over the shenanigans of international bureaucracy.

It is almost 10pm and the iron gates of Ely Place are about to close. Until recently, the night watchman used to call out the hours all night through. The tradition was stopped after the residents complained of the noise, and now the quirky little lane basks in silence when darkness falls.

A one-person human 'enclave' of sorts, I am always reluctant to leave this dislocated place, but it is late. Time to return to the real world.

In my pocket, I am carrying a Swiss Army penknife, bought in Campione (or was it in Busingen?), with tiny specks of old European dust stuck to its rocket-shaped shiny blades.

Microstates

It is common knowledge that in all 270-odd years of its history, Liechtenstein, a tiny, twenty-five-kilometre-long, sovereign principality, squeezed between Austria and Switzerland, was spared foreign invasions. Like so many other commonly accepted stereotypes about the world's and Europe's smallest sovereign countries, however, it is not entirely true. Let me explain.

To begin with, the principality has no army, and its last military engagement was in 1866, when Prussia declared war on Austria. All eighty Liechtenstein soldiers were deployed on the frontier between Tyrol and Italy for one week, during which they witnessed a blizzard (in August), but never set eyes on the enemy. They returned to Liechtenstein safe and sound (in fact, there were eighty-one of them to return; they gained a new recruit on the way back), were welcomed by a band, given refreshments at Vaduz castle and then sent home.

Liechtenstein's last soldier died in 1939.

And yet, two episodes in the principality's twentieth century history could indeed qualify as peaceful invasions of sorts. The second happened in October 1992, when a group of Swiss recruits tried by mistake to set up an observation post in the Liechtenstein village of Triesenberg on the Swiss border. A local woman, who had never seen a soldier before and was obviously unnerved by their rifles and gas-masks, simply shooed them away across the frontier back into Switzerland, which had to apologise officially for the incident.

The first episode, however, deserves a much more detailed description. In fact, it is one of the most inspiring real-life stories I had come across in all my nearly forty years in journalism. I stumbled upon it while researching one of my travel books.

> On the night of 2 May 1945, 500 fully armed Russian soldiers, under the command of Major Genera Holmston-Smyslovsky, crossed the Austrian frontier into Liechtenstein near the village of Schellenberg.
>
> The Russians, remnants of the First Russian Army of the German Wehrmacht, had entered Liechtenstein in search of political asylum. Unlike two and a half million other Russian soldiers and Cossacks, who fought on the German side and were captured by the Allies only to be handed over to Stalin for execution under the ignominious Yalta agreement, they were not extradited and were allowed to stay!
>
> The tiny Ruritanian principality was firmly committed to its status of neutrality during the last war. Near the village of Malbun, there is a church, built in 1950, 'to thank God for sparing Liechtenstein the terrors of the Second World War.' In actual fact, it was thanks not to God but to the political prowess of Prince Franz Joseph II (ironically, he was the nephew of

> Archduke Franz Ferdinand, whose assassination in Sarajevo precipitated the 1914-1918 war), who bravely paid a surprise visit to Berlin in May 1939.
>
> As the Prince himself later recalled, Hitler 'was visibly ill at ease and didn't make any impression at all' during their ninety-minute meeting in the Reich Chancellery, but since his visit 'flattered Hitler's ego,' the Nazis decided to leave Liechtenstein alone.
>
> Having come back from Germany, the Prince ordered Liechtenstein's two political parties, the Reds (the Patriotic Union) and the Blacks (the Progressive Citizens' Party), to form a coalition and join forces to protect Liechtenstein's independence …

Let us interrupt the narrative here and talk about a rather confusing and ill-defined concept of a modern mini (or micro)-state. Unlike the so-called 'micronations,' (see the next section of this book) mini-states are all fully sovereign and self-governing small entities, recognised as such by the UN, the IOM and other international organisations. According to the *Webster's College Dictionary* succinct definition a mini-state is just 'a small independent nation.' And *The Free Internet Dictionary* defines microstate (synonym of mini-state) as 'A very small nation that is an internationally-recognised sovereign state.' The obvious question here is: how small is small?

Indeed, 'small' is a relative concept when applied to countries. The UK is small compared to, say, China or Russia, but Malta is very small in relation to the UK. Or take Iceland – relatively small in population (350,000), yet vast in its area (40,000 square miles). What should we take into account: area, population or, as suggested by the *Wikipedia* article on microstates, both? My favourite definition, quoted by geographer Zbigniew Dumienski in his paper 'Microstates as Modern Protected States,' comes from E Warrington, who described a microstate as being of a size 'so small as to invite comment.'

When researching my own book on the mini-states of Europe, I arbitrarily introduced a half-a-million population as the upper limit for this or that country's inclusion which allowed me to incorporate both Malta and Luxembourg, while excluding Iceland, whose sheer vastness simply did not fit in with the general perception of a mini-state and therefore would not 'invite comment' as such.

For the purposes of this piece, I suggest the bracket be narrowed even further – to the maximum of 100,000 population, which leaves us with ten amazingly diverse sovereign countries – in Oceania (Nauru, Tuvalu, Palau and Marshall Islands), the Caribbean (St Kitts & Nevis, Antigua and Barbuda) and Europe (San Marino, Monaco, Liechtenstein and Andorra).

There is also Niue (population 1,600) – an island nation in the South Pacific, considered an associated state (a minor partner) of New Zealand.

How about the Vatican, by far the world's smallest state, with the population of under 900 and the area of just forty-four hectares, you may ask? Well, I consciously chose to leave the Papal State out both from my book and from the above list, for to me it did not quite meet the traditional criteria of a state. And not just for myself, it appears: writer Thomas Eccardt in his recent book *Secrets of the Seven Smallest States of Europe* referred to the Vatican as being more similar to 'the headquarters of international organisations' than to a state in its own right. Hopefully, His Holiness will forgive us both!

Now back to Liechtenstein and the amazing war-time story I discovered there – a brilliant real-life illustration to the much-debated concept of national sovereignty.

> … The First Russian Army of the Wehrmacht was made of Russian émigrés and freedom-fighters, most of whom were not even Soviet citizens. Its main objective was not to contribute to Russia's occupation, but rather to help it to get rid of Bolshevism, which was seen as the greater of two evils. Hitler never fully trusted the Army, and even had Holmston-Smyslovsky, a former Russian count, imprisoned and his unit disbanded for a couple of years. The army didn't commit any atrocities and its involvement in combat action was minimal.
>
> As soon as the news reached Vaduz of the 500 Russians in German uniforms, with all their arms and equipment, crossing the border, the Prince sent his representatives to Schellenberg. Baron Eduard von Falz-Fein, a long-time Liechtenstein resident of Russian extraction, from whom I first learned this story in 1993 (he passed away at the venerable age of 106 in November 2018), was asked to act as a translator.
>
> The negotiations with Holmston-Smyslovsky took place in the Zum Lowen Inn on the border. 'It was a curious sight for our peaceful Liechtenstein,' the Baron told me. 'Hundreds of heavily armed men, with their horses and vehicles, camping on the lawn behind the inn … Later we built barracks for them in the town of Ruggel …'

… Modern Liechtenstein (area 160 square kilometres, population 39,000), with its per capita GDP of over $140,000 is, by some estimates, the world's richest country. And not only due to its tax haven status and its countless letterbox companies (their number is higher than that of the principality's population!), but also because of its proportionally extensive infrastructure, with over 1,800 industrial enterprises specialising in electronics, precision engineering, metal finishing, textile and ceramic industries, which explains why it is often called a 'mini-industrial giant.'

We find a very different picture in Monaco (population 37,000) , effectively an enclave in France, whose economy – apart from banking – heavily relies on the services sector rather than manufacturing, or in San Marino (34,000), which thrives on exporting its wines, souvenirs and highly collectable postage stamps.

The very existence of the prospering microstates is a not-so-small miracle in our immensely globalised world. But their most remarkable feature, to my mind, is their frantic, yet entirely peaceful, clinging to their treasured sovereignty (read independence from their much larger and much more belligerent neighbours). As P Christiaan Klieger rightly noted in his book *The Microstates of Europe*, 'Microstates recognise the crucial importance of recognition in sovereignty and self-determination.'

Despite their minuscule size, modern mini-states are ruled in a plethora of different ways – from parliamentary and constitutional monarchy (Monaco and Liechtenstein) and unitary parliamentary republic (Palau, Marshall Islands) to San Marino's unique arrangement whereby it is governed jointly by two (!) Captains Regent, nominated by the Grand and General Council – the so-called –'diarchic directorial republic' (see below). Andorra, a tiny Catalan-speaking principality in the Pyrenees, which has been enjoying independence since 1298, while remaining a parliamentary democracy, run by the Council General (Andorra's parliament, democratically elected since 1419), also preserves an element of diarchy by maintaining its two co-Princes, one of whom is traditionally the incumbent President of France, and the other – the Bishop of Urgel, but unlike in San Marino, their role is largely ceremonial … And in St Kitts & Nevis – a mini-federation of two island states – the same minister can hold several different portfolios – both in the local island government and in the federal one, like, for example Rt Hon Mark Brantley, Nevis's Deputy Premier, whom I met in Charlestown, who holds ten.

During my short visit to Liechtenstein some years ago, I was lucky to have an audience with Prince Hans Adam II (see below), the principality's head of state and Europe's last remaining full-power monarch, who can single-handedly veto laws, call referenda and dissolve the Diet (parliament), as he did last time in September 1993. Hans Adam II then went on to declare general elections and to reject the no-confidence vote against his then Prime Minister Markus Buchel – an event normally associated with the seventeenth century, not the late twentieth …

And in 2003, he called a referendum on the expansion of his own powers and threatened to leave the country if the people voted against it. They didn't and refused to curtail them again in 2012, when an anti-monarchists' proposal to do was resolutely voted down … Not too democratic, you may say … Yet, as the story with the asylum-seeking Russian soldiers has demonstrated, at times it takes a bit of dictatorial toughness to keep the aggressor at bay … Where the world's greatest democracies – USA, Britain and France – failed to deliver and effectively capitulated in the face of a gun-brandishing bully, tiny Liechtenstein stayed unperturbed.

> … In the end, asylum was granted to all the Russians, but shortly afterwards the Prince found himself under considerable pressure from the Soviets. Unlike his British, French and American counterparts, the ruler of the tiny

> Liechtenstein firmly resisted all attempts to have the asylum-seekers extradited. 'Despite strong pressure, and in contrast to the bad example set by other countries, these unfortunate refugees were not handed over to the executioners,' the valiant Prince Franz Joseph II wrote in 1980.
> The only thing the Prince had to agree to was to allow a Soviet delegation to come to Liechtenstein and interview the asylum-seekers. By stick and carrot, Stalin's emissaries managed to dupe 300 into returning to the USSR.
> Notwithstanding generous guarantees of safety, each of them was executed on arrival ...
> Most of the remaining 200, including Holmston-Smyslovsky himself, stayed for two years before moving on, most of them to the safety of Argentina. One soldier, named Sokhin, married a local girl and lived a happy life in Liechtenstein until his death in the early 1990s ...

Thus two hundred human lives were saved by the tiny principality's faithfulness to its historical and humanitarian principles (pun unintended). Liechtenstein might be small indeed, but, like all other mini-states, it can teach the modern world an important lesson of true sovereignty and pride.

I'd like to finish with the words by Gabriel Ollivier, former General Commissioner for the Principality of Monaco:

'All these states (meaning microstates – VV) – which have proudly retained their independence in the course of many centuries – would appear to be anachronisms in a world which has seen so much political upheaval, so many changes in frontiers. Yet, they differ greatly from one another, historically, geographically and economically, and each has its own special charm ...'

* * *

Audience with Hans Adam II

The Prince's office inside the castle was unexpectedly modest and totally unguarded. A sprightly smiling man strode in. We shook hands, and I immediately felt at ease. The Prince had a warm disarming smile. On his wrist, he was wearing a simple electronic watch.

'Our country is indeed a happy one,' he said in impeccable English, with a slight German accent. 'We've got hundred per cent literacy, high living standards and practically no crime. There are problems, of course. In the last couple of years unemployment has grown from 0.1 per cent to 0.7 per cent.'

I made some hasty calculations on a piece of paper: 0.1 per cent of Liechtenstein's population was (at the time of the interview) thirty people.

'Our world has become much smaller of late, and we all live in a global village, where people are keen to find their roots, their own community,' continued the Prince. 'On the other hand, the world has become more vulnerable: a major conflict in any part of the planet now means war in your own backyard. Small countries these days can flourish only in an atmosphere of peace and trade … We strongly believe in free enterprise. We also work very hard, having the longest working week in Europe. The working day here, and my working day too, starts at 8am. There is no lunchbreak culture …'

Having spent several years as a London banker in his youth, the Prince knew what he was talking about …

'What else makes Liechtenstein tick? We have strong democracy, where people can really influence their own future. Taxes are low. Even after the war, when the state had little revenue, we preferred to lower taxes instead of increasing them, to let our businesses survive. The more you increase taxes – the less people buy. So, I think, we have found quite a good balance for our mini-state. Our slogan is 'stability through monarchy,' and the fact that we are so small makes us nearer to the people.

'Our monarchy works because it has much to do with the family. We try to promote family values and live a normal family life without getting too much into the public eye. I try to keep my family out of the press, although we are not inaccessible. All my children went to an ordinary school in Vaduz, and I walk around the town unguarded.'

* * *

Who is in charge in San Marino?

While in San Marino, I was somewhat puzzled to discover that the world's oldest republic ascribing its foundation to the fourth century AD, with a well-deserved reputation of haven of peace and liberty (during the Second World War, the republic opened its borders to more than 100,000 refugees from the Nazi-occupied countries) now had three separate voluntary armies – the Territorial Army, the Fortification Guards and the Noble Guards, not to mention its traditional Crossbowmen Corps. Spared the never-ending turmoil of neighbouring Italy, San Marino, with its zero crime rate and one prison of just four cells (from where, by the time of my visit, the last and only prisoner escaped in 1986), nevertheless boasted of two police forces – the gendarmerie and the civil police.

The republic's ruling hierarchy, modestly calling itself 'Serenissima' (Most Serene),' probably to imitate the Venetian Republic, seems cumbersome to the point of madness. It is made up of six bodies: the Arengo, the Grand and General Council (another modest name), the Captains Regent, the Council of the Twelve, the Sindaci (high officials) and the State Congress.

The Arengo, or the assembly of the heads of families, used to be the country's parliament. Nowadays it has only one (and pretty vague) function – the right of petition, whatever that means.

The sixty-seat-strong Grand and General Council, San Marino's highest legislative body, nominates two Captains Regent who jointly rule for six months and then get re-elected (what if the two heads of this ruling Push-Me-Pull-You disagree on a certain matter, I wondered?). Executive power was wielded by the Suite Congress, composed of three secretaries and seven ministers, among them the minister for culture and universities, even though at the time of my visit there was not a single university in the country!

The Council of Twelve's main role was 'to authorise the sale and transfer of dowry possessions by the wife' – a very important matter. As to the mysterious Sindaci, it is just the body of government inspectors representing the state.

There was also the Castle Board, presided over by the Captain of the Castles and comprising delegates of San Marino's nine districts (Castles).

The structure of the judiciary system was no less complicated. And all this for just 23,000 people (now the population of San Marino has grown to 34,000)!

It became clear to me why twenty-five per cent of San Marino's workforce were then employed in 'public administration.' Could that bureaucratic nightmare, at least partially, be the result of the fact that Communists and pro-Communist 'Socialists' had been in power in San Marino throughout most of the post-war period? As I know only too well after my thirty-five years in the USSR, Communism and bureaucracy go together like two legs of one and the same pair of trousers.

I felt that bureaucratic touch on my very first contact with San Marino. The leaflet, published by the Sammarinese State Tourist office, that I picked up at Rimini station while waiting for a bus to San Marino (which was late), helpfully listed winter, summer, spring and autumn under the headline 'Suitable times of the year for holidays and excursions in San Marino.' It also had a separate section 'Frontier Formalities' with only one sentence in it: 'There are no frontier formalities.'

Nice and simple!

And to crown it all, a venerable middle-aged waiter serving me at my hotel restaurant confessed to just making an extra buck by waitressing, with his main job being … the country's Foreign Minister!

He could have been fibbing me of course … But somehow I don't think so …

Micronations of the World

The Prince was running late.

'His Serene Highness offers his apologies: he is presently busy pruning flowers,' said Marco – a smiley young man with gentle brown eyes, who, despite his young age was already carrying the title of the Counsellor for Welfare and Free Time. The latter sounded like a wonderful job that I myself wouldn't mind having …

The year was 1993, the venue – the main (and only) square of the village of Seborga, population 320, empty except for a couple of dishevelled village chickens chased by a lop-eared puppy, and a parked van, inscribed '*Seborga Fiori*' (Seborga Flowers), belonging to the local flower cooperative, the country's only industrial enterprise …

The word 'country' in the previous sentence is not a typo, for that small village on the border of France and Italy proclaimed itself an independent nation, the Principality of Seborga, in 1963 on the initiative of Giorgio Carbone, a flower farmer, who then became known as Prince Giorgio I.

At the time of my visit, Seborga remained undiscovered outside the neighbouring French and Italian regions. Believe it or not, but I can seriously claim to have put it on the map: after my article on Seborga was published in the *Spectator* magazine, I was contacted by the compilers of one of the first online atlases, who wanted more information on it, which I was happy to provide, and soon the self-proclaimed Principality – for the first time in its recent history – appeared on maps and in atlases (and still does!) if not as a sovereign country, then at least as a tiny and curious geopolitical maverick – a differently coloured dot on the green Italian background …

The very fact of featuring in an atlas proved encouraging enough for Prince Giorgio to start minting Seborga's own coins – *luigino*. Apart from being nice souvenirs, they were accepted as monetary units at the village's only general store …

But seriously speaking, by legitimising Seborga cartographically, the compilers of the atlas went a bit too far, for by definition – and by recognition, or rather by the lack of it Seborga was (and still is) not a mini-state (like its neighbour Monaco, or, say Liechtenstein, but a 'micronation,' of which there are now nearly seventy all over the world, ie a **small area, or political entity that claims sovereignty but is not recognised by any other sovereign states or international organisations.**

The key word in this definition is 'any,' for there exist another group of nations – the so-called 'partially recognised states,' like, for example, the breakaway post-Soviet republics of Transdnistria and South Ossetia (recognised only by each other and a handful of other uncertain entities) which are often incorrectly referred to as micronations or mini-states.

The first recorded micronation was probably the English island of Lundy, whose owner Martin Coles Harman proclaimed himself King and started issuing coins and stamps in the beginning of the twentieth century. Among the latest additions, I could name Liberland – a patch of disputed land on the western bank of the Danube, and the 'Space Kingdom of Asgardia', based entirely in outer space, on board a small satellite.

Legally, starting a micronation is relatively easy and takes just several steps:

1. Set a goal (we'll talk about the types and goals of micronations a bit later).
2. Choose a name and a territory, be it a discarded oil platform, like in the case of Sealand, or a teenager's messy cubbyhole of the Kingdom of Talossa, founded in 1979 by then fourteen-year-old Robert Ben Madison of Milwaukee (who, incidentally, claims to have coined the very term 'micronation'), and initially confined to his own bedroom.
3. Find citizens (that shouldn't be a problem: the recently formed Asgardia has already got nearly 300,000).
4. Try to stick to the four general principles of statehood, defined by the 1933 Montevideo Convention: permanent population (even if just of one person), defined territory, government and capacity to enter into relations with the other states.

It is the latter point that stops micronations from becoming 'proper' countries, for one cannot effectively 'enter into relations' without being recognised first. That, however, does not stop micronations from holding their own regular inter-micronational gatherings, the so-called, microcons, and signing their own inter-micronational treaties, like, for example the Alcatraz Environmental Treaty of 2015, whose full text can found in the peculiar volume *The Law of Micronations 2018*, compiled and published 'by the people of the Cyanocitta Isopod Republic,' no less.

> … Back in the 1993 Seborga, a small group of tourists, with their cameras ready, suddenly materialised out of nowhere and gathered in the village centre. 'The Prince is about to arrive,' Marco announced solemnly.
> A tattered black Mercedes, flying a white-and-blue Seborga's flag, crawled into the square. A bulky bearded man, dressed in pitch-black gleaming shoes, black trousers, blue shirt with Seborga's crest on its pocket and white blazer (to match Seborga's flag colours?), got out of the car, blowing air-kisses to the waiting crowd. This was the Prince. He was followed by another man in a plain black suit. 'He is the governor of San Remo's prison, the Prince's personal friend,' Marco whispered respectfully.' Prince Giorgio I seems to have friends in the right places,' I thought to myself …

… Eccentric as he appeared, Georgio Carbone, aka, Prince Giorgio I, had a valid historical point: Seborga first became a sovereign state as far back as in the year 954 as one of the many post-Roman mini-states on the territory of the present-day Italy. Independence was bestowed on the village by Guido, the Count of Ventimiglia, the nearest coastal town.

A principality from 1040, for several hundred years prior to its incorporation into the Austro-Hungarian Empire Seborga had been under Vatican protection and even had its own mint until it was forced to close in 1686 for making too many counterfeit ecus.

After the defeat of Napoleon, when inter-European borders underwent considerable redrawing under the Treaty of Vienna, Seborga and the neighbouring Monaco were simply forgotten due to their insignificance and minuscule size. Monaco was soon remembered, but Seborga wasn't and automatically became part of Italy. So Carbone's claims of Seborga's sovereignty, like those of several other micronations, were far from trivial and rested on solid historical grounds.

Having studied these peculiar entities for years and having visited some of them too, I would provisionally divide all existing micronations into the following categories:

- **Started as a Joke**, eg: British comedian Danny Wallace's **Kingdom of Lovely**; **Republic of Kugelmugel** – a ball-shaped house in Vienna, built without planning permission; **Molossia**; **Whangamomona** – a jokey entity, founded to boost tourism in the eponymous rural New Zealand town, which at some point had a goat as its president, and many more.

- **Based on valid (and not-so-valid) Historical Claims**, eg: **Seborga**; the **Free Republic of Liberland**, founded in 2015 and claiming a long-disputed patch of land, called Siga, on the Western bank of the Danube; **Sealand**; **The Imperial Throne**, formerly the Russian Empire; **the Crown Dependency of Forvik** – an island in Shetland, which, like Seborga, claims to have been an independent nation in the Middle Ages; **the Kingdom of Tavolara** – a small table-shaped island off the north east coast of Sardinia claiming independence, allegedly sanctioned by Charles Albert, the King of Sardinia (1831-1849), from the middle of the nineteenth century, and several others.

- **Started by Squatters**, eg: **Republic of Frestonia –** which staged a 'secession' of the whole of London's Freston Road from the UK. In a real-life *Passport to Pimlico*' scenario, it even appointed its own ambassador to Great Britain in 1977, but eventually evolved into a 'normal' housing co-operative.

- **Started as a Learning Aid or an Arts Project**, eg: **Grand Dutchy of the Lagoan Islands** – created in 2005 by a school teacher from Portsmouth, UK, and consisting of a pond and three tiny islands in it; **Neue Slowenische Kunst**, or NSK – a political art collective from Slovenia which claimed to be a sovereign state in 1991 and started issuing passports and postage stamps as part of an ongoing art project; **Hay-on-Wye's Kingdom of Books** (Wales, UK), ruled by King Richard the Book-Hearted, aka local bookseller Richard Booth, who back in the 1970s declared Hay-on-Wye an international Book Town, independent from the British Crown, and some others.

- **Started as a Social Experiment or a Political Protest Gesture**, eg: **Gay and Lesbian Kingdom of the Coral Sea Islands** – declared in 2004 in response to the Australian government's failure to recognise same-sex marriages, claiming the territory of the uninhabited Coral Sea Islands and dissolved in 2017 when gay marriages were finally legalised; **Other World Kingdom** – a Czech Republic-based matriarchy, in which women rule over men; **North Dumpling** – an island off the New York State coast which declared independence as a sign of protest against the State authorities' decision not to build a wind turbine on it, and many more, including a handful of micronations in Antarctica, the only continent with areas still unclaimed by any existing government.

- **Started as a Legal or Scientific Statement**, eg: **Asgardia** and **Celestia**, founded in 1949 and claiming the whole of the universe, except for the Earth, as its territory with the aim of stopping all other entities from requesting any part of outer space.

… Carbone welcomed me warmly. 'We didn't feel like paying high Italian taxes any longer,' he told me in confidence as we were drinking in one of the two village restaurants in the company of Marco and several other members of the Prince's own Crown Council, including the Counsellor for Foreign Affairs and the Counsellor for Defence in charge of the part-time army of five. That 'army' played a pivotal role in Seborga's 'independence,' officially announced in August 1963, when three Seborgan soldiers (ie three-fifths of its army's personnel) in Napoleonic uniforms sneaked unnoticed through the nearby Passo del Bandito mountain and nailed Seborga's flag to the door of the church of San Michele, one of the three parish churches Giorgio I wanted to reclaim (together with the parishes, of course). They managed to get away with that too!

'Why should we keep paying taxes to a foreign power?' the Prince carried on. 'Our citizens want to work for the benefit of their native Seborga!'

'How are you going to survive on your own?' I asked.

'Easy! We already export our flowers to Germany, Sweden and the United States. We can declare ourselves a tax haven. Just look at San Marino – they are doing well. And we are older than they!'

After the second glass, Carbone solemnly offered me the job of Seborga's Extraordinary and Plenipotentiary Ambassador in the UK – a truly 'extraordinary' honour which I chose to refuse.

He also granted me citizenship and himself signed and stamped my brand-new Seborgan passport, fresh out of the souvenir shop (or so it looked). Not willing to complicate the Seborga-British, or possibly even Seborga-Ukrainian non-existent relationships, I didn't dare refuse it …

Prince Giorgio I passed away in 2009 and was succeeded by Marcello Menegatto, a local building contractor, elected Prince Marcello I, who, according to some sources, still reigns supreme. According to other reports, which I so far was unable to verify, he was replaced as Seborga's monarch by a French writer Nicolas Mutte in 2016.

Looking back, I come to realise that by being among the first to write about the unrecognised Principality and thus effectively putting it on the map, I have fulfilled my strictly unofficial 'ambassadorial' mission.

Moreover, I tend to regard this as an achievement of mine, for micronations – alongside enclaves, mini-states and other geopolitical curiosities – add colour, charm and diversity to the world geography and through it – to our hectic lives.

* * *

The Principality of Sealand

One of the best-known micronations, Sealand, located in the North Sea (twelve kilometres off the coast of Suffolk and hence outside the five-kilometre limit of British territorial waters) was established by the former British Army Major Paddy Bates, who proclaimed himself the Prince, and his family members – then the platform's only residents – the royalty, in 1967. Sealand occupies an offshore oil platform, originally called HM Fort Roughs and built as an anti-aircraft gun fort during World War II. In 1975, Bates introduced a constitution, as well as a national flag and an anthem and started issuing Sealand's own coins and passports, of which over 150,000 were printed only to be revoked in 1997.

In the early 2000s, Sealand, claiming to be outside the UK government's regulations, signed an agreement with an online company to host a number of dodgy websites, and in 2004 formed the Royal Bank of Sealand, with offices in Geneva.

Sealand's short history is rife with controversies which include gun shots, fired from the platform at some British workmen who tried to service a navigational buoy near the platform, and even suppressing a real *coup d'état* by Sealand's self-proclaimed prime minister AG Achenbach, who tried – with the help of several foreign mercenaries – to take over the platform while the royal family were all away in England. The defeated plotter was charged with treason and subsequently established his own government-in-exile.

Bates passed away in 2012 at the age of ninety-one, having named his son Michael as a regent.

The Space Kingdom of Asgardia

Unlike most other micronations, which claim possession of at least a patch of the earth's territory, Asgardia does not hold one single inch of the *terra firma*. Started in 2016 by a group of people who shortly afterwards, on 12 November 2017, launched a 2.8kg 2U CubeSat-type satellite 'Asgardia-1' into orbit, it only claims sovereignty over the space inside that very satellite measuring ten by ten by twenty centimetres. However, Asgardia's founding fathers, including the 'Head of Nation' Russian-Azeri scientist and businessman Igor Azhurbeyli and the 'Chairman of Parliament' Lembit Opik, a former British MP, are planning a massive expansion by launching many more satellites and then establishing a space colony in orbit. To quote Asgardia's Constitution, it 'shall be a nation of the supremacy of science and technology, and a nation of ideas.'

To become an Asgardian citizen, of whom there are already nearly 300,000, is easy: you simply have to fill in your details on the country's website and tick the box saying that you agree with its Constitution, a copy of which can be viewed online.

So far, however, Asgardia remains a micronation, for the only state that has partially recognised it is the State of Nevada (probably due to Molossiya's pressure), which has agreed to regard it as 'an unincorporated non-profit association' – not a huge achievement for human history's first 'Space Kingdom.'

The Imperial Throne (aka the new Russian Empire, aka the Romanov Empire).

In May 2016, Russian millionaire businessman Anton Bakov held talks with the government of Kiribati, a sovereign mini-state in Micronesia, about his plans to set up an 'alternative Russian Empire,' no less, on some of Kiribati's thirty-two atolls and reef islands. Bakov's plans included investing a lot of money into Kiribati's economy and encouraging residents of Russia, disappointed with Putin's rule, to move to his 'New Russian Empire.' The Kiribati government initially agreed to lease to Bakov three uninhabited islands. Thus encouraged, Bakov declared himself prime minister, announced a constitution and state symbols and claimed small bits of territory all over the globe, including Antarctica, effectively turning his creation into a micronation.

But in early 2017, the Kiribati rulers changed their mind and refused to lease their islands to Bakov, who since then was reported to be conducting negotiations with Gambia and several other undisclosed countries. His latest gesture was to invite the Russian Olympic athletes, denied participation in the 2018 Olympic Games for taking the banned performance-enhancing drugs, to compete in future as part of his highly hypothetical Romanov Empire team.

The Republic of Molossiya

'The most delightful micronation on Earth,' according to *The Lonely Planet Guide to Home-Made Nations*, Molossiya, founded in 1999 by Kevin Baugh from Nevada, with his house as the country's headquarters, is run as a witty parody of a totalitarian state. Unlike other micronations with their own constitutions, Molossiya's legislation rests on a number of official, duly numbered and dated spoof 'Presidential Proclamations.' I've managed to get hold of some them:

- It is illegal to cause a catastrophe.
- Torpedoes may not be set off in the country.
- It is illegal to wear cowboy boots unless you already won at least two cows.
- It is illegal to hunt moths under a street light and to play percussion instruments in any bathroom.
- Sunshine is guaranteed to the masses.
- Inasmuch as FHM magazine has snubbed Molossia by bumping a planned article about Molossia and has replaced it with an article about men who catch catfish with their bare hands, catfish and catfish 'noodling' are henceforth banned in Molossia.
- Inasmuch as bagged spinach from the United Sates has recently been shown to be contaminated with E coli, bagged spinach is now banned in Molossiya. Canned spinach is allowed, in deference to the popular influence of Popeye.
- His Excellency The President has decreed that Molossiya will have its own time zone, 'Molossian Standard Time.' This time zone will be 19 minutes ahead of Pacific Standard Time and 41 minutes behind Mountain Standard Time …

Jungholz, the World's Wealthiest Spot

Here's a one-million-euro question: what is the world's wealthiest spot?

No, neither Kuwait, nor the Cayman Islands, nor even the country estate of the Russian multi-billionaire and former Chelsea FC owner Roman Abramovich …

Do you feel like asking the audience, or perhaps phoning a friend? No need to do so, for I am going to tell you the answer: Jungholz – a tiny Austrian village (population 300), surrounded by Germany and all but lost in the Bavarian Alps, boasts the world's highest rate of deposited money per person and hence the world's highest concentration of capital – all due to being home to three big Austrian banks. In plain words, it is officially the world's wealthiest spot.

I visited Jungholz one snowy winter.

Free 'please pick up one' electronic euro-converters (I did pick up three as souvenirs for my friends: what the hell, it was the world's wealthiest place, after all!) were neatly stacked on a table at the plush (marble, wooden sculptures, winter gardens, original old masters, indoor fountains, etc) and totally empty reception hall of *Reiffeisenbank*, where I had an appointment with a young executive called Wolfgang. He told me that the attraction of Jungholz for investors lay in the fact that it had all the benefits of an offshore haven and many more.

'Here we have three one-hundred-per cent Austrian banks operating within the German financial system – the best of both worlds, so to speak. All three banks have permanent seats at Frankfurt Stock Exchange, and our clients are mostly German.'

The real allure for investors and money-launderers was that Austrian banking secrecy regulations, laid down in the country's Constitution, were among the world's strictest, second only to Swiss. Wolfgang showed me an English copy of his bank's 'Private Banking' portfolio – the document that I found darkly fascinating.

It began on a somewhat philosophical note: 'There are moments in life when you can't compromise on confidentiality (like, say, when having an affair? – VV). For instance, when it comes to your money. Our Goldfinger Numbered Account makes absolute confidentiality a reality.'

I rather liked the straightforwardness of the account name – 'Goldfinger,' bringing about direct associations with James Bond, gangsters, international fraudsters, etc. Confidentiality made reality, indeed. Or vice versa: reality made complete confidentiality.

'The name and address of the account holder(s) are not entered in the computer system and thus do not appear on the account statements or invoices. Only selected management-level employees and those vested with special power of attorney have access to this data.'

As I was reading, the mystery kept deepening:

'We hold the copyright on the Goldfinger Numbered Account – the only one of its kind in the world. When you open your account, your electronic fingerprint (this was where 'Goldfinger' came from! – VV), stored in your account, gives you that extra margin of security.'

The most amazing – and rather spooky – feature of the account was that the transactions did not have to stop even with the account holder's sudden demise (eg murder by a rival gang or Mafia clan, etc – VV):

'*Raiffeisenbank* in Jungholz has no obligation to report the death of a foreign account holder to the probate courts. You can make your own individual arrangements right away by naming additional individuals authorised to sign. That way you can grant authorisation now for someone to sign even after your death.'

The late Captain Bob, alias Robert Maxwell, would have loved this financial immortality. As for myself, living off modest book advances and occasional bank loans, which I was finding harder and harder to repay, the whole 'Goldfinger' scenario was as relevant as a pair of skis for a camel.

'Why can't I see any clients?' I asked Wolfgang, when we returned to the fountain-ridden reception lounge.

'They seldom come here, as most of our transactions are done either by phone or by the Internet,' he smiled and added: 'Some of our clients come from Eastern Europe.'

By saying that, he was obviously trying to please me. Possibly, even to reassure me that I could still make it big, if I wanted to, like some of my former compatriots did. To be absolutely honest, I was not interested. I knew precisely what their East European 'clients' did for a living, and that sort of 'Goldfinger' lifestyle was certainly not my cup of tea. At least, I had a much better chance to die of natural causes.

Being poor in the world's wealthiest place did not feel awkward. In fact, figuratively speaking, I was wealthier that many – having discovered Jungholz.

Packing up in my hotel room half an hour later, I remembered that I forgot to ask Wolfgang how they were able to verify electronic fingerprints by phone or by the Internet.

Not that it really mattered ...

Samnaun

'*Umniy v goru ne poidiot – umniy goru oboidiot*' is a wise Russian proverb translating simply as 'He who is clever won't climb the mountain, but would walk around it.' I had a chance to fully appreciate its wisdom during my foolhardy attempt at walking across the Alps (without skis) one February. As part of the research trip, which involved visiting all existing enclaves[30] of Europe, my plan was to go across the Alps from the Austrian ski resort of Ischgl to the village of Samnaun, a Swiss semi-enclave in Austria.

Even and orderly formations of German skiers – skis on their shoulders and hangover on their faces – were marching purposefully to Silveretta Bahn cable car station. As they were boarding – in a rush, yet without fuss, I suddenly realised that I was the only person around without skis.

I squeezed myself inside the cabin, crowded to the extent of a Moscow rush-hour tram. As it was climbing higher and higher up, I couldn't help registering how hostile and forbidding the Alps looked from close by. I thought of the daring smugglers, who used to criss-cross these treacherous slopes on primitive skis, with bags of cheap Swiss sugar (or flour) behind their backs.

With relief, I jumped out of the cabin at Idalp and immediately fell up to my knees through the snow. As I was trying to extricate my feet from its tight ice-cold grip, skiers were whooshing past me indifferently: the snow was 'consolidated' enough to support the skis, but not my wrinkled M&S boots. Above my head, cable-car ropes criss-crossed on different levels, like roads at a spaghetti junction.

Eventually, I found the Flimjochbahn station about a hundred yards away. It was a chairlift, and the cabins were much smaller than Silveretta's: each had only two seats. Apart from the plastic roof, they were open to the elements, with passengers' legs hanging precariously above the abyss. Pressing my shoulder-bag to my chest, I travelled further up in the company of a sexless creature, wearing a helmet and a thick ski-suit and pressing a ski-board to his (her) chest. He (she, it) was also wearing skis, and so did everybody else in the cabins travelling in the opposite direction. They stared at my dangling boots with a mixture of pity and disdain, as if I had no feet.

Soon, I got off on the very top of the mountain, where a heavy blizzard was raging. It suddenly became bitterly cold. My next chairlift station was about 300 yards away. I crawled towards it on my belly to stop myself from falling through the snow. Having reached it in a mere forty minutes, I learnt that they were about to close it down because of a blizzard.

[30] By 'enclaves' I mean bits of one sovereign country, totally surrounded and landlocked by another sovereign country.

The chair lift operator must have pitied me, for after about five minutes, during which I kept cursing myself for being so stupid as to have ventured across the Alps without skis, he briskly walked out of his booth and pushed me into an open cabin with a plastic screen in front. I was shivering all the way down to Altrida – either with bone-piercing cold or with fear that they would stop the chairlift any moment and I would be left dangling in the air above the precipice until the blizzard died down, or, possibly, until spring arrived, like a frozen turkey left to thaw on a balcony of a sky-scraper.

Sinisterly, I seemed to be the only passenger going down or up. At times, my cabin would screech to a near-complete halt ('This is it! The end of the line!'), but after some shilly-shallying, it would reluctantly resume its slow downwards progress.

I was frozen stiff by the time I reached Altrida. Of course, the moment I stepped out of the chairlift, I fell through the snow again and was nearly run over by a passing skier. In the distance, about 200 yards away, I saw a large log cabin, with the word 'Restaurant' on top. I needed some warming up, or rather defrosting, before I could proceed to Samnaun (there were two more chairlifts to go!). Using my freshly acquired crawling skills and propelled by a hallucinatory vision of a steaming espresso cup, I reached the log-cabin in record time of less than half an hour.

'It is not easy without skis,' a young man who sold me the coffee commented gravely in broken English after a quick sorrowful look at my boots. 'I did not see somebody do it here …'

He was obviously telling the truth, for even the daring smugglers of yesteryear crossed the Alps on skis. I was probably the first fool to undertake a ski-less crossing after Suvorov's soldiers in 1799. I promised to myself that I would go back to Ischgl by bus, even if took me a week.

Samnaun was tiny: just a cluster of restaurants and duty-free shops plus a minuscule church of St Jakobus looking so neat and bright that it could pass for a duty-free item, too.

I took shelter in a small tourism office next to the PostBus station, not knowing what a blow was waiting for me there. The office was empty, except for a young female tourism official, who was about to close it down to go home. She was clearly annoyed by my intrusion. She was even further irritated when I asked her to tell me a couple of words about Samnaun's history. Yet, being Swiss, she had a high sense of duty. With a deep sigh, she told me that the duty-free status, bestowed on the village in 1892, was an object of contention for the other four villages of the area, which were desperate for the same status, but were never granted it. Like some jealous Soviet housewives, unable to cope with their neighbour's well-being and hence writing letters of slanderous complaints to a local party committee, the residents of the four 'deprived' villages were bombarding the Swiss parliament with demands of either giving the same status to them or withdrawing it from Samnaun, using the logic of a spoilt brat: if I cannot have the sweetie, then no one can!

'The Swiss government, however, stays firm. And although Samnaun is no longer considered a semi-enclave, it keeps refusing to revoke our duty-free ...'

'Wait a moment!' I interrupted her quite rudely. 'What do you mean 'no longer considered a semi-enclave?' Considered by whom?!'

'The thing is that a way has been discovered to reach Samnaun by road from Switzerland without entering Austria. This is a bad country road, but, if you follow it, you can actually arrive here without leaving Switzerland. Besides, it is only open in summer, so theoretically in winter time Samnaun remains a pene-enclave ...'

'Do you mean to say that I have crawled across the Alps on my belly all for nothing?' I yelled.

The young woman seemed unaffected by my emotional outburst. Like the Swiss government, she 'stayed firm' ...

Livigno

Those interested in Europe's little-known geopolitical curios, I invite to Livigno – a thirteen-kilometre-long Alpine valley in the Italian province of Sondrio – and a so-called 'duty-free area,' excluded from the EU membership by a special protocol.

Livigno, located high in the Retiche Alps, between the valleys of Valtellina and Engadina, is officially part of the Danube Basin economic area, which is hundreds of miles away, and as such enjoys the right of free mooring in the Black Sea ports – although the number of its maritime vessels is 'zero!'

With its 5,000 residents, 105 hotels, 900 B&B apartments, fourteen petrol stations (duty-free petrol was one of Livigno's main trading items) and thirty-three chair lifts, Livigno had gone through numerous attempts to achieve sovereignty, starting from 1355, where it was effectively administered by two nominees of the Mayor of Bormio. In the early seventeenth century, the valley enjoyed a short period of complete independence, when ruled by the Grigioni family, and a hundred years later it was given customs benefits by Napoleon (these were later confirmed by the Austro-Hungarian Empire in 1818, by Italy in 1910 and by the EEC in 1960), who effectively made it into what it was now – a duty-free area within Italy.

My first impression of Livigno was that of an amazingly flat and long valley, lined with ski-slopes and dotted with duty-free shops.

Before dropping me at my hotel, Gianluca, my driver, showed me directions to the tourism office and told me that all buses in Livigno were free for skiers. 'But I am not a skier, I am a smoker,' I said, gasping from considerable oxygen deficiency, also known as 'altitude sickness' or 'altitude dizziness.' Gianluca reassured me that buses were free for non-skiers too – a touch of high-altitude Alpine 'communism.'

Skiers in their fancy snowsuits were cheerfully falling out of free 'communist' buses outside my hotel. Slipping over snowdrifts, I trudged up the street to the first duty-free shop, selling, among other things, vodka and grappa for astounding €2 a litre. And although I had all but given up drinking spirits, I was unable to resist such amazing bargain and bought a litre of grappa to keep me warm.

Across the road was a duty-free food shop, where I saw what could pass for the world's largest Mortadella sausage, the size of the leading wheel of a steamroller. Next to the deli was a *Lavateria* – 'Launderette' (not a lavatory). I wondered whether it was duty-free too.

More duty-free shops, separated by several metres of snow, were further up the street, their stock being roughly the same: perfumes, electronics, toiletries, clothes, rather expensive tobacco and extraordinarily cheap alcoholic drinks. Not a single customer (I didn't count myself as one) was to be found in any of them.

Loud bangs of church bells from a hidden *basilica* were floating over this snow-covered hub of consumerism. They sounded bizarre and out of place – like Chopin's funereal march played at a wedding. My poor oxygen-deficient head was tolling in unison with the bells.

Church bells above duty-free shops … Could there be a scene more Italian?

My local guide was called Mladenka. A young and tall Bosnian Serb, with the looks of a supermodel, she came to Livigno two years before. Bright, outgoing and fluent in four languages, she was a delight to be with, even if I made sure I kept at least a metre away from her when we walked the streets – to prevent her from towering above me, like a railway signal above a points man's hut.

Mladenka seemed to know everyone in Livigno. At least she greeted almost everybody, and they greeted her. She introduced me to a lady from a perfume shop who was a member of the town council, and to another lady from a clothes store who was also the town's librarian. It looked as if everybody in Livigno doubled as either a duty-free-shop owner or a duty-free-shop assistant. Everybody, except, perhaps Giuseppe Longa, a local linguist and amateur historian, who had to make his living working as a … hairdresser.

According to Giuseppe, the duty-free status was initially granted to the valley due to its poverty as the only recipe for its survival. Even so, it did not bring any real benefits to the locals until 1951, when the first road that could be used in winter was built from Switzerland under the protection of Italy's then Minister of Finance – himself a native of Valtellina. The first hotel in the valley was built in 1880, and a year later Livigno had its first tourist – an American, no doubt. It took another thirty-four years for the second hotel to be constructed.

With all its hotels and duty-free shops operating at present, Livigno could be safely regarded as the hub of commercialism in the Retiche Alps. All the shops were open from morning till late at night (with a two-hour lunch break), seven days a week, 365 days a year. Some time ago, one local shop owner, a devout Roman Catholic, wanted to have her store closed on Sundays, but Livigno authorities did not allow her to do so. 'Duty-free' obviously came before religious (or any other) duty in Livigno, where shops employed over 3,000 people – more than half of all its residents thus making them the community's main (and only) life-line, no less. Theoretically, a visitor (read shopper) could only take out of Livigno goods with total value of under €175. But, as I myself had a chance to make sure, customs controls on the Swiss border were lenient, if not to say non-existent. Livigno had become a sinecure for the no-longer-needed customs inspectors from the now defunct German-French border who were all sent to Livigno as an alternative to being sacked. 'Our customs offices are very well staffed, yet there is nothing to worry about,' Giuseppe Longa concluded with a cackle.

I was actually not at all worried: my only Livigno purchase was the bottle of extraordinarily cheap grappa – already one third empty, by the way.

Verenahof

I knew that Verenahof – a tiny bit of Germany that used to belong to Switzerland until 1964 and the only European enclave to lose its status in the second half of the twentieth century – was now part of the Swiss village of Buttenhardt somewhere near Schaffhausen. It would have been a shame not to visit it while being so close.

The problem was that I had failed to locate either Verenahof or Buttenhardt on any maps. My only hope of finding it was therefore in the hands of Gunnar Lang, the Mayor of Busingen (a nearby German enclave in Switzerland), who had mentioned attending the disenclavement ceremony there in 1967 – three years after the enclave's handover to Switzerland was officially agreed upon. Herr Lang was kind enough to offer me a lift to Verenahof the day after our meeting. He also promised to try and find some local contacts for me to talk to.

As for the ex-enclave's (or ex-exclave's, if you look at it from Germany) history, I was lucky to have found a couple of pages on Verenahof in *The Exclave Problem of Western Europe* by my fellow rootless cosmopolitan Honore M Catudal, Jr from the University of Alabama – the book that I had come to call my 'Enclavian Bible' (I – or rather my suitcase 'Sally' – carried it all through the journey).

According to the omniscient Dr Catudal, Verenahof, a patch of farmland, approximately eighteen acres in area, used to be part of the German commune Wiechs am Randen near Buttenhardt, about five hundred yards away from the German border. Its origins go back to the Middle Ages, when the Verena church (or a nunnery, according to another source – VV) owned this portion of uncultivated land.

Verenahof's highly unusual status was the product of the extreme irregularity (if not to say madness) of the German-Swiss border, which – unlike most 'normal' frontiers – does not seem to follow the features of the landscape, but bends and zigzags at unexpected intervals.[31] Through the ages, there have been numerous futile attempts by both countries to straighten it up somehow, and it was then that the status of Verenahof would inevitably become an issue.

Schaffhausen did have two chances to acquire Verenahof – in 1516 and in 1522, when Count Christoph von Tengen offered to sell it at bargain prices. But on both occasions the city elders 'for reasons which are now unclear' (*pace* Dr Catudal) refused the offers. As it often happens, when they changed their minds several years later, the train had already gone, to use the jargon of Russian market traders: the von Tengen family was longer keen on selling.

[31] Isn't it ironic that two most 'regular' and meticulous nations in Europe should share the continent's most deviant border?

In the aftermaths of the Napoleonic wars, when Talleyrandt – one of Napoleon's most trusted lieutenants – pressurised the fragmented German states to merge into the Confederation of the Rhine in 1806, Verenahof fell under jurisdiction of the Grand Duchy of Baden. With the creation of a united Germany in 1871, it became an outlying part of the German Reich, whilst being completely owned by its Swiss residents (farmers), who were required by Swiss authorities to register as 'overseas Swiss' at the Swiss consulate in Freiburg (Germany), despite the fact that the 'overseas' territory in question was, in actual fact, part of the small Swiss village of Buttenhardt in the centre of the Swiss canton Schaffhausen!

Since 1854, when Verenahof was excluded from the German Customs area and up until its disenclavement in 1964, its status was not dissimilar to that of modern Busingen: its residents – three families of farmers – paid high German taxes on their Swiss franc earnings. The main difference was that, being Swiss – not German – citizens, Verenahof farmers and their family members could not vote in German elections. On the other hand, as 'overseas Swiss,' they were not allowed to participate in Swiss municipal elections or to be elected to local (village and/or town) councils.

Also, due to endless red tape, required for arranging a routine German police visit to Verenahof[32], the minuscule German exclave ended up being *de facto* administered by the village authorities of Buttenhardt. By November 1964 when, after eight years of painstaking negotiations, Germany and Switzerland finally signed a treaty providing for Verenahof's absorption by Switzerland (the treaty went into effect in 1967), its dwellers had come to refer to themselves neither as German or Swiss, but as 'Buttenhardters!'

As I myself learned later in Verenahof, for the disenclavement to come into effect, a swap had to be agreed between Germany and Switzerland, whereby the latter had to donate eighteen acres of its precious territory to Germany in exchange for Verenahof. After years of deliberation, an unpopulated, infertile and rock-strewn patch, directly adjoining the German border, was offered. The Germans, naturally, were not happy with such exchange, and the difference in the quality of land had to be compensated with the sum of 600,000 Swiss francs, reluctantly coughed up by the Swiss government.

This little known peaceful 'annexation' signified the first and only (even if ever so slight) redrawing of Germany's border since World War II.

At the time of Dr Catudal's visit in the early 1970s, Verenahof was 'owned and inhabited by some twenty Swiss nationals' and consisted of 'merely three farms and adjacent forest land.'

[32] In each case, this entailed hard-to-obtain permissions from Swiss authorities for armed 'foreign' policemen to cross the Swiss territory, even if just a couple of hundred yards of it: the Swiss have always been extremely touchy about foreigners with weapons on their neutral terrain.

'I keep missing the right turn,' the visibly embarrassed Mayor of Busingen was mumbling from behind the wheel. 'It's been a long time …'

By any standards, thirty-five years were long enough to forget directions to a tiny unmapped (and unsignposted) former enclave. I didn't blame Gunnar Lang for getting lost while driving me to Verenahof, where, as I have said already, he had been only once before – in 1967.

To find the ex-enclave, we had to locate Buttenhardt first. That was proving unexpectedly difficult. There were no signs (in more than one sense) of Buttenhardt in the area, where, according to Gunnar's vague recollections, the village had to be located. Having circled around all suburbs of Schaffhausen, we kept finding ourselves in the same haunted spot we had already driven through at least twice.

At last, when, having despaired of applying any logic to his search (a gesture of real anguish for a German), Gunnar – in the best traditions of London black-cab drivers – randomly dived into some barely visible forest path, we saw the sought-after sign for Buttenhardt, nailed to a semi-rotten wooden pole.

It was the most amazing road sign I had ever come across, with arrows to 'Buttenhardt' pointing in two opposite directions!

As you can understand, the sign did little to facilitate our search for the elusive little village.

To cut a long story (or rather journey) short, we did find Buttenhardt in the end – quite by accident. It was a totally unremarkable one-shop village, which looked clinically dead on that early Friday afternoon.

We stopped near the tiny and permanently shut village post office. As if to underline the smallness of the place, a minuscule yellow post motorbike (a 'post-moto?'), a baby brother of the famous Swiss 'post-auto,' was parked at its entrance. A plastic tray for mail was secured to the motorbike's leathery back seat.

Gunnar made his apologies and drove away. The trip took much longer that he had expected, and he was now running late for a meeting. He was the Mayor, after all. And the Mayor, even if that of Busingen, was supposed to keep himself busy.

As a true German, however, he had carried out his promise of putting me in touch with the locals – a lovely elderly couple of retired schoolteachers by the name of Gertrud and Werner Brutsch. Married for thirty-eight years and well into their sixties, the Brutschs were slim, active and, judging by the affectionate looks they would furtively exchange from time to time, still very much in love. A living proof that mature age could still be fun, they were a pleasure to be with.

The only problem was that their English was not much better than my non-existent German; although whenever Gertrude uttered an English word, I couldn't help feeling she did it with a slight Scottish accent. In the end, we managed to get along by discovering that all three of us could speak some basic French.

The Brutschs, who had spent all their lives in Buttenhardt, took me on a tour of their deserted and sleepy (if not to say comatose) village, with Verenahof as a starting point.

The last disenclaved bit of Europe was hiding at the end of the village's main street, behind the school, doubling as Buttenhardt's community hall. It was marked with a modest signpost in the middle of the school playground saying simply 'Verenahof' and pointing at a cluster of solid freshly-painted farmhouses across the playground. These were, in fact, Verenahof.

'Prior to the disenclavement, the border ran along the edge of the playground, so that the school itself was in Switzerland and the playground – in Verenahof that was Germany,' said Gertrud.

'It was an ideal place for committing an offence, for Swiss police were barred from accessing the playground,' her husband added.

I snapped a couple of shots of the unremarkable ex-German playground and of even more unremarkable farm-houses, and Gertrud took a picture of me looking up at the 'Verenahof' sign in feigned excitement.

To be absolutely fair, I WAS rather excited to have finally located this virtually unknown European curio, even if Buttenhardt felt like the most unlikely place on earth where any sort of discovery could be made.

'Is there any memorable story connected with Verenahof?' I asked my escorts.

As it turned out, there was.

In April 1945, three German soldiers, led by *Oberst* von Hartlein, a senior SS officer, took refuge in Verenahof and claimed they were in Germany (which they were indeed!) and hence out of reach of the French occupational forces, stationed across the German border several hundred yards away. A mini-diplomatic crisis ensued. The Swiss authorities in Berne were tipped off, and they alerted the French, who quickly realised that they had no power to extract the Germans, for to 'occupy' Verenahof, they had to cross the territory of neutral Switzerland. To make matters worse, the Swiss farmers of Verenahof did not mind harbouring the Germans at all and were staunchly refusing all demands from Berne to extradite them or, at least, to stop giving them food – a request that clashed with their notion of hospitality. 'We are farmers, and we will always feed our guests, no matter where they come from,' they were reported as saying.

In the end, an agreement was reached between the French and the Swiss, whereby the French would allow a small contingent of Swiss policemen to enter the German Verenahof (of which the former were theoretically in control, yet couldn't set their feet onto it) to arrest the Nazis and to frogmarch them across five hundred yards of Swiss territory to the German border, where they would be handed over to the French occupational forces. And that was precisely what happened. The locals later reminisced that the farmers were not at all pleased with the incursion. The Nazis, naturally, were pleased even less, and the well-groomed Colonel (*Oberst*) von Hertlein was, allegedly, rather pissed off by the fact that his Swiss police escort was of a lower rank than he was. Indeed, how very irregular and insubordinate!

We retraced our footsteps to the school/village-hall building along the deserted village street that once used to mark the Swiss-German border. In the schoolyard, I spotted a couple of withered flowerbeds. They were framed with moss-covered grey stones, carved with faded, yet still clearly visible letters and numbers: 'S,' 'D,' 'CS,' '1935' and so on. I recalled seeing similar old stones lining the Swiss-German border outside Busingen.

'These stones used to mark the border near the school and went all around the playground,' confirmed Gertrud and explained that 'S' stood for *Schweiz* (Switzerland), 'D' – for *Deutschland* (Germany), and 'CS,' as I already knew, for Canton Schaffhausen.

'Rammed into the ground and nailed to it by special wedge-like "witness stones," the border posts were very hard to excavate in 1967,' added Weiner.

True, the old European borders were supposed to be impregnable and ever lasting. Yet too many of them, as I had discovered during my travels in Enclavia, were unnecessary, superfluous and at times totally ridiculous. It was good to see at least some of old border posts turned into flowerbed linings – a sight that alone made my short visit to Buttenhardt worthwhile. It gave hope that one day all European borders would be scrapped and their solid and silent markers recycled and put to a more meaningful use.

Gertrud pointed to a nearby lawn, where a big tent, erected for the Disenclavement celebrations of 1967, used to stand.

'It was a very windy day in November,' she recalled. 'The wind was so strong that it eventually blew the tent away, but this did not spoil the villagers' festive mood.'

From my point of view, there was a lot to celebrate for both Germany and Switzerland on that day, for the 1967 Disenclavement had proved not just that European borders could be redrawn outside military conflicts, but also that age-long territorial disputes between countries could be resolved peacefully and to mutual satisfaction – an important lesson, taught to Europe and the world by the tiny patch of farmland called Verenahof.

It was purely coincidental that my visit to Buttenhardt fell on one of the three days during which Switzerland was facing another momentous choice: whether or not to join the UN. It was a very 'comfortist' and unmistakably Swiss decision to extend the Referendum to three days (Friday, Saturday and Sunday) to make sure everybody, who so wished, could go to the polls at his/her own convenience.[33] Incidentally, the previous 1986 referendum rejected the UN membership by three to one, but it was held at the time when Cold War was still raging, and every Swiss household was required by law to have a nuclear bomb shelter. Now, as opinion polls indicated, there were grounds to believe that the traditional Swiss 'isolationism' (it was the world's only UN non-member country, except for Vatican) was coming to an end.

The 'No' campaigners, however, were still strong.

We went inside Buttenhardt's own polling station, conveniently situated in ... the village school building, where else? A '*NEIN*' poster on one of the walls depicted Wilhelm Tell, a legendary fourteenth-century Swiss patriot and the country's defender against foreign invaders, embracing a blond (and, no doubt, Swiss) boy, as if indeed protecting him from all corruptive 'foreign' influences.[34] On the opposite wall – in a truly pluralistic fashion – there hung a '*JA*' poster, only, instead of hooded wild-looking Wilhelm, with a crossbow on his shoulder, it carried a boring photo of some bespectacled Swiss MP.

Apart from the Brutschs and myself, the polling station was totally deserted – not counting Wilhelm Tell, the boy and the boring bureaucrat on the posters.

'Are you going to cast your ballots?' I asked Gertrud and Weiner.

'We have voted already,' they replied in chorus.

I didn't ask them whether they voted '*JA*' or '*NEIN*,' but one thing was certain: whatever their votes were, they were definitely the same.

I picked up a clean ballot from an unattended stack on an equally unattended table. It was a neatly bound brochure, with twenty-four (!) pages of text, the actual removable voting paper modestly occupying pages 22 and 23. The remaining twenty-two pages were thickly covered with small print of some mysterious rules and regulations (probably explaining how to mark your option correctly and how to fold the ballot before dropping it into an urn). I thought I could understand a certain lack of enthusiasm towards the referendum: Swiss voters, with their high sense of civic duty[35], would feel obliged to read through all the pages before casting their votes – not a very exciting prospect.

[33] The Swiss 'comfortist' voting regulations also provide for filling in the ballots at home and then dropping them at the station, if one so wishes.

[34] My second guess was that the boy could just as well be the Austrian governor's son, on whose head, as the legend goes, Wilhelm Tell put an apple to be shot through with his crossbow. He did it without mishap, and the poster could well be depicting Wilhelm Tell pacifying his living target after the shot, or else trying to cajole the boy into putting the apple onto his blond curly head before it.

[35] A couple of days before, a Swiss newspaper wrote about a (Swiss) train driver, who gave three passengers a lift back home in his car after he forgot to stop at their station. 'He made a mistake and felt his duty to amend it,' a Swiss railways spokesman was reported as saying.

The Brutschs then invited me for a quick cup of tea in their house at 1 Dorfstrasse (One Village Street) – a charming rural address. Weiner showed me a souvenir Disenclavement board, with two original 'witness stones': brown (German) and green (Swiss) – glued to it. It was revealing to see that the wedge-like stone nails, never intended to be seen above the ground, were nevertheless not only differently coloured, but also clearly marked with small letters 'S' and 'D' – a testimony to a shared Swiss-German obsession with old frontiers.

The couple talked about their village, which had just one shop, open for one hour a day and selling mostly milk, bread and butter. Buttenhardt didn't have a church, but had a church choir (!), of which both Gertrud and Weiner were members.

'Do you know that Buttenhardt is the highest village in canton Schaffhausen?' Gertrud asked me.

I confessed my complete ignorance about this truly distinctive feature of Buttenhardt which brought about recollections of my travels in America, where some small Midwest towns liked to advertise themselves to passing motorists in clumsy road-sign doggerels of the type 'Climate best by government test!' or by claiming to be 'The Biggest Small Town In The United States.' The Brutsch's 'European' patriotism, however, was different: un-rhymed, quiet (almost subdued) and totally devoid of a small-town conceit, better known as inferiority complex.

Gertrud was throwing frequent glances at her watch. To me, it was unthinkable that anyone could ever be in a hurry in Buttenhardt, but she said she had to drive to Schaffhausen to babysit for her daughter and offered me a lift. 'PostBuses are rare guests in Buttenhardt,' she remarked.

The couple kissed goodbye, and for as long as it took us to drive to the end of the wind-swept Village Street, Weiner stood outside the house and waved to his wife. Well, possibly, to me, too …

Mount Athos

The mountain path was steep and narrow. Strewn with rough shapeless rocks and mule droppings, it wound mercilessly uphill along the edge of an abyss, and it seemed endless. Cicadas chirred deafeningly, as if they were laughing at me. The white-hot disc of the midday sun with several fluffy clouds around it – like a giant freshly cooked portion of bacon and eggs – glared from the blue sizzling frying pan of the Hellenic sky.

Puffing like an early steam engine, I trudged higher and higher up the track, scaring tiny agile lizards from under my trainers. My feet felt stiff, as if I was walking on stilts, and streams of hot, salty sweat were pouring down my forehead …At last when I thought I wouldn't be able to take another step for a million pounds, I looked up and saw HIM. In his monastic *klobuk* hat he was standing on the path, blue robes and black beard flying in the breeze, and pointing at the square building of the nearby *skites*, resembling an obscure Cyrillic letter. In loose, worn sandals, he could have passed for a mirage or an Old Testament apparition, were it not for the inscription on the fringe of the grey satin trousers showing from under his habit: 'Property of the Mount Sinai Military Hospital.'

It was Father Spiridon, the chief monk of St Anna mountain *skites* (small monastery), to where we were heading. He brought mules, one for each of us, and for the last several hundred metres to the *skites* we rode on their uncomplaining backs – a sensation similar to a slow levitation and a huge relief for us, if not for the mules …

Such was the start of my previous journey to Mount Athos in 1996. The same climb today would have been very different. Firstly, we would have most likely been driven up the mountain. Secondly, there wouldn't have been any mules, for there are hardly any left on the Holy Mountain …

April 2012. Outside the walls of Great Lavra, Mouth Athos' main monastery, a row of solar panels stare up at the sky. Against the backdrop of the medieval monastery walls, the panels appeared alien and out of place – like bikini-clad models at a black-tie dinner – and I felt like pinching myself to make sure I was indeed in Mouth Athos, the 1,000-year-old all-male Orthodox monastic republic in the north of Greece, notorious for its stubborn resistance to any whiff of modernity …

It is my third visit to Mount Athos, one of the world's most spiritual places, where Orthodox monks spend their lives in prayers and contemplation. For over a thousand years – in accordance with a special edict of the Patriarch – 'no smooth-faced person' has stepped on its rocky, sunburnt shores. 'Mount Athos is one of the few places in the world that does not change with time,' I wrote after my previous 'pilgrimage' to the Holy Mountain (another name for it) in 1996 – see above.

I was wrong. The change began in 1997 – in the aftermath of the ill-fated exhibition of the artistic treasures of the Holy Mountain (priceless icons and frescoes, Ptolemy's first map of the world etc etc) held in Salonika. It was the first – and most certainly the last – attempt on the part of the monks to establish closer contacts with outside world. Titillated by the unspeakable treasures on display, a group of feminists filed a suit in the European Court of Human Rights demanding to rescind the male-only status of the Holy Mountain. The suit was eventually thrown out, yet the monks got a big scare, and as so often happens to a frightened person (or country), withdrew even deeper into themselves. It was then that the decision was taken to start modernising Mount Athos – for the first time in over 1,000 years.

I knew about the changes from the rare articles in the media and from first-hand impressions of some British visitors – as rare as the articles, for entry to Mount Athos is still conditional on a '*diamonitirion*' – an impressive-looking special visa (resembling an honorary diploma) issued sparingly, reluctantly and slowly by Macedonia's government and signed by all four members of Iera Epistasia (the Holy Administration) of Mount Athos. With disbelief, I would browse websites, claiming to be Mouth Athos-based and offering pricey (over €50 a piece) 'virtual tours' of some monasteries and no-less pricey lightings of a no-less-virtual candle. I also heard about the growing commercialisation of the country's small wine-making and icon-painting industries and of the famous monk chef Father Epiphanios of Mylopotamos, whose cookbook of Mount Athos cuisine (of which I myself had a copy!) was a best-seller in several countries, including the USA.

Frankly, I was finding all of the above hard to imagine in a place where just fifteen years ago there was hardly any heating, the electricity supply was both erratic and sporadic, and means of public transportation were limited to a fleet of reliable and low-maintenance mules and only one car, an ancient Unimog truck, driven by the legendary Father Makarios – a chain-smoking monk wearing greasy jeans under his grimy habit. Reeking of rakia and cheap Karelia cigarettes, Father Makarios was then Mount Athos' only driver, and his vehicle, with the character of a mule, carried Virgin Mary icons, instead of pin-up girls, on the windscreen and a shot-gun on the passenger seat – to blast an occasional unwary snake luxuriating on the track. There were no proper roads, just holes and bumps, and I remembered bouncing in the tarpaulin-covered back of Father Makarios's Unimog like a ping-pong ball inside an empty lunch box …

The Holy Mountain's modernisation caught up with me still on the mainland, in the Greek village of Ouranopolis – the gateway to Mount Athos, from where there was now a regular ferry connection. Caught in the all-male crowd of would-be pilgrims, I noted with wonder that the village's only couple of dusty streets had become an open-air supermarket of Mount Athos-related paraphernalia – mostly kitsch. Yet the biggest shock was inside the visa-issuing office where the coveted '*diamonitirions*' (visas) were now churned out by three LEXM RK laser printers, with the 'Iera Epistasia' members' signatures reproduced as facsimiles!

At the ferry's first stop – the monastery of Dochiariu – a couple of pick-up trucks were waiting on the pier. A handful of disembarked monks and pilgrims boarded them to be driven up the hill.

The next on the ferry's coastal route was the Russian monastery of St Panteleimon – so huge it looked like a medieval fortified city, with numerous secular buildings and blue onion domes of churches sticking out among them. In the early 1900s, it was the Holy Mountain's biggest and richest abbey, with the world's largest bell and over 3,000 prosperous monks. One of them was allegedly so rich that he had accumulated Europe's biggest private collection of telescopes which he himself had never used! By 1996, however, St Panteleimon had (for obvious reasons) degraded to the point when it was semi-ruined and had just twelve monks, with one of whom – stocky and freckled Father Filaret – I then had a short conversation in Russian.

In April 2012, the monastery looked thriving again, with neat freshly painted facades and masts of construction cranes stretching up towards the skies. Standing on the ferry's deck, I overhead the following verbal exchange between two young Russian monks.

'Look at this monastery: like everywhere else, we Russians have the biggest presence on the Holy Mountain!' commented the first monk pointing at the domes of St Panteleimon.

'Yes, our boys are doing well,' agreed the second. 'Even the largest Greek monasteries could all fit inside the guesthouse of ours!'

More cars and minibuses were waiting for our ferry in Dafni, the Holy Mountain's tiny port of entry where we all went ashore. I noticed that some disembarking monks were carrying crates with herbs, fruit and veggies – another novelty: fifteen years earlier all the monasteries and *skites* (no matter how small) were trying to be entirely self-sufficient.

I could also hear mobile phones ringing with peculiar Orthodox chant-like or prayer ring-tones! A monk then would ferret the gadget out from underneath his loose black robes – like some circus trickster, and, having finished the conversation, would drop it back – almost imperceptibly – into the seemingly bottomless dark recesses of his clothing. That was a significant change for the place where the first public phone cabin was installed as recently as in 1995 causing a heated debate and controversy comparable to the introduction of steam power in the early nineteenth-century Europe …

Unlike in 1996, the Holy Mountain now boasted of several stretches of proper road – near Dafni and around Karies, the capital. Occasionally, one could spot a timid freshly painted road sign pointing to a nearby monastery. There was even one brand new (and, no doubt, freshly painted) bus shelter, made of wood! Apart from those, driving (and riding) was still very slow and extremely bumpy, with an additional risk of a collision with another monastic vehicle. With tracks generously strewn with sharp pebbles, flat tires were common, and Father Ignatius, the driver of our Mercedes minivan, had to pull over repeatedly to help a fellow monk driver to change the wheel, while we were patiently waiting inside the van. Yes, one could now speak of a traffic flow in Mount Athos!

At the '*Archondariki*' (guest quarters) of Great Lavra where I spent the first night, a batteries recycling bank had been installed next to a public phone cabin. A strict sign in the corridor called on pilgrims and monks alike not just to refrain from exposing any bits of their 'naked flesh' (apart from the face that is) even in the washrooms (!), but also to make sure their mobile phones were permanently switched off when anywhere inside the monastery. Well, there's no denying the fact: modern technology often brings with it noise and pollution.

Understandably, there is no consensus about the ongoing Mount Athos modernisation. According to some, instead of a place for meditation and prayer which it had been for over 1,000 years, Mount Athos has now turned into a vast secularised construction site, with trucks, machinery and land cruisers. The ever-growing number of visitors is causing inconvenience to the brotherhoods, some of which are no longer able to provide their traditional hospitality (a one-night free stay, free meals and a welcome tray of coffee, rakia and sweets) to each pilgrim. Indeed, there was no welcome set waiting for us at Great Lavra, but that could have been due to the fast which was on …

Our driver monk, Father Ignatius, however, was very much in favour of the change saying that new machinery and new roads were helping to restore old monasteries at reduced costs – and the results were obvious to everyone. The chef monk Father Epiphanios, who was my host for the last two nights on Mount Athos, was in total agreement with Father Ignatius, but went even further asserting that anything that helps a monk in carrying out his monastic duties, and those include all sorts of chores and little daily jobs, should be welcome.

One area that stays untouched by modern technology, however, is the liturgy. The only tools that were used by monks during the majestic eight-hour long all-night Easter vigil at the '*katholikon*' (main temple) of Iviron monastery were long sticks with small candle-extinguishing bellows at the end. At some point during the service, all candles inside the temple were put out, and the magnificent monastic chants sounded for some time in pitch darkness until all the lights were suddenly back on, and massive brass chandeliers were being swung in celebration of Jesus Christ's resurrection.

Then, after a celebratory Easter meal (eggs, fish soup, goat cheese and wine) with the monks inside the monastery's refectory, where tables were set for 300 people at 5am, I watched the breaking of a new dawn on the balcony above the monastery yard overlooking the sea.

It was still pitch dark, and the lonely light of a detached mountain *skites* – a hermit's dwelling – was blinking in the distance, like an unknown star. Soon I heard the rhythmic and monotonous sounds of '*talantos*,' wooden drums calling brothers to another liturgy. I looked down: the black-hooded monks were sliding across the monastery yard towards the church in treacherous semi-darkness, like white-shrouded ghosts in a slow-motion picture, shown in the negative by the erroneous cinema operator of dawn.

An invisible multi-voiced choir inside the church was chanting psalms with amazing synchrony and grace as the red-robed monk of the rising sun was descending slowly from his heavenly '*skites*' above the sea and covering the world with his pink see-through cassock.

Suddenly, everything around me was full of harmony and light. Life no longer seemed purposeless and hectic. The grief that I might have inflicted on others was forgiven; my own suffering, joys and misdemeanours were all forgotten, and even death itself was no longer frightening …

The fact that – in line with the Holy Mountain's ongoing modernisation – the call for the prayer was simultaneously broadcast on the monastery's radio system did not make the magic moment I was experiencing – or the divine liturgy itself – less meaningful and less spiritual.

And that was my silent answer to the question of whether technology has changed the Holy Mountain …

Part Eleven
Chasing Ghosts: My Literary Journeys

Alexandr Solzhenitsyn

It was like chasing a ghost … At least, it felt like that in the beginning, as I was driving through the forests of the Black River Valley which, according to New England tourism officials, were past their much-publicised 'fall-foliage' peak. This ghost-hunting feeling was enhanced by schizophrenic pre-Halloween displays of grinning carved pumpkins and plastic skeletons on the porches of clapboard country houses along the highway – as if they were smirking disdainfully at the sheer futility of my quest.

I was trying to find the former abode of Alexander Solzhenitsyn, this century's greatest Russian writer, near the town of Cavendish, tucked away among the hills of Vermont – the place where he had spent seventeen nostalgic and highly prolific years of exile before returning to Russia in 1994.

I always wanted to see this house. Why? The answer can probably be found in the spirit of mystery and mass hysteria which surrounded Solzhenitsyn's name in the Soviet Union of my youth. All his books were confiscated from shops and public libraries, and one could easily end up in prison for simply possessing (let alone reading) any of his works. Bans and fatwas have always been the best publicity for writers, and I shall never forget the peculiar ticklish feeling of danger while reading a tattered copy of *One Day in the Life of Ivan Denisovich*, aged sixteen. Hiding the book under the blanket in my bed, I read (or rather swallowed) it in one sleepless night (next morning I had to pass it on to the next person in line) in the treacherous light of a small torch. My full awareness of all the dangers involved only added to the joy of reading. The book described one routine day of a prisoner of Stalin's Gulag, where Solzhenitsyn himself had served a stretch. And while heroic Soviet workers and peasants all joined in the well-rehearsed propaganda chorus of 'unanimous condemnation' ('We haven't read his books, but we furiously reject Solzhenitsyn's views …'), I treasured an old copy of *Novi Mir* magazine, with one of the writer's early short stories, which they 'forgot' to confiscate from our school library.

Later we learnt that, 'in accordance with the Soviet people's demands,' Solzhenitsyn was 'thrown out' of the country and, after a spell in Switzerland, settled in Vermont, USA, where he, allegedly, lived the life of a reclusive O'Reilly, penning down his 'anti-Soviet drivels' in a palace, surrounded with barbed wire.

And here I was in autumn-ridden Vermont, on my way to that mysterious 'palace,' whose famous dweller, now eighty, was no longer there. He was back in his ungrateful motherland, where, his prophet-like beard and his laughable attempts at teaching the Russian people 'how they should rebuild' their country became subjects of bitter comments and open ridicule. 'There's no prophet in one's own fatherland,' goes an old Russian proverb. Solzhenitsyn should have known better …

After the village of Plymouth, birthplace of America's mediocre ex-president Calvin Coolidge, the road wound through desolate countryside, dotted here and there with broken agricultural machinery, left to rust in the field, and forlorn uninhabited houses in different stages of disrepair – as if I had left prosperous New England and was driving through some dreary time-frozen landscape, only slightly brightened up by the exquisite palette of autumn forests. It was not long before I spotted the first weather-beaten 'Cavendish' sign, and shortly the town itself came into view.

To call Cavendish a town was a typically American overstatement: by European standards, it was but a medium-size village stretching for a couple of miles along the track. Walking in its deserted main (and only) street was like going back seventy years, to the times of the Great Depression. Nearly half of the houses were abandoned. Shabby wooden sheds of 'The Black River Medical Centre' and the 'Mammoth Hobbies Full Line Hobby Store' looked permanently closed down. The only town service that seemed to be still running (at least, its sign had a phone number) was 'Chimney Care.'

In the town square, next to a firmly locked hut of the 'town hall,' I spotted a granite obelisk, which – from a distance – could be mistaken for a regulation countryside war memorial. It was a memorial indeed, but not to the fallen of Cavendish (the town lost only nine men in all the wars of the twentieth century), but to a nineteenth century local railway foreman called Phineas Gage, who, as it transpired from the carved inscription, once had his tamping iron accidentally blown through his skull and out the top of his head – and survived.

My first port of call was Joe Allan's general store, made world famous by the hand-written sign 'No Directions to the Solzhenitsyns' that used to adorn one of its walls. In accordance with New Englanders' traditional respect for other people's privacy, the locals had been unconditionally protective of their own eminent exile and stayed mum about his whereabouts, although few of them were able to comprehend who exactly he was and from whom he was hiding in Cavendish.

The sign was no more, and a stocky blonde woman, unhurriedly frying burgers behind the counter, initially claimed complete ignorance not only of Solzhenitsyn, but of Joe Allan, too. It took her half-a-dozen burgers to recall that the latter had sold the shop a couple of years before and had moved out of town. Well, the first pancake is always a lump, as they say in Russia (I am not so sure about the first burger).

Apart from the store, the only other Cavendish establishment which wasn't shut down on that Saturday morning was a small bungalow, insisting it be called Cavendish Fletcher Community Library. There I had a sudden stroke of luck. Joyce Fuller, the librarian, not exactly inundated with customers and whiling away her time in the company of a fashion magazine, was genuinely happy to see a fellow human. She pointed to a near-empty shelf with thirteen Solzhenitsyn volumes in English translation, presented to the library by the writer himself shortly before his departure. The glossy hardbacks were neatly spread out along the shelf to give the impression of abundance.

She confessed to having been present at both of Solzhenitsyn's public appearances before the townsfolk: in February, 1977 – to say hello and to apologise for the fence (a sacrilege, by Vermont standards) he had to build around his property to protect himself from 'the reporters and the idle types,' and in February, 1994 – to thank the people of Cavendish for their 'kindness and hospitality' and to bid farewell. She then kindly offered to photocopy the text of both addresses for just 10 cents each, with a pamphlet on the extraordinary survival of Phineas Gage thrown in. From the latter, it turned out that the Phineas Gage Historic Festival and Anniversary Commemoration took place in Cavendish in 1998. The events of this Rod-Through-the-Head Commemoration Festival included: 'pancake breakfast; parade; BBQ chicken lunch, hosted by American Legion Post; and Hot Dogs & Hamburgers by Cavendish Boy Scout Troop 211.'

'Are there any plans to commemorate Solzhenitsyn's seventeen years in Cavendish?' I asked her. She was not sure and suggested I call up Rich Speck, the town clerk, which I did without leaving the library.

The town clerk sounded suspicious, as if Solzhenitsyn was still there and waited to be protected. He assured me that there were no plans for a Solzhenitsyn memorial and added that his presence 'had no day-to-day impact on the Cavendish community.' Unlike that of Phineas Gage, no doubt …

According to Mr Speck, Solzhenitsyn's house was now owned by his two sons, but he was not sure whether they were in town.

Using a sophisticated, almost spy-like, map, drawn by Joyce Fuller, the librarian, on the margins of the hapless Phineas Gage brochure, I set out in search of the old Hoffman house and farm, bought by Solzhenitsyn in 1976 for $150,000. From the reminiscences of those few 'reporters and idle types' who did manage to worm themselves on to the fifty-acre property, I knew that it consisted of a two-storey main house; a library-cum-study, where Solzhenitsyn wrote from 8am to 9-10pm every day (without a single holiday in seventeen years!) standing at a lectern; a guest house; a small pond; a vegetable garden; and a tennis court, where he would 'gracefully but slowly and inexpertly' (to quote one of his biographers) hit the ball during rare intervals in his writing.

Whoever Solzhenitsyn was hiding from, he couldn't have hidden better.

I turned off the paved road into a dirt track, snaking through the thick forest alongside a bubbly creek. After an umpteenth zigzag, I finally saw it. Not the house itself, but the notorious fence and the gate with an imposing 'No Trespassing. Police Take Notice' sign. Several closed circuit security cameras were staring at me blankly from nearby trees. The rusty intercom button got stuck in its socket when pressed, and there was no reply. It was evident that no one was inside the compound.

Three polythene-covered parcels with books lay on the ground, on the other side of the gate. They were addressed to Ignat Solzhenitsyn, the writer's elder son, a one-time child-prodigy musician.

For a while, I stood in front of the locked gate, listening to the jolly chatter of the creek and to the soft rustling of falling leaves, as if nature itself was shedding the leafy luggage of the crazy epoch, when authors were either imprisoned or had to encage themselves behind fences and security cameras only because they wanted to keep writing the truth.

But, somehow, there was no finality about the scene. A leaf-carpeted path led from the gate towards Solzhenitsyn's house, which could not be seen from where I stood. The path climbed up the hill before disappearing from view. That was probably why – just like my quest – it seemed incomplete, as if cut in the middle. But it also implied continuation.

What was going to happen next? Vermont forest was offering no answers. Only the fallen leaves slowly pirouetted in the air, as if trying to delay the ultimate moment of dying. And the snow-white trunks of 'Russian' birches were bursting through the red-brown sylvan setting – like piercing screams of discord through the harmonious symphony of autumn …

Joseph Heller

Here's a quote from Joseph Heller's *Something Happened,* a scathingly hilarious literary catalogue of modern complexes and anxieties:

> 'I hate funerals – I hate funerals passionately because there is always something morbid about them – and I do my best to avoid going to any (especially my own, ha, ha).'

I always found this 'ha, ha' a bit spooky. A dead man's chuckle from the grave …

I first met Joseph Heller only several months before his death, in summer 1999, at Simon & Schuster's lunch in his honour. His latest (and last as it turned out) autobiographical book *Now and Then* was about to be released in the UK, and he was in London to promote it.

I was invited to this lunch because two of my books: *Borders Up!* and *Dreams on Hitler's Couch* – were coming out simultaneously with his as part of the launch list of Simon & Schuster's new imprint 'Scribner UK.'

As always, I turned up early and settled down to wait on a bench near the restaurant's entrance.

I was soon joined by a tired-looking old man whose sallow face looked vaguely familiar.

His younger self – smiley, curly-haired and known to the whole world from the back cover of his masterpiece *Catch-22* (I read the smuggled paperback of it while still a student in Kharkov) – was showing through the badly fitting camouflage of ailment and age. He was suffering from an incurable debilitating illness that had left him partially paralysed only a couple of years before and was to kill him by the end of the year.

But I didn't know it then. And neither did he.

'You must be Joseph Heller,' I said.

We shook hands. His movements were slow and appeared forced, as if his every small gesture or a slight turn of his head were painful. They probably were. Yet his warm brown eyes were lively and full of youthful glimmer.

The eyes of an eternal Coney Island teenager who grew up in the shadow of a Ferris wheel – curious, mischievous and hungry for adventures.

He asked me a lot of questions about my life in the Soviet Union and was nodding knowingly as I was answering.

He had a peculiar squint that made him look as if he knew everything about you.

I told him I was about to start researching a book on America and was very interested in Coney Island, where knish and hot dog were invented and part of which was now known as 'Little Odessa,' for 150,000 Soviet emigrants, mostly former inhabitants of Odessa, settled there in the last twenty-five years.

I heard they had radically altered the face of that 'old world' New York neighbourhood, nicknamed 'a retired poor man's Miami Beach' in the 1930s, where Joseph Heller was born and grew up.

Our next meeting was a couple of months later, at the Cheltenham Festival of Literature.

In the Cheltenham Festival Programme (in November of the same year), our photos – Joseph Heller's and mine – were printed on the same page, next to each other.

Our talks occurred on the same day, at precisely the same time, but at different Festival venues.

We stayed at the same hotel and agreed to meet up for breakfast one morning, before our respective book-signing sessions.

'I hate book signings,' Heller muttered sipping his tea. He then told me how he was once invited to sign some books in the Mall of America.

'There were three people at my table. And next to me, the lady from *The Wheel of Fortune* who never says a word in the programme – just rotates the wheel – was signing copies of her autobiography. And you know, Vitali: the queue to her table was stretching for over a mile!'

With *Catch-22* as his very first book, he became a living classic who had been trying to catch up (no pun intended) with its resounding success for the rest of his writing career.

'You know what, come to New York and I'll show you my Coney Island,' he said when we were saying goodbye in the lobby. He gave me his phone number and asked me to call him several days in advance. 'I'll have to come over from Long Island where I now live,' he explained almost apologetically.

With his publicist in tow, he then went off to sign his books.

I was not destined to see him ever again.

Several weeks later, having agreed with the *Daily Telegraph* to do a feature on Joseph Heller's Coney Island, I was about to fly to New York and called him at home.

The phone was ringing for what seemed an eternity, and as I was ready to replace it, he finally answered.

In semi-whisper he said he was not feeling very well, but didn't cancel our 'excursion' and asked me to call him again from New York.

I did. We agreed to meet inside the Grand Central Station in the morning of 13 December.

In the afternoon of 12 December, I was on a Subway train when a man next to me opened an early edition of *New York Post.*

Joseph Heller's haggard face was on the front page.

The man hardly looked at it and flicked over to the Sports section.

I got off at the next station and bought the paper, although I already knew what must have happened.

You can see a photo of a writer, even of a great American writer, on the front page of a US tabloid on two occasions: if he wins the Nobel Prize for Literature or if he dies.

I knew that the 1999 Nobel Prize for Literature had been awarded to Gunter Grass. Therefore …

A later edition of *New York Post* for the same day had Joseph Heller's obituary moved from page one to page twenty-six.

I kept our 'appointment' inside the Grand Central next morning hoping not just against hope (my habitual Soviet past-time) but also against reason that he would somehow turn up … At times, it felt I could almost see his light-grey (nearly white) curly hairstyle and his stooping frame in the crowd.

And then I decided to go to Coney Island on my own.

Heller's Coney Island, 'with its beaches, crowds, commotion and couple of hundred entertainments,' to where 'people came from everywhere,' would have been different of course – the neighbourhood of the Amusement Park, the 1920s Cyclone rollercoaster, the Parachute Jump from which Joseph had wanted to leap but never did – and now never will, and Nathan's Stand, the birthplace of the hot dog.

From Brighton Beach, the tram took me to Mermaid Avenue – the area where Joseph Heller lived.

Or 'had lived' – as I should have been writing from then on.

I found his school, still a school now.

At Major Prime Meats butcher's shop, I had a brief chat with an elderly man called Stanley, who said he went to the same class with Joseph, and I had to break the news of Heller's death to him.

It stopped raining and the area brightened up (bright-brighter-Brighton?) a bit. Muffled music could be heard from empty fun fair rides.

The Luna Park often mentioned in *Now and Then* was no longer there. Blocks of three-storeyed red-brick buildings, populated mostly by Soviet immigrants and still known as 'Luna Park,' were in its place.

At Nathan's Hot Dogs, now a spacious emporium rather than a stand, I had a knish, a hot potato pie, reminiscent of *kartophelnik* – a flat potato pancake of my Ukrainian childhood – both of my grannies made excellent ones.

A black waitress who had never heard of Joseph Heller, told me that it was Charles Feltman, a Jewish immigrant from Germany, who actually invented the hot dog in the 1870s and served it for the first time in his restaurant where Nathan Handwerker was a waiter. In 1916, Nathan opened his own stand, lowered the price of a hot dog from ten to five cents and hired people dressed as doctors and nurses to promote his product …

I wandered into an empty circus tent and spoke with the owner called Dick. He had never heard of Joseph Heller either.

Dick complained that his business was not doing very well.

'It is hard to find people who can do what we need, sword swallowers, for example,' he said.

That could have come straight from one of Joseph Heller's books …

Somehow I felt that by visiting Coney Island on the day after Joseph Heller's death and by adding my own memories to his, I had paid my last respects to the superb writer and satirist with whom we could have become good friends.

I suddenly understood where the amazing humour (or was it 'humor?') and the sense of the absurd of *Catch-22* and Heller's other novels might have come from. Growing up in America's largest (prior to the appearance of Disneyland) amusement park must have played a role …

When I returned to London several days later and was checking my phone messages, there was one that made me freeze.

Joseph Heller's feeble voice was apologising for not being able to see me tomorrow due to not feeling well. He knew I did not carry a mobile and was hoping I would check my London answer phone from New York.

It must have been one of the last (if not the very last) phone call he had made in his life …

Oscar Wilde

'To give an accurate description of what has never occurred is ... the inalienable privilege of any man of ... culture,' a friend said to me once.

'Wait a moment,' a knowledgeable reader would exclaim. 'The quote comes from Oscar Wilde, who died in 1900 and therefore cannot possibly be a friend of yours, for even an ancient fifty-year-old wreck like yourself is not antiquated enough for that!'

With respect, allow me to disagree. For what IS a friend? He is someone, to whom you address your joys and sorrows; who stands by you in grief and trouble; who is always there to reassure and to cheer up. If so (and it IS so!), I can earnestly count long-deceased Oscar as one of my closest soul mates and confidants.

I am sure I wouldn't have survived my latest (the last of many) personal crisis, had it not been for a postcard, pinned to the wall above my writing desk, with just one sentence on it:

'We are all in the gutter, but some of us are looking at the stars.'

One of the most beautiful things ever written (or said), this sentence is worth volumes and volumes of modern prose and poetry.

And about ten years before – recovering from yet another massive setback – I was eventually able to replace Prozac with the following hourly mantra:

'A society can forgive a murderer, but never a dreamer.'

God knows how many times – facing a pile of unpaid bills, feeling cornered or suffering writer's block – I was taken out of limbo and forced to smile by recalling my friend's sardonic pronouncements of the type:

'I was working on the proof of one of my poems all the morning, and took out a comma. In the afternoon I put it back again.'

Or: 'History is an account of events that did not happen written by the people who weren't there.'

I cannot remember whether the latter 'wisdoms' were also received as postcards from Oscar, but the return address on the first 'we-are-all-in-the-gutter' one was:

'21, Westland Row, Dublin 2, Ireland.'

That was where baby Oscar was born exactly 150 years ago. If the deceased have any permanent 'address' at all, it should not be of the place where they died, but of the house where they were born. For it is there that we materialise out of 'nothingness' (I am a convinced agnostic, you know), so it is only logical that it is also there that we eventually re-join this very 'nothingness.'

While in Dublin, I always felt surrounded by Oscar.

To begin with, the 'Village' offices are right across the road from 21, Westland Row. Having my morning espresso and a cigarette outside 'Caffé Napoli' next door, I look at the windows of the fine Georgian house and can almost discern the silhouette of little Oscar, wearing – in full accordance with Victorian children's fashion – a blue velvet dress (wasn't it from then that Wilde's obsession with velvet had begun?), peeping out from behind the curtains. What he saw was probably not that different from the present-day scene, except for cars, 'Caffé Napoli' and myself.

One can rearrange furniture and replace wallpaper in the house of one's childhood, but one can never alter the view from its window.

No matter where we are, it is through that window that we look at the outside world.

What was the first work by Oscar that I read? It was probably *The Canterville Ghost*. Later – at school – we studied (as a 'scathing satire of the capitalist society,' of course) *The Importance of Being Earnest.* Interestingly, in the Soviet Union, the play's title was translated as *The Importance of Being SERIOUS*.

The word 'earnest' (read 'honest') in the title of a popular play that was constantly performed in many a theatre and hence featured prominently on posters all over the country was deemed too subversive by the ever-vigilant (and ever-so-dumb) Soviet censorship.

Having died seventeen years before the Bolshevik *coup d'etat*, Oscar was privileged enough to be censored by the 'socialist' state he had himself so craved. He would have loved the irony of that …

Round the corner from Westland Row is a much plusher house (1, Merrion Square), where Oscar spent his formative years. It now accommodates Dublin's 'American College' – another irony, if we remember Oscar's tongue-in-cheek comment from *The Picture of Dorian Gray*: 'Perhaps, after all, America never has been discovered. I myself would say that it had merely been detected.'

He himself certainly *was* 'detected' in America, where they now award 'Oscars' for artistic excellence to people who do not always deserve them. I bet Oscar would have made a great pun out of this!

And in a small leafy park opposite his Merrion Square house, Oscar himself – a self-absorbed and decadent aesthete, clad in his favourite velvet smoking jacket with floating tie – is reclining comfortably against the rock. In this exceptionally brilliant sculpture by Danny Osborne (the eccentric charm of which is strangely enhanced by the fact that it was commissioned by 'Guinness Ireland Group'), my friend appears extremely relaxed. So *natural* in fact that I am tempted to write – and remember: 'I can resist anything but temptation?' – that he looks as if he is about to step off the pedestal and dash off for a pint of 'Guinness' (if only out of gratitude to his 'sponsors') to a nearest pub – just 'to keep body and soul apart,' no doubt. On the other hand, in reality he is probably not that relaxed, for 'being natural is simply a pose' …

He sits under a branchy rowan tree (the berries on it are deep purple, the colour of freshly spilled human blood, which, according to an old Russian superstition, foretells a cold winter) inside 'a little tent of blue that prisoners call the sky.' Oscar had earned the right to coin such seemingly 'sentimental' metaphor after two years in Reading gaol.

There is another Oscar's 'home' in North Dublin, although he had never lived in it. I mean the small and cosy Dublin Writers Museum in Parnell Square.

Unlike his two other Dublin abodes, this is not a mansion but rather a Soviet-style communal flat, where one has to share bathroom and kitchen with several other tenants. For Oscar, at least, it is. The space allocated to him in the Museum is tiny – and not just in proportion to his own ego. He does have to share – not a bathroom, thankfully, but one and the same glass case with Bernard Shaw. Why? A possible explanation can be found on the 'interpretation plate' above the exhibits:

'He (Oscar – VV) never took Ireland as his subject and for that reason is usually classed as an English writer.'

What a load of nonsense!

Firstly, geniuses are by and large stateless: they belong everywhere and nowhere – all at the same time. And Oscar, like no one else, would hate the idea of being labelled, or 'classed.' Secondly, he was born in Ireland and therefore can be safely regarded as Irish by definition. I am sure he would have much preferred that to being branded as belonging to the country that actually destroyed him.

And lastly, he did write a lot about Ireland and Irishness and could easily enter into a dialogue on these subjects with his glass case neighbour Bernard Shaw (I wouldn't be surprised if this was precisely what they were doing during the Museum's closing hours):

> Oscar: 'Don't you think, my dear Bernard, that there are some who will welcome with delight the idea of solving the Irish question by doing away with the Irish people – just like they tried to do with the Jews?'

Bernard: 'I am not sure, dear boy. I may be a tolerably good European in the Nietzschean sense, but a very bad Irishman in the Sinn Fein or Chosen People sense …'
Oscar: 'Nevertheless, even you can't deny that what captivity was to the Jews, exile has been to the Irish …'

And so on …

At a first glance, Bernard Shaw appears a suitable 'neighbour': a fellow playwright and wit, he was born just two years after Oscar, in 1856, yet outlived him by fifty years and died at the 'venerable' age of ninety-four in 1950.

'He whom the gods love dies young.'

Can you imagine Oscar living into his nineties? You can't? And neither can I. Unlike, it has to be said, Malcolm Muggeridge: 'I have little doubt that if Oscar Wilde had lived into his nineties … he would have been considered a benign, distinguished figure suitable to preside at a school prize-giving or to instruct and exhort scoutmasters at their jamborees. He might even have been knighted.'

'Sir Oscar Wilde, OBE' … How incongruous! One thing I am sure of, however, is that, unlike elderly Bernard Shaw, Oscar would have never been duped by Stalin into believing that communism was the best thing after sliced bread.

Or, maybe, he would, who knows …

One other writer, playwright and wit strikes me as being the closest to Oscar – in life, in literature and even in death: Anton Chekhov. The two had never met of course, but the coincidences are striking. They lived at almost exactly the same time, albeit in different countries. Chekhov was born six years later and died at forty-four in 1904 – four years later than Oscar.

Chekhov was a practising physician, and Oscar, although not a doctor himself, was the son of Ireland's best-known ophthalmologist.

They both worked in the same genres, although Chekhov never wrote poetry.

Even their sexual preferences were, allegedly, not that dissimilar.

Like Oscar in English, Chekhov is by far the most quoted writer in the Russian language. 'I dreamt that what I had thought was reality was a dream, and what I had thought was a dream was reality,' – this entry from Chekhov's *Diaries* can easily be nominated for an Oscar, ie pass for something Oscar Wilde has written or said.

Their tragically parallel lives ended on largely the same note – a joke.

Looking at the particularly naff and faded wallpaper in need of replacement in the Paris hotel room where he was dying, Oscar said: 'One of us will have to go …'

Chekhov on his deathbed asked for a glass of champagne. 'Champagne *Ich Sterbe…*'[36] were his last words.

They both wrote their lives and lived their writing. I am sure they would have enjoyed each other's company.

An imaginary conversation with a person (or an object) that cannot be interviewed in reality has always been my favourite literary device. In the course of my journalistic career, spanning over many countries and four continents, I was able to secure exclusive 'interviews' with Hitler and Napoleon, with Chekhov's favourite writing desk (!) and with John Paul II. The latter was conducted during the Pope's visit to Melbourne:

'What is your biggest nightmare, your Holiness?'

'A pregnant female priest about to have an abortion …'

And so on.

It would have been therefore very tempting to include here my imaginary conversation with Oscar. This is probably what you are expecting me to do now.

But this particular temptation I am going to resist. As Oscar himself once observed: 'It is always nice to be expected and not to arrive.'

Having re-read what I had written so far, I realised there was need to invent a conversation that had already taken place in reality.

And keeps happening as we speak.

How can that be?

I wish I knew … 'Poets, you know, are always ahead of science' …

* * *

My main point of interest in the small Northern Ireland town of Enniskillen was Portora Royal School for Boys, where Oscar Wilde, one of my all-time favourite writers and personalities, studied in 1864-71.

Oscar's Enniskillen 'home' – his *alma mater*, where he spent all his 'formative years,' from ten to seventeen – sits on top of a hill overlooking the town. I approach it with trepidation – as if about to visit a dear, long lost friend.

Wilde and his older brother ended up studying and boarding here because their father was friendly with Portora's drawing master, who promised to keep an eye on the boys.

Oscar's nickname at the school was Grey Crow – most likely because he was different from other boys. To begin with, he did not like sports. Most certainly, he

[36] I am dying (German).

was bullied and that must have helped to mould his writer's personality. Creativity is often a product of suffering and injustice.

Walking Portora's dark and echoey corridors, ascending the worn-out (by Oscar's feet, too!) marble grand staircase and lingering in the gloomy vaulted dining room, I can almost sense the pain, frustration and claustrophobia Oscar must have experienced within these walls.

In a sense, the bullying of Oscar went on in Portora long after his death – until the 1930s, when the modest memorial plate, OSCAR WILDE, 1854-1900, WRITER & WIT, was replaced on the assembly hall's wall, having been angrily taken off due to the 'scandal' of his homosexuality.

Oscar would have been pleased to know that his old school has now become one of the venues for Enniskillen's annual Oscar Wilde Festival. This reminds me of the story the great Russian ballet dancer Rudolf Nureyev recounted to me in one of his last interviews in 1993. Like Oscar, Nureyev was mercilessly bullied – by pupils and teachers alike! – at school in the Soviet city of Ufa because of his passion for dancing. Just as in late-nineteenth-century Britain, homosexuality was a serious crime in the USSR. When Nureyev visited the school in the early 1990s on his first and only trip to his motherland after his defection (he was 'allowed' to return for a couple of days to attend his mother's funeral), he was amazed to see that the building now housed a ballet school.

Art always triumphs over prejudice in the end.

The long and forbidding corridors of Portora are overhung with portraits of obscure long-dead graduates and sombre headmasters, but Oscar's refined face is nowhere to be seen. This is bizarre, for, even if you forget his greatness as a writer, he was a Royal Scholar, with exceptional academic achievements. On the faded Royal Scholars board in the assembly hall I finally find Oscar's name. Restored in the 1930s (after being painted over in the wake of his infamous trial), it stands out on the board and looks fresher and more prominent than the rest. And in the corner of the school library (former dormitory), under Portora's new Anti-Bullying Charter (what an irony!) on the wall, I spot a glass case containing several dog-eared books that used to belong to Oscar. Among them, *The Analogy of Religion* by Joseph Butler, 1868, and the Bible, which contains the dedication: 'This prize and Holy Scripture was given by the Rev W Steele to Oscar Wilde, midsummer, 1869.'

My guide Anne tells me that Reverend William Steele was the headmaster, whose own son drowned in Erne Lake three days after finishing school and being accepted to Trinity College Dublin.

I finally find Oscar's portrait, too. It is locked away in a smallish side-room of the former headmaster's residence. With a cigarette in his mouth, my friend Oscar looks lost and anonymous. There are no names under the painting – neither of him nor of the artist. Next to him hangs a pompous portrait of a 'Mr Justice George Wright.'

A school brass band is rehearsing behind the wall, the discordant funereal sounds adding to Portora's depressing atmosphere on this dull winter afternoon.

As I smoke outside the main entrance door, several uniformed freckled boys in their early teens run out of the building. Waiting to be picked up by their parents in shiny cars (the school is no longer a boarding one), they keep yap-yapping happily into their mobile phones.

Oscar would have been amused …

AG Macdonell

Listen to this:

> 'Briefly, what I think is that it (Scotland – VV) has suffered in the past, and is suffering now, from too much England. The choice before Scotland today is whether in the future to suffer from less England, or from still more … I am now convinced that Scotsmen must decide … whether they wish to be citizens of a free country or citizens of a rather stale music-hall joke … Fundamentally, there is no halfway between freedom and slavery. In the end, there is no such thing as a free and enlightened provincialism … It is all very well for the ostrich to hide its head in the sand, but we Scots must remember what happens to the ostrich. He ends up in a farm where his owner plucks out his feathers and makes money by selling them …'
> (*My Scotland*, 1937)

Or this:

> 'Edinburgh has been called the New Athens. It cannot be allowed to be a very happy description. The framework is there, the city, the education, the history, all is there, except the divine spark. Edinburgh is the greatest dead thing in the world. Athens was the greatest alive thing in the world.'
> (Ibid)

Or how about this:

> 'It is one of the peculiarities of the Grand Central Station in New York City that whereas it is possible to buy hats, oysters, diamonds, umbrellas, shoes, flowers, silk stockings, caviar and toys under its hospitable roof, and probably, for all I know, artificial teeth, battle cruisers, and parrots, nevertheless it is almost impossible to find any trains.'
> (*A Visit to America*, 1935)

I could quote endlessly from the works of AG Macdonell, one of my favourite writers of all time, almost totally forgotten both in England and in his native Scotland.

I first learned about him by accident, having rescued *A Visit to America* from an unconquered dust-ridden bookshelf in Hay-on-Wye in 1999. It was only because I was then researching my own book on the USA that I picked up the tattered pale-blue volume with such an unpretentious, even boring, title. I opened the book at random and … Three hours later, when the shop was about to close, I was still standing there, glued to the floor and unable to stop reading the sharpest, the wittiest, the clearest and the most evocative (as well as provocative) prose I had ever come across.

On returning to London, I started questioning my literary-world contacts about Macdonell. No one had ever heard his name, conspicuous by its absence from reference sources – as if the man had never actually existed.

As the last resort, I went to the British Library, where – finally – I had a stroke of luck. In an obscure late 1940s *Writers Directory*, I found a short biographical note, according to which Archibald Gordon Macdonell was born in Aberdeen in 1895, 'the son of William Robert Macdonell, LLD, and Alice Elizabeth (White) Macdonell; the name is accented on the final syllable (*sic* – VV).' After childhood in Aberdeen, he studied at Winchester, was a lieutenant in the Royal Field Artillery during World War I, then worked for the League of Nations and was a Liberal candidate for Parliament in 1923-24.

Macdonell's short literary career was amazingly prolific and versatile, particularly during the last several years of his life, when he would publish two to three books annually, as if consciously running against his final God-set deadline. He wrote novels, award-winning thrillers (under the pseudonyms 'John Cameron' and 'Neil Gordon'), travel books, plays, journalism, reviews, short stories, historical studies. According to the *Directory*, he was killed in an air-raid in Oxford in January 1941, 'two months after his forty-fifth birthday.'

One thing led to another. Soon I managed to dig up *The Glasgow Herald* obituary, dated 18 January 1941, which claimed that Macdonell was born … at Poona, India and died not in an air-raid, but … in the bath in his Oxford flat, where his body was discovered by a maid. By the end of 2001, I was in possession of half-a-dozen short biographical articles, half of which asserted that the writer was born in India and died during the Blitz, the other half – that he was born in Aberdeen and died peacefully in his flat, except for one source claiming that he actually committed suicide.

I had also managed to get hold of several of his other books: *England, their England* – a scathing heart-felt satire of warfare and the English upper classes; *My Scotland*, where Macdonell comes through as an ardent Scottish nationalist, believing (somewhat naively) that it is the Lowland Scottish writers and – especially – poets, who represent the country's main driving force in its struggle for independence; and *How Like an Angel* – a brilliant satirical expose of budding Hollywood culture describing the escapades of an American film star in London (among other things, she insists on being driven to a station in a carriage drawn by members of European royalty). I was particularly taken by *The Autobiography of a Cad* – a spoof political memoir of Edward Fox-Ingleby, a Tory MP, an aristocrat and a vile hypocrite of a politician. Written in a deliberately highbrow style, the book, published in 1939, sounded extremely topical and modern. When I read, for example, how Fox-Ingleby's 'Buy British' campaign was undermined by the fact that all three of his cars were foreign, it immediately brought about parallels with the two Jaguars of John Prescott, portraying himself as a champion of public transport.

One thing all scanty biographical sources were in agreement on was that Macdonell had spent his formative years (childhood and early teens) in Aberdeen. Being familiar with the peculiar Aberdonian humour, I thought that the writer's incisive and punchy wit had been clearly influenced by it.

Aberdeen looked as grey and uninviting as only Aberdeen could look on a dull January afternoon: grey granite houses, grey satin skies, grey seagulls. There seemed to be three shades of grey in the spectrum: light-grey, dark-grey and Aberdeen-grey. Despite all cliches, the city staunchly refused to sparkle during short spells of sunshine. The only sparkling bits were the eyes of two Professors of Scottish Literature – David Hewitt and Derek McLure – whom I met on the medieval campus of Aberdeen University. No, they had never heard of AG Macdonell, but were kind enough to give me an insight into literary Aberdeen of the early 1900s, dominated by locally bred poets writing in Scots. Wasn't this a reason for Macdonell's life-long fascination with Scottish poetry? Prof Hewitt took me on a tour of Old Aberdeen and showed me the spectacular St Marchar's Cathedral. None of us knew that, once inside the Cathedral, we had come as close to Macdonell's childhood and his family as we could be: the following day I learned that the Macdonells, who had lived nearby, in Brig o' Balgownie, used to pray there, that Archibald's sister Margaret Rachel, who died at seventeen, had been buried in the Cathedral's graveyard; that Daniel Cottier, a Glasgow-born nineteenth-century artist, who decorated Macdonell's family home, was also a creator of the Cathedral's stained glass windows, which we admired.

Aberdeen City Archives and the Registrar's Office had no records of AG Macdonell's birth, but at least I now knew that Archibald was born NOT in Aberdeen, but, most likely, indeed in India, where his father was a one-time president of Bombay Merchant Company.

With my search looking more and more like chasing a ghost, I had a sudden breakthrough in Aberdeen's Central Library. Having found nothing, I was about to leave, when a helpful librarian suggested I looked through back issues of *Aberdeen Leopard* magazine. There, in the 1987 April/May issue, was a large article on AG Macdonell, calling him 'a star of most individual brightness.' It also had a photo of Bridgefield – a Georgian house in Bridge of Don, where he grew up.

An omniscient local joiner pointed out Bridgefield to me from his street shed next morning. To my great relief, not only the house was still there, but it was now inhabited by a highly artistic lady, whose multi-sided talents were on a par with those of AG Macdonell himself. Sculptor, artist, interior decorator and maker of unique 'designer cakes,' Seona Mason-Chadburn moved into Bridgefield ten years ago. Since then, she had been single-handedly restoring the damp and disintegrating 'C-listed' house, of which she felt an integral part. Under layers of plaster and paint, she was able to uncover elements of the original Cottier decor and other Georgian and Victorian features. She conducted guided tours of Bridgefield and wanted to have it classified as a 'B-listed' structure.

The view of the sea from Bridgefield's grand drawing room was now somewhat blocked by new trees, but otherwise it was the same as seen by little Archie. It is impossible to fully understand a writer (or any other person, for that matter) without visiting the house of his childhood and looking out at the world through HIS eyes. One can rearrange furniture and replace wallpaper inside such a house, but the view from its window is irreplaceable.

'Manuscripts do not burn,' wrote Mikhail Bulgakov. Likewise, no real talent disappears without a trace. The trees of oblivion will eventually wither away …

Seona showed me another amazing find of hers. On one of the walls, there was a faded Indian-ink cartoon of a long-nosed and arrogant early twentieth-century 'aristocrat' in flannels. The naughty childish drawing was on a twelve- to thirteen-year-old eye-level. We were both quite sure that it was done by young Archie Macdonell. Born into the family of prominent Scottish aristocrats, who wanted to be more English than the English and even made sure their purely Scottish names were anglicised by being 'accented on the final syllable,' he came to rebel against that very aristocracy and spent a large part of his literary career satirising it. A life-long quest that started with a simple childish drawing on the house wall.

After my visit to Bridgefield, Macdonell no longer felt like a ghost. I now saw him as a flesh-and-blood Aberdonian – superficially grim and blunt, yet sardonic and sentimental beneath the surface.

One surviving description of AG Macdonell's appearance comes from the USA, where, strangely enough, he is better known than in Scotland. In 1934, they saw him as 'a tall, athletic, energetic young Scot, with a close-cropped moustache.' Several years later, in his obituary, they called him 'the most picturesque, dashing and talented figure' that had ever graced 'Fleet Street and literary London.'

But I would rather remember him simply as an 'energetic young Scot,' who had lived a short life of talent, laughter and controversy.

George Orwell

The Hertfordshire village of Wallington (only a short drive away from the town where I live) is where George Orwell had spent the happiest and the most prolific several years of his life. It is tiny, pristine and perennially quiet.

If you stare at Orwell's cottage's low and narrow front door for long enough, you can almost discern a tall dishevelled man emerging from it (he has to bend down to fit through the door). He is holding a letter which he carries across the road to the village's only pillar box before disappearing inside the cottage again …

When Orwell first came to Wallington in 1936, he was fairly hard up and had to run a small grocery store in that very cottage, which has had a number of tenants and owners since then, but remains virtually unchanged.

I first read *Nineteen Eighty-Four* in Moscow in the late 1980s. A dog-eared and soiled paperback was lent to me for one night only, and next morning I was to pass it to the next person in line.

The book, like all other works by George Orwell, was strictly banned in the USSR where I was born and then lived. A huge scandal erupted when an American publisher tried to display it on his stand during the International Book Fair in Moscow in the early 1980s. I worked as an interpreter at the Mitchell Beazley stand and remember an irate Soviet official shouting at the hapless publisher: 'Take this book away from your stand this very moment! You can display anything – even bloody Golda Meir (*sic*), if you wish, but not Orwell – this anti-Soviet filth!'

The punishment for being caught in possession of *Nineteen Eighty-Four* could be a prison term. Curiously, that only added to the clandestine pleasure of reading.

In the Soviet Union of my childhood and youth, it was not just honest writing but honest reading too that was a risky, dangerous and hence a highly creative occupation, an art form of sorts …

I was savouring the book until dawn, and by the time the last page was turned, I was close to tears. How could someone who had never been in the Soviet Union and had never lived in a totalitarian state, describe our life with such poignant precision?

We had a real-life 'Ministry of Truth,' the KGB. One of its departments was called Glavlit, the state censorship agency. The word in itself (an abbreviated merger of '*Glavnoye Upravleniye Literaturi*' – Chief Directorate of Literature') is Orwell's 'Newspeak' *par excellence*. From the moment of taking power, the Bolsheviks were meticulously destroying the Russian language by simplifying its grammar and littering it with thousands of meaningless neologisms.

Each week, Glavlit released a constantly updated thick instruction manual listing books to be confiscated from all libraries and bookshops of the USSR.

A student of mine who worked as a bookseller used to show me these censorship bulletins regularly – at considerable risk to herself. Alongside the works of Orwell,

Solzhenitsyn and other 'enemy' or émigré writers, they contained thousands of seemingly innocuous titles in physics, chemistry, engineering and technology. The whole 'danger' of those books lay in the fact that they had mentions of Khruschev, Stalin and/or other political figures who had by then fallen out of favour with the system and hence become unmentionable, in the introductions.

They constituted a huge part of the list, since every book, no matter how scholarly and esoteric, was supposed to begin with a quote from a 'great leader' in power.

On one of the shelves in my garden office stands a large light-brown folio of *Kniga o vkusnoi I zdorovoi pishche – The Book of Tasty and Wholesome Cuisine*, published in Moscow in 1952. I remember leafing through its pages with coloured pictures of alluring and not necessarily 'wholesome' Russian foods (never seen in reality and therefore exotic) at the age of five or six. The 'subversive' book of recipes (with all but imaginary ingredients) which had miraculously withstood all my life's wanderings (Kharkov-Moscow-Melbourne-London-Melbourne-Edinburgh-Folkestone-Dublin-London-Letchworth etc) begins with a huge-lettered quote from Stalin on a special flap preceding the title page:

> '*One of the peculiarities of our revolution lay in the fact that it gave the Soviet people not just freedom but also material well-being and a possibility of a plentiful and cultured life.*'

It would have certainly been banned in Brezhnev's times when the names of Stalin or Khrushchev were not supposed to be mentioned in print in any context. My mother told me how, in the early 1950s when the head of the Soviet secret police and Stalin's henchman Beria was exposed as a 'British spy' and subsequently shot, all subscribers of the multi-volume *Great Soviet Encyclopedia* received in the post several printed sheets to be glued into the letter 'B' volume where the article on Beria was printed.

The enclosed instruction requested that all the Beria pages be cut out of the book and the new ones, with a disproportionately lengthy article on the Bering Strait (!), inserted instead. Special Glavlit inspectors would conduct random house checks to make sure everybody had complied.

Wasn't it precisely what Orwell's O'Brien meant when confiding to Winston Smith during the latter's Room 101 interrogation that if a single mention of person or event could not be found in print it was as if they had never existed or taken place?

The other indisputable reason for banning technical – as well as children's and all other – books in Brezhnev's times was the emigration of the author.

No wonder *Nineteen Eighty-Four* was one of the Soviet system's biggest bugaboos: it explained the technology of totalitarian power.

Amazingly though, those who controlled the printed word found it quite proper to read the banned books themselves (remember 'All animals are equal but some are more equal than others?').

Not too many people in the West know that, in a brilliant case of Orwellian doublethink, all major Soviet publishing houses had secret departments producing limited editions of prohibited books for the elite's exclusive consumption. I've seen such books (each individually numbered and with the word 'Classified' prominently stamped on the cover) a number of times thanks to a friend's mother-in-law who worked in the CPSU Central Committee library. One of them was *Nineteen Eighty-Four* – in impeccable Russian translation.

The number on the plain white cover was '59,' and underneath it the word '*Sekretno*' ('classified') was printed.

Another 'special edition' that I saw was *Secrets of Eternal Life* by C Northcope Parkinson (again, rather conscientiously translated into Russian). The senile octogenarians who ruled our poor country were naturally – and exclusively – curious about the secrets of 'eternal life,' since it was they – not the oppressed voiceless crowds they controlled – who were supposed to live forever.

By the year 1984, Orwell's dystopian *Nineteen Eighty-Four* had been all but translated into reality in the Soviet Union …

* * *

> *'We knocked on the door of a little cottage, and it was opened by a tall figure, face and clothes covered with coal smuts, who peered at us through the billowing cloud of smoke; Blair had been trying to light his first fire of the season, to find that the chimney was in some way defective …'*

That was how writer Mark Benney (quoted by Bernard Crick in *George Orwell. A Life*) described his visit to Wallington in 1936. This is probably why whenever I try to visualise George emerging from The Stores cottage in 2009, I see him 'with coal smuts' smudged all over his face …

Orwell was happy in Wallington clattering away on his typewriter (he was finishing *The Road to Wigan Pier*) when there were no customers in his cottage-cum-shop which was for most of the time: for some reason, the shop was not very popular among the locals (were they somewhat put off by Orwell's refined and aristocratic – even if occasionally coal-stained – face, his posh Etonian accent and his 'classy' lanky frame?), not counting the pilfering village children (to watch them Orwell had to drill four holes in the door!).

George/Eric went on long walks around the village, and the very few descriptions of nature in his books (he was hardly a lyricist) can be easily traced to Wallington, like this one from *Nineteen Eighty-Four* describing Winston's pastoral secret tryst with Julia:

'Winston picked his way up the lane through the dappled light and shade, stepping into pools of gold whenever the boughs parted. Under the trees to the left of him the ground was misty with bluebells … It was the second of May. From somewhere deeper in the heart of the wood came the droning of ring doves.'

Most rural landscapes hardly change with time.

It was probably during one of these walks that he spotted the dark wooden buildings of the nearby Manor Farm that he used as his model for *Animal Farm* in the eponymous classic novel set, incidentally, near the fictitious village of Willingdon (where the farmer kept the pigs)!

The large black sheds and barns of the Manor Farm are still there. Looking at them I don't stop praising fortune for the mere fact that no enterprising developer had yet come up with the idea of digging up the uncomplaining Hertfordshire countryside and building an Animal Farm Theme Park on that spot …

Such an oversight is surprising if we remember that *Animal Farm* is one of the best known, best loved and most prophetic books in human history …

It has to be said, however, that in many respects the Soviet reality had outstripped even George Orwell's insightful fantasy.

* * *

It was there, in Wallington, that Orwell married Eileen Shaughnessy in the old and eternally open parish church of St Mary.

With my wife, we often come to the church which is permanently empty and freezing inside in winter. We read the new entries to the Visitors' Book that always surprise us with their geographical versatility.

When do all these people come here, we wonder? We have never bumped into anyone else inside the church …

On the table next to the Visitors' Book is a pencil holder with reading glasses which suit my slightly presbyopic eyes perfectly – as if left there specifically for me. There's also the first scary sign of a potential Animal Farm Theme Park – a stack of photocopied George and Eileen's marriage certificates – two pounds fifty each …

One of the most treasured books in my collection is *The Penguin Essays of George Orwell.*

And not just because Orwell's essays, to my mind, are unsurpassable in their originality, clarity of thought and lucidity of language. This book was given to me as a gift in Moscow by my first ever British friend Martin Walker, then *the Guardian's* Moscow correspondent.

'For Vitali. My favourite journalist of all time, Orwell, to the first Soviet investigative journalist,' reads a faded dedication.

Andrei Makine

Andrei Makine snubs word processors.

He writes his novels in longhand, agonising over every word, every metaphor.

'Can you really write poetry on a computer screen?' he asks rhetorically, squinting at me through his small Chekhovian spectacles. And without waiting for a reply he shakes his head: 'No, you can't. Poetic novels must be handwritten too. It is only thrillers that you can type!'

Andrei loves writing. Literature and France are his main – his only – passions. 'My perception of France is literary,' he says. 'While in Russia, I learned France like a subject from a school curriculum.'

We are sitting in a small bistro in Boulevard St-Germain; outside Paris lies resplendent in soft wintry sunshine. We speak Russian, but I can't help noticing the genuine delight with which Andrei addresses a waiter in his flawless French.

What happened to Andrei Makine is a miracle, a real-life fairy tale. He had lived in Paris in poverty and despair for seven years, since his defection from the Soviet Union (he came to France on a teacher exchange scheme and simply did not return). Then one evening the phone rang in his tiny attic flat in Montmartre. Simone Gallimard, one of the top French publishers, was on the line.

'I have read your novel,' she said. '*C'est tres bien*!'

A phone call can sometimes, albeit extremely rarely, be a purveyor of good news too. Remember: we are talking about a **miracle** here!

By the time of that phone call, the novel, *Le Testament Francais*, had been rejected by dozens of publishers. Like all his previous novels, Andrei had written it in French, 'my grandmother tongue,' as he calls it.

Why a 'grandmother tongue?' Read on.

His previous three books did come out, but only after he pretended that they were translations from Russian (he invented a non-existent Russian writer whose works he, allegedly, had been translating into French). His tiny attic was brimming with piles of rejected manuscripts on which, unable to afford a bed, he slept fitfully during the night. His days were devoted to writing, to posting his manuscripts ('French publishers have a nasty habit of putting cups of coffee on the manuscripts leaving brown circles on their pages which make it impossible to send them to anyone else'), and to trying to survive on one baguette a day. The attic was still an improvement on the first couple of years in Paris, when he had to sleep in a cemetery vault and write on park benches …

Or did the miracle happen much earlier, in the 1960s, when Andrei, a romantic Soviet boy from the smoky Siberian town of Krasnoyarsk, was sitting on the balcony with his displaced French granny, Charlotte Lemonier? She taught him to speak fluent French (hence 'the grandmother tongue') and fed him real-life fairy tales about

France in her tiny flat in the outskirts of Penza, where Andrei and his sister used to spend their summer holidays.

'That evening we joined our grandmother on the little balcony of her apartment; covered in flowers, it seemed suspended above the hot blaze of the steppes. A copper sun nudged the horizon, remained undecided for moment, then plunged rapidly. The first stars trembled in the sky. Powerful, penetrating scents rose up to us with the evening breeze.'

Andrei Makine made history in France by snapping up the country's three biggest literary awards – the Prix Goncourt, Prix Medici and Prix Goncourt de Lyceens – all in a single year, 1995.

It took Andrei twenty-eight years (he was born in 1959) to reach the country of his dreams, this mysterious and remote 'Atlantis' called France, where presidents die 'in the arms of their mistresses,' the land whose melodious language 'throbbed within us, like a magical graft implanted in our hearts.'

With a couple of hours to spare before our meeting, I was wondering around Saint-Germain-des-Prés until I found a Russian bookshop. It was there that I suddenly spotted Andrei – a tall bespectacled man in a short-sleeve blue shirt. I recognised him from the photo on the cover of *Le Testament Francais,* which had been translated into twenty-seven languages, had sold a million copies in France alone, and had just been published in Britain (under the same French title – *Le Testament Francais).*

Despite his height and his resolute behaviour (he snapped several Russian newspapers from the shelf in one brisk movement – just like his literary awards), there was something deeply vulnerable about him.

Was it the burden of his sudden wealth and fame? As he told me later, he was buying these newspapers for his Russian friend who couldn't afford them.

Now – after his 'self-fiction' novel's unimaginable success, after thousands of readers' letters ('I am about to lose my eyesight, but I am so happy that your book is the last one that I have read'), after a long lunch with President Chirac, after a phone call from the dying Francois Mitterand – Andrei could afford not just the newspapers.

'My financial life hasn't changed,' he says, sipping his coffee. 'All my money is kept by the publisher, and I take only as much as is absolutely necessary. I don't need a country cottage or a car. Just like before, I never use public transport, but walk everywhere. I have walked all over France. My main luxury is to enter an unknown French town in the early hours of the morning … The only difference is that now I've got a bed.'

The most amazing writer's manifesto I had ever heard.

I thought that, with some reservations, I could put my name under it too: only 'French town' would have to be replaced with 'English,' or – better – 'European' one …

An archetypal member of Russian intelligentsia (who, by Chekhov's definition, feels his own personal guilt for every single injustice in the world), Andrei seems to agree with Tolstoy that 'a writer must suffer' (he even takes it further asserting that a writer has no right to have a family or children and keeps quoting his favourite Proust: 'Happy days are lost days for a writer'). And there is no pretence here: his ten years in France had been a continuous, if subconscious, attempt to translate this masochistic Tolstovian principle into reality.

'I've been cheated and humiliated many times,' he says. 'No one wanted to know me, let alone publish. I would sit in my attic at 4am thinking: what am I doing to myself? It was only my belief in having something important to say that kept me struggling on. It was probably insane, but **isn't the logic of writing insane in itself?** But you know what: I look at these years with nostalgia.'

I will be remembering these words for as long as I live. They will keep reassuring me in the most hopeless situations in the future …

Andrei's other persisting dream was to bring his grandmother Charlotte back to France. To invite her he needed French citizenship, which was being denied to him. Charlotte died in her dusty Russian Saranza (a fictitious town, invented by Andrei) without ever seeing her grandson, or her native France, again. The last pages of *Le Testament Francais*, where he describes his emotions on learning about her death, are the most poignant in the book:

'When I thought of Charlotte, her presence in these drowsy [Paris] streets had the reality, quiet and spontaneous, of life itself; what I still had to find were the words to tell it with.'

Andrei did find words, and his long-suffering granny could be proud of him. Yet he stops short of labelling *Le Testament Francais* autobiography, preferring to call it a legend.

'A legend is often more truthful than life itself. It is only today that we can really understand what happened yesterday. We all live in a mythical environment, and we tend to mythologise our past.'

I would also characterise its genre as 'pseudo-autobiography' or 'self-fiction.'

'To write a good book about one's native country, one has to leave it first, said a Russian literary critic.

Andrei takes this notion even further.

'Yes, to look back you need a distance. You even need death. And emigration is partial death …'

If emigration is partial death, defection can sometimes be a second birth …

Andrei is reluctant to talk about the circumstances of his defection from Russia in 1987 (in Soviet legalese, it was – just like in my case – a 'failure to return' punishable by many years in prison or execution).

'I was never a dissident. I simply could not cope with the new mafia-run Russia. I wouldn't have survived there. My country is the land of literature, my romanticism is living in between two worlds. No, I don't feel like going back to Russia. They don't understand me there. They think I am showing off by writing in French.'

Do they understand him in his adopted France? Not always, it appears.

Bestowing the highest literary award upon a 'foreigner' was quite a blow to the arrogant and conservative French literary establishment. The Prix Medici, as Andrei asserts, was but an attempt to stop him from receiving the more prestigious Prix Goncourt.

'Some people still refer to me as "this Russian writing in French, a sort of a clown." But I am a French writer, whether they want it or not …'

'My nationality is the language I write in,' Joseph Conrad once noted.

We part in a quaint fifteenth-century courtyard near Palais St Sulpice which Andrei volunteered to show me.

'Very few people, even Parisians, know about this courtyard, which is one of my favourites,' he says with pride, the same sort of pride I feel when showing my friends my favourite little-known nook of central London that is geographically part of Cambridgeshire – Ely Place.

I look at his receding lanky figure standing out in the boisterous Paris crowd. He walks turning his head right and left constantly – as if still finding it hard to believe that he is indeed in Paris.

And I suddenly realise that in his heart of hearts he will always remain a little Siberian dreamer-boy floating on his granny's balcony above the steppe …

Andrei Makine, a French writer, is walking to his next appointment in the opposite end of Paris.

He has a long way to go.

PS. When my youngest son was born shortly after that meeting in Paris, I named him Andrei – after Makine.

Peter Ustinov

A horrible phone call pierced my life in March 2004.

It was from BBC Radio 5 Live.

'Can you comment on Sir Peter Ustinov's death? You were friends, weren't you?'

Learning about his death from Radio 5 **Live ...** Ustinov would have cackled at this ...

I knew it was coming: Piotr Ionovich, as I had been politely addressing him Russian-style, by first name and patronymic (his father was called 'Iona'), since our first meeting in 1990, was approaching eighty-three.

Yet the news still came as a shock.

I remembered him telling me in Melbourne in 1992: 'I've just received a new passport that expires in 2002, so my aim now is not to expire before my passport ...'

He had succeeded. He always did.

It was hard to imagine that he would never call me again and, pretending he was Mikhail Gorbachev or President Bush Senior, wouldn't ask me to come and see him at his favourite London hotel – the Berkeley, or to have lunch.

Having lunch with him was like sharing a meal with a whole crowd of people – actors, drunks, priests, politicians – whom he mimicked tirelessly and relentlessly. While our food was served, he impersonated the waiter.

He was also in the habit of mimicking my accent, and would address me in heavily accented Russian as 'Comrade Colonel.'

His biggest reward was people's laughter. 'I was irrevocably betrothed to laughter, the sound of which has always seemed to me the most civilised music in the universe,' he wrote in his best-selling autobiography *Dear Me*.

At times, it felt as if he was afraid to stop performing even for a second, because for him that would be on a par with stopping to breathe. And the size of his audience – be it the Barbican, the Royal Festival Hall or just one person, whom he had just met in the street – did not matter.

Once, having come to see Piotr Ionovich in Berkeley Hotel, I found him alone in his suite, piled with clothes, books, letters, manuscripts and whatnots. He waved me in without stopping to talk over the phone and offered me a vodka.

Reclining in a leather armchair, so deep and soft that it negatively affected the sitter's self-esteem, I couldn't help overhearing his conversation. He was obviously being interviewed – and, as always, he was brilliant: wise, quick, funny and irreverent.

'Who is it on the other end of the line?' I was musing an hour later, downing my fifth shot. 'The *Guardian* or, maybe, the *New York Times*?'

'Who was the interview for?' I asked Ustinov when he finally (and rather reluctantly, it has to be said) got off the phone. 'Oh, it was some little university newspaper from Essex,' he replied.

One of his most beautiful human qualities was complete lack of arrogance or pomposity – the traits that could be easily forgiven in a winner of two Oscars and the only foreign member of the French Academy of Arts.

He was extremely – almost excessively – accessible and, despite being terribly busy with all his shows, plays, films, books, columns, charities and so on, found it hard to refuse favours to anyone.

'Friends are not necessarily the people you love most – they are simply the ones who got there first,' he joked.

Needless to say, people often used him for self-promotion, but he had no regrets (except, of course, for *House of Regrets* – the West End play that he wrote and starred in at the age of 21!). 'If you do good things, then good things will come to you,' he said to Terence Stamp, his co-star in *Billy Budd* – the film that Piotr Ionovich also produced and directed. And they did. Frank Muir was right when he called Ustinov 'one of the best-loved people in the world.'

Ustinov's friendship changed my life.

I often wondered why he singled me out of thousands of people he had come across and 'took me under his wing.'

Was it because we both had Russian names (although by then I had defected from Russia, and Ustinov himself was only conceived in St Petersburg and born in London, to where he 'defected' inside his mother's womb), yet in actual fact combined lots of ethnicities ('Ethnically, I am filthy,' he liked to repeat)?

His French wife Helene once confided in me that I reminded Peter of the way he himself used to be (and to look) in his younger days.

'For Vitali – Brother, Nephew, Son – in Spirit, in Laughter, in Rotundity, and in a tranquil earnestness of purpose.' – he wrote on the dedication page of his book *My Russia*.

Was 'Rotundity' the main reason for singling me out, I sometimes wondered uneasily?

In mid-November 2004, I flew to London from Dublin (where I was then temporarily based) for my last meeting with Piotr Ionovich.

In fact, I was invited to two of his 'memorial services': at the University of Durham, of which he had been Chancellor from 1992 ('Can you believe it, Vitali, I've only just been appointed Chancellor of Durham University and have already received a letter, addressed to 'Dear Mr Rectum?'') and in London – at the Church of St Martin-in-the-Fields. Due to my very busy schedule, I was only able to attend one – in London.

I felt considerable guilt at having to refuse an invitation from my 'Brother, Uncle, Father,' even if deceased. One thing I was sure about, however, was that he himself would have taken his own demise in his stride.

'Life without death is like a map without a scale,' he once observed.

Piotr Ionovich was with me constantly during this trip. He squeezed his bulk into the seat next to mine (no chair was ever big enough for him – in more than one sense) on my Aer Lingus flight.

In reality, he ended up sitting next to me on a trip once before – inside my brand-new Mazda 121.

'What a lovely little car you've got there! I have never seen a car like that before!' he exclaimed on spotting it in front of my Melbourne house in early 1991. Like a perennial teenager refusing to grow up (his face always struck me as not that of an elderly man, but rather of a long-suffering youngster, and the mane of grey hair – paradoxically – made it look even younger) had a great passion for cars and even collected them. I knew he also had a personal jet, but was not sure whether he collected planes too.

'I'd like to have a ride in your car!' he insisted.

I could not share Ustinov's enthusiasm. It was only one day before that I had got my first driving license, and my recent collision with an unsuspecting street fire hydrant, the memories of which were still fresh, did not bode well for my driving future. Besides, I had never driven the car on my own, without an instructor.

'I want you to drive me to the restaurant in this lovely car of yours!' he repeated.

We were supposed to have dinner in one of Melbourne's Russian restaurants.

I tried to talk Ustinov out of it by explaining what an awful tyro driver I was. I told him about the tragic fate of the fire hydrant, but he stayed firm.

He pushed himself inside my 'droplet' of a Mazda – knees first, and the tiny car sagged under his weight. I climbed onto the driver's seat (remember: a 'brother … in rotundity?') – and the Mazda's metallic underbelly touched the ground. Off we drove, striking sparks from the asphalt …

I sat behind the wheel trembling like an aspen leaf. If something happens, I'll go down in history as the man who killed Peter Ustinov, I was thinking obsessively. The thought in itself was not conducive to safe driving …

By the time we reached the restaurant, I was covered in cold sweat and had totally lost my appetite.

'Your driving was perfect!' Ustinov reassured me as he slowly levered himself out of the car. He had survived the experience, and his genius had been preserved for humankind. It was spared by the then world's worst driver (myself) to allow us many more meetings – in Melbourne, Sydney, London, Paris, Rome, Manchester – for thirteen more years to come.

As I flashed my passport in the poker face of an immigration officer at Heathrow, I recalled Peter Ustinov's innate dislike of borders and immigration controls.

A compulsive traveller, he was puzzled and offended by old immigration forms he had to fill on entering Australia ('One of the questions was 'when was the last time you had indigestion?' and the next 'whether or not you are insane?') and the USA ('In the space for 'Your Skin Colour' I always write 'pink'). A true internationalist, he took pride in having Italian, French, Russian, Swiss, German and even Ethiopian blood in him, but – contrary to what many people thought – not a drop of English. When he directed an opera at the Bolshoi Theatre in 1998, one Russian newspaper printed an article headlined 'Englishman Saves the Bolshoi' which prompted him to say: 'I've never been accused of being English before.'

Kofi Annan, who knew Ustinov well as a roving UNICEF goodwill ambassador for over twenty years, once remarked that Piotr Ionovich could easily 'double as permanent representative of all the UN member states.'

I thought Ustinov would have been pleased to see me waving my *European* passport. And although we first met when I lived in Australia, he kept saying (not in a didactic but rather in an avuncular manner) that my place was in Europe.

I was having dinner with Piotr Ionovich and Helene in Rome on a hot summer evening in 1992. Earlier in the day we all had an audience with the Pope, and, of course, afterwards Piotr Ionovich started mimicking the Pontiff too.

At the restaurant, Ustinov was drawing caricatures on serviettes (a brilliant cartoonist was one of his lesser-known multiple incarnations). He was joking with the waiter in fluent Italian ('How many languages do you speak?' I asked him. 'I make mistakes in eight,' he replied). Halfway through the meal, Helene told me it was the twentieth anniversary of their marriage. I was extremely touched and rushed out to buy flowers for her.

'Listen, Vitali, it is time for you to move back to Europe,' Ustinov said when I returned. 'The editor of *The European*, for which I write a weekly column, knows your work. Why don't you go and talk to him?'

We ended up writing for the same newspaper, and our respective columns often appeared on the same page, next to each other.

Ustinov adored writing his *European* column and was very proud of it. He once opted out of taking part in a top-rated BBC chat show saying he had his column to write. Having published over twenty books, he still felt he was undervalued as a writer, particularly in Britain, where he thought they perceived him only as a funny fat man, or a 'dancing bear.' Political views he expressed in his columns were sometimes naïve (great artists seldom make good politicians), but always honest, well-written and highly humanitarian. He was extremely saddened when *The European* had to wrap up in 1997.

The bells of St Martin-in-the-Fields were tolling cheerfully, not mournfully, above Trafalgar Square. The day was as dark and chilly as only London can be in mid-November. Street lanterns were burning well into the morning, and in their treacherous light the rain-soaked air looked like a condensed yellow ganglia suspended from the sky. One could almost scoop it by handfuls and cut it into pieces …

A line of black-clad people, hiding under umbrellas, was snaking into the church for Peter Ustinov's last performance. Yes, it did feel more like a performance than a 'memorial.' The church entrance was besieged by paparazzi and autograph-hunters who had come here to spot a royal or a celebrity. Even after his death Ustinov didn't stop attracting crowds.

Young boys and girls in sailors' uniforms, the so-called 'London Sea Cadets,' guarded the church entrance. I thought that was moving and somehow conveyed two very prominent streaks in Piotr Ionovich's character – childishness and romanticism. Yes, he was an unlikely modern celebrity – too sensitive, too kind and too approachable.

He was a dreamer – a lucky dreamer who had managed to have almost every dream of his realised.

Looking at the kids, I had a flashback to my own Ukrainian childhood, when I wanted to become an engine driver and a sailor, too, no doubt. Playing truant, I used to hide in a small cinema, round the corner from my school. It was there that I first saw Stanley Kubrick's *Spartacus*, where Ustinov played a character called Batiatus – the role for which he won one of his Oscars. I had watched that movie over a dozen times …

Inside the church, one could indeed observe a curious mixture of celebrities, royalty (like, say Prince Michael of Kent – a relative and complete look-alike of the unfortunate last Russian tsar Nicholas II) and 'ordinary people' like me. Many of the latter, like young actor Nick Atkinson, were 'singled out,' helped and advised by Ustinov – just like I was.

I sat next to an empty space with a nametag 'Countess Madeleine Douglas.' Ustinov would have loved that and would have immediately come up with a joke. I remembered how much he laughed when I told him the story of a German woman, who wrote for *The European* and had 'Countess Tatiana von Dunhoff' printed on her … credit card. She was probably indeed a countess: there are plenty of them in Germany.

Ustinov disliked hereditary and other 'titles' and regarded his own belated knighthood with a good deal of irony. I could never seriously think of him as of Sir Peter Ustinov, OBE (apart from his natural and rather charming OBEsity that is).

It was a highly unusual church service, with lots of laughter, theatre and music. Piotr Ionovich adored classical music, particularly Mozart, for 'the most profound superficiality' the composer possessed. He could imitate the sounds of most musical instruments and one evening, on a bet (as recalled at the service by his American friend Theodore Steinway Chapin), wrote down from memory the names of forty (!) Swiss (!!) composers.

He had extraordinary brain power, and once, having spotted some dictionaries on a shelf in my Melbourne study, noted: 'Vitali, you are the last person who needs dictionaries. Writers don't need dictionaries. Get rid of them.' And I did.

Piotr Ionovich did come up with a surprise for me during the service, the 'script' of which, as I was told, he had written himself. It happened when his daughter, actress Tamara Ustinov, and Malcolm Rennie came out to the altar (I nearly wrote 'on stage') to perform a short extract from his play *The Love of Four Colonels*.

'It was raining in Kharkov last Sunday,' were the words of Malcolm Rennie's character, 'the Russian Colonel.'

Out of all Ustinov's huge literary heritage, this one sentence, mentioning my native Ukrainian city (he knew I grew up there), was read out in the church on that day!

It was also a gentle reminder of his humorous way of addressing me as 'Comrade Colonel.'

Spasibo, Piotr Ionovich … I've heard your greeting …

I was sure his every friend in the 'audience' had received his or her own greeting, too.

After all, we didn't turn up there 'to pay our last respects,' as London newspapers reported the following morning. We came to express our ongoing love for 'one of the best-loved people in the world' – a friend, an actor, a writer, a columnist, a dramatist, a wit, a mimic, a cartoonist, a raconteur, a film-maker, a director, a producer, a musicologist, a satirist, a playwright, a polyglot, a peacemaker, a goodwill ambassador and, first and foremost, a wonderful human being whose name WAS, IS and WILL always BE 'Peter Ustinov.'

Until love, joy and laughter die out completely on this small and lonely planet of ours …

Back in Dublin, I called my childhood friend in Kharkov and asked him whether it rained there the previous Sunday.

He confirmed that it did.

Anton Chekhov

There are some interesting coincidences in the lives of Anton Chekhov and Oscar Wilde.

They lived at almost exactly the same time, albeit in different countries. Chekhov was born six years later and died at forty-four in 1904 – four years later than Oscar.

Chekhov was a practicing physician, and Oscar, although not a doctor himself, was the son of Ireland's best-known ophthalmologist.

They both worked in the same genres, although Chekhov never wrote poetry.

Even their sexual preferences were, allegedly, not that dissimilar.

Like Oscar in English, Chekhov is by far the most quoted writer in the Russian language. 'I dreamt that what I had thought was reality was a dream, and what I had thought was a dream was reality,' – this entry from Chekhov's *Diaries* can easily be nominated for an Oscar, ie pass for something Oscar Wilde has written or said.

Their tragically parallel lives ended on largely the same note – a joke.

Looking at the particularly naff and faded wall paper in need of replacement in the Paris hotel room, where he was dying, Oscar said: 'One of us will have to go …'

Chekhov on his deathbed asked for a glass of champagne. He was dying in Germany, in the rather posh spa town of Badenweiler, and was looked after by a German doctor called Swerer. It was the latter whom he asked for a glass of champagne.

According to an old German tradition, a doctor who had given a lethal diagnosis for a colleague (Chekhov, of course, was a practicing physician too) was to treat the dying man to a glass of champagne.

He injected Chekhov with camphor and asked a servant to bring champagne.

'I haven't had champagne for ages,' said Chekhov in Russian and smiled.

Then he turned over to his left side and added in German:

'Champagne Ich Sterbe…'[37] These were his last words.

Both Wilde and Chekhov wrote through their lives and lived through their writing. I am sure they would have enjoyed each other's company …

37 I am dying (German).

'Dear Venerable Table'

Once in Australia, the editor of the large daily newspaper where I worked asked me to write an article about Chekhov. Its publication was to coincide with the first night of Melbourne Theatre Company's new production of *Uncle Vanya*'

Chekhov is one of my favourite writers of all time and I keep re-reading (in Russian and in English!) his novels, short stories, plays and letters.

Alongside Chekhov's works, I had gone through a lot of the 'Chekhoviana,' ie memoirs of Chekhov written by his artist brother Mikhail, his actress wife Olga Knipper, his mistress Lika Mizinova etc Surely, I could not say anything new about Chekhov and that was why I eventually decided to write a feature not about Chekhov himself, but about his co-author, with whose unflinching solid assistance Anton Pavlovich wrote some of his best plays, novels and short stories …

Wait a moment … Did Chekhov really have a co-author? This sound like a small revolution in the Chekhoviana …

Yes, he did! Moreover, one of my last assignments in Russia was to secure an interview with this little-known Chekhov's co-author who, despite being well over a hundred years old, was still alive and amazingly well.

CURRICULUM VITAE
FAMILY NAME: Table
GIVEN NAME: Writing
SOCIAL ORIGIN: Piece of furniture
PLACES OF RESIDENCE: 1889-1892, Moscow; 1892-1899, Melikhovo; 1899-1957, Yalta; 1957-present time, permanently registered in Melikhovo
OCCUPATION: Exhibit
PRINTED WORKS: *Uncle Vanya*, *The Seagull*, *Ionich*, *The Man Who Lives in a Shell*, *The Darling*, *Gooseberry*, *Ward Number 6* etc – all written in collaboration with AP Chekhov
DISTINCTIVE FEATURES: Since 1897 – covered with green cloth

This was not an attempt at eccentricity on my part, albeit I own up to having penned an amazingly peripatetic 'life story' of an antique Biedermeier couch that used to belong to Hitler in the book called *Dreams on Hitler's Couch*.

Chekhov himself liked breathing life into furniture. In the Chekhovs' Taganrog house, where he was born and spent his childhood, there stood a cupboard where Evgenia Yakovlevna, the future writer's mother, used to keep sweets. Walking past this cupboard, young Anton would stop, bow and exclaim with reverence: 'Dear venerable cupboard!' Later he used this mocking address form in *The Cherry Orchard* …

Alone in Chekhov's modest study in the village of Melikhovo (about fifty miles away from Moscow), I was touching with trepidation the gleaming door handles that Chekhov used to touch and polished with his hands.

'A good memorial museum starts with authentic door handles,' Yuri Avdeev, the museum's director, told me.

Behind the window, I could see the kitchen garden the Chekhovs loved and called 'The South of France' …

And here it was – Chekhov's authentic writing desk, still upholstered with original green leather (not dissimilar to the one I am now writing at inside Pegasus Cottage).

There's nothing more intimate for a writer, nothing that can evoke his (or her) spirit better than the writing desk, behind which hours, days, weeks and years of struggle, elation, hard work, inspiration, tedium and whatnot are spent …

If pieces of furniture had personalities, then a writing table should be the most engrossing of them all. And by far the best interlocutor … Streets ahead of a couch, a cupboard or even a bed …

To breathe life into the legendary table I repeated Chekhov's own magic mantra: 'I dreamt that what I thought was reality was a dream, and what I thought a dream was reality' before whispering reverently:

'How do you do, my dear venerable table?'

A floorboard creaked, the table stirred slightly, as if acknowledging my greeting, and started its unhurried narrative:

'We were inseparable with Anton Pavlovich – in woes and in feasts, and my master recognised only one sort of feast and one sort of woe – they were both called 'writing.' Here my participation was indispensable.

' "I can't help thinking every moment that I must write … Write, write and write," he confessed in one of his letters to Lika written with my help, ie on top of me, of course …

'Before me, he didn't have a permanent table. The Chekhov's were poor, they kept roaming from flat to flat and using landlords' furniture. True, Anton Pavlovich's brother, Nikolai, who was an artist, once got a writing table as a royalty (or rather instead of a royalty) from publisher Utkin. That table now lives in Moscow, at Chekhov's Museum, but Anton Pavlovich worked at it only sporadically …

'I will never forget how happy Chekhov was when he bought me. "I am writing another short story now. I am totally engrossed and practically do not leave my writing table. By the way, I have bought myself a new one," he wrote proudly to his publisher Suvorin in March 1889.

'In three years' time, together with other members of Chekhov's family, I moved to Melikhovo, our country retreat.

'In Melikhovo, the Chekhovs used to get up early – very much in a peasant way. Peasantry was in Chekhov's blood: his grandfather was a serf of landowner Chertkov.

'At 5am Anton Pavlovich would already be sitting at me, unless he was to receive his patients that morning. Yes, he was a doctor, too, and was treating local peasants in this very study where we are now.

'The daily routine was meticulously observed by the Chekhovs. Anton Pavlovich bought a discarded church bell, hung it in the courtyard, and precisely at noon someone from the servants would strike it twelve times. This was the signal not only for the Chekhovs, but for the whole neighbourhood to go for lunch …

'During lunch, Anton Pavlovich would leave the dining table from time to time and would run up to me to jot down a couple of lines. He then returned to his favourite seat in the dining room, next to the door of his study – as close to me as he could be. After lunch, the Chekhovs rested, and in the evening they had music, guests and lively discussions …

'But even then Chekhov did not forget about me and did some writing. That was not easy for it was a democratic household and the visitors were allowed to move around the rooms freely; they could also enter Chekhov's study whenever they wished, and Anton Pavlovich never told them off for having disturbed him …. "It was very easy to be his guest," V Giliarovsky, a well-known Moscow writer and journalist, recalled. True, it was easy indeed for the guests but not necessarily for the host!

'Chekhov, however, never expressed his irritation aloud; only on paper he did sometimes let go … I remember clearly him writing on me to Suvorin in December 1892; "Oh, if you could only know how tired I am! Exhausted to the bursting point. Guests, guests, guests … My estate stands on Kashirsky High Road, and every passing intellectual thinks it is OK to stop at my place and warm up, and sometimes even stay overnight. The whole legion of doctors alone has visited me of late! Yes, it's pleasing to be hospitable, but there must be a limit. It was because of the guests that I fled from Moscow, after all!"

'Such bitterness was rare for Chekhov. More often he tried to be ironic about his home's popularity. "They play and sing romances in the living room next to my study all day long, that's why I am constantly in elegiac mood," he joked in his letter to L Avilova in March 1893.

'In 1884, however, fleeing the incessant stream of visitors, Chekhov moved his study to the newly built outhouse.[38] I moved with him – for summer only. Here Chekhov and I wrote *The Seagull.*

38 Chekhov's equivalent of my Pegasus Cottage! VV

On the balcony of this garden office there was a flagpole. When Anton Pavlovich was at home, a red flag was hoisted on it to let the entire neighbourhood know that Doctor Chekhov was available to receive patients!

'Now let's look at the objects on my green cloth top: an ink-pot with a lid, a pen, a candle in a candlestick, a bottle with glue, envelopes for letters. These all are fairly uninteresting, yet some other things resting on my surface do deserve separate descriptions:

'**French seed catalogue**. The Chekhovs loved to work in their garden. They ordered seeds from the South of Russia, from St Petersburg and from abroad. Having returned form his trip to Sakhalin Island where he had conducted the first ever census, Chekhov brought back the rhizomes of Sakhalin buckwheat and planted them in his Melikhovo garden, whence this plant has gradually spread all over Central Russia.

'In the garden, you can now see Chekhov-planted Berlin poplars, cherry trees and lilac. They all start blooming in spring. The Chekhovs also grew artichokes, asparagus, aubergines, watermelons, which, when they ripened, were given to guests and to the Melikhovo peasant kids. During the last years of his life, Chekhov would often say: "I think that if it were not for literature, I would have been a gardener."

'**Pince-nez**. It is hard to imagine Chekhov without a pince-nez. In actual fact, however, he started wearing glasses only in 1897, when eye-surgeon P Radzvitsky visited Melikhovo, diagnosed Chekhov with astigmatism and selected a pince-nez for him.

'**Medicine chest.** This is one of the most interesting of Chekhov's possessions. If you open the chest and sniff it, you will feel that a weak odour of medicines still lingers in it … The longevity of smells is impressive … Stories still circulate in Melikhovo district about experienced and unselfish Doctor Chekhov. He could be contacted for help any time of day and night and he had never refused anyone – not once …

'I could also tell you about a village school for Melikhovo kids Anton Pavlovich built with his own money, albeit he was far from rich. Chekhov himself acquired wooden desks for that school, and they are still there – my junior brothers and sisters. Ask them – and they may tell you much more about my famous owner and co-author …'

When it came out, my 'interview' with Chekhov's writing table was sent to the Melikhovo Museum and became one of its exhibits. I am extremely proud of this, of course …

As for *Uncle Vanya*, its Melbourne production was appalling. The actors shouted a lot on stage, as if they thought that the louder they yelled, the better their acting was, and – encouraged by the director, no doubt – had turned this rather tragic play into a farce. The audience was laughing their pants off (according to my observations, many Australians went the theatre primarily to have a good laugh). As a result, Chekhov's characters on stage talked, moved and behaved artificially – like pre-programmed robots, not living people.

During the interval, I was approached by my newspaper's theatre critic – a tall elderly man of Serbian extraction.

'What do you think of it all, Vitali?' he asked me.

I honestly told the critic that the company had fallen into a trap by trying to act a Chekhov's play 'as it was written,' by concentrating on its uppermost superficial layer, whereas Chekhov's plays existed not on one, but on several – at times, four or five – different levels that had to be kept firmly in mind and reflected in the acting …

Having opened the paper the following morning, I saw the review signed by the critic: 'The company had fallen into a trap by trying to act a Chekhov's play 'as it was written,' by concentrating on its uppermost superficial layer, whereas Chekhov's plays existed not on one, but on several – at times, four or five – different levels that had to be kept firmly in mind and reflected in the acting,' it ran.

It was my first (and, hopefully, last) piece of writing neither in the first, nor in the third, but in (or rather by) the SECOND PERSON.

'Private Love' and World War I Poets

A dried poppy flower fell out of my dog-eared memo pad as I was perusing the notes made during my two recent tours with Holts. Once scarlet and now crimson – the colour of curdled blood, it marked the page describing the Bailleul Road East Cemetery at St Laurent-Blancy, one of a thousand British memorial cemeteries in France. It is there that a regulation stone obelisk with the Star of David marks the last resting spot of 'Private I. Rosenberg, Royal Lancaster Regiment, 1st April, 1918, aged 27.'

Isaac Rosenberg was a faint Jewish boy from East London, a soldier of the Great War and one of Britain's most sophisticated and promising poets, whose life was cruelly cut short on April Fool's Day in 1918. He lies there, under vast Normandy skies, between 'Lance Corporal LF Donovan' on his left and 'Private TN Bancroft' on his right – the gruesome 'multiculturalism' of death.

Bending down for a pebble to be left on Rosenberg's grave in accordance with an ancient Jewish tradition, I picked up a red poppy and put it between the pages of my notebook. And, having straightened up, I noticed the epitaph on a twin obelisk nearby: **'Private A.A. Love, age 20, 23 April 1917**.' There came an urge to write a poem about Private Love, who died so young that he had no time to experience what his beautiful family name really meant; about Love that always carries the rank of a Private, not of a General; about the sheer absurdity of wars.

I did write a poem in the end of this four-day-long 'Poetry and Prose of the Great War' tour , but not about Private Love. The complete poem about him was already there – engraved on his tomb-stone. There was no need to add anything to it.

In the course of my eight days with Holts 'Battlefields and History' Tours, I underwent an incredible transformation – from scepticism bordering on boredom to fascination and rediscovery of my love for Britain, my adopted country.

The first tour was called 'The Dambusters.' I signed up for it reluctantly, simply because military history has never been my cup of tea. Growing up in the offensive jingoism and hooray-patriotism of the Soviet Union made me instinctively suspicious of all sorts of the militaria. I used to do badly at the compulsory military training classes at school and at the university – both in theory (which regiment stood where in the battle of Kursk) and in practice. Assembling Kalashnikov rifles, I kept losing bayonets and other 'essential' spare parts, and once nearly shot an instructor during a shooting exercise – inadvertently of course. My thinking was (and still is) that only a nation with uncertain present and even more uncertain future could wallow endlessly in the 'glorious' battles of its 'glorious' past.

Embarking on my first 'Battlefields' tour, I was also wary of noisy Soviet-style patriotism, of endless eulogies for 'our valiant boys,' sent to their deaths by 'our wise and noble government,' which I had heard so many times before. This last apprehension proved totally superfluous: not once during the tours did I hear our guides and guest speakers use the adjective 'great' to describe British soldiers, commanders and politicians, which made me conclude that British patriotism was quieter and less aggressive than its Russian or American counterparts.

My first hours on the green Holts bus taking us to Germany via France, Belgium and Holland were not very encouraging. My fellow passengers were mostly elderly couples, and some had a disturbing obsessive sparkle, characteristic of eccentrics and train-buffs, in their eyes. Both the guide and the guest speaker were ex-military, and their impeccably pressed suits sat like uniforms on their lean sprightly frames. After each 'comfort stop,' 'Plan B' was announced which meant looking around yourself to make sure all your bus neighbours were 'present and correct.'

The very concept of 'The Dambusters' was a mystery to me, the nearest association being 'The Ghostbusters,' and I couldn't help thinking that we were probably on the way to chase war-time ghosts nestling among the ruins of German dams (which turned out to be fairly close to reality).

The moment we re-boarded our bus at Calais after the Channel crossing, the guest-speaker, armed with a microphone, began showering us with verbal shrapnel of biographic details, technical characteristics and dates of battles. The only intervals in his extremely knowledgeable, yet much too militarised for my civilian ears, monologue came when he would put on a deafening video-tape depicting yet another combat scene. We watched the videos on the monitors suspended from the ceiling as we rode through France and Belgium to the non-stop sounds of cannonade. When the screens went blank, we could see our own puzzled reflections in them, as if we all had somehow become part of this never-ending video battle.

I could hardly contain my annoyance. Even buxom French toilet ladies accepting 'all European coins' at 'comfort stops' felt colourful and exciting compared to the bellicose boredom reigning inside the bus. The only sights pointed to us on the way were some 'war-time bunkers' on the outskirts of Ghent.

I can't remember at which point I – quite unexpectedly – started taking interest. Was it while watching a video documentary on Barnes Wallis, the inventor of the spinning cylindrical bomb, bouncing off the water like a tennis-ball off the lawn? To get his invention approved, Wallis had to endure a long battle with red tape, with aloof Whitehall *apparatchiks*, instinctively scared of everything new – a saga of almost Soviet proportions. That was probably why, when asked what he wanted to be remembered for, Wallis replied: 'As a grandfather of ten grandchildren.' A human story was breaking through the technicalities of warfare, like a new-born chicken through an eggshell.

Or was it during our first 'non-comfort' stop at the toy-like Dutch village of Steenbergen, where Guy Gibson, the Dambusters Wing Commander, had his fatal crash in September 1944? A small timber mill was now on the crash site, and we stood there in silence staring at stacks of wooden planks in a lifelessly clean courtyard. All of a sudden, I could clearly see the burning carcass of Gibson's Mosquito KB 267 transpire through the neat stacks of wood. Having survived the dam raids and his subsequent fame, twenty-six-year-old Guy was shot down over this sleepy Dutch village, where one of the streets is now called Gibsonstraat, and Albert Postma, a local pensioner, is looking after his grave.

Another revelation came a day later, when we were taken to see Mohne Dam, one of the six attacked by the Dambusters in May 1943. The clever spinning bombs, invented by Wallis, blew a huge hole in Mohne Dam and released a thirty-metre high wall of water. In the resulting flood, dozens of towns and villages were wiped off the face of the earth, and thousands of innocent people, including 769 Polish and Russian 'slave-labourers,' mostly women, lost their lives. The pastoral Ruhr Valley was covered in carcasses of animals and human bodies for weeks to come.

There are no reminders of that horrible night on the tree-lined banks of the Mohne River these days. Ducks and white swans, not bombs, are now bouncing off its silvery surface. It was there that I learnt one of Holts' main principles – always to give a truthful and balanced account of historic events, no matter how unpleasant this truth can be. Mohne Dam was fully restored by the Germans within four months. Water supplies to the steel factories of the Ruhr and the surviving towns were back in place three days after the raid. Within a week or so, according to survivors, life was more or less back to normal. So was Operation Chastise (the code name for the Dambusters raid) worthwhile?

Holts did not try to give us a definitive answer, but made sure the victims as well as the winners had their silent say.

In our green bus, with the Lancaster's bombing route conspicuously (and as I thought somewhat provocatively (we were in Germany, after all) drawn on its side, we drove to the memorial cemetery in the forest at Neheim, where Russian and Polish women, the victims of the raid, were buried. A simple bas-relief on their mass grave depicted troubled (or doomed?) women's faces looking up anxiously at the disproportionately huge British Lancasters above them. I suddenly came to understand why Wallis might have preferred being remembered as a granddad, not as the inventor of the deadly and undiscriminating bomb.

A large group of 'refugees' from the former Soviet Union – fat, semi-naked and foul-mouthed, were having a barbecue on the lawn next to the memorial, a sacred place where no German would ever think of picnicking. They did not look or behave like refugees, but rather like petty crooks, taking advantage of Germany's lenient asylum-seeking laws. Vodka was flowing. The nauseating stench of fried lard was hanging in the air above the spot where some of the picnickers' grandmothers could have been buried. 'Look, bloody foreigners!' one of them yelled in slurred Russian, pointing at our group.

Dinner conversation was stilted that night, and the guest speaker was not displaying his collection of model British planes and toy soldiers as he did happily the night before.

'The Dambusters' tour left me thinking about the futility of wars. It also left me willing to go on another Holts tour that would be less specialised and closer to my heart. So, when I learnt there was a vacancy on the 'Poetry and Prose of the Great War' tour, I signed up immediately.

Having started my literary career as a poet, I was always of the opinion that the best examples of poetry were triggered by suffering. That was probably why Russia's twentieth-century poetic palette was so rich and colourful: suffering was the only commodity of which the Russian people had never been short.

I boarded the Holts bus once again feeling like an old-timer. Not to the extent of the man who took 123 Holts tours within ten years (an absolute record), or even of a 'Holts Harrier' (a title bestowed on a person who had completed ten tours with Holts), but at least I knew what 'Plan B' was about. And, not being a 'Harrier,' I did harry a little about how my second experience with Holts was going to work out.

Despite my loathing of such 'totalitarian' superlatives as 'great' and 'brilliant,' I feel obliged to use them in the next sentence. The 'Poetry' tour with Holts **was** great, our guest speaker, Barry Webb, an Oxford don and a biographer of Edmund Blunden, **was** brilliant, and the whole experience could be best described as an intellectual and emotional feast on wheels.

A detailed account of it defies the powers of the pen. How can one describe High Poetry, made even more poignant by the fact that most of its creators had been killed in their twenties?

Poetry itself was our main guest-speaker on this trip. And our guides were World War I poets: Wilfred Owen and Siegfried Sassoon, Edmund Blunden and Isaac Rosenberg, Edward Thomas and AP Herbert, David Jones and WN Hodgson – twenty altogether. We learnt about their lives and deaths, we read their poems aloud on the bus and at their graves, we wandered with them across grassy fields and weed-covered old trenches retracing their final footsteps towards eternity. They were of diverse backgrounds and social standings, of different physique (from athletic Sassoon to flaxen Rosenberg and emotionally disturbed Owen), of miscellaneous poetic trends. It was World War I, the bloodiest military conflict in human history, that had brought them together, having unleashed the 'hurricane of poetry,' whose powerful gusts kept stirring our hair eighty-five years later as we trudged uneasily through forests and dirt-tracks of Normandy.

'There are no stereotypical World War I poets – they come in all shapes and sizes. But they were all particularly sensitive people,' Barry Webb told us in the beginning of the trip. It was probably their extreme 'sensitivity' that prompted many of them to write prophetic heart-rending verses hours before they were killed. I don't quote them here, because poetry is not a treatise. It is rather a deep sigh, an intimate whisper into the reader's ear. Poems should either be reproduced in full, or left alone, for a sigh and a whisper cannot be cut into pieces.

My travel companions on this tour were middle-aged British folks, whose faces were ennobled and rejuvenated by poetry. 'We assume that all the people on the bus are poets,' said Barry Webb. And so we were.

Our dinner conversations were hushed and evocative, with no small talk. Here are just a couple of randomly overheard snippets: 'We British should be ashamed of lots of things we did – like bombing Germany in the end of the Second World War …'; 'Why don't they have a grudge against us in Germany, and we do? Isn't it because we are still afraid of them?' I remember Ron, a robust elderly man with tragic blue eyes, who had recently suffered a personal tragedy, telling the only American on the tour: 'We British are not militaristic. We have simply come here to honour our sacrifice …'

Self-criticism is an admirable British quality. As a national characteristic it bodes well for the country's tomorrow, for only those who can objectively assess the past stand a chance of a better future. Holts' Battlefields & History Tours, a unique British institution, did not try to celebrate the past, but quietly encouraged us to learn from it.

One thing I have learnt from my two short trips with Holts is that a poem makes much more sense than an air-raid or a battle.

I would want to get back on the Holts bus one day and to learn some more …

* * *

PS

Below is a poem I wrote during the last tour:

Wild Poppies

Above the trenches, grass and mud
Wild poppies glisten – like drops of blood,
Squeezed from the scarred body of the Earth,
They smell of death,
They scream of birth.

But washed by the rain during the night,
They start looking like clots
Of condensed sunlight,
Like belated smiles of the dead –
These wild poppies – bright and red.

Kafka's Prague

There's something unmistakably Kafkaesque about Prague – a fact I was able to reconfirm again during my umpteenth brief visit there recently.

But what exactly is 'Kafkaesque?' The dictionary defines this adjective as .' . . of, relating to, or suggestive of Franz Kafka or his writings; especially: having a nightmarishly complex, bizarre, or illogical quality.'

If so, then Prague is indisputably Kafkaesque, for Franz Kafka himself was born there in 1883. It was in Prague that he worked as an insurance clerk and wrote – outside office hours, no doubt – most of his stories, including the famous *Metamorphosis*, in which a man called Gregor Samsa wakes up one morning as a giant repulsive insect.

The memories of Kafka, who was snubbed as a writer during his lifetime and whose works were banned by the communist rulers in both Czechoslovakia and the USSR, are being carefully preserved in Prague. A visitor to the Czech capital can go on a 'Kafka's Prague' tour, the highlight of which is the Franz Kafka Museum, with a model of the horrific torture machine from his story *The Penal Colony* among the exhibits. The Museum's courtyard is decorated with David Cerny's animatronic sculpture featuring two men (who, as some tend to believe, represent Stalin and Hitler) urinating into a small pool in the shape of the Czech Republic.

That same technology-prone sculptor David Cerny more recently created a kinetic statue of Kafka, made of forty-two chrome-plated layers of reflective stainless steel, thirty-eight of which keep rotating constantly – both synchronically and in opposing directions, with the resulting wild grimaces and sinister rictus-like grins on the writer's uncomplaining face. Ironically, the sculpture is facing a city government building, as if making faces at the whole of global bureaucracy …

Cerny's initial idea for a sculpture in that very spot was of a robot to commemorate the Czech writer Karel Capek, who coined the word ('robot' means 'worker' in Czech) in 1920, next to a Golem – a much more ancient mythical 'robot,' created, as the legend goes, by Judah Loew ben Bezalel, the sixteenth-century rabbi of Prague. He built the Golem, an animated anthropomorphic being, out of clay from the banks of the Vltava River and brought it to life by inserting a '*shtem*' – a capsule with a magic formula (an equivalent of a modern-day electronic card-key to your hotel room?) into its mouth. The Golem had of course to be deactivated on Friday evenings by having the *shtem* removed, for no one was supposed to work or to function on Saturdays. Once the rabbi forgot to remove the *shtem* – and disaster struck: the humanoid turned against its own creators …

Sipping an espresso in an al fresco café overlooking the Kafka sculpture, I was recalling my own encounters with Prague's multiple 'Golems' – the inescapable

Kafkaesque manifestations, so 'specialised' and peculiar that I was tempted to refer to them as 'technologies.'

A stone's throw from the Kafka statue was another unusual – and rather Kafkaesque – techno attraction: the Film Special Effects Museum featuring the works of world-famous Czech filmmaker Karel Zeman, responsible for all the very special special effects in such Hollywood blockbusters as *The Adventures of Sindbad the Sailor*, *Journey to the Beginning of Time* and many others. The museum was hugely interactive: visitors were encouraged to experience Zeman's at times spooky special effect technologies using their own photo and video cameras. The Museum's (and Zeman's) Kafkaesque side could be highlighted by the following words of the great filmmaker: 'Man has created a grandiose world of technology, of which dread and fear are often the result …'

Sad, but true. And the proof was not far away. In the Russian bookshop off Vaclavske Namesti I picked up the latest issue of the Czech edition of the Moscow tabloid *Komsomol'skaya Pravda*, the first page of which was dominated by the photos of the freshly unveiled by Putin 'Sarmat' and 'Kinzhal' (Dagger) intercontinental ballistic and hypersonic missiles. 'Our 'Dagger' has been sharpened and made ready for battle. May our enemies all over the globe tremble!' screamed the headlines. In the small country only fifty years ago trampled by Soviet tanks, they did sound both 'nightmarish' and 'bizarre' (read Kafkaesque).

Prague can safely claim a patent for another highly Kafkaesque 'invention' – 'defenestration' (from the German word 'Fenster' – window). I would define it as 'chucking an undesirable politician out of a window and making it look as if he has taken his own life.'

My latest visit coincided with the seventieth anniversary of the tragic death of Jan Masaryk, the former Foreign Minister of Czechoslovakia and the son of the country's first democratically elected President Tomas Masaryk. I walked past the freshly and lavishly decorated monument to Jan Masaryk near the former Foreign Ministry building in the Castle area. The body of Mr Masaryk was found in the Ministry's courtyard, beneath an open window, on 10 March 1948. It was officially announced that he had killed himself by jumping to his death. Interestingly, the first doctor to arrive at the scene also committed suicide a fortnight later.

The death of Masaryk was the final episode in the communist takeover of Czechoslovakia. Rather than a suicide, it was almost certainly the case of the centuries-old Czech political 'technology' of defenestration. The first – a collective one – happened in 1419 when several over-zealous Prague town councillors were hurled out of their office windows by a group of bullish religious reformers. Since then, there have been three more (including Masaryk's) and yet another – incomplete – one, in 1996, when two Chinese men, who weren't politicians, were tied up and thrown from the ninth floor of a Prague block of flats, but both survived.

Who is going to be the victim of the next great defenestration of Prague? Only God and probably Kafka know. Yet one thing is certain: the Kafkaesque spirit is very much alive. And here's another fresh proof: an entrepreneurial Prague businessman likes to invite the guests of his suburban villa to take a dip into a small private swimming pool, converted from one of the giant bronze ears of the dismantled statue of Stalin – the world's highest statue of the dictator that used to dominate Prague's cityscape in the 1950s.

Not sure about you, but I definitely wouldn't venture to swim in a Stalin's ear, even if made of bronze, lest I should be mysteriously sucked into some dark inner depths of the dictator's body.

Kafka would have loved this, I am sure.

* * *

The moment I entered my warm and cosy room in the Domus Henrici boutique hotel near the Prague Castle, I felt an urge to rub my eyes or to pinch myself, or both: its windows were overlooking … the Eiffel Tower on top of a hill! Could it be that I boarded a wrong plane in Stansted?

Having taken a better look at the Tower, however, I calmed down: despite a certain similarity of the cross-beams at the foundation, unlike its famous Parisian 'sister,' the Prague Tower had an octagonal, as opposed to a square, cross-section. Nor was it resting comfortably on the familiar four lattice steel columns. It also looked much smaller than the iconic creation of engineer Gustav Eiffel.

I soon found out that the sixty-three-metre-tall Petrin Lookout Tower of Prague behind my window was indeed inspired by the Eiffel Tower. Built in 1891 (two years after the latter), it had a TV broadcasting antenna, installed in it in 1953, and remained the city's main radio and television tower until the opening of a much taller and much much uglier Zhizhkov TV Tower in the opposite end of Prague. It is here that the inescapable Franz Kafka's associations began to kick in.

The Zhizhkov Tower, with its 216-metre-tall antenna spire, was built between 1985 and 1992 by the structural engineer Jiri Kozak. Nicknamed 'Jakes Finger' – after Milos Jakes, the country last communist leader, this brilliant example of the megalomaniac communist-style architecture has been known for two main reasons:

1. In 2009, one Australian website named it the world's second ugliest building (they didn't specify what the first ugliest building was, but I think I know the answer: the offices of the newspaper where I worked while living in Australia).
2. In 2000, David Cerny, a maverick Czech sculptor, the creator of the peculiar stainless-steel statue of Kafka, added ten fibreglass sculptures of babies crawling up and down the tower's pillars.

Why babies? In an interview, David Cerny explained that an old Jewish cemetery was destroyed during the construction of the Zhizhkov Tower, and the exhumed remains (which, as some believe, included those of the writer Franz Kafka, also buried there – VV) were relocated to another cemetery in the outskirts of Prague. For the sculptor, the babies therefore symbolised commemoration of the dead as well as the continuation of life above the ruins. Yet to myself, they carried another strong connotation – with Kafka's short story *Unhappiness*, in which the author is visited during the night by an apparition of a small child. From the subsequent conversation, it transpires that the child had come to represent the writer's loneliness and alienation not just from the outside world, but also from himself …

A rather sad story – one of the countless Kafkaesque tales of Prague, where arts and technology often go hand in hand with the Kafka-style dark symbolism, which I was able to feel as far back as twenty years ago while researching my book *Borders Up!* there.

Already a devoted Kafka fan, I couldn't help noticing the city's never-ending Kafkaesque landmarks, like, say the then freshly unveiled memorial plate to student Jan Palach, who set himself on fire and died on 16 January 1969 in protest against the Soviet invasion of Czechoslovakia. I could not ignore the sad irony in the fact that '*palach*' was Czech for 'flame.' . .

To my consternation, the chief brewer of the famous Staropramen brewery, which I visited as part of my research, was an exact look-alike of … Lenin, complete with the late Soviet dictator's regulation polka-dot tie and the pseudo-intellectual 'social-democratic' goatee, which trembled nervously as he spoke. I caught myself half-expecting the respected engineer to raise his hand and to cry out suddenly in a high-pitched voice (Lenin could not pronounce 'r' and had to say 'g' instead): 'Comgades! The ggeat ghevolution has happened! Hoogay!' But instead, he showed me four 'unique and precious' (in his words) conical copper tanks, the so-called brew-kettles, which had to be hidden by being buried (Kafka again!) in the brewery's courtyard during the Nazi occupation of Prague.

Yet the truly cathartic experience was spotting a thirty-metre-high statue of the 'King of Pop' Michael Jackson towering above the Vltava River, at the very spot where the giant statue of Stalin used to stand (the same statue, whose huge bronze ear is now being used as a swimming pool by one entrepreneurial Prague businessman). Initially, I thought that the latter had miraculously reappeared in Prague nearly a decade after the collapse of communism – the thought that gave me creeps.

I soon realised that it was not Stalin's but Michael Jackson's inflatable statue that he used to carry with him on international tours.

On the same day, I nearly fell victim to Jacko-mania, when one of the singer's hand-written 'I-love-you' notes, thrown down from the balcony of his Inter-Continental hotel, under which I was inadvertently passing, having briefly pirouetted in the air, landed on my unsuspecting head. In a split second, the roaring mob of Jackson's teenage fans pawed at me like the proverbial seventh wave at a flimsy sinking boat, their hands stretching towards my head (or rather towards the note). They would have definitely torn me into thousands of tiny Vitalis, had I not taken to my heels and ran away for all I was worth, my footsteps echoing loudly in the narrow streets of the Kafka's Old Town.

Sweating and breathing heavily, I came to a stop at a drinks kiosk in Argentinska Street. I was dying of thirst, but the brightly-lit sign inside the kiosk nearly made me take to my heels again. 'TIME FOR ENERGY DRINK. SEMTEX FORTE,' it ran.

Having just visited the Synthesia factory in the nearby Czech city of Pardubice (see Part Two of this book), the factory that used to produce the infamous terrorist-friendly explosive Semtex, a piece of which the size of a fist, according to experts, could blow a hole in the side of an aircraft, I was not at all tempted to test its explosive power internally.

It was of course just an ad for the eponymous fizzy drink Semtex, then popular in the Czech Republic. But as an avid reader of Kafka, I was not prepared to take chances. Would you?

Part Twelve
My Three Faraway Favourites

The Funfair of Life (South Korea)

'There are some 8,000 North Korean cannons and rocket launchers aimed at Seoul, in effect holding the inhabitants of the city hostage …'
New York Times, 4 December 2017

My first indirect impression of South Korea goes back to 1988, when a Moscow journalist colleague of mine became one of the very few lucky Soviet reporters to be sent to Seoul to cover that year's summer Olympics. On his return, he was unusually taciturn and withdrawn, and when I asked him how he liked South Korea, he pondered for a minute or so looking in front of himself, as if mesmerised, and then said: 'It was amazing: all those cars, buildings, people … It was like a funfair of life!'

Many years lapsed since then. I became a political defector from the USSR, then a journalist and travel writer in the West. Remembering my ex-colleague's metaphor, I kept looking for that mysterious 'funfair of life' in all my wanderings. And, finally, the opportunity arose to try and locate it at its very origins. I was invited to join a group of journalists and travel agents for a quick visit to the site of the 2018 Winter Olympic Games in PyeongChang and afterwards to spend some time in South Korea's capital.

* * *

On the day of my Korean Air flight from London to Seoul, North Korea launched another, more powerful than ever, ballistic missile – the first in seventy days. On the same day, another North Korean soldier escaped to the South by dashing across the border. He was shot at by North Korean border guards, but survived … It was probably not a good time to look for a 'funfair of life,' and yet I decided to start there and then.

It is an astounding fact, but the annual per capita GDP in South Korea, a nation that has no mineral resources and always had to import them, has grown 300 times since 1967 and now exceeds $27,000. In just fifty years, the country's economy has grown more than the economy of Europe in two centuries. That boom was largely the result of its citizens' devotion, hard work and technological innovation. Wherever you go in South Korea, you see technology in action – starting from the immigration control at the Seoul airport where every arriving passenger is subjected to quick biometric tests while he or she minces from one foot to the other in front of a TV screen with pictures of sumptuous Korean cuisine dishes, the images that are supposed to help you relax your facial muscles while being photographed by a mini-camera on the officer's desk – and finishing with electronic state-of-the art (and scarily excessive for a novice user) toilets, with buttons like 'wash,' 'massage,' 'rhythm' and 'enema' (*sic!*) on special control panels above the seats.

My first port of call was the city of PyeongChang in Gangwon Province to the north- east of Seoul, the site of the 2018 Winter Olympics, where we were supposed to look at some of the Olympic structures and venues.

We were met at the airport by a minivan and a gregarious female guide called Kim HyeSook, or Sooki. 'Are you concerned about the latest North Korean missile launch?' I asked her straight away. 'Yes, but not half as much as you are in Europe … ' That was a typical attitude of South Koreans towards the unending provocations of their troublesome northern neighbour: quiet awareness without fear. It was largely nurtured by dignity – a vital element of a traditional Korean character, and also by '*anshim*' –a Korean term for 'calm' and 'peace of mind,' inspired by both Confucianism and Buddhism, Korea's second leading philosophy, teaching to keep one's sangfroid in the face of the most unsettling circumstances.

The landscape of the Gangwon Province, dissected by the Taebaek mountain range, was stunning, and I had to pinch myself from time to time – not just to beat the severe nine-hour jet lag but also to remind myself that I was not in Switzerland. Despite the jet lag, I was able to register that most of the Olympic structures and objects were all ready (in the words of Yeo HyungKoo, secretary general of the Olympic Organising Committee, 'ninety-six per cent ready') and the tickets were selling well, albeit the continuing provocations by North Korea were not helping. The organisers were taking those occasional setbacks with calmness and a good deal of '*anshim*,' and carried on adding the last touches to the Olympic structures meticulously.

Like so many other places in Korea – and not just on the Olympic site – my hotel in Hanwha Resort, with both normal 'Western' and traditional Korean (no furniture, warmed up floor to sleep on) bedrooms, appeared perfect, yet not quite finished. That did not mean 'abandoned,' but rather 'fully functioning while still under construction.' This permanent incompleteness was in itself the sign of continuing development and progress, and by the end of my trip I was tempted to start referring to the whole of South Korea as a permanently unfinished country.

In short, the Olympic PyeongChang came close to becoming my sought-for 'funfair of life,' but to see it all completed I had to wait for the Olympics.

* * *

After a couple of days, I split up from the group, and since the high-speed KTX rail link was still nearing completion, took a slow – very slow – Korail train to Seoul from Jeongdongjin, an East Sea coastal town, to where people from all over the country – following another age-long tradition – flock to watch the sunrise on the New Year Day.

Next morning, I woke up to the view of skyscrapers, not mountains, in my hotel window. My room in 'Shilla Stay' was looking after me: lights would automatically come on and off, curtains would part and close, the bed would get warmed up. The room felt like part of a theme park – a Disneyland of life? – and I decided to try hard to find my 'funfair' while in Seoul.

On several occasions, I thought I was coming close.

My breath was taken away by the ancient ceremony of the changing of guard at the fourteenth-century Gyeongbokgung Palace in downtown Seoul, when very young Korean 'warriors' in colourful period robes and with moustaches, painted under their noses to give them a more fearful look, were marching solemnly across the spacious courtyard and under the pagoda-shaped arches – in the shadow of skyscrapers, and to the sounds of the Janggo – the traditional hourglass drum, drowned by the unceasing din of traffic behind the Palace fence.

With Kim Minseon, Seoul's up-and-coming celebrity chef, we were shopping for my cooking class ingredients at the Yangnyeong and Gyeongdong herb and food markets. Describing them simply as a horn of plenty would be like calling London's Shard a fairly tall building – a gross understatement: I had to shut my eyes to avoid being blinded by the pallet of colours and cover my nose not to be overwhelmed by the delicious cacophony of smells. Under Minseon's expert supervision, I ended up cooking an Oyster soup, followed by Yusa Fruit Dessert, consumed there and then in the kitchen, and washed down with generous quantities of home-made Soju – Korean rice wine.

Using Seoul's underground, or Subway, was like getting a glimpse of a transport funfair of the future. Endless white-marble corridors, moving walkways, palatial stations, trains that are always on time, and animated signs behind the train windows merging into a short movie … Returning to my hotel after midnight one morning, I was pleasantly shocked to see lots of unattended and unguarded underground stalls, with goods like perfumes, cosmetics and designer clothes piled on them and left unattended for the night, with no fear of theft. One of Buddhism's main precepts – not to take something that is not yours – was obviously at play there. In the words of Seung-mook, senior monk at the Seoul's Jogyesa Temple, 'in South Korea, pretty much everything is a little bit Buddhist. Including politics.' To me, that partially explained the Koreans' keep-calm-and-carry-on attitude to the ongoing danger from the North. They might have simply resorted to the so-called Middle Way principle, preached by the Buddha, which calls for moderation and not taking sides in conflicts.

And how can I forget the evening I spent in Seoul's 'Little Russia' in Dongdaemun area? 'A Little Central Asia,' however, would be a more fitting name for this predominantly Russian-speaking 'Seoul's Brighton Beach,' populated with migrants from Uzbekistan, Kazakhstan and Mongolia and ethnic Koreans from Russia. I had a multicultural dinner of *Shurpa* (Uzbek), *Vinegret* (Russian), *Lavash* and *Shashlik* (Georgian), *Manti* (Uzbek) and vodka (international) at the lavishly decorated

Samarkand City restaurant, run by a seemingly distinguished Uzbek manager, 'President Sanat' (as his business card said) – a culinary 'funfair' of my Soviet past.

Yet, underneath all those bustling places, the city was full of calm, quiet and serenity which stopped me from categorising Seoul as the 'funfair of life.'

My visit coincided with the Korean Buddhism Jogyesa Chrysanthemum Fragrance Sharing Festival, and all Jogye Order temples were decorated with flowers. As someone who practises a different, Western, style of Mahayana Buddhism, I was nevertheless honoured to take part in the prolonged *Moktak* (monk)-led *Yebul* (chanting ceremony). Chants and hapjangs (semi-bows) in the company of several hundred people underneath the three golden statues of the Buddha couldn't fail to generate mindfulness and peace.

As for the Hanok, a traditional Korean house, where I spent one night, it was exuding peace and calm too – from its very structure and its curvilinear shaped roof, imitating Korea's landscape and terrain. Built according to the Confucian principles, its wooden-lattice windows pasted over with Korean traditional paper, the house blended with nature. At times, it felt as if it was alive and could breathe, yawn and snore …

* * *

With just a couple of days left in Korea, I was coming to grips with the fact that I might never find the 'funfair of life' there. I still had one important place to visit – the so-called DMZ – the Demilitarized Zone, only fifty kilometres north of Seoul.

Myself a defector, I was both willing and fearful to see the world's last remaining Cold War border, to come close to my own totalitarian past for the first time in nearly thirty years. Since the collapse of the Berlin Wall, it was the North-South Korean divide that had acquired a dubious moniker of The Mother of All Borders.

My first surprise was how touristy the trip was promising to be. Coachloads of people: Koreans and foreigners – were heading towards the JSA (Joint Security Area) across the pristine landscapes of the no-man's land – a four-kilometre-wide watch-tower-ridden buffer zone, with lush vegetation and thriving undisturbed wildlife. On the way, I ticked off flocks of exterritorial herons, wild geese and majestic Siberian eagles, floating in the sky in huge numbers like some benign wide-winged fighter bombers.

Our passports were checked four times on the way to the JSA, and our guide, with a smile glued to his face, was announcing lunch arrangements (lunch was included in the tour) finishing with a tactlessly facetious rhetorical question: 'Is anyone planning to ignore lunch and to starve themselves like the North Korean people?'

No one laughed.

We soon reached Camp Bonifas, a USA Army base, named after Captain Bonifas, an American officer killed by axe-wielding North Korean border guards in 1976.

The Camp had a visitor Centre, with a regulation souvenir shop selling DMZ chocolates, DMZ vinegar (!), laminated North Korean banknotes, and 'I've Done the DMZ' t-shirts. Before being escorted to the MDL (Military Demarcation Line) inside the so-called 'Peace House' – the Military Armistice Commission building, where both sides used to meet to resolve disputes – we had to listen to a short introductory talk by two US Military Police privates, both speaking with a characteristic Mid-Western drawl. They told us we were not allowed to wear flip-flops, ripped jeans and shorts, exposing the buttocks. We then had to sign a peculiar 'Visitor Declaration,' point D of which read: 'Visitors will not point, make gestures, or expressions like scoffing, abnormal action which could be used by the North Korean side as propaganda material against the United Nations Command.'

In a disorderly formation, we proceeded to the Peace House, from where we were allowed to ogle (and to take photos of) a couple of stern-looking and motionless North Korean officers who were ogling us in return. Private Earp, our escort, told us that they nicknamed one of the North Koreans Jack, and the other one – Bob. Several tourists, including myself, ventured across the MDL that ran through the middle of a small negotiations table and momentarily ended up in North Korea *de facto*. Despite the touristy touch, the sensation was ticklish …

We looked at some other DMZ attractions: The Bridge of No Return, where POW exchanges used to be conducted; the Third Infiltration Tunnel, secretly built by North Koreans and discovered by the South after a tip by a defector; the Dora Observatory, a look-out platform, from where – through special pay-as-you-view binoculars – we were able to see bits of the North Korean territory, including the permanently empty buildings of Kijong-dong, better known as the 'propaganda village.'

Contrary to its intentions, the North was making money for South Korea by the very fact of its existence and by its precarious proximity too!

The last – and the most moving – stop on our itinerary was Dorasan train station, built during the temporary thaw in the North-South relations, the so-called 'Sunshine Policy,' under Kim Jon Il.

The empty long-disused station had an eerie feel. It spelled the end of hope. Only platform tickets were on sale at the station's ticket office. When on the platform, the tourists could examine the solitary sign 'Seoul – 56km; Pyongyang – 237km.'

'Hope this railway will reunite Korean families,' George W Bush said at the official station opening in 2002. It didn't …

* * *

I did find my 'funfair of life' in the end! Our last stop inside the DMZ was in the middle of a real-life Korean funfair right on the border with North.

It was a proper 'Western' funfair, complete with roller-coasters, merry-go-rounds and crowds of laughing ice-cream-gobbling visitors.

The wind was bringing in the muffled near-orgiastic snippets of the North Korean propaganda, continuously broadcast by the loudspeakers from across the border. Those ecstatic, almost inhuman in their insane aggressiveness, sounds, mixing with the jolly carefree bleeps and jingles of the funfair rides and merry-go-rounds, merged into an amazing and seemingly inane, yet, in actual fact, extremely meaningful, cacophony of South Korea's daily reality – exciting, inspiring and somewhat schizophrenic.

I felt suddenly as if I had indeed been visiting not just another free Western country, but a thriving, defiant and super-courageous 'funfair of life' straight under the barrel of a gun.

* * *

After my cardiologist's recommendation that I reduce the amount of long-haul flying, several months of my life were marked by a couple of spectacular train rides – in Europe and in East Asia.

The first one – an overnight journey from Krakow to Budapest on board the legendary 'Chopin' sleeper train had a touch of sadness and nostalgia. Nostalgia was due to the fact that, having lived for a number of years in Australia and then in Britain, one of the things I missed most from my Ukrainian childhood and Russian youth were overnight train journeys – to Kiev, to Moscow, to Leningrad and occasionally for holidays to the Crimea. While in Australia, I did take the Indian Pacific Express from Sydney to Perth, but the ambiance of that three-day-long journey, with nothing but red desert behind the windows of my match-box-size compartment and shift meals in the swish restaurant car, were so different from the European train routine that it did little to quench my longing …

Sadness kicked in half an hour after our PKP DK 407 Intercity train left Krakow Glowny and smoothly came to a stop at the seemingly small and dark Oswiecim (or Auschwitz, in German) station, having thus covered the exact route of the last cattle-truck journeys of the thousands of the Krakow Ghetto dwellers in March 1943 … I couldn't go to sleep in my comfortable birth for a long time after that. European train journeys are often wrought with the continent's tempestuous history unveiling silently behind the train windows …

I had a very different train journey while in South Korea last December.

Having looked at the 2018 Winter Olympics facilities in Pyongchang, I took a slow – very slow – Korail train to Seoul from Jeongodongjin, an East Sea coastal town, to where people from all over the country flock to watch the sunrise on the

New Year Day. According to the *Guinness Book of World Records*, the tracks at its station were closer to the beach than anywhere else in the world. Indeed, walking along the platform towards my carriage, I could see and hear the surf of the East Sea only several metres away …

The five-and-a-half-hour-long journey in a spacious and faultlessly clean carriage of a standard Mugunghwa-ho cross-country train, with soft freshly upholstered seats reclining almost to a bed level, was one of the most calm and comforting in my life. The second class carriage had separate male and female toilets (perhaps a tribute to Confucianism, Korea's leading philosophy, with its strict segregation of men and women in public places?), a bespoke washing room and a handful of passengers who all kept extremely quiet throughout the journey. Intercom announcements in Korean and English periodically reminded the passengers not to raise their voices, and no one did, including a baby boy with a young Mum and even younger (or so it seemed) granny in the seat in front of me – well-behaved and serene, like a little incarnation of the Buddha. The whole experience was a reminder of what a great invention railway was – something easy to forget in Britain. I even came to understand the hidden meaning of the Korail logo, rendered – rather clumsily, as I had thought – in English on the carriage's notice board: 'Refresh your life with a train.'

We were travelling along the Yeongdong Line – one of the twenty Korail lines criss-crossing the country. The line was opened in 1940, and the first ever train in Korea departed from Seoul to the sea port of Incheon in 1899, much later than in most European countries and the USA. The route was just thirty-two kilometres long, and the maximum train speed did not exceed fifty-five kilometres per hour. By 1906, however, a through railroad across the whole of the Korean Peninsula was completed. It was run by Japanese managers and engineers, with Koreans mostly doing hard manual jobs. Since Korea was then a colony of Japan, its railways' structure and organisation had been largely Japanese, and some of those features are still obvious today: as opposed to all other means of public transport, traffic on South Korean railways is still predominantly left-handed, like in Japan!

I was soon lulled into a snooze by the rhythmic rattling of train wheels. I slept for a couple of hours to the accompaniment of multiple intercom announcements in English and Korean. In my dream, one of them said that South Korea was reunited with the North, and the train's next stop will be Pyongyang. I woke up in cold sweat … We were rolling through the suburbs of Seoul, one of the world's largest and most densely populated cities, with clusters of boringly numbered (104, 105, 206, 207 etc) high-rise residential towers which reminded me of mushrooms, springing up in batches after an August rain in a Russian forest. The existence of these human anthills in the city, where in 1960 there was not a single building of over twenty storeys, was another sign of the unprecedented economic boom, known as 'South Korean Miracle': by 1970, Seoul already had eight high-rise buildings, and by 1990 –

sixty-six! Nowadays, such buildings are simply countless, and one of them was the glass-and-concrete bulk of Seoul's Cheongnyangni station, at which we soon safely arrived …

At this point you may ask: why did I choose to take a slow train to Seoul, instead of using one of Korea's famous KTX high-speed ones, based on the French TGVs – the trains that do not only run like clockwork, with 99.9 per cent punctuality (2015), but also, with the rate of 0.058 accidents per one million kilometres, are officially the world's safest?

The answer is simple: the long-awaited KTX high-speed link between PyeongChang and Seoul was opened on 22 December 2017 – three weeks after my journey. But despite the fact that a KTX train, with all its onboard technological gadgets (LTE-R communications systems, wi-fi and power points, as well as USB ports at every seat etc) could cover the same 222.7-kilometre distance in just one hour and forty minutes, I do not regret it a bit.

One huge advantage of slow train journeys is that they allow you ample time to relax, to learn, to look back at your life, and, as in my case, at your childhood too.

The Korail motto of refreshing one's life with trains, may not be that offbeat, after all …

Migrants of the Caribbean (Nevis)

It is hard to find a stone, let alone a pebble, on the sun-drenched cracked patch of land which is the old Jewish cemetery in Charlestown, the tiny capital of Nevis, an East Caribbean island with the population of 10,000. After several minutes of searching, I manage to spot a small piece of gravel, pick it up and, in accordance with an old Jewish custom, place it on the nearest tombstone as a token of respect for the once vibrant and important and now-defunct Jewish community of Nevis whose records include the invention of Muscovado sugar and educating Alexander Hamilton, one of the USA's founding fathers, who was born on the island in 1755. It is not a well-known fact that the creator of the USA's first bank and George Washington's closest aide attended the West Indies' then only Jewish school – in Charlestown.

The history of the Jews of Nevis, who migrated to the island from Spain and Portugal while fleeing the Inquisition in the 1670s, is one of the most amazing real-life stories I had come across during my thirty-seven years in journalism. It is also a tale of exile, hardship and perseverance – the story that the modern world desperately needs to know.

A Tropical Heaven

'Paradise' was the wi-fi access password at Nisbet Plantation Resort, where I stayed while on Nevis. And tropical heaven it was indeed. A former sugar plantation and the only beach-side plantation property in the Caribbean, it was there that Admiral Nelson met the young widow Fanny Nisbet, who later became his wife. Nowadays, the estate had thirty-six comfy cottages, scattered over a coconut palm grove, and an excellent colonial-style restaurant, presided over by Maitre D' Patterson Fleming, whose main duty was to make everyone feel welcome. On request, the ever-smiling Patterson (many first names of local men are derived from the last names of the former planters) would take you on a pub crawl around the island, or demonstrate his extraordinary collection of 3,000 outrageously bright ties that earned him the nickname of the island's 'Minister of Tie-rism.'

It was my first visit to the Caribbean, and the resort, with its palm trees, monkeys, exotic birds, string bands playing on the beach during the day and replaced after dark by the orchestras of melodiously squeaking, as if flute-playing, crickets, was like a widely accepted notion of the Caribbean coming to life. It could be a cliché, yes, but stereotypes can be beautiful too.

'We are not quite in the twenty-first century here,' Tim Thuell, the resort's general manager, told me.

My favourite pastime on the beach was watching the abundant brown pelicans, locally known as boobies, fishing in the sea. With complete abandon, these large graceful birds, with powerful wings and aquiline profiles, would drop vertically – and often synchronically in twos or threes – into the water, heads down, to emerge with a sparkly fish wriggling in their beaks. Never before had I seen such graceful creatures, fully immersed in their own mysterious reality …

Mystery was never far away in Nevis. Since 1628, when the island was colonised by the British, the latter used to refer to it as a jewel in the British Crown. By the onset of the eighteenth century, Nevis had become a centre of British social life rivalling many places in England itself. Some even claimed that Nevis was more important for Britain than the whole state of New Jersey … How come that this tiny island had managed to produce the best sugar in the whole of the Caribbean? How come that – for several centuries – it had been much more economically advanced and more upmarket than the neighbouring St Kitts, which is almost four times bigger, both in territory and in population?

Hon Mark Brantley, Nevis's Deputy Premier, whom I met in Charlestown, told me about the island's impressive economic development, its ambitious plans to progress from relying mostly on tourism to being the exporter of renewable energy, its toughening immigration policy, good schools and social housing. But as a true politician, who was also a senior cabinet member of the federal government of St Kitts & Nevis and the holder of ten (!) different ministerial portfolios, he declined to comment on Nevis' seeming lead over its neighbours.

Secrets of the Old Burial Ground

No amount of brown pelican watching could give me an explanation, but a possible answer came up unexpectedly during the tour of Charlestown from my driver-cum-guide, a dedicated local historian John Paris.

'Our economy is stronger due to the Jewish influence,' he said as we were walking past the old, yet well-maintained, Jewish cemetery in the centre of the town. 'Due to the Jewish settlers, for centuries – up to the 1980s when the whole of the sugar industry came to a stop – we had made the best sugar in the Caribbean, because they brought to the island the technology of crystallisation …'

'There was a slave market in Charlestown, but the Nevisian Jews never had slaves or took part in slave trade; they excelled in business and technology,' he carried on. 'It was they who taught young Alexander Hamilton to hate slavery and to be good with counting and money …'

'Wait a moment!' I interrupted looking at the time-beaten tomb stones. 'Jewish influence? How did that come about? How big is the Jewish community of Nevis these days?'

'There is no such thing any longer,' John replied. 'The last Jewish migrants left the island over 200 years ago ... We don't know where they had gone to and what happened to them afterwards ...'

More moss-covered stone fragments of the once thriving Jewish community were to be found in a small narrow lane that led from the cemetery to the town centre.

'We locals call this lane Jews Walk, albeit this is not its official name,' John explained. He then showed me the spot where Alexander Hamilton's Jewish school used to be located, now part of an old garage, and a crumbling stone building that used to be a *mikvah*, the Sephardic Jews' ritual bath.

'I went to school past these ruins,' he said. 'Until 1971, when the cemetery was officially rededicated, no one knew what they were. Some believed they could be the remains of a synagogue, the first in the Caribbean, but later they established it was probably just the school, and the synagogue must have been elsewhere ...'

We finished the tour at the two-storeyed Georgian house, built on the foundations of the structure where Hamilton was born in 1755, and now housing his museum. It was there, with the help of Nicole Liburd, the museum's curator and the executive director of the Nevis Historical and Conservation Society, that I started my quest for the mysterious Jewish enclave of Nevis. Miss Liburd was kind enough to give me access to the island's archives. The story that unveiled was extraordinary.

The Rabbi's Discoveries

The modern part of the Jews of Nevis' long saga began on a scorching Sunday afternoon of 3 February 1957, when the first ever cruise ship, SS Ryndam of the Holland-America line, visited the island.

The gleaming white ocean liner was so huge that her crew included an onboard rabbi, whose name was Malcolm Stern. The rabbi couldn't wait to get ashore for one simple reason: during the cruise, he heard from Captain John Smith, who had visited Nevis before, that Alexander Hamilton, one of the greatest Americans ever, was not only born on that island, but also received his early education in the local synagogue. When Mr Stern asked the Captain why Hamilton, who was not Jewish, had to be educated in a Jewish school, the reply was that the future USA's first Treasury Secretary, having been born out of wedlock, was denied admission to the Anglican school, but was readily accepted by the Jewish one. An avid scholar of Jewish history, the rabbi knew that the Sephardic community of Nevis was no more, but was eager to check if the Nevis synagogue, the first in the Caribbean, was still there. And how about a Jewish cemetery and other memorabilia?

Accompanied by his wife Louise, Malcolm Stern got ashore to explore Charlestown. Having turned off the main road, they stumbled upon what rabbi Stern later called 'an almost unidentifiable ruin.' A local guide told the Sterns that Nevisians called that structure 'the Jews' school.' The Sterns then spotted the remains of two characteristic columns inside the ruin and concluded that, synagogue or not, the building definitely had Jewish origins.

They proceeded down an unpaved path, to which their guide referred as 'Jews Walk' which lead them to a rather neglected lawn, overgrown with weeds, where goats grazed among hardly visible crumbling tombstones, on some of which the semi-obliterated epitaphs in Hebrew, English and Portuguese could still be discerned. 'The lot, approximately 200 feet by 75 feet, is delineated by the remains of a wire fence,' rabbi Stern recorded. To his sheer delight, he was able to read some of the epitaphs: 'The body of Benvenida Cohen Rodrigues who departed this life the 3rd of September 1684 … ' and so on – altogether nineteen markings ranging between 1684 and 1768 …

On returning to the USA, Rabbi Stern wrote several articles about his findings, thus bringing the forgotten Sephardic community of Nevis to public attention. A handful of scholars, philanthropists and plain enthusiasts visited Nevis in the following years. With the help of the government of St Kitts and Nevis, particularly the then Prime Minister the Honourable Robert L Bradshaw, some modest funds for the restoration of the historic burial ground were found, and on 25 February 1971, the old Jewish cemetery was reconsecrated (ie declared sacred again) in a special ritual which included a ceremonial procession, an official opening of the cemetery's gate by Rabbi Malcolm Stern, prayers for the dead, singing of psalms, brief address by the Premier himself and the Poem of Reconsecration, composed and read by writer and attorney Robert D Abrahams:

'Long, long ago they walked this lovely isle,
And lived and died within Mount Nevis shade;
Far was their coming, here found rest awhile,
Enjoying what their fruitful labours made.

We know not why they came, nor where they went,
But these remained, reposing in this spot -
Their wanderings at end, their voyaging spent:
A while they were remembered, then forgot.

Standing close today beside their graves,
We say the ancient prayer they would have known;
'All men are brothers' – this the truth that saves
And may the Lord of all here, bless each stone.'

* * *

Why and Where To?

The poet might have been right in saying that it was (and still is) unclear why and where to the Jews of Nevis eventually went. Some historians refer to the French invasions of 1706 and of 1782, others to the recurrent earthquakes and the economic depression, as reasons for that enigmatic mini-exodus. But the fact remains: if by the end of the seventeenth century, one fourth of the island's white population were Jewish, by the last half of the eighteenth century only three Jewish households remained. It is fair to say therefore that by the early 1800s, the once strong and vibrant Jewish community of Nevis had simply vanished from the island and from the face of the earth never to be seen again.

But the influence persisted. Armed with the traditions, attitudes and technologies introduced by the Jewish migrants, the sugar industry of Nevis became the most advanced in the Caribbean. By 1870, with over 200 plantations, mills and estates on both Nevis and St Kitts, it was the first in the West Indies to move on from wind to steam power, with sugar being the undisputed king of the island's burgeoning economy …

As for 'why they [The Jews – VV] came' to Nevis in the first place, the reason was obvious – religious persecution. The choice they were facing back in Spain and Portugal under the Inquisition was simple: convert to Christianity or die.

Their way to Nevis was long and full of hardship. Many first went to Brazil, where they learned the secrets of sugar-making, or to Barbados, before turning up on Nevis in 1677-78, when the census listed four Jewish families there. Their wanderings reminded me of the Russian Old Believers in Alaska. Driven out of Russia by so-called 'Great Schism' of the 1650s and by severe persecution under Peter the Great, whom they saw as the Antichrist, they had to flee first to the outskirts of the vast Russian empire and then farther afield – to Brazil (just like the Jews of Nevis!) and to Oregon, where they survived by growing wheat and corn, before settling down in Alaska in 1968.

Hamilton's Predicament

The difference, however, is that whereas the happy colonies of the Russian outcasts in Alaska are still thriving (as I could see for myself, having visited them), the Jews of Nevis disappeared over 200 years ago, having left a remarkable, if little-known legacy, which, alongside the technological breakthroughs in sugar-making which are still in use today, had helped to shape modern America. By that I mean their indisputable strong influence on the outlook of young Alexander Hamilton, who, as one of the USA's founding fathers, a hero of the American revolution and the First Secretary of the Treasury, had a huge effect on the state of his adopted country, the USA, and hence eventually on the future of the whole world.

For reasons unknown, yet easily guessable, the Jewish part of Hamilton's life and education has remained obscure and has been silenced by many a biographer. One of the current Broadway hits, *Hamilton: An American Musical*, while looking at Hamilton's life in some detail, does not mention it either. According to a recent issue of *Tablet Magazine*, '… something the musical doesn't explore is the founding father's early connections to Judaism …' Even Hamilton himself, according to his son, rarely alluded to his personal history – the fact that didn't stop Alan Burr, a one-time US Vice-President who killed Hamilton at a duel in 1804, from calling him 'Jew bastard.'

So, what did the Jewish school of Nevis give to young Alexander, apart from opening its doors to the bright little boy, ostracised for being the son of an unmarried woman? According to rabbi Malcolm Stern, there, 'by the age of ten, he had acquired his love of reading, his skill in mathematics (*sic* – VV), and the ability to recite the Decalogue (the Ten Commandments – VV) in Hebrew.' His son later related that Hamilton often mentioned with a smile how he was repeating the Decalogue in Hebrew when so small that he was placed standing by his teacher's side upon a table …

While at the school, Hamilton had also become fluent in French, learned to love freedom and to hate slavery of which his headmistress was a staunch opponent.

All through his life, Hamilton harboured reverence for Jewish people. In later years, he wrote that .' . . the progress of the Jews from their earliest history to the present time has been and is entirely out of the ordinary course of human affairs. Is it not then a fair conclusion that the cause also is an extraordinary one – in other words, that it is the effect of some great providential plan?' And once, speaking in court, he challenged the opposing council by saying: 'Why distrust the evidence of the Jews? Discredit them – and you destroy the Christian religion' – the thought later echoed in the works of the exiled twentieth century Russian philosopher Nikolai Berdyaev.

* * *

'Well, what can I say? They just left, after 200 years here,' shrugged Nicole Liburd, executive director of the Nevis Historical Society, when I asked her if as a historian she had her own version of why the Jews had not stayed in Nevis. She then smiled and added: 'The Jewish migrants left – and the community briefly went into decline … They played a great role here, were fine merchants, inventors and helped the economy …'

That 'help' can still be felt in Nevis where all the locals I spoke with expressed genuine affection towards Jewish people, both 'their own' and in general. Good deeds and people behind them are always remembered warmly, and that memory never fades …

This story, first published in Geographical Magazine, won the Caribbean Tourism Organisation Best Feature Award in 2018.

Old Believers (Alaska)

She was sitting on the pavement (or, as they say in America, 'sidewalk'), next to a 'Paws for Coffee' coffee-shop for dogs, in a wind-swept suburb of Anchorage, Alaska's biggest city. Her slanting Inupiaq eyes stared straight in front of her, across the buzzing freeway and further – past a McDonald's outlet and a grey modernistic bungalow of an 'Alaska Cremation Center' – into nowhere. She was drunk. Or stoned. Or, most likely, both – alcoholism and drug-addiction are still rife among Alaska's natives. A soiled Russian Orthodox cross, carved out of whale's bone, was dangling round her dried-out parchment-like neck.

I spotted her while trying to walk off my jet-lag on my first afternoon in Alaska, although my first encounter with what is known as 'Russian Alaska,' or 'Russian America in Alaska,' occurred several hours earlier, on the flight from Minneapolis to Anchorage, where I sat next to a taciturn Alaskan Indian dressed in the black robes of a Russian Orthodox priest.

Peaceful Russian Orthodox missionaries were eventually much more successful in Alaska than bellicose communist preachers in Russia itself: communism in Russia is no more, whereas Orthodoxy in Alaska (and in Russia, for that matter) is stronger than ever, and three-bar Russian Orthodox crosses are still scratching the vast, stormy and pinkish (as if chronically inflamed and itchy) Alaskan skies from the tops of missile-shaped church domes. They have become an inseparable part of Alaska's ever-dramatic landscape, so brilliantly conveyed in the paintings of Norman Lowell, an Alaskan artist who lives on the Kenai Peninsula. His canvas *In the Stillness of the Night* features a solitary Russian church in the shadow of a snow-capped mountain, with *Aurora Borealis* ablaze above its roof. This artistic image is a true reflection of modern Alaska, where ethnic Russians are few and far between, but Russian Orthodoxy remains the dominant religion.

When the first Russian colonists started arriving in Alaska in the middle of the eighteenth century under the banner 'For God and Tsar,' they brought their religion with them. The locals, who used to believe in supreme divine force, proved easy converts. They eagerly took to Orthodoxy not only because of its kindness and its impressive rituals, but also because many Russian priests were highly educated people, who shared their medical knowledge with the Indians and helped them create their own alphabets by translating psalms and gospels into local languages. Soon, it became common practice for the natives to adopt the names (first and last) of their Russian Godparents after baptism. Leafing through a bulky 1999 Anchorage White Pages, I kept coming across Russian names: 'Olin,' 'Oleksa,' 'Oleksyk,' 'Oskolkoff.' Among them, there were three 'Ivanovs' and six, somewhat Westernised, 'Ivanoffs.'

After the sale of Alaska to America in 1867 (at $7.2 million, it was USA's best-ever bargain), many locals chose to keep their Russian names, whereas others opted for easier-to-spell Anglo-Saxon ones for secular purposes. Camille Fergusson, a young Tlingit woman in Sitka, the ex-capital of Russian Alaska, told me that her real church name was Yelizaveta. And although some aspects of the Orthodox mass are becoming increasingly Americanised (I couldn't believe my eyes when I saw pews in the Holy Resurrection Church in Kodiak, for one is supposed to stand or to kneel on the floor during the fairly Spartan Orthodox service), and most of the liturgies are now conducted in English, some hymns and psalms are still sung in Old Church Slavonic.

Nowhere else in Alaska is this peculiar fusion of cultures so obvious as in Eklutna – a native Athabascan Indian village twenty-six miles north-east of Anchorage. On entering the graveyard of the Old St Nicholas Orthodox Church, I was momentarily blinded by a sudden riot of bright colours emanating from the graves – the last thing one would expect at a normally sombre Orthodox cemetery. Each burial was marked not only by a traditional three-bar cross, but also by a multi-coloured 'spirit house' – a transitional Wendy-house-like 'dwelling' for the deceased in accordance with an ancient Athabascan system of beliefs which has no concept of physical death. The colours of these toy-houses – complete with gabled roofs, doors and tiny window-frames – differed from clan to clan, and their size was in proportion to the age of the deceased, but each of them was radiant, cheerful and (indeed!) death-defying. Any child would love to have one in a toy-box ...

Travelling in Alaska, I often thought what it would have looked like, had it not been sold to 'the Boston Men' (a Russian nickname for the Americans) in 1867 and remained part of the Russian Empire – not a far-fetched historical alternative, if we remember that the sale was debated in the US Senate for over six months. There would have certainly been many more Russian names in phone directories, but fewer churches, which would have been replaced by Stalinist wedding-cake skyscrapers, with stars – not crosses – on their cheeky spires. There wouldn't have been a lot of 'No Touch Laser Car Wash' stations, Aircraft Parts centres selling spare parts for privately owned hydro-planes, and ubiquitous 'drive-thru' Espresso coffee shops (Espresso is America's new consumerist idol), routinely offering forty-odd types of coffee, including a 'half-caf' – a cross between a proper espresso and a de-caffeinated one.

One thing is certain, however: had Alaska stayed Russian (and then Soviet), it – paradoxically – would have never become home to the world's most obscure community of Russian outcasts confined to a handful of small villages (Nikolaevsk, Voznesenka, Razdolna, Kachemak-Selo, Port Graham and Nanwalek – no more than two to three thousand people altogether) in the south-west of the Kenai Peninsula. Visitors are not welcome there, but I was lucky (my name must have helped).

* * *

The road to the village of Nikolaevsk was overgrown with fireweed, an endemic bright-red wild flower, and *pushki*, a cauliflower-like poisonous plant. The latter's name was distinctively un-English and must have originated from Alaska's Russian settlers (*'pushki'* is Russian for 'canons'). In vain, I was trying to spot a road sign for Nikolaevsk: there were none. Finally, following the instructions given to me in Homer, the nearest town, I turned onto an unpaved dirt-track. After a half-hour-long bumpy ride, I was overtaken by a battered old Rover with a bearded man behind the wheel. A woman in strange Mennonite-style headwear was sitting next to him. It was my first glimpse of Nikolaevsk residents, the Russian Old Believers – a much-persecuted and therefore extremely reclusive religious group, who first came to Alaska in the 1960s.

The origins of the Old Believers' movement go back to the so-called 'Great Schism' of 1650s, when Nikon, a strong-minded Russian Orthodox Patriarch and a strict disciplinarian, decided to correct the Church-Slavonic holy texts and the method of worship practised by the Russian masses. His reforms were opposed by a section of the Orthodox church, who accused Nikon of heresy and vowed to stick to the old ways. Nikon's reforms were far from iconoclastic and concerned such seemingly insignificant issues as how many fingers (two or three) would be used to make the sign of the cross; whether 'Alleluia' should be sung two or three times; whether the priests should walk around the altar with or against the passage of the sun, and so on. But in the eyes of the more conservative believers this constituted a huge change in their faith. Organically opposed to any reform, the Old Believers (as they became to be known) suffered severe persecution under Peter the Great, whom they saw as the Antichrist. As a result, many had to flee to the outskirts of the vast Russian Empire. After the Communist *coup d'etat* of 1917, a considerable number escaped over the border to China, where they stayed until the Chinese revolution of 1949 forced them even farther away from home – to South America and Australia.

The majority of Nikolaevsk residents came to Alaska (in 1968) from Brazil, via Oregon, where they survived by growing wheat and corn. In the words of Father Kondratiy Fefelov, with whom I spoke inside the village church of St Nicholas, they left Brazil because of its poverty ('We couldn't sell our crops') and Oregon – in fear of the 'corruptive influence' the American media, mainly television, could have on their children, traditionally brought up in strict accordance with the Old Believers' religious values. 'We wanted to get away from Western civilisation, with all its drugs and sexes (*sic*), and to be on our own …'

'How come you allow this?' I asked him, pointing at a satellite dish on the roof of a neighbouring house. The priest waved his hand nervously: 'We had to slacken up eventually. You ban television – and the kids run to our American neighbours, or go to the cinema, which is even more dissipating …' He pronounced 'cinema' with disgust – in precisely the same way the Old Believers of Peter the Great times must have uttered the hated word 'reform.'

With eleven children and thirty-six grandchildren, Father Kondratiy, to whom the villagers reverentially referred to as Batiushka (Little Father), knew what he was talking about.

Children were everywhere in Nikolaevsk, where each family had ten to fifteen offspring (it is not unusual for a girl to get married at fourteen or fifteen). They were all serious, quiet and too shy to talk to a stranger like myself – particularly the girls in their traditional long dresses ('*talichkas*') and coloured kerchiefs, which they were bound to change for a more sophisticated headwear ('*shashmura*') – a cap covered with a scarf – after getting married and becoming 'khoziaiki' ('house-hostesses'), preoccupied mainly with cooking and child-bearing. Marriages in Nikolaevsk have still to be approved and blessed by the '*Batiushka*' (little father).

And yet, the feared Western civilisation has crept its way into this closed anachronistic world. 'We have a problem with young Russian village guys who are in the habit of getting drunk and driving their pick-up trucks at breakneck speed across the town,' a tourism official in Homer confided in me. When I asked the '*Batiushka*' about it, he pretended he didn't hear the question.

In a challenge to the age-long traditions of male domination, several Nikolaevsk women found themselves jobs in Homer, whereas a couple of others chose to leave the community altogether and moved into the 'real world,' where, as one Nikolaevsk resident told me with horror, 'they wear shorts and even use make-up.' On the other hand, three American families came to live in Nikolaevsk and seem to be getting along well with the Russians.

Yet even the most conformist of the Old Believers cannot dismiss all the fruits of Western civilisation as harmful. The '*Batiushka*' himself was telling me with pride about the villagers' own small fleet of ultra-modern fishing vessels, with the latest electronic equipment (fishing consitutes their main source of income). Nikolaevsk boasts an excellent secondary school, one of the best in Alaska, where all the subjects, except for Russian, are taught in English. No wonder the village teenagers prefer communicating in English, although most of them retain a reasonably good command of their melodious old-fashioned Russian language. As for smaller kids, they hardly speak any Russian at all. 'They don't want to learn Russian,' complained Nina Fefelova, at whose house I was put up for the night. Nina, herself an Old Believer, came to Nikolaevsk from the Russian Far East seven years ago and married one of the '*Batiushka*'s sons, a deacon called Denis. She taught Russian at the village school.

A bubbly and outgoing character, Nina was not devoid of a business streak and ran a tiny Russian gift-shop from her own back-yard. She made me wear a traditional Russian '*rubakha*' (a collar-less silk shirt) and a '*kushak*' (sash), both borrowed from her shop, and kept snapping pictures of me in this ridiculous (from my point of view) outfit, now only worn by dancers of Russian folk ensembles when on stage.

In the evening, I was invited to watch fish-canning in the courtyard of Feopent Ivanovich Reutov, a thick-set elderly man, who was born in Russia ('My parents didn't tell me where') and grew up in Brazil. The canning was done in an antediluvian way: tins of pink salmon were placed into a capacious iron barrel with water and boiled for four hours on a powerful bonfire – 'to kill all the microbes.' Two youngsters, Iona and Flegon, both duly bearded (the Old Believers' men are not allowed to cut their facial hair) and wearing baseball caps, came to help.

A neighbour, Father Deacon Josip, popped in, allegedly to borrow a scythe, and stayed.

I felt at ease in the company of my fellow outcasts, who seemed to accept my 'Western' attire, my 'modernised' Russian language, my shaven beard-less face, even my camera (the Old Believers are notoriously camera-shy). There was only one thing about me that they could not come to grips with: smoking. 'In Voznesenka, they would attack you with an axe, if they saw you with a cigarette in your mouth,' Iona told me with a grimace of disapproval on his face. I made a mental note never to come close to the village of Voznesenka, which had a reputation of being even more reclusive and more conservative than Nikolaevsk.

They told me off, when I inadvertently dropped a cigarette end on the grass: 'Pick it up and hide it somewhere. If the *Batiushka* finds it, you are in trouble …'

'Don't you realise that smoking is a sin?' Josip, the Deacon, persisted. I mumbled something to the effect that we were all sinners in one way or another. 'This is true,' Josip said pensively, and the subject of smoking was dropped for the rest of the night, although the word 'sin' came up again, when Flegon mentioned his girlfriend, an American divorcee with a child.

'We must ask the *Batiushka* to marry you and to take you out of sin as soon as possible, in the name of Jesus Christ, our saviour,' Iona, who himself was properly married to an Old Beliver Russian girl, commented. 'He must be joking,' I thought, but Iona's face was dead serious, and his dark-brown eyes were full of sad reproach.

A warm and velvety summer night fell upon Nikolaevsk fast, as if the smallish village was suddenly covered with an oversized black and fluffy *ushanka* (a traditional Russian fur hat with ear-flaps) from Nina's gift-shop. The fire was burning brightly in Feopent Ivanovich's courtyard tearing the darkness into shreds, dagger-like. Iona produced a bottle of raspberry-flavoured (we were in America, after all!) Smirnoff. All the men, except for me, crossed themselves before every drink.

Deacon Josip was telling us about his childhood in Brazil. And although he had never been to Russia, his Russian speech was amazing: it was the language of Tolstoy and Turgenev, free of foreign borrowings and clumsy modern abbreviations. Like their lifestyle and customs, the Old Believers' mother-tongue was frozen in the time warp of 1917-1920, when their grandparents, with bags and baggages and under cover of darkness, crossed the Russian-Chinese border into Manchuria.

Merciless and insatiable Alaskan mosquitoes were buzzing above our heads, and some big dark shadows were moving in the bushes, behind the lawn. Could they be the moose? I felt as though I was watching a perfectly directed (by Andrei Tarkovsky?) Russian movie set in in the middle of the last century. Only this 'movie' was for real, and I myself was among the cast …

It was already past midnight, when Josip and Iona burst into a heart-rending Russian folksong which I had never heard before. They sang about long farewells, dusty roads and a hard life in a foreign land, which in Russian is called 'chuzhbina' – a word that doesn't have a direct equivalent in English. Contained in it are willows rustling soothingly above the winding creek, the wind whistling through a birch grove, and an endless snow-covered Russian steppe glistening like marble under the moon.

I suddenly understood why, after centuries of wanderings, these people chose to settle in Alaska, which looks so deceptively similar to their cruel, yet dear, homeland – the country that most of them have never been to and will never see. Like Russia, Alaska has willows above creeks, snow-covered plains, and birch-groves. It used to be a part of Russia and, in a sense, it still is, for the genuine Russian spirit destroyed by the Bolsheviks and no longer found in Russia itself, has been smuggled out and kept intact here by the Old Believers.

Looking at their faces, lit by the last flashes of the dying bonfire, I knew: they had found their new home for many years to come. I remembered a memorial plate which I had seen earlier at the Nikolaevsk School Assembly Hall:

'In Commemoration of the Old Believers Who Became United States Citizens,' it said.

Dozens of old-fashioned Russian names followed.

Part Thirteen
My Worst Journey Ever

My travels were not always idyllic …

It was autumn 2001 and I was all set to go to the Island of St Helena – one of the world's remotest and most obscure places.

The reason for the trip was the recent arrival of television on the island – for the first time in its history. I wanted to establish whether the fact that St Helena boasted the world's most cultured and well-behaved children (according to numerous sociological surveys) had anything to do with the islanders' total lack of exposure to the 'small screen.'

The answer was fairly obvious even without going to the island, but, to be perfectly honest, I simply wanted to get there and to add St Helena to the already impressive list of obscure destinations I had visited.

Getting to St Helena was not easy.

The island was one of the few remaining places in the world that didn't have an airport, and the only way of reaching from the UK was first flying to Cape Town and then taking the *Royal Mail Ship St Helena* – the only means of reaching the island. The sailing time from Cape Town was five days. On the morning of the sixth day, if you were lucky, the RMS would drop the mail (and yourself) on St Helena.

The whole trip, including an even lengthier return journey, was supposed to take me just over a month. My trip had been booked throughout including a cabin on board RMS *St Helena.* I had even exchanged emails with the man whom I was to share that cabin with – a UK government official travelling to the island to resolve some minor taxation issues.

In the afternoon before my departure day, when I was busy packing my suitcase with books and video cassettes (the latter, I thought, could prove nice souvenirs for the TV-hungry islanders), the *Daily Telegraph's* Travel Editor phoned me asking to cancel the trip.

'We've got something else in mind for you,' he said. 'Something no less exciting …'

'But I have everything ready for St Helena,' I tried to object. 'Why don't you ask someone else to do that mysterious "something?" '

'Because you are the only one of us who can do it,' he replied.

From the explanation that followed, it transpired that The *Telegraph* had been approached by one of London's poshest travel agencies, who wanted to invite a writer to join for eight days what was officially the world's most expensive package tour.

With the average cost of $70,000 per person for twenty-eight days (drinks were not included!), it was called 'Around the World by a Private Jet' – a fairly self-explanatory name.

The editor's point was that whereas a 'native' British journalist, when confronted with such a generous invite, would feel instinctively obliged to write something positive about the tour, I as the only 'un-English' writer in the Section, wouldn't feel such a moral obligation and would actually be able to bring back an impartial piece of journalism ...

Besides, coming (as I did) from the hardship-ridden Soviet background, was bound to invite some revealing comparisons and flashbacks ...

His logic didn't strike me as particularly sound, but having weighed up all pros and cons (among the pros were visits – even if extremely brief – to India and Thailand plus natural curiosity as to what the world's most expensive package tour might involve), I called him back and accepted the offer.

The TV-starved islanders of St Helena were not destined to get hold of my carefully selected set of video cassettes that included such all-time favourites of mine as *Once Upon a Time in America*, Andrei Tarkovsky's *Solaris* and *Battleship Potemkin*, too ...

* * *

'For Monks Only' ran a peremptory sign above the only row of empty seats in the Domestic Terminal of Bangkok airport, where I was shifting from one foot to the other waiting for a connecting flight to Chiang Mai.

I had to beat the temptation to lower my aching jet-lagged frame onto a seat: for all my debts and bank overdrafts, I could hardly pass for an impoverished over-ascetic Buddhist monk. To begin with, I was wearing shoes. Also, I was on the way to joining in one of the world's ultimate hedonistic experiences – a twenty-eight-day-long 'Around the World by Private Jet' tour.

The 'Private jet' was originally meant to be Concorde, but after all Concordes were grounded last August, it had to be replaced with a Boeing 747, specially refitted to provide the clients with 'ultra-First Class luxury unavailable from any commercial source,' according to a glossy promotional brochure. There were eight stopovers, each of two to three days duration, in this round-the-globe hop, starting and finishing in New York: Hawaii, Shanghai, Chiang Mai (Thailand), Jaipur (India), Dubai, Florence, Tunisia and Lisbon. I was supposed to join the group of forty-nine tourists, mostly Americans, in Chiang Mai and to fly back to London from Dubai a week later.

Yet, so far the experience was far from hedonistic. My back was sore after being repeatedly stabbed by the sharp knees of some long-legged and fidgety British teenager, who sat behind me on the economy-class flight from Heathrow.

I bought a copy of *The Nation*, a Thai daily. 'Artificial legs are presented to disabled people at a public charity event to mark the one hundredth birthday of the late Princess mother,' read the caption underneath the front-page cover photo. With my legs feeling numb and almost artificial, I trudged to Departures ...

On the plane to Chiang Mai, I had another read of the A&K glossy brochure with promises of 'six-star tours,' which made me wonder what kind of 'six-star' hotels they were going to put me up at.

I would probably be at a loss if asked to name the best hotel I have stayed in. But, after many years as a travelling journalist in the former Soviet Union, I knew for sure where the world's worst hotel was – in the Turkmenistan town of Mari on the Afghan border.

I remember a bearded Turkmen woman solemnly giving me the key to the hotel's only 'luxury suite.' The room was full of flies and smelt like a mortuary. It was forty-two degrees of heat, but the air-conditioner did not work. Nor did the shower. The biggest surprise, however, was that I was supposed to share my room and the only medium-sized bed with a male Communist party official from Ashkhabad. He was snoring and fretting on his side of the bed all night, and when I finally managed to nod off, I dreamt of an earthquake. Also, I got severely poisoned at the hotel's restaurant (it only had eggs and cucumbers on offer, but this was enough) and nearly died.

Regent Resort, my Chiang Mai hotel, was built in the style of a traditional peaked-roof northern Thai village. It was a cluster of luxury villas, blending effortlessly into the surrounding landscape of rice fields and tropical forest.

The moment I approached the Reception, a stunning-looking and constantly bowing Thai girl put an orchid wreath around my stiffened neck. Another girl, also a stunner, was trying (in vain) to relieve me of my shoulder bag, whereas a third smiling beauty was filling in my registration form kneeling in front of me in what I thought was a rather suggestive manner …

My villa was a mere hundred yards away, but they didn't allow me to walk: a buggy truck with a smiling and bowing male driver materialised from nowhere, and I was politely, yet firmly, offered a lift.

Shedding orchid petals with every move, I climbed into the buggy.

Inside my teakwood-fitted villa, goldfish swam in circles in round water-filled flowerpots. To my relief, there was no Party *apparatchik* snoring on my enormous bed, the size of a medieval European town square.

But the biggest surprise in the form of a thick portfolio awaited me on the desk. Apart from welcoming letters and useful tips, the folder contained an envelope with some pocket money in local currency and half-a-dozen picture postcards with stamps lovingly affixed!

They didn't allow me to walk to the restaurant: I was picked up halfway by a buggy truck. While ordering an exquisite four-course Thai meal I had to remind myself not to worry about the prices: all food was included in the package.

It was at the dinner that I had the first glimpse of my travel companions from the Abercrombie & Kent round-the-world tour. They looked ordinary and were engaged in the usual touristy babble of the 'what-are-we-going-to-see-tomorrow' type. It was hard to imagine that each of them had paid the equivalent of my two-year earnings for the trip.

Having firmly decided to walk back, I sneaked out of the restaurant unnoticed and I had to hide behind the trees to avoid the ubiquitous buggies. Of course, I got lost and had to be escorted back to my villa by a white-clad security guard, who was lighting my path with a torch. On depositing me at my door, he saluted with what sounded like a New Zealand rugby team war-cry, turned about-face and goose-stepped back to his booth. Looking at his receding back from the porch, I felt like a military ruler of a small banana republic watching his troops on parade.

Next morning, I met the members of the travel agency's staff travelling with our group: a tour director, two tour managers and a luggage master – a soft-spoken Peruvian man, who went with us everywhere. There were all helpful, efficient and seemed to be enjoying what they did.

For the sightseeing, our group was split between two air-conditioned buses – 'red' and 'blue.'

'What do you do?' I asked my blue-bus neighbour, a stocky ruddy-faced man in a baseball cap. 'I manage money,' he said. In the following days, I noticed that most of my companions were fairly evasive when it came to their occupations. 'I own a business,' or 'I am a retired financier,' were the most common replies.

Each bus had its own 'bus-boy,' obsessively plying us with cold drinks and distributing special refresher towels. I thought it would be nice to have one back in London on my erratic 100 bus route from Wapping to Liverpool Street (I lived in Tower Hamlets then).

First, we went on a bicycle rickshaw ride across Chiang Mai. My rickshaw was pulled by a dried-out sinewy old man, so thin that he was almost transparent. Pressing the pedals of his rusty antediluvian bike for all he was worth, he was constantly lagging behind the rest of the procession. The members of the Thai royal family were grinning at us condescendingly from ubiquitous street posters.

Few things make you look so silly as luxuriating in a cart pulled by an elderly cyclist in torn, worn-down slippers.

A boat ride on the Ping River was next. Snacks and fresh fruit were waiting for us on the deck. 'This is your lunch, ha-ha!' joked our facetious Thai guide. She knew only too well that it wasn't. And so did we (which didn't stop us from emptying our plates, by the way).

We chugged along the river, its banks lined with shabby wooden huts.

'Surely, in the rainy season these houses would be flooded and all the poor people's valuables washed away,' an omniscient woman from our group commented loudly, with her mouth full.

'What valuables?!' our tour manager interjected angrily, but cut himself short.

After a huge lunch, we drove outside Chiang Mai to visit a hill tribe village, where we were quickly led through dimly-lit shacks, past knitting women and playing kids, none of whom acknowledged our presence. They must have been used to such flying visits by foreigners.

The stone-age nature of the village life was somewhat undermined by satellite dishes on some of the roofs.

'Up to fourteen people live in each little house here,' our guide commented.

'Did she say people or chickens?' asked the same American woman. Everyone in the group laughed. The guide bit her lip.

It was scorching hot. 'Three showers a day wouldn't be enough here, especially if you only have five a year,' another American mumbled. And everyone, including the guide, had to laugh again …

My first evening with the tour was truly spectacular.

Halfway through a sumptuous open-air dinner, somewhere between live Thai dancing and fireworks, servants started launching *Kom Loy* – small hot-air balloons, made of *Sa* (Mulberry) paper. The air inside the *Kom Loy* was heated from underneath by candles installed in their baskets. As the balloons were climbing higher and higher, the candles kept burning until their tiny flickering lights and the multiple pimple-like stars in the velvety tropical sky became indistinguishable from each other, and it was no longer possible to tell which stars were real and which weren't …

'We are fulfillers of dreams!' a senior travel agency official, who had come from Bangkok for the occasion, shouted into the night sky, where the coloured rockets suddenly took the shape of two huge fire-spitting letters –'A' and 'K'.

At that moment, I was ready to believe him, although he forgot to mention that the price of a single-supplement dream was just under $70,000, whereas a twin-share dream was worth a meagre $62,000 …

Prices aside, can one live in a fantasy world for more than a day or two, after which even your wildest desires tend to shrink and lose their sparkle, like a cluster of charred burnt-out fireworks?

I asked myself this question next morning, when the very thought of breakfast was unbearable after the previous day's sophisticated gluttony. There was no time to answer it, though, for we had to go for more Thai meals, briefly interrupted by shopping, bamboo-rafting and elephant-riding.

One thing was certain, though: from day two I started slowly but surely losing the plot. And the mind-boggling luxury of the chartered Boeing 747, which we boarded the following day for a flight to Delhi, only added to my confusion.

My name was embroidered on a starched white napkin covering the headrest on one of my First Class seats.

Yes, I had four seats at my disposal with enough combined legroom to accommodate a couple of basketball teams. My fifth – smoking – seat was at the back of the plane, where I would often retreat to have my dessert followed by an after-meal cigarette.

Between leisurely puffs, I would get a glimpse of two youngish American women from our group jogging around the cabin's perimeter. They calculated that one full circle constituted approximately 0.2 miles.

Strict 'Do not throw foreign articles into the toilet' signs were hardly visible behind bunches of fresh flowers and piles of French perfumes, with which all the plane's bathrooms were stuffed almost to the ceiling. On board this jet, I felt very much like a foreign article in constant peril of being flushed down the loo.

We had a huge 'Hot Lunch' on the way to Delhi.

My name was duly printed on the cover of a glossy five-page menu (I was getting fed up with seeing my name everywhere, as if they were worried that I would somehow forget it and kept reminding me of it every two minutes).

When, halfway through the feast, the captain announced that we were approaching Everest, I was tempted to ask whether it came with rice, vegetables or French fries.

The on-board 'wine of the day' was Chateaux Beaux, 1996. I asked one of the fourteen cabin crew for Errazuriz – my favourite Chilean Chardonnay. His face fell, as if he had just learnt of a sudden failure of all the plane's engines. They didn't have it in stock! How outrageous! As a consolation I was given a leather-bound notepad, with a silver Parker pen thrown in, and a glass of Dom Perignon.

A survivor of hundreds of super-austere Aeroflot flights, where the only drink (and food) they served was tepid mineral water in plastic cups with fossilised imprints of previous users' teeth, I felt like asking for political asylum in this flying first-class restaurant.

In Jaipur (India), we stayed at Rajvillas, built to resemble a Rajastani fort. The level of luxury there was pretty much the same as at Regent Resort, only the welcome wreaths were made of marigolds.

My villa was again full of flowers, but unlike in Thailand, it had a four-poster bed (sleeping on it alone felt like a minor offence) and a white marble bath, the size of a swimming pool.

And, of course, the magic welcome portfolio, with money and stamped postcards, was also there, only this time I took it almost for granted. I was half-expecting to find some hasty 'Love from India' messages scribbled for me on the postcards.

Unlike Regent Resort, discreetly hidden among the hills, the stone-walled complex of Rajvillas was across the road from a poverty-ridden Jaipur neighbourhood. The contrast was striking: the cost of an overnight stay in Rajvillas was much higher than an average annual salary of an Indian ($300).

Most of my travel companions didn't like India, whose penury they found irritating.

Their animosity could not be quite shaken off by the beauties of the Pink City and Taj Mahal, nor by yet another elephant ride – the second one within three days.

They remained seemingly unimpressed by the opulent reception at the palace of the Maharajah of Jaipur, where we were met by dancing elephants with our agency banners on their backs.

I thought it wouldn't be long before, similar to a madness-faking (in an attempt to avoid a purge) accountant Berlaga from Ilf and Petrov's *Little Golden Calf*, I started shouting at the top of my voice: 'I am the Viceroy of India! Where are my trusty *nabobs*, my *maharajahs*, my *abreks*, my *kunaks*, my elephants?!'

The Americans squealed with delight when we boarded our faithful snow-white jet in Delhi for a three-hour hop to the UAE. Suffering from Delhi belly (countless bottles of the agency's bespoke mineral water for washing our faces and cleaning our teeth hadn't saved us from catching the bug), I could remember very little of Dubai, except for gleaming marble-fitted bathroom of my Ritz Carlton Hotel room.

Back in London, I was finding it hard to recall the details of the trip. I could evoke what we had for lunches and dinners, but was unable – for love or money – to recollect where exactly we had been served this or that yummy soup or curry – in Agra? In Jaipur? Or was it on the plane?

And I wasn't alone in suffering from amnesia after that journey.

'We feel as if we are in the movies,' my stoic travel companions often commented while yet another foreign scene was unveiling behind the windows of our air-conditioned bus.

According to my calculations, the proportion of sightseeing to eating and moving from place to place was roughly one to ten. It was seldom that we had a chance to walk more than two to three hundred yards a day. To repeat Hemingway's famous description of Paris as a 'moveable feast,' our trip was a 'moveable feast' in its own right, only 'feast' in its context meant not a 'celebration of the soul,' but a huge hedonistic meal.

One good thing is that now I know the difference between travelling the world and 'doing the world' in a luxury jet. It is like the difference between the real stars and the lit-up hot-air balloons.

Hedonism is the enemy of a traveller. It makes his eyes oily and unable to see things for what they are.

Our Chiang Mai guide told us about Thai boxing – a local sport where you are allowed to use any part of your body, except for your teeth. It sounded like an antithesis of our tour, during which we were not allowed to exercise any parts of our bodies, apart from our teeth.

No wonder my thirty-year-old stainless-steel dental bridge, a memento of my Soviet past (one London dentist used to call it 'Lenin Bridge'), broke in two and fell out of my mouth during one of the lunches. I brought it back to London in my pocket as a souvenir of all the wonderful food I had eaten on this trip …

It was actually useful in one sense: from then on when confronted with the question of what my best ever trip was, I could answer:

'Well, I am not so sure about the best one, but the worst was definitely …'

Part Fourteen
My Geography of Healing

After years of travels, I had developed a simple rule of quick familiarisation with a hitherto unknown to me city or town by visiting three places: a bookshop (even if I didn't speak the local language: you can tell a lot about a place by simply looking at the books they publish and the people who buy them); a coffee shop (obvious and doesn't require an explanation); and a train station (to make sure there's an escape route in case I actively dislike the place and feel like moving away fast).

In the aftermaths of open-heart surgery, with lots of subsequent complications, I – reluctantly – had to add another, fourth, venue, to this list – a hospital.

Until then, there hadn't been lots of hospitals in my life. The very first was in my native Ukrainian city of Kharkiv, then better known by its Russified name 'Kharkov,' where at the age of seven I had my cold-prone adenoids removed in a rather crude procedure. Wearing my best and only little suit, I was tied to a chair, and the surgeon, armed with huge blood-stained forceps, had managed – after six goes – to drag some resilient intestines (that's how those slimy red bits looked and felt) out of my throat. No anaesthetic was used. 'What a brave little boy!' the surgeon said afterwards. 'He didn't even cry!'

I didn't cry for one simple reason. One of the nurses had promised to give me an ice-cream after the operation if I didn't … She hadn't seriously meant it of course. It was the first time that the Soviet system, represented by the lying nurse, showed its true face to me, and I will never forget how miserable and let down it made me feel. The experience was useful in a way, for it prepared me for all the multiple future lies I was to endure during my thirty-five years in the USSR. So, yes, hospitals sometimes do reflect the nature of the society they serve …

Here it would be relevant to note that geographical units: countries, cities, villages, islands, deserts, etc – are themselves capable of making you ill. Or stressed. Or both.

A couple of examples.

I had come to Las Vegas in the middle of my eleven-month-long American journalistic assignment. In a way, I liked the place for its boisterous and unadulterated Kitsch – Las Vegas' euphemism for 'culture,' spelt with a capital 'K' – and for its total lack of pretence, as if the city was constantly taking the mickey out of itself. 'Mechanic on duty. Free aspirin and tender sympathy,' ran a sign on top of a city garage. One certainly needed a lot of aspirin and even more 'sympathy' to cope with Las Vegas.

Another city that is certain to give you a headache and make you crave an aspirin is Rome, Europe's only metropolis that – honestly and truly – never sleeps. Yevgeny Yevtushenko, a recently deceased Russian poet, aptly compared it to a giant alarm clock buzzing constantly in your ear.

What else? Moscow, where I had lived for over twelve years, polluted and full of uncertain menace, gives you asthma and panic attacks. And New York, according to Jan Morris, is the best place in the world to have a heart attack. And not just because of the city's 'various spasms.' 'If I had to have a heart attack, the best place would be on Fifth Avenue. There'd be more good people coming to help than in any other city,' she noted after calling New York 'in some ways the nastiest city on earth,' but also possibly 'the kindest.'

I remember asking a permanently stressed New York friend of mine why she kept crossing the road on red pedestrian lights and stopped at green. 'We New Yorkers love our freedom. No one is telling us when to cross the road!' she snapped.

To me, the world's 'kindest' city is certainly Budapest, where crowds of genuinely worried locals, offering help, surrounded me after I inadvertently slipped, fell and broke my ribs in one of its icy streets one winter …

Well, I was lucky not to have a heart attack in New York, but came close to having it during my recuperation trip to Majorca.

'What you need is complete rest and a bit of Mediterranean sun,' my cardiologist told me a couple of months after the operation. I followed his advice and made arrangements for a week-long holiday in Bon Sol, a beautiful hotel-cum-resort in Illetas, one of the suburbs of Palma de Majorca, the Balearics' capital.

Mind you, Palma itself is not a tranquiliser city. It is rather an energiser – a glass of intense Majorcan red wine for breakfast … A relatively small metropolis of under 500,000 people, it appears at least twice as large due to its boundless energy, noise and bustle. The city where one can indeed pick up a bottle of wine in an excellent bookshop called 'Babel' in which the world's literary classics and wine bottles share the same spaces – part bookshelves, part wine racks …

I had been to Palma many times before and thought I had known it well, to the point that my latest novel, *Out of the Blu*, is partially set there. In accordance with my tested travel rules (see above), I had repeatedly visited the city's cafés, bookshops and its small and old-fashioned railway station, from where one can catch an electric train (or tram) to Soller. This time I, sadly, had to add a hospital to that list.

On my first night in Majorca, I suffered an attack of acute pericarditis (you can look up this cardio condition, sounding a bit like a Greek last name, if you wish) and ended up in the emergency department ('Urgencias') of the island's main hospital – Son Espaces, my latest hospital experience so far.

The interesting thing is that we Brits do not associate the normally cheerful, talkative and robust Mediterranean dwellers with disease. Books have been written about some Greek and other islands famous for their healthy diets and the islanders' incredible longevity. So one can be forgiven for assuming that all Greeks, Italians or, say, Majorcans are generally healthy, and seeing them being sick ruins the stereotype.

It was surprising to see the ailing locals in Son Espaces, and some of those swarthy southerners were very poorly indeed …

To cut a long story short, I was received and treated with an amazing (by British standards) speed and didn't have to wait in the queue. Several hours later I was discharged back to Bon Sol, my dilemma being either to fly back to the UK the following morning, or to recover in the resort.

'People come to us to heal, that's what Bon Sol is for,' Lorraine and Martin Xamena, who own and run the resort, told me.

'This is a healing place, and we guarantee that by the end of the week you will fully recover,' they added.

They proved right. Places do not just make you ill; they can also be healing.

In my travels, I was lucky to find myself in the spots that looked and felt like meditations coming to life. They were mostly islands, for large expanses of water are calming in themselves, and that calm spreads onto the chunks of land, surrounded by seas and oceans. I found both the Falklands and the Faroe Islands profoundly relaxing and, yes, healing too, after spending some of the most peaceful days of my life there.

I came to the Hebridean island of Tiree (see Part Six of this book) in October 2001, to recover from the shock of 9/11 which I had narrowly escaped, having stayed on the thirty-second floor of one of the World Trade Center hotels, which collapsed shortly after the Twin Towers, only weeks before the attack.

Autumn in the Hebrides is the time when quiet and stillness reign supreme, when most tourists are gone and the strong winter gales that are known to have lifted schoolkids off the ground have not yet arrived. It is the season of crisp sunny mornings, of vast all-embracing skies mixing with granite-coloured sea, of stunning sunsets – exorbitant and over-the-top for a viewer having no one to share them with … I cycled around the island humming the unsophisticated doggerel of my own making: 'Life is totally stress-free, on the island of Tiree' to the accompaniment of the wind whistling in my ears like a hooligan and cleansing my soul …

At various points of my peripatetic life, full of crises and hardship, I found myself temporarily appeased in Tasmania, with its quiet nostalgia for good old Europe; in Melbourne, Australia, where I recovered from a PTSD, caused by overworking and a relationship breakdown; and in Folkestone, Kent, where – day after day – I chilled out by pacing endlessly along the permanently deserted promenade above the cliffs, overlooking the Channel …

Bon Sol was vaguely reminiscent of Folkestone in its ubiquitous sea views and its hilly location. Only the sea was the deep-blue Mediterranean as opposed to the uninviting granite-coloured waters of La Manche.

'Take time to reflect and to nourish your soul' ran the sign on one of Bon Sol's viewing terraces. I spent hours on them breathing deeply and looking at the sea with a regulation yacht sail on the horizon – a living illustration to one of my favourite poems of all time, *The Lonely Sail* by Mikhail Lermontov:

'A white sail shows for an instant
Where gleams the sea, an azure streak.

What left it in its homeland distant?
In alien parts what does it seek?

The billows play, the mast bends creaking,
The wind, impatient, moans and sighs …
It is not joy that it is seeking,
Nor is it happiness it flies.

The blue waves dance, they dance and tremble,
The sun's bright rays caress the seas.
And yet for storm it begs, the rebel,
As if in storm lurks calm and peace!'

The utterly peaceful and tranquil sea views were inescapable in this amazing family-run resort, where all the staff and all the guests felt and behaved as if they were part of the family too.

It was also calming to discover that the hotel owners were champions of clean energy, and that several years ago Bon Sol was voted one of the world's top ten greenest resorts …

A cheerful chorus of birds greeted me in the morning, instead of the 'chorus of drips' in the hospital in Stevenage where I was recovering from a post-surgery complication several weeks earlier. Litres of antibiotics were pumped into my uncomplaining veins for hours on end from two drips, which I monikered Doris and Dorothy. With time, I learned to walk, even to 'dance,' with the drips, turning them around in the long hospital corridor. Having finished their drippings, they screamed like peahens in mating season …

And of an evening, the chorus of birds was replaced by a no-less-melodious choir of frogs, so familiar to me from my Ukrainian childhood and hence profoundly calming …

From my balcony, I often watched white cruise ships leaving the Palma Harbour at dusk and accumulating the last rays of the sun as they moved away – those floating sun magnets. I would then close my eyes and repeat, like a mantra, the meditative and prayer-like Bon Sol's logo: '*Paz en el espiritu. Sol para el cuerpo. Calor en el Corazon*' – 'Peace for the soul. Sun for the body. Warmth for the heart.'

With every passing day, I was feeling better and better.

'Peace, sun and warmth … ' How little one needs to be happy …

How little and how very very much!

My Perfect Day

(instead of an epilogue)

At sunrise, I would be on Mount Athos, self-governing republic of Orthodox monks in Northern Greece, where I once had an unforgettable sun-worshipping experience.

To say that my Greek guide, who accompanied me on that particular pilgrimage to the Holy Mountain, was a snorer would have been a gross understatement. Had Oscars been awarded for snoring, he would have definitely snatched up the one for the best and loudest soundtrack. Since the accommodation for visitors on Mount Athos is little more than basic, we had to share one and the same cell in the monastery of Philotheu.

After several hours of gentle whistling and diplomatic coughing, I had to resort to far less gentle pushes and far less diplomatic Russian swear words which I shouted at the top of my voice. The magnificent, Oscar-winning snores continued unaffected. I got dressed, picked up my cigarettes and went out onto the monastery's balcony hanging precariously above the cliff.

It was still pitch dark, and the lonely light of a detached mountain *skites* – a hermit's dwelling – was blinking in the distance, like an unknown star. Soon I heard the rhythmic and monotonous sounds of semantrons, the wooden drums calling monks to the morning liturgy.

I looked down: the black-hooded monks were sliding across the monastery yard towards the church in treacherous semi-darkness, like white-shrouded ghosts in a slow-motion picture, shown in the negative by the erroneous cinema operator of dawn.

An invisible multi-voiced choir inside the church was chanting psalms with amazing synchrony and grace.

The red-robed monk of the rising sun was descending slowly from his heavenly *skites* above the sea and covering the world with his pink see-through cassock.

Suddenly, everything around me was full of light, harmony and meaning. And although out of three main virtues of a Mount Athos monk – chastity, obedience and lack of personal possessions – I could only boast the third one, for a fleeting moment I felt like taking a monastic vow, and spending the rest of my days in that truly divine part of the world.

'Thank you for snoring last night!' I said to my guide at breakfast.

For breakfast, I would go across the globe, to Melbourne.

One can easily put on a couple of kilos by simply staring at the mind-boggling displays of cakes and biscuits in the windows of countless cafés in Ackland Street in its cosmopolitan seaside suburb of St Kilda. No other city in the world comes close to Melbourne in quantity (if not always in quality) of food: I once saw a burger stall doing brisk trade in the lobby of a local cardiology hospital.

As a four-double-espresso-per-day person, I like having breakfast in one of the Ackland Street coffee shops, most of which are either Jewish or Italian. Trying to watch my weight, I sip my coffee, breathing salty sea air and gaping at the cream-capped culinary Everests in the shop windows. The view in itself is so hedonistic and so filling that it often helps me forsake my regulation morning croissant.

At lunchtime, I would be back in Europe, in Malta.

The Oleander restaurant in the village of Xaghra on Gozo, the second largest island of the Maltese archipelago, overlooks the Nativity of the Virgin church with a marvellous *trompe l'oeil* of a painted clock on its ornate façade. The clock is designed to confuse the devil when he starts dealing with the souls of the dead – an old Maltese tradition.

I am not sure about the devil, but these painted clocks all over the country must be very effective in confusing unwary tourists, of whom there are many – too many in Malta, if not yet in Xaghra – into missing their flights back home..

It is probably due to the painted clock that lunch at the Oleander is normally long and unhurried.

I would start with stuffed squid; the world's best squid can be found on Gozo, followed by bean soup and *fenek* – rabbit casseroled in red wine and garlic. The restaurant is usually buzzing with locals gobbling on their beloved *gbejniet*, Gozo's homemade goat cheese, and washing it down with plenty of beer. Watching them, one comes to understand a popular Maltese joke. The Gozitans are the butt of jokes in Malta, like Newfoundlanders in Canada, Tasmanians in Australia, Georgians in Russia, and the Irish all over the English-speaking world. This goes to the effect that the Gozitans are 'cheese-headed' and should incorporate *gbejniet* into their coat of arms …

There is no better place for my dream afternoon than Hay-on-Wye, a small town in the county of Powys on the border of England and Wales. As a passionate bookworm, I absolutely adore browsing through the stocks of the town's thirty-odd second-hand bookshops.

Books in Hay are literally strewn all over the town. Apart from the bookshops, they can be found on numerous unattended open-air bookstalls, exposed to the elements: sun-beaten and often soaked with rainwater. Looking for a book you need is similar to digging for gold bullion in the sand: you never know what you might come across and whether you are going to find anything at all. It is precisely this uncertainty that makes the search so exciting and so similar to a treasure hunt. I remember ferreting out a thick Victorian monograph *Social History of British Sea-Weeds* one day and agonising for half-an-hour whether to buy it or not. In the end, I decided against it: seaweeds, no matter how socially active, were not exactly within the sphere of my interests.

And you know what: I have been regretting it ever since …

Come dinnertime – and my imagination transfers me to Vaduz, the tiny capital of the pocket-handkerchief alpine principality of Liechtenstein.

I remember how Felix Real, an acclaimed Liechtenstein hotelier and restaurateur, got upset one evening when I, being a teetotaller, refused the offer of Vaduse Rose from his cellars.

'But it is so good, so good – um-m-m …' he was saying, kissing his own fingers as proof. The old man was so distraught that I became seriously worried about his health, and, possibly, even his life. Grief-stricken, he stumbled out of his 'Real' restaurant in Vaduz to continue suffering in the privacy of his house (or so I thought), and I was left in the hands of three buxom blonde waitresses who immediately brought me a menu the size of the Gutenberg Bible.

The names of the dishes sounded like a French prayer – '*Homard, langoustines et coquille St Jaques grilles a l'estragon*' … Amen!

As soon as I had coped with the starter of wonderfully delicate smoked eel, they brought me a set of six knives and forks (plus a special little spoon for the sauce) and threateningly placed them on a wooden board on my table. My main course of lamb fillet was delivered on a gleaming trolley, which resembled a gun carriage carrying the body of a Soviet General Secretary of the eighties to be buried near the Kremlin Wall. Stainless steel lids covering the plates looked like brass cymbals, and I could almost hear the sounds of Chopin's Funeral March (was it mourning the contents of my wallet?), when the waitresses synchronically lifted them.

The trolley was then solemnly driven back to its kitchen stable. It didn't want to go and was kicking the waitresses with its obnoxious wheels.

At this point, Felix Real reappeared in the restaurant. He was smiling. My mounting appetite must have cured his distress.

Approaching night would find me in Venice, the city that I will never stop loving. I know it is banal to fall in love with Venice, but isn't it more banal not to fall in love with it?

At sunset, when the water in its canals gleams with a magic translucent light of its own, as if slowly, almost reluctantly, discharging the sunlight it has accumulated during the day; when blinds fall like thick black eyelids on the gaping eye-sockets of tired old houses; when the gentle tolling of distant church bells mingles with the soft smacking sound of lovers' kisses – there suddenly comes a whiff of fresh sea breeze, a reminder of the days when Venice meant ships, spices and trade routes to be explored.

At dusk, I like sitting on the bank of the Grand Canal listening to the soft splashes of water against the ancient Venetian stones. It is then that I start seeing Venice as an ageing but still graceful woman suffering from insomnia and shuffling restlessly around the house in her loose-fitting slippers in the night.

After a full and tiring globe-trotting day, I would have little problem falling asleep in my bed in the North London suburb of Muswell Hill – the place where I belong and where my home is.

It will always be there, even if I don't live there any longer …

* * *

A NOTE OF THANKS

VITALI VITALIEV AND THRUST BOOKS are grateful to the *Guardian*, the *Herald*, *The European*, the *Daily/Sunday Telegraph* and the *Age* newspapers as well as to *Village Weekly*, *Geographical* and *E&T* magazines and Random House publishers.

Special thanks to Christine Bohling, Fiona Craig, Francesca di Franco, Dmitri Vitaliev and Ian Mayes.

Of Travel Writing As a Genre

(hitherto unpublished tips for an aspiring travel scribe)

Strictly speaking, travel writing as a literary genre does not exist. It is only in the English-speaking countries that the so-called 'travel literature' is sold in separate 'travel sections' of big bookshops (in the USA, the section is normally called 'Travel Memoirs'). In German or, say in Russian, there is no special term to denote 'travel writing,' and books about voyages are classified as 'adventure literature,' 'memoirs' or even 'autobiography.' The latter makes a lot of sense to me. Indeed, were Chekhov, Dickens and Mark Twain 'travel writers?' True, they all felt the need to travel at certain stages of their lives and careers (Chekhov – to the island of Sakhalin, Dickens – to America, Mark Twain – to Europe and around the globe), but, while doing so, they remained what they always had been – great writers and masters of a number of 'proper' literary genres: novelists, essayists, playwrights etc.

Modern times have created a new breed of scribes, whose one and only speciality is writing about their travels. They think that travelling in foreign lands is more likely to offer interesting observations that are hard to find in their normal daily routine. But literature, and that includes 'travel literature,' is very much about discovering beautiful and exotic things in the familiar and seemingly unexciting environment.

The best 'travel writers' of modern times: Jan Morris, Eric Newby, Patrick Lee Fermor, Colin Thubron etc – despite devoting a disproportionate amount of their time to writing about their travels, have considerable achievements in other literary genres.

Conclusion: a true writer is always an artist, whether he spends his life on the road, or never leaves his town or village.

Many aspiring young writers these days are willing to write about nothing else but travel. This desire is normally dictated by a shortage of life experience and the delusion that writing about travel is not only easy, but also allows for all sorts of lucrative freebies – luxury hotels, first-class flights, sumptuous (and, no doubt, free) meals in best restaurants. This self-deception is largely due to the extraordinary popularity of Bill Bryson's amusing and irreverent travelogues. One literary critic aptly called this new 'Brysonesque' style of writing '**cheerful laddism**.' Such books are but collections of jokes and puns ('it was so quiet in the pub that one could hear a fly fart' – Bill Bryson), but have little – if anything – to do with literature or quality journalism. And, contrary to what most people think, they actually do not sell that well. Unless you are Bill Bryson, of course.

In short, before you start wandering the globe in the hope that this will provide you with new experience, make sure you already have plenty to share and to say.

For the reasons I've just explained, from now on I will refer to 'travel literature' as travel journalism. I am using the latter term without quotes, for, unlike the illusionary eponymous literary genre, travel journalism does exist and takes a lot of space on book shelves as well as in newspapers, magazines and online. Below, I will try to share with you some of my thoughts on how to write, to structure and to sell such material. If the examples I will be quoting are not from my own writing, their sources will be named in the text.

The Importance of Getting Lost

At my Creative Writing seminars and Travel Journalism workshops, I am often asked what the most important skill of a travel journalist is. My answer is the ability to get lost. It is only when you have lost direction and are getting seriously concerned about where the next road turn is going to take you that you start noticing some really important details about a town/city or a landscape. That is why a good sense of direction can be a liability rather than a merit for a travel journalist – just as , at times, a too thorough knowledge of a foreign language becomes an impediment for a translator of poetry, who – most importantly – has to be a poet himself.

One of my most evocative travel experiences was getting (seriously!) lost in the Alps and, without realising it, wandering from Liechtenstein, where I was based, into Austria. It was only when I was sitting in a country pub, still being sure I was in Liechtenstein, that I started noticing strange things: a portrait of the Austrian Chancellor on the wall, huge Wiener schnitzels on the patrons' plates and so on. But only when they calculated my bill in Austrian schillings (it was before the euro) and not in Swiss francs, the currency of Liechtenstein, did I realise that I was in Austria.

Travel writing is indeed like poetry, for which, if we believe Boris Pasternak, you don't have to look high up in the mountains, since there is plenty of it scattered in the grass under your feet; you only have to go to the trouble of bending down and picking it up. This also means that to come up with a good travel article, you don't have to travel to the jungles of Equatorial Africa, the Amazon River delta or other remote corners of the world. Write about places nearer to home, but try to find in them something that no one has seen before. At my seminars, I often give students the task of writing a travel article about the street they live in. 'Open your eyes wide, get lost in your own street, imagine you've never been in it before – and you'll be genuinely surprised by what you'll find.' Their first reaction is usually rather sceptical: 'There's nothing in my little lane to attract a tourist …' Yet, after looking at it with the eyes of a perceptive first-time visitor, most manage to discover very interesting things.

In short, it doesn't really matter where you travel to. What **does** matter is **what you see.** 'We see only what we have the gift of seeing,' wrote Henry Longfellow. And your vision gets much sharper, if you are not sure where you are going to …

'A good traveller is one who doesn't know where he is going to,' wrote Chinese novelist Lin Yutang. The same applies to a good travel journalist.

Descriptions

As Jerome K. Jerome noted in his travel book *Three Men on a Bummel*, descriptions of places never work on paper. The great English humourist was of the opinion that even the worst of picture postcards could give you a better idea of a landscape or a monument than the very best of literary descriptions.

I think that he was right. But only to an extent. Impersonal and clichéd descriptions, overloaded with adjectives, are indeed pretty useless. If you write: 'The little mountain church was beautiful,' it means absolutely nothing to the reader, for beauty **is** in the eyes of the beholder, and concepts of it differ from person to person. On the other hand, if you were to say: 'The church, nestling in the valley underneath me, looked so light and fragile that I felt like putting it on the palm of my hand and carrying it back home,' the reader would see a much clearer picture. That is why, rather than saying: 'My hotel was overlooking the sea,' write: 'I fell asleep to the soothing sounds of the surf behind my hotel room window.'

The conclusion is: describe by all means, but do it through **INTERACTION** with yourself and/or other people. The only meaning of a site or a landscape lies in the way they are perceived by a traveller, ie yourself.

As for the **adjectives**, or epithets, one has to be very sparing: try not to use more than one adjective at a time and make sure it is the only right one. The travel journalist here has to act like an experienced pharmacist and allow no more than one drop of an adjective per noun (two – in rare cases: one descriptive and one qualitative; see 'frail wooden scaffolding' or 'sharp black rocks' in the quote below). If it is right, the effect of the medicine (or, in this case, the image) will be enhanced. On the other hand, if you apply too much of it, there's a serious risk of counter-effects due to an overdose.

Here's how I chose to describe the monastery of Simonopetra in Mount Athos – the fourteenth-century skyscraper, sitting on a tower-like rock high above the sea:

> 'The monastery's guest quarters were situated along the perimeter of the top of the monastery building. To get to the bathroom, one had to pass through a circular terrace, clinging to the monastery walls. This frail wooden scaffolding was precariously suspended above the bottomless precipice. It

shook under your feet like an unsteady ship deck during a sea-storm. Through gaps between squeaky floorboards sagging under your feet, sharp black rocks licked by the foamy sea were clearly visible a good hundred metres below. In short, it was an ideal place for committing suicide, even if you didn't feel particularly suicidal. It was also ideal for deterring you from using the bathroom too often.'

Another important element of description is **getting one's reference points right**. If you say: 'I went out onto the deck at 3am.,' the immediate question is: how did you know it was 3am. and not 3.30 or 4? Write instead: 'I woke up and looked at my watch. It was 3 o'clock in the morning. I got dressed and went out onto the deck.' Similarly: 'The castle was over 600 years old.' How did you know that, the reader would wonder? A more authoritative (and honest) way of expressing the same thought would be: 'According to a local tourism brochure, the castle was over 600 years old.'

The Power of Detail

Nothing brings a travel feature to life better than a precise, unusual and telling little detail. Always keep your eyes open for seemingly unimportant little things – be it a persistent Alpine flower bursting through the rock or a hardly visible mark on a person's face. Mark Twain was a master of detail. In the opening chapter of his book *Innocents Abroad*, describing the world's first package tour from America to Europe, the tourists are standing on the deck of the ship about to sail off to the Old World and waving to the people on the pier who came to see them off. The latter are waving back, of course. The writer then notes: 'The flag on the ship's mast tried to wave but failed.' – and the whole scene immediately comes alive. One can even feel the gentle sea breeze on the faces of the intrepid would-be travellers …

Once in Moldova, I went on a tour of the forty-two-kilometre-long old wine cellars in Novie Maleshti. My escort in that underground city, complete with streets, lanes and crossroads – so wide that lorries drove freely along them – was a local wine-maker, whose face carried an amazing little detail: he had a clearly visible scar, left by a wine glass, on the bridge of his nose – the result of years and years of daily (and often hourly) wine-tasting. That little trait was so evocative that I was able to write in my feature: 'I was escorted around the cellars by a local man, with a professional wine-taster's corn on the bridge of his nose.' The reader does not need to know much more about that person and can still see him very clearly. **One precise little detail can be worth pages and pages of description.**

The most evocative details are often found off the beaten track. That is why I always encourage my students to **get off the main tourist drags and venture into**

back lanes (in a city) and dirt-tracks (in the countryside), with their eyes and notebooks wide open.

Also, no matter how tired and rushed you may be, make sure that the first thing you do on arrival to a new destination is pop into a coffee shop, buy a cuppa and observe the locals. Listen to what they say (knowledge of foreign tongues would come handy, if you are abroad). Watch their body language. Browse through a local rag. Local newspapers often carry useful tips and information that you won't get anywhere else. These first impressions of a new place are invaluable. My experience shows that the details spotted on the first day, when one's perception of a place is fresh and one's mind is open, are particularly memorable and revealing. A good travel writer should strive to become a **master of first impressions.**

Taking a Plunge

How do we structure a travel article or a book? The obvious temptation is to build up your narrative in a strictly chronological order: arriving, looking around, describing, departing. Yet this is not always the best way to grab the reader's attention. In quality travel journalism, it is 'bad manners' to start an article with 'The train was approaching Moscow' or with 'I fastened my seat belt in preparation for landing.' The editors of the travel section of the *Daily Telegraph*, where I used to work, would always cross out such clichéd openings.

Where to start from then? From the middle! Take a plunge into the narrative, begin with the climax (if any), and then reverse to the chronological beginning. This ancient literary device is known as *in media res* – 'in the middle of things,' the expression first coined by Horace commenting on the works of Homer.

'My boat overturned in the middle of the river' as the first sentence of a travel article is a good example of 'taking a plunge.' In more than one sense, in this particular case.

I applied the *in media res* approach while writing a long and all-encompassing travel feature (which later became part of one of my travel books) on Mount Athos, the unique self-governing monastic mini-state on the Halkidiki peninsula in Northern Greece, the first paragraph of which was as follows:

> 'The mountain path was steep and narrow. Strewn with rough shapeless rocks and mule droppings, it wound mercilessly uphill along the edge of an abyss, and it seemed endless. Cicadas chirred deafeningly, as if they were laughing at me. The white-hot disc of the midday sun with several fluffy clouds around it – like a giant freshly-cooked portion of bacon-and-eggs – glared from the blue sizzling frying pan of the Hellenic sky. Puffing like an early steam engine, I trudged higher and higher up the track, scaring tiny agile lizards from under

my trainers. My feet felt alien, as if I was walking on stilts, and streams of hot, salty sweat were pouring down my forehead …'

I did it again in another *Daily Telegraph* feature on travelling among the indigenous ethnic minorities of Alaska:

'She was sitting on the pavement (or, as they say in America, 'sidewalk'), next to a 'Paws for Coffee' coffee-shop for dogs, in a wind-swept suburb of Anchorage, Alaska's biggest city. Her slanting Inupiaq eyes stared straight in front of her, across the buzzing freeway and further – past a McDonald's outlet and a grey modernistic bungalow of an 'Alaska Cremation Center' – into nowhere. She was drunk. Or stoned. Or, most likely, both – alcoholism and drug-addiction are still rife among Alaska's natives. A soiled Russian Orthodox cross, carved out of whale's bone, was dangling round her dried-out parchment-like neck …'

In media res (or taking a plunge) is my favourite way of starting a travel feature. I never had reasons to regret choosing it. Refreshed by the initial 'plunge,' the narrative as a rule develops easily and runs ahead freely.

Avoiding 'Props'

There is a growing tendency among modern travel journalists/writers to make up for their lack of knowledge and insight with unorthodox means of transport and curious objects (or subjects) they carry. It has become 'fashionable' to travel around the world by bicycles, to criss-cross it in old jalopies, to fly over it in colourful balloons, or walk across it on their hands. One scribe travelled to Eastern Europe with a pig. Another roamed Ireland carrying an old fridge. Yet another one went across America with … Einstein's brain in the boot of his car! Such articles and books can trigger a couple of laughs, some of them may even sell, yet whatever the commercial outcome, this is not literature or journalism, but a sort of literary (or journalistic) scam. By diverting the reader's attention from important realities they are unable (or unwilling) to observe, these writers confess to their own laziness and incompetence.

Avoid using props, for, as I have said repeatedly ('and I will say it again' – *pace* Tony Blair), the only 'luggage' you need is a pair of sharp and compassionate eyes. Observe, research, describe and report **without ever getting arrogant or patronising to the locals**. Otherwise, you may end up with something resembling the following passage, a spoof extract from a stereotypical travel book on Eastern Europe that I put together, having studied a number of failed travel-writing endeavours:

'On a dull rainy morning, my Hungarian (Polish, Czech) unemployed friend Gyula (Stanislaw, Bohumil) kindly – for just a hundred US dollars, the equivalent of his salary for ten years – offered me a lift to Warsaw (Bucharest, Bratislava) in his dilapidated Skoda (Dacia, Polish Fiat). We are chugging towards the drab capital city along a bumpy, pot-holed dirt-track, lined with destitute prostitutes, prostituting destitutes and corrupt, bribe-seeking policemen in their grey uniforms. We drive past gloomy apartment blocks with peeling stucco on their façades and filthy washing hanging from the balconies. Hungry, skeleton-like children, dressed in rags, play in the debris and follow with their sad eyes the gleaming BMWs of the new rich and the Mafiosi – with sub-machine-guns and rockets launchers sticking out of their bullet-proof windows …'

And so on …

One Last Thought:

Despite popular beliefs, travel journalism is a difficult and highly competitive genre. Don't go into it for the sake of freebies and exciting journeys, for being a travel journalist is an extremely demanding, tiring and lonely profession. During my long travel assignment in the USA, when I had visited thirty-nine states within five months and had to be on the road every day (while filing a newspaper column as I went), I came close to having a nervous breakdown due to over-exhaustion. At times, I had just a couple of hours to make sense of a big city, like Boston or Santa Fe, and to write about it, having found something that other writers had so far failed to spot. It was one of the most trying experiences of my life.

Having said that, travel journalism can be great fun for those who are able and willing – above anything – to observe.

Photos From Vitali's Travels

Approaching Haymaey Island, Iceland

Haymaey Harbour, Iceland

Beware Hot Springs, Iceland

Breakfast cooked Iceland style!

Geothermal Park in Hveragerdi, Iceland

Fragments of former empire – Clock Tower in Piccadilly Circus, the centre of Basseterre, St Kitts

St Kitts scenic railway

Ithaca – the Greek island to where travellers do return

Embracing Venice

A street market in Vitali's favourite French town – Montreuil-sur-Mer

Climbing the walls in a Berlin book shop

Straddling borders (Slovenia/Italy)

On early morning train in Switzerland

Rattling through Switzerland

PostBus on a lonely road to Grindlewald in Swiss Alps

Steepest bus route in Europe – 28-degree gradient – from Reichenbach to Griesalp, Switzerland

Alpine call for tea break!

George Orwell's old house in Kitts Lane, Wallington, Hertfordshire

Hazy early morning view where the Atlantic Ocean and the Caribbean Sea meet, St, Kitts & Nevis

Rest in peace – an old Jewish cemetery in Charlestown, Nevis

When in Prague…

Traveller at home

About the Author

Vitali Vitaliev was born in 1954 in Kharkiv, Ukraine and studied French and English at Kharkiv University. He then became the first investigative journalist in the Soviet Union. As a result, he was forced to defect from the USSR by the KGB in January 1990. He has become widely known in the West for his regular appearances on TV and radio. Vitaliev has published thirteen books which have been translated into a number of languages. He has contributed regularly to the *Guardian*, the *European*, the *Daily Telegraph*, the *Australian* and others, and has also made several TV documentaries. He has lived and worked in Russia, England, Scotland, Australia and Ireland and is a Fellow of the Royal Geographical Society and the Royal Literary Fund.

'Vitali Vitaliev is a star in the making.'
TIME MAGAZINE

'Vitaliev has an irrepressible sense of humour'
THE GUARDIAN

'With the charm of Michael Palin, the wit of Clive Anderson, this man is adorable.'
TIME OUT

'Vitaliev is a very amusing writer.'
SUNDAY TIMES

'Vitali Vitaliev is streets ahead of any other journalist.'
CLIVE JAMES

'Imagine Michael Palin, Clive Anderson and Bill Bryson all rolled into one and you'll have some idea of what to expect'
EGO

Also by Vitali Vitaliev from Thrust Books

Little is the Light
Nostalgic travels in the mini-states of Europe

Four years after his escape from the Soviet Union in 1990, award-winning journalist and author Vitali Vitaliev went in search of surviving pockets of freedom, autonomy and self-government. He found eleven countries, each with a population of less than half a million, each one of them beautiful and each one described in this book with sparkling humour, wisdom, and an unmatchable sense of irony. His travels take him to Liechtenstein, San Marino, Mount Athos, the Isle of Man, Luxembourg, the Faroe Islands, Gibraltar, Andorra, Malta, Monaco and Seborga.

'Little is the light will be seen far in a murky night' reads a proverb the author finds relevant. This book is his exploration of the small lights shining from Europe's mini states.

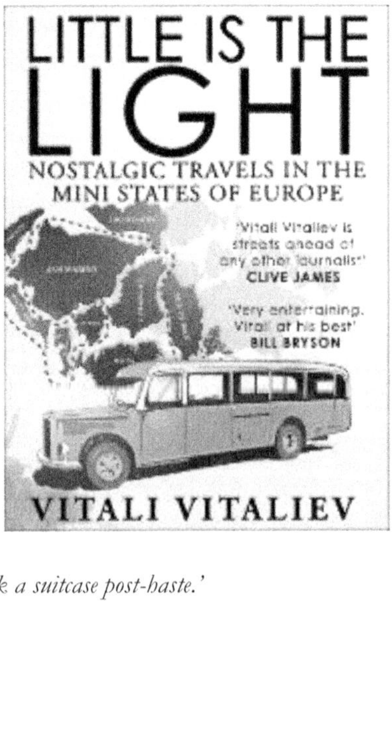

'It makes you want to pack a suitcase post-haste.'
SUNDAY HERALD SUN

'Vitali is a jokey, quizzical, irrepressible wanderer full of bounce and self-confidence. I love this book.'
JOHN SIMPSON, WORLD AFFAIRS EDITOR OF THE BBC

'Vitali takes pleasure in playing the uncivilised alien . . . An unreconstructed male who yawns in church, puffs his way up Mount Athos on the lungs of a lifetime smoker and can't quite see the point of fancy wines, when a shot of vodka would do the job much faster. His very name seems to spell "life-force".'
OBSERVER

'Very entertaining. Vitali at his best.'
BILL BRYSON

Available from Amazon for the Kindle and in paperback.

For more information and to read sample chapters go to the Thrust Books website: www.thrustbooks.com.

Borders Up!
Eastern Europe through the bottom of a glass

One would assume that with the collapse of Communism, East Europeans would drink much less than before: a democratic society should surely be able to provide many more means of escape than alcohol. The reality, however, is very different. *Borders Up!* is Vitali Vitaliev's sharp and sardonic travelogue, an attempt to find out why drinking in post-Communist Eastern Europe has increased dramatically since the fall of the Berlin Wall. Informative and very, very funny.

'Border's Up! by renowned Russian/British journalist Vitali Vitaliev quickly became one of my favourites… the humour of Vitaliev's anecdotes and the brilliant use of the English language in conveying them will have any reader on the floor laughing – and longing for a drink. For those with a background in Central and Eastern Europe, the book is even more hilarious, because it presents a truth that is often confined only to insiders' jokes… Vitaliev belongs to a rare group of people who can write with brilliance and style in a second language… I must say I have re-read this book several times, and have fallen off my chair laughing at the same passages time and time again. The book is one of the funniest I have ever read'
CENTRAL EUROPE REVIEW

'Vitaliev drinks his way through Eastern Europe with surprising focus, each draught redolent of the company, and community, it is drunk in. Fuelled more by the author's gift of observation rather than his penchant for Riesling, Vitaliev's travelogue cultivates a pacy, empassioned style that turns what is essentially an excuse for a long-haul pub crawl into an incisive portrait of post-Communist Europe. A prolonged moment of clarity'
OBSERVER

'He has a sharp and sardonic eye; and his observations are informed by his humanity and compassion. He has written a funny and sad book which seems to be about drinking, but is really about people, suffering, tyranny and foolishness. He is an engaging fellow and his book puts you at his companionable elbow'
DAILY TELEGRAPH

'An ironic and witty commentator on life. He writes with a humanist's appetite, and an outsider's discrimination, for social oddity. There is great charm in his emotional roller-coasting'
SPECTATOR

'Vitaliev transcends his genre, producing a new travel-writing of the soul, a journey with lessons about what really matters in life. That makes it literature'
LITERARY REVIEW

'I admire his writing which gets better and better. We're both interested in the history of the 20th century, but he's lived it, and I've been a spectator'
CLIVE JAMES

'Intoxicating stuff. Extraordinarily funny account of travels in Eastern Europe, seen through the bottom of a vodka glass. Vitali, a former Soviet Journalist of the Year who was expelled from the USSR, is a wonderful raconteur and has the true humourist's genius for illuminating darkness with laughter'
AMAZON.CO.UK – A reader in Sussex, England

Available from Amazon for the Kindle and in paperback.

For more information and to read sample chapters go to the Thrust Books website: www.thrustbooks.com.

Vitali's Ireland:
Time Travels in the Celtic Tiger

A unique perspective on 21st century Irish cultural identity, delivered in a style rich with his typical sardonic wit.

Ukrainian-born Vitali Vitaliev, an award-winning travel writer and journalist, uses his outsider's perspective to recount his Irish adventures. A renowned cultural observer, he muses on the nation's quirks and stereotypes, whilst his reference to mid-19th century guide books provides an insightful historical comparison. The result is an affectionate if slightly perplexed portrait of a nation in transition.

'This is a book that will perplex and infuriate some but appear quite humorous to others . . . Eccentric guide to a land of contradictions . . . A rather eclectic mixture of farce, travel guide and personal observation . . . This book should be required reading for those executives who run our tourist authorities.'
COLIN LENIHAN, MINISTER FOR INTEGRATION, IN THE IRISH TIMES

'Slightly eccentric and highly enjoyable . . . Slightly cranky, sometimes bewildered, often meandering back across his life and generally highly entertaining, Vitali's Ireland is very much an

outsider's look into our country. If he doesn't know what to make of us, it is maybe because he is viewing us at a junction where we don't know what to make of ourselves.'
DERMOT BOLGER, IN SUNDAY BUSINESS

'Vitali is big hearted, broad minded and smart as a whip . . . A Ukranian-born Russian exile whose worldwide perambulations have produced a string of fine, intelligent works of idiosyncratic reportage, this somewhat unusual visitor offers a valuable gift to us Irish readers: The outside perspective . . . Vitaliev wanders the 32 counties like some kind of gormless, amiable pilgrim, half-Mr Bean, half-Socrates. . . . (His) observations on the folly of the Northern conflict are heartbreaking in their simplicity and world-weary resignation . . . I could fill this paper with quotable extracts.'
HUGH TYNAN, IN THE IRISH EXAMINER WEEKEND

Available from Amazon for the Kindle and in paperback.

For more information and to read sample chapters go to the Thrust Books website: www.thrustbooks.com.

Life as a Literary Device:
A Writer's Manual of Survival

Both a summation and a new beginning for Vitaliev, *Life as a Literary Device* is an analysis of how literature has bound his life and an exploration of how to survive in the modern world.

'Like "Tristram Shandy", this is a text that begins everywhere, goes everywhere and carries the reader back to the ground of his own heart. A journey I was delighted to make.'
IAIN SINCLAIR

'I read LIFE AS . . . over the holidays. What a brilliant read - and I loved the quirky originality of the structure, Vitali's humanity, and his view of life as a major ongoing dramatic event. Vitaliev is very damn good.'
DOUGLAS KENNEDY

'Vitaliev has finally got around to putting his witty way with a crisis onto the page by explaining – in amusingly circuitous routes – how literature has saved him over the years. Along with Haruki Murakami's running memoir and Martin Amis' experience – it's a memoir, an exercise in attitude and a fascinating window onto the creative process.'
MONOCLE MAGAZINE

'Vitaliev is a genial companion. His tone is immensely likeable. He relishes his successes without arrogance and suffers disappointment without self-pity. He is a genuinely comic writer – not a

sabre-toothed satirist, despite the Krokodil years, but friendly and slightly melancholy. His English is fluent and idiomatic. For all the zaniness, there is a good deal of humanity and common sense in this miscellany. I was sorry when the journey ended, and wanted to start the rolling, rocking ride all over again.'
THE INDEPENDENT

'An honest and fact-filled memoir.'
SCOTLAND ON SUNDAY

'A highly absorbing memoir that grips the reader from the very first pages . . .'
HERTFORDSHIRE LIFE

'Vitali offers a unique perspective on even the most mundane things. And despite the atypical narrative style, the stuff he writes about certainly makes for a good read.'
THE KATMANDU POST

'A celebration of books and their authors . . . full of unpredictable twists and turns . . . A tale of how life and literature are linked . . . This book is an inspiration to anyone who feels a need to write.'
BOOKDEALER

'This book has joy, vivacity and humour . . . A delightful experience of which Vitali can be justly proud.'
OXFORD PROSPECT

'A life bound by literature and informed by "mauvism" . . . Vitali stops where he started: in the middle of things and defined by his heart . . . A fascinating new book which defies categorization, meandering between memoir, novel and diary.'
SUNDAY HERALD

Available from Amazon for the Kindle.

For more information and to read sample chapters go to the Thrust Books website: www.thrustbooks.com.

Passport to Enclavia:
Travels in Search of a European Identity

Acclaimed investigative journalist Vitali Vitaliev explores the idiosyncrasies of Europe's forgotten enclaves, and uncovers the ten year old roots of the current EU crisis, providing a timelessly topical perspective on one of recent history's key events, the birth of the Euro.

'Vitali Vitaliev is that rare thing: a comic writer who is also serious. And what he says about the shifting currents of an Europe trying to redefine its identity in the wake of so many changed geo-political realities is never less than compelling. Read this book for the pleasure of Vitaliev's wry take on human folly and for his penetrating analysis of a continent grappling with manifold dilemmas. He is, as always, a great traveling companion.'
DOUGLAS KENNEDY

'This exploration of European identity makes for a fascinating, often very funny, journey; and like all the best travellers, Vitaliev can also be magnificently grumpy.'
GEOGRAPHICAL

'Vitaliev's good book is about the nature of enclaves, the futility of frontiers and the ingenious and amusing ways that people bothered by customs, border guards, permits and forms manage to swat them away with minimum fuss.'
EUROPEAN VOICE

Available from Amazon for the Kindle and in paperback.

For more information and to read sample chapters go to the Thrust Books website: www.thrustbooks.com.

Printed in Great Britain
by Amazon

70390619R10373